Best Jobs for the 21st Century

J. Michael Farr and LaVerne L. Ludden, Ed.D.

With database work by Paul Mangin

jist

Best Jobs for the 21st Century

© 1999 JIST Works, Inc.

Published by JIST Works, Inc.
720 North Park Avenue
Indianapolis, IN 46202-3490
Phone: 317-264-3720   Fax: 317-264-3709
E-Mail: jistworks@aol.com
World Wide Web Address: http://www.jist.com

See the back of this book for additional JIST titles. Quantity discounts are available.

Printed in the United States of America

02 01 00 99   5 4 3 2 1

We have been careful to provide accurate information throughout this book, but it is possible that errors and omissions have been introduced. Please consider this when making any career plans or other important decisions. Trust your own judgment above all else and in all things.

Please consider that the occupational information in this book has its limitations. It should not be used in legal settings as a basis for occupational injuries or other matters. This is because occupational information contained in this book reflects jobs as they have been found to occur in general, but they may not coincide in every respect with the content of jobs as performed in particular establishments or at certain localities. Users of this information demanding specific job requirements should supplement this data with local information detailing jobs within their community.

ISBN 1-56370-486-2

Credits and Acknowledgments

The occupational information used in this book is based on data obtained from both the U.S. Department of Labor and the U.S. Department of Commerce. These sources provide the most authoritative source of occupational information available. The job descriptions in Section 2 are based on information obtained from the Occupational Information Network (O*NET). The O*NET database of occupational information was developed by researchers and developers working under the direction of the U.S. Department of Labor. They, in turn, were assisted by thousands of employers who gave details on the nature of work provided in the many thousands of job samplings that were used in the development of the database.

While the O*NET database has been released recently, it is based on the substantial work done on an earlier occupational database that was used to develop the *Dictionary of Occupational Titles* and other information sources. That database was first used in the 1939 edition of the *Dictionary of Occupational Titles* and has been continuously updated since. All of this work, over many years, has formed the basis for much of the occupational information used by employers, job seekers, career counselors, education and training institutions, researchers, policy makers, and many others.

About This Book

The "best" job for you is a personal decision. But objective criteria can be used to identify jobs that are, for example, better paying than other jobs with similar duties. This book provides that type of information. We have sorted through the data for *all* major jobs and selected only those that meet one of the following parameters:

▲ Have average annual earnings of $40,000 or more

▲ Are expected to increase the number of people employed in that occupation by 10 percent or more by 2006

▲ Are large enough occupations to create 100,000 or more job openings each year

There were 686 jobs that met this criteria, and descriptions for all of them appear in Section 2. We are not suggesting that all of these jobs are good ones for you to consider—they are not. But we present such a wide range of jobs that you are likely to find one or more that will stand out. These are the jobs you should consider most in your future career planning.

The jobs are arranged into a variety of useful lists in Section 1. For example, you can find lists for the best-paying jobs at various levels of education or training, which is very useful if you are considering additional training or education. You can use these same lists to find jobs that pay you more without requiring additional education. We have also arranged the jobs in groupings based on interests and in other ways that are useful for career planning.

We hope you find this book as interesting as we did while putting it together. We have tried to make it easy to use and as interesting as occupational information can be.

We wish you well in your career and in your life.

Table of Contents

Summary of Major Sections

Introduction. *Starts on page 1.*

Section 1: Lists of the Best Jobs for the 21st Century. *Starts on page 9.*

▲ **The Best of the Best—Jobs with the Highest Pay, Fastest Growth, and Largest Number of Openings:** Includes The 50 Best Jobs for the 21st Century and other lists of the best of all jobs based on pay, growth, and number of openings. *Starts on page 10.*

▲ **The Best Jobs Lists for Different Types of Workers:** The best jobs for youth, older workers, part-time workers, the self-employed, and for men and women. *Starts on page 20.*

▲ **The Best Jobs Lists Based on Levels of Education, Training, and Experience:** The best jobs organized by level of training, experience, and education—from jobs requiring only short-term training or experience to those requiring graduate degrees plus substantial experience. *Starts on page 57.*

▲ **The Best Jobs Lists Based on Interests:** The best jobs within 12 major areas of interest including artistic, scientific, plants and animals, protective/law enforcement, mechanical, industrial, business detail, selling, accommodating/personal service, humanitarian/ helping people, leading/influencing, and physical performing/sports. *Starts on page 74.*

Career Planning Guide to Selecting Occupations Based on Interests. Following the lists is a very helpful guide for exploring career options. It is based on a system developed by the U.S. Department of Labor called the Guide for Occupational Exploration (GOE). *Starts on page 89.*

Section 2: The Best Jobs Directory—Descriptions of the 686 Best Jobs for the 21st Century. Each of the jobs described in this section meet our criteria for fast growth, high pay, or a large number of openings. The descriptions include details on what a person does in the job, the knowledge and abilities required, pay, projected growth rate, training and education required, and other information. The 279 major job titles are arranged in alphabetical order. *Starts on page 115.*

Bibliography of Best Career Resources, Including Internet Sites: A thorough listing of the best resources on career planning, job search, education, and related topics. *Starts on page 557.*

The Best Jobs Directory

Contents

Contents

Contents

Contents

Contents

Contents

Contents

Introduction

The beginning of a new millennium comes around only once in a thousand years, and it motivates many of us to think about the future. This book uses employment projections through 2006 to help you identify jobs with the best possibilities for fast growth, high pay, and the most openings. We hope that you find our approach interesting and that the book encourages you to uncover possibilities that you may not have considered.

This introduction is designed to help you better understand and use the rest of the book. We've kept it short and nontechnical in hopes that you will read it.

How Occupations Were Selected

We gave some information on how occupations were selected in the "About This Book" statement earlier. Here are a few more details about the occupations selected for this book:

1. We started with the jobs included in the new O*NET database. The O*NET is a new database of occupational information first released by the U.S. Department of Labor shortly before the release of this book. It includes information on about 1,200 occupations and is now the primary source of detailed information on occupations, replacing the earlier *Dictionary of Occupational Titles* database. We used the O*NET as a basis for this book because it is the newest and most reliable occupational information available from any source.

2. Because we wanted to include pay data that was not included in the O*NET, we cross-referenced information on earnings developed by the U.S. Census Bureau. This information is the most reliable information we could obtain, but the census uses a different system of job titles than the O*NET. We were able to link the two systems and tie census earnings information to many of the O*NET job titles.

3. We then went through the resulting list of occupations and included those that met one or more of the following criteria:

   ▲ Have earnings of $40,000 or more a year (the average earnings for all workers is about $26,500 a year)

▲ Are expected to increase the number of people employed in that occupation by 10 percent or more by 2006

▲ Are a large enough occupation to create 100,000 or more job openings each year

There were 686 O*NET occupations that met the criteria, and these are the ones in this book. They are arranged within 279 more general Census Bureau titles.

Section 1: Lists of the Best Jobs for the 21st Century

We had some fun in putting together the lists that we think are most likely to interest you. The lists are easy to understand; simply find the lists that interest you and browse them. We added notes to the lists as needed to help you understand how we developed them or to provide tips on using them.

The lists are arranged into groupings that seemed helpful to us. For example, one group arranges the best jobs at different levels of education and training—information that many will find useful. In reviewing the lists, keep in mind that the primary measures for selection as a "best" job on any list is a combination of high pay, high growth, and high number of openings. For example, the best occupations for college graduates are those that have the highest total ranking for pay, growth, and number of openings.

The list titles are provided in the table of contents and are repeated here, along with a few additional comments. As in the table of contents, we have arranged the lists into groupings.

The Best of the Best—Jobs with the Highest Pay, Fastest Growth, and Largest Numbers of Openings

These lists used criteria most people consider important in selecting a "best" job—high pay, high growth, and large numbers of openings. Of all 686 jobs that met our criteria for inclusion in this book, the ones on these lists had the highest overall ratings.

▲ **The 50 Best Jobs for the 21st Century:** Provides a list of occupations with the highest combination scores for pay, growth, and number of openings.

▲ **Best-Paying Jobs:** The jobs with the highest average earnings per year.

▲ **Fastest-Growing Jobs:** The jobs with the highest percentage growth rates projected through 2006.

▲ **Jobs with the Largest Number of Annual Openings**

The Best Jobs Lists for Different Types of Workers

We did some special analysis to create these lists. For example, we sorted all 686 occupations included in this book in order of the percentage of part-time workers employed in each. We then used those with a higher percentage of part-time workers and ranked them on a combination of pay, growth, and number of openings to find those with the highest total scores. We provide more details on the criteria we used for creating these lists in Section 1. The lists include

▲ Best Jobs for Younger Workers Ages 16-24

▲ Best Jobs for Older Workers 55 and Over

▲ Best Jobs for Part-Time Workers

▲ Best Jobs for Self-Employed People

▲ Best Jobs Employing 70 Percent or More Women

▲ Best Jobs Employing 70 Percent or More Men

The Best Jobs Lists Based on Levels of Education, Training, and Experience

We used the same categories for training and education that the U.S. Department of Labor assigns to each occupation. These lists will help you identify jobs that pay more or that are more interesting to you at your current level of education. These lists also can help you identify occupations on the level of education you are willing to pursue:

▲ Best Jobs Requiring Graduate or Professional Degrees

▲ Best Jobs Requiring Four-Year Bachelor's Degrees

▲ Best Jobs Requiring Bachelor's Degrees Plus Experience

▲ Best Jobs Requiring Two-Year Associate's Degrees

▲ Best Jobs Requiring Postsecondary Vocational Training

▲ Best Jobs Requiring Work Experience in a Related Job

▲ Best Jobs Requiring Long-Term, On-the-Job Training

▲ Best Jobs Requiring Moderate-Term, On-the-Job Training

▲ Best Jobs Requiring Short-Term On-the-Job Training

The Best Jobs Lists Based on Interests

These lists are very helpful for career exploration. They arrange all 279 occupations in this book into groupings of jobs based on interests. These groupings use a system called the Guide for Occupational Exploration, or GOE, developed by the U.S. Department of Labor to assist in career exploration. It is very helpful for identifying occupations related to one that you are familiar with or simply for exploring career alternatives. Note: This is the only place where all 279 jobs appear. The other lists only include those with the highest ratings. Additional information on using the GOE system to help you make career decisions is included in a section of this book titled "Career Planning Guide to Selecting Occupations Based on Interests," and we encourage you to review this. The interest groupings include the following:

▲ Best Artistic Jobs

▲ Best Scientific Jobs

▲ Best Plant and Animal Jobs

▲ Best Protective/Law Enforcement Jobs

▲ Best Mechanical Jobs

▲ Best Industrial Jobs

▲ Best Business Detail Jobs

▲ Best Selling Jobs

▲ Best Accommodating/Personal Service Jobs

▲ Best Humanitarian/Helping Others Jobs

▲ Best Leading and Influencing Jobs

▲ Best Physical Performing/Sports Jobs

Best Jobs for the 21st Century™ © 1999, JIST Works, Inc., Indianapolis, IN

Section 2: The Best Jobs Directory— Descriptions of the 686 Best Jobs for the 21st Century

The second section provides job descriptions for the 686 occupations that were selected for this book. The descriptions are organized under 279 titles of major jobs.

As a reminder, the occupations included in this section were selected because they met one or more of the following three criteria:

▲ The number of job openings for the occupation is expected to increase by 10 percent or more by 2006. This is an indicator of jobs offering high potential for entry and advancement.

▲ The average annual earnings for the job are equal to or greater than $40,000. This pay rate is far higher than the average earnings of about $26,500 annually.

▲ The occupation has 100,000 or more job openings each year. Occupations that meet this criteria are included because they provide more opportunities for employment.

The main job titles in Section 2 are listed in alphabetical order. This makes it easy to look up a job that you've identified in a list from Section 1 and want to learn more about. Note that descriptions are arranged under the 279 general job titles used by the Census Bureau; we did this so that we could include earnings data.

The information provided for each occupation was obtained from the new O*NET database. As mentioned earlier, this data was developed by the U.S. Department of Labor and is the most recent and reliable data available. Each of the descriptions includes the following information:

▲ **Job Title.** The title commonly used to describe the occupation

▲ **Growth.** The percentage increase in the number of people employed in the occupation through 2006

▲ **Annual Job Openings.** The number of job openings projected per year

▲ **Yearly Earnings.** The average total pay received by all workers in this occupation

▲ **Education Required.** The amount of training, education, or work experience typically required for entry into this occupation. The letters *O-J-T* stand for on-the-job training.

▲ **Self-Employed.** The percentage of self-employed workers in the occupation

▲ **Part-Time.** The percentage of part-time workers employed in the occupation

Following this labor market information are the O*NET job descriptions for related jobs. There may only be one description, or there may be several. Each job description contains the following information:

▲ **Summary Description and Tasks.** The first lines, in bold, provide a summary description of the occupation. This is followed by a listing of tasks that are generally performed by people who work in the job.

▲ **Knowledge.** Lists the special knowledge typically required to do the job well. In many cases, this will give you a good idea of the types of specific courses or education needed for the job. In other cases, it may simply tell you the types of knowledge that would be helpful to have.

▲ **Abilities.** Lists the mental, physical, and sensory abilities typically required to perform the job.

Job Title ⟶ # Accountants and Auditors

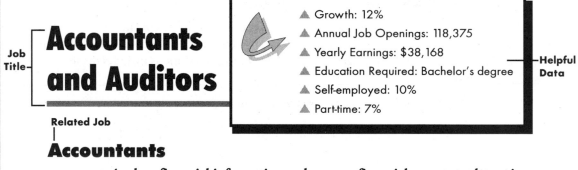

▲ Growth: 12%
▲ Annual Job Openings: 118,375
▲ Yearly Earnings: $38,168
▲ Education Required: Bachelor's degree
▲ Self-employed: 10%
▲ Part-time: 7%

⟵ **Helpful Data**

Related Job
Accountants

Summary Description ⟶ **Analyze financial information and prepare financial reports to determine or maintain record of assets, liabilities, profit and loss, tax liability, or other financial activities within an organization.** Exclude auditors. Analyzes

Task List ⟶ operations, trends, costs, revenues, financial commitments, and obligations incurred, to project future revenues and expenses, using a computer. Develops, maintains, and analyzes budgets, and prepares periodic reports comparing budgeted costs to actual costs. Analyzes records of financial transactions to determine accuracy and completeness of entries, using computer. Prepares balance sheet, profit and loss statement, amortization and depreciation schedules, and

Task List — other financial reports, using calculator or computer. Reports finances of establishment to management, and advises management about resource utilization, tax strategies, and assumptions underlying budget forecasts. Develops, implements, modifies, and documents budgeting, cost, general, property, and tax accounting systems. Predicts revenues and expenditures, and submits reports to management. Computes taxes owed; ensures compliance with tax payment, reporting, and other tax requirements; and represents establishment before taxing authority. Surveys establishment operations to ascertain accounting needs. Establishes table of accounts, and assigns entries to proper accounts. Audits contracts and prepares reports to substantiate transactions prior to settlement. Prepares forms and manuals for workers performing accounting and bookkeeping tasks. Appraises, evaluates, and inventories real property and equipment, and records description, value, location, and other information. Adapts accounting and recordkeeping functions to current technology of computerized accounting systems. Directs activities of workers performing accounting and bookkeeping tasks.

Knowledge Required — **Knowledge:** Administration and Management; Clerical; Economics and Accounting; Personnel and Human Resources; Computers and Electronics; Mathematics; Sociology and Anthropology; Education and Training; English Language; Philosophy and Theology; Law, Government, and Jurisprudence

Abilities Needed — **Abilities:** Written Comprehension; Written Expression; Fluency of Ideas; Originality; Deductive Reasoning; Mathematical Reasoning; Number Facility; Memorization; Speed of Closure; Flexibility of Closure; Perceptual Speed; Finger Dexterity; Near Vision

Caveat Datum (or, loosely translated, beware of data)

One of the problems with data is that it is true on the average. But just as there is no precisely average person, there is no such thing as a statistically average example of a particular job. We say this because data, while helpful, can also be misleading.

Take, for example, the yearly earnings information in this book. This is highly reliable information obtained from a very large U.S. working population sample by the Census Bureau. It tells us the average annual pay received by people in various job titles (actually, it is the "mean" annual pay, which means that half earned more and half less).

This sounds great, except that you have to realize that half of all people in that occupation earned less than that average amount. For example, people just entering the occupation or with a few years of work experience will often earn much less. People who live in rural areas or who work for smaller employers typically earn less than those who do similar work in cities (where the cost of living is higher) or for bigger employers. People in certain areas of the country earn less than those in others. In some jobs, such as bartending, a large percentage of the workforce is part-time (in this case, a whopping 43 percent), and the lower annual pay of these workers reduces the "average" pay for this occupation to a paltry $13,395, even though most full-time bartenders earn much more.

So, in reviewing the information in Section 2, please understand the limitations of data. You still need to use common sense in career decision-making as in most other things in life. Even so, we hope that you find the information helpful and interesting.

Thanks for reading the introduction. You are surely a more thorough person than those who jumped into the book without reading this. The truth is, at least one of the authors is the type of person who never reads documentation before trying to use software. That same type of person turns to a book's good parts and skips the introduction. This is an example of the same point that we were trying to make earlier: All of us are different, but there is always something for each us.

We wish you a satisfying career and, more importantly, life.

Lists of the Best Jobs for the 21st Century

We've tried to make the lists in this section both fun to use and informative. Use the table of contents to find the lists that most interest you, or simply browse the lists that follow. Most, such as the list of jobs with the highest pay, are very easy to understand and require little explanation. We provide comments as needed on the lists to inform you of the selection criteria we used or other details we think you may want to know.

As you review the lists, one or more of the occupations may appeal to you enough to seek additional information. As this happens, mark that occupation (or, if someone else will be using this book, write it on a separate sheet of paper) so that you can look up its description in Section 2.

All lists emphasize occupations with high pay, high growth, or large numbers of openings because many people consider one of these factors important in selecting a desirable job. These measures are also easily quantified and are, therefore, often presented in lists of best jobs you read about in the newspapers and other media.

While earnings, growth, and openings are important, there are other factors to consider. For example, location, liking the people you work with, having an opportunity to serve others, and enjoying your work are a few of many factors that may define the ideal job for you. These measures are difficult or impossible to quantify based on the data we have available and so are not used in this book. You will need to consider the importance of these issues yourself. We suggest that you refer to the bibliography for additional resources to help in your career planning.

Having said this, the lists do include measures that are easily quantified, can be easily sorted, and can be put into list form. All data used in this book comes from government sources including the U.S. Department of Labor and the Census Bureau.

The earnings figures are based on the average annual pay received by full-time workers. Since some occupations have high percentages of part-time workers, those workers would receive, of course, relatively less pay on a weekly or annual basis. The earnings also represent the national averages and actual pay rates can vary greatly by location, amount of previous work experience, and other factors.

The Best of the Best—Jobs with Highest Pay, Fastest Growth, and Largest Number of Openings

We've created four lists of occupations in this grouping. Three list jobs with the highest earnings, growth, and job openings, and a fourth combines scores from the other three lists to create a listing of occupations with the highest combined rankings.

The 50 Best Jobs for the 21st Century

This is our premier list—the list that most people will want to know about. Here are some observations about this list:

▲ A quick review of the best jobs for the 21st century reveals the importance of education. Eighteen of the top 20 jobs require at least a bachelor's degree. Nine of the top 20 jobs are in technical or health-related occupations. Systems analysts, computer engineers, and engineering, mathematical, and natural science managers top the list.

▲ Many jobs in the top 20 require advanced technology skills and training but, among the top 50, there are jobs in most major occupational groups and industries including the arts, education, health care and other helping professions, business, management, and others.

▲ Many of these jobs are in the service and information industries but, contrary to what we often hear, these are not dead-end jobs with low pay and status.

▲ While pay is only one of three factors determining what jobs were included in this list, about 80 percent of the jobs pay more than the average for all workers, which is just above $26,000 a year—and 42 percent of the jobs on the list pay $40,000 or more per year.

The main point that comes through is that opportunities abound for jobs with good pay in the 21st century, but to get them you may need to learn new skills and to continually update them in the future.

Details on the selection process: We began with the 279 jobs that met our criteria for inclusion in this book: high pay, fast growth, or large numbers of openings. We sorted these jobs into three lists in order of highest pay, fastest growth, and largest number of openings. The occupation with the highest pay was given a score of 279; the one with the next highest pay was given a score of 278.

This scoring process was continued for each occupation on each of the three lists, resulting in a total score for each occupation. Then a new list was created based on the total score given to each occupation based on its ranking on all three measures. Systems analysts was the occupation with the highest combined score, and it is on the top of the list that follows. The other occupations follow, in descending order based on their total scores.

The 50 Best Jobs for the 21st Century

Job	Earnings	Annual Job Openings	Percent of Growth
1. Systems analysts	$48,360	87,318	103
2. Computer engineers	$54,912	34,884	109
3. Engineering, mathematical, and natural science managers	$65,686	37,494	45
4. Securities and financial services sales workers	$59,634	40,568	38
5. Marketing, advertising, and public relations managers	$53,602	54,600	29
6. Computer scientists	$48,630	26,732	118
7. Service managers	$48,339	171,229	21
8. Physical therapists	$52,811	19,122	71
9. Special education teachers	$37,104	49,029	59
10. General managers and top executives	$58,344	288,825	15
11. Computer programmers	$48,360	58,990	23
12. Management support workers	$35,339	154,129	26
13. Registered nurses	$40,310	165,362	21
14. Lawyers	$70,117	45,929	19
15. Secondary school teachers	$36,784	168,392	22
16. Electrical and electronics engineers	$53,227	19,098	29
17. Physicians	$96,637	29,681	21
18. Financial managers	$54,392	74,297	18
19. Social workers	$31,221	75,554	32
20. College and university faculty	$44,800	126,584	19

(continued)

(continued)

Job	Earnings	Annual Job Openings	Percent of Growth
21. Dental hygienists	$42,432	18,373	48
22. Management analysts	$48,194	46,026	21
23. Management support specialists	$38,251	124,342	20
24. Occupational therapists	$46,779	9,543	66
25. Speech-language pathologists and audiologists	$42,702	12,202	51
26. Musicians	$30,888	49,350	33
27. Artists and commercial artists	$33,114	46,893	28
28. Vocational education and training instructors	$33,800	82,354	23
29. Loan officers and counselors	$37,419	29,989	28
30. Paralegals	$32,032	21,705	68
31. Sales specialists and support workers	$24,502	765,025	23
32. Correction officers	$28,787	48,102	32
33. Writers and editors	$38,355	41,449	21
34. Sports instructors and coaches	$22,901	82,035	41
35. Food service and lodging managers	$26,562	68,207	29
36. Adjustment clerks	$22,422	80,643	46
37. Clerical supervisors and managers	$31,013	143,806	19
38. Designers	$30,867	42,478	26
39. Health care support specialists	$31,054	45,719	24
40. Home health aides	$16,286	156,127	77
41. Bill and account collectors	$22,402	68,308	42
42. Receptionists and information clerks	$18,075	336,852	30
43. Teacher aides and educational assistants	$15,974	353,119	38
44. Insurance adjusters, examiners, and investigators	$38,230	21,662	23
45. Customer service representatives	$27,061	29,751	36
46. Flight attendants	$36,442	9,844	35
47. Physician assistants	$40,414	5,090	47
48. Personal service workers	$17,202	279,051	31
49. Physical and corrective therapy assistants	$23,587	26,479	79
50. Respiratory therapists	$32,781	9,453	46

Best-Paying Jobs

We know that many people will turn to this list first. Like most people, you probably consider the amount of money you can earn at a job to be important in selecting a career. That is one of the reasons we provide the Best-Paying Jobs list. Keep in mind that the earnings reflect the national average earnings for all workers in the occupation. This is an important consideration because starting pay in the job is usually a lot less than what can be earned with several years of experience. Earnings also vary significantly by region of the country, so actual pay in your area could be substantially different.

The highest-paying job on this list is physician, with average annual earnings of $96,636. All top 25 jobs have average annual earnings greater than $52,000. The average annual earnings for all workers is slightly more than $26,000, so the top 25 jobs on this list earn more than double the national average.

Most of the best-paying jobs require at least a four-year college degree. This isn't surprising, since the lifetime earnings of someone with a bachelor's degree is more than double that of a high school graduate. Six of the top 10 best-paying jobs require a professional degree, which normally requires three or more years of education beyond a bachelor's degree. Workers with professional degrees have lifetime earnings four times greater than those of high school graduates.

Other lists later in this section present high-paying jobs at all levels of education. While it is clear that higher levels of education and training are often required for jobs with high earnings, there remain opportunities for higher-than-average pay at all levels of education.

Best-Paying Jobs

Job	Average Annual Earnings
1. Physicians	$96,636
2. Dentists	$85,508
3. Podiatrists	$85,134
4. Lawyers	$70,116
5. Aircraft pilots and flight engineers	$69,097
6. Petroleum engineers	$68,224
7. Actuaries	$66,352
8. Engineering, mathematical, and natural science managers	$65,686
9. Optometrists	$64,209
10. Chiropractors	$63,211
11. Physicists and astronomers	$62,774
12. Aerospace engineers	$59,633
13. Securities and financial services sales workers	$59,633
14. General managers and top executives	$58,344
15. Nuclear engineers	$57,740
16. Medical scientists	$56,659
17. Chemical engineers	$55,764
18. Pharmacists	$55,328
19. Computer engineers	$54,912
20. Financial managers	$54,392
21. Production engineers	$54,329
22. Marketing, advertising, and public relations managers	$53,601
23. Electrical and electronics engineers	$53,227
24. Veterinarians and veterinary inspectors	$52,936
25. Physical therapists	$52,811

Fastest-Growing Jobs

This is a list of occupations that are projected to have the highest percentage increase in the numbers of people employed through 2006. The three fastest-growing jobs are computer scientists, computer engineers, and systems analysts. These jobs are all expected to more than double by 2006. It is not surprising to find that computer and technology-related jobs lead this list—just like computers are leading the advances in this information age. Health-related professions also dominate the list, which is consistent with the increasing health needs of the aging baby boom generation. Twelve—almost 50 percent—of the top 25 fastest-growing jobs are in health-related occupations. Both computer- and health-related jobs will provide many opportunities for finding employment in the 21st century. But, as this list demonstrates, computer- and health-related jobs are not the only ones with potential for strong growth.

Fastest-Growing Jobs

Job	Percent of Growth
1. Computer scientists	118
2. Computer engineers	109
3. Systems analysts	103
4. Personal and home care aides	85
5. Physical and corrective therapy assistants	79
6. Home health aides	77
7. Desktop publishing workers	74
8. Medical assistants	74
9. Physical therapists	71
10. Occupational therapy assistants and aides	69
11. Paralegals	68
12. Therapeutic services and administration	67
13. Occupational therapists	66
14. Special education teachers	59
15. Human services workers	55
16. Data processing equipment repairers	52
17. Medical records technicians	51
18. Speech-language pathologists and audiologists	51
19. Amusement and recreation attendants	48
20. Dental hygienists	48
21. Physician assistants	47
22. Adjustment clerks	46
23. Respiratory therapists	46
24. Manicurists	45
25. Engineering, mathematical, and natural science managers	45

Jobs with Largest Number of Annual Openings

Occupations with the most annual openings often provide easier entry for new workers and the ability to move from one job to another with relative ease. Such jobs are also attractive to people reentering the labor market, part-time job seekers, and workers who want to move from one employer to another. Many of these occupations are also used as a second job by people wanting to supplement their income.

Note that an occupation with large numbers of openings does not mean it will be high paying or attractive in other ways. It simply means that it is a large occupation that employs many people. For example, the top 25 occupations on this list pay an average of under $20,000 a year—less than the $26,500 a year average paid to all workers. And the average growth rate of these jobs is less than 16 percent, a bit higher than the 14 percent average growth rate projected for all occupations through the year 2006.

Jobs with Largest Number of Annual Openings

Job	Annual Openings
1. Retail salespersons	1,236,273
2. Cashiers	1,109,571
3. Janitors, cleaners, and maids	818,941
4. Sales specialists and support workers	765,025
5. Food counter and fountain workers	727,389
6. Waiters and waitresses	714,482
7. General office clerks	661,333
8. Helpers and laborers	586,697
9. Food preparation workers	573,079
10. Secretaries	433,901
11. Teacher aides and educational assistants	353,119
12. Stock clerks	346,772
13. Truck drivers light and heavy	346,612
14. Receptionists and information clerks	336,852
15. Child care workers	328,078
16. Bookkeeping, accounting, and auditing clerks	327,125
17. Marketing and sales worker supervisors	305,545
18. Nursing aides, orderlies, and attendants	304,868
19. General managers and top executives	288,825
20. Guards	283,077
21. Personal service workers	279,051
22. Hand packers and packagers	271,086
23. Hand workers	267,301
24. Short order and fast food cooks	237,301
25. Freight, stock, and material movers	232,034

The Best Jobs Lists for Different Types of Workers

These lists examine the best jobs for younger workers, older workers, part-time workers, self-employed workers, and jobs dominated by men and women.

There are actually five lists for each of the categories we included in this list group. For example, the best jobs lists for younger workers includes

▲ Jobs with the Highest Percentage of Younger Workers Ages 16-24

▲ Best Jobs for Younger Workers Ages 16-24

▲ Best-Paying Jobs for Younger Workers Ages 16-24

▲ Fastest-Growing Jobs for Younger Workers Ages 16-24

▲ Jobs with the Most Annual Openings for Younger Workers Ages 16-24

As in previous groupings, the Best Jobs for Younger Workers Ages 16-24 list—and the lists that are similarly named—are based on a combined score for pay, growth, and number of openings.

The Potential Controversy

We considered excluding the best jobs lists for women to avoid upsetting some readers. But we know that people can handle the facts. So we asked our computer to tell us which jobs employed the highest percentages of men and women.

The computer told us that most nurses are women and most bricklayers are men and made other similar revelations. Many of these facts should not come as a surprise to anyone who lives in the real world. We also found that most ski patrol officers and lifeguards are young and that most lawn service managers are over 55. Some findings will make sense, like the lifeguards, but others are simply interesting, like the lawn service managers.

We think that you can learn some interesting information from these lists, perhaps something you can use to plan your career. As needed, we provide additional comments prior to each list.

The Best Jobs Lists for Younger Workers Ages 16-24

We sorted our list of included occupations to find those with the highest percentage of workers 16 through 24 years of age. While these folks represent about 16 percent of the total workforce, we included only those occupations that employ 30 percent of more of these young workers—about twice the average for all occupations.

While young workers are employed in virtually all major occupations, the ones with the highest percentage tend to be in entry-level, part-time, seasonal, or service jobs. This makes sense in that many young workers have not yet settled into careers or are working while going to school. The jobs they get tend to be relatively easy to obtain but have relatively low wages.

More than 50 percent of the jobs on these lists pay the minimum wage and only three pay more than $6.50 an hour. These low-paying jobs are often referred to as entry-level jobs because they offer inexperienced workers an opportunity to enter the labor market. Many young people work in them to earn some money, gain basic job skills, and then use their experience to move up to better-paying jobs.

While these are the jobs that employ the highest percentage of young workers, other lists in this section provide jobs with higher long-term earnings, opportunities for advancement, and other career advantages.

Jobs with Highest Percentage of Younger Workers Ages 16-24

Job	Percent
1. Ski patrol workers and life guards	76
2. Dining room, cafeteria, and bar helpers	56
3. Private household child care workers	53
4. Cashiers	52
5. Food counter and fountain workers	51
6. Waiters and waitresses	47
7. Freight, stock, and material movers	46
8. Amusement and recreation attendants	46
9. Ushers, lobby attendants, and ticket takers	46
10. Counter and rental clerks	45
11. Construction trades helpers	44
12. Food preparation workers	40
13. Specialty food workers	39
14. Vehicle washers and equipment cleaners	39
15. Library assistants and bookmobile drivers	38
16. Bread and pastry bakers	38
17. Short order and fast food cooks	38
18. Restaurant cooks	38
19. Institution or cafeteria cooks	38
20. Bank tellers	34

Best Jobs for Younger Workers Ages 16-24

Job	Percent	Earnings	Percent Growth	Openings
1. Helpers and laborers	30	$20,509	16	586,697
2. Short order and fast food cooks	38	$18,491	22	237,301
3. Cashiers	52	$17,472	17	1,109,571
4. Retail salespersons	33	$19,302	10	1,236,273
5. Amusement and recreation attendants	46	$17,222	48	130,390
6. Food preparation workers	40	$17,181	19	573,079
7. Bread and pastry bakers	38	$19,178	26	61,382
8. Freight, stock, and material movers	46	$18,678	5	232,034
9. Restaurant cooks	38	$17,118	15	224,725
10. Specialty food workers	39	$16,536	27	82,637
11. Counter and rental clerks	45	$15,496	23	129,889
12. Food counter and fountain workers	51	$14,643	14	727,389
13. Vehicle washers and equipment cleaners	39	$16,078	25	103,946
14. Construction trades helpers	11	$18,075	9	137,805
15. Ski patrol workers and life guards	76	$17,202	17	53,969
16. Waiters and waitresses	47	$13,998	11	714,482
17. Veterinary assistants	31	$14,685	28	7,248
18. Sprayers applicators	30	$16,182	21	5,889
19. Gardeners and groundskeepers	30	$15,038	0	188,023
20. Ushers, lobby attendants, and ticket takers	46	$13,354	28	25,394

Best-Paying Jobs for Younger Workers Ages 16-24

Job	Percent	Average Annual Earnings
1. Helpers and laborers	30	$20,509
2. Retail salespersons	33	$19,302
3. Bread and pastry bakers	38.	$19,178
4. Freight, stock, and material movers	46	$18,678
5. Short order and fast food cooks	38	$18,491
6. Construction trades helpers	44	$18,075
7. Cashiers	52	$17,472
8. Amusement and recreation attendants	46	$17,222
9. Ski patrol workers and lifeguards	76	$17,202
10. Food preparation workers	40	$17,181
11. Restaurant cooks	38	$17,118
12. Specialty food workers	39	$16,536
13. Sprayers applicators	30	$16,182
14. Vehicle washers and equipment cleaners	39	$16,078
15. Counter and rental clerks	45	$15,496
16. Gardeners and groundskeepers	30	$15,038
17. Veterinary assistants	31	$14,685
18. Food counter and fountain workers	51	$14,643
19. Library assistants and bookmobile drivers	38	$14,581
20. Animal caretakers	31	$14,414

Fastest-Growing Jobs for Younger Workers Ages 16-24

Job	Percent	Percent Growth
1. Amusement and recreation attendants	46	48
2. Veterinary assistants	31	28
3. Ushers, lobby attendants, and ticket takers	46	28
4. Specialty food workers	39	27
5. Bread and pastry bakers	38	26
6. Vehicle washers and equipment cleaners	39	25
7. Counter and rental clerks	45	23
8. Short order and fast food cooks	38	22
9. Sprayers applicators	30	21
10. Animal caretakers	31	21
11. Food preparation workers	40	19
12. Cashiers	52	17
13. Ski patrol workers and lifeguards	76	17
14. Helpers and laborers	30	16
15. Restaurant cooks	38	15
16. Library assistants and bookmobile drivers	38	15
17. Food counter and fountain workers	51	14
18. Dining room, cafeteria, and bar helpers	56	14
19. Waiters and waitresses	47	11
20. Retail salespersons	33	10

Jobs with the Most Annual Openings for Younger Workers Ages 16-24

Job	Percent	Annual Job Openings
1. Retail salespersons	33	1,236,273
2. Cashiers	52	1,109,571
3. Food counter and fountain workers	51	727,389
4. Waiters and waitresses	47	714,482
5. Helpers and laborers	30	586,697
6. Food preparation workers	40	573,079
7. Short order and fast food cooks	38	237,301
8. Freight, stock, and material movers	46	232,034
9. Restaurant cooks	38	224,725
10. Gardeners and groundskeepers	30	188,023
11. Private household child care workers	53	146,546
12. Construction trades helpers	44	137,805
13. Dining room, cafeteria, and bar helpers	56	132,882
14. Amusement and recreation attendants	46	130,390
15. Counter and rental clerks	45	129,889
16. Institution or cafeteria cooks	38	120,220
17. Bank tellers	34	109,086
18. Vehicle washers and equipment cleaners	39	103,946
19. Specialty food workers	39	82,637
20. Bread and pastry bakers	38	61,382

The Best Jobs Lists for Older Workers 55 and Over

We sorted the occupations in this book to include those with 15 percent or more of workers who are 55 or older. These workers account for approximately 12.5 percent of the workforce. The participation in the workforce for people 55 and over is less than that of other age groups as workers begin to retire. This is also an age group that had been particularly affected by layoffs during the 80s and 90s.

One use of these lists is to help identify careers that might be interesting as you decide to change careers or approach retirement. Some occupations are on the lists because they are attractive to older workers wanting part-time work to supplement their retirement income. For example, we think that lawn service managers are on the list because it pays pretty well, can be done less than full-time and on a flexible schedule, and lends itself to self-employment. Other occupations on the list such as clergy, physicians, and musicians take many years of training and experience. Once a person is established in that career, the person often works in that occupation until retirement.

Jobs with the Highest Percentage of Workers 55 and Older

Job	Percent
1. Lawn service managers	35.2
2. Nursery and greenhouse managers	35.2
3. Clergy	31.2
4. Property and real estate managers	27.0
5. Real estate appraisers	26.8
6. Real estate agents	26.8
7. Bus drivers	23.3
8. Management analysts	22.3
9. Human services workers	21.7
10. Private detectives	21.7
11. Guards	21.7
12. Personal and home care aides	21.7
13. Curators, archivists, museum technicians, and restorers	20.1
14. Musicians	19.4
15. College and university faculty	19.0
16. Bookkeeping, accounting, and auditing clerks	18.3
17. Physicians	18.0
18. Pest controllers and assistants	17.7
19. Janitors, cleaners, and maids	17.6
20. Recreation workers	17.3

 Best Jobs for the 21st Century™ © 1999, JIST Works, Inc., Indianapolis, IN

Best Jobs for Older Workers 55 and Over

Job	Percent	Earnings	Growth	Openings
1. Chiropractors	17	$63,211	27	2,595
2. Veterinarians and veterinary inspectors	17	$52,936	23	2,381
3. Physicians	18	$96,637	21	29,681
4. Musicians	19	$30,888	33	49,350
5. Director of religious education and activities	17	$24,170	36	10,781
6. Human services workers	22	$21,112	55	42,907
7. Management analysts	22	$48,194	21	46,026
8. Personal and home care aides	22	$13,832	85	58,134
9. Lawn service managers	35	$25,917	22	4,637
10. College and university faculty	19	$44,800	19	126,584
11. Civil engineers	17	$49,920	18	15,979
12. Pest controllers and assistants	18	$21,507	22	16,835
13. Guards	22	$16,640	23	283,077
14. Nursery and greenhouse managers	35	$26,104	19	2,575
15. Recreation workers	17	$17,139	22	29,800
16. Dietitians and nutritionists	15	$32,406	18	4,079
17. Property and real estate managers	27	$33,114	16	29,483
18. Construction and building inspectors	15	$35,381	15	5,878
19. Private detectives	22	$24,648	19	17,441
20. Optometrists	17	$64,210	12	1,630

Best-Paying Jobs for Older Workers 55 and Over

Job	Percent	Average Annual Earnings
1. Physicians	18.0	$96,637
2. Dentists	17.3	$85,509
3. Podiatrists	17.3	$85,134
4. Optometrists	17.3	$64,210
5. Chiropractors	17.3	$63,211
6. Veterinarians and veterinary inspectors	17.3	$52,936
7. Education administrators	15.3	$52,437
8. Civil engineers	17.3	$49,920
9. Management analysts	22.3	$48,194
10. Real estate agents	26.8	$45,219
11. College and university faculty	19.0	$44,800
12. Real estate appraisers	26.8	$38,334
13. Construction and building inspectors	15.2	$35,381
14. Property and real estate managers	27.0	$33,114
15. Dietitians and nutritionists	15.3	$32,406
16. Musicians	19.4	$30,888
17. Curators, archivists, museum technicians, and restorers	20.1	$30,035
18. Clergy	31.2	$28,870
19. Nursery and greenhouse managers	35.2	$26,104
20. Tutors and instructors	15.0	$26,000

Fastest-Growing Jobs for Older Workers 55 and Over

Job	Percent	Percent Growth
1. Personal and home care aides	22	85
2. Human services workers	22	55
3. Director of religious education and activities	17	36
4. Musicians	19	33
5. Chiropractors	17	27
6. Veterinarians and veterinary inspectors	17	23
7. Guards	22	23
8. Lawn service managers	35	22
9. Pest controllers and assistants	18	22
10. Recreation workers	17	22
11. Physicians	18	21
12. Management analysts	22	21
13. College and university faculty	19	19
14. Nursery and greenhouse managers	35	19
15. Private detectives	22	19
16. Civil engineers	17	18
17. Dietitians and nutritionists	15	18
18. Property and real estate managers	27	16
19. Construction and building inspectors	15	15
20. Curators, archivists, museum technicians, and restorers	20	15

Jobs with the Most Annual Openings for Older Workers 55 and Over

Job	Percent	Annual Job Openings
1. Janitors, cleaners, and maids	18	818,941
2. Bookkeeping, accounting, and auditing clerks	18	327,125
3. Guards	22	283,077
4. Tutors and instructors	15	149,064
5. College and university faculty	19	126,584
6. Personal and home care aides	22	58,134
7. Musicians	19	49,350
8. Management analysts	22	46,026
9. Human services workers	22	42,907
10. Real estate agents	27	41,554
11. Education administrators	15	39,333
12. Library assistants and bookmobile drivers	17	32,759
13. Bus drivers	23	31,905
14. Recreation workers	17	29,880
15. Physicians	18	29,681
16. Property and real estate managers	27	29,483
17. Messengers	17	25,352
18. Private detectives	22	17,441
19. Pest controllers and assistants	18	16,835
20. Civil engineers	17	15,979

The Best Jobs Lists for Part-Time Workers

Many people prefer to work less than full time, and some end up doing so because they can't find good full-time jobs. For example, people who are going to school or who have young children may prefer part-time work so that they can attend classes or spend more time with their family. There are also money-related reasons, such as working a second job to supplement income or working two or more part-time jobs because one desirable full-time job was not available.

If you want to work part-time, these lists will be helpful in identifying where most others are finding opportunities for this kind of work. Many of the jobs, particularly those with lower pay, can be learned quickly, offer flexible work schedules, are easy to obtain, and offer other advantages desirable for many people in certain situations.

While many people think of part-time jobs as requiring low skill and providing low pay, this is not always the case. For example, 5 of the 10 best-paying part-time jobs require professional credentials or substantial experience, such as university faculty and musicians, and 6 of the 20 best jobs are in teaching and education.

The occupations in these lists were those where 30 percent of more of the workers were part-time. Note that the these are the only lists where earnings are reported as hourly earnings—we thought this made more sense for evaluating these jobs.

Jobs with Highest Percentage of Part-Time Workers

Job	Percent Part-Time
1. Food counter and fountain workers	62.9
2. Library assistants and bookmobile drivers	61.7
3. Dining room, cafeteria, and bar helpers	59.5
4. Specialty food workers	58.2
5. Food preparation workers	57.4
6. Cashiers	57.2
7. Waiters and waitresses	57.0
8. Musicians	53.5
9. Ski patrol workers and life guards	51.4
10. Private household child care workers	51.0
11. Counter and rental clerks	50.8
12. Amusement and recreation attendants	48.8
13. Ushers, lobby attendants, and ticket takers	48.8
14. Teacher aides and educational assistants	46.8
15. Flight attendants	45.7
16. Child care workers	43.4
17. Bus drivers	43.3
18. Bartenders	43.1
19. Vocational education and training instructors	42.5
20. Adult education instructors	42.5

Best Jobs for the 21st Century™ © 1999, JIST Works, Inc., Indianapolis, IN

Best Jobs for Part-Time Workers

Job	Percent Part-Time	Earnings	Growth	Openings
1. Receptionists and information clerks	35	$ 8.69	30	336,852
2. Sports instructors and coaches	43	$11.01	41	82,035
3. Teacher aides and educational assistants	47	$ 7.68	38	353,119
4. Personal service workers	40	$ 8.27	31	279,051
5. College and university faculty	32	$21.54	19	126,584
6. Vocational education and training instructors	43	$16.25	23	82,354
7. Musicians	54	$14.85	33	49,350
8. Physical and corrective therapy assistants	35	$11.34	79	26,479
9. Tutors and instructors	40	$12.50	15	149,064
10. Human services workers	42	$10.15	55	42,907
11. Dental assistants	40	$10.37	38	45,487
12. Adult education instructors	43	$13.16	21	81,219
13. Child care workers	43	$ 6.73	36	328,078
14. Flight attendants	46	$17.52	35	9,844
15. Retail salespersons	40	$ 8.26	10	1,236,273
16. General office clerks	31	$ 9.27	7	661,333
17. Preschool and kindergarten teachers	32	$11.16	20	77,151
18. Amusement and recreation attendants	49	$ 6.42	48	130,390
19. Travel agents	32	$10.56	24	38,234
20. Bookkeeping, accounting, and auditing clerks	33	$10.95	-5	327,125

Best-Paying Jobs for Part-Time Workers

Job	Percent Part-Time	Average Hourly Earnings
1. Farm and home management advisors	43	$23.32
2. College and university faculty	32	$21.54
3. Flight attendants	46	$17.52
4. Vocational education and training instructors	43	$16.25
5. Musicians	54	$14.85
6. Adult education instructors	43	$13.16
7. Tutors and instructors	40	$12.50
8. Bus drivers	43	$11.76
9. Physical and corrective therapy assistants	35	$11.34
10. Preschool and kindergarten teachers	32	$11.16
11. Sports instructors and coaches	43	$11.01
12. Bookkeeping, accounting, and auditing clerks	33	$10.95
13. Travel agents	32	$10.56
14. Dental assistants	40	$10.37
15. Pest controllers and assistants	30	$10.34
16. Human services workers	42	$10.15
17. Freight, stock, and material movers	38	$ 9.28
18. General office clerks	31	$ 9.27
19. Ski patrol workers and lifeguards	51	$ 8.98
20. Receptionists and information clerks	35	$ 8.69

Best Jobs for the 21st Century™ © 1999, JIST Works, Inc., Indianapolis, IN

Fastest-Growing Jobs for Part-Time Workers

Job	Percent Part-Time	Percent Growth
1. Personal and home care aides	42	85
2. Physical and corrective therapy assistants	35	79
3. Human services workers	42	55
4. Amusement and recreation attendants	49	48
5. Manicurists	37	45
6. Sports instructors and coaches	43	41
7. Dental assistants	40	38
8. Teacher aides and educational assistants	47	38
9. Ambulance drivers and attendants	35	37
10. Child care workers	43	36
11. Flight attendants	46	35
12. Musicians	54	33
13. Personal service workers	40	31
14. Receptionists and information clerks	35	30
15. Veterinary assistants	38	28
16. Ushers, lobby attendants, and ticket takers	49	28
17. Specialty food workers	58	27
18. Bread and pastry bakers	39	26
19. Travel agents	32	24
20. Vocational education and training instructors	43	23

Jobs with the Most Annual Openings for Part-Time Workers

Job	Percent Part-Time	Annual Job Openings
1. Retail salespersons	40	1,236,273
2. Cashiers	57	1,109,571
3. Janitors, cleaners, andmaids	32	818,941
4. Food counter and fountain workers	63	727,389
5. Waiters and waitresses	57	714,482
6. General office clerks	31	661,333
7. Food preparation workers ·	57	573,079
8. Teacher aides and educational assistants	47	353,119
9. Receptionists and information clerks	35	336,852
10. Child care workers	43	328,078
11. Bookkeeping, accounting, and auditing clerks	33	327,125
12. Personal service workers	40	279,051
13. Short order and fast food cooks	39	237,301
14. Freight, stock, and material movers	38	232,034
15. Restaurant cooks	39	224,725
16. Tutors and instructors	40	149,064
17. Private household child care workers	51	146,546
18. Dining room, cafeteria, and bar helpers	60	132,882
19. Amusement and recreation attendants	49	130,390
20. Counter and rental clerks	51	129,889

The Best Jobs Lists for Self-Employed People

About 11 percent of all working people are self-employed or own their own business. This is a substantial part of our workforce, yet they get little mention in most career books. That is one reason we have included these lists.

Many occupations in these lists, such as greenhouse managers or bicycle repairers, are held by people who operate one- or two-person businesses and who may also do this work part-time. Others, such as carpet installers, will often work on a per-job basis under the supervision of others.

While the lists do not show it, older workers and women make up a rapidly growing part of the self-employed. With the large-scale layoffs of the 1980s and 90s, some highly experienced older workers had difficulty finding employment and set up consulting and other small businesses as a result. Large numbers of women are now forming small businesses or creating self-employment opportunities as an alternative to traditional employment.

Some occupations, such as many physicians and lawyers, have a high percentage of self-employment, but they have set up structures where they technically work for a corporation rather than themselves. These workers are not included in these lists.

We sorted our database of occupations and included in the lists that follow occupations where 30 percent or more of the workers were self-employed. Eleven of the 20 best jobs for self- employment require at least a bachelor's degree, and most of the remaining jobs require postsecondary education or long-term, on-the-job training.

The 20 best-paying jobs show that self-employed workers can have very high earnings—all top 20 jobs pay well above average, and two-thirds of the top 35 earned above the national average. It would seem that self-employment can be a good career move for those with highly sought skills.

Jobs with Highest Percentage of Self-Employed People

Job	Percent Self-Employed
1. Nursery and greenhouse managers	85
2. Bicycle repairers	70
3. Real estate agents	70
4. Carpet installers	67
5. Artists and commercial artists	61
6. Lawn service managers	59
7. Chiropractors	58
8. Child care workers	58
9. Service managers	49
10. Adult education instructors	49
11. Dentists	49
12. Podiatrists	47
13. Management analysts	46
14. Interior designers	46
15. Hairdressers, hairstylists, and cosmetologists	46
16. Painters and paperhangers	46
17. Camera and photographic equipment repairers	45
18. Photographers	44
19. Psychologists	44
20. Property and real estate managers	40

Best Jobs for the 21st Century™ © 1999, JIST Works, Inc., Indianapolis, IN

Best Jobs for Self-Employed People

Job	Percent Self-Employed	Earnings	Percent Growth	Openings
1. Service managers	49	$48,339	21	171,229
2. Artists and commercial artists	61	$33,114	28	46,893
3. Lawyers	36	$70,117	19	45,929
4. Management analysts	46	$48,194	21	46,026
5. Food service and lodging managers	38	$26,562	29	68,207
6. Designers	32	$30,867	26	42,478
7. Marketing and sales worker supervisors	37	$32,718	11	305,545
8. Adult education instructors	49	$27,373	21	81,219
9. Writers and editors	31	$38,355	21	41,449
10. Interior designers	46	$32,094	28	9,238
11. Architects	31	$46,883	20	10,404
12. Carpenters	37	$30,139	6	167,617
13. Child care workers	58	$13,998	06	328,078
14. Painters and paperhangers	46	$26,062	15	71,544
15. Chiropractors	58	$63,211	27	2,595
16. Property and real estate managers	40	$33,114	16	29,483
17. Real estate agents	70	$45,219	6	41,554
18. Manicurists	37	$15,392	45	8,973
19. Hairdressers, hairstylists, and cosmetologists	46	$16,744	10	90,496
20. Psychologists	44	$48,090	8	10,914

Best-Paying Jobs for Self-Employed People

Job	Percent Self-Employed	Average Annual Earnings
1. Dentists	49	$85,509
2. Podiatrists	47	$85,134
3. Lawyers	36	$70,117
4. Optometrists	38	$64,210
5. Chiropractors	58	$63,211
6. Veterinarians and veterinary inspectors	40	$52,936
7. Service managers	49	$48,339
8. Management analysts	46	$48,194
9. Psychologists	44	$48,090
10. Architects	31	$46,883
11. Real estate agents	70	$45,219
12. Writers and editors	31	$38,355
13. Artists and commercial artists	61	$33,114
14. Property and real estate managers	40	$33,114
15. Marketing and sales worker supervisors	37	$32,718
16. Interior designers	46	$32,094
17. Designers	32	$30,867
18. Carpenters	37	$30,139
19. Carpet installers	67	$29,973
20. Camera and photographic equipment repairers	45	$29,182

Best Jobs for the 21st Century™ © 1999, JIST Works, Inc., Indianapolis, IN

Fastest-Growing Jobs for Self-Employed People

Job	Percent Self-Employed	Percent Growth
1. Manicurists	37	45
2. Child care workers	58	36
3. Bicycle repairers	70	34
4. Food service and lodging managers	38	29
5. Artists and commercial artists	61	28
6. Interior designers	46	28
7. Dancers and choreographers	37	28
8. Chiropractors	58	27
9. Designers	32	26
10. Camera and photographic equipment repairers	45	24
11. Veterinarians and veterinary inspectors	40	23
12. Lawn service managers	59	22
13. Service managers	49	21
14. Management analysts	46	21
15. Writers and editors	31	21
16. Adult education instructors	49	21
17. Architects	31	20
18. Lawyers	36	19
19. Nursery and greenhouse managers	85	19
20. Photographers	44	17

Jobs with the Most Annual Openings for Self-Employed People

Job	Percent Self-Employed	Annual Job Openings
1. Child care workers	58	328,078
2. Marketing and sales worker supervisors	37	305,545
3. Service managers	49	171,229
4. Carpenters	37	167,617
5. Hairdressers, hairstylists, and cosmetologists	46	90,496
6. Adult education instructors	49	81,219
7. Painters and paperhangers	46	71,544
8. Food service and lodging managers	38	68,207
9. Artists and commercial artists	61	46,893
10. Management analysts	46	46,026
11. Lawyers	36	45,929
12. Designers	32	42,478
13. Real estate agents	70	41,554
14. Writers and editors	31	41,449
15. Property and real estate managers	40	29,483
16. Photographers	44	20,243
17. Psychologists	44	10,914
18. Architects	31	10,404
19. Interior designers	46	9,238
20. Manicurists	37	8,973

Best Jobs for the 21st Century™ © 1999, JIST Works, Inc., Indianapolis, IN

The Best Jobs Lists for Women

As stated earlier, the next group of lists is not meant to restrict women from considering job options. Our reason for including these lists is exactly the opposite. We hope that it helps people see possibilities that they might not otherwise have considered. For example, we suggest that women browse the lists that employ high percentages of men. Many of those occupations pay quite well and could be handled by women who want to do them—and who get the necessary education and training.

We created the lists by sorting the database of occupations in this book to include occupations where 70 percent or more of the workers were either men or women. We then excluded any occupation with a growth rate of zero or lower. That left 96 jobs for men and 67 for women.

The lists that follow present the occupations employing high percentages of women. In comparing these lists to those with a high percentage of men, it struck us that there were distinct differences beyond the obvious. For example, jobs employing high percentages of women are growing much faster than the similar lists for men. The average job growth for the top 20 jobs for women is 59 percent while it is less than half that rate for men—28 percent. The number of annual job openings shows a similar pattern. Occupations with the highest percent of men average 160,388, while those for women are almost double, at 313,218 openings.

This might explain why men have had more problems than women in adapting to an economy dominated by service and information-based jobs—many women may simply be better prepared, with more appropriate skills, for the jobs that are now growing rapidly. Economists have long noticed that men over 50 who are laid off their jobs find it very difficult to locate new jobs. Looking over our lists based on gender, you can see how this might be so. Older males, traditionally employed in manufacturing, trade, and other "male" jobs, may have developed few skills needed in the most occupations that are now rapidly growing. If they lose these jobs due to downsizing or any other reason, there are fewer similar jobs available. The result is longer lengths of unemployment, new employment in lower-paying jobs, forced withdrawal from the labor market, and other fates not suffered by many women who have skills that are in more demand.

Perhaps you can come to other conclusions, but there is a variety of evidence that women with good technical training and education are doing quite well in the labor market. And it is increasingly true that either gender, without these skills, are less likely to find the best jobs.

Jobs with Highest Percentage of Women

Job	Percent Women
1. Legal secretaries	99
2. Medical secretaries	99
3. Preschool and kindergarten teachers	98
4. Dental assistants	97
5. Child care workers	95
6. Licensed practical nurses	95
7. Receptionists and information clerks	94
8. Registered nurses	94
9. Teacher aides and educational assistants	93
10. Dietitians and nutritionists	92
11. Hairdressers, hairstylists, and cosmetologists	91
12. Manicurists	91
13. Bank tellers	91
14. Nursing aides, orderlies, and attendants	89
15. Home health aides	89
16. Travel agents	88
17. Hotel desk clerks	87
18. Cost estimators	87
19. Pharmacists	86
20. Physician assistants	86

Best Jobs for the 21st Century™ © 1999, JIST Works, Inc., Indianapolis, IN

Best Jobs Employing 70 Percent or More Women

Job	Percent Women	Annual Earnings	Percent Growth	Job Openings
1. Special education teachers	84	$37,104	59	49,029
2. Physical therapists	74	$52,811	71	19,122
3. Registered nurses	94	$40,310	21	165,362
4. Dental hygienists	82	$42,432	48	18,373
5. Paralegals	80	$32,032	68	21,705
6. Occupational therapists	74	$46,779	66	9,543
7. Speech-language pathologists and audiologists	74	$42,702	51	12,202
8. Adjustment clerks	75	$22,422	46	80,643
9. Physical and corrective therapy assistants	79	$23,587	79	26,479
10. Home health aides	89	$16,286	77	156,127
11. Physician assistants	86	$40,414	47	5,090
12. Health care support specialists	78	$31,054	24	45,719
13. Medical assistants	82	$19,864	74	34,511
14. Human services workers	85	$21,112	55	42,907
15. Personal and home care aides	85	$13,832	85	58,134
16. Respiratory therapists	74	$32,781	46	9,453
17. Customer service representatives	76	$27,061	36	29,751
18. Therapeutic services and administration	74	$31,866	67	1,767
19. Teacher aides and educational assistants	93	$15,974	38	353,119
20. Insurance adjusters, examiners, and investigators	75	$38,230	23	21,662

Best-Paying Jobs Employing 70 Percent or More Women

Job	Percent Women	Average Annual Earnings
1. Pharmacists	86	$55,328
2. Physical therapists	74	$52,811
3. Occupational therapists	74	$46,779
4. Speech-language pathologists and audiologists	74	$42,702
5. Dental hygienists	82	$42,432
6. Insurance claims examiners	75	$41,142
7. Physician assistants	86	$40,414
8. Registered nurses	94	$40,310
9. Cost estimators	87	$39,894
10. Nuclear medicine technologists	74	$38,605
11. Insurance adjusters, examiners, and investigators	75	$38,230
12. Special education teachers	84	$37,104
13. Flight attendants	82	$36,442
14. Elementary teachers	86	$35,280
15. Cardiology technologists	82	$33,696
16. Respiratory therapists	74	$32,781
17. Dietitians and nutritionists	92	$32,406
18. Paralegals	80	$32,032
19. Radiologic technologists	74	$31,970
20. Therapeutic services and administration	74	$31,866

Fastest-Growing Jobs Employing 70 Percent or More Women

Job	Percent Women	Percent Growth
1. Personal and home care aides	85	85
2. Physical and corrective therapy assistants	79	79
3. Home health aides	89	77
4. Medical assistants	82	74
5. Physical therapists	74	71
6. Occupational therapy assistants and aides	81	69
7. Paralegals	80	68
8. Therapeutic services and administration	74	67
9. Occupational therapists	74	66
10. Special education teachers	84	59
11. Human services workers	85	55
12. Speech-language pathologists and audiologists	74	51
13. Medical records technicians	82	51
14. Dental hygienists	82	48
15. Physician assistants	86	47
16. Respiratory therapists	74	46
17. Adjustment clerks	75	46
18. Emergency medical technicians	82	45
19. Manicurists	91	45
20. Dental assistants	97	38

Jobs with the Most Openings Employing 70 Percent or More Women

Job	Percent Women	Annual Job Openings
1. Cashiers	80	1,109,571
2. Food counter and fountain workers	73	727,389
3. Waiters and waitresses	79	714,482
4. General office clerks	80	661,333
5. Food preparation workers	74	573,079
6. Teacher aides and educational assistants	93	353,119
7. Receptionists and information clerks	94	336,852
8. Child care workers	95	328,078
9. Nursing aides, orderlies, and attendants	89	304,868
10. Registered nurses	94	165,362
11. Elementary teachers	86	164,163
12. Home health aides	89	156,127
13. Bank tellers	91	109,086
14. Clerical support workers	75	105,566
15. Hairdressers, hairstylists, and cosmetologists	91	90,496
16. Licensed practical nurses	95	81,622
17. Adjustment clerks	75	80,643
18. Preschool and kindergarten teachers	98	77,151
19. Billing, cost, and rate clerks	82	67,231
20. Personal and home care aides	85	58,134

Best Jobs for the 21st Century™ © 1999, JIST Works, Inc., Indianapolis, IN

The Best Jobs Lists for Men

We suggest you read the introductory material to "The Best Job Lists for Different Types of Workers" to better understand the purpose for publishing the following lists. As stated earlier, we are not suggesting that the best jobs lists for men include the only jobs that men should consider.

For example, male nurses and elementary school teachers are in short supply, and the few available are highly recruited and often find jobs quickly. Just as many women should consider careers typically held by men, many men should consider career opportunities among occupations typically held by women. This is particularly true now, since occupations with high percentages of women workers are growing more rapidly than our similar lists for men.

Note that nine of the best jobs employing high percentages of men are in the mechanical field, while 14 of the best jobs with a high percentage of women are in the humanitarian fields—primarily health and social service. This confirms the concern that many educators, counselors, and social advocates have about sexual stereotyping. In many cases, both men and women would be well advised to consider occupations typically held by the opposite gender.

Another thing we noticed is that the 20 best-paying jobs for men have earnings significantly higher than the women's best-paying jobs. You have to go to the 14th position on the men's list before finding a job that earns less than the highest-paying job for women. Ten of the highest-paying jobs for men are in the production field, while 13 of the highest-paying jobs for women are in the humanitarian fields. This indicates that women interested in improving their earnings might want to seriously consider jobs traditionally dominated by men.

Jobs with Highest Percentage of Men

Job	Percent Men
1. Excavation and loading machine operators	100
2. Automotive body and related repairers	99
3. Automotive mechanics	99
4. Bricklayers and stone masons	99
5. Carpenters	99
6. Heat, air conditioning, and refrigeration mechanics and installers	99
7. Mineral extraction workers	99
8. Carpet installers	98
9. Operating engineers	98
10. Paving and surfacing equipment operators	98
11. Plasterers	98
12. Aircraft pilots and flight engineers	97
13. Construction trades helpers	97
14. Construction installation workers	97
15. Electrical and electronic equipment mechanics and installers	97
16. Painters and paperhangers	97
17. Specialty mechanics, installers, and repairers	97
18. Truck drivers light and heavy	96
19. Insulation workers	95
20. Wood machinists	95

   Best Jobs for the 21st Century™ © 1999, JIST Works, Inc., Indianapolis, IN

Best Jobs Employing 70 Percent or More Men

Job	Percent Men	Annual Earnings	Percent Growth	Openings
1. Engineering, mathematical, and natural science managers	72	$65,686	45	37,494
2. Securities and financial services sales workers	70	$59,634	38	40,568
3. Physicians	78	$96,637	21	29,681
4. Lawyers	75	$70,117	19	45,929
5. Computer programmers	71	$48,360	23	58,990
6. General managers and top executives	72	$58,344	15	288,825
7. Electrical and electronics engineers	94	$53,227	29	19,098
8. Correction officers	81	$28,787	32	48,102
9. Construction managers	72	$46,301	18	22,043
10. Civil engineers	92	$49,920	18	15,979
11. Police patrol officers	87	$35,485	18	22,701
12. Chiropractors	79	$63,211	27	2,595
13. Architects	84	$46,883	20	10,404
14. Data processing equipment repairers	82	$29,453	52	8,843
15. Mechanical engineers	95	$48,901	16	14,290
16. Production engineers	90	$54,330	14	19,706
17. Electrical and electronic technicians	85	$33,800	16	31,145
18. Specialty mechanics, installers, and repairers	97	$28,080	18	34,082
19. Veterinarians and veterinary inspectors	79	$52,936	23	2,381
20. Guards	84	$16,640	23	283,077

Best-Paying Jobs Employing 70 Percent or More Men

Job	Percent Men	Average Annual Earnings
1. Physicians	78	$96,637
2. Dentists	79	$85,509
3. Podiatrists	79	$85,134
4. Lawyers	75	$70,117
5. Aircraft pilots and flight engineers	97	$69,098
6. Engineering, mathematical, and natural science managers	72	$65,686
7. Optometrists	79	$64,210
8. Chiropractors	79	$63,211
9. Securities and financial services sales workers	70	$59,634
10. Aerospace engineers	92	$59,634
11. General managers and top executives	72	$58,344
12. Nuclear engineers	92	$57,741
13. Chemical engineers	92	$55,765
14. Production engineers	90	$54,330
15. Electrical and electronics engineers	94	$53,227
16. Veterinarians and veterinary inspectors	79	$52,936
17. Judges and magistrates	75	$51,667
18. Industrial engineers	85	$51,064
19. Civil engineers	92	$49,920
20. Materials engineers	92	$49,566

Best Jobs for the 21st Century™ © 1999, JIST Works, Inc., Indianapolis, IN

Fastest-Growing Jobs Employing 70 Percent or More Men

Job	Percent Men	Percent Growth
1. Data processing equipment repairers	82	52
2. Engineering, mathematical, and natural science managers	72	45
3. Securities and financial services sales workers	70	38
4. Bicycle repairers	93	34
5. Correction officers	81	32
6. Paving and surfacing equipment operators	98	30
7. Electrical and electronics engineers	94	29
8. Chiropractors	79	27
9. Numerical control machine tool operators and tenders	85	27
10. Parking lot attendants	89	26
11. Vehicle washers and equipment cleaners	88	25
12. Camera and photographic equipment repairers	94	24
13. Veterinarians and veterinary inspectors	79	23
14. Computer programmers	71	23
15. Guards	84	23
16. Water and liquid waste treatment plant and system operators	95	23
17. Lawn service managers	76	22
18. Landscape architects	84	21
19. Physicians	78	21
20. Telephone and cable TV line installers and repairers	85	21

Jobs with the Most Annual Openings Employing 70 Percent or More Men

Job	Percent Men	Annual Job Openings
1. Helpers and laborers	87	586,697
2. Truck drivers light and heavy	96	346,612
3. General managers and top executives	72	288,825
4. Guards	84	283,077
5. Freight, stock, and material movers	80	232,034
6. General utility maintenance repairers	93	192,097
7. Carpenters	99	167,617
8. Traffic, shipping, and receiving clerks	72	163,214
9. Blue collar worker supervisors	91	142,666
10. Construction trades helpers	97	137,805
11. Automotive mechanics	99	118,300
12. Vehicle washers and equipment cleaners	88	103,946
13. Industrial truck and tractor operators	93	74,968
14. Painters and paperhangers	97	71,544
15. Computer programmers	71	58,990
16. Machine operators, tenders, setters, and set-up operators	70	55,263
17. Driver sales workers	90	49,513
18. Correction officers	81	48,102
19. Lawyers	75	45,929
20. Securities and financial services sales workers	70	40,568

 Best Jobs for the 21st Century™ © 1999, JIST Works, Inc., Indianapolis, IN

The Best Jobs Lists Based on Levels of Education, Training, and Experience

A very clear relationship exists between education and earnings—the more education you have, the more you are likely to earn. The lists that follow arrange all the jobs that met our criteria for inclusion in this book (see the introduction) by level of education, training, and work experience. These are the levels typically required for a new entrant to begin work in the occupation.

Unlike many of the other lists, we did not include separate lists for highest pay, growth, or number of openings. Instead, we included on one list *all* the occupations in our database that fit into each of the education levels. For example, one list includes all the jobs that require a bachelor's degree, rather than just the ones with the highest ratings. We then arranged these occupations based on their total scores for earnings, growth, and number of openings. We think this list will be more helpful than separate but limited lists.

Once again, our lists use the same categories now used by the U.S. Department of Labor for entry into various occupations. We've provided comments on the lists themselves that define the categories and provide other fascinating details.

Use the Lists to Locate Better Job Opportunities

We used an example on the back cover of a real person who used these lists to identify a job with higher pay but with a similar level of education to the job held now. Doing this can be very helpful, since it will tell you how to leverage your present skills and experience into better paying or more interesting opportunities. As we mentioned in the introduction to the book, doing this could, with just a bit of effort, result in big advances in pay for doing similar work.

You can also use these lists to figure out the possibilities if you were to get additional training, education, or work experience. For example, maybe you are a high school graduate interested in the field of medicine. You will find jobs related to this at most levels of training and education and can consider what jobs you might get, say, if you were to get a year or so of training. You could then work in that field and, later, get more training for an even better paying job in the medical area. Or maybe you are enrolled or considering a four-year college degree. Looking over the lists will help you identify a possible area of study (or eliminate one you were considering).

The list of jobs by education should also help you when planning your education. For example, a job as restaurant cook requires long-term, on-the-job training and pays an average of $16,182 a year. However, a flight attendant requires the same level of education, but the job pays $36,442 a year. This looks like a good reason to be a flight attendant until you note that for every 23 job openings for restaurant cook there is only one job opening for a flight attendant—and a flight attendant must be away from home often.

Caveat Datum, Revisited

We warned you in the introduction to beware the data, and we want to do it again here. The occupational data we used in this book is the most accurate available anywhere, but it has its limitations. For example, a four-year college degree in accounting, finance, or a related area is typically required for entry into the accounting profession. But some people working as accountants don't have such a degree, and others have much more education than the "minimum" required for entry.

In a similar way, people with a bachelor's degree will typically earn considerably more than a high school dropout, but some high school dropouts earn much more than the average for the highest paid occupation in this book. And, as you know, some college grads, particularly recent grads, work in jobs where the pay is much lower than the average for all college grads.

So, as you browse the lists that follow, please use them as a way to be encouraged rather than discouraged. Education and training are very important for success in the labor market of the future, but so is ability, drive, initiative and, yes, luck.

Having said this, we encourage you to get as much education and training as you can. It used to be that you got your schooling and never went back, but this is not a good attitude to have now. You will probably need to continue learning new things throughout your working life. This can be done by going to school, and this is a good thing for many people to do. But there are also many other ways to learn such as workshops, certification programs, employer training, night schools, Internet learning programs, reading related books and magazines, and many others. Upgrading your computer and other technical skills is particularly important in our rapidly changing workplace, and you avoid doing so at your peril.

As one of our grandfathers used to say, "The harder you work, the luckier you get." It was just as true then as it is now.

Best Jobs Requiring Graduate or Professional Degrees

Jobs requiring a degree beyond the bachelor's degree have been combined in this list. The education levels include the following:

First professional degree. This type of degree normally requires a minimum of two years of education beyond the bachelor's degree and frequently requires three years. Physician and attorney are two such occupations.

Doctoral degree. This degree normally requires at least three years of full-time academic work beyond the bachelor's degree. An example is medical scientist.

Master's degree. Completion of a master's degree usually requires one to two years of full-time study beyond the bachelor's degree. An example is urban and regional planner.

There are 21 jobs included in this group. The average earnings for the group are $54,069. The average rate of growth is 16 percent, and the average number of job openings annually is 16,638.

Best Jobs Requiring Graduate or Professional Degrees

Job	Level of Education	Earnings	Percent Growth	Annual Job Openings
1. Physicians	First professional degree	$96,637	21	29,681
2. Lawyers	First professional degree	$70,117	19	45,929
3. Management analysts	Master's degree	$48,194	21	46,026
4. Chiropractors	First professional degree	$63,211	27	2,595
5. College and university faculty	Doctor's degree	$44,800	19	126,584
6. Speech-language pathologists and audiologists	Master's degree	$42,702	51	12,202
7. Medical scientists	Doctor's degree	$56,659	25	3,333
8. Dentists	First professional degree	$85,509	8	5,073
9. Veterinarians and veterinary inspectors	First professional degree	$52,936	23	2,381
10. Biological scientists	Doctor's degree	$41,829	25	7,110
11. Counselors	Master's degree	$36,566	19	27,181
12. Optometrists	First professional degree	$64,210	12	1,630
13. Psychologists	Master's degree	$48,090	8	10,914
14. Podiatrists	First professional degree	$85,134	10	616
15. Clergy	First professional degree	$28,870	13	14,514
16. Operations research analysts	Master's degree	$45,760	8	5,316
17. Physicists and astronomers	Doctor's degree	$62,774	-2	1,073
18. Mathematicians	Doctor's degree	$46,342	9	960
19. Curators, archivists, museum technicians, and restorers	Master's degree	$30,035	15	2,367
20. Urban and regional planners	Master's degree	$40,934	5	3,856
21. Life scientists	Doctor's degree	$44,138	-3	53

Best Jobs Requiring Four-Year Bachelor's Degrees

The bachelor's degree normally requires four to five years of full-time academic work beyond high school. There are 60 jobs on our list that require a bachelor's degree.

The average earnings for the group is $42,245. The average rate of growth is 24 percent, and the average number of openings annually is 30,946.

Best Jobs Requiring Four-Year Bachelor's Degrees

Job	Earnings	Percent Growth	Openings
1. Computer engineers	$54,912	109	34,884
2. Systems analysts	$48,360	103	87,318
3. Physical therapists	$52,811	71	19,122
4. Computer scientists	$48,630	118	26,732
5. Electrical and electronics engineers	$53,227	29	19,098
6. Computer programmers	$48,360	23	58,990
7. Special education teachers	$37,104	59	49,029
8. Secondary school teachers	$36,784	22	168,392
9. Management support workers	$35,339	26	154,129
10. Management support specialists	$38,251	20	124,342
11. Loan officers and counselors	$37,419	28	29,989
12. Occupational therapists	$46,779	66	9,543
13. Writers and editors	$38,355	21	41,449
14. Social workers	$31,221	32	75,554
15. Civil engineers	$49,920	18	15,979
16. Economists	$50,544	19	11,343
17. Production engineers	$54,330	14	19,706
18. Physical scientists	$47,632	28	4,131
19. Physician assistants	$40,414	47	5,090
20. Residential counselors	$19,261	41	38,516
21. Construction managers	$46,301	18	22,043
22. Designers	$30,867	26	42,478

(continued)

Job	Earnings	Percent Growth	Openings
23. Pharmacists	$55,328	13	13,826
24. Mechanical engineers	$48,901	16	14,290
25. Architects	$46,883	20	10,404
26. Public relations specialists and publicity writers	$33,862	27	17,954
27. Insurance claims examiners	$41,142	22	7,281
28. Accountants and auditors	$38,168	12	118,375
29. Personnel, training, and labor relations specialists	$36,566	18	36,049
30. Preschool and kindergarten teachers	$23,216	20	77,151
31. Chemists	$43,306	18	10,572
32. Elementary teachers	$35,280	10	164,163
33. Industrial production managers	$50,710	-3	14,917
34. Therapeutic services and administration	$31,866	67	4,767
35. Director of religious education and activities	$24,170	36	10,781
36. Aerospace engineers	$59,634	8	3,771
37. Chemical engineers	$55,765	15	1,434
38. Recreation workers	$17,139	22	29,880
39. Interior designers	$32,094	28	9,238
40. Tutors and instructors	$26,000	15	149,064
41. Industrial engineers	$51,064	14	3,554
42. Geologists, geophysicists, and oceanographers	$52,083	15	1,687
43. Property and real estate managers	$33,114	16	29,483
44. Landscape architects	$38,875	21	1,593
45. Actuaries	$66,352	0	1,165
46. Nuclear engineers	$57,741	5	715
47. Budget analysts	$42,058	12	8,204
48. Credit analysts	$36,962	16	5,454
49. Clinical laboratory technologists	$30,805	15	23,944
50. Petroleum engineers	$68,224	-14	549

(continued)

(continued)

Job	Earnings	Percent Growth	Openings
51. Employment interviewers	$35,090	16	10,430
52. Agricultural and food scientists	$35,942	20	2,016
53. Foresters and conservation scientists	$36,650	17	3,200
54. Materials engineers	$49,566	7	933
55. Recreational therapists	$26,770	21	3,414
56. Dietitians and nutritionists	$32,406	18	4,079
57. Farm and home management advisors	$48,506	-38	3,078
58. Meteorologists	$47,674	8	421
59. Mining engineers	$49,837	-13	130
60. Statisticians	$47,507	1	937

Best Jobs Requiring Bachelor's Degrees Plus Experience

Jobs in this category are often management-related and require some experience in a related nonmanagerial position.

The average earnings for the 12 jobs in this group are $49,793. The average rate of growth is 19 percent, and the average number of job openings annually is 65,285.

Best Jobs Requiring Bachelor's Degrees Plus Experience

Job	Earnings	Percent Growth	Openings
1. Engineering, mathematical, and natural science managers	$65,686	45	37,494
2. General managers and top executives	$58,344	15	288,825
3. Marketing, advertising, and public relations managers	$53,602	29	54,600
4. Financial managers	$54,392	18	74,297
5. Service managers	$48,339	21	171,229
6. Artists and commercial artists	$33,114	28	46,893
7. Education administrators	$52,437	12	39,333
8. Personnel, training, and labor relations managers	$45,989	18	20,995
9. Communication, transportation, and utilities managers	$48,818	15	10,840
10. Administrative services managers	$44,200	11	24,605
11. Judges and magistrates	$51,667	2	3,558
12. Purchasing managers	$40,934	8	10,746

Best Jobs Requiring Two-Year Associate's Degrees

It usually requires two years of full-time academic work beyond high school to obtain this degree.

There are 12 jobs on our list that require an associate's degree, and their average earnings is $33,199. The average rate of growth is 31 percent, and the average number of job openings annually is 29,324.

Best Jobs Requiring Two-Year Associate's Degrees

Job	Earnings	Percent Growth	Openings
1. Dental hygienists	$42,432	48	165,362
2. Paralegals	$32,032	68	45,719
3. Radiologic technologists	$31,970	29	31,145
4. Respiratory therapists	$32,781	46	12,865
5. Registered nurses	$40,310	21	9,453
6. Health care support specialists	$31,054	24	23,270
7. Science and mathematics technicians	$34,466	13	18,373
8. Electrical and electronic technicians	$33,800	15	13,258
9. Cardiology technologists	$33,696	35	866
10. Medical records technicians	$20,488	51	8,181
11. Nuclear medicine technologists	$38,605	13	1,686
12. Law clerks	$26,749	12	21,705

Best Jobs Requiring Postsecondary Vocational Training

This requirement can vary from training that involves a few months but is usually less than one year. In a few instances, as many as four years of training may be required.

There are 16 jobs on the list for this group. The average earnings for the group are $27,104, average rate of growth is 23 percent, and the average number of job openings annually is 52,874.

Best Jobs Requiring Postsecondary Vocational Training

Job	Earnings	Percent Growth	Openings
1. Data processing equipment repairers	$29,453	52	41,554
2. Surgical technologists	$25,002	32	433,901
3. Dancers and choreographers	$28,018	28	49,667
4. Commercial and industrial electronic equipment repairers	$33,800	12	81,622
5. Aircraft mechanics	$35,422	14	18,841
6. Licensed practical nurses	$26,021	21	39,871
7. Emergency medical technicians	$21,362	45	9,140
8. Broadcast technicians	$31,034	15	6,642
9. Legal secretaries	$29,349	13	38,234
10. Secretaries	$23,130	0	90,496
11. Travel agents	$21,965	24	8,973
12. Medical secretaries	$21,757	32	8,843
13. Electrical and electronic equipment mechanics and installers	$29,994	13	4,727
14. Real estate agents	$45,219	6	4,283
15. Manicurists	$15,392	45	5,893
16. Hairdressers, hairstylists, and cosmetologists	$16,744	10	3,301

Best Jobs Requiring Work Experience in a Related Job

This type of job requires a worker to have experience in a related occupation. An example is police detectives who are selected based on their experience as police patrol officers

Some of these jobs will require special training or education (but not a bachelor's degree) in order to qualify for the related jobs. There are 17 jobs on the list for this group, and their average earnings are $33,455. The average rate of growth is 14 percent, and the average number of job openings annually is 67,956.

Best Jobs Requiring Work Experience in a Related Job

Job	Earnings	Percent Growth	Openings
1. Vocational education and training instructors	$33,800	23	143,806
2. Construction and building inspectors	$35,381	15	305,545
3. Clerical supervisors and managers	$31,013	19	279,051
4. Real estate appraisers	$38,334	12	82,354
5. Police detectives	$41,267	8	68,207
6. Police and detective supervisors	$44,928	-1	81,219
7. Nursery and greenhouse managers	$26,104	19	142,666
8. Fire fighting and prevention supervisors	$40,981	1	5,878
9. Ship captains and pilots	$40,810	-2	23,870
10. Adult education instructors	$27,373	21	4,637
11. Food service and lodging managers	$26,562	29	2,575
12. Cost estimators	$39,894	16	1,049
13. Blue collar worker supervisors	$35,110	3	7,984
14. Personal service workers	$17,202	31	1,525
15. Aircraft assemblers	$31,346	10	3,216
16. Marketing and sales worker supervisors	$32,718	11	1,203
17. Lawn service managers	$25,917	22	470

Best Jobs Requiring Long-Term, On-the-Job Training

This type of training requires more than 12 months of on-the-job training or combined work experience and formal classroom instruction. This includes occupations that use formal apprenticeships that may take up to four years. It also includes intensive occupation-specific, employer-sponsored training like police academies.

Furthermore, it includes occupations that require natural talent that must be developed over many years. There are 32 jobs in this group. The average earnings for the group are $31,824. The average rate of growth is 19 percent, and the average number of job openings annually is 37,885.

Best Jobs Requiring Long-Term, On-the-Job Training

Job	Earnings	Percent Growth	Openings
1. Securities and financial services sales workers	$59,634	38	40,568
2. Musicians	$30,888	33	49,350
3. Flight attendants	$36,442	35	9,844
4. Insurance adjusters, examiners, and investigators	$38,230	23	21,662
5. Correction officers	$28,787	32	48,102
6. Police patrol officers	$35,485	18	22,701
7. Producers, directors, actors, and entertainers	$35,339	24	17,112
8. Bricklayers and stone masons	$36,171	14	26,880
9. Aircraft pilots and flight engineers	$69,098	14	6,641
10. General utility maintenance repairers	$23,234	18	192,097
11. Specialty mechanics, installers, and repairers	$28,080	18	34,082
12. Heat, air conditioning, and refrigeration mechanics and installers	$29,162	17	22,587
13. Carpenters	$30,139	6	167,617
14. Desktop publishing workers	$27,706	74	4,117
15. Restaurant cooks	$16,182	15	224,725
16. Athletes, coaches, and umpires	$28,995	16	8,407
17. Water and liquid waste treatment plant and system operators	$28,766	23	5,419
18. Automotive mechanics	$27,643	12	118,300
19. Automotive body and related repairers	$28,184	13	28,792
20. Telephone and cable TV line installers and repairers	$31,533	21	465
21. Food and beverage production workers	$22,214	29	6,257
22. Elevator installers and repairers	$45,843	8	2,695
23. Plasterers	$29,806	13	4,579
24. Air traffic controllers and airplane dispatchers	$45,739	0	3,310
25. Plant and system operators	$23,566	15	4,753
26. Electromedical and biomedical equipment repairers	$32,718	12	1,427
27. Institution or cafeteria cooks	$16,078	5	120,220
28. Dispensing opticians	$22,547	14	7,780
29. Power distributors and dispatchers	$45,906	-4	756
30. Office machine and cash register servicers	$24,898	18	1,267
31. Furniture finishers	$19,635	12	7,479
32. Wood machinists	$19,718	14	2,342

Best Jobs Requiring Moderate Term, On-the-Job Training

Occupations that require this type of training can be performed adequately after a one month to one year of combined on-the-job and informal training. Typically workers observe experienced workers perform tasks and are gradually moved into progressively more difficult assignments.

There are 48 jobs in this group. The average earnings for the group are $24,255. The average rate of growth is 25 percent, and the average number of job openings annually is 44,204.

Best Jobs Requiring Moderate-Term, On-the-Job Training

Job	Earnings	Percent Growth	Openings
1. Sales specialists and support workers	$24,502	23	765,025
2. Sports instructors and coaches	$22,901	41	82,035
3. Insulation workers	$27,373	19	22,457
4. Physical and corrective therapy assistants	$23,587	79	26,479
5. Painters and paperhangers	$26,062	15	71,544
6. Numerical control machine tool operators and tenders	$26,645	27	12,786
7. Dental assistants	$21,570	38	45,487
8. Occupational therapy assistants and aides	$28,683	69	3,684
9. Paving and surfacing equipment operators	$25,334	30	13,012
10. Human services workers	$21,112	55	42,907
11. Medical assistants	$19,864	74	34,511
12. Transportation equipment painters	$30,181	19	7,029
13. Mineral extraction workers	$27,082	12	27,481
14. Operating engineers	$35,027	14	12,085
15. Bread and pastry bakers	$17,222	26	61,382
16. Electroneurodiagnostic technologists	$30,992	24	818
17. Private detectives	$24,648	19	17,441
18. Bus drivers	$24,461	15	31,905

(continued)

(continued)

Job	Earnings	Percent Growth	Openings
19. Transportation and material moving operators	$24,794	15	22,268
20. Insurance claims clerks	$23,795	26	15,014
21. Camera and photographic equipment repairers	$29,182	24	1,158
22. Machine operators, tenders, setters, and set-up operators	$24,731	11	55,263
23. Dispatchers	$26,562	11	19,239
24. Metal and plastic machine setters and operators	$24,107	16	20,091
25. Construction installation workers	$25,626	13	19,001
26. Photographers	$23,379	17	20,243
27. Packaging and filling machine operators	$19,698	16	74,811
28. Pharmacy technicians	$31,054	11	9,841
29. Pest controllers and assistants	$21,507	22	16,835
30. Carpet installers	$29,973	12	6,420
31. Laundry and drycleaning machine operators	$14,581	22	30,822
32. Combination machine tool setters and operators	$22,568	18	16,451
33. Bookkeeping, accounting, and auditing clerks	$22,776	-5	327,125
34. Typists and word processors	$21,403	0	120,405
35. Excavation and loading machine operators	$28,558	11	4,626
36. Locksmiths and safe repairers	$26,270	15	2,054
37. Television and movie camera operators	$25,792	15	2,440
38. Plastic molding machine operators and setters	$19,760	18	15,111
39. Bicycle repairers	$15,766	34	5,525
40. Sprayers applicators	$20,509	21	5,889
41. Title examiners and searchers	$26,000	13	3,107
42. Printing related setters and operators	$25,314	14	1,499
43. Electronic semiconductor processors	$24,336	12	3,801
44. Bindery workers	$21,154	14	5,529
45. Metal fabricators	$23,379	11	5,701
46. Extruding and forming machine operators	$24,253	10	3,021
47. Electrolytic plating machine setters and operators	$21,278	10	6,553
48. Textile bleaching and dyeing machine operators	$18,886	10	3,881

Best Jobs Requiring Short-Term, On-the-Job Training

It is possible to work in these occupations and achieve an average level of performance within a few days or weeks through on-the-job training. There are 61 jobs in this group.

The average earnings for the group are $22,422. The average rate of growth is 46 percent, and the average number of job openings annually is 80,643.

Best Jobs Requiring Short Term, On-the-Job Training

Job	Earnings	Percent Growth	Openings
1. Adjustment clerks	$22,422	46	80,643
2. Bill and account collectors	$22,402	42	68,308
3. Receptionists and information clerks	$18,075	30	336,852
4. Truck drivers light and heavy	$24,274	15	346,612
5. Teacher aides and educational assistants	$15,974	38	353,119
6. Customer service representatives	$27,061	36	29,751
7. Home health aides	$16,286	77	156,127
8. Helpers and laborers	$19,178	16	586,697
9. Guards	$16,640	23	283,077
10. Nursing aides, orderlies, and attendants	$16,120	25	304,868
11. Clerical support workers	$21,757	19	105,566
12. Child care workers	$13,998	36	328,078
13. General office clerks	$19,282	7	661,333
14. Retail salespersons	$17,181	10	1,236,273
15. Billing, cost, and rate clerks	$22,027	17	67,231
16. Correspondence clerks	$22,110	31	4,614
17. Industrial truck and tractor operators	$24,565	12	74,968
18. Brokerage clerks	$28,766	19	16,901
19. Library technical assistants	$20,946	28	10,919
20. Hand packers and packagers	$14,560	23	271,086
21. Stock clerks	$19,344	3	346,772
22. Traffic, shipping, and receiving clerks	$21,882	9	163,214
23. Amusement and recreation attendants	$13,354	48	130,390
24. Short order and fast food cooks	$14,414	22	237,301
25. Cashiers	$13,686	17	1,109,571
26. Food preparation workers	$13,770	19	573,079

(continued)

(continued)

Job	Earnings	Percent Growth	Openings
27. Freight, stock, and material movers	$19,302	5	232,034
28. Specialty food workers	$15,038	27	82,637
29. Construction trades helpers	$19,864	9	137,805
30. Personal and home care aides	$13,832	85	58,134
31. Janitors, cleaners, and maids	$16,432	4	818,941
32. Vehicle washers and equipment cleaners	$14,685	25	103,946
33. Counter and rental clerks	$14,581	23	129,889
34. Pruners	$22,880	16	9,030
35. Ski patrol workers and life guards	$18,678	17	53,969
36. Specialty records clerks	$22,568	10	34,193
37. Driver sales workers	$20,342	12	49,513
38. Food counter and fountain workers	$12,293	14	727,389
39. Hand workers	$17,826	1	267,301
40. Postal mail carriers	$28,371	11	6,160
41. Ambulance drivers and attendants	$16,474	37	3,864
42. Loan and credit clerks	$22,090	10	34,251
43. Gardeners and groundskeepers	$18,491	0	188,023
44. Wholesale and retail sales order fillers	$18,886	12	38,294
45. Interviewing clerks	$18,075	18	19,262
46. Hotel desk clerks	$14,643	21	51,216
47. Veterinary assistants	$15,787	28	7,248
48. Waiters and waitresses	$11,690	11	714,482
49. Library assistants and bookmobile drivers	$17,472	15	32,759
50. Animal caretakers	$15,496	21	31,339
51. Meat, poultry, and fish cutters and trimmers	$15,309	23	26,398
52. Solderers and brazers	$16,910	21	4,882
53. Parking lot attendants	$14,352	26	12,214
54. Bank tellers	$16,536	1	109,086
55. Ushers, lobby attendants, and ticket takers	$12,230	28	25,394
56. Dining room, cafeteria, and bar helpers	$12,210	14	132,882
57. Messengers	$17,118	11	25,352
58. Painting, coating, and decorating workers	$18,928	10	5,584
59. Farm workers	$14,248	-9	217,762
60. Private household child care workers	$13,998	-9	146,546
61. Bartenders	$13,395	0	103,325

The Best Jobs Lists Based on Interests

These lists organize occupations into groupings based on interests. The system using these Interest Areas was developed by the U.S. Department of Labor as an intuitive way to assist in career exploration. The system is called the *Guide for Occupational Exploration*, or GOE. Additional information on the GOE system is provided following the lists.

Within each interest grouping, occupations are arranged in order of their total scores based on earnings, pay, and number of openings. These are the only lists in Section 1 to include all 279 occupations described in Section 2. The lists also provide a useful way to identify jobs that are related to ones you have had in the past or that require similar skills to those you want to use in the future.

Best Artistic Jobs: These occupations involve an interest in the creative expression of feelings or ideas.

Job	Annual Earnings	Percent Growth	Annual Job Openings
1. Musicians	$30,888	33	49,350
2. Artists and commercial artists	$33,114	28	46,893
3. Writers and editors	$38,355	21	41,449
4. Designers	$30,867	26	42,478
5. Producers, directors, actors, and entertainers	$35,339	24	17,112
6. Interior designers	$32,094	28	9,238
7. Desktop publishing workers	$27,706	74	4,117
8. Dancers and choreographers	$28,018	28	4,283
9. Photographers	$23,379	17	20,243
10. Television and movie camera operators	$25,792	15	2,440

Best Scientific Jobs: These occupations involve an interest in discovering, collecting, and analyzing information about the natural world, and in applying scientific research findings to problems in medicine, the life sciences, and the natural sciences.

Job	Annual Earnings	Percent Growth	Annual Job Openings
1. Physicians	$96,637	21	29,681
2. Speech-language pathologists and audiologists	$42,702	51	12,202
3. Chiropractors	$63,211	27	2,595
4. Medical scientists	$56,659	25	3,333
5. Physical scientists	$47,632	28	4,131
6. Pharmacists	$55,328	13	13,826
7. Veterinarians and veterinary inspectors	$52,936	23	2,381
8. Chemists	$43,306	18	10,572
9. Biological scientists	$41,829	25	7,110
10. Dentists	$85,509	8	5,073
11. Veterinary assistants	$15,787	28	7,248
12. Clinical laboratory technologists	$30,805	15	23,944
13. Geologists, geophysicists, and oceanographers	$52,083	15	1,687
14. Optometrists	$64,210	12	1,630
15. Science and mathematics technicians	$34,466	13	23,270
16. Foresters and conservation scientists	$36,650	17	3,200
17. Podiatrists	$85,134	10	616
18. Agricultural and food scientists	$35,942	20	2,016
19. Physicists and astronomers	$62,774	-2	1,073
20. Mathematicians	$46,342	9	960
21. Nuclear medicine technologists	$38,605	13	866
22. Meteorologists	$47,674	8	421
23. Life scientists	$44,138	-3	53

Best Plant and Animal Jobs: These occupations involve an interest in working with plants and animals, usually outdoors.

Job	Annual Earnings	Percent Growth	Annual Job Openings
1. Pest controllers and assistants	$21,507	22	16,835
2. Lawn service managers	$25,917	22	4,637
3. Animal caretakers	$15,496	21	31,339
4. Pruners	$22,880	16	9,030
5. Sprayers applicators	$20,509	21	5,889
6. Nursery and greenhouse managers	$26,104	19	2,575
7. Gardeners and groundskeepers	$18,491	0	188,023
8. Farm workers	$14,248	-9	217,762

Best Jobs for the 21st Century™ © 1999, JIST Works, Inc., Indianapolis, IN

Best Protective/Law Enforcement Jobs: These occupations involve an interest in using authority to protect people and property.

Job	Annual Earnings	Percent Growth	Annual Job Openings
1. Correction officers	$28,787	32	48,102
2. Guards	$16,640	23	283,077
3. Police patrol officers	$35,485	18	22,701
4. Ski patrol workers and lifeguards	$18,678	17	53,969
5. Private detectives	$24,648	19	17,441
6. Police detectives	$41,267	8	3,216
7. Police and detective supervisors	$44,928	-1	1,203
8. Fire fighting and prevention supervisors	$40,981	1	470

Best Mechanical Jobs: These occupations involve an interest in applying mechanical principles to practical situations by use of machines or hand tools.

Job	Annual Earnings	Percent Growth	Annual Job Openings
1. Engineering, mathematical, and natural science managers	$65,686	45	37,494
2. Computer engineers	$54,912	109	34,884
3. Electrical and electronics engineers	$53,227	29	19,098
4. Civil engineers	$49,920	18	15,979
5. Construction managers	$46,301	18	22,043
6. Architects	$46,883	20	10,404
7. Cost estimators	$39,894	16	23,870
8. Mechanical engineers	$48,901	16	14,290
9. Production engineers	$54,330	14	19,706
10. Electrical and electronic technicians	$33,800	15	31,145
11. Data processing equipment repairers	$29,453	52	8,843
12. Aircraft pilots and flight engineers	$69,098	14	6,641
13. Specialty mechanics, installers, and repairers	$28,080	18	34,082
14. Bricklayers and stone masons	$36,171	14	26,880
15. General utility maintenance repairers	$23,234	18	192,097
16. Heat, air conditioning, and refrigeration mechanics and installers	$29,162	17	22,587
17. Insulation workers	$27,373	19	22,457
18. Short order and fast food cooks	$14,414	22	237,301
19. Bread and pastry bakers	$17,222	26	61,382
20. Paving and surfacing equipment operators	$25,334	30	13,012
21. Transportation equipment painters	$30,181	19	7,029
22. Helpers and laborers	$19,178	16	586,697
23. Truck drivers light and heavy	$24,274	15	346,612
24. Food preparation workers	$13,770	19	573,079
25. Vehicle washers and equipment cleaners	$14,685	25	103,946
26. Painters and paperhangers	$26,062	15	71,544
27. Landscape architects	$38,875	21	1,593

(continued)

Best Jobs for the 21st Century™ © 1999, JIST Works, Inc., Indianapolis, IN

(continued)

Job	Annual Earnings	Percent Growth	Annual Job Openings
28. Chemical engineers	$55,765	15	1,434
29. Construction and building inspectors	$35,381	15	5,878
30. Water and liquid waste treatment plant and system operators	$28,766	23	5,419
31. Blue collar worker supervisors	$35,110	3	142,666
32. Operating engineers	$35,027	14	12,085
33. Industrial engineers	$51,064	14	3,554
34. Carpenters	$30,139	6	167,617
35. Automotive mechanics	$27,643	12	118,300
36. Aircraft mechanics	$35,422	14	5,893
37. Restaurant cooks	$16,182	15	224,725
38. Automotive body and related repairers	$28,184	13	28,792
39. Transportation and material moving operators	$24,794	15	22,268
40. Broadcast technicians	$31,034	15	4,727
41. Industrial production managers	$50,710	-3	14,917
42. Camera and photographic equipment repairers	$29,182	24	1,158
43. Commercial and industrial electronic equipment repairers	$33,800	12	9,140
44. Telephone and cable TV line installers and repairers	$31,533	21	465
45. Aerospace engineers	$59,634	8	3,771
46. Industrial truck and tractor operators	$24,565	12	74,068
47. Mineral extraction workers	$27,082	12	27,481
48. Pharmacy technicians	$31,054	11	9,841
49. Bicycle repairers	$15,766	34	5,525
50. Ambulance drivers and attendants	$16,474	37	3,864
51. Construction installation workers	$25,626	13	19,001
52. Construction trades helpers	$19,864	9	137,805
53. Carpet installers	$29,973	12	6,420
54. Stock clerks	$19,344	3	346,772
55. Freight, stock, and material movers	$19,302	5	232,034
56. Janitors, cleaners, and maids	$16,432	4	818,941
57. Plasterers	$29,806	13	4,579

(continued)

Job	Annual Earnings	Percent Growth	Annual Job Openings
58. Wholesale and retail sales order fillers	$18,886	12	38,294
59. Electrical and electronic equipment mechanics and installers	$29,994	13	3,301
60. Elevator installers and repairers	$45,843	8	2,695
61. Locksmiths and safe repairers	$26,270	15	2,054
62. Office machine and cash register servicers	$24,898	18	1,267
63. Nuclear engineers	$57,741	5	715
64. Plant and system operators	$23,566	15	4,753
65. Dispensing opticians	$22,547	14	7,780
66. Electromedical and biomedical equipment repairers	$32,718	12	1,427
67. Materials engineers	$49,566	7	933
68. Air traffic controllers and airplane dispatchers	$45,739	0	3,310
69. Institution or cafeteria cooks	$16,078	5	120,220
70. Petroleum engineers	$68,224	-14	549
71. Bindery workers	$21,154	14	5,529
72. Excavation and loading machine operators	$28,558	11	4,626
73. Printing related setters and operators	$25,314	14	1,499
74. Furniture finishers	$19,635	12	7,479
75. Ship captains and pilots	$40,810	-2	1,049
76. Power distributors and dispatchers	$45,906	-4	756
77. Mining engineers	$49,837	-13	130
78. Metal fabricators	$23,379	11	5,701
79. Wood machinists	$19,718	14	2,342

Best Industrial Jobs: These occupations involve an interest in repetitive, concrete, organized activities done in a factory setting.

Job	Annual Earnings	Percent Growth	Annual Job Openings
1. Numerical control machine tool operators and tenders	$26,645	27	12,786
2. Machine operators, tenders, setters, and set-up operators	$24,731	11	55,263
3. Food and beverage production workers	$22,214	29	6,257
4. Metal and plastic machine setters and operators	$24,107	16	20,091
5. Combination machine tool setters and operators	$22,568	18	16,451
6. Hand packers and packagers	$14,560	23	271,086
7. Packaging and filling machine operators	$19,698	16	74,811
8. Meat, poultry, and fish cutters and trimmers	$15,309	23	26,398
9. Laundry and drycleaning machine operators	$14,581	22	30,822
10. Plastic molding machine operators and setters	$19,760	18	15,111
11. Electronic semiconductor processors	$24,336	12	3,801
12. Aircraft assemblers	$31,346	10	1,525
13. Hand workers	$17,826	1	267,301
14. Electrolytic plating machine setters and operators	$21,278	10	6,553
15. Solderers and brazers	$16,910	21	4,882
16. Extruding and forming machine operators	$24,253	10	3,021
17. Painting, coating, and decorating workers	$18,928	10	5,584
18. Textile bleaching and dyeing machine operators	$18,886	10	3,881

Best Business Detail Jobs: These occupations involve an interest in organized, clearly defined activities requiring accuracy and attention to details, primarily in an office setting.

Job	Annual Earnings	Percent Growth	Annual Job Openings
1. Clerical supervisors and managers	$31,013	19	143,806
2. Adjustment clerks	$22,422	46	80,643
3. Bill and account collectors	$22,402	42	68,308
4. Customer service representatives	$27,061	36	29,751
5. Receptionists and information clerks	$18,075	30	336,852
6. Legal secretaries	$29,349	13	49,667
7. Insurance claims examiners	$41,142	22	7,281
8. Medical secretaries	$21,757	32	39,871
9. Brokerage clerks	$28,766	19	16,901
10. Secretaries	$23,130	0	433,901
11. Insurance claims clerks	$23,795	26	15,014
12. Clerical support workers	$21,757	19	105,566
13. Counter and rental clerks	$14,581	23	129,889
14. Billing, cost, and rate clerks	$22,027	17	67,231
15. Bookkeeping, accounting, and auditing clerks	$22,776	-5	327,125
16. Cashiers	$13,686	17	1,109,571
17. Medical records technicians	$20,488	51	13,258
18. Traffic, shipping, and receiving clerks	$21,882	9	163,214
19. Correspondence clerks	$22,110	31	4,614
20. General office clerks	$19,282	7	661,333
21. Dispatchers	$26,562	11	19,239
22. Hotel desk clerks	$14,643	21	51,216
23. Law clerks	$26,749	12	8,181
24. Specialty records clerks	$22,568	10	34,193
25. Postal mail carriers	$28,371	11	6,160
26. Loan and credit clerks	$22,090	10	34,251
27. Title examiners and searchers	$26,000	13	3,107
28. Typists and word processors	$21,403	0	120,405
29. Interviewing clerks	$18,075	18	19,262
30. Library assistants and bookmobile drivers	$17,472	15	32,759
31. Bank tellers	$16,536	1	109,086
32. Messengers	$17,118	11	25,352

Best Selling Jobs: These occupations involve an interest in bringing others to a particular point of view by personal persuasion, using sales and promotional techniques.

Job	Annual Earnings	Percent Growth	Annual Job Openings
1. Securities and financial services sales workers	$59,634	38	40,568
2. Sales specialists and support workers	$24,502	23	765,025
3. Retail salespersons	$17,181	10	1,236,273
4. Driver sales workers	$20,342	12	49,513
5. Real estate agents	$45,219	6	41,554
6. Travel agents	$21,965	24	38,234

Best Accommodating/Personal Service Jobs: These
occupations involve an interest in catering to the wishes and needs of others, usually on a one-to-one basis.

Job	Annual Earnings	Percent Growth	Annual Job Openings
1. Personal service workers	$17,202	31	279,051
2. Amusement and recreation attendants	$13,354	48	130,390
3. Flight attendants	$36,442	35	9,844
4. Bus drivers	$24,461	15	31,905
5. Specialty food workers	$15,038	27	82,637
6. Food counter and fountain workers	$12,293	14	727,389
7. Recreation workers	$17,139	22	29,880
8. Manicurists	$15,392	45	8,973
9. Hairdressers, hairstylists, and cosmetologists	$16,744	10	90,496
10. Parking lot attendants	$14,352	26	12,214
11. Waiters and waitresses	$11,690	11	714,482
12. Dining room, cafeteria, and bar helpers	$12,210	14	132,882
13. Ushers, lobby attendants, and ticket takers	$12,230	28	25,394
14. Bartenders	$13,395	0	103,325

Best Jobs for the 21st Century™ © 1999, JIST Works, Inc., Indianapolis, IN

Best Humanitarian/Helping Others Jobs: These occupations involve an interest in helping others with their mental, spiritual, social, physical, or vocational needs.

Job	Annual Earnings	Percent Growth	Annual Job Openings
1. Physical therapists	$52,811	71	19,122
2. Special education teachers	$37,104	59	49,029
3. Registered nurses	$40,310	21	165,362
4. Dental hygienists	$42,432	48	18,373
5. Occupational therapists	$46,779	66	9,543
6. Home health aides	$16,286	77	156,127
7. Social workers	$31,221	32	75,554
8. Physical and corrective therapy assistants	$23,587	79	26,479
9. Personal and home care aides	$13,832	85	58,134
10. Physician assistants	$40,414	47	5,090
11. Medical assistants	$19,864	74	34,511
12. Therapeutic services and administration	$31,866	67	4,767
13. Respiratory therapists	$32,781	46	9,453
14. Child care workers	$13,998	36	328,078
15. Health care support specialists	$31,054	24	45,719
16. Human services workers	$21,112	55	42,907
17. Preschool and kindergarten teachers	$30,181	20	77,151
18. Dental assistants	$21,570	38	45,487
19. Counselors	$30,566	19	27,181
20. Occupational therapy assistants and aides	$28,683	69	3,684
21. Nursing aides, orderlies, and attendants	$16,120	25	304,868
22. Licensed practical nurses	$26,021	21	81,622
23. Radiologic technologists	$31,970	29	12,865
24. Emergency medical technicians	$21,362	45	18,841
25. Cardiology technologists	$33,696	35	1,686
26. Director of religious education and activities	$24,170	36	10,781
27. Surgical technologists	$25,002	32	6,642
28. Private household child care workers	$13,998	-9	146,546
29. Clergy	$28,870	13	14,514
30. Electroneurodiagnostic technologists	$30,992	24	818
31. Recreational therapists	$26,770	21	3,414

Best Leading and Influencing Jobs: These occupations involve an interest in leading and influencing others by using high-level verbal or numerical abilities.

Job	Annual Earnings	Percent Growth	Annual Job Openings
1. Systems analysts	$48,360	103	87,318
2. Marketing, advertising, and public relations managers	$53,602	29	54,600
3. Service managers	$48,339	21	171,229
4. General managers and top executives	$58,344	15	288,825
5. Computer scientists	$48,630	118	26,732
6. Lawyers	$70,117	19	45,929
7. Financial managers	$54,392	18	74,297
8. Computer programmers	$48,360	23	58,990
9. Secondary school teachers	$36,784	22	168,392
10. Management support workers	$35,339	26	154,129
11. College and university faculty	$44,800	19	126,584
12. Management analysts	$48,194	21	46,026
13. Teacher aides and educational assistants	$15,974	38	353,119
14. Management support specialists	$38,251	20	124,342
15. Education administrators	$52,437	12	39,333
16. Loan officers and counselors	$37,419	28	29,989
17. Economists	$50,544	19	11,343
18. Vocational education and training instructors	$33,800	23	82,354
19. Food service and lodging managers	$26,562	29	68,207
20. Insurance adjusters, examiners, and investigators	$38,230	23	21,662
21. Paralegals	$32,032	68	21,705
22. Personnel, training, and labor relations managers	$45,989	18	20,995
23. Residential counselors	$19,261	41	38,516
24. Adult education instructors	$27,373	21	81,219

(continued)

(continued)

Job	Annual Earnings	Percent Growth	Annual Job Openings
25. Communication, transportation, and utilities managers	$48,818	15	10,840
26. Accountants and auditors	$38,168	12	118,375
27. Public relations specialists and publicity writers	$33,862	27	17,954
28. Marketing and sales worker supervisors	$32,718	11	305,545
29. Elementary teachers	$35,280	10	164,163
30. Personnel, training, and labor relations specialists	$36,566	18	36,049
31. Tutors and instructors	$26,000	15	149,064
32. Administrative services managers	$44,200	11	24,605
33. Library technical assistants	$20,946	28	10,919
34. Psychologists	$48,090	8	10,914
35. Property and real estate managers	$33,114	16	29,483
36. Budget analysts	$42,058	12	8,204
37. Judges and magistrates	$51,667	2	3,558
38. Actuaries	$66,352	0	1,165
39. Credit analysts	$36,962	16	5,454
40. Employment interviewers	$35,090	16	10,430
41. Real estate appraisers	$38,334	12	7,984
42. Purchasing managers	$40,934	8	10,746
43. Operations research analysts	$45,760	8	5,316
44. Farm and home management advisors	$48,506	-38	3,078
45. Dietitians and nutritionists	$32,406	18	4,079
46. Urban and regional planners	$40,934	5	3,856
47. Statisticians	$47,507	1	937
48. Curators, archivists, museum technicians, and restorers	$30,035	15	2,367

Best Physical Performing/ Sports Jobs: These occupations involve an interest in physical activities performed before an audience.

Job	Annual Earnings	Percent Growth	Annual Job Openings
1. Sports instructors and coaches	$22,901	41	82,035
2. Athletes, coaches, and umpires	$28,995	16	8,407

Career Planning Guide to Selecting Occupations Based on Interests

> *The lists of best jobs based on interests give details on occupations in similar interest areas. The information that follows provides more information on the "system" of interests that those lists use.*
>
> *You can use the information to help you identify career interests. While it is not a career assessment test, it provides data that can help you clarify your career goals. This material is particularly helpful if you are considering new career options, getting additional training or education, looking to advance in your current career area, or seeking new job targets in a job search.*

To meet the needs of career counselors and others, the U.S. Department of Labor developed a system to organize jobs into major interest areas. This is a useful and intuitive way for people to explore career options. The system was used in a book published by the Department of Labor titled the *Guide for Occupational Exploration* (GOE). Since then, occupational reference books, career assessment tests, and career information software have used the GOE system for organizing occupations. You may use some of these GOE-based materials and, even if you don't, the information in this section can help you clarify your career objectives.

The GOE organizes all jobs into just 12 major Interest Areas. These 12 Interest Areas are then divided into more specialized subgroups. Look over the 12 descriptions for the GOE Interest Areas that follow. As you do, decide which areas seem most interesting to you.

1. **Artistic:** *An interest in the creative expression of feelings or ideas.* You can satisfy this interest in several of the creative or performing arts. For example, if you enjoy literature, writing or editing might appeal to you. If you prefer work in the performing arts, you could direct or perform in drama, music, or dance. If you especially enjoy the visual arts, you could become a critic in painting, sculpture, or ceramics. You may prefer to use your hands to create or decorate products. Or you may like to model clothes or develop stage sets for plays.

2. **Scientific:** *An interest in discovering, collecting, and analyzing information about the natural world, and in applying scientific research findings to problems in medicine, the life sciences, and the natural sciences.* You can satisfy this interest by working with the knowledge and processes of the sciences. You may enjoy researching and developing new knowledge in mathematics, or perhaps solving problems in the physical or life sciences would appeal to you. You may wish to study medicine and help people or animals. If you want to work with scientific equipment and procedures, you could seek a job in a research or testing laboratory.

3. **Plants and Animals:** *An interest in working with plants and animals, usually outdoors.* You can satisfy this interest by working in farming, forestry, fishing, or related fields. You may like doing physical work outdoors, such as on a farm. You may enjoy animals; perhaps training or taking care of animals would appeal to you. If you have management ability, you could own, operate, or manage a farm or related business.

4. **Protective/Law Enforcement:** *An interest in using authority to protect people and property.* You can satisfy this interest by working in law enforcement, fire fighting, and related fields. For example, if you enjoy mental challenge and intrigue, you could investigate crimes or fires for a living. You may prefer to fight fires and respond to other emergencies. Or, if you want more routine work, perhaps a job in guarding or patrolling would appeal to you. If you have management ability, you could seek a leadership position in law enforcement and protective services.

5. **Mechanical:** *An interest in applying mechanical principles to practical situations by use of machines or hand tools.* You can satisfy your mechanical interest in a variety of careers, ranging from routine jobs to complex professional positions. If you enjoy working with ideas about things, you could seek a job in engineering or in a related technical field. You may instead prefer to deal directly with things: you could find a job in the crafts or trades, building, making, or repairing objects. You may like to drive or operate vehicles and special equipment. If you prefer routine or physical work in settings other than factories, perhaps work in mining or construction would appeal to you.

6. **Industrial:** *An interest in repetitive, concrete, organized activities done in a factory setting.* You can satisfy this interest by working in one of many industries that mass-produce goods. You may enjoy manual work, using your hands or hand tools. Perhaps you prefer to operate or take care of machines. You may like to inspect, sort, count, or weigh products. Using your training and experience to set up machines or supervise other workers may appeal to you.

7. **Business Detail:** *An interest in organized, clearly defined activities requiring accuracy and attention to details, primarily in an office setting.* You can satisfy this interest in a variety of jobs in which you attend to the details of a business operation. You may enjoy using your math skills; if so, perhaps a job in billing, computing, or financial record-keeping would satisfy you. If you prefer to deal with people, you may want a job in which you

meeting the public, talk on the telephone, or supervise other workers. You may like to operate computer terminals, typewriters, or bookkeeping machines. Perhaps a job in filing or recording would satisfy you. Or you may wish to use your training and experience to manage an office.

8. **Selling:** *An interest in bringing others to a particular point of view by personal persuasion, using sales and promotional techniques.* You can satisfy this interest in a variety of sales jobs. You may enjoy selling technical products or services, or perhaps a selling job requiring less technical knowledge. You may work in stores, sales offices, or customers' homes. You may wish to buy and resell products to make a profit. You can also satisfy this interest in legal work, business negotiations, advertising, and related fields.

9. **Accommodating/Personal Service:** *An interest in catering to the wishes and needs of others, usually on a one-to-one basis.* You can satisfy this interest by providing services for the convenience of others in hotels, restaurants, airplanes, and other locations. If you enjoy improving the appearance of others, perhaps working in the hair and beauty care field would satisfy you. Or you may wish to provide personal services such as taking tickets, carrying baggage, or ushering.

10. **Humanitarian/Helping People:** *An interest in helping others with their mental, spiritual, social, physical, or vocational needs.* You can satisfy this interest by work in which caring for people's welfare is important. Perhaps the spiritual or mental well-being of others concerns you. If so, you would prepare for a job in religion or counseling. If you wish to help others with physical problems, you could work in the nursing, therapy, or rehabilitation fields. You may like to provide needed but less complicated care by working as an aide, orderly, or technician.

11. **Leading and Influencing:** *An interest in leading and influencing others by using high-level verbal or numerical abilities.* You can satisfy this interest through study and work in a variety of professional fields. You may enjoy the challenge and responsibility of leadership. You may like to help others learn, in which case working in education may appeal to you.

12. **Physical Performing/Sports:** *An interest in physical activities performed before an audience.* You can satisfy this interest through jobs in athletics, sports, and the performance of physical feats. Perhaps a job as a professional player or official would appeal to you. You may wish to develop and perform special acts such as acrobatics or wire walking.

GOE Interest Areas and Subgroups, Including Related *OOH* and *DOT* Jobs, Self-Employment Jobs, and Related Education and Training

The 12 major GOE Interest Areas are further divided into 66 work groups and 348 even more specific subgroups of related jobs. All jobs are organized within these increasingly specific clusters of related jobs.

The GOE uses a system of number codes for the various groupings. Called "GOE Codes," these numbers can be used to cross-reference you to other occupational information systems that use the same organizational structure.

The information that follows provides you with a variety of useful information. For each of the 12 major GOE Interest Areas it gives the following:

GOE Subgroups. Each of the 12 major GOE Interest Areas are further organized into subgroups of related jobs. Each of these subgroups has a four-digit GOE number that allows you to cross-reference it to information systems using the GOE structure.

Related *OOH* Occupations. For each GOE subgroup, we have provided a listing of job titles found in the *Occupational Outlook Handbook,* the *OOH.* The *OOH* is a book published by the U.S. Department of Labor and updated every two years. It provides thorough descriptions for the 250 largest jobs in our economy and is widely used in schools, libraries, and other settings. This listing will give you a good idea of the major job titles that are related to each GOE Interest Area and subgroup. Note any *OOH* job titles that interest you and read the descriptions provided in the *OOH* for these jobs.

Related *DOT* Jobs. This is a listing of jobs found in the *Dictionary of Occupational Titles (DOT)* that are related to the GOE Interest Area. The *DOT* is also published by the U.S. Department of Labor and provides brief descriptions for over 12,000 jobs. Many of these job titles are more specialized than the job titles used in the *OOH,* and we included them here to give you an idea of the wide range of job titles available within the various GOE Interest Areas. Once again, you can identify job titles of particular interest and obtain more information on these jobs from the *DOT.*

Self-Employment Options. This list provides some jobs that offer self-employment opportunities related to each GOE Interest Area.

Related Education and Training. Provides a partial listing of education and training programs, courses, majors, or topical areas that are related to the occupations in each GOE Interest Area.

01 ARTISTIC: An interest in the creative expression of feelings or ideas.

GOE Subgroups

01.01 Literary Arts

01.02 Visual Arts

01.03 Performing Arts: Drama

01.04 Performing Arts: Music

01.05 Performing Arts: Dance

01.06 Craft Arts

01.07 Elemental Arts

01.08 Modeling

Related *OOH* Occupations

01.01 Literary Arts—Social Scientists and Urban Planners; Radio and Television Announcers and Newscasters; Writers and Editors; Actors, Directors, and Producers

01.02 Visual Arts—Marketing, Advertising, and Public Relations Managers; Adult Education Teachers; Designers; Photographers and Camera Operators; Visual Artists; Broadcast Technicians; Blue-Collar Worker Supervisors; Prepress Workers; Apparel Workers

01.03 Performing Arts: Drama—Adult Education Teachers; Radio and Television Announcers and Newscasters; Actors, Directors, and Producers; Secretaries

01.04 Performing Arts: Music—Adult Education Teachers; Actors, Directors, and Producers; Musicians

01.05 Performing Arts: Dance—Adult Education Teachers; Dancers and Choreographers

01.06 Craft Arts—Social Scientists and Urban Planners; Adult Education Teachers; Archivists and Curators; Designers; Photographers and Camera Operators; Visual Artists; Barbers and Cosmetologists; Industrial Machinery Repairers; Carpenters; Blue-Collar Worker Supervisors; Inspectors, Testers, and Graders; Jewelers; Prepress Workers; Bindery Workers; Apparel Workers; Shoe and Leather Workers and Repairers; Woodworking Occupations; Photographic Process Workers; Handlers, Equipment Cleaners, Helpers, and Laborers

01.07 Elemental Arts—Actors, Directors, and Producers

01.08 Modeling—Adult Education Teachers; Actors, Directors, and Producers

Related *DOT* Occupations

Actor/actress, announcer, art appraiser, art director, art teacher, artist, architect, biographer, cartoonist, choreographer, clothes designer, color expert, columnist, comedian, commentator, commercial artist, commercial designer, communications technician, composer, continuity writer, copyist, copy editor, copy writer, costuming supervisor, critic, crossword puzzle maker, dance instructor, dancer, delineator, director, disk jockey, display designer, drama teacher, editor, editorial assistant, editorial writer, English teacher, engraver, fashion artist, film editor, freelance writer, furniture designer, graphic arts technician, graphic designer, graphologist, greeting card editor, humorist, illustrator, interior designer, interpreter, jeweler, literature instructor, lyricist, magician, make-up artist, memorial designer, mime, model, model maker, music teacher, musician, novelist, offset-plate maker, orchestrator, package designer, painter, playwright, producer, photoengraving etcher, photographer, photojournalist, poet, print maker, producer, puppeteer, quick sketch artist, radio director, reader, reporter, screen writer, sculptor, set decorator, set designer, singer, story editor, taxidermist, technical writer, translator, writer.

Self-Employment Options

Advertising person, aerial photography, airbrush artist/retoucher, art consultant/dealer, artist, art gallery, art instruction, artist's representative, arts and crafts instructor, book designer, eulogy writer, fashion designer, jewelry designer, mural maker, oil and water painting restorer, paste-up artist, short story author, sign painter, stained glass artist, tole painter.

Related Education and Training

Art, craft arts, drama, graphic arts, music, photography, modern dance, architecture, art history, theater arts, performing arts, commercial art, interior design, commercial photography, visual arts, illustration design, literature, journalism, humanities, English, creative writing, communications studies, language, philosophy, classics, broadcasting, and composition.

02 SCIENTIFIC: An interest in discovering, collecting, and analyzing information about the natural world, and in applying scientific research findings to problems in medicine, life sciences, and natural sciences.

GOE Subgroups

02.01 Physical Sciences

02.02 Life Sciences

02.03 Medical Sciences

02.04 Laboratory Technology

OOH Occupations

02.01 Physical Sciences—Engineering, Science, and Data Processing Managers; Metallurgical, Ceramic, and Materials Engineers; Surveyors; Mathematicians; Chemists; Geologists and Geophysicists; Meteorologists; Physicists and Astronomers; Social Scientists and Urban Planners; Science Technicians

02.02 Life Sciences—Inspectors and Compliance Officers, except Construction; Agricultural Scientists; Biological and Medical Scientists; Foresters and Conservation Scientists; Chemists; Physicists and Astronomers; Social Scientists and Urban Planners; Veterinarians; Dietitians and Nutritionists; Science Technicians; Farm Operators and Managers

02.03 Medical Sciences—Health Services Managers; Chiropractors; Dentists; Optometrists; Physicians; Podiatrists; Veterinarians; Speech-Language Pathologists and Audiologists

02.04 Laboratory Technology—Engineering, Science, and Data Processing Managers; Health Services Managers; Biological and Medical Scientists; Chemists; Pharmacists; Photographers and Camera Operators; Clinical Laboratory Technologists and Technicians; Radiologic Technologists; Engineering Technicians; Science Technicians; Medical Assistants; Inspectors, Testers, and Graders; Textile Machinery Operators; Photographic Process Workers

DOT Occupations

Aerial photograph interpreter, agronomist, anesthesiologist, animal scientist, archaeologist, astronomer, animal scientist, anthropologist, audiologist, biochemist, biologist, biological aide, biomedical engineer, botanist, chemist, chiropractor, coroner, crystallographer, cytologist, dairy scientist, dental hygienist, dentist, embalmer, environmental analyst, environmental research project manager, food chemist, food technologist, forest ecologist, geneticist, geodesist, geographer, geologist, geophysical prospector, geophysicists, hydrologist, laboratory assistant, laboratory technician, laboratory tester, mathematician, materials scientist, medical officer, medical laboratory assistant, medical technologist, metallurgist, meteorologist, microbiologist, mineralogist, nematologist, neurologist, nurse aide, optometrist, paleontologist, perfumer, petrologist, pharmacist, pharmacologist, physical metallurgist, physical science teacher, physical therapist, physician, physiologist, physicist, plant breeder, poultry scientist, radiologist, range manager, research dietitian, scientific helper, seismologist, soil conservationist, soil scientist, speech pathologist, stratigrapher, veterinarian, zoologist.

Self-Employment Options

Audiologist, biological laboratory operation, chiropractor, dentist, doctor, environmental services, geological consultant, herbalist, home health agency, home-visit nurse, medical lab technician, microscope rental/repair, personal home care, plant breeder, recycling services, solar consultant, solar systems designer, speech pathologist.

Related Education and Training

Biology, chemistry, anatomy, pharmacology, anesthesiology, radiology, biochemistry, toxicology, microbiology, nursing, chiropractic, human nutrition, dentistry, allied health professions, medical technology, physical therapy, physician assistant, astronomy, earth science, physics, geology, meteorology, archeology, mining/minerals engineering, geophysics, aerospace science, pure mathematics, planetary science, and paleontology.

03 PLANTS AND ANIMALS: An interest in working with plants and animals, usually outdoors.

GOE Subgroups

03.01 Managerial Work

03.02 General Supervision

03.03 Animal Training and Service

03.04 Elemental Work

OOH Occupations

03.01 Managerial Work: Plants and Animals—Construction Contractors and Managers; General Managers and Top Executives; Industrial Production Managers; Inspectors and Compliance Officers, except Construction; Foresters and Conservation Scientists; Science Technicians; Gardeners and Groundskeepers; Farm Operators and Managers; Fishers, Hunters, and Trappers

03.02 General Supervision: Plants and Animals—Science Technicians; Forestry and Logging Occupations; Blue-Collar Worker Supervisors

03.03 Animal Training and Service—Animal Caretakers, except farm; Handlers, Equipment Cleaners, Helpers, and Laborers

03.04 Elemental Work: Plants and Animals—Science Technicians; Material Recording, Scheduling, Dispatching, and Distributing Occupations; Firefighting Occupations; Gardeners and Groundskeepers; Fishers, Hunters, and Trappers; Forestry and Logging Occupations; Blue-Collar Worker Supervisors; Butchers and Meat, Poultry, and Fish Cutters; Inspectors, Testers, and Graders; Woodworking Occupations; Material Moving Equipment Operators; Handlers, Equipment Cleaners, Helpers, and Laborers

DOT Occupations

Agriculture scientist, animal breeder/caretaker, animal keeper, animal trainer, animal trapper, artificial-breeding technician, barn boss, botanist, budder, cemetery worker, Christmas tree farm manager, comp tender, cowpuncher, cruiser, dairy farm manager, dog catcher, dog groomer, electric-fork operator, farm machine operator, farm worker, farming supervisor, field contractor, fish farmer, fish hatchery supervisor, forest nursery supervisor, forestry aide, forestry worker, game warden, greens superintendent, horse exerciser, fisher, forest ecologist, forester, game farm worker, gamekeeper, game preserve manager, greenskeeper, horse trainer, horseshoer, horticulture worker, landscape gardener, lawn service worker, livestock rancher, logger, logging supervisor, nursery manager, park ranger, plant propagator, park naturalist, parks and grounds groundskeeper, poultry breeder, poultry farm worker, range manager, seedling sorter, shellfish grower, soil conservationist, special effects gardener, stable attendant, tree cutter and trimmer, tree cutter, tree planter, tree surgeon, veterinarian assistant, wildlife biologist, wildlife control agent, woods boss, yard worker, zoo director, zoologist.

Self-Employment Options

Animal boarder, animal breeder, animal clipper, animal dipper, animal food depot owner, animal groomer, animal sitter, bee keeper, cattle farmer, dairy farmer, duck boarder and breeder, exterminator, greenhouse owner, farmer, florist, florist sales and service, flower arranger, flower bulb sales, gardener, gardening service owner, goat keeper, goldfish breeding, green plant maintenance, herb farming, horticulturist, landscape contractor, lawn maintenance service, mink farmer, pet groomer, pig farmer, poultry farmer, seed shop owner, sheep farmer, tack shop owner, taxidermist, trapper, tree maintenance service, vegetable farmer, veterinarian.

Related Education and Training

Wildlife technology, zoology, animal science, botany, landscaping, horticulture, agriculture, fisheries and wildlife services, wastewater technology, water resources, animal nutrition, environmental sciences, oceanography, farm management, animal grooming, biology, forestry, soil science, botany, agronomy, life sciences, agricultural economics, forest recreation, forestry and wildlife resources, environmental conservation, industrial forestry, and plan pathology.

04 PROTECTIVE: An interest in using authority to protect people and property.

GOE Subgroups

04.01 Safety and Law Enforcement

04.02 Security Services

OOH Occupations

04.01 Safety and Law Enforcement—General Managers and Top Executives; Inspectors and Compliance Officers, except Construction; Social Scientists and Urban Planners; Adult Education Teachers; Firefighting Occupations; Police Detectives, and Special Agents

04.02 Security Services—Inspectors and Compliance Officers, except Construction; Adjusters, Investigators, and Collectors; Dispatchers; Correction Officers; Firefighting Occupations; Guards; Police detectives, and Special Agents

DOT Occupations

Alarm investigator, airline security agent, armed services personnel, armored-car guard, bailiff, border guard, bodyguard, bouncer, chaperon, correctional officer, court deputy, customs inspector, customs patrol officer, deputy sheriff, detective, dispatcher, equal-opportunity representative, fire chief's aide, fire inspector, fire fighter, fire marshall, fire prevention bureau captain, fire ranger, fire warden, fish and gambling monitor, food and drug inspector, game warden, gate tender, house officer, immigration guard, internal security manager, jailer, lifeguard, merchant patroller, motorized squad commanding officer, narcotics investigator, parking enforcement office, park ranger, parking enforcement officer, patroller, police academy instructor, police inspector, police officer, protective officer, repossessor, safety inspector, security guard, security guard dispatcher, school bus monitor, sheriff, ski patroller, smoke jumper, smoke jumper supervisor, special agent, state highway police officer, traffic sergeant, undercover operator, wildlife agent.

Self-Employment Options

Bodyguard, burglar alarm sales, collections agent, fire alarm system sales, fire extinguisher sales, fire investigator, firearms instructor, firearms repair/service, firearms safety instructor, firearms sales, fireworks manufacturing, investigative services, law-for-the-layperson instructor, loss adjustment services, martial arts training school, military equipment, private detective, security systems designer.

Related Education and Training

Criminology, law enforcement, fire science, political science, army ROTC, physical education, economics, correctional justice, state police academy, history, police science, correctional administration, and protective services.

05 MECHANICAL: An interest in applying mechanical principles to practical situations by use of machines or hand tools.

GOE Subgroups

05.01 Engineering

05.02 Managerial Work: Mechanical

05.03 Engineering Technology

05.04 Air and Water Vehicle Operation

05.05 Craft Technology

05.06 Systems Operation

05.07 Quality Control

05.08 Land and Water Vehicle Operation

05.09 Material Control

05.10 Crafts

05.11 Equipment Operation

05.12 Elemental Work: Mechanical

OOH Occupations

05.01 Engineering—Engineering, Science, and Data Processing Managers; Management Analysts and Consultants; Aerospace Engineers; Chemical Engineers; Civil Engineers; Electrical and Electronics Engineers; Industrial Engineers; Mechanical Engineers; Metallurgical, Ceramic, and Materials Engineers; Mining Engineers; Nuclear Engineers; Petroleum Engineers; Architects; Landscape Architects; Surveyors; Computer Scientists and Systems Analysts; Geologists and Geophysicists; Physicists and Astronomers; Designers; Engineering Technicians; Science Technicians; Manufacturers' and Wholesale Sales Representatives; Retail sales workers; Machinists and Tool Programmers

05.02 Managerial Work: Mechanical—Construction Contractors and Managers; Engineering, Science, and Data Processing Managers; General Managers and Top Executives; Industrial Production Managers; Inspectors and Compliance Officers, except Construction; Marketing, Advertising, and Public Relations Managers; Property and Real Estate Managers; Purchasers and Buyers; Industrial Engineers; Petroleum Engineers; Science Technicians; Services Sales Representatives; Dispatchers; Blue-Collar Worker Supervisors

05.03 Engineering Technology—Construction and Building Inspectors; Cost Estimators; Engineering, Science, and Data Processing Managers; Inspectors and Compliance Officers, except Construction; Purchasers and Buyers; Industrial Engineers; Mechanical Engineers; Surveyors; Aircraft Pilots; Air Traffic Controllers; Broadcast Technicians; Drafters; Engineering Technicians; Science Technicians; Material Recording, Scheduling, Dispatching, and Distributing Occupations; Blue-Collar Worker Supervisors; Inspectors, Testers, and Graders; Apparel Workers; Rail Transportation Workers

05.04 Air and Water Vehicle Operation—Inspectors and Compliance Officers, except Construction; Adult Education Teachers; Aircraft Pilots; Science Technicians; Fishers, Hunters, and Trappers; Water Transportation Occupations

05.05 Craft Technology—Health Services Managers; Industrial Production Managers; Management Analysts and Consultants; Adult Education Teachers; Dietitians and Nutritionists; Engineering Technicians; Chefs, Cooks, and Other Kitchen Workers; Aircraft Mechanics and Engine Specialists; Automotive Body Repairers; Automotive Mechanics; Diesel Mechanics; Commercial and Industrial Electronic Equipment Repairers; Communications Equipment Mechanics; Computer and Office Machine Repairers; Electronic Home Entertainment Equipment Repairers; Telephone Installers and Repairers; Elevator Installers and Repairers; Farm Equipment Mechanics; General Maintenance Mechanics; Heating, Air-Conditioning, and Refrigeration Technicians; Home Appliance and Power Tool Repairers; Industrial machinery repairers; Line Installers and Cable Splicers; Millwrights; Mobile Heavy Equipment Mechanics; Motorcycle, Boat, and Small Engine Mechanics; Musical Instrument Repairers and Tuners; Bricklayers and Stonemasons; Carpenters; Concrete Masons and Terrazzo Workers; Drywall Workers and Lathers; Electricians; Painters and Paperhangers; Plasterers; Plumbers and Pipefitters; Sheetmetal Workers; Structural and Reinforcing Ironworkers; Tilesetters; Precision assemblers; Blue-Collar Worker Supervisors; Inspectors, Testers, and Graders; Boilermakers; Jewelers; Machinists and Tool Programmers; Metalworking and Plastics-Working Machine Operators; Tool and Die Makers; Welders, Cutters, and Welding Machine Operators; Prepress Workers; Printing press operators; Bindery Workers; Apparel Workers; Shoe and Leather Workers and Repairers; Upholsterers; Woodworking Occupations; Dental Laboratory Technicians; Ophthalmic Laboratory Technicians; Handlers, Equipment Cleaners, Helpers, and Laborers

05.06 Systems Operation—Adult Education Teachers; Dispatchers; Blue-Collar Worker Supervisors; Inspectors, Testers, and Graders; Electric Power Generating Plant Operators and Power Distributors and Dispatchers; Stationary Engineers; Water and Wastewater Treatment Plant Operators; Material Moving Equipment Operators; Water Transportation Occupations; Handlers, Equipment Cleaners, Helpers, and Laborers

05.07 Quality Control—Construction and Building Inspectors; Inspectors and Compliance Officers, except Construction; Engineering Technicians; Clerical Supervisors and Managers; Material Recording, Scheduling, Dispatching, and Distributing Occupations; Firefighting Occupations; Forestry and Logging Occupations; Automotive Body Repairers; Communications Equipment Mechanics; Elevator Installers and Repairers; Line Installers and Cable Splicers; Inspectors, Testers, and Graders; Handlers, Equipment Cleaners, Helpers, and Laborers

05.08 Land and Water Vehicle Operation—Blue-Collar Worker Supervisors; Inspectors, Testers, and Graders; Rail Transportation Workers; Taxi Drivers and Chauffeurs; Truckdrivers; Water Transportation Occupations; Handlers, Equipment Cleaners, Helpers, and Laborers

05.09 Material Control—Cost Estimators; Inspectors and Compliance Officers, except Construction; Counter and Rental Clerks; Retail sales workers; Adjusters, Investigators, and Collectors; Clerical Supervisors and Managers; Material Recording, Scheduling, Dispatching, and Distributing Occupations; Dispatchers; Traffic, Shipping, and Receiving Clerks; Billing Clerks; Bookkeeping, Accounting, and Auditing Clerks; Library Assistants and

Bookmobile Drivers; Industrial Machinery Repairers; Blue-Collar Worker Supervisors; Inspectors, Testers, and Graders; Handlers, Equipment Cleaners, Helpers, and Laborers

05.10 Crafts—Photographers and Camera Operators; Dispensing Opticians; Broadcast Technicians; Engineering Technicians; Clerical Supervisors and Managers; Material Recording, Scheduling, Dispatching, and Distributing Occupations; Order Clerks; Chefs, Cooks, and Other Kitchen Workers; Private Household Workers; Fishers, Hunters, and Trappers; Automotive Body Repairers; Automotive Mechanics; Commercial and Industrial Electronic Equipment Repairers; Communications Equipment Mechanics; Electronic Home Entertainment Equipment Repairers; Farm Equipment Mechanics; General Maintenance Mechanics; Heating, Air-Conditioning, and Refrigeration Technicians; Home Appliance and Power Tool Repairers; Industrial machinery repairers; Line Installers and Cable Splicers; Motorcycle, Boat, and Small Engine Mechanics; Vending Machine Servicers and Repairers; Bricklayers and Stonemasons; Carpenters; Carpet Installers; Concrete Masons and Terrazzo Workers; Drywall Workers and Lathers; Electricians; Glaziers; Insulation Workers; Painters and Paperhangers; Plumbers and Pipefitters; Roofers; Roustabouts; Precision assemblers; Blue-Collar Worker Supervisors; Butchers and Meat, Poultry, and Fish Cutters; Inspectors, Testers, and Graders; Metalworking and Plastics-Working Machine Operators; Welders, Cutters, and Welding Machine Operators; Prepress Workers; Printing Press Operators; Shoe and Leather Workers and Repairers; Woodworking Occupations; Painting and Coating Machine Operators; Photographic Process Workers; Handlers, Equipment Cleaners, Helpers, and Laborers

05.11 Equipment Operation. Janitors and Cleaners; Insulation Workers; Blue-Collar Worker Supervisors; Material Moving Equipment Operators; Rail Transportation Workers; Truckdrivers

05.12 Elemental Work: Mechanical—Clerical Supervisors and Managers; Stock Clerks; Chefs, Cooks, and Other Kitchen Workers; Janitors and Cleaners; Private Household Workers; Forestry and Logging Occupations; Aircraft Mechanics and Engine Specialists; Automotive Body Repairers; Automotive Mechanics; Farm Equipment Mechanics; Industrial Machinery Repairers; Line Installers and Cable Splicers; Carpenters; Insulation Workers; Roofers; Roustabouts; Tilesetters; Blue-Collar Worker Supervisors; Inspectors, Testers, and Graders; Boilermakers; Metalworking and Plastics-Working Machine Operators; Welders, Cutters, and Welding Machine Operators; Water and Wastewater Treatment Plant Operators; Prepress Workers; Printing Press Operators; Bindery Workers; Photographic Process Workers; Material Moving Equipment Operators; Rail Transportation Workers; Water Transportation Occupations; Handlers, Equipment Cleaners, Helpers, and Laborers

DOT Occupations

Aeronautical test engineer, air conditioning mechanic, aircraft mechanic, architect, automatic door mechanic, automobile body repairer, automobile mechanic, baggage handler, battery repairer, boilermaker, bookbinder, brake coupler, bricklayer, cabinetmaker, cable splicer, cable tester, carpenter, cleaner, clerical methods analyst, die designer, distribution field engineer, drafter, engraver, electrician, electronics assembler, engineer, estimator, excavator, facilities planner, film developer, floor layer, heavy equipment operator, janitor, land surveyor, laser technician, laundry worker, lodging facilities attendant, logistics engineer, machinist, maintenance mechanic, management analyst, mechanic, millwright, miner, offset press operator, optician, painter, pipe fitter, plasterer, plumber, production planner, quality control directory, refrigeration unit repairer, rug dyer, safety clothing and equipment developer, safety inspector, sales engineer, school plant consultant, scrap sorter, sewing machine operator, shore hand, silk screen repairer, stonemason, surveyor, tool and die maker, television/cable installer, tool designer, tool planner, welder, truck driver, vacuum cleaner repairer, warehouse worker, welder, welding technician.

Self-Employment Options

Appliance repairer, auto body rebuilder, auto mechanic, backhoe operator, cabinet maker, car wash owner, ceiling specialist, charter boat operator, chimney sweep, computer repair service, contractor, electronics repair shop, floor specialist, furniture maker, home remodeling service, investor, mason, mobile auto window service, mobile designer, motor bike repair and sales, plasterer, plumber, quick oil change shop, radio repairer, remodeler, restoration specialist, roofer, vacuum sales and service shop, vehicle tester.

Related Employment and Training

Auto mechanics, engineering, mechanical drawing, electronics, industrial arts, shops/crafts, welding, architecture, heating and air conditioning, carpentry, masonry, pipe fitting, major appliance repair, heavy equipment maintenance, and building maintenance.

06 INDUSTRIAL: An interest in repetitive, concrete, organized activities done in a factory setting.

GOE Subgroups

06.01 Production Technology

06.02 Production Work

06.03 Quality Control

06.04 Elemental Work: Industrial

OOH Occupations

06.01 Production Technology—Material Recording, Scheduling, Dispatching, and Distributing Occupations; Dispatchers; Commercial and Industrial Electronic Equipment Repairers; Computer and Office Machine Repairers; Industrial machinery repairers; Motorcycle, Boat, and Small Engine Mechanics; Musical Instrument Repairers and Tuners;

Precision assemblers; Blue-Collar Worker Supervisors; Inspectors, Testers, and Graders; Jewelers; Metalworking and Plastics-Working Machine Operators; Tool and Die Makers; Welders, Cutters, and Welding Machine Operators; Printing Press Operators; Bindery Workers; Apparel Workers; Textile Machinery Operators; Woodworking Occupations; Ophthalmic Laboratory Technicians

06.02 Production Work—Adult Education Teachers; Clerical Supervisors and Managers; Aircraft Mechanics and Engine Specialists; Commercial and Industrial Electronic Equipment Repairers; Computer and Office Machine Repairers; Farm Equipment Mechanics; Industrial Machinery Repairers; Musical Instrument Repairers and Tuners; Carpenters; Painters and Paperhangers; Plumbers and Pipefitters; Precision Assemblers; Blue-Collar Worker Supervisors; Butchers and Meat, Poultry, and Fish Cutters; Inspectors, Testers, and Graders; Metalworking and Plastics-Working Machine Operators; Welders, Cutters, and Welding Machine Operators; Water and Wastewater Treatment Plant Operators; Prepress Workers; Printing press operators; Bindery Workers; Apparel Workers; Shoe and Leather Workers and Repairers; Textile Machinery Operators; Upholsterers; Woodworking Occupations; Dental Laboratory Technicians; Ophthalmic Laboratory Technicians; Painting and Coating Machine Operators; Photographic Process Workers; Material Moving Equipment Operators; Handlers, Equipment Cleaners, Helpers, and Laborers

06.03 Quality Control—Material Recording, Scheduling, Dispatching, and Distributing Occupations; Traffic, Shipping, and Receiving Clerks; Industrial Machinery Repairers; Blue-Collar Worker Supervisors; Butchers and Meat, Poultry, and Fish Cutters; Inspectors, Testers, and Graders; Metalworking and Plastics-Working Machine Operators; Prepress Workers; Apparel Workers; Handlers, Equipment Cleaners, Helpers, and Laborers

06.04 Elemental Work: Industrial—Adult Education Teachers; Material Recording, Scheduling, Dispatching, and Distributing Occupations; Janitors and Cleaners; Forestry and Logging Occupations; Aircraft Mechanics and Engine Specialists; Industrial Machinery Repairers; Musical Instrument Repairers and Tuners; Carpenters; Drywall Workers and Lathers; Painters and Paperhangers; Blue-Collar Worker Supervisors; Butchers and Meat, Poultry, and Fish Cutters; Inspectors, Testers, and Graders; Metalworking and Plastics-Working Machine Operators; Welders, Cutters, and Welding Machine Operators; Prepress Workers; Printing Press Operators; Bindery Workers; Apparel Workers; Textile Machinery Operators; Woodworking Occupations; Painting and Coating Machine Operators; Photographic Process Workers; Material Moving Equipment Operators; Handlers, Equipment Cleaners, Helpers, and Laborers

DOT Occupations

Alloy weigher, bakery worker, bench hand, bicycle assembler, binder, box tender, bowling ball grader and maker, butcher, carpet cutter, cloth grader supervisor, color matcher, electronics tester, furnace helper, gear-shover set-up operator, grinder operator, inspector and tester, kiln worker, knitting-machine operator, linen grader, locket maker, loom setter, machine setter, machinist, mannequin-mold maker, mixer, mill operator, picker, plumbing systems tester, punch-press operator, roller maker, rug inspector, sander, saw operator, sewing supervisor, solderer, spark tester, speedometer inspector, spring inspector, stocking inspector, stitcher, testing-machine operator, tire repairer, umbrella examiner, upholstery sewer, watch repairer, weaver, welder setter, zipper cutter.

Self-Employment Options

Accessories manufacturer, bookbinder, carpet cleaning service, carpet sales and installation store, customized draper, electronics consultant, film processor, gem engraver, house painting, industrial catalog preparation, industrial supplies rental, leather products sales, linen products manufacturer, luggage manufacturer, magazine binding, mobile locksmith, plastics designer, scrap dealer, sewing machine operator, silk screen printer, tool maker, toy designer, trucker, upholstery business, watch repair service.

Related Education and Training

Management training, supervision, mechanical shop, blueprint reading, math computing/shop math, machine shop, graphic processes (printing and bindery), sheetmetal shop, chemistry, forging/heat treating, sewing or upholstery, watch repair, foundry, glass blowing, wood shop or machining, electronics, auto body repair, electrical shop, diesel and auto mechanics, photographic laboratory production, printing press operations, leatherworking, meatcutting

07 BUSINESS DETAIL: An interest in organized, clearly defined activities requiring accuracy and attention to details, primarily in an office setting.

GOE Subgroups

07.01 Administrative Detail

07.02 Mathematical Detail

07.03 Financial Detail

07.04 Oral Communications

07.05 Records Processing

07.06 Clerical Machine Operation

07.07 Clerical Handling

OOH Occupations

07.01 Administrative Detail—Administrative Services Managers; Education Administrators; Inspectors and Compliance Officers, except Construction; Personnel, Training, and

Labor Relations Specialists and Managers; Human Services Workers; Archivists and Curators; Counselors; Adjusters, Investigators, and Collectors; Clerical Supervisors and Managers; Credit Clerks and Authorizers; General Office Clerks; Material Recording, Scheduling, Dispatching, and Distributing Occupations; Postal Clerks and Mail Carriers; Billing Clerks; Bookkeeping, Accounting, and Auditing Clerks; Brokerage Clerks and Statement Clerks; Personnel Clerks; Secretaries; Teacher Aides; Police Detectives, and Special Agents

07.02 Mathematical Detail—Mathematicians; Cashiers; Counter and Rental Clerks; Adjusters, Investigators, and Collectors; Bank Tellers; Clerical Supervisors and Managers; General Office Clerks; Reservation and Transportation Ticket Agents and Travel Clerks; Material Recording, Scheduling, Dispatching, and Distributing Occupations; Stock Clerks; Traffic, Shipping, and Receiving Clerks; Billing Clerks; Bookkeeping, Accounting, and Auditing Clerks; Brokerage Clerks and Statement Clerks; Payroll and Timekeeping Clerks

07.03 Financial Detail—Cashiers; Counter and Rental Clerks; Retail Sales Workers; Adjusters, Investigators, and Collectors; Bank Tellers; Clerical Supervisors and Managers; Reservation and Transportation Ticket Agents and Travel Clerks; Mail Clerks and Messengers; Postal Clerks and Mail Carriers; Bookkeeping, Accounting, and Auditing Clerks

07.04 Oral Communications—Adult Education Teachers; Cashiers; Counter and Rental Clerks; Adjusters, Investigators, and Collectors; Clerical Supervisors and Managers; Credit Clerks and Authorizers; General Office Clerks; Hotel and Motel Clerks; Interviewing and New Accounts Clerk; Receptionists; Reservation and Transportation Ticket Agents and Travel Clerks; Mail Clerks and Messengers; Material Recording, Scheduling, Dispatching, and Distributing Occupations; Dispatchers; Library Assistants and Bookmobile Drivers; Order Clerks; Personnel Clerks; Telephone Operators; Firefighting Occupations; Police Detectives, and Special Agents; Blue-Collar Worker Supervisors

07.05 Records Processing—Writers and Editors; Medical Record Technicians; Adjusters, Investigators, and Collectors; Clerical Supervisors and Managers; Credit Clerks and Authorizers; General Office Clerks; Receptionists; Reservation and Transportation Ticket Agents and Travel Clerks; Mail Clerks and Messengers; Material Recording, Scheduling, Dispatching, and Distributing Occupations; Dispatchers; Stock Clerks; Traffic, Shipping, and Receiving Clerks; Postal Clerks and Mail Carriers; Bookkeeping, Accounting, and Auditing Clerks; File Clerks; Library Assistants and Bookmobile Drivers; Order Clerks; Personnel Clerks; Stenographers and Court Reporters; Typists, Word Processors, and Data Entry Keyers

07.06 Clerical Machine Operation—Clerical Supervisors and Managers; Computer and Peripheral Equipment Operators; Receptionists; Billing Clerks; Stenographers and Court Reporters; Typists, Word Processors, and Data Entry Keyers; Blue-Collar Worker Supervisors; Prepress Workers

07.07 Clerical Handling—Cashiers; Clerical Supervisors and Managers; General Office Clerks; Mail Clerks and Messengers; Material Recording, Scheduling, Dispatching, and Distributing Occupations; Traffic, Shipping, and Receiving Clerks; Billing Clerks; File Clerks; Library Assistants and Bookmobile Drivers; Inspectors, Testers, and Graders; Handlers, Equipment Cleaners, Helpers, and Laborers

DOT Occupations

Accountant, accounting analyst, accounting clerk, actuary, adding machine operator, administrative clerk, administrative secretary, admissions evaluator, admitting officer, advertising clerk, advice clerk, appraiser, archivist, audit clerk, auditor, bank teller, billing clerk, bond clerk, bookkeeper, brokerage clerk, budget clerk, bursar, buyer, cashier, checker, claims examiner, clerk typist, collator, collection clerk, collector, computer operator, controller, copyreader, credit analyst, credit counselor, court clerk, curator, data typist, dispatcher, examiner, field cashier, file clerk, financial aid counselor, financial analyst, information clerk, insurance adjuster, insurance clerk, keypunch operator, labor expediter, layaway clerk, legal assistant, legal secretary, librarian, loan counselor, loan officer, loan interviewer, mail censor, mail clerk, mail handler, market research analyst, medical records clerk, medical secretary, new accounts clerk, night auditor, officer helper, payroll clerk, personnel clerk, phototypesetter operator, postal clerk, procurement clerk, programmer, purchasing agent, radio officer, reader, real estate clerk, receptionist, reservation clerk, routing clerk, secretary, securities clerk, securities trader, shipping clerk, statistical clerk, statistician, stenographer, switchboard operator, systems analyst, tax clerk, telephone operator, test technician, ticket agent, title examiner, toll collector, tourist information assistant, travel clerk, typist, underwriter, vault cashier, word processor.

Self-Employment Options

Answering service, bookkeeping service, data processor, dictating/transcribing service, financial aid service, information broker, income tax preparer, indexer, mail order business, mail sorting service, medical claims processing, office equipment and supply sales, office permanent and temporary help agency, office record storage and shredding, secretarial service, utility/telephone bill auditing.

Related Education and Training

Secretarial science, legal assistance, data processing, typing, library science, computer science, stenography, legal secretary, court reporting, clerk-typist, general office practice, bookkeeping, accounting, banking, finance, insurance, real estate, business law, investments and securities, database management, and income tax.

08 SELLING: An interest in bringing others to a particular point of view by personal persuasion, using sales and promotional techniques.

GOE Subgroups

08.01 Sales Technology

08.02 General Sales

08.03 Vending

OOH Occupations

08.01 Sales Technology—Property and Real Estate Managers; Purchasers and Buyers; Insurance Agents and Brokers; Manufacturers' and Wholesale Sales Representatives; Retail sales workers; Securities and Financial Services Sales Representatives; Services Sales Representatives; Bank Tellers

08.02 General Sales—Manufacturers' and Wholesale Sales Representatives; Real Estate Agents, Brokers, and Appraisers; Retail Sales Workers; Securities and Financial Services Sales Representatives; Services Sales Representatives; Travel Agents; Blue-Collar Worker Supervisors; Truckdrivers

08.03 Vending—Photographers and Camera Operators; Retail Sales Workers

DOT Occupations

Advertising agent, auctioneer, auto sales worker, marketing consultant, business services sales agent, buyer, cigarette vendor, communications consultant, comparison shopper, computer and equipment systems sales representatives, demonstrator, estate planner, field contact technician, field representative, foreign banknote teller/trader, fund raiser, grain buyer, group-sales representative, hardware supplies salesperson, insurance agent, jewelry salesperson, leasing agent, lounge car attendant, membership solicitor, outside property agent, pawn broker, peddler, pharmaceutical dealer, placer, public relations specialist, real estate sales agent, sales agent, sales representative, shoe salesperson, song plugger, sporting goods salesperson, sales exhibitor, sales route driver, sandwich-board carrier, subscriptions crew leader, telephone solicitor, traffic agent, travel agent, vendor, wedding consultant, wholesale sales representative.

Self-Employment Options

Antiques dealer, bridal consultant, carpet sales, direct mail sales, direct sales from home, discount store owner, display specialties service, flea market, mutual fund sales, off-price retailing store, pawn shop, public relations service, real estate broker, sales instructor, sales representative, salesperson, telephone sales and service, travel agency, travel consultant, tour service manager, tourist guide/escort, video rental shop, vitamin sales, wedding service.

Related Education and Training

Public relations, advertising, marketing, retail management, public affairs, consumer behavior, sales force management, real estate, and industrial sales.

09 ACCOMMODATING: An interest in catering to the wishes and needs of others, usually on a one-to-one basis.

GOE Subgroups

09.01 Hospitality Services

09.02 Barber and Beauty Services

09.03 Passenger Services

09.04 Customer Services

09.05 Attendant Services

OOH Occupations

09.01 Hospitality Services—Recreation Workers; Social Workers; Adult Education Teachers; Archivists and Curators; Food and Beverage Service Occupations; Flight Attendants; Private Household Workers; Rail Transportation Workers

09.02 Barber and Beauty Services—Barbers and Cosmetologists

09.03 Passenger Services—Adult Education Teachers; Blue-Collar Worker Supervisors; Busdrivers; Rail Transportation Workers; Taxi Drivers and Chauffeurs

09.04 Customer Services—Retail Managers; Cashiers; Counter and Rental Clerks; Retail Sales Workers; Material Recording, Scheduling, Dispatching, and Distributing Occupations; Stock Clerks; Food and Beverage Service Occupations; Vending Machine Servicers and Repairers; Blue-Collar Worker Supervisors; Truckdrivers; Handlers, Equipment Cleaners, Helpers, and Laborers

09.05 Attendant Services—Clerical Supervisors and Managers; Reservation and Transportation Ticket Agents and Travel Clerks; Chefs, Cooks, and Other Kitchen Workers; Food and Beverage Service Occupations; Barbers and Cosmetologists; Private Household Workers; Handlers, Equipment Cleaners, Helpers, and Laborers

DOT Occupations

Alpine guide, automobile rental clerk, bagger, baker, bar attendant, barber, bartender, bellhop, bicycle rental clerk, bridge instructor, bus attendant, bus driver, butler, cab supervisor, caddie, cafeteria attendant, camp counselor, car wash attendant, cardroom attendant, caterer helper, chauffeur, clerk, cook, cosmetologist, counter attendant, curb attendant, delivery route drive, desk clerk, drive-in theater attendant, driving instructor, doorkeeper, elevator operator, escort, food service worker, flight attendant, funeral attendant, gate attendant, group worker, hair stylist, host/hostess, maid, manicurist, masseur/masseuse, newspaper carrier, page, parking-lot attendant, passenger service representative, pay station attendant, personal shopper, plant guide, platform attendant, porter, pullman conductor, real estate guide, recreation leader, sales attendant, scalp-treatment operator, skate shop attendant, social director, steward/stewardess, streetcar operator, taxi driver, ticket taker, usher, vault attendant, waiter/waitress.

Self-Employment Options

Beautician, beauty consultant, bed and breakfast inn, building/office cleaner, caterer, coffee and tea store, convenience food store, driver/chauffeur, gift basket store, hair care service, hair removal service, health food store owner, home economist, home shopper, hot meals provider, ice cream store, lunch cart operator, maid service, massage service, party planner, pool cleaning service, restaurant owner, sandwich delivery service, tour guide/escort.

Related Education and Training

Home economics, food service, cosmetology, dietetics, textiles/clothing, nutrition, consumer science, clothing and textile management, travel/tourism, catering, tailoring and alteration, food service, executive housekeeping.

10 HUMANITARIAN: An interest in helping others with their mental, spiritual, social, physical, or vocational needs.

GOE Subgroups

10.01 Social Services

10.02 Nursing, Therapy, and Specialized Teaching Services

10.03 Child and Adult Care

OOH Occupations

10.01 Social Services—Education Administrators; Personnel, Training, and Labor Relations Specialists and Managers; Psychologists; Human Services Workers; Social Workers; Protestant Ministers; Rabbis; Roman Catholic Priests; Counselors

10.02 Nursing, Therapy, and Specialized Teaching Services— Education Administrators; Health Services Managers; Personnel, Training, and Labor Relations Specialists and Managers; Recreation Workers; Adult Education Teachers; School Teachers—Kindergarten, Elementary, and Secondary; Occupational Therapists; Physical Therapists; Physician Assistants; Recreational Therapists; Registered Nurses; Respiratory Therapists; Cardiovascular Technologists and Technicians; Dental Hygienists; Licensed Practical Nurses; Nuclear Medicine Technologists; Radiologic Technologists; Preschool Workers

10.03 Child and Adult Care—Cardiovascular Technologists and Technicians; EEG Technologists; Emergency Medical Technicians; Surgical Technologists; Dental Assistants; Medical Assistants; Nursing Aides and Psychiatric Aides; Preschool Workers; Homemaker-Home Health Aides; Private Household Workers

DOT Occupations

Ambulance attendant, anthropologist, astrologer, athletic trainer, blind aide, companion, athletic trainer, blind aide, companion, case aide, caseworker, caseworker supervisor, child monitor, child welfare caseworker, child-care worker, children's tutor, clergy member, community health nursing director, counselor, Dean of Students, dental assistant, director of religious activities, Director of Placement, educational therapist technician, emergency medical technician, first-aid attendant, foreign student advisor, group work program aide, historian, home attendant, hypnotherapist, inservice coordinator, job analyst, manual-arts therapist, marriage counselor, music therapist, nurse, nurse's aide, occupational therapist, orderly, orientation therapist for the blind, parole officer, physical therapist, physician assistant, playroom attendant, preschool teacher, principal, program aide, radiologic technologist, recreational therapist, recreational worker, rehabilitation counselor, residence counselor, respiratory therapist, social worker, sociologist, teacher, teacher's aide, university professor, urban planner, veteran's contact representative.

Self-Employment Options

Baby-sitter, camp director, child therapist, child-care specialist, diet consultant, elderly care specialist, exceptional needs counselor, family counselor, foster parent, growth counselor, hypnotist, individual psychotherapist, instructor for the handicapped, marriage broker, nursery/daycare operator, nursing home operation, senior day care, stress management consultant, tutor, vocational advice.

Related Education and Training

Family studies, psychology, sociology, human development, social work, education, religious studies, teacher education, education administration, child care studies, special education, counseling, recreational therapy, geriatrics, human resources, and curriculum and instruction.

11 LEADING-INFLUENCING: An interest in leading and influencing others by using high-level verbal or numerical abilities.

GOE Subgroups

11.01 Mathematics and Statistics

11.02 Educational and Library Services

11.03 Social Research

11.04 Law

11.05 Business Administration

11.06 Finance

11.07 Services Administration

11.08 Communications

11.09 Promotion

11.10 Regulations Enforcement

11.11 Business Management

11.12 Contracts and Claims

OOH Occupations

11.01 Mathematics and Statistics—Engineering, Science, and Data Processing Managers; General Managers and Top Executives; Management Analysts and Consultants; Actuaries; Computer Scientists and Systems Analysts; Operations Research Analysts; Statisticians; Computer Programmers; Science Technicians

11.02 Educational and Library Services—Education Administrators; Personnel, Training, and Labor Relations Specialists and Managers; Adult Education Teachers; Archivists and Curators; College and University Faculty; Librarians; School Teachers—Kindergarten, Elementary, and Secondary; Dietitians and Nutritionists; Library Technicians; Clerical Supervisors and Managers; General Office Clerks; Stock Clerks; Library Assistants and Bookmobile Drivers; Order Clerks; Teacher Aides; Homemaker-Home Health Aides

11.03 Social Research—Employment Interviewers; Personnel, Training, and Labor Relations Specialists and Managers; Social Scientists and Urban Planners; Economists and Marketing Research Analysts; Psychologists; Sociologists; Urban and Regional Planners; Archivists and Curators

11.04 Law—Personnel, Training, and Labor Relations Specialists and Managers; Lawyers and Judges; Paralegals

11.05 Business Administration—Administrative Services Managers; Engineering, Science, and Data Processing Managers; Financial Managers; General Managers and Top Executives; Health Services Managers; Industrial Production Managers; Inspectors and Compliance Officers, except Construction; Loan Officers and Counselors; Marketing, Advertising, and Public Relations Managers; Personnel, Training, and Labor Relations Specialists and Managers; Property and Real Estate Managers; Purchasers and Buyers; Restaurant and Food Service Managers; Retail Managers; Archivists and Curators; Public Relations Specialists; Writers and Editors; Actors, Directors, and Producers; Retail sales workers; Blue-Collar Worker Supervisors

11.06 Finance—Accountants and Auditors; Budget Analysts; Financial Managers; Loan Officers and Counselors; Management Analysts and Consultants; Purchasers and Buyers; Underwriters; Economists and Marketing Research Analysts; Real Estate Agents, Brokers, and Appraisers; Securities and Financial Services Sales Representatives; Credit Clerks and Authorizers; Billing Clerks

11.07 Services Administration—Education Administrators; General Managers and Top Executives; Health Services Managers; Management Analysts and Consultants; Personnel, Training, and Labor Relations Specialists and Managers; Foresters and Conservation Scientists; Recreation Workers; Social Workers; Archivists and Curators; Counselors; Librarians; School Teachers—Kindergarten, Elementary, and Secondary; Public Relations Specialists

11.08 Communications—Mathematicians; Librarians; Radio and Television Announcers and Newscasters; Reporters and Correspondents; Writers and Editors; Actors, Directors, and Producers

11.09 Promotion—Education Administrators; General Managers and Top Executives; Marketing, Advertising, and Public Relations Managers; Personnel, Training, and Labor Relations Specialists and Managers; Public Relations Specialists; Actors, Directors, and Producers; Manufacturers' and Wholesale Sales Representatives; Services Sales Representatives; Police Detectives and Special Agents

11.10 Regulations Enforcement—General Managers and Top Executives; Health Services Managers; Inspectors and Compliance Officers, except Construction; Personnel, Training, and Labor Relations Specialists and Managers; Science Technicians; Firefighting Occupations; Blue-Collar Worker Supervisors

11.11 Business Management—Financial Managers; Funeral Directors; Hotel Managers and Assistants; Marketing, Advertising, and Public Relations Managers; Personnel, Training, and Labor Relations Specialists and Managers; Property and Real Estate Managers; Restaurant and Food Service Managers; Retail Managers; Recreation Workers; Blue-Collar Worker Supervisors; Rail Transportation Workers

11.12 Contracts and Claims—Administrative Services Managers; Construction Contractors and Managers; Engineering, Science, and Data Processing Managers; Property and Real Estate Managers; Purchasers and Buyers; Lawyers and Judges; Services Sales Representatives; Adjusters, Investigators, and Collectors; Clerical Supervisors and Managers

DOT Occupations

Academic dean, account executive, actuary, administrative assistant, adult education teacher, advertising agent, airport manager, anthropologist, applied statistician, appraiser, arbitrator, audiovisual librarian, auditor, bibliographer, branch manager, business manager, career-guidance counselor, city planning aide, classifier, commissary manager, credit analyst, curator, or, department store manager, director of employment research and planning, director of vital statistics, district attorney, economist, education specialist, educational institution president, employment interviewer, education supervisor, ethnologist, executive director, fashion coordinator, federal aid coordinator, financial analyst, food service director, forms analyst, funeral director, genealogist, historian, historic sites supervisor, hospital administrator, hotel manager, information scientist, information system programmer, intelligence specialist, investigator, job analyst, judge, lawyer, library director, librarian, lobbyist, magistrate, maintenance supervisor, manager, mathematical statistician, mathematical technician, media specialist, membership director, newscaster, office manager, operations director, paralegal assistant, patent agent, pawnbroker, personnel manager, politician, postmaster, principal, production manager, program director, project director, psychologist, public relations specialist, records management director, reporter, reports analyst, retail store manager, risk and insurance manager, school administrator, securities trader, social welfare administrator, sociologist, special agent, sports director, supervisor, systems analyst, teacher, teacher's aide, ticket broker, traffic manager, training representative, translator, treasurer, underwriter, vocational training instructor, warden, wholesale sales representative.

Self-Employment Options

Auctioneer, audiovisual production, commodity broker, communications consultant, educational consultant, educational researcher, importer/exporter, information broker, information service, instruction-book preparation, insurance agent, insurance sales, investment consultant, language translator service, paralegal assistance service, researcher, seminar promotions, special projects coordinator.

Related Education and Training

Management science, business administration, economics, labor relations, international management, finance, law/ethics, public administration, small business management, hotel/motel management, urban planning, health care administration, computer science, banking, finance, business law, and investments and securities.

12 PHYSICAL PERFORMING: An interest in physical activities performed before an audience.

GOE Subgroups

12.01 Sports

12.02 Physical Feats

OOH Occupations

12.02 Actors, Directors, and Producers

DOT Occupations

Acrobat, aerialist, athletic trainer, automobile racer, charter, coach, dog track kennel manager, dude wrangler, flagger, golf course ranger, golf pro, head coach, health club worker, horse identifier, horse-race starter, horse-race timer, hunting guide, jockey, jockey-room custodian, juggler, lead pony rider, marshall, motorcycle racer, patrol judge, physical educational teacher, pit steward, professional athlete, professional athletes coach, professional sports scout, racetrack steward, recreation leader, rodeo performer, scorer, sports psychologist, sports instructor, stunt performer, sulky driver, tour guide, umpire, wire walker.

Self-Employment Options

Aerobics instructor, children's fitness center, coach, developing training/exercise equipment, gymnastics instructor, health spa director, horseback riding instructor, personal trainer, physical fitness center, sports equipment salesperson, sporting goods store, sports memorabilia shop, sports instructor, umpire/referee, yoga instructor.

Related Education and Training

Sports psychology, sports physiology, physical education, leisure studies, recreational administration, coaching, sports medicine, health and wellness, athletic training, outdoor recreation, driver education, and sports education.

The Best Jobs Directory

Descriptions of the 686 Best Jobs for the 21st Century

This section of the book provides useful information on many occupations. Among them are the jobs with the highest pay, fastest growth, and largest number of openings.

If you have not read the introduction to this book, please consider doing so because it provides important information on the selection criteria for the descriptions in this directory. It also gives details on the descriptions so that you will better understand them.

As you review the descriptions, keep in mind the criteria we used. Each selected occupation features one of the following criteria.

▲ Has earnings of $40,000 or more a year (the average earnings for all workers is about $26,500 a year)

▲ Is expected to increase the number of people employed in that occupation by 10 percent or more by 2006

▲ Is a large enough occupation to create 100,000 or more job openings each year

Notice that only one criteria needs to be met for a job to be included in this book. If an occupation has, for example, over 100,000 new openings a year, it would be included even though its pay and growth rate are below average. You might ask, doesn't this mean that some "bad" jobs may appear in this section? The answer is yes and no.

We say this because systems analysts—the job with the highest total score for high pay, fast growth, and large number of openings—would be a *very bad* job for people who hate to do or are not good at that sort of work. On the other hand, many people love working as a bartender, even though its projected growth rate is 0 percent and average annual earnings are a paltry $13,395. Yet both jobs are described in the directory that follows.

The fact is that, somewhere, a systems analyst works as a bartender and loves it. Maybe this person likes the work a bartender does—the interaction with people; the physical activity; the ability to counsel customers on personal matters. Maybe the person likes the change of pace at a part-time job after doing the systems analyst gig as a day job. Maybe this individual got tired of being a systems analyst and is making a transition to something else. Or maybe the person found a way to make more money as a bartender (with tips, some bartenders can do quite well) than as a systems analyst.

So, our point is, that all the occupations are "just right" for the right people, at the right times in their lives. We are all likely to change our careers and jobs several times during our lives, and it's not always money that motivates us to do so. Browse the occupations in the lists in Section 1 and review the descriptions that follow. Somewhere, a place for you exists, and we hope you find it.

Accountants and Auditors

▲ Growth: 12%
▲ Annual Job Openings: 118,375
▲ Yearly Earnings: $38,168
▲ Education Required: Bachelor's degree
▲ Self-employed: 10%
▲ Part-time: 7%

A

Accountants

Analyze financial information and prepare financial reports to determine or maintain record of assets, liabilities, profit and loss, tax liability, or other financial activities within an organization. Exclude auditors. Analyzes operations, trends, costs, revenues, financial commitments, and obligations incurred, to project future revenues and expenses, using a computer. Develops, maintains, and analyzes budgets, and prepares periodic reports comparing budgeted costs to actual costs. Analyzes records of financial transactions to determine accuracy and completeness of entries, using computer. Prepares balance sheet, profit and loss statement, amortization and depreciation schedules, and other financial reports, using calculator or computer. Reports finances of establishment to management, and advises management about resource utilization, tax strategies, and assumptions underlying budget forecasts. Develops, implements, modifies, and documents budgeting, cost, general, property, and tax accounting systems. Predicts revenues and expenditures, and submits reports to management. Computes taxes owed; ensures compliance with tax payment, reporting, and other tax requirements; and represents establishment before taxing authority. Surveys establishment operations to ascertain accounting needs. Establishes table of accounts, and assigns entries to proper accounts. Audits contracts and prepares reports to substantiate transactions prior to settlement. Prepares forms and manuals for workers performing accounting and bookkeeping tasks. Appraises, evaluates, and inventories real property and equipment, and records description, value, location, and other information. Adapts accounting and recordkeeping functions to current technology of computerized accounting systems. Directs activities of workers performing accounting and bookkeeping tasks.

Knowledge: Administration and Management; Clerical; Economics and Accounting; Personnel and Human Resources; Computers and Electronics; Mathematics; Sociology and Anthropology; Education and Training; English Language; Philosophy and Theology; Law, Government, and Jurisprudence

Abilities: Written Comprehension; Written Expression; Fluency of Ideas; Originality; Deductive Reasoning; Mathematical Reasoning; Number Facility; Memorization; Speed of Closure; Flexibility of Closure; Perceptual Speed; Finger Dexterity; Near Vision

Auditors

Examine and analyze accounting records to determine financial status of establishment and prepare financial reports concerning operating procedures. Reviews data about material assets, net worth, liabilities, capital stock, surplus, income, and expenditures. Analyzes annual reports, financial statements, and other records, using accepted accounting and statistical procedures to determine financial condition. Evaluates reports from commission regarding solvency and profitability of company. Inspects account books and system for efficiency, effectiveness, and use of accepted accounting procedures to record transactions. Inspects cash on hand, notes receivable and payable, negotiable securities, and canceled checks. Reports to management about asset utilization and audit results, and recommends changes in operations and financial activities. Reviews taxpayer accounts, and conducts audits on-site, by correspondence, or by summoning taxpayer to office. Analyzes data for deficient controls, duplicated effort, extravagance, fraud, or noncompliance with laws, regulations, and management policies. Audits records to determine unemployment insurance premiums, liabilities, and compliance with tax laws. Examines payroll and personnel records to determine worker's compensation coverage. Examines records, tax returns, and related documents pertaining to settlement of decedent's estate. Verifies journal and ledger entries by examining inventory. Studies costs and revenue requirements, and designs new rate structure. Confers with company officials about financial and regulatory matters. Evaluates taxpayer finances to determine tax liability, notifies taxpayer of liability, and advises taxpayer of appeal rights. Examines records and interviews workers to ensure recording of transactions and compliance with laws and regulations. Supervises auditing of establishments and determines scope of investigation required. Prepares and presents testimony to regulatory commission hearings. Directs activities of personnel engaged in filing, recording, compiling, and transmitting financial records.

Knowledge: Administration and Management; Clerical; Economics and Accounting; Computers and Electronics; Mathematics; English Language; Philosophy and Theology; Law, Government, and Jurisprudence

Abilities: Written Comprehension; Oral Expression; Written Expression; Problem Sensitivity; Deductive Reasoning; Inductive Reasoning; Mathematical Reasoning; Number Facility; Memorization; Speed of Closure; Flexibility of Closure; Perceptual Speed; Selective Attention; Near Vision

Data Processing Auditors

Plan and conduct audits of data processing systems and applications to safeguard assets, ensure accuracy of data, and promote operational efficiency. Gathers data by interviewing workers, examining records, and using computer. Analyzes data to evaluate effectiveness of controls, accuracy of reports, and efficiency and security of operations. Establishes objectives and plan for audit, following general audit plan and previous audit reports. Writes audit report and recommendations using computer. Devises, writes, and tests computer program to obtain information needed for audit. Devises controls for new or modified computer application, for error detection, and to prevent inaccuracy and data loss.

Knowledge: Administration and Management; Clerical; Economics and Accounting; Computers and Electronics; Mathematics; Philosophy and Theology; Telecommunications

Abilities: Written Comprehension; Problem Sensitivity; Information Ordering; Category Flexibility; Speed of Closure; Flexibility of Closure; Perceptual Speed; Wrist-Finger Speed

Actuaries

▲ Growth: 0%
▲ Annual Job Openings: 1,165
▲ Yearly Earnings $66,352
▲ Education Required: Bachelor's degree
▲ Self-employed: 0%
▲ Part-time: 5%

Actuaries

Apply knowledge of mathematics, probability, statistics, and principles of finance and business to problems in life, health, social, and casualty insurance, annuities, and pensions. Determines mortality, accident, sickness, disability, and retirement rates. Constructs probability tables regarding fire, natural disasters, and unemployment, based on analysis of statistical data and other pertinent information. Designs or reviews insurance and pension plans and calculates premiums. Determines equitable basis for distributing surplus earnings under participating insurance and annuity contracts in mutual companies. Ascertains premium rates required and cash reserves and liabilities necessary to ensure payment of future benefits.

Knowledge: Clerical; Economics and Accounting; Mathematics; Sociology and Anthropology; History and Archeology; Philosophy and Theology; Law, Government, and Jurisprudence

Abilities: Written Expression; Deductive Reasoning; Mathematical Reasoning; Number Facility; Speed of Closure; Flexibility of Closure

Adjustment Clerks

▲ Growth: 46%

▲ Annual Job Openings: 80,643

▲ Yearly Earnings $22,422

▲ Education Required: Short-term O-J-T

▲ Self-employed: 0%

▲ Part-time: 12%

Adjustment Clerks

Investigate and resolve customers' inquiries concerning merchandise, service, billing, or credit rating. Examine pertinent information to determine accuracy of customers' complaints and responsibility for errors. Notify customers and appropriate personnel of findings, adjustments, and recommendations, such as exchange of merchandise, refund of money, credit to customers' accounts, or adjustment to customers' bills. Reviews claims adjustments with dealer, examines parts claimed to be defective, and approves or disapproves of dealer's claim. Notifies customer and designated personnel of findings and recommendations, such as exchanging merchandise or refunding money, or adjustment of bill. Examines weather conditions and number of days in billing period, and reviews meter accounts for errors which might explain high utility charges. Writes work order. Prepares reports showing volume, types, and disposition of claims handled. Compares merchandise with original requisition and information on invoice, and prepares invoice for returned goods. Orders tests to detect product malfunction, and determines if defect resulted from faulty construction. Trains dealers or service personnel in construction of products, service operations, and customer service.

Knowledge: Economics and Accounting

Abilities: None above average

Administrative Services Managers

▲ Growth: 11%
▲ Annual Job Openings: 24,605
▲ Yearly Earnings $44,200
▲ Education Required: Work experience, plus degree
▲ Self-employed: 0%
▲ Part-time: 6%

Property Officers and Contract Administrators

Coordinate property procurement and disposition activities of a business, agency, or other organization. Administer contracts for purchase or sale of equipment, materials, products, or services. Directs activities concerned with unclaimed property, and contracts for purchase of equipment, materials, products, or services. Authorizes obtaining and purchase of materials, supplies and equipment, and equipment maintenance. Prepares plans for selling and maintaining materials and property. Prepares, reviews, and negotiates bids and estimates with firms, bidders, and customers. Recommends disposal of materials and property. Examines performance requirements, property-related data, delivery schedules, and estimates of costs of material, equipment, and production. Advises company departments concerning contractual rights and obligations. Inspects inventory and transfers or fills material and equipment requests. Examines and evaluates materials and property to ensure conformance to company standards. Coordinates work of sales department.

Knowledge: Administration and Management; Economics and Accounting; Sales and Marketing; Law, Government, and Jurisprudence; Transportation

Abilities: Written Comprehension; Oral Expression; Written Expression; Problem Sensitivity; Deductive Reasoning; Inductive Reasoning; Category Flexibility; Mathematical Reasoning; Number Facility; Perceptual Speed; Gross Body Equilibrium; Near Vision; Speech Recognition

Administrative Services Managers

Plan, direct, and coordinate supportive services of an organization, such as recordkeeping, mail distribution, telephone reception, and other office support services. May oversee facilities planning and maintenance and custodial operations. Include facilities managers. Exclude procurement managers. Coordinates activities of clerical and administrative personnel in establishment or organization. Analyzes and organizes office operations, procedures, and production to improve efficiency. Recommends cost-saving methods, such as supply changes and disposal of records to improve efficiency of department. Prepares and reviews reports and schedules to ensure accuracy and efficiency. Formulates budgetary reports. Hires and terminates clerical and administrative personnel. Conducts classes to teach procedures to staff.

Knowledge: Administration and Management; Clerical; Economics and Accounting; Personnel and Human Resources; Mathematics; Psychology; Education and Training; English Language

Abilities: Oral Comprehension; Oral Expression; Written Expression; Fluency of Ideas; Originality; Mathematical Reasoning; Number Facility; Memorization; Time Sharing; Wrist-Finger Speed; Near Vision; Speech Recognition; Speech Clarity

Adult Education Instructors

- ▲ Growth: 21%
- ▲ Annual Job Openings: 81,219
- ▲ Yearly Earnings $27,372
- ▲ Education Required: Work experience in a related occupation
- ▲ Self-employed: 36%
- ▲ Part-time: 42%

Instructors—Nonvocational Education

Teach or instruct out-of-school youths and adults in courses other than those that normally lead to an occupational objective and are less than the baccalaureate level. Subjects may include self-improvement and nonvocational courses such as Americanization, basic education, art, drama, music, bridge, homemaking, stock market analysis, languages, modeling, flying, dancing, and automobile driving. Teaching may take place in public or private schools or in an organization whose primary business is other than education. Conducts classes, workshops, and demonstrations to teach principles, techniques, procedures, or methods of designated subject. Presents lectures and conducts discussions to increase students' knowledge and competence. Administers oral, written, and performance tests and issues grades in accordance with performance. Plans course content and method of instruction. Prepares outline of instructional program and lesson plans, and establishes course goals. Selects and assembles books, materials, and supplies for courses or projects. Observes students to determine and evaluate qualifications, limitations, abilities, interests, aptitudes, temperament, and individual characteristics. Observes and evaluates students' work to determine progress, and makes suggestions for improvement. Adapts course of study and training methods to meet students' needs and abilities. Conducts seminars or workshops for other teachers to demonstrate methods of using institution facilities and collections to enhance school programs. Directs and supervises student project activities, performances, tournaments, exhibits, contests, or plays. Evaluates success of instruction, based on number and enthusiasm of participants, and recommends retaining or eliminating course in future. Plans and conducts field trips to enrich instructional programs. Confers with leaders of government and other groups to coordinate training or to assist students to fulfill required criteria. Maintains records, such as student grades, attendance, and supply inventory. Confers with parents of students or students to resolve problems. Writes instructional articles on designated subjects. Orders, stores, and inventories books, materials, and supplies.

Knowledge: Economics and Accounting; Sociology and Anthropology; Education and Training; English Language; Foreign Language; Fine Arts; History and Archeology; Philosophy and Theology

Abilities: Oral Comprehension; Oral Expression; Written Expression; Speech Clarity

Aerospace Engineers

- ▲ Growth: 8%
- ▲ Annual Job Openings: 3,771
- ▲ Yearly Earnings $59,633
- ▲ Education Required: Bachelor's degree
- ▲ Self-employed: 0%
- ▲ Part-time: 1%

Aerospace Engineers

Perform a variety of engineering work in designing, constructing, and testing aircraft, missiles, and spacecraft. May conduct basic and applied research to evaluate adaptability of materials and equipment to aircraft design and manufacture. May recommend improvements in testing equipment and techniques. Include aeronautical and astronautical engineers. Develops design criteria for aeronautical or aerospace products or systems, including testing methods, production costs, quality standards, and completion dates. Analyzes project requests and proposals and engineering data to determine feasibility, producibility, cost, and production time of aerospace or aeronautical product. Formulates conceptual design of aeronautical or aerospace products or systems to meet customer requirements. Formulates mathematical models or other methods of computer analysis to develop, evaluate, or modify design according to customer engineering requirements. Plans and conducts experimental, environmental, operational, and stress tests on models and prototypes of aircraft and aerospace systems and equipment. Evaluates product data and design from inspections and reports for conformance to engineering principles, customer requirements, and quality standards. Directs and coordinates activities of engineering or technical personnel designing, fabricating, modifying, or testing aircraft or aerospace products. Directs research and development programs to improve production methods, parts, and equipment technology and to reduce costs. Reviews performance reports and documentation from customers and field engineers, and inspects malfunctioning or damaged products to determine problem. Plans and coordinates activities concerned with investigating and resolving customers reports of technical problems with aircraft or aerospace vehicles. Writes technical reports and other documentation, such as handbooks and bulletins, for use by engineering staff, management, and customers. Maintains records of performance reports for future reference. Evaluates and approves selection of vendors by study of past performance and new advertisements.

Knowledge: Administration and Management; Economics and Accounting; Customer and Personal Service; Personnel and Human Resources; Production and Processing; Computers and Electronics; Engineering and Technology; Design; Building and Construction; Mechanical; Mathematics; Physics; English Language; Telecommunications; Communications and Media

Abilities: Oral Comprehension; Written Comprehension; Oral Expression; Written Expression; Fluency of Ideas; Originality; Deductive Reasoning; Inductive Reasoning; Information Ordering; Mathematical Reasoning; Number Facility; Speed of Closure; Visualization

Agricultural and Food Scientists

- ▲ Growth: 20%
- ▲ Annual Job Openings: 2,016
- ▲ Yearly Earnings $35,942
- ▲ Education Required: Bachelor's degree
- ▲ Self-employed: 8%
- ▲ Part-time: 6%

Animal Scientists

Research or study selection, breeding, feeding, management, and marketing of livestock, pets, or other economically important animals. Studies nutritional requirements of animals and nutritive value of feed materials for animals and poultry. Studies effects of management practices, processing methods, feed, and environmental conditions on quality and quantity of animal products, such as eggs and milk. Researches and controls selection and breeding practices to increase efficiency of production and improve quality of animals. Develops improved practices in incubation, brooding, and artificial insemination. Develops improved practices in feeding, housing, sanitation, and parasite and disease control of animals and poultry. Determines generic composition of animal population and heritability of traits, utilizing principles of genetics. Crossbreeds animals with existing strains, or crosses strains to obtain new combinations of desirable characteristics.

Knowledge: Food Production; Chemistry; Biology; Medicine and Dentistry; History and Archeology

Abilities: Oral Comprehension; Written Comprehension; Written Expression; Fluency of Ideas; Originality; Problem Sensitivity; Deductive Reasoning; Inductive Reasoning; Information Ordering; Category Flexibility; Mathematical Reasoning; Number Facility; Memorization; Flexibility of Closure

Plant Scientists

Conduct research in breeding, production, and yield of plants or crops, and control of pests. Conducts research to determine best methods of planting, spraying, cultivating, and harvesting horticultural products. Experiments to develop new or improved varieties of products having specific features, such as higher yield, resistance to disease, size, or maturity. Studies crop production to discover effects of various climatic and soil conditions on crops. Develops methods for control of noxious weeds, crop diseases, and insect pests. Conducts experiments and investigations to determine methods of storing, processing, and transporting horticultural products. Studies insect distribution and habitat, and recommends methods to prevent importation and spread of injurious species. Aids in control and elimination of agricultural, structural, and forest pests by developing new and improved pesticides. Conducts experiments regarding causes of bee diseases and factors affecting yields of nectar pollen on various plants visited by bees. Identifies and classifies species of insects and allied forms, such as mites and spiders. Prepares articles and gives lectures on horticultural subjects. Improves bee strains, utilizing selective breeding by artificial insemination.

Knowledge: Food Production; Chemistry; Biology; Geography; Education and Training; English Language; History and Archeology; Communications and Media

Abilities: Oral Comprehension; Written Comprehension; Written Expression; Fluency of Ideas; Deductive Reasoning; Inductive Reasoning; Information Ordering; Category Flexibility; Mathematical Reasoning; Number Facility; Memorization; Flexibility of Closure

Food Scientists

Apply scientific and engineering principles in research, development, production, packaging, and processing of foods. Conducts research on new products and development of foods, applying scientific and engineering principles. Develops new and improved methods and systems for food processing, production, quality control, packaging, and distribution. Studies methods to improve quality of foods, such as flavor, color, texture, nutritional value, and convenience. Studies methods to improve physical, chemical, and microbiological composition of foods. Develops food standards, safety and sanitary regulations, and waste management and water supply specifications. Confers with process engineers, flavor experts, and packaging and marketing specialists to resolve problems in product development. Tests new products in test kitchen.

Knowledge: Production and Processing; Food Production; Chemistry; Biology; Law, Government, and Jurisprudence

Abilities: Written Comprehension; Fluency of Ideas; Originality; Deductive Reasoning; Inductive Reasoning; Category Flexibility

Soil Scientists

Research or study soil characteristics, map soil types, and investigate responses of soils to known management practices to determine use capabilities of soils and effects of alternative practices on soil productivity. Studies soil characteristics and classifies soils according to standard types. Investigates responses of specific soil types to soil management practices, such as fertilization, crop rotation, and industrial waste control. Conducts experiments on farms or experimental stations to determine best soil types for different plants. Performs chemical analysis on micro-organism content of soil to determine microbial reactions and chemical mineralogical relationship to plant growth. Provides advice on rural or urban land use.

Knowledge: Food Production; Chemistry; Biology; Geography

Abilities: Oral Comprehension; Written Comprehension; Fluency of Ideas; Originality; Deductive Reasoning; Inductive Reasoning; Category Flexibility; Mathematical Reasoning; Number Facility; Flexibility of Closure

Air Traffic Controllers and Airplane Dispatchers

▲ Growth: 0%
▲ Annual Job Openings: 3,310
▲ Yearly Earnings $45,739
▲ Education Required: Long-term O-J-T
▲ Self-employed: 0%
▲ Part-time: 11%

Airplane Dispatchers and Air Traffic Controllers

Control air traffic on and within vicinity of airport and movement of air traffic between altitude sectors and control centers, according to established procedures and policies. Authorize, regulate, and control commercial airline flights, according to government or company regulations, to expedite and ensure flight safety. Communicates with, relays flight plans to, and coordinates movement of air traffic between control centers. Determines timing of and procedure for flight vector changes in sector. Issues landing and take-off authorizations and instructions, and communicates other information to aircraft. Controls air traffic at and within vicinity of airport. Recommends flight path changes to planes traveling in storms or fog or in emergency situations. Relays air traffic information, such as altitude, expected time of arrival, and course of aircraft, to control centers. Transfers control of departing flights to traffic control center and accepts control of arriving flights from air traffic control center. Analyzes factors, such as weather reports, fuel requirements, and maps, to determine flights and air routes. Directs radio searches for aircraft, and alerts control centers emergency facilities of flight difficulties. Inspects, adjusts, and controls radio equipment and airport lights. Completes daily activity report and keeps record of messages from aircraft. Reviews records and reports for clarity and completeness and maintains records and reports.

Knowledge: Computers and Electronics; Physics; Geography; Telecommunications; Transportation

Abilities: Number Facility; Memorization; Speed of Closure; Flexibility of Closure; Perceptual Speed; Spatial Orientation; Selective Attention; Time Sharing; Response Orientation; Reaction Time; Gross Body Equilibrium; Near Vision; Hearing Sensitivity; Auditory Attention; Sound Localization; Speech Clarity

Aircraft Assemblers

- ▲ Growth: 10%
- ▲ Annual Job Openings: 1,525
- ▲ Yearly Earnings $31,345
- ▲ Education Required: Work experience in a related occupation
- ▲ Self-employed: 0%
- ▲ Part-time: 3%

Aircraft Structure Assemblers, Precision

Assemble tail, wing, fuselage, or other structural section of aircraft, space vehicles, and missiles from parts, subassemblies, and components; and install functional units, parts, or equipment, such as landing gear, control surfaces, doors, and floorboards. Installs units, parts, equipment, and components in structural assembly, according to blueprints and specifications, using hand tools and power tools. Bolts, screws, or rivets accessories to fasten, support, or hang components and subassemblies. Drills holes in structure and subassemblies, and attaches brackets, hinges, or clips to secure installation or to fasten subassemblies. Locates and marks reference points and holes for installation of parts and components, using jigs, templates, and measuring instruments. Aligns structural assemblies. Cuts, trims, and files parts, and verifies fitting tolerances to prepare for installation. Positions and aligns subassemblies in jigs or fixtures, using measuring instruments, following blueprint lines and index points. Inspects and tests installed units, parts, and equipment for fit, performance, and compliance with standards, using measuring instruments and test equipment.

Knowledge: Production and Processing; Engineering and Technology; Design; Building and Construction; Mechanical

Abilities: Perceptual Speed; Spatial Orientation; Visualization; Arm-Hand Steadiness; Manual Dexterity; Finger Dexterity; Multilimb Coordination; Rate Control; Wrist-Finger Speed; Speed of Limb Movement; Explosive Strength; Trunk Strength; Stamina; Extent Flexibility; Dynamic Flexibility; Gross Body Coordination; Gross Body Equilibrium; Depth Perception

Aircraft Systems Assemblers, Precision

Lay out, assemble, install, and test aircraft systems, such as armament, environmental control, plumbing and hydraulic systems. Aligns, fits, and assembles system components, such as armament, structural, and mechanical components, using jigs, fixtures, measuring instruments, hand tools, and power tools. Lays out location of parts and assemblies, according to specifications. Assembles and installs parts, fittings, and assemblies on aircraft, using layout tools, hand tools, power tools, and fasteners. Tests systems and assemblies for functional performance, and adjusts, repairs, or replaces malfunctioning units or parts. Installs mechanical linkages and actuators, and verifies tension of cables, using tensiometer. Examines parts for defects and for conformance to specifications, using precision measuring instruments. Reworks, replaces, realigns, and adjusts parts and assemblies according to specifications. Cleans, oils, assembles, and attaches system components to aircraft, using hand tools, power tools, and measuring instruments. Reads and interprets blueprints, illustrations, and specifications to determine layout, sequence of operations, or identity and relationship of parts. Measures, drills, files, cuts, bends, and smoothes materials to ensure fit and clearance of parts.

Knowledge: Production and Processing; Engineering and Technology; Design; Building and Construction; Mechanical

Abilities: Visualization; Arm-Hand Steadiness; Manual Dexterity; Multilimb Coordination; Rate Control; Reaction Time; Wrist-Finger Speed; Speed of Limb Movement; Static Strength; Explosive Strength; Dynamic Strength; Trunk Strength; Extent Flexibility; Dynamic Flexibility; Gross Body Equilibrium; Depth Perception

Aircraft Rigging Assemblers

Fabricate and assemble aircraft tubing or cable components or assemblies. Sets up and operates machines and systems to crimp, cut, bend, form, swage, flare, bead, burr, and straighten tubing, according to specifications. Assembles and attaches fittings onto cable and tubing components, using hand tools. Measures, cuts, and inspects cable and tubing, using master template, measuring instruments, and cable cutter or saw. Welds tubing and fittings, and solders cable ends, using tack-welder, induction brazing chamber, or other equipment. Swages fittings onto cable, using swaging machine. Forms loops or splices in cables, using clamps and fittings, or reweaves cable strands. Marks location of cutouts, holes, and trim lines of parts and relationship of parts, using measuring instruments. Fabricates cable templates. Reads and interprets blueprints, work orders, data charts, and specifications to determine operations, and type, quantity, dimensions, configuration, and finish of tubing, cable, and fittings. Verifies dimensions of cable assembly and position of fittings, using measuring instruments, and repairs and reworks defective assemblies. Selects and installs accessories in swaging machine, using hand tools. Marks identifying information on tubing or cable assemblies, using electro-chemical etching device, label, rubber stamp, or other methods. Tests tubing and cable assemblies for defects, using pressure testing equipment and proofloading machines. Cleans, lubricates, and coats tubing and cable assemblies.

Knowledge: Production and Processing; Engineering and Technology; Design; Physics

Abilities: Arm-Hand Steadiness; Manual Dexterity; Finger Dexterity; Multilimb Coordination; Rate Control; Speed of Limb Movement; Explosive Strength; Dynamic Strength; Stamina; Dynamic Flexibility; Gross Body Equilibrium

Aircraft Mechanics

- ▲ Growth: 14%
- ▲ Annual Job Openings: 5,893
- ▲ Yearly Earnings $35,422
- ▲ Education Required: Postsecondary vocational training
- ▲ Self-employed: 0%
- ▲ Part time: 2%

Aircraft Mechanics

Inspect, test, repair, maintain, and service aircraft. Adjusts, aligns, and calibrates aircraft systems, using hand tools, gauges, and test equipment. Examines and inspects engines or other components for cracks, breaks, or leaks. Tests engine and system operations, using testing equipment, and listens to engine sounds to detect and diagnose malfunctions. Disassembles and inspects parts for wear, warping, or other defects. Repairs, replaces, and rebuilds aircraft structures, functional components, and parts, such as wings and fuselage, rigging, and hydraulic units. Services and maintains aircraft systems by performing tasks, such as flushing crankcase, cleaning screens, greasing moving parts, and checking brakes. Assembles and installs electrical, plumbing, mechanical, hydraulic, and structural components and accessories, using hand tools and power tools. Removes engine from aircraft or installs engine, using hoist or forklift truck. Reads and interprets aircraft maintenance manuals and specifications to determine feasibility and method of repairing or replacing malfunctioning or damaged components. Modifies aircraft structures, space vehicles, systems, or components, following drawings, engineering orders, and technical publications.

Knowledge: Engineering and Technology; Design; Building and Construction; Mechanical

Abilities: Deductive Reasoning; Memorization; Speed of Closure; Flexibility of Closure; Perceptual Speed; Arm-Hand Steadiness; Manual Dexterity; Finger Dexterity; Control Precision; Multilimb Coordination; Rate Control; Reaction Time; Wrist-Finger Speed; Speed of Limb Movement; Static Strength; Explosive Strength; Dynamic Strength; Trunk Strength; Stamina; Extent Flexibility; Dynamic Flexibility; Gross Body Coordination; Gross Body Equilibrium; Visual Color Discrimination; Depth Perception; Hearing Sensitivity; Sound Localization

Aircraft Body and Bonded Structure Repairers

Repair body or structure of aircraft according to specifications. Reinstalls repaired or replacement parts for subsequent riveting or welding, using clamps and wrenches. Repairs or fabricates defective section or part, using metal fabricating machines, saws, brakes, shears, and grinders. Trims and shapes replacement section to specified size, and fits and secures section in place, using adhesives, hand tools, and power tools. Reads work orders, blueprints, and specifications, or examines sample or damaged part to determine repair or fabrication procedures and sequence of operations. Locates and marks dimension and reference lines on defective or replacement part, using templates, scribes, compass, and steel rule. Removes or cuts out defective part, or drills holes to gain access to internal defect or damage, using drill and punch. Positions and secures damaged part or structure, and examines to determine location and extent of damage or defect. Communicates with other workers to fit and align heavy parts or to expedite processing of repair parts. Cleans, strips, primes, and sands structural surfaces and materials prior to bonding. Cures bonded structure, using portable or stationary curing equipment. Spreads plastic film over area to be repaired to prevent damage to surrounding area.

Knowledge: Design; Building and Construction; Mechanical

Abilities: Information Ordering; Manual Dexterity; Finger Dexterity; Multilimb Coordination; Rate Control; Wrist-Finger Speed; Speed of Limb Movement; Explosive Strength; Dynamic Strength; Trunk Strength; Stamina; Extent Flexibility; Dynamic Flexibility; Gross Body Coordination; Gross Body Equilibrium; Depth Perception

Aircraft Engine Specialists

Repair and maintain the operating condition of aircraft engines. Include helicopter engine mechanics. Exclude electrical system specialists and aircraft mechanics whose primary duties do not involve engine repair. Replaces or repairs worn, defective, or damaged components, using hand tools, gauges, and testing equipment. Disassembles and inspects engine parts, such as turbine blades and cylinders, for wear, warping, cracks, and leaks. Reassembles engine and installs engine in aircraft. Listens to operating engine to detect and diagnose malfunctions, such as sticking or burned valves. Tests engine operation—using test equipment such as ignition analyzer, compression checker, distributor timer, and ammeter—to identify malfunction. Removes engine from aircraft, using hoist or forklift truck. Services and maintains aircraft and related apparatus by performing activities such as flushing crankcase, cleaning screens, and lubricating moving parts. Reads and interprets manufacturers' maintenance manuals, service bulletins, and other specifications to determine feasibility and methods of repair. Adjusts, repairs, or replaces electrical wiring system and aircraft accessories. Services, repairs, and rebuilds aircraft structures, such as wings, fuselage, rigging, and surface and hydraulic controls, using hand or power tools and equipment.

Knowledge: Engineering and Technology; Building and Construction; Mechanical; Physics

Abilities: Written Comprehension; Problem Sensitivity; Inductive Reasoning; Information Ordering; Speed of Closure; Flexibility of Closure; Finger Dexterity; Multilimb Coordination; Static Strength; Explosive Strength; Extent Flexibility; Dynamic Flexibility; Gross Body Equilibrium; Night Vision; Peripheral Vision; Depth Perception; Hearing Sensitivity; Auditory Attention; Sound Localization

Aircraft Pilots and Flight Engineers

- ▲ Growth: 14%
- ▲ Annual Job Openings: 6,641
- ▲ Yearly Earnings $69,097
- ▲ Education Required: Long-term O-J-T
- ▲ Self-employed: 1%
- ▲ Part-time: 23%

Airplane Pilots, Commercial

Pilot airplane to transport passengers, mail, or freight for other commercial purposes. Must have commercial pilot's license. Starts engines, operates controls, and pilots airplane to transport passengers, mail, or freight, adhering to flight plan and regulations and procedures. Obtains and reviews data, such as load weight, fuel supply, weather conditions,. and flight schedule. Plots flight pattern and files flight plan with appropriate officials. Orders changes in fuel supply, load, route, or schedule to ensure safety of flight. Conducts preflight checks and reads gauges to verify that fluids and pressure are at prescribed levels. Operates radio equipment and contacts control tower for takeoff, clearance, arrival instructions, and other information. Coordinates flight activities with ground crew and air-traffic control, and informs crew members of flight and test procedures. Holds commercial pilot's license issued by Federal Aviation Administration. Conducts in-flight tests and evaluations, at specified altitudes, in all types of weather to determine receptivity and other characteristics of equipment and systems. Logs information, such as flight time, altitude flown, and fuel consumption. Plans and formulates flight activities and test schedules and prepares flight evaluation reports. Gives training and instruction in aircraft operations for students and other pilots.

Knowledge: Computers and Electronics; Engineering and Technology; Mechanical; Physics; Geography; Medicine and Dentistry; Education and Training; Foreign Language; Public Safety and Security; Law, Government, and Jurisprudence; Telecommunications; Transportation

Abilities: Oral Expression; Information Ordering; Mathematical Reasoning; Number Facility; Speed of Closure; Flexibility of Closure; Perceptual Speed; Spatial Orientation; Selective Attention; Time Sharing; Control Precision; Multilimb Coordination; Response Orientation; Rate Control; Reaction Time; Wrist-Finger Speed; Speed of Limb Movement; Far Vision; Visual Color Discrimination; Night Vision; Peripheral Vision; Depth Perception; Glare Sensitivity; Hearing Sensitivity; Auditory Attention; Sound Localization; Speech Recognition; Speech Clarity

Small Airplane Pilots

Pilot airplane or helicopter to perform activities such as crop dusting and aerial photography. Pilots airplane or helicopter to photograph areas of earth's surface or to dust or spray fields. Adjusts controls to hold aircraft on course and to ensure coverage of area to be sprayed or photographed. Holds aircraft in level flight to eliminate forward and lateral tilt of aircraft. Sights along pointers on aircraft to topographical landmarks. Studies maps to become acquainted with topography, obstacles, or hazards, such as air turbulence, hedgerows, and hills. Notifies livestock owners to move livestock from property to be sprayed or dusted, and arranges for warning signals to be posted.

Knowledge: Food Production; Physics; Geography; Fine Arts; Public Safety and Security; Telecommunications; Transportation

Abilities: Information Ordering; Flexibility of Closure; Perceptual Speed; Spatial Orientation; Selective Attention; Time Sharing; Arm-Hand Steadiness; Control Precision; Multilimb Coordination; Response Orientation; Rate Control; Reaction Time; Gross Body Equilibrium; Far Vision; Night Vision; Peripheral Vision; Depth Perception; Glare Sensitivity; Hearing Sensitivity; Auditory Attention; Sound Localization

Flight Instructors

Train new and experienced pilots seeking licenses or experience on new aircraft. Instructs new pilots in company regulations and procedures and in operation of company's aircraft. Conducts training and review courses in use of equipment, flight procedures, and techniques. Observes and evaluates performance, knowledge, and skills of pilots, using manuals, check lists, or proficiency tests. Explains operation of aircraft components, such as altimeter, tachometer, rudder, and flaps. Demonstrates techniques for controlling aircraft during taxiing, takeoff, spins, stalls, turns, and landings. Notes pilot's compliance with or infringement of company or Federal Aviation Administration flight regulations. Compiles and issues reports on findings to appropriate company and FAA officials. Holds commercial pilot's certificate, with instructor's rating, issued by Federal Aviation Administration.

Knowledge: Personnel and Human Resources; Computers and Electronics; Geography; Education and Training; Public Safety and Security; Law, Government, and Jurisprudence; Telecommunications; Transportation

Abilities: Written Comprehension; Oral Expression; Information Ordering; Mathematical Reasoning; Number Facility; Speed of Closure; Flexibility of Closure; Perceptual Speed; Spatial Orientation; Selective Attention; Time Sharing; Control Precision; Multilimb Coordination; Response Orientation; Rate Control; Reaction Time; Speed of Limb Movement; Gross Body Equilibrium; Far Vision; Visual Color Discrimination; Night Vision; Peripheral Vision; Depth Perception; Glare Sensitivity; Hearing Sensitivity; Auditory Attention; Sound Localization; Speech Clarity

Flight Navigators

Locate position and direct course of airplane in flight, using navigational aids such as charts, maps, sextant, and slide rule. Establishes position of airplane, using navigation instruments and charts, celestial observation, or dead reckoning. Directs course of airplane and deviations from course required by weather conditions, such as wind drifts and forecasted atmospheric conditions. Utilizes navigation aids, such as radio beams and beacons, to locate position and direct course of airplane. Records and maintains flight log, including time in flight, altitude flown, and fuel consumed.

Knowledge: Physics; Geography; Foreign Language; Public Safety and Security; Telecommunications; Transportation

Abilities: Deductive Reasoning; Mathematical Reasoning; Number Facility; Speed of Closure; Flexibility of Closure; Perceptual Speed; Spatial Orientation; Selective Attention; Time Sharing; Response Orientation; Rate Control; Near Vision; Far Vision; Night Vision; Peripheral Vision; Depth Perception; Glare Sensitivity; Auditory Attention; Sound Localization; Speech Recognition

Flight Engineers

Make preflight, inflight, and postflight inspections, adjustments, and minor repairs to ensure safe and efficient operation of aircraft. Inspects aircraft for defects, such as fuel or oil leaks and malfunctions in electrical, hydraulic, and pressurization systems. Adjusts instruments and makes minor repairs, such as replacing fuses and freeing jammed controls, to ensure safe operation of aircraft. Monitors fuel gauges and control panel to verify aircraft performance, and regulates engine speed according to instructions. Verifies passenger and cargo distribution and amount of fuel to ensure conformance to weight and balance specifications. Reports needed repairs to ground maintenance personnel. Keeps log of rate of fuel consumption, engine performance, and uncorrected malfunctions.

Knowledge: Computers and Electronics; Engineering and Technology; Design; Mechanical; Physics; Geography; Public Safety and Security; Telecommunications; Transportation

Abilities: Oral Comprehension; Written Comprehension; Problem Sensitivity; Deductive Reasoning; Mathematical Reasoning; Number Facility; Speed of Closure; Flexibility of Closure; Perceptual Speed; Spatial Orientation; Selective Attention; Time Sharing; Finger Dexterity; Control Precision; Multilimb Coordination; Response Orientation; Rate Control; Reaction Time; Far Vision; Visual Color Discrimination; Night Vision; Peripheral Vision; Hearing Sensitivity; Auditory Attention; Sound Localization

Helicopter Pilots

Pilot helicopter for commercial purposes, such as transporting passengers and cargo. Pilots helicopter to transport passengers and cargo, conduct search and rescue missions, fight fires, report traffic conditions, or for other purposes. Plans flight, following government and company regulations, using aeronautical charts and navigation instruments. Inspects helicopter prior to departure to detect malfunctions or unsafe conditions, using check list. Writes specified information in flight record, such as time in flight, altitude flown, and fuel consumption. Instructs students in operation of helicopter and equipment, and flight procedures and techniques.

Knowledge: Computers and Electronics; Engineering and Technology; Geography; Medicine and Dentistry; Therapy and Counseling; Education and Training; Public Safety and Security; Law, Government, and Jurisprudence; Telecommunications; Transportation

Abilities: Number Facility; Flexibility of Closure; Perceptual Speed; Spatial Orientation; Selective Attention; Time Sharing; Arm-Hand Steadiness; Control Precision; Multilimb Coordination; Response Orientation; Rate Control; Reaction Time; Speed of Limb Movement; Gross Body Equilibrium; Far Vision; Night Vision; Peripheral Vision; Depth Perception; Glare Sensitivity; Hearing Sensitivity; Auditory Attention; Sound Localization

Ambulance Drivers and Attendants

▲ Growth: 37%

▲ Annual Job Openings: 3,864

▲ Yearly Earnings $16,473

▲ Education Required: Short-term O-J-T

▲ Self-employed: 0%

▲ Part-time: 34%

Ambulance Drivers and Attendants, Except Emergency Medical Technicians

Drive ambulance or assist ambulance driver in transporting sick, injured, or convalescent persons. Assist in lifting patients and rendering first aid. May be required to have Red Cross first-aid training certificate. Transports sick or injured persons to hospital, or convalescents to destination, avoiding sudden motions detrimental to patients. Places patient on stretcher and loads stretcher into ambulance, usually with help of ambulance attendant. Administers first aid as needed. Reports facts concerning accident or emergency to hospital personnel or law enforcement officials. Changes soiled linens on stretcher. Shackles violent patients.

Knowledge: Customer and Personal Service; Biology; Geography; Medicine and Dentistry; Therapy and Counseling; Foreign Language; Transportation

Abilities: Memorization; Speed of Closure; Flexibility of Closure; Spatial Orientation; Selective Attention; Time Sharing; Control Precision; Multilimb Coordination; Response Orientation; Rate Control; Reaction Time; Wrist-Finger Speed; Speed of Limb Movement; Static Strength; Explosive Strength; Stamina; Dynamic Flexibility; Gross Body Coordination; Gross Body Equilibrium; Far Vision; Night Vision; Peripheral Vision; Depth Perception; Glare Sensitivity; Hearing Sensitivity; Auditory Attention; Sound Localization

Amusement and Recreation Attendants

▲ Growth: 48%
▲ Annual Job Openings: 130,390
▲ Yearly Earnings $13,353
▲ Education Required: Short-term O-J-T
▲ Self-employed: 1%
▲ Part-time: 48%

Amusement and Recreation Attendants

Perform variety of attending duties at amusement or recreation facility. May schedule use of recreation facilities, maintain and provide equipment to participants of sporting events or recreational pursuits, or operate amusement concessions and rides. Schedules use of recreation facilities, such as golf courses, tennis courts, bowling alleys, and softball diamonds. Rents, sells, and issues sports equipment and supplies, such as bowling shoes, golf balls, swimming suits, and beach chairs. Sells tickets and collects fees from customers, and collects or punches tickets. Operates or drives mechanical riding devices in amusement parks or carnivals, or explains use of devices. Receives, retrieves, replaces, and stores sports equipment and supplies; arranges items in designated areas; and erects or removes equipment. Provides information about facilities, entertainment options, and rules and regulations. Assists patrons on and off amusement rides, boats, or ski lifts, and in mounting and riding animals; and fastens or directs patrons to fasten safety devices. Directs patrons of establishment to rides, seats, or attractions, or escorts patrons on tours of points of interest. Monitors activities to ensure adherence to rules and safety procedures to protect environment and maintain order, and ejects unruly patrons. Tends automatic equipment in funhouse to amuse, excite, or mystify patrons, and ski lift to transport skiers. Launches, moors, and demonstrates use of boats, such as rowboats, canoes, and motorboats, or caddies for golfers. Provides entertainment services, such as guessing patron's weight, conducting games, or explaining use of arcade game machines, and photographing patrons. Announces and describes amusement park attractions to patrons to entice customers to games and other entertainment. Sells and serves refreshments to customers. Verifies winning bingo cards and awards prizes or pays money to winning players. Cleans sporting equipment, vehicles, rides, booths, facilities, and grounds. Inspects, repairs, adjusts, tests, fuels, and oils sporting and recreation equipment, game machines, and amusement rides. Records details of attendance, sales, receipts, reservations, and repair activities. Attends animals, performing such tasks as harnessing, saddling, feeding, watering, and grooming, and drives horse-drawn vehicle for entertainment or advertising purposes.

Knowledge: Sales and Marketing; Customer and Personal Service; Mechanical; Public Safety and Security

Abilities: Perceptual Speed; Spatial Orientation; Time Sharing; Control Precision; Response Orientation; Rate Control; Reaction Time; Static Strength; Dynamic Strength; Trunk Strength;

Stamina; Extent Flexibility; Dynamic Flexibility; Gross Body Coordination; Gross Body Equilibrium; Far Vision; Night Vision; Peripheral Vision; Depth Perception; Glare Sensitivity; Hearing Sensitivity; Auditory Attention; Sound Localization; Speech Recognition

Games-of-Chance Attendants

Perform a variety of duties associated with games of chance. Conduct gambling tables, such as dice, roulette, or cards, collect fees, pay winnings, and explain rules. Conducts gambling table or game, such as dice, roulette, cards, or keno, and ensures that game rules are followed. Exchanges paper currency for playing chips or coin money, and collects game fees or wagers. Verifies, computes, and pays out winnings. Participates in card game for gambling establishment to provide minimum complement of players at table. Prepares collection report for submission to supervisor. Seats cardroom patrons at tables. Sells food, beverages, and tobacco to players.

Knowledge: Sales and Marketing; Customer and Personal Service; Foreign Language; Law, Government, and Jurisprudence

Abilities: Memorization; Perceptual Speed; Selective Attention; Time Sharing; Response Orientation; Wrist-Finger Speed; Night Vision; Peripheral Vision; Auditory Attention; Sound Localization; Speech Recognition

Animal Caretakers

Growth: 21%
Annual Job Openings: 31,339
Yearly Earnings $15,496
Education Required: Short-term O-J-T
Self-employed: 26%
Part-time: 38%

Animal Caretakers, except Farm

Feed, water, and exercise or otherwise care for small or large animals in establishments such as zoos, pounds, animal hospitals, or kennels. Feeds and waters animals according to schedule and feeding instructions. Mixes food, liquid formulas, medications, or food supplements according to instructions, prescriptions, and knowledge of animal species. Exercises animals to maintain their fitness and health, or trains animals to perform certain tasks. Adjusts controls to regulate specified temperature and humidity of animal quarters, nursery, or exhibit area. Examines and observes animals for signs of illness, disease, or injury, and provides treatment or informs veterinarian. Washes, brushes, clips, trims, and grooms animals. Cleans and disinfects animal quarters, such as pens, stables, cages, and yards, and surgical or other equipment, such as saddles and bridles. Anesthetizes and inoculates animals, according to instructions. Transfers animals between enclosures for breeding, birthing, shipping, or rearranging exhibits. Records information about animals, such as weight, size, physical condition, diet, medications, and food intake. Orders, unloads, and stores feed and supplies. Saddles and shoes animals. Responds to questions from patrons and provides information about animals, such as behavior, habitat, breeding habits, or facility activities. Observes and cautions children petting and feeding animals in designated area. Installs equipment in animal care facility, such as infrared lights, feeding devices, or cribs. Repairs fences, cages, or pens.

Knowledge: Medicine and Dentistry

Abilities: Dynamic Strength

Farriers

Fit, shape, and nail protective shoes to animals' hooves. Trims and shapes hoof, using knife and snippers. Shapes shoe to fit hoof, using swage, forge, and hammer. Nails shoe to hoof and files hoof flush with shoe. Removes worn or defective shoe from animal's hoof, using nail snippers and pincers. Examines hoof to detect bruises and cracks and to determine trimming required. Measures hoof, using calipers and steel tape. Selects aluminum or steel shoe from stock, according to hoof measurements and purpose and requirements of use. Places leather pad, sponge, or pine tar mixture onto bruised or cracked hoof for protection.

Knowledge: None above average

Abilities: Wrist-Finger Speed; Speed of Limb Movement; Explosive Strength; Dynamic Strength; Gross Body Equilibrium; Peripheral Vision

Animal Groomers and Bathers

Comb, clip, trim, bathe, and shape animals' coats to groom animals. Trims animal's toenails, and clips hair and fur according to determined pattern, using clippers, comb, and shears. Combs and brushes animal to remove matting, dead skin, and burrs, and to shape coat, using animal brush and comb. Draws and regulates water for bath, and washes animal, using perfumed soap or shampoo and handbrush. Places and secures animal on grooming table and studies proportions of animal to determine cutting pattern that will achieve desired style. Dries animal, using towel and electric dryer. Determines desired clipping pattern for animal, according to written or oral instructions. Calms animal by talking or employing other techniques. Cleans animal quarters.

Knowledge: None above average

Abilities: Speed of Limb Movement

Aquarists

Perform a variety of duties, such as feeding, cleaning tanks, monitoring temperature, and treating sick or injured fish, to care for aquatic life in aquarium exhibits. Prepares food and feeds fish and other aquatic life according to schedule. Monitors thermometers to determine water temperature in tanks, and adjusts thermostats to maintain specified temperature. Collects water samples, compares samples to chart for acid analysis, and adds chemicals to maintain specified water conditions. Cleans tanks and removes algae from tank windows. Observes fish and aquatic life to detect and treat disease, injury, and illness, according to instructions. Maintains aquatic plants and decorations in aquatic displays. Fires sedation gun and assists crew in collection of aquatic specimens during expeditions.

Knowledge: Chemistry; Biology

Abilities: None above average

Architects

▲ Growth: 20%
▲ Annual Job Openings: 10,404
▲ Yearly Earnings $46,883
▲ Education Required: Bachelor's degree
▲ Self-employed: 28%
▲ Part-time: 8%

Architects, Except Landscape and Marine

Plan and design structures, such as private residences, office buildings, theaters, factories, and other structural property. Prepares information regarding design, structure specifications, materials, color, equipment, estimated costs, and construction time. Plans layout of project. Integrates engineering element into unified design. Prepares scale drawings. Consults with client to determine functional and spatial requirements of structure. Estimates costs and construction time. Conducts periodic on-site observation of work during construction to monitor compliance with plans. Directs activities of workers engaged in preparing drawings and specification documents. Prepares contract documents for building contractors. Represents client in obtaining bids and awarding construction contracts. Administers construction contracts. Prepares operating and maintenance manuals, studies, and reports.

Knowledge: Administration and Management; Economics and Accounting; Sales and Marketing; Customer and Personal Service; Personnel and Human Resources; Engineering and Technology; Design; Building and Construction; Mathematics; Physics; Geography; English Language; Fine Arts; History and Archeology; Public Safety and Security; Law, Government, and Jurisprudence; Communications and Media

Abilities: Oral Comprehension; Written Comprehension; Oral Expression; Written Expression; Fluency of Ideas; Originality; Problem Sensitivity; Deductive Reasoning; Inductive Reasoning; Information Ordering; Category Flexibility; Mathematical Reasoning; Number Facility; Memorization; Speed of Closure; Flexibility of Closure; Spatial Orientation; Visualization; Selective Attention; Time Sharing; Gross Body Equilibrium; Near Vision; Far Vision; Visual Color Discrimination; Night Vision; Speech Recognition

Artists and Commercial Artists

- ▲ Growth: 28%
- ▲ Annual Job Openings: 46,893
- ▲ Yearly Earnings $33,113
- ▲ Education Required: Work experience, plus degree
- ▲ Self-employed: 57%
- ▲ Part-time: 24%

Painters and Illustrators

Paint or draw subject material to produce original artwork or provide illustrations to explain or adorn written or spoken word, using watercolors, oils, acrylics, tempera, or other paint mediums. Renders drawings, illustrations, and sketches of buildings, manufactured products, or models, working from sketches, blueprints, memory, or reference materials. Paints scenic backgrounds, murals, and portraiture for motion picture and television production sets, glass artworks, and exhibits. Etches, carves, paints, or draws artwork on material, such as stone, glass, canvas, wood, and linoleum. Develops drawings, paintings, diagrams, and models of medical or biological subjects for use in publications, exhibits, consultations, research, and teaching. Integrates and develops visual elements, such as line, space, mass, color, and perspective, to produce desired effect. Brushes or sprays protective or decorative finish on completed background panels, informational legends, exhibit accessories, or finished painting. Confers with professional personnel or client to discuss objectives of museum exhibits, develop illustration ideas, and theme to be portrayed. Selects colored glass, cuts glass, and arranges pieces in design pattern for painting. Integrates knowledge of glass cutting, stresses, portraiture, symbolism, heraldry, ornamental and historical styles, and related factors with functional requirements to conceptualize idea. Photographs person, artifacts, scenes, plants, or other objects, and develops negatives to obtain prints to be used in exhibits. Studies style, techniques, colors, textures, and materials used by artist to maintain consistency in reconstruction or retouching procedures. Cuts, carves, scrapes, molds, or otherwise shapes material to fashion exhibit accessories from clay, plastic, wood, fiberglass, and papier-mache. Performs tests to determine factors, such as age, structure, pigment stability, and probable reaction to various cleaning agents and solvents. Removes painting from frame or paint layer from canvas to restore artwork, following specified technique and equipment. Applies select solvents and cleaning agents to clean surface of painting and remove accretions, discolorations, and deteriorated varnish. Examines surfaces of paintings and proofs of artwork, using magnifying device, to determine method of restoration or needed corrections. Assembles, leads, and solders finished glass to fabricate stained glass article. Installs finished stained glass in window or door frame.

Knowledge: Design; Chemistry; Fine Arts; History and Archeology

Abilities: Fluency of Ideas; Originality; Visualization; Gross Body Equilibrium; Visual Color Discrimination

Sketch Artists

Sketch likenesses of subjects according to observation or descriptions either to assist law enforcement agencies in identifying suspects or for entertainment purposes of patrons, using mediums such as pencil, charcoal, and pastels. Draws sketch, profile, or likeness of posed subject or photograph, using pencil, charcoal, pastels, or other medium. Assembles and arranges outlines of features to form composite image, according to information provided by witness or victim. Alters copy of composite image until witness or victim is satisfied that composite is best possible representation of suspect. Interviews crime victims and witnesses to obtain descriptive information concerning physical build, sex, nationality, and facial features of unidentified suspect. Prepares series of simple line drawings conforming to description of suspect and presents drawings to informant for selection of sketch. Poses subject to accentuate most pleasing features or profile. Classifies and codes components of image, using established system, to help identify suspect. Measures distances and develops sketches of crime scene from photograph and measurements. Adjusts strong lights to cast subject's shadow on backdrop to aid in viewing subject's profile. Cuts profile from photograph or cuts freehand outline of profile from paper. Glues silhouette on paper of contrasting color or mounts silhouette in frame or folder. Operates photocopy or similar machine to reproduce composite image. Searches police photograph records, using classification and coding system, to determine if existing photograph of suspect is available.

Knowledge: Design; Fine Arts

Abilities: Visualization; Arm-Hand Steadiness; Finger Dexterity

Graphic Designers

Design art and copy layouts for material to be presented by visual communications media, such as books, magazines, newspapers, television, and packaging. Draws sample of finished layout and presents sample to art director for approval. Draws and prints charts, graphs, illustrations, and other artwork, using computer. Arranges layout based upon available space, knowledge of layout principles, and aesthetic design concepts. Marks up, pastes, and assembles final layouts to prepare layouts for printer. Keys information into computer equipment to create layouts for client or supervisor. Determines size and arrangement of illustrative material and copy, and selects style and size of type. Prepares illustrations or rough sketches of material according to instructions of client or supervisor. Produces still and animated graphic formats for on-air and taped portions of television news broadcasts, using electronic video equipment. Studies illustrations and photographs to plan presentation of material, product, or service. Reviews final layout and suggests improvements as needed. Prepares series of drawings to illustrate sequence and timing of story development for television production. Confers with client regarding layout design. Photographs layouts, using camera, to make layout prints for supervisor or client. Prepares notes and instructions for workers who assemble and prepare final layouts for printing. Develops negatives and prints, using negative and print developing equipment and tools and work aids, to produce layout photographs.

Knowledge: Computers and Electronics; Design; Fine Arts; Telecommunications; Communications and Media

Abilities: Fluency of Ideas; Originality; Visualization; Visual Color Discrimination; Speech Recognition

Cartoonists and Animators

Draw cartoons or other animated images by hand for publication, motion pictures, or television. May specialize in creating storyboards, laying out scenes, painting, in-betweening, developing characters, or clean up. Sketches and submits cartoon or animation for approval. Renders sequential drawings of characters or other subject material which, when photographed and projected at specific speed, becomes animated. Creates and prepares sketches and model drawings of characters, providing details from memory, live models, manufactured products, or reference material. Develops personal ideas for cartoons, comic strips, or animations, or reads written material to develop ideas. Makes changes and corrections to cartoon, comic strip, or animation as necessary. Develops color patterns and moods and paints background layouts to dramatize action for animated cartoon scenes. Labels each section with designated colors when colors are used. Discusses ideas for cartoons, comic strips, or animations with editor or publisher's representative.

Knowledge: Sales and Marketing; Fine Arts; Communications and Media

Abilities: Fluency of Ideas; Originality; Visualization; Arm-Hand Steadiness; Visual Color Discrimination

Sculptors

Design and construct three-dimensional artworks, using materials such as stone, wood, plaster, and metal and employing various manual and tool techniques. Carves objects from stone, concrete, plaster, wood, or other material, using abrasives and tools such as chisels, gouges, and mall. Constructs artistic forms from metal or stone, using metal-working, welding, or masonry tools and equipment. Cuts, bends, laminates, arranges, and fastens individual or mixed raw and manufactured materials and products to form works of art. Models substances, such as clay or wax, using fingers and small hand tools to form objects.

Knowledge: Design; Fine Arts

Abilities: Originality; Visualization; Manual Dexterity

Glass Blowers, Molders, Benders, and Finishers

Shape molten glass according to patterns. Shapes, bends, or joins sections of glass, using paddles, pressing and flattening hand tools, or cork. Blows tubing into specified shape, using compressed air or own breath. Places glass into die or mold of press and controls press to form products, such as, glassware components or optical blanks. Dips end of blowpipe into molten glass to collect gob on pipe head or cuts gob from molten glass, using sheers. Preheats or melts glass pieces or anneals or cools glass products and components, using ovens and refractory powder. Heats glass to pliable stage, using gas flame or oven. Cuts length of tubing to specified size, using file or cutting wheel. Inspects and measures product to verify conformance to specifications, using instruments, such as micrometers, calipers, magnifier, and ruler. Examines gob of molten glass for imperfections, utilizing knowledge of molten glass characteristics. Strikes neck of finished article to separate article from blowpipe. Determines type and quantity of glass required to fabricate product. Adjusts press stroke length and pressure, and regulates oven temperatures according to glass type processed. Develops sketch of glass product into blueprint specifications, applying knowledge of glass technology and glass blowing.

Knowledge: Production and Processing

Abilities: None above average

Throwers

Mold clay into ware as clay revolves on potter's wheel. Raises and shapes clay into ware, such as vases, saggers, and pitchers, on revolving wheel, using hands, fingers, and thumbs. Smoothes surfaces of finished piece, using rubber scrapers and wet sponge. Adjusts speed of wheel according to feel of changing firmness of clay. Positions ball of clay in center of potters wheel. Starts motor, or pumps treadle with foot to revolve wheel. Pulls wire through base of article and wheel to separate finished piece. Verifies size and form, using calipers and templates. Moves piece from wheel to dry.

Knowledge: Fine Arts

Abilities: Arm-Hand Steadiness; Manual Dexterity; Rate Control

Model and Mold Makers

Construct molds or models, using fiberglass, plaster, or clay. Shapes sculptured clay surfaces to form details of mold or model, using various sculptor's tools, hands, and scrapers. Pours plaster or compound over model and spreads evenly over surface, using brush or spatula. Builds layers of material, such as fiberglass, resin, or rubber paint around model to form mold or cast, and shield around cast. Cuts and removes sections of hardened mold or cast, using hand or power tools. Reassembles sections of shield and cast to form complete mold, using shellac or concrete. Mixes water and powder or catalytic compound, and clay, according to specifications, to form plaster or other compound. Punches holes in surface of model to assure plaster will adhere. Smoothes surface of cast to remove excess materials, using electric grinder, polishing wheel, file, or sandpaper. Cuts templates of model according to blueprints or layout drawings. Constructs frame to support figure while modeling. Verifies uniformity and smoothness of curved surfaces. Brushes liquid soap or wax onto model or frame to prevent adhesion of plaster or fiberglass. Duplicates completed model half to make measurements of unfinished half symmetrical. Covers specified portions of model with aluminum foil or transparent media trim to identify or detail. Repairs molds using carpenter tools.

Knowledge: Building and Construction; Fine Arts

Abilities: Visualization; Arm-Hand Steadiness; Manual Dexterity; Wrist-Finger Speed; Speed of Limb Movement; Explosive Strength

Precision Painters

Paint decorative free-hand designs on objects, such as pottery, cigarette cases, and lampshades, using hand brushes. Applies paint or metallic leaf to workpiece, using handbrush, airbrush, or roller. Sketches or traces design or lettering onto workpiece or pattern material to prepare pattern or stencil, using measuring and drawing instruments. Designs pattern or lettering to paint workpieces, such as signs, glassware, pottery, or zinc plates, using measuring and drawing instruments. Removes excess paint, using brush or cotton swab. Mixes paint according to established formulas to obtain specified color and desired consistency. Examines workpiece to compare with pattern and to detect imperfections. Applies preservative coating to workpiece. Reads work order to determine work procedures and materials required. Positions and aligns workpiece on work area. Uses wheel equipment to hold and revolve workpiece while applying paint. Cuts out letters or designs using hand or powered cutting tools. Hangs workpieces on rack to dry or places workpieces on conveyor. Maintains daily production records.

Knowledge: Design; Fine Arts

Abilities: Originality; Arm-Hand Steadiness; Manual Dexterity; Finger Dexterity; Wrist-Finger Speed; Visual Color Discrimination

Silk Screen Process Decorators

Apply lettering, designs, or coloring to products, using silk screen process. Applies ink or glaze to screen or pattern over drawing or plate and prints design. Positions mask or applies protective coating over parts not to be shaded. Selects and prepares color glaze or ink. Cleans ink, glaze, or protective coating from parts of drawing not to be shaded. Cuts stencil by hand, using cutting tools, or photographs design on film. Reads job order and examines drawing or design to determine method of making stencil. Catalogs and stores screens for future orders.

Knowledge: Production and Processing; Fine Arts

Abilities: Arm-Hand Steadiness; Visual Color Discrimination

Engravers/Carvers

Engrave or carve designs or lettering onto objects, using hand-held power tools. Holds workpiece against outer edge of wheel and twists and turns workpiece to grind glass according to marked design. Carves design on workpiece, using electric hand tool. Cuts outline of impression with graver and removes excess material with knife. Traces, sketches, or presses design or facsimile signature on workpiece by hand, or by using artist equipment. Selects and mounts wheel and miter on lathe, and equips lathe with water to cool wheel and prevent dust. Polishes engravings using felt and cork wheels. Prepares workpiece to be engraved or carved, such as glassware, rubber, or plastic product. Attaches engraved workpiece to mount, using cement. Dresses and shapes cutting wheels by holding dressing stone against rotating wheel. Suggests original designs to customer or management.

Knowledge: Production and Processing; Fine Arts

Abilities: Originality; Arm-Hand Steadiness; Manual Dexterity; Finger Dexterity; Rate Control; Wrist-Finger Speed; Dynamic Flexibility; Near Vision; Depth Perception

Etchers

Etch or cut artistic designs in glass articles, using acid solutions, sandblasting equipment, and design patterns. Immerses waxed ware in hydrofluoric acid to etch design on a glass surface. Sandblasts exposed area of glass, using spray gun, to cut design in surface. Places template against glassware surface and sprays with sand to cut design in surface. Positions pattern against waxed or taped ware and sprays ink through pattern to transfer design to wax or tape. Removes wax or tape, using stylus or knife, to expose glassware surface to be etched. Coats glass in molten wax or masks glassware with tape. Immerses ware in hot water to remove wax or peels off tape.

Knowledge: Production and Processing; Chemistry; Fine Arts

Abilities: Arm-Hand Steadiness; Manual Dexterity; Wrist-Finger Speed; Gross Body Equilibrium

Tracers and Letterers

Lay out and trace lettering and designs on various surfaces, using stylus or writing instruments and master copies. Draws designs, letters, and lines by hand, according to specifications, using artist and drafting tools. Traces lettering or designs on workpiece, using light box, opaque projector, and artist and drafting equipment. Designs letters, borders, scrollwork, characters, or script, according to specifications. Positions design on workpiece and lays out reference points on design, using measuring instruments. Reads work order or manuscript to determine words and symbols needed. Measures width, thickness, and spacing of characters and design, using optical or measuring instruments. Cuts out letters or designs, using cutting tools. Applies colors to patterns, using stylus, pen, brush, sponge, opaque, India ink, and paints. Applies coatings to workpiece, such as metallic leaf, shellac, oil, glue, or lacquer, using brush, spray, roller, or hand tools. Positions and secures work piece. Rubs metallic leaf with burnishing agate, cotton pad, or gloved hand to polish leaf or simulate worn metal finish. Assembles composite design to determine accuracy for final approved form. Corrects errors in design to make ready for printing. Determines availability of characters specified on order. Reproduces reference copies, using automatic film developer or duplication equipment. Types lines and characters, such as letters, musical notations, Braille symbols, using typewriter or computer. Maintains detailed records of jobs and reference sources.

Knowledge: Production and Processing; Design; Fine Arts

Abilities: Visualization; Arm-Hand Steadiness; Manual Dexterity; Finger Dexterity; Visual Color Discrimination

Gilders

Cover surfaces of items, such as books, furniture, and signs, with metal leaf, using hand tools. Picks up leaf with brush or felt-edged tool and lays leaf over sizing. Smoothes leaf over surface and removes excess, using brush. Presses sheets or ribbons of leaf onto sizing by hand. Brushes sizing (thin glue) on sections of items to be covered with leaf, according to design. Rubs leaf with polished burnishing agent or cotton pad to polish leaf or simulate worn metal finish. Transfers leaf from supply book onto pallet.

Knowledge: Fine Arts

Abilities: Arm-Hand Steadiness; Manual Dexterity; Wrist-Finger Speed; Dynamic Strength

Athletes, Coaches, and Umpires

- ▲ Growth: 16%
- ▲ Annual Job Openings: 8,407
- ▲ Yearly Earnings $28,995
- ▲ Education Required: Long-term O-J-T
- ▲ Self-employed: 31%
- ▲ Part-time: 25%

Coaches and Scouts

Analyze performance or instruct athletes of professional sporting events. May evaluate athletes' strengths and weaknesses as possible recruits or to improve the athletes' technique to prepare them for competition. Analyzes athletes' performance and reviews game statistics or records to determine fitness and potential for professional sports. Plans and directs physical conditioning program for athletes to achieve maximum athletic performance.

Observes athletes to determine areas of deficiency and need for individual or team improvement. Evaluates team and opposition capabilities to develop and plan game strategy. Instructs athletes, individually or in groups, demonstrating sport techniques and game strategies. Evaluates athletes' skills and discusses or recommends acquisition, trade, or position assignment of players. Prepares scouting reports detailing information, such as selection or rejection of athletes and locations identified for future recruitment. Negotiates with professional athletes or representatives to obtain services and arrange contracts.

Knowledge: Administration and Management; Sales and Marketing; Personnel and Human Resources; Psychology; Therapy and Counseling; Education and Training

Abilities: Oral Expression; Fluency of Ideas; Originality; Problem Sensitivity; Deductive Reasoning; Inductive Reasoning; Category Flexibility; Memorization; Speed of Closure; Flexibility of Closure; Perceptual Speed; Spatial Orientation; Visualization; Selective Attention; Time Sharing; Response Orientation; Reaction Time; Speed of Limb Movement; Explosive Strength; Stamina; Dynamic Flexibility; Gross Body Coordination; Gross Body Equilibrium; Far Vision; Night Vision; Peripheral Vision; Depth Perception; Glare Sensitivity; Auditory Attention; Sound Localization

Athletic Trainers

Evaluate, advise, and treat athletes to maintain physical fitness. Evaluates physical condition of athletes and advises or prescribes routines and corrective exercises to strengthen muscles. Recommends special diets to improve health, increase stamina, and reduce weight of athletes. Wraps ankles, fingers, wrists, or other body parts with synthetic skin, gauze, or adhesive tape to support muscles and ligaments. Administers emergency first aid, treats minor chronic disabilities, or refers injured person to physician. Massages body parts to relieve soreness, strains, and bruises.

Knowledge: Customer and Personal Service; Biology; Psychology; Medicine and Dentistry; Therapy and Counseling

Abilities: Problem Sensitivity; Speed of Closure; Speed of Limb Movement; Static Strength; Stamina; Extent Flexibility; Dynamic Flexibility; Gross Body Coordination; Gross Body Equilibrium

Professional Athletes

Participate in physical, competitive athletic events. Participates in athletic events and competitive sports, according to established rules and regulations. Plays professional sport and is identified according to sport played, such as football, basketball, baseball, hockey, or boxing. Exercises and practices under direction of athletic trainer or professional coach to prepare and train for competitive events. Represents team or professional sports club, speaking to groups involved in activities, such as sports clinics and fund raisers.

Knowledge: None above average

Abilities: Spatial Orientation; Visualization; Selective Attention; Time Sharing; Arm-Hand Steadiness; Manual Dexterity; Multilimb Coordination; Response Orientation; Rate Control; Reaction Time; Speed of Limb Movement; Static Strength; Explosive Strength; Dynamic Strength; Trunk Strength; Stamina; Extent Flexibility; Dynamic Flexibility; Gross Body Coordination; Gross Body Equilibrium; Far Vision; Peripheral Vision; Depth Perception; Glare Sensitivity; Auditory Attention; Sound Localization; Speech Recognition

Motor Racers

Drive automobiles or ride motorcycles in competitive races. Drives car or motorcycle over track, course, or natural terrain to participate in trial, qualifying, and competitive races. Maneuvers vehicle to avoid accident, barrier, or other emergency situation. Watches for warning flags and other signals indicating emergency situation and responds to instructions given by track officials. Listens to engine and observes fuel, oil, compression, and other gauges to ensure vehicle is operating efficiently. Evaluates speed, maneuverability, and position of other vehicles during competitive race to determine appropriate racing strategy. Performs maintenance work on car or motorcycle.

Knowledge: Mechanical; Transportation

Abilities: Perceptual Speed; Spatial Orientation; Visualization; Selective Attention; Time Sharing; Arm-Hand Steadiness; Manual Dexterity; Control Precision; Multilimb Coordination; Response Orientation; Rate Control; Reaction Time; Speed of Limb Movement; Stamina; Extent Flexibility; Gross Body Coordination; Far Vision; Peripheral Vision; Depth Perception; Glare Sensitivity; Hearing Sensitivity; Auditory Attention; Sound Localization

Jockeys and Sulky Drivers

Ride racehorses or drive sulkies in horse or harness race. Drives and controls speed of horse or horse-drawn sulky to race from starting gate to finish line. Monitors speed and position of horses or sulkies to determine how to challenge for lead position in race. Mounts horse after weighing-in, and rides horse to specified numbered stall of starting gate. Studies performance record of competing horses to plan race strategy. Confers with training personnel to discuss ability and peculiarities of horses, and to analyze performance of horses for competitive races. Trains or directs other workers involved in training and grooming, feeding, stabling, handling, and transporting race horses.

Knowledge: None above average

Abilities: Spatial Orientation; Visualization; Selective Attention; Time Sharing; Multilimb Coordination; Response Orientation; Rate Control; Reaction Time; Speed of Limb Movement; Dynamic Strength; Trunk Strength; Stamina; Gross Body Coordination; Gross Body Equilibrium; Far Vision; Peripheral Vision; Depth Perception; Glare Sensitivity

Horse Riders/Exercisers

Ride horses to exercise, condition, or lead other horses. Rides horse to exercise, condition, and train horse for racing, following specific instructions of training personnel. Leads procession of riders in post position order onto track to starting gate area. Leads horses to and from receiving barn or paddock before and after race. Informs trainer of horse's behavior and physical condition to modify training or conditioning in preparation for race. Rides horse to chase and restrain runaway horses to prevent disruption of race and injury to horse or thrown rider. Grooms and feeds horses. Diverts riders from competitor involved in accident on racetrack. Assists horse ambulance workers to remove injured horse from track, using block and tackle.

Knowledge: Medicine and Dentistry

Abilities: Rate Control; Speed of Limb Movement; Dynamic Strength; Trunk Strength; Stamina; Gross Body Coordination; Gross Body Equilibrium; Far Vision; Peripheral Vision

Umpires, Referees, and Other Sports Officials

Officiate at competitive athletic or sporting events. Detect infractions of rules and decide penalties according to established regulations. Include all sporting officials, referees, and competition judges. Observes actions of participants at athletic and sporting events to regulate competition and detect infractions of rules. Resolves claims of rule infractions, or complaints lodged by participants, and assesses penalties based on established regulations. Clocks events according to established standards for play, or to measure performance of participants. Makes qualifying determinations regarding participants, such as qualifying order or handicap. Signals participants or other officials to facilitate identification of infractions or otherwise regulate play or competition. Directs participants to assigned areas such as starting blocks or penalty areas. Inspects sporting equipment or examines participants to ensure compliance to regulations and safety of participants and spectators. Records and maintains information regarding participants and sporting activities. Confers with other sporting officials and facility managers to provide information, coordinate activities, and discuss problems. Prepares reports to regulating organization concerning sporting activities, complaints, and actions taken or needed, such as fines or other disciplinary actions.

Knowledge: None above average

Abilities: Memorization; Perceptual Speed; Selective Attention; Time Sharing; Response Orientation; Rate Control; Reaction Time; Speed of Limb Movement; Stamina; Gross Body Coordination; Gross Body Equilibrium; Far Vision; Peripheral Vision; Depth Perception; Glare Sensitivity; Hearing Sensitivity; Auditory Attention; Speech Clarity

Automotive Body and Related Repairers

▲ Growth: 13%
▲ Annual Job Openings: 28,792
▲ Yearly Earnings $28,184
▲ Education Required: Long-term O-J-T
▲ Self-employed: 19%
▲ Part-time: 8%

Automotive Glass Installers and Repairers

Replace or repair broken windshields and window glass in motor vehicles. Installs precut replacement glass to replace curved or custom-shaped windows. Removes broken or damaged glass windshield or window glass from motor vehicles, using hand tools to remove screws from frame holding glass. Applies moisture-proofing compound along glass edges and installs glass into windshield- or glass-frame in door or side panel of vehicle. Installs rubber-channeling strip around edge of glass or frame to weather-proof and to prevent rattling. Cuts flat safety glass according to specified pattern, using glass-cutter. Holds cut or uneven edge of glass against automated abrasive belt to shape or smooth edges. Obtains windshield for specific automobile make and model from stock and examines for defects prior to installation. Replaces or adjusts motorized or manual window-raising mechanisms.

Knowledge: None above average

Abilities: Arm-Hand Steadiness; Static Strength; Trunk Strength; Stamina; Extent Flexibility; Dynamic Flexibility; Gross Body Coordination; Gross Body Equilibrium

Automotive Body Repairers

Repair and customize automotive bodies and frames. Positions dolly block against surface of dented area and beats opposite surface to remove dents, using hammer. Straightens bent automobile or other vehicle frames, using pneumatic frame-straightening machine. Fills depressions with body filler and files, grinds, and sands repaired surfaces, using power tools and hand tools. Paints and sands repaired surface, using paint spraygun and motorized sander. Cuts opening in vehicle body for installation of customized windows, using templates and power shears or chisel. Fits and secures windows, vinyl roof, and metal trim to vehicle body, using caulking gun, adhesive brush, and mallet. Removes damaged fenders and panels, using wrenches and cutting torch, and installs replacement parts, using wrenches or welding equipment. Measures and marks vinyl material and cuts material to size for roof installation, using rule, straightedge, and hand shears. Cuts away damaged fiberglass from automobile body, using air grinder. Soaks fiberglass matting in resin mixture and applies layers of matting over repair area to specified thickness. Mixes polyester resin and hardener to be used in restoring damaged area. Peels separating film from repair area and washes repaired surface with water. Examines vehicle to determine extent and type of damage. Cuts and tapes plastic separating film to outside repair area to avoid damaging surrounding surfaces during repair procedure. Removes upholstery, accessories, electrical window- and seat-operating equipment, and trim to gain access to vehicle body and fenders. Reads specifications or confers with customer to determine custom modifications to alter appearance of vehicle. Adjusts or aligns headlights, wheels, and brake system. Cleans work area, using air hose to remove damaged material and discarded fiberglass strips used in repair procedures.

Knowledge: Engineering and Technology; Mechanical; Foreign Language

Abilities: Visualization; Selective Attention; Finger Dexterity; Wrist-Finger Speed; Speed of Limb Movement; Static Strength; Dynamic Strength; Trunk Strength; Stamina; Extent Flexibility; Dynamic Flexibility; Gross Body Equilibrium; Visual Color Discrimination

Truck and Trailer Body Repairers

Repair and service truck bodies and trailers. Replaces and repairs worn and defective parts on used metal trailers. Constructs and repairs metal truck bodies and trailers, using hand tools and power tools. Overhauls used and wrecked trailer bodies, following shop orders or specifications. Installs metal or wood flooring on trailers. Installs interiors, insulation, and fixtures, using hand tools—such as hammer, file, and screwdriver—and power tools, such as bandsaw, sander, and drill. Installs electrical wiring for dome lights, tail lights, brake lights, and other equipment, according to specified procedures. Fits and assembles components, using hand tools and portable power tools, such as drill, riveter, and welding apparatus. Installs, adjusts, and services motor-cooling systems in refrigerated trailers. Lays out dimensions on metal stock according to specifications, using square, rule, and punch. Sprays or brushes paint, primer, or protective coating on wood and metal surfaces. Examines completed new trailers and tests, adjusts, and repairs wheel alignments, bearings, lights, and brake assemblies.

Knowledge: Mechanical

Abilities: Visualization; Finger Dexterity; Multilimb Coordination; Speed of Limb Movement; Stamina; Extent Flexibility; Dynamic Flexibility; Gross Body Coordination; Gross Body Equilibrium; Visual Color Discrimination; Hearing Sensitivity

Automotive Body Repair Estimators

Estimate cost of repairing damaged automobile and truck bodies. Examines damaged vehicle for dents, scratches, broken glass, and other areas requiring repair, replacement, or repainting. Examines interior for evidence of fire or water damage to upholstery and appointments. Determines feasibility of repair or replacement of parts, such as bumpers, fenders, and doors, according to relative costs and damage. Computes cost of replacement parts and labor to restore vehicle, using standard labor and parts cost manuals. Estimates cost of repainting, converting vehicles to special purposes, or customizing undamaged vehicles, depending on specialty of shop. Sights along fenders to detect frame damage, or positions vehicle in frame-aligning rig to locate misalignment. Explains estimate to customer, and answers customer's questions regarding estimate. Enters itemized estimate on job order card or estimate form.

Knowledge: Nove above average

Abilities: Gross Body Equilibrium; Near Vision

Automotive Mechanics

▲ Growth: 12%
▲ Annual Job Openings: 118,300
▲ Yearly Earnings $27,643
▲ Education Required: Long-term O-J-T
▲ Self-employed: 20%
▲ Part-time: 6%

Automotive Master Mechanics

Repair automobiles, trucks, buses, and other vehicles. Master mechanics repair virtually any part on the vehicle or specialize in the transmission system. Repairs and overhauls defective automotive units, such as engines, transmissions, or differentials. Repairs or replaces parts, such as pistons, rods, gears, valves, and bearings. Overhauls or replaces carburetors, blowers, generators, distributors, starts, and pumps. Repairs manual and automatic transmissions. Repairs, relines, replaces, and adjusts brakes. Rewires ignition system, lights, and instrument panel. Repairs or replaces shock absorbers. Installs and repairs accessories, such as radios, heaters, mirrors, and windshield wipers. Repairs radiator leaks. Replaces and adjusts headlights. Examines vehicles and discusses extent of damage or malfunction with customer. Aligns front end. Rebuilds parts, such as crankshafts and cylinder blocks. Repairs damaged automobile bodies.

Knowledge: Computers and Electronics; Engineering and Technology; Mechanical

Abilities: Originality; Problem Sensitivity; Inductive Reasoning; Information Ordering; Memorization; Perceptual Speed; Spatial Orientation; Visualization; Selective Attention; Time Sharing; Manual Dexterity; Finger Dexterity; Control Precision; Response Orientation; Rate Control; Reaction Time; Wrist-Finger Speed; Speed of Limb Movement; Static Strength; Explosive Strength; Trunk Strength; Extent Flexibility; Dynamic Flexibility; Gross Body Equilibrium; Visual Color Discrimination; Depth Perception; Hearing Sensitivity; Auditory Attention; Sound Localization

Automotive Specialty Technicians

Repair only one system or component on a vehicle, such as brakes, suspension, or radiator. Repairs, installs, and adjusts hydraulic and electromagnetic automatic lift mechanisms used to raise and lower automobile windows, seats, and tops. Repairs and replaces automobile leaf springs. Removes and replaces defective mufflers and tailpipes from automobiles. Repairs and aligns defective wheels of automobiles. Repairs and rebuilds clutch systems. Repairs, overhauls, and adjusts automobile brake systems. Installs and repairs automotive air-conditioning units. Rebuilds, repairs, and tests automotive injection units. Converts vehicle fuel systems from gasoline to butane gas operations, and repairs and services operating butane fuel units. Aligns and repairs wheels, axles, frames, torsion bars, and steering mechanisms of automobiles. Repairs, replaces, and adjusts defective carburetor parts and gasoline filters. Repairs and replaces defective balljoint suspension, brakeshoes, and wheel bearings. Inspects and tests new vehicles for damage, records findings, and makes repairs. Inspects, tests, repairs, and replaces automotive cooling systems and fuel tanks. Tunes automobile engines and tests electronic computer components. Examines vehicle, compiles estimate of repair costs, and secures customer approval to perform repairs.

Knowledge: Customer and Personal Service; Computers and Electronics; Engineering and Technology; Design; Mechanical; Physics; Chemistry

Abilities: Information Ordering; Flexibility of Closure; Perceptual Speed; Visualization; Manual Dexterity; Multilimb Coordination; Response Orientation; Rate Control; Reaction Time; Wrist-Finger Speed; Static Strength; Explosive Strength; Trunk Strength; Extent Flexibility; Dynamic Flexibility; Gross Body Equilibrium; Visual Color Discrimination; Peripheral Vision; Hearing Sensitivity; Auditory Attention; Sound Localization

Bank Tellers

▲ Growth: 1%

▲ Annual Job Openings: 109,086

▲ Yearly Earnings $16,536

▲ Education Required: Short-term O-J-T

▲ Self-employed: 0%

▲ Part-time: 34%

Tellers

Receive and pay out money. Keep records of money and negotiable instruments involved in a financial institution's various transactions. Receives checks and cash for deposit, verifies amount, and examines checks for endorsements. Cashes checks and pays out money after verification of signatures and customer balances. Counts currency, coins, and checks received for deposit, shipment to branch banks, or Federal Reserve Bank, by hand or currency-counting machine. Prepares daily inventory of currency, drafts, and travelers' checks. Examines coupons and bills presented for payment to verify issue, payment date, and amount due. Enters customers' transactions into computer to record transactions and issues computer-generated receipts. Issues checks to bond owners in settlement of transactions. Balances currency, coin, and checks in cash drawer at end of shift and calculates daily transactions. Quotes unit exchange rate, following daily international rate sheet or computer display. Removes deposits from automated teller machines and night depository, and counts and balances cash in them. Gives information to customer about foreign currency regulations, and computes exchange value and transaction fee for currency exchange. Explains, promotes, or sells products or services, such as travelers' checks, savings bonds, money orders, and cashier's checks. Composes, types, and mails correspondence relating to discrepancies, errors, and outstanding unpaid items.

Knowledge: Clerical; Economics and Accounting; Sales and Marketing; Customer and Personal Service; Foreign Language; Law, Government, and Jurisprudence

Abilities: Number Facility; Memorization; Perceptual Speed; Wrist-Finger Speed; Near Vision; Speech Recognition

Bartenders

▲ Growth: 0%
▲ Annual Job Openings. 103,325
▲ Yearly Earnings $13,395
▲ Education Required: Short-term O-J-T
▲ Self-employed: 1%
▲ Part-time: 43%

B

Bartenders

Mix and serve to patrons alcoholic and nonalcoholic drinks, following standard recipes. Mixes ingredients, such as liquor, soda water, sugar, and bitters, to prepare cocktails and other drinks. Serves wine and draft or bottled beer. Collects money for drinks served. Arranges bottles and glasses to make attractive display. Slices and pits fruit for garnishing drinks. Orders or requisitions liquors and supplies. Cleans glasses, utensils, and bar equipment. Prepares appetizers, such as pickles, cheese, and cold meats.

Knowledge: Sales and Marketing; Customer and Personal Service; Psychology; Philosophy and Theology; Law, Government, and Jurisprudence

Abilities: Memorization; Wrist-Finger Speed; Speed of Limb Movement; Trunk Strength; Stamina; Extent Flexibility; Gross Body Equilibrium; Visual Color Discrimination; Night Vision; Peripheral Vision; Auditory Attention; Speech Recognition

Bicycle Repairers

▲ Growth: 34%
▲ Annual Job Openings: 5,525
▲ Yearly Earnings $15,766
▲ Education Required: Moderate-term O-J-T
▲ Self-employed: 0%
▲ Part-time: 9%

Bicycle Repairers

Repair and service bicycles, using hand tools. Installs, repairs, and replaces equipment or accessories, such as handle bars, stands, lights, and seats. Aligns wheels. Disassembles axle to repair, adjust, and replace defective parts, using hand tools. Installs and adjusts speed and gear mechanisms. Welds broken or cracked frame together, using oxyacetylene torch and welding rods. Repairs holes in tire tubes, using scraper and patch. Paints bicycle frame, using spray gun or brush. Shapes replacement parts, using bench grinder. Assembles new bicycles. Sells new bicycles and accessories.

Knowledge: Sales and Marketing; Engineering and Technology; Mechanical

Abilities: Finger Dexterity; Gross Body Equilibrium

Bill and Account Collectors

▲ Growth: 42%
▲ Annual Job Openings: 68,308
▲ Yearly Earnings $22,401
▲ Education Required: Short-term O-J-T
▲ Self-employed: 1%
▲ Part-time: 12%

Bill and Account Collectors

Locate and notify customers of delinquent accounts by mail, telephone, or personal visit to solicit payment. Duties include receiving payment and posting amount to customers' account; preparing statements to credit department if customer fails to respond; initiating repossession proceedings or service disconnection; and keeping records of collection and status of accounts. Exclude workers who collect money from coin boxes. Mails form letters to customers to encourage payment of delinquent accounts. Persuades customers to pay amount due on credit account, damage claim, or nonpayable check, or negotiates extension of credit. Notifies credit department, orders merchandise repossession or service disconnection, or turns over account to attorney if customer fails to respond. Receives payments and posts amount paid to customer account, using computer or paper records. Records infor-

Best Jobs for the 21st Century™ © 1999, JIST Works, Inc., Indianapolis, IN

mation about financial status of customer and status of collection efforts. Confers with customer by telephone or in person to determine reason for overdue payment and review terms of sales, service, or credit contract. Traces delinquent customer to new address by inquiring at post office or questioning neighbors. Drives vehicle to visit customer, return merchandise to creditor, or deliver bills. Sorts and files correspondence, and performs miscellaneous clerical duties.

Knowledge: Clerical; Economics and Accounting; Law, Government, and Jurisprudence

Abilities: Rate Control; Speech Recognition

Billing, Cost, and Rate Clerks

▲ Growth: 17%
▲ Annual Job Openings: 67,231
▲ Yearly Earnings $22,027
▲ Education Required: Short-term O-J-T
▲ Self-employed: 0%
▲ Part-time: 13%

Billing, Cost, and Rate Clerks

Compile data, compute fees and charges, and prepare invoices for billing purposes. Duties include computing costs and calculating rates for goods, services, and shipment of goods; posting data; and keeping other relevant records. May involve use of computer or typewriter, calculator, and adding and bookkeeping machines. Exclude workers whose primary duty is operation of special office machines or workers who calculate charges for passenger transportation. Computes amounts due from such documents as purchase orders, sales tickets, and charge slips. Compiles and computes credit terms, discounts, and purchase prices for billing documents. Keeps records of invoices and support documents. Consults manuals which include rates, rules, regulations, and government tax and tariff information. Compiles cost factor reports, such as labor, production, storage, and equipment. Verifies compiled data from vendor invoices to ensure accuracy, and revises billing data when errors are found. Types billing documents, shipping labels, credit memorandums, and credit forms, using typewriter or computer. Resolves discrepancies on accounting records. Answers mail and telephone inquiries regarding rates, routing, and procedures. Estimates market value of product or services. Updates manuals when rates, rules, or regulations are amended.

Knowledge: Clerical; Economics and Accounting; Mathematics; Law, Government, and Jurisprudence; Transportation

Abilities: Written Expression; Category Flexibility; Mathematical Reasoning; Number Facility; Perceptual Speed; Wrist-Finger Speed; Near Vision; Speech Recognition

Bindery Workers

▲ Growth: 14%
▲ Annual Job Openings: 5,529
▲ Yearly Earnings $21,153
▲ Education Required: Moderate-term O-J-T
▲ Self-employed: 0%
▲ Part-time: 5%

Bindery Machine Setters and Set-up Operators

Set up or set up and operate machines that perform some or all of the following functions in order to produce books, magazines, pamphlets, catalogs, and other printed materials: gathering, folding, cutting, stitching, rounding and backing, supering, casing-in, lining, pressing, and trimming. Installs bindery machine devices, such as knives, guides, and clamps to accommodate sheets, signatures or books of specified sizes. Sets machine controls to adjust length and thickness of folds, stitches or cuts, and to adjust speed and pressure. Mounts and secures rolls or reels of wire, cloth, paper or other material onto machine spindles and fills paper feed. Positions and clamps stitching heads on crossarms to space stitches to specified lengths. Starts machines and makes trial runs to verify accuracy of machine setup. Observes and monitors machine operations to detect malfunctions and makes required adjustments. Fills glue pot and adjusts flow of glue and speed of conveyors. Threads wire into machine to load stitcher head for stapling. Reads work order to determine work instructions. Examines product samples for defects. Cleans and lubricates machinery parts and makes minor repairs. Removes books or products from machine and stacks them. Trains workers to set up, operate, and use automatic bindery machines. Records time spent on specific tasks and number of items produced, for daily production sheet. Manually stocks supplies such as signatures, books, or paper.

Knowledge: Production and Processing

Abilities: Perceptual Speed; Arm-Hand Steadiness; Control Precision

Biological Scientists

▲ Growth: 25%
▲ Annual Job Openings: 7,110
▲ Yearly Earnings $41,828
▲ Education Required: Doctor's degree
▲ Self-employed: 4%
▲ Part-time: 6%

Biochemists

Research or study chemical composition and processes of living organisms that affect vital processes such as growth and aging, to determine chemical actions and effects on organisms, such as the action of foods, drugs, or other substances on body functions and tissues. Studies chemistry of living processes, such as cell development, breathing, and digestion, and living energy changes, such as growth, aging, and death. Researches methods of transferring characteristics, such as resistance to disease, from one organism to another. Researches and determines chemical action of substances, such as drugs, serums, hormones, and food, on tissues and vital processes. Examines chemical aspects of formation of antibodies, and researches chemistry of cells and blood corpuscles. Isolates, analyzes, and identifies hormones, vitamins, allergens, minerals, and enzymes, and determines their effects on body functions. Develops and executes tests to detect disease, genetic disorders, or other abnormalities. Develops methods to process, store, and use food, drugs, and chemical compounds. Develops and tests new drugs and medications used for commercial distribution. Prepares reports and recommendations based upon research outcomes. Designs and builds laboratory equipment needed for special research projects. Cleans, purifies, refines, and otherwise prepares pharmaceutical compounds for commercial distribution. Analyzes foods to determine nutritional value and effects of cooking, canning, and processing on this value.

Knowledge: Building and Construction; Mathematics; Chemistry; Biology

Abilities: Oral Comprehension; Written Comprehension; Oral Expression; Written Expression; Originality; Problem Sensitivity; Deductive Reasoning; Inductive Reasoning; Information Ordering; Category Flexibility; Number Facility; Memorization; Speed of Closure; Near Vision

Biologists

Study the relationship among organisms and between organisms and their environment. Studies basic principles of plant and animal life, such as origin, relationship, development, anatomy, and functions. Studies aquatic plants and animals and environmental conditions affecting them, such as radioactivity or pollution. Collects and analyzes biological data about relationship among and between organisms and their environment. Studies reactions of plants, animals, and marine species to parasites. Identifies, classifies, and studies structure, behavior, ecology, physiology, nutrition, culture, and distribution of plant and animal species. Measures salinity, acidity, light, oxygen content, and other physical conditions of water to determine their relationship to aquatic life. Studies and manages wild animal populations. Develops methods and apparatus for securing representative plant, animal, aquatic, or soil samples. Investigates and develops pest management and control measures. Communicates test results to state and federal representatives and general public. Prepares environmental impact reports for industry, government, or publication. Cultivates, breeds, and grows aquatic life, such as lobsters, clams, or fish farming. Plans and administers biological research programs for government, research firms, medical industries, or manufacturing firms. Researches environmental effects of present and potential uses of land and water areas, and determines methods of improving environment or crop yields. Develops methods of extracting drugs from aquatic plants and animals.

Knowledge: Food Production; Mathematics; Physics; Chemistry; Biology; English Language

Abilities: Oral Comprehension; Written Comprehension; Oral Expression; Written Expression; Originality; Problem Sensitivity; Deductive Reasoning; Inductive Reasoning; Information Ordering; Category Flexibility; Memorization; Speed of Closure; Flexibility of Closure; Near Vision

Biophysicists

Research or study physical principles of living cells and organisms, their electrical and mechanical energy, and related phenomena. Studies physical principles of living cells and organisms and their electrical and mechanical energy. Researches manner in which characteristics of plants and animals are carried through successive generations. Researches transformation of substances in cells, using atomic isotopes. Investigates damage to cells and tissues caused by X rays and nuclear particles. Studies spatial configuration of submicroscopic molecules, such as proteins, using X ray and electron microscope. Investigates transmission of electrical impulses along nerves and muscles. Investigates dynamics of seeing and hearing. Analyzes functions of electronic and human brains, such as learning, thinking, and memory. Researches cancer treatment, using radiation and nuclear particles. Studies absorption of light by chlorophyll in photosynthesis or by pigments of eye involved in vision.

Knowledge: Mathematics; Physics; Chemistry; Biology

Abilities: Oral Comprehension; Written Comprehension; Written Expression; Originality; Problem Sensitivity; Deductive Reasoning; Inductive Reasoning; Information Ordering; Category Flexibility; Mathematical Reasoning; Number Facility; Memorization; Speed of Closure; Flexibility of Closure; Near Vision

Botanists

Research or study development of life processes, physiology, heredity, environment, distribution, morphology, and economic value of plants for application in such fields as agronomy, forestry, horticulture, and pharmacology. Studies development, life processes, and economic value of plants and fungi for application in such fields as horticulture and pharmacology. Studies behavior, internal and external structure, mechanics, and biochemistry of plant or fungi cells, using microscope and scientific equipment. Investigates effect of rainfall, deforestation, pollution, acid rain, temperature, climate, soil, and elevation on plant or fungi growth. Studies and compares healthy and diseased plants to determine agents responsible for diseased conditions. Investigates comparative susceptibility of different varieties of plants to disease, and develops plant varieties immune to disease. Studies rates of spread and intensity of plant diseases under different environmental conditions, and predicts disease outbreaks. Inspects flower and vegetable seed stocks and flowering bulbs, to determine presence of diseases, infections, and insect infestation. Identifies and classifies plants or fungi based on study and research. Tests disease control measures under laboratory and field conditions for comparative effectiveness, practicality, and economy. Plans and administers environmental research programs for government, research firms, medical industries, or manufacturing firms. Devises methods of destroying or controlling disease-causing agents. Prepares reports and recommendations based upon research outcomes. Develops drugs, medicines, molds, yeasts, or foods from plants or fungi, or develops new types of plants. Develops practices to prevent or reduce deterioration of perishable plant products in transit or storage. Develops improved methods of propagating and growing edible fungi.

Knowledge: Chemistry; Biology

Abilities: Oral Comprehension; Written Comprehension; Written Expression; Originality; Problem Sensitivity; Deductive Reasoning; Inductive Reasoning; Information Ordering; Category Flexibility; Speed of Closure; Flexibility of Closure; Near Vision

Microbiologists

Research or study growth, structure, development, and general characteristics of bacteria and other micro-organisms. Studies growth, structure, development, and general characteristics of bacteria and other micro-organisms. Examines physiological, morphological, and cultural characteristics, using microscope, to identify micro-organisms. Studies growth structure and development of viruses and rickettsiae. Observes action of micro-organisms upon living tissues of plants, higher animals, and other micro-organisms, and on dead organic matter. Isolates and makes cultures of bacteria or other micro-organisms in prescribed media, controlling moisture, aeration, temperature, and nutrition. Conducts chemical analyses of substances, such as acids, alcohols, and enzymes. Researches use of bacteria and micro-organisms to develop vitamins, antibiotics, amino acids, grain alcohol, sugars, and polymers. Prepares technical reports and recommendations based upon research outcomes. Plans and administers biological research program for government, private research centers, or medical industry.

Knowledge: Mathematics; Chemistry; Biology; English Language

Abilities: Oral Comprehension; Written Comprehension; Oral Expression; Written Expression; Fluency of Ideas; Originality; Problem Sensitivity; Deductive Reasoning; Inductive

Reasoning; Information Ordering; Category Flexibility; Mathematical Reasoning; Number Facility; Memorization; Speed of Closure; Flexibility of Closure; Perceptual Speed; Visualization; Selective Attention; Near Vision

Geneticists

Research or study inheritance and variation of characteristics on forms of life to determine laws, mechanisms, and environmental factors in origin, transmission, and development of inherited traits. Conducts experiments to determine laws, mechanisms, and environmental factors in origin, transmission, and development of inherited traits. Analyses determinants responsible for specific inherited traits, such as color differences, size, and disease resistance. Studies genetic determinants to understand relationship of heredity to maturity, fertility, or other factors. Devises methods for altering or producing new traits, using chemicals, heat, light, or other means. Prepares technical reports and recommendations based upon research outcomes. Counsels clients in human and medical genetics. Plans and administers genetic research program for government, private research centers, or medical industry.

Knowledge: Administration and Management; Mathematics; Chemistry; Biology; Medicine and Dentistry; Therapy and Counseling; Foreign Language

Abilities: Oral Comprehension; Written Comprehension; Oral Expression; Written Expression; Originality; Deductive Reasoning; Inductive Reasoning; Information Ordering; Category Flexibility; Mathematical Reasoning; Flexibility of Closure; Near Vision

Physiologists and Cytologists

Research or study cellular structure and functions, or organ-system functions, of plants and animals. Studies cells, cellular structure, cell division, and organ-system functions of plants and animals. Studies functions of plants and animals, such as growth, respiration, movement, and reproduction, under normal and abnormal conditions. Conducts experiments to determine effects of internal and external environmental factors on life processes and functions. Studies physiology of plants, animals, or particular human body area, function, organ, or system. Utilizes microscope, X ray equipment, spectroscope, and other equipment to study cell structure and function and to perform experiments. Studies glands and their relationship to bodily functions. Analyzes reproductive cells and methods by which chromosomes divide or unite. Studies formation of sperm and eggs in animal sex glands, and studies origin of blood and tissue cells. Researches physiology of unicellular organisms, such as protozoa, to ascertain physical and chemical factors of growth. Studies influence of physical and chemical factors on malignant and normal cells. Assesses and evaluates hormonal status and presence of atypical or malignant changes in exfoliated, aspirated, or abraded cells. Selects and sections minute particles of animal or plant tissue for microscopic study, using microtome and other equipment. Stains tissue sample to make cell structures visible or to differentiate parts. Prepares technical reports and recommendations based upon research outcomes. Plans and administers biological research programs for government, private research centers, or medical industry.

Knowledge: Administration and Management; Chemistry; Biology

Abilities: Oral Comprehension; Written Comprehension; Oral Expression; Written Expression; Fluency of Ideas; Originality; Problem Sensitivity; Deductive Reasoning; Inductive Reasoning; Information Ordering; Category Flexibility; Memorization; Speed of Closure; Flexibility of Closure; Near Vision

Zoologists

Research or study origins, interrelationships, classification, habits, life histories, life processes, diseases, relation to environment, growth, development, genetics, and distribution of animals. Studies origins, interrelationships, classification, life histories, diseases, development, genetics, and distribution of animals. Analyzes characteristics of animals to identify and classify animals. Studies animals in their natural habitats, and assesses effects of environment on animals. Collects and dissects animal specimens and examines specimens under microscope. Prepares collections of preserved specimens or microscopic slides for species identification and study of species development or animal disease. Conducts experimental studies, using chemicals and various types of scientific equipment. Raises specimens for study and observation or for use in experiments.

Knowledge: Chemistry; Biology

Abilities: Oral Comprehension; Written Comprehension; Written Expression; Fluency of Ideas; Originality; Problem Sensitivity; Deductive Reasoning; Inductive Reasoning; Information Ordering; Category Flexibility; Memorization; Speed of Closure; Flexibility of Closure; Perceptual Speed; Spatial Orientation; Selective Attention; Time Sharing; Response Orientation; Gross Body Equilibrium; Far Vision; Night Vision; Glare Sensitivity; Hearing Sensitivity; Auditory Attention; Sound Localization

Toxicologists

Research or study the effects of toxic substances on physiological functions of humans, animals, and plants. Researches effects of toxic substances on physiological functions of humans, animals, and plants for consumer protection and industrial safety programs. Designs and conducts studies to determine physiological effects of various substances on laboratory animals, plants, and human tissue. Interprets results of studies in terms of toxicological properties of substances and hazards associated with their misuse. Collects and prepares samples of toxic materials for analysis or examination. Dissects dead animals, using surgical instruments, and examines organs for toxic substances. Applies cosmetic or ingredient onto skin, or injects substance into animal, and observes animal for abnormalities, inflammation, or irritation. Analyzes samples of toxic materials to identify compound and develop treatment. Tests and analyzes blood samples for presence of toxic conditions, using microscope and laboratory test equipment. Reviews toxicological data for accuracy, and suggests clarifications or corrections to data. Writes and maintains records and reports of studies and tests for use as toxicological resource material. Informs regulatory agency personnel and industrial firms concerning toxicological properties of products and materials. Advises governmental and industrial personnel on degree of hazard of toxic materials and on precautionary labeling. Testifies as expert witness on toxicology in hearings and court proceedings.

Knowledge: Mathematics; Chemistry; Biology; English Language

Abilities: Oral Comprehension; Written Comprehension; Oral Expression; Written Expression; Fluency of Ideas; Originality; Problem Sensitivity; Deductive Reasoning; Inductive Reasoning; Information Ordering; Category Flexibility; Mathematical Reasoning; Number Facility; Memorization; Speed of Closure; Flexibility of Closure; Perceptual Speed; Visualization; Selective Attention; Time Sharing; Manual Dexterity; Near Vision; Far Vision; Visual Color Discrimination; Peripheral Vision; Glare Sensitivity; Speech Clarity

Blue Collar Worker Supervisors

▲ Growth: 3%
▲ Annual Job Openings: 142,666
▲ Yearly Earnings $35,110
▲ Education Required: Work experience in a related occupation
▲ Self-employed: 9%
▲ Part-time: 2%

First Line Supervisors and Manager/Supervisors—Mechanics, Installers, and Repairers

Directly supervise and coordinate activities of mechanics, repairers, and installers and their helpers. Managers/supervisors are generally found in smaller establishments, where they perform both supervisory and management functions, such as accounting, marketing, and personnel work, and may also engage in the same repair work as the workers they supervise. Exclude work leaders who spend 20 percent or more of their time at tasks similar to those of employees under their supervision. These are included in the occupations which are most closely related to their specific work duties. Assigns workers to perform activities, such as service appliances, repair and maintain vehicles, and install machinery and equipment. Directs, coordinates, and assists in performance of workers' activities, such as engine tune-up, hydroelectric turbine repair, or circuit breaker installation. Recommends or initiates personnel actions, such as employment, performance evaluations, promotions, transfers, discharges, and disciplinary measures. Confers with personnel—such as management, engineering, quality control, customers, and workers' representatives—to coordinate work activities and resolve problems. Examines object, system, or facilities—such as telephone, air-conditioning, or industrial plant—and analyzes information to determine installation, service, or repair needed. Interprets specifications, blueprints, and job orders, and constructs templates and lays out reference points for workers. Monitors operations, and inspects, tests, and measures completed work, such as hand tools, gauges, and specifications to verify conformance to standards. Establishes or adjusts work methods and procedures to meet production schedules, using knowledge of capacities of machines, equipment, and personnel. Computes estimates and actual costs of factors, such as materials, labor, and outside contractors, and prepares budgets. Requisitions materials and supplies, such as tools, equipment, and replacement parts for work activities. Completes and maintains reports, such as time and production records, inventories, and test results. Trains workers in methods, procedures, and use of equipment and work aids, such as blueprints, hand tools, and test equipment. Recommends measures, such as procedural changes, service manual revisions, and equipment purchases, to improve work performance and minimize operating costs. Patrols work area and examines tools and equipment to detect unsafe conditions or violations of safety rules.

Knowledge: Administration and Management; Economics and Accounting; Sales and Marketing; Personnel and Human Resources; Design; Building and Construction; Mechanical; Public Safety and Security

Abilities: Information Ordering

First Line Supervisors and Manager/Supervisors—Construction Trades

Directly supervise and coordinate activities of construction trades workers. Supervises and coordinates activities of construction trades workers. Directs and leads workers engaged in construction activities. Assigns work to employees, using material and worker requirements data. Confers with staff and workers to ensure production and personnel problems are resolved. Suggests and initiates personnel actions, such as promotions, transfers, and hires. Analyzes and resolves worker problems and recommends motivational plans. Examines and inspects work progress, equipment, and construction sites to verify safety and ensure that specifications are met. Estimates material and worker requirements to complete job. Reads specifications, such as blueprints and data, to determine construction requirements. Analyzes and plans installation and construction of equipment and structures. Locates, measures, and marks location and placement of structures and equipment. Records information, such as personnel, production, and operational data, on specified forms and reports. Trains workers in construction methods and operation of equipment. Recommends measures to improve production methods and equipment performance to increase efficiency and safety. Assists workers engaged in construction activities, using hand tools and equipment.

Knowledge: Administration and Management; Personnel and Human Resources; Design; Building and Construction; Psychology

Abilities: Originality; Problem Sensitivity; Information Ordering; Category Flexibility; Memorization; Speed of Closure; Flexibility of Closure; Perceptual Speed; Spatial Orientation; Visualization; Time Sharing; Arm-Hand Steadiness; Manual Dexterity; Finger Dexterity; Control Precision; Multilimb Coordination; Response Orientation; Rate Control; Reaction Time; Wrist-Finger Speed; Speed of Limb Movement; Static Strength; Explosive Strength; Dynamic Strength; Trunk Strength; Stamina; Extent Flexibility; Dynamic Flexibility; Gross Body Coordination; Gross Body Equilibrium; Peripheral Vision; Glare Sensitivity

First Line Supervisors and Manager/Supervisors—Extractive Workers

Directly supervise and coordinate activities of extractive workers. Supervises and coordinates activities of workers engaged in the extraction of geological materials. Directs and leads workers engaged in extraction of geological materials. Assigns work to employees, using material and worker requirements data. Confers with staff and workers to ensure production personnel problems are resolved. Analyzes and resolves worker problems and recommends motivational plans. Analyzes and plans extraction process of geological materials. Trains workers in construction methods and operation of equipment. Examines and inspects equipment, site, and materials to verify specifications are met. Recommends measures to improve production methods and equipment performance to increase efficiency and safety. Suggests and initiates personnel actions, such as promotions, transfers, and hires. Records information, such as personnel, production, and operational data on specified forms. Assists workers engaged in extraction activities, using hand tools and equipment. Locates, measures, and marks materials and site location, using measuring and marking equipment. Orders materials, supplies, and repair of equipment and machinery.

Knowledge: Administration and Management; Personnel and Human Resources; Engineering and Technology; Education and Training

Abilities: Problem Sensitivity; Deductive Reasoning; Information Ordering

First Line Supervisors and Manager/Supervisors—Production and Operating Workers

Directly supervise and coordinate activities of production and operating workers, such as testers, precision workers, machine setters and operators, assemblers, fabricators, or plant and system operators. Manager/supervisors are generally found in smaller establishments, where they perform both supervisory and management functions, such as accounting, marketing, and personnel work, and may also engage in the same production work as the workers they supervise. Exclude work leaders who spend 20 percent or more of their time at tasks similar to those of employees under their supervision. These are included in the occupations which are most closely related to their specific

work duties. Directs and coordinates the activities of employees engaged in production or processing of goods. Plans and establishes work schedules, assignments, and production sequences to meet production goals. Calculates labor and equipment requirements and production specifications, using standard formulae. Determines standards, production, and rates based on company policy, equipment and labor availability, and workload. Reviews operations and accounting records or reports to determine feasibility of production estimates and to evaluate current production. Confers with management or subordinates to resolve worker problems, complaints, or grievances. Confers with other supervisors to coordinate operations and activities within departments or between departments. Reads and analyzes charts, work orders, or production schedules to determine production requirements. Maintains operations data, such as time, production, and cost records and prepares management reports. Recommends or implements measures to motivate employees and improve production methods, equipment performance, product quality, or efficiency. Requisitions materials, supplies, equipment parts, or repair services. Interprets specifications, blueprints, job orders, and company policies and procedures for workers. Inspects materials, products, or equipment to detect defects or malfunctions. Demonstrates equipment operations or work procedures to new employees, or assigns employees to experienced workers for training. Monitors or patrols work area and enforces safety or sanitation regulations. Monitors gauges, dials, and other indicators to ensure operators conform to production or processing standards. Sets up and adjusts machines and equipment.

Knowledge: Administration and Management; Economics and Accounting; Sales and Marketing; Personnel and Human Resources; Production and Processing; Mathematics; Psychology; Education and Training

Abilities: Oral Comprehension; Problem Sensitivity; Number Facility; Selective Attention; Time Sharing; Response Orientation; Auditory Attention; Sound Localization; Speech Clarity

First Line Supervisors and Manager/Supervisors—Transportation and Material Moving Machine and Vehicle Operators

Directly supervise and coordinate activities of transportation and material-moving machine and vehicle operators. May supervise helpers assigned to these workers. Manager/supervisors are generally found in smaller establishments where they perform both supervisory and management functions, such as accounting, marketing, and personnel work, and may also engage in the same work as the workers they supervise. Exclude work leaders who spend 20 percent or more of their time at tasks similar to those of employees under their supervision. These are included in the occupations which are most closely related to their specific work duties. Reviews orders, production schedules, and shipping/receiving notices to determine work sequence and material shipping dates, type, volume, and destinations. Plans and establishes transportation routes, work schedules, and assignments and allocates equipment to meet transportation, operations, or production goals. Directs workers in transportation or related services, such as pumping, moving, storing, and loading/unloading of materials or people. Maintains or verifies time, transportation, financial, inventory, and personnel records. Explains and demonstrates work tasks to new workers, or assigns workers to experienced workers for further training. Resolves worker problems or assists workers in solving problems. Computes and estimates cash, payroll, transportation, personnel, and storage requirements, using calculator. Requisitions needed personnel, supplies, equipment, parts, or repair services. Recommends and implements measures to improve worker motivation, equipment performance, work methods, and customer service. Prepares, compiles, and submits reports on work activities, operations, production, and work-related accidents. Inspects or tests materials, stock, vehicles, equipment, and facilities to locate defects, meet maintenance or production specifications, and verify safety standards. Interprets transportation and tariff regulations, shipping orders, safety regulations, and company policies and procedures for workers. Recommends or implements personnel actions, such as hiring, firing, and performance evaluations. Receives telephone or radio reports of emergencies, and dispatches personnel and vehicle in response to request. Confers with customers, supervisors, contractors, and other personnel to exchange information and resolve problems. Assists workers in performing tasks, such as coupling railroad cars or loading vehicles. Repairs or schedules repair and preventive maintenance of vehicles and other equipment. Examines, measures, and weighs cargo or materials to determine specific handling requirements. Drives vehicles or operates machines or equipment.

Knowledge: Administration and Management; Economics and Accounting; Sales and Marketing; Personnel and Human Resources; Production and Processing; Mathematics; Physics; Psychology; Geography; Education and Training; Public Safety and Security; Transportation

Abilities: Mathematical Reasoning; Number Facility; Speech Recognition

First Line Supervisors and Manager/Supervisors—Helpers, Laborers, and Material Movers, Hand

Directly supervise and coordinate activities of helpers, laborers, and material movers. Manager/supervisors are generally found in smaller establishments, where they perform both supervisory and management functions, such as accounting, marketing, and personnel work, and may also engage in the same hand labor as the workers they supervise. Exclude work leaders who spend 20 percent or more of theirtime at tasks similar to those of employees under their supervision. These are included in the occupations which are most closely related to their specific work duties. Supervises and coordinates activities of workers performing assigned tasks. Assigns duties and work schedules.

Determines work sequence and equipment needed, according to work order, shipping records, and experience. Observes work procedures to ensure quality of work. Trains and instructs workers. Records information, such as daily receipts, employee time and wage data, description of freight, and inspection results. Verifies materials loaded or unloaded against work order, and schedules times of shipment and mode of transportation. Examines freight to determine sequence of loading and equipment to determine compliance with specifications. Inspects equipment for wear and completed work for conformance to standards. Inventories and orders supplies. Informs designated employees or department of items loaded, or reports loading deficiencies. Quotes prices to customers. Resolves customer complaints.

Knowledge: Administration and Management; Economics and Accounting; Sales and Marketing; Customer and Personal Service; Personnel and Human Resources; Production and Processing; Mathematics; Psychology; Education and Training

Abilities: None above average

Bookkeeping, Accounting, and Auditing Clerks

▲ Growth: -5%
▲ Annual Job Openings: 327,125
▲ Yearly Earnings $22,776
▲ Education Required: Moderate-term O-J-T
▲ Self-employed: 9%
▲ Part-time: 32%

Tax Preparers

Prepare tax returns for individuals or small businesses, but do not have the background or responsibilities of an accredited accountant or certified public accountant. May work for established tax return firm. Reviews financial records, such as income statements and documentation of expenditures, to determine forms needed to prepare return. Computes taxes owed, using adding machine, and completes entries on forms, following tax form instructions and tax tables. Consults tax law handbook or bulletins to determine procedure for preparation of atypical returns. Interviews client to obtain additional information on taxable income and deductible expenses and allowances. Verifies totals on forms prepared by others to detect errors in arithmetic or procedure, as needed. Calculates form preparation fee according to complexity of return and amount of time required to prepare forms.

Knowledge: Clerical; Economics and Accounting; Mathematics; Law, Government, and Jurisprudence

Abilities: Deductive Reasoning; Mathematical Reasoning; Number Facility

Bookkeepers

Classify, record, and summarize numerical data to compile and maintain financial records. Computes and/or records financial transactions and other account information (such as interest) to update or maintain accounting records. Classifies items on reports for bookkeeping purposes. Posts records. Compiles statistical reports of cash receipts, expenditures, accounts payable and receivable, profit and loss, and other items pertinent to business operation. Examines accuracy of balances, figures, calculations, postings, and other records pertaining to business or operating transactions, and reconciles or notes any discrepancies. Calculates such items as amounts due, balances, costs, discounts, dividends, equity, interest, net charges, outstanding balances, principal, profits, ratios, taxes, and wages. Debits or credits accounts. Compiles information from financial records into reports for organizational and regulatory personnel or customers. Complies with federal, state, and company policies, procedures, and regulations. Receives, processes, or transfers negotiable instruments, such as checks, drafts, coupons, and vouchers. Files and sorts documents. Types vouchers, invoices, account statements, and reports, using typewriter or computer. Prepares and processes billing statements and investigates billing irregularities. Prepares budgets and compiles budgetary reports containing statistics and other data. Verifies terms of credit, such as amount, insurance coverage, and shipping conditions, to determine compliance with standards. Handles inquiries and complaints, using account information and transition records. Coordinates customer credit information and collateral papers, complying with bank credit standards. Prepares letters. Examines collateral or appraises retirement value of equipment.

Knowledge: Clerical; Economics and Accounting; Computers and Electronics; Mathematics; Law, Government, and Jurisprudence

Abilities: Written Expression; Deductive Reasoning; Category Flexibility; Mathematical Reasoning; Number Facility; Memorization; Perceptual Speed; Wrist-Finger Speed; Near Vision; Speech Recognition

Accounting Clerks

Compute, calculate, and post financial, statistical, and numerical data to maintain accounting records. Computes and/or records financial transactions and other account information (such as interest) to update or maintain accounting records. Calculates such items as amounts due, balances, costs, discounts, dividends, equity, interest, net charges, outstanding balances, principal, profits, ratios, taxes, and wages. Posts records. Examines accuracy of balances, calculations, postings, and other records pertaining to business or operating transactions, and reconciles or notes discrepancies. Classifies items on reports for bookkeeping purposes. Compiles statistical reports of cash receipts, expenditures, accounts payable and receivable, profit and loss, and other items pertinent to business operation. Compiles information from financial records into reports for organizational and regulatory personnel or customers. Receives, processes, or transfers negotiable instruments, such as checks, drafts, coupons, and vouchers. Prepares financial application forms. Files and sorts documents.

Types vouchers, invoices, account statements, and reports, using typewriter or computer. Prepares letters.

Knowledge: Clerical; Economics and Accounting; Computers and Electronics; Mathematics; English Language

Abilities: Written Expression; Deductive Reasoning; Category Flexibility; Mathematical Reasoning; Number Facility; Memorization; Speed of Closure; Perceptual Speed; Wrist-Finger Speed; Near Vision

Bread and Pastry Bakers

▲ Growth: 26%
▲ Annual Job Openings: 61,382
▲ Yearly Earnings $17,222
▲ Education Required: Moderate-term O-J-T
▲ Self employed: 9%
▲ Part-time: 38%

Bakers, Bread and Pastry

Mix and bake ingredients according to recipes to produce small quantities of breads, pastries, and other baked goods for consumption on premises or for sale as specialty baked goods. Weighs and measures ingredients, using measuring cups and spoons. Mixes ingredients to form dough or batter by hand, or using electric mixer. Rolls and shapes dough, using rolling pin, and cuts dough in uniform portions with knife, divider, and cookie cutter. Molds dough in desired shapes, places dough in greased or floured pans, and trims overlapping edges with knife. Mixes and cooks pie fillings, pours fillings into pie shells, and tops filling with meringue or cream. Checks production schedule to determine variety and quantity of goods to bake. Spreads or sprinkles toppings on loaves or specialties and places dough in oven, using long-handled paddle (peel). Covers filling with top crust; places pies in oven; and adjust drafts or thermostatic controls to regulate oven temperatures. Mixes ingredients to make icings, decorates cakes and pastries, and blends colors for icings, shaped ornaments, and statuaries. Cuts, peels, and prepares fruit for pie fillings.

Knowledge: Food Production

Abilities: None of the above

Bricklayers and Stone Masons

- ▲ Growth: 14%
- ▲ Annual Job Openings: 26,880
- ▲ Yearly Earnings $36,171
- ▲ Education Required: Long-term O-J-T
- ▲ Self-employed: 22%
- ▲ Part-time: 8%

Brick Masons

Lay building materials—such as brick, structural tile, concrete, cinder, glass, gypsum, and terra cotta block (except stone)—to construct or repair walls, partitions, arches, sewers, and other structures. Include refractory brick masons. Lays and aligns bricks, blocks, or tiles to build or repair structures or high-temperature equipment, such as cupolas, kilns, ovens, or furnaces. Applies and smooths mortar or other mixture over work surface and removes excess, using trowel and hand tools. Examines brickwork or structure to determine need for repair. Measures distance from reference points and marks guidelines to lay out work, using plumb bobs and levels. Calculates angles and courses, and determines vertical and horizontal alignment of courses. Mixes specified amount of sand, clay, dirt, or mortar powder with water to form refractory mixture. Applies primer to work surface and fuses plastic liner to primed surface, using torch. Fastens or fuses brick or other building material to structure with wire clamps, anchor holes, torch, or cement. Breaks or cuts bricks, tiles, or blocks to size, using edge of trowel, hammer, or power saw. Positions frame over casings on kiln frame to lay arches or to build new kilns. Cleans working surface to remove scale, dust, soot, or chips of brick and mortar, using broom, wire brush, or scraper. Removes burned or damaged brick or mortar, using sledgehammer, crowbar, chipping gun, or chisel. Sprays or spreads refractories over brickwork to protect against deterioration.

Knowledge: Building and Construction

Abilities: Information Ordering; Visualization; Manual Dexterity; Static Strength; Explosive Strength; Dynamic Strength; Trunk Strength; Stamina; Extent Flexibility; Dynamic Flexibility; Gross Body Equilibrium

Stone Masons

Build stone structures, such as piers, walls, and abutments. Lay walks, curbstones, or special types of masonry for vats, tanks, and floors. Shapes, trims, faces, and cuts marble or stone preparatory to setting, using power saws, cutting equipment, and hand tools. Sets stone or marble in place, according to layout or pattern. Aligns and levels stone or marble, using measuring devices such as rule, square, and plumbline. Lays out wall pattern or foundation of monument, using straightedge, rule, or staked lines. Mixes mortar or grout and pours or spreads mortar or grout on marble slabs, stone, or foundation. Finishes joints between stones, using trowel. Cleans excess mortar or grout from surface of marble, stone, or monument, using sponge, brush, water, or acid. Smooths, polishes, and bevels surfaces, using hand tools and power tools. Lines interiors of molds with treated paper and fills molds with composition-stone mixture. Positions mold along guidelines of wall, presses mold in place, and removes mold and paper from wall. Repairs cracked or chipped areas of ornamental stone or marble surface, using blow-torch and mastic. Removes sections of monument from truck bed, and guides stone onto foundation, using skids, hoist, or truck crane. Drills holes in marble or ornamental stone and anchors bracket. Digs trench for foundation of monument, using pick and shovel.

Knowledge: Building and Construction

Abilities: Wrist-Finger Speed; Speed of Limb Movement; Static Strength; Explosive Strength; Dynamic Strength; Trunk Strength; Stamina; Dynamic Flexibility; Gross Body Equilibrium

Stone Cutters and Carvers

Cut or carve stone according to diagrams and patterns. Guides nozzle over stone following stencil outline or chips along marks to create design or work surface down to desired finish. Drills holes, or cuts molding and grooves in stone. Studies artistic objects or graphic materials, such as models, sketches, or blueprints and plans carving or cutting technique. Lays out designs or dimensions on stone surface, by freehand or transfer from tracing paper, using scribe or chalk and measuring instruments. Selects chisels, pneumatic or surfacing tools, or sandblasting nozzles and determines sequence of their use according to intricacy of design or figure. Removes or adds stencil during blasting to create differences in depth of cuts, intricate designs, or rough, pitted finish. Loads sandblasting equipment with abrasive, attaches nozzle to hose, and turns valves to admit compressed air and activate jet. Verifies depth and dimensions of cut or carving, using measuring instruments, to ensure adherence to specifications. Moves fingers over surface of carving to ensure smoothness of finish.

Knowledge: Design; Building and Construction; Physics; Fine Arts

Abilities: Visualization; Arm-Hand Steadiness; Depth Perception

Broadcast Technicians

▲ Growth: 15%

▲ Annual Job Openings: 4,727

▲ Yearly Earnings $31,033

▲ Education Required: Postsecondary vocational training

▲ Self-employed: 3%

▲ Part-time: 11%

Broadcast Technicians

Set up, operate, and maintain electrical and electronic equipment used in radio and television broadcasts. Lays electrical cord and audio and video cables between vehicle, microphone, camera, and reporter or person to be interviewed. Aligns antennae with receiving dish to obtain clearest signal for transmission of news event to station. Sets up, operates, and maintains radio and television production equipment to broadcast programs or events. Monitors transmission of news event to station and adjusts equipment as needed to maintain quality broadcast. Previews scheduled program to ensure that signal is functioning and program is ready for transmission. Performs preventive and minor equipment maintenance, using hand tools. Observes monitors and converses with station personnel to set audio and video levels and to verify station is on-air. Selects source, such as satellite or studio, from which program will be recorded. Reads television programming log to ascertain program to be recorded or aired. Maintains log, as required by station management and Federal Communications Commission. Edits manuals, schedules programs, and prepares reports outlining past and future programs, including content. Instructs trainees in how to use television production equipment, to film events, and to copy/edit graphics or sound onto videotape. Produces educational and training films and videotapes, including selection of equipment and preparation of script. Drives news van to location of news events.

Knowledge: Computers and Electronics; Geography; Education and Training; Telecommunications; Communications and Media; Transportation

Abilities: Deductive Reasoning; Information Ordering; Selective Attention; Time Sharing; Control Precision; Response Orientation; Rate Control; Reaction Time; Gross Body Coordination; Gross Body Equilibrium; Far Vision; Visual Color Discrimination; Night Vision; Peripheral Vision; Depth Perception; Glare Sensitivity; Hearing Sensitivity; Auditory Attention; Sound Localization; Speech Recognition

Transmitter Engineers

Operate and maintain radio transmitter to broadcast radio and television programs. Operates and maintains radio transmitter to broadcast radio and television programs. Monitors console panel and signal emission and makes adjustments as needed to maintain quality of transmission. Operates microwave transmitter and receiver to receive or send program to and from other broadcast stations. Tests components of malfunctioning transmitter to diagnose trouble, using test equipment, such as oscilloscope, voltmeters, and ammeters. Disassembles and repairs equipment, using hand tools. Notifies broadcast studio when ready to transmit. Converses with studio personnel to determine cause of equipment failure and to solve problem. Maintains log of programs transmitted, as required by Federal Communications Commission.

Knowledge: Computers and Electronics; Telecommunications; Communications and Media

Abilities: Problem Sensitivity; Selective Attention; Time Sharing; Response Orientation; Rate Control; Reaction Time; Hearing Sensitivity; Auditory Attention; Sound Localization

Brokerage Clerks

- ▲ Growth: 19%
- ▲ Annual Job Openings: 16,901
- ▲ Yearly Earnings $28,766
- ▲ Education Required: Short-term O-J-T
- ▲ Self-employed: 0%
- ▲ Part-time: 19%

Brokerage Clerks

Perform clerical duties involving the purchase or sale of securities. Duties include writing orders for stock purchases and sales, computing transfer taxes, verifying stock transactions, accepting and delivering securities, informing customers of stock price fluctuations, computing equity, distributing dividends, and keeping records of daily transactions and holdings. Records and documents security transactions, such as purchases, sales, conversions, redemptions, and payments, using computers, accounting ledgers, and certificate records. Prepares reports summarizing daily transactions and earnings for individual customer accounts. Computes total holdings, dividends, interest, transfer taxes, brokerage fees, and commissions, and allocates appropriate payments to customers. Prepares forms, such as receipts, withdrawal orders, transmittal papers, and transfer confirmations, based on transaction requests from stockholders. Corresponds with customers and confers with coworkers to answer inquiries, discuss market fluctuations, and resolve account problems. Schedules and coordinates transfer and delivery of security certificates between companies, departments, and customers. Monitors daily stock prices and computes fluctuations to determine the need for additional collateral to secure loans. Verifies ownership and transaction information and dividend distribution instructions to ensure conformance with governmental regulations, using stock records and reports. Files, types, and operates standard office machines.

Knowledge: Clerical; Economics and Accounting; Sales and Marketing; Computers and Electronics; Mathematics; Communications and Media

Abilities: Written Comprehension; Mathematical Reasoning; Number Facility; Wrist-Finger Speed

Budget Analysts

▲ Growth: 12%

▲ Annual Job Openings: 8,204

▲ Yearly Earnings $42,057

▲ Education Required: Bachelor's degree

▲ Self-employed: 0%

▲ Part-time: 7%

Budget Analysts

Examine budget estimates for completeness, accuracy, and conformance with procedures and regulations. Examine requests for budget revisions, recommend approval or denial, and draft correspondence. Analyze monthly department budgeting and accounting reports for the purpose of maintaining expenditure controls. Provide technical assistance to officials in the preparation of budgets. Analyzes accounting records to determine financial resources required to implement program, and submits recommendations for budget allocations. Reviews operating budgets periodically to analyze trends affecting budget needs. Analyzes costs in relation to services performed during previous fiscal years to prepare comparative analyses of operating programs. Recommends approval or disapproval of requests for funds. Advises staff on cost analysis and fiscal allocations. Correlates appropriations for specific programs with appropriations for divisional programs, and includes items for emergency funds. Directs preparation of regular and special budget reports to interpret budget directives and to establish policies for carrying out directives. Consults with unit heads to ensure adjustments are made in accordance with program changes to facilitate long-term planning. Directs compilation of data based on statistical studies and analyses of past and current years to prepare budgets. Testifies regarding proposed budgets before examining and fund-granting authorities to clarify reports and gain support for estimated budget needs. Administers personnel functions of budget department, such as training, work scheduling, promotions, transfers, and performance ratings.

Knowledge: Administration and Management; Economics and Accounting; Personnel and Human Resources; Computers and Electronics; Mathematics; Education and Training

Abilities: Written Comprehension; Deductive Reasoning; Mathematical Reasoning; Number Facility

Bus Drivers

▲ Growth: 15%
▲ Annual Job Openings: 31,905
▲ Yearly Earnings $24,460
▲ Education Required: Moderate-term O-J-T
▲ Self-employed: 1%
▲ Part-time: 43%

Bus Drivers

Drive bus, transporting passengers over specified routes to local or distant points, according to a time schedule. Assist passengers with baggage. Collect tickets or cash fares. Drives vehicle over specified route or to specified destination, according to time schedule, to transport passengers, complying with traffic regulations. Assists passengers with baggage, and collects tickets or cash fares. Parks vehicle at loading area for passengers to board. Loads and unloads baggage in baggage compartment. Regulates heating, lighting, and ventilating systems for passenger comfort. Advises passengers to be seated and orderly while on vehicle. Records cash receipts and ticket fares. Inspects vehicle and checks gas, oil, and water before departure. Reports delays or accidents. Makes minor repairs to vehicle and changes tires.

Knowledge: Geography; Public Safety and Security; Transportation

Abilities: Spatial Orientation; Control Precision; Response Orientation; Reaction Time; Far Vision; Night Vision; Peripheral Vision

Camera and Photographic Equipment Repairers

Growth: 24%
Annual Job Openings: 1,158
Yearly Earnings $29,182
Education Required: Moderate-term O-J-T
Self-employed: 53%
Part-time: 7%

Camera and Photographic Equipment Repairers

Repair and adjust cameras and photographic equipment, including motion picture cameras and equipment, using specialized tools and testing devices. Measures parts to verify specified dimensions/settings, such as camera shutter speed and light meter reading accuracy, using measuring instruments. Examines cameras, equipment, processed film, and laboratory reports to diagnose malfunction, using work aids and specifications. Disassembles equipment to gain access to defect, using hand tools. Adjusts cameras, photographic mechanisms, and equipment, such as range and view finders, shutters, light meters, and lens systems, using hand tools. Calibrates and verifies accuracy of light meters, shutter diaphragm operation, and lens carriers, using timing instruments. Fabricates or modifies defective electronic, electrical, and mechanical components, using bench lathe, milling machine, shaper, grinder, and precision hand tools, according to specifications. Tests equipment performance, focus of lens system, alignment of diaphragm, lens mounts, and film transport, using precision gauges. Reads and interprets engineering drawings, diagrams, instructions, and specifications to determine needed repairs, fabrication method, and operation sequence. Assembles aircraft cameras, still and motion picture cameras, photographic equipment, and frames, using diagrams, blueprints, bench machines, hand tools, and power tools. Installs film in aircraft camera and electrical assemblies and wiring in camera housing, following blueprints and using hand tools and soldering equipment. Lays out reference points and dimensions on parts and metal stock to be machined, using precision measuring instruments. Cleans and lubricates cameras and polishes camera lenses, using cleaning materials and work aids. Records test data and documents fabrication techniques on reports. Requisitions parts and materials. Demonstrates operation and servicing of equipment to customers. Recommends design changes or upgrades of micro-filming, film-developing, and photographic equipment. Schedules service calls according to customer location and priority. Interviews prospective buyers and provides informational leads to sales personnel.

Knowledge: Sales and Marketing; Computers and Electronics; Engineering and Technology; Design; Mechanical; Physics; Chemistry; Fine Arts

Abilities: Written Comprehension; Arm-Hand Steadiness; Finger Dexterity; Control Precision; Dynamic Flexibility; Gross Body Equilibrium; Near Vision; Visual Color Discrimination; Night Vision; Depth Perception; Glare Sensitivity; Hearing Sensitivity; Sound Localization; Speech Clarity

Cardiology Technologists

▲ Growth: 35%
▲ Annual Job Openings: 1,686
▲ Yearly Earnings $33,696
▲ Education Required: Associate degree
▲ Self-employed: 0%
▲ Part-time: 22%

Cardiology Technologists

Conduct tests on pulmonary and/or cardiovascular systems of patients for diagnostic purposes. May conduct or assist in electrocardiograms, cardiac catheterizations, and pulmonary function, lung capacity and similar tests. Operates diagnostic imaging equipment to produce contrast-enhanced radiographs of heart and cardiovascular system. Injects contrast medium into blood vessels of patient. Activates fluoroscope and 35 mm motion picture camera to produce images used to guide catheter through cardiovascular system. Conducts electrocardiogram, phonocardiogram, echocardiogram, stress testing, and other cardiovascular tests, using specialized electronic test equipment, recording devices, and laboratory instruments. Conducts tests of pulmonary system, using spirometer and other respiratory testing equipment. Observes gauges, recorder, and video screens of multichannel data analysis system, during imaging of cardiovascular system. Operates multichannel physiologic monitor to measure and record functions of cardiovascular and pulmonary systems, as part of cardiac catheterization team. Records variations in action of heart muscle, using electrocardiograph. Records two-dimensional ultrasonic and Doppler flow analyses of heart and related structures, using ultrasound equipment. Observes ultrasound display screen and listens to Doppler signals to acquire data for measurement of blood flow velocities. Compares measurements of heart wall thickness and chamber sizes to standard norms to identify abnormalities. Assesses cardiac physiology and calculates valve areas from blood flow velocity measurements. Enters factors such as amount and quality of radiation beam, and filming sequence, into computer. Alerts physician to abnormalities or changes in patient responses. Adjusts equipment and controls according to physicians' orders or established protocol. Explains testing procedures to patient to obtain cooperation and reduce anxiety. Reviews test results with physician. Records test results and other data into patient's record. Prepares and positions patients for testing.

Knowledge: Clerical; Computers and Electronics; Physics; Chemistry; Biology; Psychology; Medicine and Dentistry; Therapy and Counseling; English Language; Foreign Language

Abilities: Hearing Sensitivity

Electrocardiograph Technicians

Record electromotive variations in heart muscle using electrocardiograph, to provide data for diagnosis of heart ailments. Moves electrodes along specified area of chest to produce electrocardiogram and record electromotive variations occurring in different areas of heart muscle. Connects electrode leads to EKG machine and starts machine to record pulse from electrodes. Monitors electrocardiogram to identify abnormal heart rhythm patterns. Keys information into machine or presses button to mark tracing paper to indicate positions of chest electrodes. Obtains information from patient for electrocardiograph (EKG) records, including patient identification, brief history, and medication used. Attaches electrodes to specified locations on patient, such as chest, arms, and legs. Enters patient data into computer for analysis of tracing. Attaches electrodes of Holter monitor (electrocardiograph) to patient to record data over extended period of time. Explains test procedures and gives instructions to patient. Directs patient to perform physical exercise as specified by physician. Edits and forwards final test results to attending physician for analysis and interpretation. Maintains patient comfort and privacy, using such methods as draping and bed screens. Pastes and labels tracings on mounting cards. Notifies physicians of emergencies and assists physicians in emergencies. Escorts patient to treatment room or wheels equipment to patient bedside. Cleans and maintains equipment and supplies.

Knowledge: Clerical; Customer and Personal Service; Computers and Electronics; Biology; Psychology; Medicine and Dentistry; Therapy and Counseling; Philosophy and Theology

Abilities: Oral Comprehension; Oral Expression; Problem Sensitivity; Inductive Reasoning; Information Ordering; Memorization; Speed of Closure; Flexibility of Closure; Perceptual Speed; Spatial Orientation; Selective Attention; Finger Dexterity; Response Orientation; Reaction Time; Hearing Sensitivity; Speech Recognition

Carpenters

- ▲ Growth: 6%
- ▲ Annual Job Openings: 167,617
- ▲ Yearly Earnings $30,139
- ▲ Education Required: Long-term O-J-T
- ▲ Self-employed: 31%
- ▲ Part-time: 8%

Construction Carpenters

Construct, erect, install, and repair structures and fixtures of wood, plywood, and wallboard, using carpenter's hand tools and power tools. Shapes or cuts materials to specified measurements, using hand tools, machines, or power saw. Assembles and fastens materials, using hand tools and wood screws, nails, dowel pins, or glue, to make framework or props. Builds or repairs cabinets, doors, frameworks, floors, and other wooden fixtures used in buildings, using woodworking machines, carpenter's hand tools, and power tools. Installs structures and fixtures (such as windows, frames, floorings, and trim), or hardware, using carpenter's hand and power tools. Fills cracks and other defects in plaster or plasterboard and sands patch, using patching plaster, trowel, and sanding tool. Finishes surfaces of woodworking or wallboard in houses and buildings, using paint, hand tools, and paneling. Removes damaged or defective parts or sections of structure, and repairs or replaces, using hand tools. Measures and marks cutting lines on materials, using ruler, pencil, chalk, and marking gauge. Verifies trueness of structure, using plumb bob and level. Studies specifications in blueprints, sketches, or building plans to determine materials required and dimensions of structure to be fabricated. Prepares layout according to blueprint or oral instructions, using rule, framing square, and calipers. Inspects ceiling or floor tile, wall coverings, siding, glass, or woodwork to detect broken or damaged structures. Estimates amount and kind of lumber or other materials required, and selects and orders them.

Knowledge: Design; Building and Construction

Abilities: Spatial Orientation; Visualization; Arm-Hand Steadiness; Manual Dexterity; Finger Dexterity; Control Precision; Multilimb Coordination; Wrist-Finger Speed; Speed of Limb Movement; Static Strength; Explosive Strength; Dynamic Strength; Trunk Strength; Stamina;

Extent Flexibility; Dynamic Flexibility; Gross Body Coordination; Gross Body Equilibrium; Peripheral Vision; Depth Perception; Glare Sensitivity

Rough Carpenters

Build rough wooden structures—such as concrete forms, scaffolds; tunnel, bridge, or sewer supports; billboard signs; and temporary frame shelters—according to sketches, blueprints, or oral instructions. Assembles and fastens material together to construct wood or metal framework of structure, using bolts, nails, or screws. Studies blueprints and diagrams to determine dimensions of structure or form to be constructed or erected. Measures materials or distances—using square, measuring tape, or rule—to lay out work. Cuts or saws boards, timbers, or plywood to required size, using handsaw, power saw, or woodworking machine. Bores bolt-holes in timber with masonry or concrete walls, using power drill. Erects prefabricated forms, framework, scaffolds, hoists, roof supports, or chutes, using hand tools, plumb rule, and level. Installs rough door and window frames, subflooring, fixtures, or temporary supports in structures undergoing construction or repair. Anchors and braces forms and other structures in place, using nails, bolts, anchor rods, steel cables, planks, wedges, and timbers. Examines structural timbers and supports to detect decay, and replaces timber, using hand tools, nuts, and bolts. Fabricates parts, using woodworking and metal-working machines. Digs or directs digging of post holes, and sets pole to support structure.

Knowledge: Building and Construction

Abilities: Visualization; Manual Dexterity; Speed of Limb Movement; Static Strength; Trunk Strength; Gross Body Equilibrium

Tank Builders and Coopers

Construct or assemble and erect wooden tanks for storing liquids. Determines dimensions of wooden parts of tank from blueprints, diagrams, and other specifications, using measuring instruments. Cuts tank parts from lumber, using power tools and carpenter's hand tools. Assembles and fastens cut or precut parts together, using hammer and staple gun. Shapes parts, using hand tools to trim and bevel edges and to form bottoms, headings, and ends of tanks. Positions hoops or rods around tank and tightens them, using hand tools, to secure them in place. Measures or marks position of wooden parts on foundation. Levels parts, using leveling shims, carpenter's level, and hand tools. Places or directs placement of assembled tank on foundation, using powered hoist, and secures it on foundation, using hand tools. Tests tanks to determine leaks and holding properties, and adjusts tank sections to repair lead, using caulking. Removes and replaces defective parts of tank or hogshead mat, using windlass to compress staves and loosen hoops, and hand tools. Inspects parts for fit or to detect damage or defect. Plugs holes with wooden plugs.

Knowledge: Building and Construction

Abilities: Arm-Hand Steadiness; Manual Dexterity; Finger Dexterity; Control Precision; Multilimb Coordination; Wrist-Finger Speed; Speed of Limb Movement; Static Strength;

Explosive Strength; Dynamic Strength; Trunk Strength; Stamina; Dynamic Flexibility; Gross Body Coordination; Gross Body Equilibrium

Carpenter Assemblers and Repairers

Perform a variety of tasks requiring a limited knowledge of carpentry, such as applying siding and weatherboard to building exteriors or assembling and erecting prefabricated buildings. Measures and marks location of studs, leaders, and receptacle openings, using tape measure, template, and marker. Cuts sidings and moldings, sections of weatherboard, and openings in platerboard, and lumber, using hand tools and power tools. Aligns and fastens materials together, using hand tools and power tools, to form building or bracing. Lays out and aligns materials on work table or in assembly jig according to specified instructions. Installs prefabricated windows and doors, insulation, walls, and ceiling and floor panels or siding, using adhesives, hoists, hand tools, and power tools. Trims overlapping edges of wood, and weatherboard, using portable router or power saw and hand tools. Removes surface defects, using knife, scraper, wet sponge, electric iron, and sanding tools. Repairs or replaces defective locks, hinges, cranks, and pieces of wood, using glue, hand tools, and power tools. Realigns windows and screens to fit casements, and oils moving parts. Measures cut materials to determine conformance to specifications, using tape measure. Examines wood surfaces for defects, such as nicks, cracks, or blisters. Fills cracks, seams, depressions, and nail holes with filler. Studies blueprints, specification sheets, and drawings to determine style and type of window or wall panel required. Moves panel or roof section to other work stations or to storage or shipping area, using electric hoist. Directs crane operator in positioning floor, wall, ceiling, and roof panels on house foundation. Applies stain, paints or crayons to defects and filter to touch up the repaired area.

Knowledge: Building and Construction

Abilities: Spatial Orientation; Visualization; Arm-Hand Steadiness; Manual Dexterity; Multilimb Coordination; Speed of Limb Movement; Static Strength; Explosive Strength; Dynamic Strength; Trunk Strength; Stamina; Extent Flexibility; Dynamic Flexibility; Gross Body Coordination; Gross Body Equilibrium; Depth Perception; Glare Sensitivity

Boat and Ship Builders

Construct and repair ships or boats, according to blueprints. Cuts and forms parts, such as keel, ribs, sidings, and support structures and blocks, using woodworking hand tools and power tools. Constructs and shapes wooden frames, structures, and other parts according to blueprint specifications, using hand tools, power tools, and measuring instruments. Assembles and installs hull timbers and other structures in ship, using adhesive, measuring instruments, and hand tools or power tools. Attaches metal part—such as fittings, plates, and bulkheads—to ship, using brace and bits, augers, and wrenches. Cuts out defect, using power tools and hand tools, and fits and secures replacement part, using caulking gun, adhesive, or hand tools. Smooths and finishes ship surfaces, using power sander, broadax, adze, and paint, and waxes and buffs surface to specified finish. Establishes dimensional reference points on layout and hull to make template of parts and to locate machinery and equipment. Measures and marks dimensional lines on lumber, following template and using scriber. Positions and secures support structures on construction area. Inspects boat to determine location and extent of defect. Marks outline of boat on building dock, shipway, or mold loft according to blueprint specifications, using measuring instruments and crayon. Attaches hoist to sections of hull, and directs hoist operator to align parts over blocks, according to layout of boat. Consults with customer or supervisor, and reads blueprint to determine necessary repairs.

Knowledge: Production and Processing; Engineering and Technology; Design; Building and Construction; Mechanical

Abilities: Information Ordering; Visualization; Arm-Hand Steadiness; Manual Dexterity; Speed of Limb Movement; Static Strength; Dynamic Strength; Extent Flexibility; Gross Body Equilibrium

Ship Carpenters and Joiners

Fabricate, assemble, install, or repair wooden furnishings in ships or boats. Reads blueprints to determine dimensions of furnishings in ships or boats. Shapes and laminates wood to form parts of ship, using steam chambers, clamps, glue, and jigs. Assembles and installs hardware, gaskets, floors, furnishings, or insulation, using adhesive, hand tools, and power tools. Repairs structural woodwork and replaces defective parts and equipment, using hand tools and power tools. Cuts wood or glass to specified dimensions, using hand tools and power tools. Constructs floors, doors, and partitions, using woodworking machines, hand tools, and power tools. Shapes irregular parts and trims excess material from bulkhead and furnishings to ensure that fit meets specifications. Transfers dimensions or measurements of wood parts or bulkhead on plywood, using measuring instruments and marking devices. Greases gears and other moving parts of machines on ship.

Knowledge: Design; Building and Construction

Abilities: Visualization; Manual Dexterity; Speed of Limb Movement; Stamina; Dynamic Flexibility; Gross Body Equilibrium

Brattice Builders

Build doors or brattices (ventilation walls or partitions) in underground passageways to control the proper circulation of air through the passageways and to work areas. Installs rigid and flexible air ducts to transport air to work areas. Erects partitions to support roof in areas unsuited to timbering or bolting. Drills and blasts obstructing boulders to reopen ventilation shafts.

Knowledge: Building and Construction

Abilities: Explosive Strength; Dynamic Strength; Trunk Strength; Stamina; Extent Flexibility; Gross Body Equilibrium

Exhibit Builders

Construct and install exhibits or displays for museums or other commercial exhibitions. Sets up display in designated site, such as exhibit gallery or commercial location. Cuts glass, wood, plastic, plexiglas, or sheet metal parts for framework of exhibit or display, using hand and power tools. Assembles parts with nails, screws, bolts, and glue, to fabricate panels, shelves, and other exhibit components, using hand tools. Installs electrical wiring for illumination, audio, video, or control equipment in framework of exhibit or display, according to design specifications. Paints enamel, varnish, or other finish on structures of exhibit, using spray, brush, cloth, sponge, or fingers. Designs displays or exhibits according to pictures, sketches or verbal instructions from customer. Affixes murals, photographs, mounted legend materials, and graphics in framework or on fixtures. Studies sketches or scale drawings for displays or exhibits to determine type, amount, and cost of material needed. Tests electrical, electronic, and mechanical components of exhibit structure to verify operation. Disassembles and reassembles display to make working drawings for production, or to send to prospective customers. Confers with exhibit personnel, designer, customer, or salesperson to discuss refinement, additions, or adjustments to exhibit or display. Maintains inventory of building materials, tools, and equipment, and orders supplies. Supervises assigned duties of carpentry, electrical, and other workers assisting in construction of exhibit or display.

Knowledge: Administration and Management; Personnel and Human Resources; Engineering and Technology; Design; Building and Construction; Fine Arts

Abilities: Originality; Spatial Orientation; Visualization; Arm-Hand Steadiness; Manual Dexterity; Finger Dexterity; Wrist-Finger Speed; Speed of Limb Movement; Static Strength; Explosive Strength; Dynamic Strength; Trunk Strength; Stamina; Extent Flexibility; Dynamic Flexibility; Gross Body Coordination; Gross Body Equilibrium; Visual Color Discrimination; Peripheral Vision; Depth Perception

Carpet Installers

▲ Growth: 12%

▲ Annual Job Openings: 6,420

▲ Yearly Earnings $29,972

▲ Education Required: Moderate-term O-J-T

▲ Self-employed: 60%

▲ Part-time: 13%

Carpet Installers

Lay carpets or rugs in homes or buildings. Exclude workers who lay linoleum.
Stretches carpet to ensure smooth surface and presses carpet in place over tack strips. Installs carpet on some floors using adhesive, following prescribed method. Cuts carpet padding to size, and installs padding, following prescribed method. Measures and cuts carpeting to size

according to floor sketches, using carpet knife. Cuts and trims carpet to fit along wall edges, openings, and projections. Joins edges of carpet that meet at openings, using tape with glue and heated carpet iron. Studies floor sketches to determine area to be carpeted and amount of material needed to complete job. Sews sections of carpeting together by hand, when necessary. Nails tack strips around area to be carpeted, or uses old strips to attach edges of new carpet. Fastens metal treads across door openings or where carpet meets flooring to hold carpet in place. Moves furniture from area to be carpeted and removes old carpet and padding.

Knowledge: None above average

Abilities: Arm-Hand Steadiness; Multilimb Coordination; Speed of Limb Movement; Static Strength; Explosive Strength; Dynamic Strength; Trunk Strength; Stamina; Extent Flexibility; Dynamic Flexibility; Gross Body Coordination; Gross Body Equilibrium

Cashiers

- ▲ Growth: 17%
- ▲ Annual Job Openings: 1109,571
- ▲ Yearly Earnings $13,686
- ▲ Education Required: Short-term O-J-T
- ▲ Self-employed: 0%
- ▲ Part-time: 57%

Cashiers, General

Receive payments, issue receipts, handle credit transactions, account for the amounts received, and perform related clerical duties in a wide variety of business establishments. Receives sales slip, cash, check, voucher, or charge payments, and issues refunds or credits to customer. Issues receipt and change due. Operates cash register or electronic scanner. Computes and records totals of transactions. Cashes checks. Keeps periodic balance sheet of amount and number of transactions. Sells tickets and other items to customer. Sorts, counts, and wraps currency and coins. Learns prices, stocks shelves, marks prices, weighs items, issues trading stamps, and redeems food stamps and coupons. Answers questions and provides information to customers. Bags, boxes, or wraps merchandise. Compiles and maintains nonmonetary reports and records. Resolves customers' complaints. Accepts bets and computes and pays winnings in gambling establishment. Monitors check-out stations, issues and removes cash as needed, and assigns workers to reduce customer delay.

Knowledge: Clerical; Sales and Marketing; Customer and Personal Service

Abilities: Memorization; Perceptual Speed; Finger Dexterity; Wrist-Finger Speed; Speech Recognition

Cash Accounting Clerks

Receive payments, issue receipts, handle credit transactions, account for the amounts received, and perform related clerical duties in a wide variety of business establishments. Operate office machines, such as typewriter; computer terminal; and adding, calculating, bookkeeping, and check-writing machines. Receives cash or checks or completes credit card transactions. Counts money to verify amounts and issues receipts for funds received. Issues change and cashes checks. Compares totals on cash register with amount of currency in register to verify balances. Endorses checks, lists and totals cash and checks, and prepares bank deposit slips. Operates office machines, such as typewriter; computer terminal; and adding, calculating, bookkeeping, and check-writing machines. Issues itemized statements to customers. Disburses cash and writes vouchers and checks in payment of company expenses. Posts data and balances accounts. Withdraws cash from bank accounts and keeps custody of cash fund. Compiles collection, disbursement, and bank-reconciliation reports. Prepares payroll paychecks. Authorizes various plant expenditures and purchases.

Knowledge: Clerical; Economics and Accounting; Computers and Electronics

Abilities: Mathematical Reasoning; Number Facility; Perceptual Speed; Wrist-Finger Speed; Near Vision

Chemical Engineers

▲ Growth: 15%

▲ Annual Job Openings: 1,434

▲ Yearly Earnings $55,764

▲ Education Required: Bachelor's degree

▲ Self-employed: 2%

▲ Part-time: 1%

Chemical Engineers

Design chemical plant equipment and devise processes for manufacturing chemicals and products such as gasoline, synthetic rubber, plastics, detergents, cement, paper, and pulp by applying principles and technology of chemistry, physics, and engineering. Devises processes to separate components of liquids or gases, using absorbent such as fuller's earth or carbons. Conducts research to develop new and improved chemical manufacturing processes. Designs and plans layout, and oversees workers engaged in constructing and improving equipment to implement chemical processes on commercial scale. Designs measurement and control systems for chemical plants based on data collected in laboratory experiments and in pilot plant operations. Develops electrochemical processes to generate electric currents, using controlled chemical reactions, or to produce chemical changes, using electric currents. Determines most effective arrangement of operations, such as mixing, crushing, heat transfer, distillation, and drying. Performs laboratory studies of steps in manufacture of new product, and tests proposed process in small-scale operation (pilot plant). Performs tests throughout stages of production to determine degree of control over variables, including temperature, density, specific gravity, and pressure. Develops safety procedures to be employed by workers operating equipment or working in close proximity to ongoing chemical reactions. Prepares estimate of production costs and production progress reports for management. Directs activities of workers who operate equipment such as absorption and evaporation towers and electromagnets to effect required chemical reaction. Directs workers using absorption method to remove soluble constituent or vapor by dissolving in a liquid.

Knowledge: Administration and Management; Economics and Accounting; Production and Processing; Computers and Electronics; Engineering and Technology; Design; Mechanical; Mathematics; Physics; Chemistry; Biology; English Language; Public Safety and Security; Law, Government, and Jurisprudence

Abilities: Oral Comprehension; Written Comprehension; Oral Expression; Written Expression; Fluency of Ideas; Originality; Problem Sensitivity; Deductive Reasoning; Inductive Reasoning; Information Ordering; Category Flexibility; Mathematical Reasoning; Number Facility; Memorization; Speed of Closure; Perceptual Speed; Spatial Orientation; Visualization; Selective Attention; Time Sharing; Control Precision; Response Orientation; Reaction Time; Gross Body Equilibrium; Near Vision; Far Vision; Visual Color Discrimination; Peripheral Vision; Depth Perception; Glare Sensitivity; Hearing Sensitivity; Auditory Attention; Speech Clarity

Chemists

▲ Growth: 18%
▲ Annual Job Openings: 10,572
▲ Yearly Earnings $43,305
▲ Education Required: Bachelor's degree
▲ Self-employed: 0%
▲ Part-time: 3%

Chemists, Except Biochemists

Conduct qualitative and quantitative chemical analyses or chemical experiments in laboratories for quality or process control or to develop new products or knowledge.
Analyzes organic and inorganic compounds to determine chemical and physical properties, composition, structure, relationships, and reactions, utilizing chromatography, spectroscopy, and spectrophotometry techniques. Induces changes in composition of substances by introducing heat, light, energy, and chemical catalysts for quantitative and qualitative analysis. Develops, improves, and customizes products, equipment, formulas, processes, and analytical methods. Compiles and analyzes test information to determine process or equipment operating efficiency and to diagnose malfunctions. Studies effects of various methods of

processing, preserving, and packaging on composition and properties of foods. Prepares test solutions, compounds, and reagents for laboratory personnel to conduct test. Confers with scientists and engineers to conduct analyses of research projects, interpret test results, or develop nonstandard tests. Writes technical papers and reports and prepares standards and specifications for processes, facilities, products, and tests. Directs, coordinates, and advises personnel in test procedures for analyzing components and physical properties of materials. Tests, or supervises workers in testing, food and beverage samples to ensure compliance with applicable laws and quality and purity standards.

Knowledge: Administration and Management; Production and Processing; Computers and Electronics; Engineering and Technology; Mathematics; Physics; Chemistry; Biology; English Language

Abilities: Oral Comprehension; Written Comprehension; Oral Expression; Written Expression; Problem Sensitivity; Deductive Reasoning; Inductive Reasoning; Information Ordering; Category Flexibility; Mathematical Reasoning; Number Facility; Speed of Closure; Flexibility of Closure; Perceptual Speed; Selective Attention; Time Sharing; Visual Color Discrimination; Speech Clarity

Child Care Workers

▲ Growth: 36%
▲ Annual Job Openings: 328,078
▲ Yearly Earnings $13,998
▲ Education Required: Short-term O-J-T
▲ Self-employed: 57%
▲ Part-time: 43%

Child Care Workers

Attend to children at schools, businesses, and institutions. Perform variety of tasks, such as dressing, feeding, bathing, and overseeing play. Exclude preschool teachers and teacher aides. Cares for children in institutional setting, such as group homes, nursery schools, private businesses, or schools for the handicapped. Organizes and participates in recreational activities, such as games. Disciplines children and recommends or initiates other measures to control behavior, such as caring for own clothing and picking up toys and books. Places or hoists children into baths or pools. Instructs children regarding desirable health and personal habits, such as eating, resting, and toilet habits. Assists in preparing food for children, serves meals and refreshments to children, and regulates rest periods. Reads to children, and teaches them simple painting, drawing, handwork, and songs. Wheels handicapped children to classes or other areas of facility, secure in equipment, such as chairs and slings. Monitors children on life-support equipment to detect malfunctioning of equipment and calls for medical assistance when needed.

Knowledge: Customer and Personal Service; Psychology; Therapy and Counseling

Abilities: Time Sharing; Sound Localization

Chiropractors

- ▲ Growth: 27%
- ▲ Annual Job Openings: 2,595
- ▲ Yearly Earnings $63,211
- ▲ Education Required: First professional degree
- ▲ Self-employed: 56%
- ▲ Part-time: 10%

Chiropractors

Adjust spinal column and other articulations of the body to prevent disease and correct abnormalities of the human body believed to be caused by interference with the nervous system. Examine patient to determine nature and extent of disorder. Manipulate spine or other involved area. May utilize supplementary measures such as exercise, rest, water, light, heat, and nutritional therapy. Examines patient to determine nature and extent of disorder. Manipulates spinal column and other extremities to adjust, align, or correct abnormalities caused by neurologic and kinetic articular dysfunction. Utilizes supplementary measures, such as exercise, rest, water, light, heat, and nutritional therapy. Performs diagnostic procedures, including physical, neurologic, and orthopedic examinations, and laboratory tests, using instruments and equipment such as X ray machine and electrocardiograph.

Knowledge: Customer and Personal Service; Physics; Chemistry; Biology; Psychology; Sociology and Anthropology; Medicine and Dentistry; Therapy and Counseling; English Language; Philosophy and Theology

Abilities: Problem Sensitivity; Deductive Reasoning; Inductive Reasoning; Perceptual Speed; Manual Dexterity; Finger Dexterity; Multilimb Coordination; Wrist-Finger Speed; Speed of Limb Movement; Dynamic Strength

Civil Engineers

- ▲ Growth: 18%
- ▲ Annual Job Openings: 15,979
- ▲ Yearly Earnings $49,920
- ▲ Education Required: Bachelor's degree
- ▲ Self-employed: 6%
- ▲ Part-time: 5%

Civil Engineers, Including Traffic

Perform engineering duties in planning, designing, and overseeing construction and maintenance of structures and facilities such as roads, railroads, airports, bridges, harbors, channels, dams, irrigation projects, pipelines, power plants, water and sewage systems, and waste disposal units. Include traffic engineers who specialize in studying vehicular and pedestrian traffic conditions. Analyzes survey reports, maps, drawings, blueprints, aerial photography, and other topographical or geologic data to plan projects. Plans and designs transportation or hydraulic systems and structures, following construction and government standards, using design software and drawing tools. Estimates quantities and cost of materials, equipment, or labor to determine project feasibility. Directs construction, operations, and maintenance activities at project site. Computes load and grade requirements, water flow rates, and material stress factors to determine design specifications. Directs or participates in surveying to lay out installations and establish reference points, grades, and elevations to guide construction. Inspects project sites to monitor progress and ensure conformance to design specifications and safety or sanitation standards. Conducts studies of traffic patterns or environmental conditions to identify engineering problems and assess the potential impact of projects. Tests soils and materials to determine the adequacy and strength of foundations, concrete, asphalt, or steel. Provides technical advice regarding design, construction, or program modifications and structural repairs to industrial and managerial personnel. Prepares or presents public reports, such as bid proposals, deeds, environmental impact statements, and property and right-of-way descriptions.

Knowledge: Administration and Management; Economics and Accounting; Computers and Electronics; Engineering and Technology; Design; Building and Construction; Mathematics; Physics; Geography; English Language; Public Safety and Security; Law, Government, and Jurisprudence; Transportation

Abilities: Oral Comprehension; Written Comprehension; Oral Expression; Written Expression; Fluency of Ideas; Originality; Problem Sensitivity; Deductive Reasoning; Inductive Reasoning; Information Ordering; Mathematical Reasoning; Number Facility; Speed of Closure; Flexibility of Closure; Visualization; Time Sharing

Clergy

▲ Growth: 13%
▲ Annual Job Openings: 14,514
▲ Yearly Earnings $28,870
▲ Education Required: First professional degree
▲ Self-employed: 0%
▲ Part-time: 10%

Clergy

Conduct religious worship and perform other spiritual functions associated with beliefs and practices of religious faith or denomination, as delegated by ordinance, license, or other authorization. Provide spiritual and moral guidance and assistance to members. Leads congregation in worship services. Conducts wedding and funeral services. Administers religious rites or ordinances. Counsels those in spiritual need. Interprets doctrine of religion. Instructs people who seek conversion to faith. Prepares and delivers sermons and other talks. Visits sick and shut-ins, and helps poor. Engages in interfaith, community, civic, educational, and recreational activities sponsored by or related to interest of denomination. Writes articles for publication. Teaches in seminaries and universities.

Knowledge: Psychology; Sociology and Anthropology; Therapy and Counseling; Education and Training; English Language; History and Archeology; Philosophy and Theology; Communications and Media

Abilities: Oral Expression; Written Expression; Fluency of Ideas; Speech Clarity

Clerical Supervisors and Managers

▲ Growth: 19%
▲ Annual Job Openings: 143,806
▲ Yearly Earnings $31,012
▲ Education Required: Work experience in a related occupation
▲ Self-employed: 0%
▲ Part-time: 3%

Postmasters and Mail Superintendents

Direct and coordinate operational, administrative, management, and supportive services of a U.S. post office; or coordinate activities of workers engaged in postal and related work in assigned post office. Organizes and supervises directly, or through subordinates, such activities as processing incoming and outgoing mail to ensure efficient service to patrons. Directs and coordinates operational, management, and supportive services of associate post offices within district area known as sectional center. Directs and co-ordinates operations of several sectional centers within district. Prepares and submits detailed and summary reports of post office activities to designated supervisors. Confers with suppliers to obtain bids for proposed purchases, requisitions supplies, and disburses funds as specified by law. Selects, trains, and evaluates performance of employees and prepares work schedules. Negotiates labor disputes. Selects, trains, and terminates postmasters and managers of associate postal units. Resolves customer complaints and informs public of postal laws and regulations.

Knowledge: Administration and Management; Clerical; Economics and Accounting; Customer and Personal Service; Personnel and Human Resources; Psychology; Geography; Education and Training; Law, Government, and Jurisprudence; Transportation

Abilities: None above average

First-Line Supervisors, Customer Service

Supervise and coordinate activities of workers involved in providing customer service. Supervises and coordinates activities of workers engaged in clerical, administrative support, or service activities. Schedules workers according to workload to meet necessary deadlines. Observes and evaluates workers' performance. Issues instructions and assigns duties to workers. Trains and instructs employees. Hires and discharges workers. Communicates with other departments and management to resolve problems and expedite work. Interprets and communicates work procedures and company policies to staff. Helps workers in resolving problems and completing work. Resolves complaints and answers questions of customers regarding services and procedures. Reviews and checks work of subordinates, such as reports, records, and applications, for accuracy and content, and corrects errors. Prepares, maintains, and submits reports and records, such as budgets and operational and personnel reports. Makes recommendations to management concerning staff and improvement of procedures. Plans and develops improved procedures. Requisitions or purchases supplies.

Knowledge: Administration and Management; Clerical; Economics and Accounting; Customer and Personal Service; Personnel and Human Resources; Psychology; Sociology and Anthropology; Therapy and Counseling; Education and Training; Law, Government, and Jurisprudence; Communications and Media

Abilities: Written Expression; Fluency of Ideas; Originality; Mathematical Reasoning; Number Facility; Memorization; Perceptual Speed; Near Vision; Speech Recognition; Speech Clarity

First-Line Supervisors, Administrative Support

Supervise and coordinate activities of workers involved in providing administrative support. Supervises and coordinates activities of workers engaged in clerical, administrative support, or service activities. Directs workers in such activities as maintaining files, compiling and preparing reports, computing figures, or moving shipments. Plans, prepares, and revises work schedules and duty assignments according to budget allotments, customer needs, problems, workloads, and statistical forecasts. Evaluates subordinate job performance and conformance to regulations, and recommends appropriate personnel action. Oversees, coordinates, or performs activities associated with shipping, receiving, distribution, and transportation. Verifies completeness and accuracy of subordinates' work, computations, and records. Interviews, selects, and discharges employees. Consults with supervisor and other personnel to resolve problems, such as equipment performance, output quality, and work schedules. Reviews records and reports pertaining to such activities as production, operation, payroll, customer accounts, and shipping. Trains employees in work and safety procedures and company policies. Participates in work of subordinates to facilitate productivity or overcome difficult aspects of work. Examines procedures and recommends changes to save time, labor, and other costs and to improve quality control and operating efficiency. Maintains records of such matters as inventory, personnel, orders, supplies, and machine maintenance. Identifies and resolves discrepancies or errors. Compiles reports and information required by management or governmental agencies. Plans layout of stockroom, warehouse, or other storage areas, considering turnover, size, weight, and related factors pertaining to items stored. Inspects equipment for defects and notifies maintenance personnel or outside service contractors for repairs. Analyzes financial activities of establishment or department and assists in planning budget. Computes figures, such as balances, totals, and commissions. Requisitions supplies.

Knowledge: Administration and Management; Clerical; Economics and Accounting; Customer and Personal Service; Personnel and Human Resources; Mathematics; Psychology; Education and Training; Philosophy and Theology; Public Safety and Security; Law, Government, and Jurisprudence; Transportation

Abilities: Oral Comprehension; Written Comprehension; Oral Expression; Written Expression; Inductive Reasoning; Category Flexibility; Mathematical Reasoning; Number Facility; Memorization; Perceptual Speed; Time Sharing; Wrist-Finger Speed; Gross Body Equilibrium; Near Vision; Speech Recognition; Speech Clarity

Clerical Support Workers

- ▲ Growth: 19%
- ▲ Annual Job Openings: 105,566
- ▲ Yearly Earnings $21,756
- ▲ Education Required: Short-term O-J-T
- ▲ Self-employed: 2%
- ▲ Part-time: 15%

Transit Clerks

Sort, record, prove, and prepare transit items for mailing to or from out-of-city banks to ensure correct routing and prompt collection. Operates machines to encode, add, cancel, photocopy, and sort checks, drafts, and money orders for collection and prove records of transactions. Places checks into machine that encodes amounts in magnetic ink, adds amounts, and cancels checks. Enters amount of each check, using keyboard. Places encoded checks in sorter and activates machine to automatically microfilm, sort, and total checks according to bank drawn on. Reads check and enters data, such as amount, bank, or account number, using keyboard. Records, sorts, and proves other transaction documents, such as deposit and withdrawal slips, using proof machine. Encodes correct amount, or prepares transaction correction record if error is found. Observes panel light to note check machine cannot read. Compares machine totals to listing received with batch of checks, and rechecks each item if totals differ. Enters commands to transfer data from machine to computer. Manually sorts and lists items for proof or collection. Bundles sorted check with tape listing each item to prepare checks, drawn on other banks, for collection. Cleans equipment and replaces printer ribbons, film, and tape. Operates separate photocopying machine.

Knowledge: Clerical; Computers and Electronics

Abilities: None above average

Clinical Laboratory Technologists

▲ Growth: 15%
▲ Annual Job Openings: 23,944
▲ Yearly Earnings $30,804
▲ Education Required: Bachelor's degree
▲ Self-employed: 1%
▲ Part-time: 19%

Medical and Clinical Laboratory Technologists

Perform a wide range of complex procedures in the general area of the clinical laboratory, or perform specialized procedures in such areas as cytology, histology, and microbiology. Duties may include supervising and coordinating activities of workers engaged in laboratory testing. Include workers who teach medical technology when teaching is not their primary activity. Cuts, stains, and mounts biological material on slides for microscopic study and diagnosis, following standard laboratory procedures. Examines slides under microscope to detect deviations from norm and to report abnormalities for further study. Analyzes samples of biological material for chemical content or reaction. Selects and prepares specimen and media for cell culture, using aseptic technique and knowledge of medium components and cell requirements. Harvests cell culture at optimum time sequence based on knowledge of cell cycle differences and culture conditions. Prepares slide of cell culture to identify chromosomes, views and photographs slide under photomicroscope, and prints picture. Cultivates, isolates, and assists in identifying microbial organisms, and performs various tests on these micro-organisms. Examines and tests human, animal, or other materials for microbial organisms. Conducts chemical analysis of body fluids, including blood, urine, and spinal fluid, to determine presence of normal and abnormal components. Performs tests to determine blood group, type, and compatibility for transfusion purposes. Studies blood cells, number of blood cells, and morphology, using microscopic technique. Cuts images of chromosomes from photograph and identifies and arranges them in numbered pairs on karyotype chart, using standard practices. Conducts research under direction of microbiologist or biochemist. Communicates with physicians, family members, and researchers requesting technical information regarding test results. Calibrates and maintains equipment used in quantitative and qualitative analysis, such as spectrophotometers, calorimeters, flame photometers, and computer-controlled analyzers. Enters analysis of medical tests and clinical results into computer for storage. Sets up, cleans, and maintains laboratory equipment.

Knowledge: Clerical; Personnel and Human Resources; Chemistry; Biology; Psychology; Medicine and Dentistry; Therapy and Counseling; Education and Training; English Language; Philosophy and Theology; Communications and Media

Abilities: Oral Comprehension; Written Comprehension; Oral Expression; Written Expression; Fluency of Ideas; Originality; Problem Sensitivity; Deductive Reasoning; Inductive Reasoning; Information Ordering; Category Flexibility; Mathematical Reasoning; Number Facility; Memorization; Speed of Closure; Flexibility of Closure; Perceptual Speed; Visualization; Selective Attention; Time Sharing; Arm-Hand Steadiness; Near Vision; Far Vision; Visual Color Discrimination; Speech Recognition; Speech Clarity

Medical and Clinical Laboratory Technicians

Perform routine tests in medical laboratory for use in treatment and diagnosis of disease. Prepare vaccines, biologicals, and serums for prevention of disease. Prepare tissue samples for pathologists, take blood samples, and execute such laboratory tests as urinalysis and blood counts. May work under the general supervision of a medical laboratory technologist. Conducts quantitative and qualitative chemical analyses of body fluids, such as blood, urine, and spinal fluid. Performs blood counts, using microscope. Incubates bacteria for specified period and prepares vaccines and serums by standard laboratory methods. Conducts blood tests for transfusion purposes. Inoculates fertilized eggs, broths, or other bacteriological media with organisms. Tests vaccines for sterility and virus inactivity. Prepares standard volumetric solutions and reagents used in testing. Draws blood from patient, observing principles of asepsis to obtain blood sample.

Knowledge: Mathematics; Chemistry; Biology; Medicine and Dentistry; Philosophy and Theology

Abilities: Oral Comprehension; Inductive Reasoning; Information Ordering; Category Flexibility; Number Facility; Memorization; Speed of Closure; Flexibility of Closure; Perceptual Speed; Selective Attention; Arm-Hand Steadiness; Finger Dexterity; Wrist-Finger Speed; Near Vision; Visual Color Discrimination

College and University Faculty

▲ Growth: 19%
▲ Annual Job Openings: 126,584
▲ Yearly Earnings $44,800
▲ Education Required: Doctor's degree
▲ Self-employed: 0%
▲ Part-time: 32%

Nursing Instructors—Postsecondary

Demonstrate and teach patient care in classroom and clinical units to nursing students. Instruct students in principles and application of physical, biological, and psychological subjects related to nursing. Conduct and supervise laboratory experiments. Issue assignments, direct seminars, etc. Participate in planning curriculum with medical and nursing personnel and in evaluating and improving teaching and nursing practices. May specialize in specific subjects, such as anatomy or chemistry, or in a type of nursing activity, such as nursing of surgical patients. Instructs and lectures nursing students in principles and application of physical, biological, and psychological subjects related to nursing. Conducts and supervises laboratory work. Issues assignments to students. Participates in planning curriculum, teaching schedule, and course outline with medical and nursing personnel. Directs seminars and panels. Supervises student nurses and demonstrates patient care in clinical units of hospital. Cooperates with medical and nursing personnel in evaluating and improving teaching and nursing practices. Prepares and administers examinations to nursing students. Evaluates student progress and maintains records of student classroom and clinical experience. Conducts classes for patients in health practices and procedures.

Knowledge: Administration and Management; Customer and Personal Service; Personnel and Human Resources; Chemistry; Biology; Psychology; Sociology and Anthropology; Medicine and Dentistry; Therapy and Counseling; Education and Training; English Language; Philosophy and Theology; Public Safety and Security; Law, Government, and Jurisprudence

Abilities: Oral Comprehension; Written Comprehension; Oral Expression; Written Expression; Fluency of Ideas; Originality; Problem Sensitivity; Deductive Reasoning; Inductive Reasoning; Information Ordering; Category Flexibility; Mathematical Reasoning; Number Facility; Memorization; Speed of Closure; Visualization; Time Sharing; Arm-Hand Steadiness; Response Orientation; Reaction Time; Static Strength; Gross Body Equilibrium; Near Vision; Far Vision; Visual Color Discrimination; Night Vision; Sound Localization; Speech Recognition; Speech Clarity

Life Sciences Teachers—Postsecondary

Teach courses pertaining to living organisms, such as biological sciences, agricultural sciences, and medical sciences. Include teachers of subjects such as botany, zoology,

agronomy, biochemistry, biophysics, soil conservation, forestry, psychiatry, surgery, and obstetrics. Prepares and delivers lectures to students. Stimulates class discussions. Compiles bibliographies of specialized materials for outside reading assignments. Compiles, administers, and grades examinations, or assigns this work to others. Advises students on academic and vocational curricula. Directs research of other teachers or graduate students working for advanced academic degrees. Conducts research in particular field of knowledge and publishes findings in professional journals. Acts as adviser to student organizations. Serves on faculty committee providing professional consulting services to government and industry.

Knowledge: Administration and Management; Clerical; Food Production; Computers and Electronics; Mathematics; Physics; Chemistry; Biology; Psychology; Medicine and Dentistry; Therapy and Counseling; Education and Training; English Language; Communications and Media

Abilities: Oral Comprehension; Written Comprehension; Oral Expression; Written Expression; Fluency of Ideas; Mathematical Reasoning; Number Facility; Speech Recognition; Speech Clarity

Chemistry Teachers—Postsecondary

Teach courses pertaining to the chemical and physical properties and compositional changes of substances. Work may include instruction in the methods of qualitative and quantitative chemical analysis. Prepares and delivers lectures to students. Stimulates class discussions. Compiles, administers, and grades examinations, or assigns this work to others. Compiles bibliographies of specialized materials for outside reading assignments. Directs research of other teachers or graduate students working for advanced academic degrees. Advises students on academic and vocational curricula. Conducts research in particular field of knowledge and publishes findings in professional journals. Acts as adviser to student organizations. Serves on faculty committee providing professional consulting services to government and industry.

Knowledge: Administration and Management; Computers and Electronics; Engineering and Technology; Mathematics; Physics; Chemistry; Biology; Psychology; Sociology and Anthropology; Education and Training; English Language; Foreign Language

Abilities: Oral Comprehension; Written Comprehension; Oral Expression; Written Expression; Fluency of Ideas; Originality; Deductive Reasoning; Inductive Reasoning; Information Ordering; Category Flexibility; Mathematical Reasoning; Number Facility; Memorization; Speed of Closure; Perceptual Speed; Selective Attention; Finger Dexterity; Far Vision; Night Vision; Speech Clarity

Physics Teachers—Postsecondary

Teach courses pertaining to the laws of matter and energy. Prepares and delivers lectures to students. Stimulates class discussions. Compiles, administers, and grades examinations, or assigns this work to others. Compiles bibliographies of specialized materials for outside reading assignments. Advises students on academic and vocational curricula. Directs research of other teachers or graduate students working for advanced academic degrees. Conducts research in particular field of knowledge and publishes findings in professional journals. Serves on faculty committee providing professional consulting services to government and industry. Acts as adviser to student organizations.

Knowledge: Administration and Management; Engineering and Technology; Mathematics; Physics; Chemistry; Psychology; Sociology and Anthropology; Therapy and Counseling; Education and Training; English Language; Foreign Language; History and Archeology; Philosophy and Theology

Abilities: Oral Comprehension; Written Comprehension; Oral Expression; Written Expression; Fluency of Ideas; Originality; Problem Sensitivity; Deductive Reasoning; Inductive Reasoning; Information Ordering; Category Flexibility; Mathematical Reasoning; Number Facility; Memorization; Speed of Closure; Flexibility of Closure; Selective Attention; Time Sharing; Far Vision; Night Vision; Sound Localization; Speech Clarity

Social Science Teachers—Postsecondary

Teach courses pertaining to human society and its characteristic elements, with economic and social relations and with scientific data relating to human behavior and mental processes. Include teachers of subjects such as psychology, economics, history, political science, and sociology. Prepares and delivers lectures to students. Stimulates class discussions. Compiles, administers, and grades examinations, or assigns this work to others. Compiles bibliographies of specialized materials for outside reading assignments. Advises students on academic and vocational curricula. Directs research of other teachers or graduate students working for advanced academic degrees. Conducts research in particular field of knowledge and publishes findings in professional journals. Serves on faculty committee providing professional consulting services to government and industry. Acts as adviser to student organizations.

Knowledge: Administration and Management; Clerical; Economics and Accounting; Personnel and Human Resources; Computers and Electronics; Mathematics; Psychology; Sociology and Anthropology; Geography; Therapy and Counseling; Education and Training; English Language; History and Archeology; Philosophy and Theology; Law, Government, and Jurisprudence; Communications and Media

Abilities: Oral Comprehension; Written Comprehension; Oral Expression; Written Expression; Fluency of Ideas; Deductive Reasoning; Mathematical Reasoning; Speech Clarity

Health Specialties Teachers—Postsecondary

Teach courses in health specialties such as veterinary medicine, dentistry, pharmacy, therapy, laboratory technology, and public health. Exclude nursing instructors and medical sciences teachers. Prepares and delivers lectures to students. Compiles bibliographies of specialized materials for outside reading assignments. Stimulates class discussions.

Compiles, administers, and grades examinations, or assigns this work to others. Advises students on academic and vocational curricula. Directs research of other teachers or graduate students working for advanced academic degrees. Conducts research in particular field of knowledge and publishes findings in professional journals. Acts as adviser to student organizations. Serves on faculty committee providing professional consulting services to government and industry.

Knowledge: Administration and Management; Clerical; Computers and Electronics; Mathematics; Chemistry; Biology; Psychology; Sociology and Anthropology; Medicine and Dentistry; Therapy and Counseling; Education and Training; English Language; Philosophy and Theology; Law, Government, and Jurisprudence; Communications and Media

Abilities: Oral Comprehension; Written Comprehension; Oral Expression; Written Expression; Mathematical Reasoning; Speech Clarity

English and Foreign Language Teachers— Postsecondary

Teach courses in English language and literature or in foreign languages and literature. Include teachers of subjects such as journalism, classics, and linguistics. Prepares and delivers lectures to students. Compiles, administers, and grades examinations, or assigns this work to others. Compiles bibliographies of specialized materials for outside reading assignments. Stimulates class discussions. Advises students on academic and vocational curricula. Directs research of other teachers or graduate students working for advanced academic degrees. Conducts research in particular field of knowledge and publishes findings in professional journals. Acts as adviser to student organizations. Serves on faculty committee providing professional consulting services to government and industry.

Knowledge: Clerical; Computers and Electronics; Sociology and Anthropology; Therapy and Counseling; Education and Training; English Language; Foreign Language; History and Archeology; Philosophy and Theology; Communications and Media

Abilities: Oral Comprehension; Written Comprehension; Oral Expression; Written Expression; Fluency of Ideas; Speech Recognition; Speech Clarity

Art, Drama, and Music Teachers— Postsecondary

Teach courses in art, drama, and music, including painting and sculpture. Prepares and delivers lectures to students. Stimulates class discussions. Compiles bibliographies of specialized materials for outside reading assignments. Compiles, administers, and grades examinations, or assigns this work to others. Advises students on academic and vocational curricula. Directs research of other teachers or graduate students working for advanced academic degrees. Conducts research in particular field of knowledge and publishes findings in professional journals. Serves on faculty committee providing professional consulting services to government and industry. Acts as adviser to student organizations.

Knowledge: Administration and Management; Clerical; Sociology and Anthropology; Therapy and Counseling; Education and Training; English Language; Fine Arts; History and Archeology; Philosophy and Theology; Communications and Media

Abilities: Oral Comprehension; Written Comprehension; Oral Expression; Written Expression; Fluency of Ideas; Originality; Flexibility of Closure; Far Vision; Visual Color Discrimination; Hearing Sensitivity; Speech Clarity

Engineering Teachers—Postsecondary

Teach courses pertaining to the application of physical laws and principles of engineering for the development of machines, materials, instruments, processes, and services. Include teachers of subjects such as chemical, civil, electrical, industrial, mechanical, mineral, and petroleum engineering. Prepares and delivers lectures to students. Stimulates class discussions. Compiles bibliographies of specialized materials for outside reading assignments. Compiles, administers, and grades examinations, or assigns this work to others. Advises students on academic and vocational curricula. Directs research of other teachers or graduate students working for advanced academic degrees. Conducts research in particular field of knowledge and publishes findings in professional journals. Serves on faculty committee providing professional consulting services to government and industry. Acts as adviser to student organizations.

Knowledge: Administration and Management; Clerical; Computers and Electronics; Engineering and Technology; Design; Building and Construction; Mathematics; Physics; Chemistry; Therapy and Counseling; Education and Training; English Language; Telecommunications; Communications and Media

Abilities: Oral Comprehension; Written Comprehension; Oral Expression; Written Expression; Fluency of Ideas; Originality; Deductive Reasoning; Mathematical Reasoning; Number Facility; Time Sharing; Speech Clarity

Mathematical Sciences Teachers— Postsecondary

Teach courses pertaining to mathematical concepts, statistics, and actuarial science and to the application of original and standardized mathematical techniques in solving specific problems and situations. Prepares and delivers lectures to students. Compiles, administers, and grades examinations, or assigns this work to others. Stimulates class discussions. Directs research of other teachers or graduate students working for advanced academic degrees. Compiles bibliographies of specialized materials for outside reading assignments. Conducts research in particular field of knowledge and publishes findings in professional journals. Advises students on academic and vocational curricula. Acts as adviser to student organizations. Serves on faculty committee providing professional consulting services to government and industry.

Knowledge: Administration and Management; Clerical; Computers and Electronics; Mathematics; Education and Training; English Language; Philosophy and Theology; Communications and Media

Abilities: Oral Comprehension; Written Comprehension; Oral Expression; Written Expression; Fluency of Ideas; Originality; Mathematical Reasoning; Number Facility; Speech Clarity

Computer Science Teachers—Postsecondary

Teach courses in computer science. May specialize in a field of computer science, such as the design and function of computers or operations and research analysis. Prepares and delivers lectures to students. Stimulates class discussions. Compiles bibliographies of specialized materials for outside reading assignments. Compiles, administers, and grades examinations, or assigns this work to others. Directs research of other teachers or graduate students working for advanced academic degrees. Conducts research in particular field of knowledge and publishes findings in professional journals. Advises students on academic and vocational curricula. Acts as adviser to student organizations. Serves on faculty committee providing professional consulting services to government and industry.

Knowledge: Administration and Management; Clerical; Computers and Electronics; Engineering and Technology; Design; Mathematics; Physics; Psychology; Sociology and Anthropology; Therapy and Counseling; Education and Training; English Language; Philosophy and Theology; Telecommunications; Communications and Media

Abilities: Oral Comprehension; Written Comprehension; Oral Expression; Written Expression; Fluency of Ideas; Originality; Deductive Reasoning; Inductive Reasoning; Category Flexibility; Memorization; Speed of Closure; Flexibility of Closure; Far Vision; Night Vision; Speech Clarity

Combination Machine Tool Setters and Operators

- ▲ Growth: 18%
- ▲ Annual Job Openings: 16,451
- ▲ Yearly Earnings $22,568
- ▲ Education Required: Moderate-term O-J-T
- ▲ Self-employed: 0%
- ▲ Part-time: 2%

Combination Machine Tool Setters and Set-Up Operators, Metal and Plastic

Set up or set up and operate more than one type of cutting or forming machine tool, such as gear hobbers, lathes, press brakes, shearing, and boring machines. Exclude workers who set up or set up and operate only one type of metal or plastic working machine. Sets up and operates lathes, cutters, borers, millers, grinders, presses, drills, and auxiliary machines to make metallic and plastic workpieces. Moves controls or mounts gears, cams, or templates in machine to set feed rate and cutting speed, depth, and angle. Monitors machine operation and moves controls to align and adjust position of workpieces and action of cutting tools. Selects, installs, and adjusts alignment of drills, cutters, dies, guides, and holding devices, using template, measuring instruments, and hand tools. Starts machine and turns handwheels or valves to engage feeding, cooling, and lubricating mechanisms. Reads blueprint or job order to determine product specifications and tooling instructions and to plan operational sequences. Measures and marks reference points and cutting lines on workpiece, using traced templates, compasses, and rules. Computes data, such as gear dimensions and machine settings, applying knowledge of shop mathematics. Inspects first-run workpieces and verifies conformance to specifications to check accuracy of machine set-up. Lifts, positions, and secures workpieces in holding devices, using hoists and hand tools. Makes minor electrical and mechanical repairs and adjustments, and notifies supervisor when major service is required. Records operational data such as pressure readings, length of stroke, feeds, and speeds. Instructs operators or other workers in machine set-up and operation.

Knowledge: Production and Processing; Design; Mechanical; Foreign Language

Abilities: Perceptual Speed; Visualization; Selective Attention; Time Sharing; Control Precision; Reaction Time; Speed of Limb Movement; Static Strength; Extent Flexibility; Gross Body Equilibrium; Visual Color Discrimination; Auditory Attention

Combination Machine Tool Operators and Tenders, Metal and Plastic

Operate or tend more than one type of cutting or forming machine tool that has been previously set up. Includes such machine tools as band saws, press brakes, slitting machines, drills, lathes, and boring machines. Exclude workers who operate or tend only one type of cutting or forming machine. Activates and tends or operates machines to cut, shape, thread, bore, drill, tap, bend, or mill metal or non-metallic material. Observes machine operation to detect workpiece defects or machine malfunction. Positions, adjusts, and secures workpiece against stops, on arbor, or in chuck, fixture, or automatic feeding mechanism manually or using hoist. Reads job specifications to determine machine adjustments and material requirements. Aligns layout marks with die or blade. Extracts or lifts jammed pieces from machine, using fingers, wire hooks, or lift bar. Inspects workpiece for defects and measures workpiece, using rule, template, or other measuring instruments, to determine accuracy of machine operation. Adjusts machine components and changes worn accessories, such as cutting tools and brushes, using hand tools. Sets machine stops or guides to specified length as indicated by scale, rule, or template. Installs machine components, such as chucks, boring bars, or cutting tools, according to specifications, using hand tools. Removes burrs, sharp edges, rust, or scale from workpiece, using file, hand grinder, wire brush, or power tools. Performs minor machine maintenance, such as oiling or cleaning machines, dies, or workpieces, or adding coolant to machine reservoir.

Knowledge: Production and Processing

Abilities: Manual Dexterity; Control Precision; Multilimb Coordination; Rate Control; Speed of Limb Movement; Dynamic Flexibility; Gross Body Equilibrium

Commercial and Industrial Electronic Equipment Repairers

- ▲ Growth: 12%
- ▲ Annual Job Openings: 9,140
- ▲ Yearly Earnings $33,800
- ▲ Education Required: Postsecondary vocational training
- ▲ Self-employed: 10%
- ▲ Part-time: 6%

Transformer Repairers

Clean and repair electrical transformers. Cleans transformer case, using scrapers and solvent. Disassembles distribution, streetlight, or instrument transformers. Drains and filters transformer oil. Reassembles transformer. Fills reassembled transformer with oil until coils are submerged. Replaces worn or defective parts, using hand tools. Dismantles lamination assembly, preparatory to cleaning and inspection. Inspects transformer for defects, such as cracked weldments. Secures input and output wires in position. Signals crane operator to raise heavy transformer component subassemblies. Winds replacement coils, using coil-winding machine.

Knowledge: Mechanical; Telecommunications

Abilities: Manual Dexterity; Dynamic Strength; Dynamic Flexibility; Gross Body Equilibrium

Armature and Salvage Repairers

Recondition and rebuild salvaged electrical parts of equipment, and wind new coils on armatures of used generators and motors. Solders, wraps, and coats wires to ensure proper insulation. Replaces broken and defective parts. Cuts insulating material to fit slots on armature core, and places material in bottom of core slots. Winds new coils on armatures of generators and motors. Disassembles salvaged equipment used in electric-power systems, such as air circuit breakers and lightning arresters, using hand tools, and discards nonrepairable parts. Inserts and hammers ready-made coils into place. Cleans and polishes parts, using solvent and buffing wheel. Bolts porcelain insulators to wood parts to assemble hot stools. Solders ends of coils to commutator segments. Tests armatures and motors to ensure proper operation.

Knowledge: Mechanical

Abilities: None above average

Electronics Mechanics and Technicians

Install, maintain, and repair electronic equipment, such as industrial controls, telemetering and missile control systems, radar systems, transmitters, and antennae. Analyzes technical requirements of customer desiring to utilize electronic equipment, and performs installation and maintenance duties. Replaces or repairs defective components, using hand tools and technical documents. Adjusts defective components, using hand tools and technical documents. Installs equipment in industrial or military establishments and in aircraft and missiles. Calibrates testing instruments and installed or repaired equipment to prescribed specifications. Tests faulty equipment, using test equipment and applying knowledge of functional operation of electronic unit and systems, to diagnose malfunction. Inspects components of equipment for defects, such as loose connections and frayed wire, and for accuracy of assembly and installation. Determines feasibility of using standardized equipment, and develops specifications for equipment required to perform additional functions. Operates equipment to demonstrate use of equipment and to analyze malfunctions. Services electrical radioactivity-detecting instruments used to locate radioactive formations in oil- or gas-well boreholes, using special testing apparatus. Studies blueprints, schematics, manuals, and other specifications to determine installation procedures. Converses with equipment operators to ascertain whether mechanical or human error contributed to equipment breakdown. Maintains records of repairs, calibrations, and tests. Enters information into computer to copy program or to draw, modify, or store schematics, applying knowledge of software package used. Consults with customer, supervisor, and engineers to plan layout of equipment and to resolve problems in system operation and maintenance. Signs overhaul documents for equipment replaced or repaired. Advises management regarding customer satisfaction, product performance, and suggestions for product improvements. Accompanies flight crew to perform in-flight adjustments and to determine and record required post-flight repair work. Supervises workers in installing, testing, tuning, and adjusting equipment to obtain optimum operating performance. Instructs workers in electronic theory.

Knowledge: Administration and Management; Personnel and Human Resources; Computers and Electronics; Engineering and Technology; Design; Mathematics; Physics; Education and Training; Telecommunications

Abilities: Oral Comprehension; Oral Expression; Deductive Reasoning; Information Ordering; Mathematical Reasoning; Visualization; Finger Dexterity

Test Card and Circuit Board Repairers

Replace and realign broken, worn, or misaligned probes on probe test cards, and repair defective surfaces and circuitry on printed circuit boards. Repairs defective circuitry and board surface faults, using hand tools and soldering or welding equipment. Removes, replaces, and resolders defective wiring and probes, using tweezers and soldering iron. Cuts and removes defective wires on PCBs, using knife. Observes probe card through microscope and aligns probes in specified position over test wafer, using tweezers. Aligns probes on even plane, using tweezers and test equipment. Positions replacement wire on circuit, using magnetic tweezers, and positions PCB's under microscope to examine circuitry. Reads specification sheets, manuals, and diagrams to determine probe card wiring and probe positions. Inspects probe cards, using microscope, to detect defects, and examines boards to determine that repairs meet specifications. Reads work orders to determine number of PCBs to be repaired, type of repairs, and method and tools required. Washes solder or liquid gold over specified areas to restore board surfaces. Cleans repaired boards with solvent, using brush and rags. Places PCBs in industrial oven to cure solder mask. Removes and stacks repaired boards on racks for movement to next work station. Maintains repair, replacement, probe, and inventory records, using computer. Prepares production reports.

Knowledge: Computers and Electronics

Abilities: Arm-Hand Steadiness; Finger Dexterity; Control Precision; Near Vision

Powerhouse, Substation, and Relay Electricians

Inspect, test, repair, and maintain electrical equipment in generating stations or powerhouses; substation equipment, such as oil circuit breakers and transformers; and in-service relays, to prevent and remedy abnormal behavior of transmission and distribution lines and equipment. Repairs, replaces, and cleans equipment, such as brushes, commutators, windings, bearings, relays, switches, controls, and instruments. Repairs or rebuilds circuit breakers, transformers, and lightning arresters by replacing worn parts. Inspects and tests equipment and circuits to identify malfunction or defect, using wiring diagrams and testing devices such as ohmmeters, voltmeters, or ammeters. Tests oil in circuit breakers and transformers for dielectric strength, and periodically refills. Tests insulators and bushings of equipment by inducing voltage across insulation, using testing apparatus and calculating insulation loss. Disconnects voltage regulators, bolts, and screws, and connects replacement regulators to high-voltage lines. Analyzes test data to diagnose malfunctions and evaluate effect of system modifications. Prepares reports of work performed. Notifies personnel of need for equipment shutdown requiring changes from normal operation to maintain service. Paints, repairs, and maintains buildings, and sets forms and pours concrete footings for installation of heavy equipment.

Knowledge: Computers and Electronics; Engineering and Technology; Mechanical; Physics

Abilities: Perceptual Speed; Selective Attention; Reaction Time; Dynamic Strength; Extent Flexibility; Dynamic Flexibility; Gross Body Equilibrium; Visual Color Discrimination; Hearing Sensitivity; Auditory Attention; Sound Localization

Station Installers and Repairers, Telephone

Install and repair telephone station equipment, such as telephones, coin collectors, telephone booths, and switching-key equipment. Installs communication equipment, such as intercommunication systems and related apparatus, using schematic diagrams, testing devices, and hand tools. Assembles telephone equipment, mounts brackets, and connects wire leads, using hand tools and following installation diagrams or work order. Repairs cables, lays out plans for new equipment, and estimates material required. Analyzes equipment operation, using testing devices to locate and diagnose nature of malfunction and ascertain needed repairs. Disassembles components and replaces, cleans, adjusts, and repairs parts, wires, switches, relays, circuits, or signaling units, using hand tools. Operates and tests equipment to ensure elimination of malfunction. Climbs poles to install or repair outside service lines.

Knowledge: Computers and Electronics; Mechanical; Telecommunications

Abilities: Dynamic Strength; Stamina; Gross Body Coordination; Gross Body Equilibrium

Aircraft Electricians

Lay out, install, repair, test, and maintain electrical systems in aircraft. Assembles components, such as switches, electrical controls, and junction boxes, using hand tools and soldering iron. Connects components to assemblies, such as radio systems, instruments, magnetos, inverters, and in-flight refueling systems, using hand tools and soldering iron. Tests components or assemblies, using circuit tester, oscilloscope, and voltmeter. Adjusts, repairs, or replaces malfunctioning components or assemblies, using hand tools and soldering iron. Lays out installation of assemblies and systems in aircraft, according to blueprints and wiring diagrams, using scribe, scale, and protractor. Installs electrical and electronic components, assemblies, and systems in aircraft, using hand tools, power tools, and soldering iron. Sets up and operates ground support and test equipment to perform functional flight test of electrical and electronic systems. Interprets flight test data to diagnose malfunctions and systemic performance problems. Fabricates parts and test aids as required.

Knowledge: Computers and Electronics; Engineering and Technology; Design; Physics; Telecommunications

Abilities: Information Ordering; Spatial Orientation; Visualization; Arm-Hand Steadiness; Manual Dexterity; Finger Dexterity; Multilimb Coordination; Wrist-Finger Speed; Speed of Limb Movement; Explosive Strength; Extent Flexibility; Dynamic Flexibility; Gross Body Coordination; Gross Body Equilibrium; Visual Color Discrimination

Ground Transportation Electricians

Install and repair electrical wiring equipment and systems in automobiles, locomotives, buses, trucks, and travel trailers. Adjusts, repairs, or replaces defective wiring and relays in ignition, lighting, air-conditioning, and safety control systems, using electrician's tools. Repairs or rebuilds starters, generators, distributors, or door controls, using electrician's tools. Installs electrical equipment, such as air-conditioning, heating, or ignition systems, generator brushes, and commutators, using hand tools. Installs fixtures, outlets, terminal boards, switches, and wall boxes, using hand tools. Measures, cuts, and installs framework and conduit to support and connect wiring, control panels, and junction boxes, using hand tools. Splices wires with knife or cutting pliers, and solders connections to fixtures, outlets, and equipment. Visually inspects and tests electrical system or equipment, using testing devices such as oscilloscope, voltmeter, and ammeter, to determine malfunctions. Cuts openings and drills holes for fixtures, outlet boxes, and fuse holders, using electric drill and router. Confers with customer to determine nature of malfunction. Estimates cost of repairs based on parts and labor charges.

Knowledge: Computers and Electronics; Building and Construction; Mechanical

Abilities: Arm-Hand Steadiness; Manual Dexterity; Finger Dexterity; Control Precision; Multilimb Coordination; Wrist-Finger Speed; Speed of Limb Movement; Explosive Strength; Trunk Strength; Stamina; Extent Flexibility; Dynamic Flexibility; Gross Body Coordination; Gross Body Equilibrium; Visual Color Discrimination

Valve and Regulator Repairers

Test, repair, and adjust mechanical regulators and valves. Replaces, repairs, or adjusts defective valve or regulator parts, and tightens attachments, using hand tools, power tools, and welder. Tests valves and regulators for leaks, temperature, and pressure settings, using precision testing equipment. Disassembles mechanical control devices or valves, such as regulators, thermostats, or hydrants, using power tools, hand tools, and cutting torch. Examines valves or mechanical control device parts for defects, dents, or loose attachments. Lubricates wearing surfaces of mechanical parts, using oils or other lubricants. Measures salvageable parts removed from mechanical control devices for conformance to standards or specifications, using gauges, micrometers, and calipers. Cleans corrosives and other deposits from serviceable parts, using solvents, wire brushes, or sandblaster. Dips valves and regulators in molten lead to prevent leakage, and paints valves, fittings, and other devices, using spray gun. Correlates testing data, performs technical calculations, and writes test reports to record data. Records repair work, inventories parts, and orders new parts. Advises customers on proper installation of valves or regulators and related equipment.

Knowledge: Mechanical; Physics

Abilities: Arm-Hand Steadiness; Manual Dexterity; Finger Dexterity; Wrist-Finger Speed; Extent Flexibility; Dynamic Flexibility; Gross Body Equilibrium

Mechanical Door Repairers

Install, service, and repair opening and closing mechanisms of automatic doors and hydraulic door closers. Installs door frames, door closers, and electronic-eye mechanisms, using power tools, hand tools, and electronic test equipment. Removes or disassembles defective automatic mechanical door closers, using hand tools. Sets in and secures floor treadle for door-activating mechanism, and connects powerpack and electrical panelboard to treadle. Repairs, replaces, or fabricates worn or broken parts, using welder, lathe, drill press, and shaping and milling machines. Studies blueprints and schematic diagrams to determine method of installing and repairing automated door openers. Covers treadle with carpeting or other floor-covering materials, and tests system by stepping on treadle. Bores and cuts holes in flooring, using hand tools and power tools. Lubricates door-closer oil chamber and packs spindle with leather washer. Cleans door-closer parts, using caustic soda, rotary brush, and grinding wheel.

Knowledge: Engineering and Technology; Building and Construction; Mechanical

Abilities: Arm-Hand Steadiness; Speed of Limb Movement; Stamina; Extent Flexibility; Gross Body Equilibrium; Visual Color Discrimination

Pump Installers and Servicers

Erect, install, and repair electric, gasoline, diesel, or turbine pumps, according to diagrams or specifications, using hand and power tools. Cuts, threads, and tightens pump parts to assemble pump section, using hand tools and power tools. Installs pump section vertically in well casing, using rig loadline and winch, hand tools, power tools, and diagrams. Dismantles, cleans, repairs, and replaces defective pump parts. Aligns pump parts to minimize friction, using hand tools and gauges. Verifies alignment of pump shaft by visually inspecting or using dial indicator. Lubricates moving parts, and adjusts valves to prevent overloading. Pumps air into well to measure water levels and capacity of well, using pressure gauge and orifice meter. Recommends repair or adjustment of motor to improve operation of pumps. Extends hoisting mast of rig, and stabilizes, using guy wires and struts. Drives rig (truck-mounted hoisting equipment) adjacent to well.

Knowledge: Building and Construction; Mechanical; Transportation

Abilities: Spatial Orientation; Arm-Hand Steadiness; Manual Dexterity; Control Precision; Multilimb Coordination; Rate Control; Reaction Time; Speed of Limb Movement; Static Strength; Explosive Strength; Dynamic Strength; Trunk Strength; Stamina; Extent Flexibility; Dynamic Flexibility; Gross Body Coordination; Gross Body Equilibrium; Depth Perception; Glare Sensitivity

Communication, Transportation, and Utilities Managers

▲ Growth: 15%
▲ Annual Job Openings: 10,840
▲ Yearly Earnings $48,817
▲ Education Required: Work experience, plus degree
▲ Self-employed: 0%
▲ Part-time: 6%

Transportation Managers

Plan, direct, and coordinate the transportation operations within an organization, or the activities of organizations that provide transportation services. Directs and coordinates, through subordinates, activities of operations department to obtain use of equipment, facilities, and human resources. Confers and cooperates with management and other in formulating and implementing administrative, operational, and customer relations policies and procedures. Analyzes expenditures and other financial reports to develop plans, policies, and budgets for increasing profits and improving services. Enforces compliance of operations personnel with administrative policies, procedures, safety rules, and government regulations. Reviews transportation schedules, worker assignments, and routes to ensure compliance with standards for personnel selection, safety, and union contract terms. Conducts investigations in cooperation with government agencies to determine causes of transportation accidents and to improve safety procedures. Oversees activities relating to dispatching, routing, and tracking transportation vehicles, such as aircraft and railroad cars. Prepares management recommendations, such as need for increasing fares, tariffs, or expansion or changes to existing schedules. Recommends or authorizes capital expenditures for acquisition of new equipment or property to increase efficiency and services of operations department. Oversees process of investigation and response to customer or shipper complaints relating to operations department. Oversees workers assigning tariff classifications and preparing billing according to mode of transportation and destination of shipment. Acts as organization representative before commissions or regulatory bodies during hearings, such as to increase rates and change routes and schedules. Inspects or oversees repairs and maintenance to equipment, vehicles, and facilities to enforce standards for safety, efficiency, cleanliness, and appearance. Oversees procurement process, including research and testing of equipment, vendor contacts, and approval of requisitions. Negotiates and authorizes contracts with equipment and materials suppliers. Participates in union contract negotiations and settlement of grievances.

Knowledge: Administration and Management; Economics and Accounting; Sales and Marketing; Personnel and Human Resources; Mathematics; Geography; Public Safety and Security, Law, Government, and Jurisprudence; Transportation

Abilities: Oral Comprehension; Written Comprehension; Oral Expression; Fluency of Ideas; Originality; Problem Sensitivity; Deductive Reasoning; Mathematical Reasoning; Time Sharing; Speech Clarity

Communications Managers

Plan, direct, and coordinate the communication operations within an organization, or the activities of organizations that provide communication services, such as radio and TV broadcasting or telecommunications. Supervises personnel directly or through subordinates, and coordinates worker or departmental activities. Directs investigation of rates, services, activities, or station operations to ensure compliance with government regulations. Prepares or directs preparation of plans, proposals, reports, or other documents. Develops operating procedures and policies and interprets for personnel. Analyzes reports, data, studies, or governmental rulings to determine status, appropriate response, or effect on operations or profitability. Confers with officials, administrators, management, or others to discuss programs, services, production, or procedures. Directs, coordinates, and inspects equipment installations to ensure compliance with regulations, standards, and deadlines. Plans work activities and prepares schedules. Directs testing and inspection of equipment for operational performance. Makes recommendations or advises personnel regarding procedures, acquisitions, complaints, or business activities. Negotiates settlements, contractual agreements, or services with company representatives or owners. Reviews and authorizes or approves recommendations, contracts, plans, or requisitions for equipment and supplies. Prepares budget for department, station, or program, and monitors expenses. Determines workforce requirement, hires and discharges workers, and assigns work. Conducts studies to determine effectiveness and adequacy of equipment, work load, or estimated equipment and maintenance costs. Reviews accounts and records and verifies accuracy of cash balances.

Knowledge: Administration and Management; Economics and Accounting; Personnel and Human Resources; Computers and Electronics; Engineering and Technology; Mathematics; Psychology; English Language; Telecommunications; Communications and Media

Abilities: Oral Comprehension; Written Comprehension; Oral Expression; Written Expression; Fluency of Ideas; Originality; Problem Sensitivity; Deductive Reasoning; Inductive Reasoning; Information Ordering; Category Flexibility; Mathematical Reasoning; Number Facility; Memorization; Speed of Closure; Flexibility of Closure; Perceptual Speed; Speech Clarity

Utilities Managers

Plan, direct, and coordinate the activities or operations of organizations that provide utility services, such as electricity, natural gas, sanitation, and water. Schedules and coordinates activities such as processing and distribution of services, patrolling and inspection of facilities, and maintenance activities. Formulates, implements, and interprets policies and procedures. Develops plans to meet expanded needs, such as increasing capacity or facilities or modifying equipment. Plans methods and sequence of operations to obtain optimum utilization of facilities and land or to facilitate system modifications. Authorizes repair, movement, installation, or construction of equipment, supplies, or facilities. Hires, discharges, supervises, and coordinates activities of workers directly or through subordinates. Confers with management, personnel, customers, and other to solve technical or administrative problems, discuss matters, and coordinate activities. Analyzes data, trends, reports, consumption, or test results to determine adequacy of facilities, system performance, or development areas. Develops test procedures, directs and schedules testing activities, and analyzes results. Investigates and evaluates new developments in materials, tools, or equipment. Forecasts consumption of utilities to meet demands or to determine construction, equipment, or maintenance requirements. Inspects project, operations, or site to determine progress, need for repair, or compliance with specifications and regulations. Prepares budget estimates based on anticipated material, equipment, and personnel needs. Determines action to be taken in event of emergencies, such as machine, equipment, or power failure. Prepares reports, directives, records, work orders, specifications for work methods, and other documents.

Knowledge: Administration and Management; Economics and Accounting; Sales and Marketing; Personnel and Human Resources; Engineering and Technology; Design; Building and Construction; Mathematics; Physics; Psychology

Abilities: Problem Sensitivity; Deductive Reasoning; Inductive Reasoning; Mathematical Reasoning; Number Facility; Time Sharing

Storage and Distribution Managers

Plan, direct, and coordinate the storage and distribution operations within an organization, or the activities of organizations that are engaged in storing and distributing materials and products. Establishes standard and emergency operating procedures for receiving, handling, storing, shipping, or salvaging products or materials. Confers with department heads to coordinate warehouse activities, such as production, sales, records control, and purchasing. Plans, develops, and implements warehouse safety and security programs and activities. Reviews invoices, work orders, consumption reports, and demand forecasts to estimate peak delivery periods and issue work assignments. Supervises the activities of workers engaged in receiving, storing, testing, and shipping products or materials. Inspects physical condition of warehouse and equipment and prepares work orders for testing, maintenance, or repair. Negotiates contracts, settlements, and freight-handling agreements to resolve problems between foreign and domestic shippers. Develops and implements plans for facility modification or expansion, such as equipment purchase or changes in space allocation or structural design. Examines invoices and shipping manifests for conformity to tariff and customs regulations, and contacts customs officials to effect release of shipments. Interviews, selects, and trains warehouse and supervisory personnel. Schedules air or surface pickup, delivery, or distribution of products or materials. Prepares or directs preparation of correspondence, reports, and operations, maintenance, and safety manuals. Interacts with customers or shippers to solicit new business, answer questions about services offered or required, and investigate complaints. Examines products or materials to estimate quantities or weight and type of container required for storage or transport.

Knowledge: Administration and Management; Economics and Accounting; Sales and Marketing; Personnel and Human Resources; Production and Processing; Design; Mathematics; Psychology; Education and Training; Public Safety and Security; Law, Government, and Jurisprudence; Communications and Media; Transportation

Abilities: Written Comprehension; Problem Sensitivity; Deductive Reasoning; Inductive Reasoning; Mathematical Reasoning; Number Facility; Speed of Closure; Visualization; Selective Attention; Time Sharing

Computer Engineers

▲ Growth: 109%

▲ Annual Job Openings: 34,884

▲ Yearly Earnings $54,912

▲ Education Required: Bachelor's degree

▲ Self-employed: 7%

▲ Part-time: 5%

Computer Engineers

Analyze data processing requirements to plan EDP system to provide system capabilities required for projected work loads. Plan layout and installation of new system or modification of existing system. May set up and control analog or hybrid computer systems to solve scientific and engineering problems. Analyzes software requirements to determine feasibility of design within time and cost constraints. Analyzes information to determine, recommend, and plan layout for type of computers and peripheral equipment modifications to existing systems. Consults with engineering staff to evaluate interface between hardware and software and operational and performance requirements of overall system. Evaluates factors such as reporting formats required, cost constraints, and need for security restrictions to determine hardware configuration. Formulates and designs software system, using scientific analysis and mathematical models to predict and measure outcome and consequences of design. Confers with data processing and project managers to obtain information on limitations and capabilities for data processing projects. Develops and directs software system testing procedures, programming, and documentation. Coordinates installation of software system. Monitors functioning of equipment to ensure system operates in conformance with specifications. Consults with customer concerning maintenance of software system. Specifies power supply requirements and configuration. Enters data into computer terminal to store, retrieve, and manipulate data for analysis of system capabilities and requirements. Recommends purchase of equipment to control dust, temperature, and humidity in area of system installation. Trains users to use new or modified equipment.

Knowledge: Administration and Management; Clerical; Economics and Accounting; Customer and Personal Service; Computers and Electronics; Engineering and Technology; Design; Mathematics; Education and Training; English Language; Telecommunications; Communications and Media

Abilities: Oral Comprehension; Written Comprehension; Oral Expression; Written Expression; Fluency of Ideas; Originality; Problem Sensitivity; Deductive Reasoning; Inductive Reasoning; Information Ordering; Category Flexibility; Mathematical Reasoning; Number Facility; Memorization; Speed of Closure; Visualization; Selective Attention; Near Vision; Speech Recognition; Speech Clarity

Computer Programmers

▲ Growth: 23%
▲ Annual Job Openings: 58,990
▲ Yearly Earnings $48,360
▲ Education Required: Bachelor's degree
▲ Self-employed: 3%
▲ Part-time: 7%

Computer Support Specialists

Provide technical assistance and training to system users. Investigate and resolve computer software and hardware problems of users. Answer clients' inquiries in person and via telephone concerning the use of computer hardware and software, including printing, word processing, programming languages, electronic mail, and operating systems. Installs and performs minor repairs to hardware, software, and peripheral equipment, following design or installation specifications. Confers with staff, users, and management to determine requirements for new systems or modifications. Reads technical manuals, confers with users, and conducts computer diagnostics to determine nature of problems and provide technical assistance. Develops training materials and procedures, and conducts training programs. Enters commands and observes system functioning to verify correct operations and detect errors. Tests and monitors software, hardware, and peripheral equipment to evaluate use, effectiveness, and adequacy of product for user. Prepares evaluations of software and hardware, and submits recommendations to management for review. Refers major hardware or software problems or defective products to vendors or technicians for service. Maintains record of daily data communication transactions, problems and remedial action taken, and installation activities. Conducts office automation feasibility studies, including workflow analysis, space design, and cost comparison analysis. Reads trade magazines and technical manuals, and attends conferences and seminars to maintain knowledge of hardware and software. Supervises and coordinates workers engaged in problem-solving, monitoring, and installing data communication equipment and software. Inspects equipment and reads order sheets to prepare for delivery to users.

Knowledge: Administration and Management; Economics and Accounting; Sales and Marketing; Customer and Personal Service; Computers and Electronics; Mathematics; Education and Training; Telecommunications

Abilities: Written Comprehension; Oral Expression; Written Expression; Originality; Deductive Reasoning; Mathematical Reasoning; Number Facility; Speed of Closure; Visualization; Selective Attention; Time Sharing; Finger Dexterity; Near Vision; Visual Color Discrimination; Speech Recognition; Speech Clarity

C

Computer Programmers

Convert project specifications and statements of problems and procedures to detailed logical flowcharts for coding into computer language. Develop and write computer programs to store, locate, and retrieve specific documents, data, and information. Analyzes, reviews, and rewrites programs, using workflow chart and diagram, applying knowledge of computer capabilities, subject matter, and symbolic logic. Converts detailed logical flowchart to language processible by computer. Resolves symbolic formulations, prepares flowcharts and block diagrams, and encodes resultant equations for processing. Develops programs from workflow charts or diagrams, considering computer storage capacity, speed, and intended use of output data. Prepares or receives detailed workflow chart and diagram to illustrate sequence of steps to describe input, output, and logical operation. Compiles and writes documentation of program development and subsequent revisions. Revises or directs revision of existing programs to increase operating efficiency or adapt to new requirements. Consults with managerial and engineering and technical personnel to clarify program intent, identify problems, and suggest changes. Enters program and test data into computer, using keyboard. Writes instructions to guide operating personnel during production runs. Observes computer monitor screen to interpret program operating codes. Prepares records and reports. Collaborates with computer manufacturers and other users to develop new programming methods. Assists computer operators or system analysts to resolve problems in running computer program. Assigns, coordinates, and reviews work of programming personnel. Trains subordinates in programming and program coding. Directs and coordinates activities of computer programmers working as part of project team.

Knowledge: Administration and Management; Clerical; Personnel and Human Resources; Computers and Electronics; Design; Mathematics; Education and Training; English Language; Communications and Media

Abilities: Oral Comprehension; Written Comprehension; Oral Expression; Written Expression; Fluency of Ideas; Originality; Problem Sensitivity; Deductive Reasoning; Inductive Reasoning; Information Ordering; Category Flexibility; Mathematical Reasoning; Number Facility; Memorization; Speed of Closure; Flexibility of Closure; Perceptual Speed; Visualization; Selective Attention; Finger Dexterity; Wrist-Finger Speed; Near Vision

Computer Scientists

▲ Growth: 118%

▲ Annual Job Openings: 26,732

▲ Yearly Earnings $48,630

▲ Education Required: Bachelor's degree

▲ Self-employed: 2%

▲ Part-time: 5%

Database Administrators

Coordinate changes to computer databases; test and implement the database, applying knowledge of database management systems. May plan, coordinate, and implement security measures to safeguard computer databases. Writes logical and physical database descriptions, including location, space, access method, and security. Establishes and calculates optimum values for database parameters, using manuals and calculator. Develops data model describing data elements and how they are used, following procedures using pen, template, or computer software. Codes database descriptions and specifies identifiers of database to management system, or directs others in coding descriptions. Tests, corrects errors, and modifies changes to programs or to database. Reviews project request describing database user needs, estimating time and cost required to accomplish project. Selects and enters codes to monitor database performance and to create production database. Directs programmers and analysts to make changes to database management system. Reviews workflow charts developed by programmer analyst to understand tasks computer will perform, such as updating records. Reviews procedures in database management system manuals for making changes to database. Confers with coworkers to determine scope and limitations of project. Revises company definition of data as defined in data dictionary. Specifies user and user access levels for each segment of database. Trains users and answers questions.

Knowledge: Administration and Management; Computers and Electronics; Mathematics; Education and Training

Abilities: Written Comprehension; Written Expression; Fluency of Ideas; Originality; Problem Sensitivity; Deductive Reasoning; Inductive Reasoning; Information Ordering; Category Flexibility; Mathematical Reasoning; Number Facility; Memorization; Speed of Closure; Flexibility of Closure; Perceptual Speed; Time Sharing; Wrist-Finger Speed; Near Vision

Construction and Building Inspectors

▲ Growth: 15%
▲ Annual Job Openings: 5,878
▲ Yearly Earnings $35,380
▲ Education Required: Work experience in a related occupation
▲ Self-employed: 1%
▲ Part-time: 2%

Construction and Building Inspectors

Inspect structures using engineering skills to determine structural soundness and compliance with specifications, building codes, and other regulations. Inspections may be general in nature or limited to a specific area, such as electrical systems or plumbing. Inspects bridges, dams, highways, building, wiring, plumbing, electrical circuits, sewer, heating system, and foundation for conformance to specifications and codes. Reviews and interprets plans, blueprints, specifications, and construction methods to ensure compliance to legal requirements. Measures dimensions and verifies level, alignment, and elevation of structures and fixtures to ensure compliance to building plans and codes. Approves and signs plans that meet required specifications. Records and notifies owners, violators, and authorities of violations of construction specifications and building codes. Issues violation notices, stop-work orders, and permits for construction and occupancy. Confers with owners, violators, and authorities to explain regulations and recommend alterations in construction or specifications. Reviews complaints, obtains evidence, and testifies in court that construction does not conform to code. Maintains daily logs, inventory, and inspection and construction records, and prepares reports. Evaluates premises for cleanliness, including garbage disposal and lack of vermin infestation. Computes estimates of work completed and approves payment for contractors.

Knowledge: Economics and Accounting; Design; Building and Construction; Mathematics; Physics; Public Safety and Security; Law, Government, and Jurisprudence

Abilities: Written Comprehension; Written Expression; Problem Sensitivity; Inductive Reasoning; Flexibility of Closure; Spatial Orientation; Stamina; Gross Body Equilibrium; Near Vision; Far Vision; Visual Color Discrimination; Speech Clarity

Elevator Inspectors

Inspect elevators and other lifting and conveying devices to verify conformance to laws and ordinances regulating design, installation, and safe operation. Inspects electrical and mechanical features of elevators and other lifting devices to validate conformance to safety regulations and procedures. Conducts tests of elevator's speed, brakes, and safety devices. Recommends corrections for unsafe conditions of elevators and lifting devices. Investigates and determines cause of accidents involving lifting devices. Consults with engineers, installers, and owners regarding corrections of unsafe conditions. Records and formulates reports of inspections and investigations of unsafe conditions or accidents. Computes maximum loads for elevators and other lifting or conveying devices. Seals operating device of unsafe elevators and other lifting devices.

Knowledge: Design; Building and Construction; Public Safety and Security; Law, Government, and Jurisprudence

Abilities: Selective Attention; Stamina; Gross Body Equilibrium; Visual Color Discrimination; Sound Localization

Construction Installation Workers

▲ Growth: 13%

▲ Annual Job Openings: 19,001

▲ Yearly Earnings $25,625

▲ Education Required: Moderate-term O-J-T

▲ Self-employed: 13%

▲ Part-time: 8%

Fence Erectors

Erect and repair metal and wooden fences and fence gates around highways, industrial establishments, residences, or farms, using hand and power tools. Sets metal or wooden post in upright position in posthole. Attaches fence rail support to post, using hammer and pliers. Inserts metal tubing through rail supports. Completes top fence rail of metal fence by connecting tube sections, using metal sleeves. Attaches rails or tension wire along bottoms of posts to form fencing frame. Stretches wire, wire mesh, or chain-link fencing between posts. Attaches fencing to frame. Nails top and bottom rails to fence posts, or inserts them in slots on posts. Nails pointed slats to rails to construct picket fence. Erects alternate panel, basket weave, and louvered fences. Mixes and pours concrete around base of post, or tamps soil into posthole to embed post. Assembles gate and fastens gate in position, using hand tools. Saws required lengths of lumber to make rails for wooden fence. Digs postholes with spade, posthole digger, or power-driven auger. Aligns posts, using line or by sighting, and verifies vertical alignment of posts with plumb bob or spirit level. Lays out fence line, using tape measure, and marks positions for postholes. Cuts metal tubing, using pipe cutter. Welds metal parts together, using portable gas welding equipment. Blasts rock formations with dynamite to facilitate digging of postholes.

Knowledge: Building and Construction

Abilities: Speed of Limb Movement; Static Strength; Explosive Strength; Dynamic Strength; Trunk Strength; Stamina; Extent Flexibility; Dynamic Flexibility; Depth Perception; Glare Sensitivity

Construction Installation Workers

Install variety of equipment or home improvement products, such as awnings, antennae, and lawn-sprinkler systems, using hand and portable power tools. Cuts materials and components to size, using power saw or hand saw. Joins component parts together or attaches components to structure or building, using screws, bolts, nails, hand tools, and power tools. Examines installation site and studies sketches or blueprints to determine materials, dimensions, position, tools, and assembly methods required. Lays out components needed to assemble unit to organize fabrication and assembly procedure. Measures and marks buildings, piping, and components to determine assembly and installation requirements and procedures. Drills holes in components or structure to facilitate installation or assembly. Installs electrical and mechanical control mechanisms. Installs piping and other plumbing-related components, using wrenches, sealants, torches, solder, and pipe cutting, threading, and bending equipment. Mixes and places cement around bases of standards. Performs necessary carpentry work. Operates completed unit to ensure proper operation and identify malfunctions. Digs trenches or excavates building site, using shovel or ditching machine.

Knowledge: Design; Building and Construction; Mechanical

Abilities: Multilimb Coordination; Static Strength; Explosive Strength; Dynamic Strength; Trunk Strength; Stamina; Extent Flexibility; Gross Body Equilibrium

Window Treatment Installers

Install venetian blinds and draperies. Hangs and arranges drapes and venetian blinds to enhance appearance of room. Measures installation site to obtain specifications for fabrication of draperies or venetian blinds. Measures and marks location for hanging brackets, using rule and pencil. Drills bracket holes in cement, plaster, or wood brackets, using hand or electric drill. Screws and bolts brackets and hangers onto wall, using hand tools. Pulls lowering, raising, and tilting cords to detect and adjust functioning defects. Delivers finished draperies to customers' homes.

Knowledge: None above average

Abilities: None above average

Swimming Pool Installers and Servicers

Install and service swimming pools. Assembles and aligns wall panel sections, edging, and drain tiles, using nuts, bolts, electric air gun, and transit. Lays out and connects pipelines for water inlets, return valves, and filters, using hand tools. Mixes, pours, spreads, and smooths concrete evenly throughout foundation, walls, and deck surrounding pool. Installs liner into pool. Assembles heater parts; connects gas, oil, or electric lines; and starts heater to verify working order of unit. Maintains and repairs pool and equipment, advises customers, and sells chemicals to prevent pool water problems. Plots length and width of pool site, according to specifications, and marks corners of site, using stakes and sledgehammer. Starts pump to fill pool with water, installs return valves, and checks pool for leaks. Dumps and spreads gravel into hollow foundation to form drain field, using wheelbarrow, shovel, and rake. Operates backhoe to dig, shape, and grade walls for pool. Confers with customer to ensure that pool location and dimensions meet customer's demands.

Knowledge: Sales and Marketing; Customer and Personal Service; Engineering and Technology; Design; Building and Construction; Physics; Chemistry

Abilities: Static Strength; Explosive Strength; Dynamic Strength; Trunk Strength; Stamina; Extent Flexibility; Gross Body Coordination; Gross Body Equilibrium

Construction Workers, Except Trade

Perform a variety of tasks in support of construction trade workers, such as cleaning, demolition, and equipment tending. Tends pumps, compressors, and generators to provide power for tools, machinery, and equipment or to heat and move materials such as asphalt. Mops, brushes, or spreads paints, cleaning solutions, or other compounds over surfaces to clean or provide protection. Cleans construction site to eliminate possible hazards. Tends machine that pumps concrete, grout, cement, sand, plaster, or stucco through spray gun for application to ceilings and walls. Lubricates, cleans, and repairs machinery, equipment, and tools. Sprays materials such as water, sand, steam, vinyl, paint, or stucco through hose to clean, coat, or seal surfaces. Mixes ingredients to create compounds used to cover or clean surfaces. Razes buildings and salvages useful materials. Loads and unloads trucks and hauls and hoists materials. Mixes concrete, using portable mixer. Erects and disassembles scaffolding, shoring, braces, and other temporary structures. Grinds, scrapes, sands, or polishes surfaces, such as concrete, marble, terrazzo, or wood flooring, using abrasive tools or machines. Builds and positions forms for pouring concrete and dismantles forms after use, using saws, hammers, nails, or bolts. Signals equipment operators to facilitate alignment, movement, and adjustment of machinery, equipment, and materials. Digs ditches and levels earth to grade specifications, using pick and shovel. Positions, joins, aligns, and seals structural components, such as concrete wall sections and pipes. Applies caulking compounds by hand or with caulking gun to seal crevices. Smooths and finishes freshly poured cement or concrete, using float, trowel, screed, or powered cement finishing tool. Measures, marks, and records openings and distances to lay out area to be graded or to erect building structures.

Knowledge: Building and Construction; Mechanical

Abilities: Speed of Limb Movement; Static Strength; Dynamic Strength; Trunk Strength; Stamina; Gross Body Equilibrium

Concrete and Utility Cutters and Drillers

Operate machines to cut and drill concrete or asphalt to facilitate installation and maintenance of utilities. Positions and lowers saw or drill over marked cutting or drilling mark. Starts motor and begins cutting or drilling operation. Guides saw along line, using handle bars attached to saw. Observes pressure gauge to maintain specified pressure on drill bit with crank. Locates and marks cutting or drilling position, using rule and chalk. Attaches diamond-edged circular blade or diamond-tipped core drill to equipment, using hand tools. Assembles components of drilling equipment and connects water hose to supply coolant to cutting blade or drill, using hand tools. Lubricates equipment, changes worn cutting blades and core drills, and makes minor repairs, using grease gun and hand tools.

Knowledge: Building and Construction

Abilities: None above average

Conduit Mechanics

Build and repair concrete underground vaults and manholes, and install ducts to provide installation and maintenance facilities for underground power cables. Installs sheeting, shoring, and bracing for excavation. Builds wooden forms and erects steel reinforcing for concrete vaults and manholes. Installs brackets and braces, and cuts apertures required for installation of electric equipment and ducts. Demolishes or trims vaults and manholes, using pneumatic tools, working in proximity to high-voltage electric cables and equipment. Cuts, threads, bends, and installs metal conduit. Lays drain pipe and connects it to sewer system. Cuts and lays tile or fiber ducts, using portable saw and grinder and brick mason's hand tools. Forces air through ducts to test for obstructions, using air compressor. Directs workers engaged in pouring concrete into forms, and removes forms after concrete has set.

Knowledge: Engineering and Technology; Building and Construction; Mechanical; Physics

Abilities: Arm-Hand Steadiness; Multilimb Coordination; Static Strength; Explosive Strength; Dynamic Strength; Trunk Strength; Stamina; Gross Body Equilibrium

Hydraulic Jack Setters and Operators

Set up and operate hydraulic jacks to raise precast concrete floors or roof slabs. Attaches precast concrete slabs to jacks, using threaded metal rods and nuts. Mounts motor to jacks, attaches hoses and electrical wiring, and sets tension on chain drive to prepare for lifting operation. Connects pump and jacks to control panel, and positions panel so that jacks and grade marks may be observed simultaneously. Starts pump and moves levers and valves on control panel to regulate action of jacks. Adjusts control valves when slab has reached predetermined position. Observes performance of jacks during lifting operation to detect malfunction. Measures and marks grade lines on support columns. Signals worker to verify grade with rule. Directs welding crew to weld supporting collars or brackets to column.

Knowledge: Engineering and Technology; Building and Construction

Abilities: Gross Body Equilibrium

Pipeline Maintenance Workers

Perform a variety of duties required in the cleaning and maintenance of pipelines. Starts engine and moves levers to control cleaning, coating, and wrapping operation. Opens valve to start flow of hot coating compounds onto pipe surface. Removes rust and foreign substances from meters and valves, using sandblasting equipment. Pours corrosion-resistant material over pipe or applies material with brush or spray gun. Wraps pipe with strips of paper or fabric to prevent corrosion and leakage. Selects, assembles, and installs scraping, brushing, coating, and wrapping apparatus. Inspects paper holders, observes flow of hot compounds into reservoir, and makes adjustments to ensure proper operation. Dismantles and restores fences, gates, water lines, and other obstructions that inhibit pipeline work. Cuts or clears brush, trees, weeds, and trash from pipeline right-of-ways, using axes and hoes. Installs connections to pipes, using wrenches and pipe tongs. Signals tractor operator to lift and move assembled apparatus into position at end of pipe. Drives and operates equipment, such as backhoes, bulldozers, and side booms, to dig ditches and lay pipe. Cleans storage tanks, using squeegees and rakes. Digs drainage ditches, using shovel. Spreads chemical pellets along right-of-way for control of tree growth. Loads and unloads trucks, and moves and positions materials and equipment for other workers.

Knowledge: Building and Construction; Mechanical; Physics

Abilities: Control Precision; Multilimb Coordination; Rate Control; Static Strength; Explosive Strength; Dynamic Strength; Stamina; Gross Body Equilibrium

Sign Erectors

Erect, assemble, and maintain signs and steel posts. Places wood or metal post in hole, and secures post in vertical position with cement. Mounts sign post onto previously constructed base, using shims, carpenter's level, and wrench. Bolts, screws, or nails plywood or metal sign panels to sign post or frame, using hand tools. Attaches poles and guy wires for hanging signs to buildings, using bolts, hammers, wrenches, and other hand tools and power tools. Raises signs and poles into position using truck-mounted hoist or hydraulic boom. Secures sign to hanging pole with hooks. Operates airhammer to drive metal post into ground. Paints or replaces worn or damaged signs. Measures, marks, and drills holes for mounting sign, using tape measure, chalk, and drill. Digs hole with posthole digger or shovel. Makes electrical connections to power source and tests sign for correct operation.

Knowledge: Building and Construction

Abilities: Static Strength; Explosive Strength; Dynamic Strength; Stamina; Gross Body Equilibrium

Construction Managers

Growth: 18%

Annual Job Openings: 22,043

Yearly Earnings $46,300

Education Required: Bachelor's degree

Self-employed: 16%

Part-time: 6%

Landscaping Managers

Plan and direct landscaping functions and sequences of work to landscape grounds of private residences, public areas, or commercial and industrial properties, according to landscape design and clients' specifications. Confers with prospective client and studies landscape designs, drawings, and bills of materials to ascertain scope of landscaping work required. Formulates and submits estimate and contract for client or bid to industrial concern or governmental agency. Calculates labor, equipment, material, and overhead costs to determine minimum estimate or bid which will provide for margin of profit. Plans landscaping functions and sequences of work at various sites to obtain optimum utilization of workforce and equipment. Inspects work at sites for compliance with terms and specifications of contract. Inspects grounds or area to determine equipment requirements for grading, tilling, or replacing top soil, and labor requirements. Directs and coordinates activities of workers engaged in performing landscaping functions in contractual agreement. Purchases and ensures that materials are on-site as needed.

Knowledge: Administration and Management; Economics and Accounting; Sales and Marketing; Customer and Personal Service; Personnel and Human Resources; Design; Chemistry; Biology

Abilities: Fluency of Ideas; Originality; Information Ordering; Visualization

Construction Managers

Plan, direct, coordinate, and budget, usually through subordinate supervisory personnel, activities concerned with the construction and maintenance of structures, facilities, and systems. Participate in the conceptual development of a construction project and oversee its organization, scheduling, and implementation. Include specialized construction fields such as carpentry or plumbing. Include general superintendents, project managers, and constructors who manage, coordinate, and supervise the construction process. Plans, organizes, and directs activities concerned with construction and maintenance of structures, facilities, and systems. Confers with supervisory personnel to discuss such matters as work procedures, complaints, and construction problems. Inspects and reviews construction work, repair projects, and reports to ensure work conforms to specifications. Studies job specifications to plan and approve construction of project. Directs and supervises workers on construction site to ensure project meets specifications. Contracts workers to perform construction work in accordance with specifications. Requisitions supplies and materials to complete construction project. Interprets and explains plans and contract terms to administrative staff, workers, and clients. Formulates reports concerning such areas as work progress, costs, and scheduling. Dispatches workers to construction sites to work on specified projects. Investigates reports of damage at construction sites to ensure proper procedures are being carried out.

Knowledge: Administration and Management; Personnel and Human Resources; Design; Building and Construction; Public Safety and Security; Law, Government, and Jurisprudence

Abilities: Speech Recognition

Construction Trades Helpers

- ▲ Growth: 9%
- ▲ Annual Job Openings: 137,805
- ▲ Yearly Earnings $19,864
- ▲ Education Required: Short-term O-J-T
- ▲ Self-employed: 0%
- ▲ Part-time: 16%

Floor-Sanding Machine Operators

Scrape and sand wooden floors to smooth surfaces, using floor scraper and floor sanding machine. Guides machine over surface of floor until surface is smooth. Scrapes and sands floor edges and areas inaccessible to floor sander, using scraper and disk-type sander. Attaches sandpaper to roller of sanding machine. Applies filler compound to floor to seal wood.

Knowledge: None above average

Abilities: Manual Dexterity; Multilimb Coordination; Rate Control; Speed of Limb Movement; Static Strength; Explosive Strength; Dynamic Strength; Trunk Strength; Stamina; Dynamic Flexibility; Gross Body Coordination; Gross Body Equilibrium

Air Hammer Operators

Use air hammer to break asphalt, concrete, stone, or other pavement; loosen earth; dig clay; break rock; trim bottom or sides of trenches or other excavations; drill holes in concrete; reduce size of large stones; or tamp earth in backfills. Inserts drill in chuck, trips trigger to start hammer, and leans on hammer to force drill into solid mass. Connects steam or compressed-air and water lines to hammer. Changes drill or adds lengths as depth of hole increases. Replaces or sharpens bits. Lays steam, compressed-air, or water pipelines used to power jackhammer. Lubricates hammer.

Knowledge: Mechanical

Abilities: Multilimb Coordination; Static Strength; Explosive Strength; Dynamic Strength; Trunk Strength; Stamina; Gross Body Coordination; Gross Body Equilibrium

Helpers—Brick and Stone Masons, and Hard Tile Setters

Help brick masons, stone masons, or hard tile setters by performing duties of lesser skill. Duties include supplying or holding materials or tools, and cleaning work area and equipment. Exclude apprentice workers (which are reported with the appropriate construction or maintenance trade occupation). Exclude construction or maintenance laborers who do not primarily assist brick masons, stone masons, or hard tile setters. Assists in the preparation, installation, repair, or rebuilding of tile, brick, or stone surfaces. Removes damaged tile, brick, or mortar, and prepares installation surfaces, using pliers, chipping hammers, chisels, drills, and metal wire anchors. Applies grout between joints of bricks or tiles, using grouting trowel. Removes excess grout and residue from tile or brick joints with wet sponge or trowel. Applies caulk, sealants or other agents to installed surface. Cleans installation surfaces, equipment, tools, worksite, and storage areas, using water, chemical solutions, oxygen lance, or polishing machines. Corrects surface imperfections or fills chipped, cracked, or broken bricks or tiles, using fillers, adhesives, and grouting materials. Modifies material moving, mixing, grouting, grinding, polishing, or cleaning procedures, according to the type of installation or materials required. Transports materials, tools, and machines to installation site, manually or using conveyance equipment. Manually or machine-mixes mortar, plaster, and grout, according to standard formulae. Selects materials for installation, following numbered sequence or drawings. Cuts materials to specified size for installation, using power saw or tile cutter. Moves or positions marble slabs and ingot covers, using crane, hoist, or dolly. Arranges and stores materials, machines, tools and equipment. Erects scaffolding or other installation structures.

Knowledge: Building and Construction

Abilities: Speed of Limb Movement; Static Strength; Dynamic Strength; Stamina; Dynamic Flexibility; Gross Body Equilibrium

Helpers—Carpenters and Related Workers

Help carpenters or carpentry-related craft workers by performing duties of lesser skill. Duties include supplying or holding materials or tools, and cleaning work area and equipment. Exclude apprentice workers (which are reported with the appropriate construction or maintenance trade occupation). Exclude construction or maintenance laborers who do not primarily assist carpenters or carpentry-related craft workers. Holds plumb bobs, sighting rods, and other equipment to aid in establishing reference points and lines. Positions and holds timbers, lumber, and paneling in place for fastening or cutting. Selects needed tools, equipment, and materials from storage and transports items to worksite. Erects scaffolding, shoring, and braces. Hews timbers. Covers surfaces with laminated plastic covering material. Cuts and installs insulating or sound-absorbing material. Drills holes in timbers or lumber. Cuts timbers, lumber, or paneling to specified dimensions. Cuts tile or linoleum to fit. Glues and clamps edges or joints of assembled parts. Smooths and sands surfaces to remove ridges, tool marks, glue, or caulking. Spreads adhesives on flooring to install tile or linoleum. Fastens timbers or lumber with glue, screws, pegs, or nails.

Knowledge: Building and Construction; Mechanical

Abilities: Spatial Orientation; Arm-Hand Steadiness; Manual Dexterity; Multilimb Coordination; Response Orientation; Reaction Time; Wrist-Finger Speed; Speed of Limb Movement; Static Strength; Explosive Strength; Dynamic Strength; Trunk Strength; Stamina; Extent Flexibility; Dynamic Flexibility; Gross Body Equilibrium; Far Vision; Peripheral Vision

Helpers—Electricians and Powerline Transmission Installers

Help electricians or powerline transmission installers by performing duties of lesser skill. Duties include supplying or holding materials or tools, and cleaning work area and equipment. Exclude apprentice workers (which are reported with the appropriate construction or maintenance trade occupation). Exclude construction or maintenance laborers who do not primarily assist electricians or powerline transmission installers. Maintains tools and equipment, washes parts, and keeps supplies and parts in order. Transports tools, materials, equipment, and supplies to worksite, manually or using handtruck or by driving truck. Raises, lowers, or positions equipment, tools, and materials for installation or use, using hoist, handline, or block and tackle. Breaks up concrete to facilitate installation or repair of equipment, using air hammer. Trims trees and clears undergrowth along right-of-way. Strips insulation from wire ends, using wire-stripping pliers, and attaches wires to terminals for subsequent soldering. Measures, cuts, and bends wire and conduit, using measuring instruments and hand tools. Drills holes for wiring, using power drill, and pulls or pushes wiring through opening. Bolts component parts together to form tower assemblies, using hand tools. Solders electrical connections, using soldering iron. Rigs scaffolds, hoists, and shoring, erects barricades, and digs trenches. Traces out short circuits in wiring, using test meter. Examines electrical units for loose connections and broken insulation and tightens connections, using hand tools. Strings transmission lines or cables through ducts or conduits, underground, through equipment, or to towers. Disassembles defective electrical equipment, replaces defective or worn parts, and reassembles equipment, using hand tools. Threads conduit ends, connects couplings, and fabricates and secures conduit support brackets, using hand tools.

Knowledge: Computers and Electronics

Abilities: Spatial Orientation; Arm-Hand Steadiness; Manual Dexterity; Finger Dexterity; Multilimb Coordination; Speed of Limb Movement; Static Strength; Explosive Strength;

Dynamic Strength; Trunk Strength; Stamina; Extent Flexibility; Dynamic Flexibility; Gross Body Coordination; Gross Body Equilibrium; Peripheral Vision; Depth Perception

Helpers—Painters, Paperhangers, Plasterers, and Stucco Masons

Help painters, paperhangers, plasterers, or stucco masons by performing duties of lesser skill. Duties include supplying or holding materials or tools, and cleaning work area and equipment. Exclude apprentice workers (which are reported with the appropriate construction or maintenance trade occupation). Exclude construction or maintenance laborers who do not primarily assist painters, paperhangers, plasterers, or stucco masons. Performs any combination of support duties to assist painter, paperhanger, plasterer, or mason. Pours specified amounts of chemical solutions into stripping tanks. Places articles to be stripped into stripping tanks. Removes articles, such as cabinets, metal furniture, and paint containers, from stripping tanks after prescribed period of time. Covers surfaces of articles not to be painted with masking tape prior to painting. Fills cracks or breaks in surfaces of plaster articles with putty or epoxy compounds. Smooths surfaces of articles to be painted, using sanding and buffing tools and equipment.

Knowledge: None above average

Abilities: Static Strength; Dynamic Strength

Helpers—Plumbers, Pipefitters, and Steamfitters

Help plumbers, pipefitters, or steamfitters by performing duties of lesser skill. Duties include supplying or holding materials or tools, and cleaning work area and equipment. Exclude apprentice workers (which are reported with the appropriate construction or maintenance trade occupation). Exclude construction or maintenance laborers who do not primarily assist plumbers, pipefitters, or steamfitters. Fits or assists in fitting valves, couplings, or assemblies to tanks, pumps, or systems, using hand tools. Disassembles and removes damaged or worn pipe. Assists in installing gas burners to convert furnaces from wood, coal, or oil. Requisitions tools and equipment and selects type and size of pipe. Fills pipes with sand or resin to prevent distortion, and holds pipes during bending and installation. Immerses pipes in chemical solution to remove dirt, oil, and scale. Cleans shop, work area, and machines, using solvent and rags. Mounts brackets and hangers on walls and ceilings to hold pipes. Cuts or drills holes in walls to accommodate passage of pipes, using pneumatic drill.

Knowledge: Building and Construction

Abilities: Arm-Hand Steadiness; Manual Dexterity; Finger Dexterity; Multilimb Coordination; Static Strength; Explosive Strength; Dynamic Strength; Trunk Strength; Stamina; Extent Flexibility; Dynamic Flexibility; Gross Body Coordination; Gross Body Equilibrium

Correction Officers

▲ Growth: 32%

▲ Annual Job Openings: 48,102

▲ Yearly Earnings $28,787

▲ Education Required: Long-term O-J-T

▲ Self-employed: 0%

▲ Part-time: 1%

Correction Officers and Jailers

Guard inmates in penal or rehabilitative institution, in accordance with established regulations and procedures. May guard prisoners in transit between jail, courtroom, prison, or other point, traveling by automobile or public transportation. Include deputy sheriffs who spend the majority of their time guarding prisoners in county correctional institutions. Monitors conduct of prisoners, according to established policies, regulations, and procedures, to prevent escape or violence. Takes prisoner into custody and escorts to locations within and outside of facility, such as visiting room, courtroom, or airport. Inspects locks, window bars, grills, doors, and gates at correctional facility, to prevent escape. Uses weapons, handcuffs, and physical force to maintain discipline and order among prisoners. Searches prisoners, cells, and vehicles for weapons, valuables, or drugs. Guards facility entrance to screen visitors. Records information, such as prisoner identification, charges, and incidences of inmate disturbance. Questions and investigates prisoner and crime to obtain information to solve crime and make recommendations concerning disposition of case. Serves meals and distributes commissary items to prisoners. Administers medical aid to injured or ill prisoners.

Knowledge: Psychology; Sociology and Anthropology; Medicine and Dentistry; Public Safety and Security; Law, Government, and Jurisprudence

Abilities: Problem Sensitivity; Spatial Orientation; Selective Attention; Time Sharing; Response Orientation; Reaction Time; Speed of Limb Movement; Static Strength; Explosive Strength; Dynamic Strength; Stamina; Gross Body Coordination; Gross Body Equilibrium; Far Vision; Night Vision; Peripheral Vision; Glare Sensitivity; Hearing Sensitivity; Sound Localization

Correspondence Clerks

▲ Growth: 31%

▲ Annual Job Openings: 4,614

▲ Yearly Earnings $22,110

▲ Education Required: Short-term O-J-T

▲ Self-employed: 0%

▲ Part-time: 12%

Correspondence Clerks

Compose letters in reply to requests for merchandise, damage claims, credit and other information, delinquent accounts, incorrect billings, or unsatisfactory services. Duties may include gathering data to formulate reply and typing correspondence. Composes letter in response to request or problem identified by correspondence. Reads incoming correspondence to ascertain nature of writer's concern and determine disposition of correspondence. Gathers data to formulate reply. Completes form letters in response to request or problem identified by correspondence. Types acknowledgment letter to person sending correspondence. Reviews records pertinent to resolution of problem for completeness and accuracy, and attaches records to correspondence for reply by others. Processes orders for goods requested in correspondence. Compiles data pertinent to manufacture of special products for customers. Routes correspondence to other departments for reply. Maintains files and control records to show status of action in processing correspondence. Confers with company personnel regarding feasibility of complying with writer's request, such as to design and manufacture special product. Investigates discrepancies in reports and records and confers with personnel in affected departments to ensure accuracy and compliance with procedures. Compiles data from records to prepare periodic reports.

Knowledge: Clerical

Abilities: Wrist-Finger Speed

Cost Estimators

- ▲ Growth: 16%
- ▲ Annual Job Openings: 23,870
- ▲ Yearly Earnings $39,894
- ▲ Education Required: Work experience in a related occupation
- ▲ Self-employed: 0%
- ▲ Part-time: 9%

Cost Estimators

Prepare cost estimates for product manufacturing, construction projects, or services, to aid management in bidding on or determining price of product or service. May specialize according to particular service performed or type of product manufactured. Analyzes blueprints, specifications, proposals, and other documentation, to prepare time, cost, and labor estimates. Prepares estimates for selecting vendors or subcontractors and determining cost effectiveness. Reviews data to determine material and labor requirements, and prepares itemized list. Prepares estimates used for management purposes, such as planning, organizing, and scheduling work. Prepares time, cost, and labor estimates for products, projects, or services, applying specialized methodologies, techniques, or processes. Computes cost factors used for preparing estimates for management and determining cost effectiveness. Conducts special studies to develop and establish standard hour and related cost data or to effect cost reduction. Consults with clients, vendors, or other individuals to discuss and formulate estimates and resolve issues.

Knowledge: Administration and Management; Economics and Accounting; Production and Processing; Building and Construction; Mathematics

Abilities: Mathematical Reasoning; Number Facility

Counselors

- ▲ Growth: 19%
- ▲ Annual Job Openings: 27,181
- ▲ Yearly Earnings $36,566
- ▲ Education Required: Master's degree
- ▲ Self-employed: 2%
- ▲ Part-time: 18%

Vocational and Educational Counselors

Counsel individuals and provide group educational and vocational guidance services. Advises counselees to assist them in developing their educational and vocational objectives.

Advises counselees to assist them in understanding and overcoming personal and social problems. Collects and evaluates information about counselees' abilities, interests, and personality characteristics, using records, tests, and interviews. Compiles and studies occupational, educational, and economic information to assist counselees in making and carrying out vocational and educational objectives. Interprets program regulations or benefit requirements and assists counselees in obtaining needed supportive services. Refers qualified counselees to employer or employment service for placement. Conducts follow-up interviews with counselees and maintains case records. Establishes and maintains relationships with employers and personnel from supportive service agencies to develop opportunities for counselees. Plans and conducts orientation programs and group conferences to promote adjustment of individuals to new life experiences. Teaches vocational and educational guidance classes. Addresses community groups and faculty members to explain counseling services.

Knowledge: Personnel and Human Resources; Psychology; Sociology and Anthropology; Therapy and Counseling; Education and Training; English Language

Abilities: Oral Expression

Vocational Rehabilitation Coordinators

Develop and coordinate implementation of vocational rehabilitation programs. Develops proposals for rehabilitation programs to provide needed services, utilizing knowledge of program funding sources and government regulations. Consults with community groups and personnel from rehabilitation agencies to identify need for new or modified vocational rehabilitation programs. Collects and analyzes data to define and resolve rehabilitation problems, utilizing knowledge of vocational rehabilitation theory and practice. Monitors program operations and recommends additional measures to ensure that programs meet defined needs. Negotiates contracts for rehabilitation program equipment and supplies. Plans and provides training for vocational rehabilitation staff.

Knowledge: Administration and Management; Personnel and Human Resources; Psychology; Sociology and Anthropology; Therapy and Counseling; Education and Training; English Language; Philosophy and Theology; Law, Government, and Jurisprudence

Abilities: None above average

Counter and Rental Clerks

▲ Growth: 23%
▲ Annual Job Openings: 129,889
▲ Yearly Earnings $14,580
▲ Education Required: Short-term O-J-T
▲ Self-employed: 1%
▲ Part-time: 50%

Counter and Rental Clerks

Receive orders for services, such as rentals, repairs, dry-cleaning, and storage. May compute cost and accept payment. Rents item or arranges for provision of service to customer. Prepares rental forms, obtains customer signature, and collects deposit. Computes charges based on rental. Receives, examines, and tags articles to be altered, cleaned, stored, or repaired. Explains rental fees and provides information about rented items, such as operation or description. Receives payment or records credit charges. Answers telephone and receives orders by phone. Recommends to customer items offered by rental facility that meet customer needs. Reserves items for requested time and keeps record of items rented. Greets customers of agency that rents items, such as apparel, tools, and conveyances, or that provide services, such as rug cleaning. Requests license for car or plane rental. Receives film for processing and loads film into automatic processing equipment. Inspects and adjusts rental items to meet needs of customer. Files processed film and photographic prints, according to name.

Knowledge: Clerical; Sales and Marketing; Customer and Personal Service; Telecommunications

Abilities: Category Flexibility; Speech Recognition

Credit Analysts

▲ Growth: 16%
▲ Annual Job Openings: 5,454
▲ Yearly Earnings $36,961
▲ Education Required: Bachelor's degree
▲ Self-employed: 0%
▲ Part-time: 7%

Credit Analysts

Analyze current credit data and financial statements of individuals or firms to determine the degree of risk involved in extending credit or lending money. Prepare reports with this credit information for use in decision making. Analyzes credit data and financial statements to determine degree of risk involved in extending credit or lending money. Generates financial ratios, using computer program, to evaluate customer's financial status. Analyzes financial data, such as income growth, quality of management, and market share, to determine profitability of loan. Compares liquidity, profitability, and credit history with similar establishments of same industry and geographic location. Evaluates customer records and recommends payment plan based on earnings, savings data, payment history, and purchase activity. Completes loan application, including credit analysis and summary of loan request, and submits to loan committee for approval. Confers with credit association and other business representatives to exchange credit information. Reviews individual or commercial customer files to identify and select delinquent accounts for collection. Consults with customers to resolve complaints and verify financial and credit transactions, and adjusts accounts as needed.

Knowledge: Economics and Accounting; Personnel and Human Resources; Computers and Electronics; Mathematics; Geography; History and Archeology; Philosophy and Theology; Law, Government, and Jurisprudence

Abilities: Deductive Reasoning; Mathematical Reasoning; Number Facility; Near Vision; Speech Recognition

Curators, Archivists, Museum Technicians, and Restorers

- ▲ Growth: 15%
- ▲ Annual Job Openings: 2,367
- ▲ Yearly Earnings $30,035
- ▲ Education Required: Master's degree
- ▲ Self-employed: 0%
- ▲ Part-time: 21%

Curators

Plan, direct, and coordinate activities of exhibiting institution, such as museum, art gallery, botanical garden, zoo, or historic site. Direct instructional, acquisition, exhibitory, safekeeping, research, and public service activities of institution. Plans and organizes acquisition, storage, and exhibition of collections and related educational materials. Develops and maintains institution's registration, cataloging, and basic recordkeeping systems. Studies, examines, and tests acquisitions to authenticate their origin, composition, history, and current value. Negotiates and authorizes purchase, sale, exchange, or loan of collections. Directs and coordinates activities of curatorial, personnel, fiscal, technical, research, and clerical staff. Confers with institution's board of directors to formulate and interpret policies, determine budget requirements, and plan overall operations. Arranges insurance coverage for objects on loan or special exhibits, and recommends changes in coverage for entire collection. Plans and conducts special research projects. Writes and reviews grant proposals, journal articles, institutional reports, and publicity materials. Attends meetings, conventions, and civic events to promote use of institution's services, seek financing, and maintain community alliances. Conducts or organizes tours, workshops, and instructional sessions to acquaint individuals with use of institution's facilities and materials. Reserves facilities for group tours and social events and collects admission fees. Inspects premises for evidence of deterioration and need for repair. Schedules special events at facility and organizes details such as refreshment, entertainment, and decorations.

Knowledge: Administration and Management; Clerical; Economics and Accounting; Sales and Marketing; Sociology and Anthropology; Geography; English Language; Foreign Language; Fine Arts; History and Archeology; Philosophy and Theology; Communications and Media

Abilities: Category Flexibility; Memorization; Speech Clarity

Archivists

Appraise, edit, and direct safekeeping of permanent records and historically valuable documents. Participate in research activities based on archival materials. Directs activities of workers engaged in cataloging and safekeeping of valuable materials and disposition of worthless materials. Directs filing and cross-indexing of selected documents in alphabetical and chronological order. Prepares document descriptions and reference aids for use of archives, such as accession lists, bibliographies, abstracts, and microfilmed documents. Directs acquisition and physical arrangement of new materials. Analyzes documents by ascertaining date of writing, author, or original recipient of letter to appraise value to posterity. Establishes policy guidelines concerning public access and use of materials. Selects and edits documents for publication and display, according to knowledge of subject, literary expression, and techniques for presentation and display. Requests or recommends pertinent materials available in libraries, private collections, or other archives. Advises government agencies, scholars, journalists, and others conducting research by supplying available materials and information.

Knowledge: Administration and Management; Clerical; Sociology and Anthropology; English Language; History and Archeology; Philosophy and Theology; Communications and Media

Abilities: Category Flexibility; Memorization

Museum Research Workers

Plan, organize, and conduct research in scientific, historical, cultural, or artistic fields to document or support exhibits in museums and museum publications. Conducts research on historic monuments, buildings, and scenes to construct exhibits. Develops plans for project or studies guidelines for project prepared by professional staff member to outline research procedures. Plans schedule according to variety of methods to be used, availability and quantity of resources, and number of personnel assigned. Conducts research, utilizing institution library, archives, and collections, and other sources of information, to collect, record, analyze, and evaluate facts. Discusses findings with other personnel to evaluate validity of findings. Prepares reports of completed projects for publication, for presentation to agency requesting project, or for use in other research activities. Monitors construction of exhibits to ensure authenticity of proportion, color, and costumes.

Knowledge: Administration and Management; Computers and Electronics; Mathematics; Psychology; Sociology and Anthropology; Geography; English Language; Foreign Language; Fine Arts; History and Archeology; Philosophy and Theology; Telecommunications; Communications and Media

Abilities: Written Comprehension; Written Expression

Museum Technicians and Conservators

Prepare specimens, such as fossils, skeletal parts, and textiles, for museum collection and exhibits. May restore documents or install, arrange, and exhibit materials. Preserves or directs preservation of objects, using plaster, resin, sealants, hardeners, and shellac. Repairs and restores surfaces of artifacts to original appearance and to prevent deterioration, according to accepted procedures. Evaluates need for repair and determines safest and most effective method of treating surface of object. Cleans objects, such as paper, textiles, wood, metal, glass, rock, pottery, and furniture, using cleansers, solvents, soap solutions, and polishes. Constructs skeletal mounts of fossils, replicas of archaeological artifacts, or duplicate specimens, using variety of materials and hand tools. Repairs or reassembles broken objects, using glue, solder, hand tools, power tools, and small machines. Studies descriptive information on object or conducts standard chemical and physical tests to determine age, composition, and original appearance. Designs and fabricates missing or broken parts. Cuts and welds metal sections in reconstruction or renovation of exterior structural sections and accessories of exhibits. Recommends preservation measures, such as control of temperature, humidity, and exposure to light, to curatorial and building maintenance staff. Installs, arranges, assembles, and prepares artifacts for exhibition. Plans and conducts research to develop and improve methods of restoring and preserving specimens. Records methods and treatment taken to repair, preserve, and restore each artifact, and maintains museum files. Prepares reports of activities. Notifies superior when restoration of artifact requires outside experts. Directs curatorial and technical staff in handling, mounting, care, and storage of art objects. Estimates cost of restoration work. Builds, repairs, and installs wooden steps, scaffolds, and walkways to gain access to or permit improved view of exhibited equipment.

Knowledge: Building and Construction; Chemistry; Sociology and Anthropology; Fine Arts; History and Archeology; Philosophy and Theology

Abilities: Flexibility of Closure; Visualization; Wrist-Finger Speed; Visual Color Discrimination

Craft Demonstrators

Demonstrate and explain techniques and purposes of historic crafts. Engages in activities such as molding candles, shoeing horses, operating looms, or working in appropriate period setting to demonstrate craft. Describes craft techniques and explains the relationship of craft to traditional lifestyle of time and area. Practices techniques involved in handicraft to ensure accurate and skillful demonstrations. Answers visitor questions, or refers visitors to other sources for information. Studies historical and technical literature to acquire information about time period and lifestyle depicted in display and craft techniques. Drafts outline of talk, assisted by research personnel, to acquaint visitors with customs and crafts associated with folk life depicted.

Knowledge: Sociology and Anthropology; Geography; Fine Arts; History and Archeology; Philosophy and Theology

Abilities: Multilimb Coordination; Speech Clarity

Customer Service Representatives

- ▲ Growth: 36%
- ▲ Annual Job Openings: 29,751
- ▲ Yearly Earnings $27,060
- ▲ Education Required: Short-term O-J-T
- ▲ Self-employed: 0%
- ▲ Part-time: 12%

Customer Service Representatives, Utilities

Interview applicants for water, gas, electric, or telephone service. Talk with customer by phone or in person, and receive orders for installation, turn-on, discontinuance, or change in services. Confers with customer by phone or in person to receive orders for installation, turn-on, discontinuance, or change in service. Completes contract forms, prepares change-of-address records, and issues discontinuance orders, using computer. Resolves billing or service complaints and refers grievances to designated departments for investigation. Determines charges for service requested and collects deposits. Solicits sale of new or additional utility services.

Knowledge: Sales and Marketing; Customer and Personal Service

Abilities: None above

Dancers and Choreographers

▲ Growth: 28%

▲ Annual Job Openings: 4,283

▲ Yearly Earnings $28,017

▲ Education Required: Postsecondary vocational training

▲ Self-employed: 30%

▲ Part-time: 25%

Dancers

Dance alone, with partners, or in a group to entertain audience. Performs classical, modern, or acrobatic dances in productions. Harmonizes body movements to rhythm of musical accompaniment. Studies and practices dance moves required in role. Rehearses solo or with partners or troupe members. Coordinates dancing with that of partner or dance ensemble. Works with choreographer to refine or modify dance steps. Devises and choreographs dance for self or others. Auditions for parts in productions.

Knowledge: Fine Arts

Abilities: Fluency of Ideas; Originality; Memorization; Spatial Orientation; Multilimb Coordination; Speed of Limb Movement; Static Strength; Explosive Strength; Dynamic Strength; Trunk Strength; Stamina; Extent Flexibility; Dynamic Flexibility; Gross Body Coordination; Gross Body Equilibrium; Peripheral Vision; Depth Perception; Auditory Attention

Choreographers

Create and teach original dances for ballet, musical, or revue to be performed for stage, television, motion picture, or nightclub production. Determines dance movements designed to suggest story, interpret emotion, or enliven show. Creates original dance routines for ballets, musicals, or other forms of entertainment. Instructs cast in dance movements at rehearsals to achieve desired effect. Studies story line and music to envision and devise dance movements. Directs and stages dance presentations for various forms of entertainment. Auditions performers for one or more dance parts.

Knowledge: Personnel and Human Resources; Education and Training; Fine Arts; Communications and Media

Abilities: Fluency of Ideas; Originality; Memorization; Spatial Orientation; Visualization; Time Sharing; Multilimb Coordination; Speed of Limb Movement; Explosive Strength; Dynamic Strength; Trunk Strength; Stamina; Extent Flexibility; Dynamic Flexibility; Gross Body Coordination; Gross Body Equilibrium; Peripheral Vision; Depth Perception

Data Processing Equipment Repairers

▲ Growth: 52%

▲ Annual Job Openings: 8,843

▲ Yearly Earnings $29,452

▲ Education Required: Postsecondary vocational training

▲ Self-employed: 4%

▲ Part-time: 6%

Data Processing Equipment Repairers

Repair, maintain, and install electronic computers (mainframes, minis, and micros), peripheral equipment, and word-processing systems. Replaces defective components and wiring. Tests faulty equipment and applies knowledge of functional operation of electronic units and systems to diagnose cause of malfunction. Tests electronic components and circuits to locate defects, using oscilloscopes, signal generators, ammeters, and voltmeters. Aligns, adjusts, and calibrates equipment according to specifications. Converses with equipment operators to ascertain problems with equipment before breakdown or cause of breakdown. Adjusts mechanical parts, using hand tools and soldering iron. Calibrates testing instruments. Maintains records of repairs, calibrations, and tests. Enters information into computer to copy program from one electronic component to another, or to draw, modify, or store schematics. Operates equipment, such as communication equipment or missile control systems in ground and flight test.

Knowledge: Customer and Personal Service; Computers and Electronics; Engineering and Technology; Design; Mechanical; Physics; Telecommunications

Abilities: Written Comprehension; Fluency of Ideas; Originality; Problem Sensitivity; Deductive Reasoning; Inductive Reasoning; Information Ordering; Mathematical Reasoning; Memorization; Speed of Closure; Perceptual Speed; Visualization; Selective Attention; Manual Dexterity; Finger Dexterity; Control Precision; Response Orientation; Wrist-Finger Speed; Explosive Strength; Extent Flexibility; Gross Body Equilibrium; Near Vision; Visual Color Discrimination; Hearing Sensitivity; Auditory Attention; Sound Localization

D

Dental Assistants

- ▲ Growth: 38%
- ▲ Annual Job Openings: 45,487
- ▲ Yearly Earnings $21,569
- ▲ Education Required: Moderate-term O-J-T
- ▲ Self-employed: 0%
- ▲ Part-time: 39%

Dental Assistants

Assist dentist at chair, set up patient and equipment, keep records, and perform related duties as required. Prepares patient, sterilizes and disinfects instruments, sets up instrument trays, prepares materials, and assists dentist during dental procedures. Takes and records medical and dental histories and vital signs of patients. Records treatment information in patient records. Assists dentist in management of medical and dental emergencies. Exposes dental diagnostic X rays. Applies protective coating of fluoride to teeth. Provides postoperative instructions prescribed by dentist. Makes preliminary impressions for study casts and occlusal registrations for mounting study casts. Pours, trims, and polishes study casts. Cleans and polishes removable appliances. Instructs patients in oral hygiene and plaque-control programs. Schedules appointments, prepares bills and receives payment for dental services, completes insurance forms, and maintains records, manually or using computer. Cleans teeth, using dental instruments. Fabricates temporary restorations and custom impressions from preliminary impressions.

Knowledge: Clerical; Medicine and Dentistry

Abilities: Control Precision

Dental Hygienists

- ▲ Growth: 48%
- ▲ Annual Job Openings: 18,373
- ▲ Yearly Earnings $42,432
- ▲ Education Required: Associate degree
- ▲ Self-employed: 0%
- ▲ Part-time: 22%

Dental Hygienists

Perform dental prophylactic treatments and instruct groups and individuals in the care of the teeth and mouth. Cleans calcareous deposits, accretions, and stains from teeth and beneath margins of gums, using dental instruments. Applies fluorides and other cavity-preventing agents to arrest dental decay. Provides clinical services and health education to improve and maintain oral health of school children. Conducts dental health clinics for community groups to augment services of dentist. Removes excess cement from coronal surfaces of teeth. Charts conditions of decay and disease for diagnosis and treatment by dentist. Places and removes rubber dams, matrices, and temporary restorations. Examines gums, using probes, to locate periodontal recessed gums and signs of gum disease. Feels lymph nodes under patient's chin to detect swelling or tenderness that could indicate presence of oral cancer. Feels and visually examines gums for sores and signs of disease. Places, carves, and finishes amalgam restorations. Makes impressions for study casts. Removes sutures and dressings. Exposes and develops X ray film. Administers local anesthetic agents.

Knowledge: Biology; Medicine and Dentistry

Abilities: Arm-Hand Steadiness

Dentists

- ▲ Growth: 8%
- ▲ Annual Job Openings: 5,073
- ▲ Yearly Earnings $85,508
- ▲ Education Required: First professional degree
- ▲ Self-employed: 44%
- ▲ Part-time: 20%

Oral Pathologists

Research or study nature, cause, effects, and development of diseases associated with mouth. Examine oral tissue specimens of patients to determine pathological conditions such as tumors and lesions. Examines oral tissue specimen to determine pathological conditions, such as tumors and lesions, using microscope and other laboratory equipment. Determines nature and cause of oral condition. Evaluates previous and future development of oral condition. Examines patient's mouth, jaw, face, and associated areas. Obtains oral tissue specimen from patient, using medical instruments. Discusses diagnosis with patient and referring practitioner.

Knowledge: Chemistry; Biology; Psychology; Medicine and Dentistry; Therapy and Counseling; English Language

Abilities: Problem Sensitivity; Arm-Hand Steadiness; Finger Dexterity

Dentists

Diagnose, prevent, and treat problems of the teeth and tissue of the mouth. Exclude orthodontists; prosthodontists; oral and maxillofacial surgeons; and oral pathologists. Fills, extracts, and replaces teeth, using rotary and hand instruments, dental appliances, medications, and surgical implements. Applies fluoride and sealants to teeth. Treats exposure of pulp by pulp capping, removal of pulp from pulp chamber, or root canal, using dental instruments. Treats infected root canal and related tissues. Fills pulp chamber and canal with endodontic materials. Eliminates irritating margins of fillings and corrects occlusions, using dental instruments. Examines teeth, gums, and related tissues to determine condition, using dental instruments, X ray, and other diagnostic equipment. Formulates plan of treatment for patient's teeth and mouth tissue. Removes pathologic tissue or diseased tissue using surgical instruments. Restores natural color of teeth by bleaching, cleaning, and polishing. Analyzes and evaluates dental needs to determine changes and trends in patterns of dental disease. Counsels and advises patients about growth and development of dental problems and preventive oral health care services. Fabricates prosthodontic appliances, such as space maintainers, bridges, dentures, and obturating appliances. Fits and adjusts prosthodontic appliances in patient's mouth. Produces and evaluates dental health educational materials. Plans, organizes, and maintains dental health programs.

Knowledge: Chemistry; Biology; Medicine and Dentistry; English Language

Abilities: Oral Expression; Problem Sensitivity; Arm-Hand Steadiness; Manual Dexterity; Finger Dexterity; Control Precision

Orthodontists

Examine, diagnose, and treat dental malocclusions and oral cavity anomalies. Design and fabricate appliances to realign teeth and jaws to produce and maintain normal function and to improve appearance. Diagnoses teeth and jaw or other dental-facial abnormalities. Plans treatment, using cephalometric, height, and weight records, dental X rays and front and lateral dental photographs. Examines patient's mouth to determine position of teeth and jaw development. Fits dental appliances in patient's mouth to alter position and relationship of teeth and jaws and to realign teeth. Adjusts dental appliances periodically to produce and maintain normal function. Designs and fabricates appliances, such as space maintainers, retainers, and labial and lingual arch wires.

Knowledge: Customer and Personal Service; Chemistry; Biology; Medicine and Dentistry; Therapy and Counseling

Abilities: Arm-Hand Steadiness; Manual Dexterity; Finger Dexterity; Control Precision

Prosthodontists

Construct oral prostheses to replace missing teeth and other oral structures; to correct natural and acquired deformation of mouth and jaws; to restore and maintain oral function, such as chewing and speaking; and to improve appearance. Designs and fabricates dental prostheses. Corrects natural and acquired deformation of mouth and jaws through use of prosthetic appliances. Records physiologic position of jaws to determine shape and size of dental prostheses, using face bows, dental articulators, and recording devices. Adjusts prostheses to fit patient. Replaces missing teeth and associated oral structures with artificial teeth to improve chewing, speech, and appearance.

Knowledge: Chemistry; Biology; Medicine and Dentistry

Abilities: Finger Dexterity

Oral and Maxillofacial Surgeons

Perform surgery on mouth, jaws, and related head and neck structure to execute difficult and multiple extractions of teeth, to remove tumors and other abnormal growths; to correct abnormal jaw relations by mandibular or maxillary revision; to prepare mouth for insertion of dental prosthesis; or to treat fractured jaws. Executes difficult and multiple extraction of teeth. Removes tumors and other abnormal growths, using surgical instruments. Performs preprosthetic surgery to prepare mouth for insertion of dental prosthesis. Corrects abnormal jaw relations by mandibular or maxillary revision. Treats fractures of jaws. Administers general and local anesthetics.

Knowledge: Chemistry; Biology; Psychology; Medicine and Dentistry; Therapy and Counseling; English Language

Abilities: Problem Sensitivity; Visualization; Arm-Hand Steadiness; Manual Dexterity; Finger Dexterity; Control Precision; Reaction Time; Near Vision

Designers

- ▲ Growth: 26%
- ▲ Annual Job Openings: 42,478
- ▲ Yearly Earnings $30,867
- ▲ Education Required: Bachelor's degree
- ▲ Self-employed: 36%
- ▲ Part-time: 20%

Fashion Designers

Design clothing and accessories. Create original garments or design garments that follow well-established fashion trends. May develop the line of color and kinds of materials. Designs custom garments for clients. Integrates findings of analysis and discussion, and personal tastes and knowledge of design, to originate design ideas. Sketches rough and detailed drawings of apparel or accessories, and writes specifications, such as color scheme, construction, or material type. Draws pattern for article designed, cuts pattern, and cuts material according to pattern, using measuring and drawing instruments, and scissors. Examines sample garment on and off model, and modifies design to achieve desired effect. Attends fashion shows and reviews garment magazines and manuals to analyze fashion trends, predictions, and consumer preferences. Confers with sales and management executives or with clients regarding design ideas. Sews together sections to form mockup or sample of garment or article, using sewing equipment. Arranges for showing of sample garments at sales meetings or fashion shows. Directs and coordinates workers who draw and cut patterns, and constructs sample or finished garment.

Knowledge: Sales and Marketing; Customer and Personal Service; Production and Processing; Design; Education and Training; Fine Arts

Abilities: Fluency of Ideas; Originality; Visualization; Time Sharing; Arm-Hand Steadiness; Manual Dexterity; Finger Dexterity; Wrist-Finger Speed; Visual Color Discrimination

Commercial and Industrial Designers

Develop and design manufactured products, such as cars, home appliances, and children's toys. Combine artistic talent with research on product use, marketing, and materials, to create the most functional and appealing product design. Confers with engineering, marketing, production, or sales department, or with customer, to establish design concepts for manufactured products. Integrates findings and concepts and sketches design ideas. Prepares detailed drawings, illustrations, artwork, or blueprints, using drawing instruments or paints and brushes. Designs packaging and containers for products, such as foods, beverages, toiletries, or medicines. Evaluates design ideas for feasibility based on factors such as appearance, function, serviceability, budget, production costs/methods, and market characteristics. Creates and designs graphic material for use as ornamentation, illustration, or advertising on manufactured materials and packaging. Presents design to customer or design committee for approval and discusses need for modification. Modifies design to conform with customer specifications, production limitations, or changes in design trends. Reads publications, attends showings, and studies traditional, period, and contemporary design styles and motifs to obtain perspective and design concepts. Directs and coordinates preparation of detailed drawings from sketches or fabrication of models or samples. Fabricates model or sample in paper, wood, glass, fabric, plastic, or metal, using hand and power tools. Prepares itemized production requirements to produce item.

Knowledge: Sales and Marketing; Production and Processing; Design; Education and Training; Fine Arts; History and Archeology

Abilities: Oral Comprehension; Written Comprehension; Oral Expression; Fluency of Ideas; Originality; Deductive Reasoning; Information Ordering; Mathematical Reasoning; Number Facility; Visualization; Arm-Hand Steadiness; Near Vision; Visual Color Discrimination; Speech Recognition

Set Designers

Design sets for theatrical, motion picture, and television productions. Integrates requirements including script, research, budget, and available locations to develop design. Prepares rough draft and scale working drawings of sets, including floor plans, scenery, and properties to be constructed. Presents drawings for approval and makes changes and corrections as directed. Designs and builds scale models of set design or miniature sets used in filming backgrounds or special effects. Selects furniture, draperies, pictures, lamps, and rugs for decorative quality and appearance. Researches and consults experts to determine architectural and furnishing styles to depict given periods or locations. Confers with heads of production and direction to establish budget and schedules, and to discuss design ideas. Estimates costs of design materials and construction, or rental of location or props. Directs and coordinates set construction, erection, or decoration activities to ensure conformance to design, budget, and schedule requirements. Reads script to determine location, set, or decoration requirements. Examines dressed set to ensure props and scenery do not interfere with movements of cast or view of camera. Assigns staff to complete design ideas and prepare sketches, illustrations, and detailed drawings of sets, or graphics and animation.

Knowledge: Design; Building and Construction; Geography; Fine Arts; History and Archeology; Communications and Media

Abilities: Fluency of Ideas; Originality; Speed of Closure; Spatial Orientation; Visualization; Selective Attention; Time Sharing; Gross Body Equilibrium; Far Vision; Visual Color Discrimination; Night Vision; Auditory Attention; Sound Localization

Exhibit Designers

Plan, design, and oversee construction and installation of permanent and temporary exhibits and displays. Prepares preliminary drawings of proposed exhibit, including detailed construction, layout, material specifications, or special effects diagrams. Designs display to decorate streets, fairgrounds, buildings, or other places for celebrations, using paper, cloth, plastic, or other materials. Designs, draws, paints, or sketches backgrounds and fixtures for use in windows or interior displays. Oversees preparation of artwork, construction of exhibit components, and placement of collection to ensure intended interpretation of concepts and conformance to specifications. Confers with client or staff regarding theme, interpretative or informational purpose, planned location, budget, materials, or promotion. Submits plans for approval, and adapts plan to serve intended purpose or to conform to budget or fabrication restrictions. Arranges for acquisition of specimens or graphics, or building of exhibit structures by outside contractors to complete exhibit. Inspects installed exhibit for conformance to specifications and satisfactory operation of special effects components.

Knowledge: Sales and Marketing; Customer and Personal Service; Computers and Electronics; Design; Building and Construction; Fine Arts

Abilities: Fluency of Ideas; Originality; Visualization; Time Sharing; Arm-Hand Steadiness; Wrist-Finger Speed; Far Vision; Visual Color Discrimination

Art Directors

Formulate design concepts and presentation approaches, and direct workers engaged in artwork, layout design, and copy writing for visual communications media, such as magazines, books, newspapers, and packaging. Assigns and directs staff members to develop design concepts into art layouts or prepare layouts for printing. Formulates basic layout design or presentation approach, and conceives material details, such as style and size of type, photographs, graphics, and arrangement. Reviews and approves art and copy materials developed by staff, and proofs of printed copy. Reviews illustrative material and confers with client concerning objectives, budget, background information, and presentation approaches, styles, and techniques. Confers with creative, art, copy writing, or production department heads to discuss client requirements, outline presentation concepts, and coordinate creative activities. Presents final layouts to client for approval. Prepares detailed storyboard showing sequence and timing of story development for television production. Writes typography instructions, such as margin widths and type sizes, and submits for typesetting or printing. Marks up, pastes, and completes layouts to prepare for printing. Draws custom illustrations for project.

Knowledge: Administration and Management; Sales and Marketing; Production and Processing; Design; Psychology; Fine Arts; Communications and Media

Abilities: Oral Expression; Fluency of Ideas; Originality; Visualization; Time Sharing; Near Vision; Visual Color Discrimination; Night Vision; Speech Recognition; Speech Clarity

Floral Designers

Design and fashion live, cut, dried, and artificial floral and foliar arrangements for events, such as holidays, anniversaries, weddings, balls, and funerals. Plans arrangement according to client's requirements, utilizing knowledge of design and properties of materials, or selects appropriate standard design pattern. Selects flora and foliage for arrangement. Trims material and arranges bouquets, wreaths, terrariums, and other items using trimmers, shapers, wire, pin, floral tape, foam, and other materials. Confers with client regarding price and type of arrangement desired. Decorates buildings, halls, churches, or other facilities where events are planned. Packs and wraps completed arrangements. Estimates costs and prices arrangements. Conducts classes, demonstrations, or trains other workers.

Knowledge: Customer and Personal Service; Fine Arts

Abilities: Gross Body Equilibrium; Visual Color Discrimination

Merchandise Displayers and Window Trimmers

Plan and erect commercial displays, such as those in windows and interiors of retail stores and at trade exhibitions. Constructs or assembles prefabricated display properties from fabric, glass, paper, and plastic, using hand tools and woodworking power tools, according to specifications. Originates ideas for merchandise display or window decoration. Develops layout and selects theme, lighting, colors, and props to be used. Prepares sketches or floor plans of proposed displays. Installs booths, exhibits, displays, carpets, and drapes, as guided by floor plan of building and specifications. Consults with advertising and sales staff to determine type of merchandise to be featured and time and place for each display. Cuts out designs on cardboard, hardboard, and plywood, according to motif of event. Arranges properties, furniture, merchandise, backdrop, and other accessories, as shown in prepared sketch. Installs decorations, such as flags, banners, festive lights, and bunting, on or in building, street, exhibit hall, or booth. Places price and descriptive signs on backdrop, fixtures, merchandise, or floor. Dresses mannequins for use in displays.

Knowledge: Sales and Marketing; Design; Sociology and Anthropology; Fine Arts; Communications and Media

Abilities: Originality; Visualization; Extent Flexibility; Dynamic Flexibility; Gross Body Equilibrium; Visual Color Discrimination; Depth Perception

Desktop Publishing Workers

- ▲ Growth: 74%
- ▲ Annual Job Openings: 4,117
- ▲ Yearly Earnings $27,705
- ▲ Education Required: Long-term O-J-T
- ▲ Self-employed: 0%
- ▲ Part-time: 19%

Electronic Pagination System Operators

Using a computer screen, call up type and art elements from computer memory and position them into a completed page, using knowledge of type styles and size and composition patterns. The composited page is then transmitted for production into film or directly into plates. Views monitors for visual representation of work in progress and for instructions and feedback throughout process. Activates options, such as masking or text processing. Enters data, such as background color, shapes, and coordinates of images; and retrieves data from system memory. Activates options, such as masking, pixel (picture element) editing, airbrushing, or image retouching. Enters data, such as coordinates of images and color specifications, into system to retouch and make color corrections. Saves completed work on floppy disks or magnetic tape. Enters digitized data into electronic prepress system computer memory, using scanner, camera, keyboard, or mouse. Studies layout or other instructions to determine work to be done and sequence of operations. Loads floppy disks or tapes containing information into system. Creates special effects, such as vignettes, mosaics, and image combining.

Knowledge: Clerical; Computers and Electronics; English Language; Fine Arts; Telecommunications; Communications and Media

Abilities: Visualization; Wrist-Finger Speed; Near Vision; Visual Color Discrimination

Dietitians and Nutritionists

▲ Growth: 18%
▲ Annual Job Openings: 4,079
▲ Yearly Earnings $32,406
▲ Education Required: Bachelor's degree
▲ Self-employed: 16%
▲ Part-time: 29%

Dietitians and Nutritionists

Organize, plan, and conduct food service or nutritional programs to assist in promotion of health and control of disease. May administer activities of department providing quantity food service. May plan, organize, and conduct programs in nutritional research. Develops and implements dietary-care plans based on assessments of nutritional needs, diet restrictions, and other current health plans. Consults with physicians and health care personnel to determine nutritional needs and diet restrictions of patients or clients. Instructs patients and their families in nutritional principles, dietary plans, and food selection and preparation. Monitors food service operations and ensures conformance to nutritional and quality standards. Plans, organizes, and conducts training programs in dietetics, nutrition, and institutional management and administration for medical students and hospital personnel. Supervises activities of workers engaged in planning, preparing, and serving meals. Evaluates nutritional care plans and provides follow-up on continuity of care. Plans, conducts, and evaluates dietary, nutritional, and epidemiological research, and analyzes findings for practical applications. Inspects meals served for conformance to prescribed diets and standards of palatability and appearance. Develops curriculum and prepares manuals, visual aids, course outlines, and other materials used in teaching. Writes research reports and other publications to document and communicate research findings. Plans and prepares grant proposals to request program funding. Confers with design, building, and equipment personnel to plan for construction and remodeling of food service units.

Knowledge: Food Production; Computers and Electronics; Chemistry; Biology; Psychology; Medicine and Dentistry; Education and Training; English Language; History and Archeology

Abilities: Written Comprehension; Oral Expression; Written Expression; Fluency of Ideas; Originality; Speed of Closure; Near Vision; Auditory Attention; Speech Clarity

Dining Room, Cafeteria, and Bar Helpers

▲ Growth: 14%
▲ Annual Job Openings: 132,882
▲ Yearly Earnings $12,209
▲ Education Required: Short-term O-J-T
▲ Self-employed: 0%
▲ Part-time: 59%

Dining Room and Cafeteria Attendants, and Bartender Helpers

Perform any combination of the following duties to facilitate food service: carry dirty dishes from dining room to kitchen; replace soiled table linens; set tables with silverware and glassware; replenish supply of clean linens, silverware, glassware, and dishes; supply service bar with food, such as soups, salads, and desserts; and serve ice water, butter, and coffee to patrons. May wash tables. Carries dirty dishes to kitchen and wipes tables and seats with dampened cloth. Carries food, dishes, trays, and silverware from kitchen and supply departments to serving counters. Replenishes supply of clean linens, silverware, glassware, and dishes in dining room. Replenishes food and equipment at steamtables and serving counters of cafeteria to facilitate service to patrons. Sets tables with clean linens, sugar bowls, and condiments. Cleans bar and equipment, and replenishes bar supplies, such as liquor, fruit, ice, and dishes. Carries trays from food counters to tables for cafeteria patrons, and serves ice water and butter to patrons. Keeps assigned area and equipment clean, makes coffee, fills fruit juice dispensers, and stocks vending machines with food in automat. Stocks refrigerating units with wines and bottled beer, replaces empty beer kegs, and slices and pits fruit used to garnish drinks. Washes glasses, bar, and equipment, polishes bar fixtures, mops floors, and removes empty bottles and trash. Circulates among diners and serves coffee. Garnishes and positions foods on table to ensure visibility to patrons and convenience in serving. Mixes and prepares flavors for mixed drinks. Transfers food and dishes between floors of establishment, using dumbwaiter. Runs errands and delivers food orders to offices.

Knowledge: None above average

Abilities: None above average

Director of Religious Education and Activities

▲ Growth: 36%

▲ Annual Job Openings: 10,781

▲ Yearly Earnings $24,169

▲ Education Required: Bachelor's degree

▲ Self-employed: 0%

▲ Part-time: 14%

Directors, Religious Activities and Education

Direct and coordinate activities of a denominational group to meet religious needs of students. Plan, organize, and direct church school programs designed to promote religious education among church membership. Provide counseling and guidance relative to marital, health, financial, and religious problems. Coordinates activities with religious advisers, councils, and university officials to meet religious needs of students. Counsels individuals regarding marital, health, financial, and religious problems. Plans congregational activities and projects to encourage participation in religious education programs. Develops, organizes, and directs study courses and religious education programs within congregation. Supervises instructional staff in religious education program. Promotes student participation in extracurricular congregational activities. Assists and advises groups in promoting interfaith understanding. Plans and conducts conferences dealing with interpretation of religious ideas and convictions. Solicits support, participation, and interest in religious education programs from congregation members, organizations, officials, and clergy. Analyzes member participation and changes in congregation emphasis to determine needs for religious education. Interprets policies of university to community religious workers. Interprets religious education to public through speaking, leading discussions, and writing articles for local and national publications. Analyzes revenue and program cost data to determine budget priorities. Orders and distributes school supplies.

Knowledge: Administration and Management; Economics and Accounting; Psychology; Sociology and Anthropology; Therapy and Counseling; Education and Training; English Language; Philosophy and Theology; Communications and Media

Abilities: Oral Expression; Speech Clarity

Dispatchers

▲ Growth: 11%
▲ Annual Job Openings: 19,239
▲ Yearly Earnings $26,561
▲ Education Required: Moderate-term O-J-T
▲ Self-employed: 1%
▲ Part-time: 8%

Dispatchers—Except Police, Fire, and Ambulance

Schedule and dispatch workers, work crews, equipment, or service vehicles for conveyance of materials, freight, or passengers or for normal installation, service, or emergency repairs rendered outside the place of business. Duties may include use of radio or telephone to transmit assignments and compiling statistics and reports on work progress. Routes or assigns workers or equipment to appropriate location, according to customer request, specifications, or needs. Determines types or amount of equipment, vehicles, materials, or personnel required, according to work order or specifications. Relays work orders, messages, and information to or from work crews, supervisors, and field inspectors, using telephone or two-way radio. Receives or prepares work orders, according to customer request or specifications. Records and maintains files and records regarding customer requests, work or services performed, charges, expenses, inventory, and other dispatch information. Confers with customer or supervising personnel regarding questions, problems, and requests for service or equipment. Orders supplies and equipment, and issues to personnel.

Knowledge: Customer and Personal Service, Geography; Telecommunications; Transportation

Abilities: None above average

Dispensing Opticians

▲ Growth: 14%
▲ Annual Job Openings: 7,780
▲ Yearly Earnings $22,547
▲ Education Required: Long-term O-J-T
▲ Self-employed: 4%
▲ Part-time: 10%

Opticians, Dispensing and Measuring

Design, measure, fit, and adapt lenses and frames for client, according to written optical prescription or specification. Assist client with selecting frames. Measure customer for size of eyeglasses and coordinate frames with facial and eye measurements and optical prescription. Prepare work order for optical laboratory containing instructions for grinding and mounting lenses in frames. Verify exactness of finished lens spectacles. Adjust frame and lens position to fit client. May shape or reshape frames. Include contact lens opticians. Measures client's bridge and eye size, temple length, vertex distance, pupillary distance, and optical centers of eyes, using measuring devices. Prepares work order and instructions for grinding lenses and fabricating eyeglasses. Verifies finished lenses are ground to specification. Determines client's current lens prescription, when necessary, using lensometer or lens analyzer and client's eyeglasses. Recommends specific lenses, lens coatings, and frames to suit client needs. Assists client in selecting frames according to style and color, coordinating frames with facial and eye measurements and optical prescription. Heats, shapes, or bends plastic or metal frames to adjust eyeglasses to fit client, using pliers and hands. Evaluates prescription in conjunction with client's vocational and avocational visual requirements. Repairs damaged frames. Fabricates lenses to prescription specifications. Instructs clients in adapting to wearing and caring for eyeglasses. Grinds lens edges or applies coating to lenses. Selects and orders frames for display. Manages one or more optical shops. Sells optical goods, such as binoculars, sunglasses, magnifying glasses, and low-vision aids. Computes amount of sale and collects payment for services.

Knowledge: Administration and Management; Economics and Accounting; Sales and Marketing; Customer and Personal Service; Personnel and Human Resources

Abilities: None above average

Driver/Sales Workers

- ▲ Growth: 12%
- ▲ Annual Job Openings: 49,513
- ▲ Yearly Earnings $20,342
- ▲ Education Required: Short-term O-J-T
- ▲ Self-employed: 2%
- ▲ Part-time: 12%

Driver/Sales Workers

Drive truck or other vehicle over established routes to deliver and sell goods, such as food products; pick up and deliver items, such as laundry; or refill, service, and collect coins from vending machines. Include newspaper delivery drivers. Drives truck to deliver such items as food, medical supplies, or newspapers. Collects coins from vending machines, refills machines, and removes aged merchandise. Sells food specialties, such as sandwiches and beverages, to office workers and patrons of sports events. Collects money from customers, makes change, and records transactions on customer receipt. Calls on prospective customers to explain company services and to solicit new business. Records sales or delivery information on daily sales or delivery record. Informs regular customers of new products or services and price changes. Reviews list of dealers, customers, or station drops, and loads truck. Writes customer orders and sales contracts according to company guidelines. Listens to and resolves customers' complaints regarding product or services. Maintains truck and food-dispensing equipment and cleans inside of machines that dispense food or beverages. Arranges merchandise and sales promotion displays, or issues sales promotion materials to customers.

Knowledge: Economics and Accounting; Sales and Marketing; Transportation

Abilities: None above average

Economists

- ▲ Growth: 19%
- ▲ Annual Job Openings: 11,343
- ▲ Yearly Earnings $50,544
- ▲ Education Required: Bachelor's degree
- ▲ Self-employed: 21%
- ▲ Part-time: 8%

Economists

Conduct research, prepare reports, or formulate plans to aid in solution of economic problems arising from production and distribution of goods and services. May collect

and process economic and statistical data using econometric and sampling techniques. **Exclude market research analysts.** Studies economic and statistical data in area of specialization, such as finance, labor, or agriculture. Reviews and analyzes data to prepare reports, to forecast future marketing trends, and to stay abreast of economic changes. Organizes research data into report format, including graphic illustrations of research findings. Compiles data relating to research area, such as employment, productivity, and wages and hours. Formulates recommendations, policies, or plans to interpret markets or solve economic problems. Devises methods and procedures for collecting and processing data, using various econometric and sampling techniques. Develops economic guidelines and standards in preparing points of view used in forecasting trends and formulating economic policy. Supervises research projects and students' study projects. Provides advice and consultation to business and public and private agencies. Testifies at regulatory or legislative hearings to present recommendations. Teaches theories, principles, and methods of economics. Assigns work to staff.

Knowledge: Economics and Accounting; Personnel and Human Resources; Production and Processing; Food Production; Computers and Electronics; Mathematics; Geography; Education and Training; History and Archeology; Philosophy and Theology; Law, Government, and Jurisprudence

Abilities: Oral Comprehension; Written Comprehension; Oral Expression; Written Expression; Fluency of Ideas; Originality; Problem Sensitivity; Deductive Reasoning; Inductive Reasoning; Category Flexibility; Mathematical Reasoning; Number Facility; Speed of Closure; Near Vision; Speech Recognition; Speech Clarity

Market Research Analysts

Research market conditions in local, regional, or national areas to determine potential sales of a product or service. May gather information on competitors, prices, sales, and methods of marketing and distribution. May use survey results to create a marketing campaign based on regional preferences and buying habits. Examines and analyzes statistical data to forecast future marketing trends and to identify potential markets. Gathers data on competitors, and analyzes prices, sales, and method of marketing and distribution. Establishes research methodology and designs format for data gathering, such as surveys, opinion polls, or questionnaires. Collects data on customer preferences and buying habits. Checks consumer reaction to new or improved products or services. Prepares reports and graphic illustrations of findings. Attends staff conferences to submit findings and proposals to management for consideration. Translates complex numerical data into nontechnical, written text.

Knowledge: Economics and Accounting; Sales and Marketing; Customer and Personal Service; Food Production; Computers and Electronics; Mathematics; Psychology; Geography; Philosophy and Theology

Abilities: Written Expression; Deductive Reasoning; Inductive Reasoning; Mathematical Reasoning; Number Facility; Speed of Closure; Selective Attention; Near Vision; Auditory Attention

Education Administrators

▲ Growth: 12%
▲ Annual Job Openings: 39,333
▲ Yearly Earnings $52,436
▲ Education Required: Work experience, plus degree
▲ Self-employed: 7%
▲ Part-time: 9%

College and University Administrators

Plan, direct, and coordinate research and instructional programs at postsecondary institutions, including universities, colleges, and junior and community colleges. Exclude college presidents. Establishes operational policies and procedures and develops academic objectives. Directs work activities of personnel engaged in administration of academic institutions, departments, and alumni organizations. Meets with academic and administrative personnel to disseminate information, identify problems, monitor progress reports, and ensure adherence to goals and objectives. Evaluates personnel and physical plant operations, student programs, and statistical and research data to implement procedures or modifications to administrative policies. Advises staff and students on problems relating to policies, program administration, and financial and personal matters, and recommends solutions. Estimates and allocates department funding based on financial success of previous courses and other pertinent factors. Completes and submits operating budget for approval, controls expenditures, and maintains financial reports and records. Consults with staff, students, alumni, and subject experts to determine needs/feasibility, and to formulate admission policies and educational programs. Represents college/university as liaison officer with accrediting agencies and to exchange information between academic institutions and in community. Determines course schedules and correlates room assignments to ensure optimum use of buildings and equipment. Confers with other academic staff to explain admission requirements and transfer credit policies, and compares course equivalencies to university/college curriculum. Negotiates with foundation and industry representatives to secure loans for university and identify costs and materials for building construction. Recruits, employs, trains, and terminates department personnel. Reviews student misconduct reports requiring disciplinary action and counsels students to ensure conformance to university policies. Coordinates alumni functions and encourages alumni endorsement of recruiting and fundraising activities. Plans and promotes athletic policies, sports events, ticket sales, and student participation in social, cultural, and recreational activities. Assists faculty and staff to conduct orientation programs, teach classes, issue student transcripts, and prepare commencement lists. Audits financial status of student organization and facility accounts, and certifies income reports from event ticket sales. Advises student organizations, sponsors faculty activities, and arranges for caterers, entertainers, and decorators at scheduled events. Selects and counsels candidates for financial aid, and coordinates issuing and collecting of student aid payments.

Knowledge: Administration and Management; Economics and Accounting; Sales and Marketing; Customer and Personal Service; Personnel and Human Resources; Mathematics; Psychology; Sociology and Anthropology; Therapy and Counseling; Education and Training; English Language; Foreign Language; History and Archeology; Philosophy and Theology; Public Safety and Security; Law, Government, and Jurisprudence; Communications and Media

Abilities: Oral Comprehension; Written Comprehension; Oral Expression; Written Expression; Fluency of Ideas; Originality; Problem Sensitivity; Deductive Reasoning; Inductive Reasoning; Category Flexibility; Mathematical Reasoning; Number Facility; Memorization; Speed of Closure; Selective Attention; Near Vision; Far Vision; Speech Recognition; Speech Clarity

Educational Program Directors

Plan, develop, and administer programs to provide educational opportunities for students. Establishes program philosophy, plans, policies, and academic codes of ethics to maintain educational standards for student screening, placement, and training. Plans, directs, and monitors instructional methods and content for educational, vocational, or student activity programs. Reviews and approves new programs or recommends modifications to existing programs. Evaluates programs to determine effectiveness, efficiency, and utilization, and to ensure activities comply with federal, state, and local regulations. Prepares and submits budget requests, or grant proposals to solicit program funding. Determines scope of educational program offerings, and prepares drafts of course schedules and descriptions to estimate staffing and facility requirements. Coordinates outreach activities with businesses, communities, and other institutions or organizations to identify educational needs and establish and coordinate programs. Collects and analyzes survey data, regulatory information, and demographic and employment trends to forecast enrollment patterns and curriculum changes. Directs and coordinates activities of teachers or administrators at daycare centers, schools, public agencies, and institutions. Determines allocations of funds for staff, supplies, materials, and equipment, and authorizes purchases. Organizes and directs committees of specialists, volunteers, and staff to provide technical and advisory assistance for programs. Plans and coordinates consumer research and educational services to assist organizations in product development and marketing. Recruits, hires, trains, and evaluates primary and supplemental staff, and recommends personnel actions for programs and services. Contacts and addresses commercial, community, or political groups to promote educational programs and services or to lobby for legislative changes. Writes articles, manuals, and other publications and assists in the distribution of promotional literature. Confers with parents and staff to discuss educational activities, policies, and student behavioral or learning problems. Counsels and provides guidance to students regarding personal, academic, or behavioral problems. Reviews and interprets government codes and develops programs to ensure facility safety, security, and maintenance. Completes, maintains, or assigns preparation of attendance, activity, planning, or personnel reports and records for officials and agencies. Teaches classes or courses to students.

Knowledge: Administration and Management; Clerical; Economics and Accounting; Sales and Marketing; Customer and Personal Service; Personnel and Human Resources; Food Production; Mathematics; Psychology; Sociology and Anthropology; Therapy and Counseling; Education and Training; English Language; History and Archeology; Philosophy and Theology; Public Safety and Security; Law, Government, and Jurisprudence; Telecommunications; Communications and Media

Abilities: Oral Comprehension; Written Comprehension; Oral Expression; Written Expression; Fluency of Ideas; Originality; Problem Sensitivity; Deductive Reasoning; Inductive Reasoning; Information Ordering; Category Flexibility; Mathematical Reasoning; Number Facility; Memorization; Speed of Closure; Selective Attention; Time Sharing; Near Vision; Far Vision; Speech Recognition; Speech Clarity

Instructional Coordinators

Develop instructional material, educational content, and instructional methods to provide guidelines to educators and instructors for developing curricula, conducting courses, and incorporating current technology. Researches, evaluates, and prepares recommendations on curricula, instructional methods, and materials for school system. Develops tests, questionnaires, and procedures to measure effectiveness of curriculum and to determine if program objectives are being met. Prepares or approves manuals, guidelines, and reports on state educational policies and practices for distribution to school districts. Orders or authorizes purchase of instructional materials, supplies, equipment, and visual aids designed to meet educational needs of students. Confers with school officials, teachers, and administrative staff to plan and develop curricula and establish guidelines for educational programs. Confers with educational committees and advisory groups to gather information on instructional methods and materials related to specific academic subjects. Advises teaching and administrative staff in assessment, curriculum development, management of student behavior, and use of materials and equipment. Observes, evaluates, and recommends changes in work of teaching staff to strengthen teaching skills in classroom. Plans, conducts, and evaluates training programs and conferences for teachers to study new classroom procedures, instructional materials, and teaching aids. Advises school officials on implementation of state and federal programs and procedures. Conducts or participates in workshops, committees, and conferences designed to promote intellectual, social, and physical welfare of students. Coordinates activities of workers engaged in cataloging, distributing, and maintaining educational materials and equipment in curriculum library and laboratory. Interprets and enforces provisions of state education codes and rules and regulations of state board of education. Prepares or assists in preparation of grant proposals, budgets, and program policies and goals. Addresses public audiences to explain and elicit support for program objectives. Recruits, interviews, and recommends hiring of teachers. Reviews student files and confers with educators, parents, and other concerned parties to decide student placement and provision of services. Inspects and authorizes repair of instructional equipment, such as musical instruments.

Knowledge: Administration and Management; Economics and Accounting; Sales and Marketing; Personnel and Human Resources; Psychology; Sociology and Anthropology; Therapy and Counseling; Education and Training; English Language; Foreign Language; Fine Arts; History and Archeology; Philosophy and Theology; Law, Government, and Jurisprudence; Communications and Media

Abilities: Oral Comprehension; Written Comprehension; Oral Expression; Written Expression; Fluency of Ideas; Originality; Memorization; Speech Recognition; Speech Clarity

Electronics Mechanics and Technicians

▲ Growth: 13%
▲ Annual Job Openings: 3,301
▲ Yearly Earnings $29,993
▲ Education Required: Postsecondary vocational training
▲ Self-employed: 3%
▲ Part-time: 2%

Electronics Mechanics and Technicians

Install, maintain, and repair electronic equipment, such as industrial controls, telemetering and missile control systems, radar systems, transmitters, and antennae. Analyzes technical requirements of customer desiring to utilize electronic equipment, and performs installation and maintenance duties. Replaces or repairs defective components, using hand tools and technical documents. Adjusts defective components, using hand tools and technical documents. Installs equipment in industrial or military establishments and in aircraft and missiles. Calibrates testing instruments and installed or repaired equipment to prescribed specifications. Tests faulty equipment, using test equipment and applying knowledge of functional operation of electronic unit and systems, to diagnose malfunction. Inspects components of equipment for defects, such as loose connections and frayed wire, and for accuracy of assembly and installation. Determines feasibility of using standardized equipment, and develops specifications for equipment required to perform additional functions. Operates equipment to demonstrate use of equipment and to analyze malfunctions. Services electrical radioactivity-detecting instruments used to locate radioactive formations in oil- or gas-well boreholes, using special testing apparatus. Studies blueprints, schematics, manuals, and other specifications to determine installation procedures. Converses with equipment operators to ascertain whether mechanical or human error contributed to equipment breakdown. Maintains records of repairs, calibrations, and tests. Enters information into computer to copy program or to draw, modify, or store schematics, applying knowledge of software package used. Consults with customer, supervisor, and engineers to plan layout of equipment and to resolve problems in system operation and maintenance. Signs overhaul documents for equipment replaced or repaired. Advises management regarding customer satisfaction, product performance, and suggestions for product improvements. Accompanies flight crew to perform in-flight adjustments and to determine and record required post-flight repair work. Supervises workers in installing, testing, tuning, and adjusting equipment to obtain optimum operating performance. Instructs workers in electronic theory.

Knowledge: Administration and Management; Personnel and Human Resources; Computers and Electronics; Engineering and Technology; Design; Mathematics; Physics; Education and Training; Telecommunications

Abilities: Oral Comprehension; Oral Expression; Deductive Reasoning; Information Ordering; Mathematical Reasoning; Visualization; Finger Dexterity

Electrical and Electronic Technicians

▲ Growth: 15%
▲ Annual Job Openings: 31,145
▲ Yearly Earnings $33,800
▲ Education Required: Associate degree
▲ Self-employed: 0%
▲ Part-time: 3%

Electronics Engineering Technicians

Lay out, build, test, troubleshoot, repair, and modify developmental and production electronic components, parts, equipment, and systems, such as computer equipment, missile control instrumentation, electron tubes, test equipment, and machine tool numerical controls, applying principles and theories of electronics, electrical circuitry, engineering mathematics, electronic and electrical testing, and physics. Reads blueprints, wiring diagrams, schematic drawings, and engineering instructions for assembling electronics units, applying knowledge of electronic theory and components. Fabricates parts, such as coils, terminal boards, and chassis, using bench lathes, drills, or other machine tools. Assembles circuitry or electronic components, according to engineering instructions, technical manuals, and knowledge of electronics, using hand tools and power tools. Tests electronics unit, using standard test equipment, to evaluate performance and determine needs for adjustments. Adjusts and replaces defective or improperly functioning circuitry and electronics components, using hand tools and soldering iron. Designs basic circuitry and sketches for design documentation, as directed by engineers, using drafting instruments and computer-aided design equipment. Assists engineers in development of testing techniques, laboratory equipment, and circuitry or installation specifications, by writing reports and recording data.

Knowledge: Production and Processing; Computers and Electronics; Engineering and Technology; Design; Building and Construction; Mathematics; Physics

Abilities: None above average

Calibration and Instrumentation Technicians

Develop, test, calibrate, operate, and repair electrical, mechanical, electromechanical, electrohydraulic, or electronic measuring and recording instruments, apparatus, and equipment. Plans sequence of testing and calibration program for instruments and equipment, according to blueprints, schematics, technical manuals, and other specifications. Sets up test equipment and conducts tests on performance and reliability of mechanical, structural, or electromechanical equipment. Modifies performance and operation of component parts and circuitry to specifications, using test equipment and precision instruments. Selects sensing, telemetering, and recording instrumentation and circuitry. Disassembles and reassembles instruments and equipment, using hand tools, and inspects instruments and equipment for defects. Sketches plans for developing jigs, fixtures, instruments, and related nonstandard apparatus. Analyzes and converts test data, using mathematical formulas, and reports results and proposed modifications. Performs preventive and corrective maintenance of test apparatus and peripheral equipment. Confers with engineers, supervisor, and other technical workers to assist with equipment installation, maintenance, and repair techniques.

Knowledge: Computers and Electronics; Engineering and Technology; Design; Mechanical; Mathematics

Abilities: Written Comprehension; Deductive Reasoning; Information Ordering; Mathematical Reasoning

Electrical Engineering Technicians

Apply electrical theory and related knowledge to test and modify developmental or operational electrical machinery and electrical control equipment and circuitry in industrial or commercial plants and laboratories. Sets up and operates test equipment to evaluate performance of developmental parts, assemblies, or systems under simulated operating conditions. Modifies electrical prototypes, parts, assemblies, and systems to correct functional deviations. Plans method and sequence of operations for testing and developing experimental electronic and electrical equipment. Assembles electrical and electronic systems and prototypes, according to engineering data and knowledge of electrical principles, using hand tools and measuring instruments. Analyzes and interprets test information. Draws diagrams and writes engineering specifications to clarify design details and functional criteria of experimental electronics units. Collaborates with electrical engineer and other personnel to solve developmental problems. Maintains and repairs testing equipment.

Knowledge: Computers and Electronics; Engineering and Technology; Design; Mathematics; Physics

Abilities: Deductive Reasoning; Information Ordering; Mathematical Reasoning; Visualization

Sound Engineering Technicians

Operate machines and equipment to record, synchronize, mix, or reproduce music, voices, and previously recorded sound effects. Records speech, music, and other sounds on recording media, using recording equipment. Mixes and edits voices, music, and taped sound effects during stage performances, using sound-mixing board. Synchronizes and equalizes prerecorded dialog, music, and sound effects with visual action of motion picture or television production, using control console. Reproduces and duplicates sound recordings from original recording media, using sound editing and duplication equipment. Regulates volume level and quality of sound during motion picture, phonograph, television, or radio production recording sessions, using control console. Sets up, adjusts, and tests recording equipment to prepare for recording session. Keeps log of recordings. Maintains recording equipment. Supervises workers preparing and producing sound effects for radio, film, and videotape productions.

Knowledge: Computers and Electronics; Engineering and Technology; Telecommunications; Communications and Media

Abilities: Flexibility of Closure; Selective Attention; Response Orientation; Hearing Sensitivity; Auditory Attention; Sound Localization

Laser Technicians

Construct, install, and test gas or solid-state laser devices, according to engineering specifications and project instructions. Sets up electronic and optical instruments to test laser device, using electrical or optical inputs. Operates controls of vacuum pump and gas transfer equipment to fill laser body with specified volume and pressure of gases, and tests laser body for pressure leaks, using leak detector. Reviews assembly layout, blueprints, and sketches, and confers with engineering personnel to interpret production details of laser for workers. Analyzes test data and prepares technical reports for engineering personnel to recommend solutions to technical problems. Installs and aligns optical parts, such as mirrors and wave plates, in laser body, using precision instruments. Assembles laser body in chassis, and installs and aligns electronic components, tubing, and wiring to connect controls.

Knowledge: Computers and Electronics; Engineering and Technology; Design; Physics

Abilities: Oral Comprehension; Written Comprehension; Oral Expression; Written Expression; Inductive Reasoning; Information Ordering; Number Facility; Visualization; Finger Dexterity; Control Precision; Near Vision

Radio Operators

Receive and transmit communications using radiotelegraph or radiotelephone equipment, in accordance with government regulations. May repair equipment. Communicates by radio with test pilots, engineering personnel, and others during flight testing to relay information. Communicates with receiving operator to give and receive instruction for transmission. Turns controls or throws switches to activate power, adjust voice volume and modulation, and set transmitter on specified frequency. Repairs transmitting equipment, using electronic testing equipment, hand tools, and power tools, to maintain communication system in operative condition. Determines and obtains bearings of source from which signal originated, using direction-finding procedures and equipment. Monitors emergency frequency for distress calls and dispatches emergency equipment. Operates sound-recording equipment to record signals and preserve broadcast for analysis by intelligence personnel. Coordinates radio searches for overdue or lost airplanes. Examines and operates new equipment prior to installation in airport radio stations. Establishes and maintains standards of operation by periodic inspections of equipment and routine tests. Reviews company and Federal Aviation Authority regulations regarding radio communications, and reports violations. Maintains station log of messages transmitted and received for activities such as flight testing and fire locations.

Knowledge: Computers and Electronics; Geography; Telecommunications; Communications and Media

Abilities: Oral Expression; Flexibility of Closure; Selective Attention; Time Sharing; Control Precision; Response Orientation; Reaction Time; Hearing Sensitivity; Auditory Attention; Sound Localization; Speech Recognition; Speech Clarity

Electrical and Electronics Engineers

- ▲ Growth: 29%
- ▲ Annual Job Openings: 19,098
- ▲ Yearly Earnings $53,227
- ▲ Education Required: Bachelor's degree
- ▲ Self-employed: 3%
- ▲ Part-time: 2%

Electrical Engineers

Design, develop, test, or supervise the manufacturing and installation of electrical equipment, components, or systems for commercial, industrial, military, or scientific use. Exclude computer engineers. Designs electrical instruments, equipment, facilities, components, products, and systems for commercial, industrial, and domestic purposes. Plans and implements research methodology and procedures to apply principles of electrical theory to engineering projects. Prepares and studies technical drawings, specifications of electrical systems, and topographical maps to ensure installation and operations conform to standards and customer requirements. Develops applications of controls, instruments, and systems for new commercial, domestic, and industrial uses. Directs operations and coordinates manufacturing, construction, installation, maintenance, and testing activities to ensure compliance with specifications, applicable codes, and customer requirements. Plans layout of electric power-generating plants and distribution lines and stations. Conducts field surveys and studies maps, graphs, diagrams, and other data to identify and correct power system problems. Performs detailed calculations to compute and establish manufacturing, construction, and installation standards and specifications. Confers with engineers, customers, and others to discuss existing or potential engineering projects and products. Inspects completed installations and observes operations for conformance to design and equipment specifications, and operational and safety standards. Evaluates and analyzes data regarding electric power systems and stations, and recommends changes to improve operating efficiency. Estimates labor, material, and construction costs, and prepares specifications for purchase of materials and equipment. Collects data relating to commercial and residential development, population, and power system interconnection to determine operating efficiency of electrical systems. Compiles data and writes reports regarding existing and potential engineering studies and projects. Operates computer-assisted engineering and design software and equipment to perform engineering tasks. Investigates customer or public complaints, determines nature and extent of problem, and recommends remedial measures.

Knowledge: Administration and Management; Economics and Accounting; Production and Processing; Computers and Electronics; Engineering and Technology; Design; Building and Construction; Mechanical; Mathematics; Physics; Public Safety and Security; Telecommunications

Abilities: Oral Comprehension; Written Comprehension; Oral Expression; Written Expression; Fluency of Ideas; Originality; Problem Sensitivity; Deductive Reasoning; Inductive Reasoning; Information Ordering; Category Flexibility; Mathematical Reasoning; Number Facility; Memorization; Speed of Closure; Flexibility of Closure; Spatial Orientation; Visualization; Finger Dexterity; Wrist-Finger Speed

Electronics Engineers, Except Computer

Research, design, develop, and test electronic components and systems for commercial, industrial, military, or scientific use, utilizing knowledge of electronic theory and materials properties. Design electronic circuits and components for use in fields such as telecommunications, aerospace guidance and propulsion control, acoustics, or instruments and controls. Exclude computer hardware engineers. Designs electronic components, products, and systems for commercial, industrial, medical, military, and scientific applications. Develops operational, maintenance, and testing procedures for electronic products, components, equipment, and systems. Plans and develops applications and modifications for electronic properties used in components, products, and systems, to improve technical performance. Plans and implements research, methodology, and procedures to apply principles of electronic theory to engineering projects. Directs and coordinates activities concerned with manufacture, construction, installation, maintenance, operation, and modification of electronic equipment, products, and systems. Evaluates operational systems and recommends repair or design modifications based on factors such as environment, service, cost, and system capabilities. Analyzes system requirements, capacity, cost, and customer needs to determine feasibility of project and to develop system plan. Conducts studies to gather information regarding current services, equipment capacities, traffic data, and acquisition and installation costs. Inspects electronic equipment, instruments, products, and systems to ensure conformance to specifications, safety standards, and applicable codes and regulations. Prepares engineering sketches and specifications for construction, relocation, and installation of transmitting and receiving equipment, facilities, products, and systems. Confers with engineers, customers, and others to discuss existing and potential engineering projects or products. Operates computer-assisted engineering and design software and equipment to perform engineering tasks. Provides technical assistance to field and laboratory staff regarding equipment standards and problems, and applications of transmitting and receiving methods. Prepares, reviews, and maintains maintenance schedules and operational reports and charts. Reviews or prepares budget and cost estimates for equipment, construction, and installation projects, and controls expenditures. Determines material and equipment needs, and orders supplies. Investigates causes of personal injury resulting from contact with high-voltage communications equipment.

Knowledge: Administration and Management; Economics and Accounting; Customer and Personal Service; Production and Processing; Computers and Electronics; Engineering and Technology; Design; Building and Construction; Mechanical; Mathematics; Physics; English Language; Telecommunications; Communications and Media

Abilities: Oral Comprehension; Written Comprehension; Oral Expression; Written Expression; Fluency of Ideas; Originality; Problem Sensitivity; Deductive Reasoning; Inductive Reasoning; Information Ordering; Category Flexibility; Mathematical Reasoning; Number Facility; Memorization; Speed of Closure; Flexibility of Closure; Visualization; Time Sharing; Finger Dexterity; Wrist-Finger Speed; Near Vision

Electrolytic Plating Machine Setters and Operators

▲ Growth: 10%
▲ Annual Job Openings: 6,553
▲ Yearly Earnings $21,278
▲ Education Required: Moderate-term O-J-T
▲ Self-employed: 0%
▲ Part-time: 1%

Electrolytic Plating and Coating Machine Setters and Set-Up Operators, Metal and Plastic

Set up or set up and operate electrolytic plating or coating machines, such as continuous multistrand electrogalvanizing machines, to coat metal or plastic products electrolytically with chromium, copper, cadmium, or other metal, to provide protective or decorative surfaces or to build up worn surfaces. Moves controls to permit electrodeposition of metal on object or to regulate movement of wire strand to obtain specified thickness. Adjusts voltage and amperage, based on observations. Determines size and composition of object to be plated and amount of electrical current and time required, following work order. Suspends object, such as part or mold, from cathode rod (negative terminal), and immerses object in plating solution. Suspends stick or piece of plating metal from anode (positive terminal), and immerses metal in plating solution. Mixes chemical solutions, fills tanks, and charges furnaces. Removes plated object from solution at periodic intervals and observes object to ensure conformance to specifications. Plates small objects, such as nuts or bolts, using motor-driven barrel. Immerses object in cleaning and rinsing baths to complete plating process. Examines object at end of process to determine thickness of metal deposit, or measures thickness, using instruments such as micrometers. Measures, marks, and masks areas excluded from plating. Grinds, polishes, or rinses object in water, and dries object to maintain clean, even surface.

Knowledge: Chemistry

Abilities: None above average

Electrolytic Plating and Coating Machine Operators and Tenders, Metal and Plastic

Operate or tend electrolytic plating or coating machines, such as zinc-plating machines and anodizing machines, to coat metal or plastic products electrolytically with chromium, zinc, copper, cadmium, or other metal to provide protective or decorative

surfaces or to build up worn surfaces. Measures or estimates amounts of electric current needed and time required to coat objects. Adjusts dials to regulate flow of current and voltage supplied to terminals to control plating process. Positions objects to be plated in frame, or suspends them from positive or negative terminals of power supply. Removes object from plating solution after specified time or when desired thickness of metal is deposited on them. Mixes and tests plating solution to specified formula and turns valves to fill tank with solution. Monitors and measures thickness of electroplating on component part to verify conformance to specifications, using micrometer. Mixes forming acid solution, treats battery plates, and removes and rinses formed plates. Immerses objects to be coated or plated into cleaning solutions, or sprays with conductive solution to prepare object for plating. Rinses coated object in cleansing liquids and dries with cloth or centrifugal driers, or by tumbling in sawdust-filled barrels. Lubricates moving parts of plating conveyor and cleans plating and cleaning solution tanks.

Knowledge: Chemistry

Abilities: None above average

Electromedical and Biomedical Equipment Repairers

▲ Growth: 12%
▲ Annual Job Openings: 1,427
▲ Yearly Earnings $32,718
▲ Education Required: Long-term O-J-T
▲ Self-employed: 0%
▲ Part-time: 9%

Electromedical and Biomedical Equipment Repairers

Test, adjust, and repair electromedical equipment, using hand tools and meters. Inspects and tests malfunctioning medical and related equipment, using test and analysis instruments and following manufacturers' specifications. Repairs and replaces defective parts, such as motors, clutches, tubes, transformers, resistors, condensers, and switches, using hand tools. Calibrates and adjusts components and equipment, using hand tools, power tools, measuring devices, and following manufacturers' manuals and troubleshooting techniques. Disassembles malfunctioning equipment and removes defective components. Safety-tests medical equipment and facility's structural environment to ensure patient and staff safety from electrical or mechanical hazards. Solders loose connections, using soldering iron. Maintains various equipment and apparatus, such as patient monitors, electrocardiographs, x-ray units, defibrillators, electrosurgical units, anesthesia apparatus, pacemakers, and sterilizers. Installs medical, dental, and related technical equipment in medical and research facilities. Fabricates hardware, using machine and power tools and hand tools. Modifies or develops instruments or devices, under supervision of medical or engineering staff. Cleans and lubricates equipment, using solvents, rags, and lubricants. Logs records of maintenance and repair work and approved updates of equipment as required by manufacturer. Consults with medical or research staff to ensure that equipment functions properly and safely. Demonstrates and explains correct operation of equipment to medical personnel. Represents equipment manufacturer as salesperson or service technician.

Knowledge: Sales and Marketing; Computers and Electronics; Engineering and Technology; Design; Mechanical; Chemistry; Medicine and Dentistry; Telecommunications

Abilities: Written Comprehension; Visualization; Selective Attention; Finger Dexterity; Explosive Strength; Hearing Sensitivity; Sound Localization; Speech Clarity

Electroneurodiagnostic Technologists

▲ Growth: 24%
▲ Annual Job Openings: 818
▲ Yearly Earnings $30,992
▲ Education Required: Moderate-term O-J-T
▲ Self-employed: 0%
▲ Part-time: 22%

Electroneurodiagnostic Technologists

Record electrical activity of the brain and other nervous system functions using a variety of techniques and equipment. May prepare patients for the test, obtain medical history, calculate results, and maintain equipment. Measures electrical activity of brain and nerves, using electroencephalograph (EEG), polysomnograph, or electromyograph to diagnose brain, sleep, and nervous system disorders. Operates recording instruments and supplemental equipment and chooses settings for optimal viewing of nervous system. Attaches electrodes to predetermined locations, and verifies functioning of electrodes and recording instrument. Records montage (electrode combination) and instrument settings, and observes and notes patient's behavior during test. Performs other physiological tests, such as electrocardiogram, electrooculogram, and ambulatory electroencephalogram. Measures patient's head and other body parts, using tape measure, and marks points where electrodes are to be placed. Conducts visual, auditory, and somatosensory-evoked-potential response tests to measure latency of response to stimuli. Writes technical reports summarizing test results to assist physician in diagnosis of brain disorders. Monitors patient during surgery, using EEG or evoked-potential instrument. Performs video monitoring of patient's actions during test.

Knowledge: Computers and Electronics; Biology; Medicine and Dentistry; English Language

Abilities: Written Expression; Selective Attention

Electronic Semiconductor Processors

- ▲ Growth: 12%
- ▲ Annual Job Openings: 3,801
- ▲ Yearly Earnings $24,336
- ▲ Education Required: Moderate-term O-J-T
- ▲ Self-employed: 0%
- ▲ Part-time: 2%

Electronic Semiconductor Processors

Process materials used in manufacture of electronic semiconductors. Measures and weighs amounts of crystal-growing materials, mixes and grinds materials, and loads materials into container, following procedures. Forms seed crystal for crystal growing or locates crystal axis of ingot, using x-ray equipment, drill, and sanding machine. Aligns photomask pattern on photoresist layer, exposes pattern to ultraviolet light, and develops pattern, using specialized equipment. Attaches ampoule to diffusion pump to remove air from ampoule, and seals ampoule, using blowtorch. Places semiconductor wafers in processing containers or equipment holders, using vacuum wand or tweezers. Monitors operation, and adjusts controls of processing machines and equipment, to produce compositions with specific electronic properties. Manipulates valves, switches, and buttons, or keys commands into control panels to start semiconductor processing cycles. Etches, laps, polishes, or grinds wafers or ingots, using etching, lapping, polishing, or grinding equipment. Operates saw to cut remelt into sections of specified size or to cut ingots into wafers. Cleans and dries materials and equipment using solvent, etching or sandblasting equipment, and drying equipment to remove contaminants or photoresist. Studies work order, instructions, formulas, and processing charts to determine specifications and sequence of operations. Loads and unloads equipment chambers and transports finished product to storage or to area for further processing. Inspects materials, components, or products for surface defects and measures circuitry, using electronic test equipment, precision measuring instruments, and standard procedures. Counts, sorts, and weighs processed items. Stamps or etches identifying information on finished component. Maintains processing, production, and inspection information and reports.

Knowledge: Production and Processing

Abilities: Control Precision

Electronic Semiconductor Wafer Etchers and Engravers

Tend or use equipment to etch or engrave semiconductor wafers. Sets and adjusts equipment controls to activate etch cycle to etch or engrave wafer surface. Places loaded container into air or spin dryer, adjusts controls, and tends machine that rinses and dries etched wafers. Monitors equipment control panels to ensure chemicals and materials meet processing specifications. Immerses containers in chemical and water baths to etch circuitry patterns into or strip excess resist from wafer surfaces. Measures dimensions of wafers, such as thickness, flatness, or diameter, using microscope measuring attachment, micrometer, or flatness or thickness gauge. Calculates etching time based on thickness of material to be removed from wafers or crystals. Scribes identifying information on designated area of wafers, following specifications and using metal stylus. Inspects etched and stripped wafers, using microscope, to detect scratches or contaminants and to ensure conformance to specifications. Replaces etching and rinsing solutions in equipment and cleans bath containers and work area. Inserts or removes semiconductor wafers from containers, such as boats or cassettes, using vacuum wand or tweezers. Records production details.

Knowledge: Chemistry

Abilities: Flexibility of Closure; Selective Attention; Manual Dexterity; Finger Dexterity; Control Precision; Speed of Limb Movement; Gross Body Equilibrium; Depth Perception

Electronic Semiconductor Test and Development Technicians

Operate variety of machines and equipment used in production and testing of electronic semiconductor wafers and chips. Operates equipment to convert integrated circuit layout designs into working photomasks, using knowledge of microelectronic processing, equipment, procedures, and specifications. Operates equipment to clean, coat, bake, expose, develop, and cure photoresist on wafers. Operates equipment to grow layers of dielectric, metal, and semiconductor material on masked areas of wafers. Operates equipment to clean, etch, or remove materials not covered by photoresist. Operates equipment to implant chemicals to selective areas of wafer substrate to alter substrate characteristics. Inspects and measures test wafer, using electronic measuring equipment and microscope, to ensure wafers meet processing and company specifications. Assembles, dices, cleans, mounts, bonds, and packages integrated circuit devices manually or using special equipment. Analyzes test results, using engineering specifications and calculator. Records test results in logbooks. Discusses production problems with workers. Writes reports on equipment repair, recalibration recommendations, test results, and operator procedure violations. Assists in technical writing of semiconductor processing specifications.

Knowledge: Production and Processing; Computers and Electronics; Engineering and Technology; Mathematics

Abilities: Information Ordering; Mathematical Reasoning; Number Facility; Near Vision

Electronic Semiconductor Crystal-Growing Technicians and Equipment Operators

Set up and operate furnaces and reactors used to grow crystals from materials—such as silicon, quartz, or gallium arsenide—used in the production of semiconductors. Sets and adjusts computerized or mechanical controls to regulate power level, temperature, vacuum, and rotation speed of furnace, according to crystal-growing specifications. Observes and monitors material meltdown and crystal growth, and readjusts equipment controls as necessary. Connects reactor to computer, using hand tools and power tools. Loads computer-controlled equipment with materials to grow layer of semiconductor material on wafer surface. Inspects wafers for defects, such as scratches, growths, and pits. Activates computer program to clean equipment or cleans by hand, using vacuum cleaner and cleaning supplies Measures and tests thickness and bow of wafer and thickness and photo-luminescence of epitaxial layer, using gauges and test equipment. Inspects equipment for leaks, diagnoses equipment malfunctions, and requests equipment repairs. Analyzes processing procedures and equipment functions to identify and resolve semiconductor crystal-growth problems. Cleans semiconductor wafers, using cleaning equipment such as chemical baths, automatic wafer cleaners, or blow-off wands. Inscribes line on wafer, using metal scribe, and breaks off sample section of wafer. Cuts line on light bar sample to isolate die, using wafer saw, and measures brightness of die, using tester. Computes production statistics, surface area of wafer, or defects per square inch, using calculator. Replaces furnace liners and reactor accessories, such as bell jar and carousel. Constructs sheet metal housing, and installs and repairs wiring, switches, gauges, and lines on reactor, using hand tools and power tools. Records production data in logbook and processing documents. Demonstrates and explains crystal-growing procedures to workers.

Knowledge: Computers and Electronics; Mechanical; Mathematics; Physics; Chemistry

Abilities: Flexibility of Closure; Perceptual Speed; Visualization; Selective Attention; Finger Dexterity; Response Orientation; Reaction Time; Gross Body Equilibrium; Hearing Sensitivity; Sound Localization

Electronic Semiconductor Sawyers, Abraders, and Polishers

Operate equipment to grind, abrade, or scribe semiconductor wafers. Adjusts equipment controls to set speed, angle, and thickness of cut. Monitors equipment cycle to verify accuracy of operation. Positions workpiece in holding fixture of sawing, drilling, grinding, or sanding equipment. Inspects sample workpiece for flaws, using x-ray machine, and measures workpiece with calipers and gauges. Readjusts controls based on inspection and measurements. Determines crystal orientations of ingot sections, using x-ray equipment, and draws orientation lines on ingot. Mounts crystal ingots or wafers on blocks or plastic laminate, using special mounting devices. Removes workpiece from equipment and cleans workpiece, using water, ultrasonic cleaner, or etching equipment. Records production information. Cleans and maintains equipment. Sorts and wraps finished workpieces in protective material.

Knowledge: Production and Processing

Abilities: Flexibility of Closure; Perceptual Speed; Selective Attention; Finger Dexterity; Control Precision; Dynamic Flexibility; Hearing Sensitivity; Sound Localization

Electronic Semiconductor Wafer Breakers, Mounters, and Packagers

Break, mount, and package crystals and wafers used in manufacture of electronic semiconductors. Breaks semiconductor wafers into individual dies, using hand tools or chemical solutions and breaking equipment. Positions, secures, and seals lids on semiconductor packages, using tweezers and heated chuck or automatic furnace. Places individual dies in carriers, using vacuum wand or brush. Positions wafers on cushion or waxed template. Tends equipment that attaches, mounts, presses, and disassembles templates and wafers. Attaches crystal ingot to graphite or epoxy backing and mounts on crystal saw block, using adhesive or wax. Sorts semiconductor crystal ingots according to size and crystal orientation. Inspects semiconductors to remove defective devices. Cleans dies and templates, using solutions and cleaning equipment. Maintains production records.

Knowledge: Computers and Electronics

Abilities: Finger Dexterity

Elementary Teachers

▲ Growth: 10%

▲ Annual Job Openings: 164,163

▲ Yearly Earnings $35,280

▲ Education Required: Bachelor's degree

▲ Self-employed: 0%

▲ Part-time: 11%

Teachers—Elementary School

Teach elementary pupils in public or private schools basic academic, social, and other formulative skills. Exclude special education teachers of the handicapped. Lectures, demonstrates, and uses audio-visual aids and computers to present academic, social, and motor skill subject matter to class. Teaches subjects such as math, science, or social studies. Prepares course objectives and outline for course of study, following curriculum guidelines or requirements of state and school. Prepares, administers, and corrects tests, and records results. Assigns lessons, corrects papers, and hears oral presentations. Teaches rules of conduct and maintains discipline and suitable learning environment in classroom and on playground. Evaluates student performance and discusses pupil academic and behavioral attitudes and achievements with parents. Keeps attendance and grade records and prepares reports as required by school. Counsels pupils when adjustment and academic problems arise. Supervises outdoor and indoor play activities. Teaches combined grade classes. Attends staff meetings, serves on committees, and attends workshops or in-service training activities. Coordinates class field trips. Prepares bulletin boards.

Knowledge: Administration and Management; Clerical; Customer and Personal Service; Mathematics; Chemistry; Biology; Psychology; Sociology and Anthropology; Geography; Medicine and Dentistry; Therapy and Counseling; Education and Training; English Language; Foreign Language; Fine Arts; History and Archeology; Philosophy and Theology; Law, Government, and Jurisprudence; Transportation

Abilities: Oral Comprehension; Written Comprehension; Oral Expression; Written Expression; Fluency of Ideas; Originality; Category Flexibility; Mathematical Reasoning; Number Facility; Memorization; Speed of Closure; Spatial Orientation; Time Sharing; Gross Body Equilibrium; Far Vision; Night Vision; Peripheral Vision; Auditory Attention; Speech Recognition; Speech Clarity

Elevator Installers and Repairers

▲ Growth: 8%

▲ Annual Job Openings: 2,695

▲ Yearly Earnings $45,843

▲ Education Required: Long-term O-J-T

▲ Self-employed: 0%

▲ Part-time: 7%

Elevator Installers and Repairers

Assemble, install, repair, and maintain electric and hydraulic freight and passenger elevators, escalators, and dumbwaiters. Assembles and installs electric and hydraulic freight and passenger elevators, escalators, and dumbwaiters. Inspects, tests, and adjusts elevators, escalators, and dumbwaiters to meet factory specifications and safety codes. Repairs or upgrades elevators, escalators, and dumbwaiters to meet safety regulations and building codes. Studies blueprints to determine layout of framework and foundations. Cuts prefabricated sections of framework, rails, and other components to specified dimensions. Completes service reports to verify conformance to prescribed standards.

Knowledge: Engineering and Technology; Building and Construction; Mechanical; Public Safety and Security

Abilities: Information Ordering; Dynamic Strength; Stamina; Extent Flexibility; Gross Body Equilibrium; Night Vision; Peripheral Vision; Depth Perception; Hearing Sensitivity

Emergency Medical Technicians

- ▲ Growth: 45%
- ▲ Annual Job Openings: 18,841
- ▲ Yearly Earnings $21,361
- ▲ Education Required: Postsecondary vocational training
- ▲ Self-employed: 0%
- ▲ Part-time: 22%

Emergency Medical Technicians

Administer first-aid treatment and transport sick or injured persons to medical facility, working as members of an emergency medical team. Administers first-aid treatment and life-support care to sick or injured persons in prehospital setting. Assists in removal and transport of victims to treatment center. Assesses nature and extent of illness or injury to establish and prioritize medical procedures. Observes, records, and reports patient's condition and reactions to drugs and treatment, to physician. Monitors cardiac patient, using electrocardiograph. Communicates with treatment center personnel to arrange reception of victims and to receive instructions for further treatment. Assists treatment center personnel to obtain and record victim's vital statistics, and to administer emergency treatment. Assists treatment center personnel to obtain information relating to circumstances of emergency. Drives mobile intensive care unit to specified location, following instructions from emergency medical dispatcher. Maintains vehicles and medical and communication equipment, and replenishes first-aid equipment and supplies.

Knowledge: Chemistry; Biology; Psychology; Geography; Medicine and Dentistry; Therapy and Counseling; Foreign Language; Telecommunications; Transportation

Abilities: Problem Sensitivity; Speed of Closure; Selective Attention; Time Sharing; Response Orientation; Rate Control; Reaction Time; Static Strength; Stamina; Gross Body Equilibrium; Night Vision; Peripheral Vision; Glare Sensitivity

Employment Interviewers

▲ Growth: 16%

▲ Annual Job Openings: 10,430

▲ Yearly Earnings $35,089

▲ Education Required: Bachelor's degree

▲ Self-employed: 0%

▲ Part-time: 6%

Employment Interviewers, Private or Public Employment Service

Interview job applicants in employment office and refer them to prospective employers for consideration. Search application files, notify selected applicants of job openings, and refer qualified applicants to prospective employers. Contact employers to verify referral results. Record and evaluate various pertinent data. Interviews job applicants to select people meeting employer qualifications. Refers selected applicants to person placing job order, according to policy of organization. Reviews employment applications and evaluates work history, education and training, job skills, compensation needs, and other qualifications of applicants. Records additional knowledge, skills, abilities, interests, test results, and other data pertinent to selection and referral of applicants. Reviews job orders and matches applicants with job requirements, utilizing manual or computerized file search. Informs applicants of job duties and responsibilities, compensation and benefits, work schedules, working conditions, promotional opportunities, and other related information. Keeps records of applicants not selected for employment. Searches for and recruits applicants for open positions. Conducts or arranges for skills, intelligence, or psychological testing of applicants. Performs reference and background checks on applicants. Evaluates selection and testing techniques by conducting research or follow-up activities and conferring with management and supervisory personnel. Contacts employers to solicit orders for job vacancies, and records information on forms to describe duties, hiring requirements, and related data. Refers applicants to vocational counseling services.

Knowledge: Administration and Management; Clerical; Sales and Marketing; Customer and Personal Service; Personnel and Human Resources; Psychology; Sociology and Anthropology; Therapy and Counseling

Abilities: Oral Comprehension

Engineering, Mathematical, and Natural Science Managers

▲ Growth: 45%
▲ Annual Job Openings: 37,494
▲ Yearly Earnings $65,686
▲ Education Required: Work experience, plus degree
▲ Self-employed: 0%
▲ Part-time: 6%

Engineering Managers

Plan, direct, and coordinate activities in such fields as architecture, engineering, and related research and development. These persons spend the greatest portion of their time in managerial work, for which a background consistent with that described for engineers is required. Exclude natural science managers; mathematical managers; computer operations, information systems, computer programming, and data processing managers; as well as managers of computer-related occupations. Establishes procedures and directs testing, operation, maintenance, and repair of transmitter equipment. Evaluates contract proposals, directs negotiation of research contracts, and prepares bids and contracts. Plans and directs installation, maintenance, testing, and repair of facilities and equipment. Directs, reviews, and approves product design and changes, and directs testing. Plans, coordinates, and directs engineering project, organizes and assigns staff, and directs integration of technical activities with products. Plans and directs oilfield development, gas and oil production, and geothermal drilling. Analyzes technology, resource needs, and market demand, and confers with management, production, and marketing staff to plan and assess feasibility of project. Plans, directs, and coordinates survey work with activities of other staff, certifies survey work, and writes land legal descriptions. Administers highway planning, construction, and maintenance, and reviews and recommends or approves contracts and cost estimates. Directs engineering of water control, treatment, and distribution projects. Confers with and prepares reports for officials, and speaks to public to solicit support.

Knowledge: Administration and Management; Economics and Accounting; Sales and Marketing; Personnel and Human Resources; Engineering and Technology; Design; Building and Construction; Mechanical; Mathematics; Physics; Chemistry; Psychology; Geography; English Language; History and Archeology; Public Safety and Security; Law, Government, and Jurisprudence; Telecommunications; Communications and Media

Abilities: Oral Comprehension; Written Comprehension; Oral Expression; Written Expression; Fluency of Ideas; Originality; Problem Sensitivity; Deductive Reasoning; Inductive Reasoning; Information Ordering; Category Flexibility; Mathematical Reasoning; Number Facility; Memorization; Speed of Closure; Spatial Orientation; Visualization; Selective

Attention; Time Sharing; Gross Body Equilibrium; Near Vision; Far Vision; Visual Color Discrimination; Peripheral Vision; Speech Recognition; Speech Clarity

Natural Sciences Managers

Plan, direct, and coordinate activities in such fields as life sciences, physical sciences, mathematics, statistics, and related research and development. These persons spend the greatest portion of their time in managerial work, for which a background consistent with that described for mathematicians or natural scientists is required. Exclude engineering managers; computer operations, information systems, computer programming, and data processing managers; as well as managers of computer-related occupations. Schedules, directs, and assigns duties to engineers, technicians, researchers, and other staff. Plans and directs research, development, and production activities of chemical plant. Coordinates successive phases of problem analysis, solution proposals, and testing. Prepares and administers budget, approves and reviews expenditures, and prepares financial reports. Reviews project activities, and prepares and reviews research, testing, and operational reports. Confers with scientists, engineers, regulators, and others to plan and review projects and to provide technical assistance. Advises and assists in obtaining patents or other legal requirements. Provides technical assistance to agencies conducting environmental studies.

Knowledge: Administration and Management; Economics and Accounting; Personnel and Human Resources; Production and Processing; Engineering and Technology; Mathematics; Physics; Chemistry; Biology; Psychology; Geography; Education and Training; English Language; Foreign Language; History and Archeology; Law, Government, and Jurisprudence

Abilities: Oral Comprehension; Written Comprehension; Oral Expression; Written Expression; Fluency of Ideas; Originality; Problem Sensitivity; Deductive Reasoning; Inductive Reasoning; Information Ordering; Category Flexibility; Mathematical Reasoning; Number Facility; Memorization; Speed of Closure; Perceptual Speed; Visualization; Selective Attention; Time Sharing; Near Vision; Far Vision; Speech Recognition; Speech Clarity

Computer and Information Systems Managers

Plan, direct, and coordinate activities in such fields as electronic data processing, information systems, systems analysis, and computer programming. These persons spend the greatest portion of their time in managerial work, for which a background consistent with that described for computer professionals—such as computer systems analysts, computer scientists, database administrators, computer programmers, and computer support specialists—would be required. Evaluates data processing project proposals and assesses project feasibility. Directs department, prepares and reviews operational reports, adjusts schedule to meet priorities, and prepares progress reports. Establishes work standards, directs training, participates in staffing and promotion decisions, and disciplines workers. Consults with users, management, vendors, and technicians to determine computing needs and system requirements. Analyzes workflow; assigns, schedules, and reviews work; and directs and coordinates with other departments. Meets with department heads, managers, supervisors, vendors, and others to solicit cooperation and resolve problems. Approves, prepares, monitors, and adjusts operational budget. Develops and interprets organizational goals, policies, and procedures, and reviews project plans.

Knowledge: Administration and Management; Clerical; Economics and Accounting; Sales and Marketing; Customer and Personal Service; Personnel and Human Resources; Computers and Electronics; Mathematics; Psychology; Education and Training; English Language; Communications and Media

Abilities: Oral Comprehension; Written Comprehension; Oral Expression; Written Expression; Fluency of Ideas; Originality; Problem Sensitivity; Deductive Reasoning; Inductive Reasoning; Information Ordering; Category Flexibility; Mathematical Reasoning; Number Facility; Memorization; Speed of Closure; Selective Attention; Time Sharing; Near Vision; Speech Recognition; Speech Clarity

Laboratory Managers

Coordinate activities of university science laboratory to assist faculty in teaching and research programs. Prepares and puts in place equipment scheduled for use during laboratory teaching sessions. Confers with teaching staff to evaluate new equipment and methods. Consults with laboratory coordinator to determine equipment purchase priorities based on budget allowances, condition of existing equipment, and scheduled activities. Demonstrates care and use of equipment to teaching assistants. Trains teaching staff and students in application and use of new equipment. Develops methods of laboratory experimentation, applying knowledge of scientific theory and computer capability. Builds prototype equipment, applying electromechanical knowledge and using hand tools and power tools. Diagnoses and repairs malfunctioning equipment, applying knowledge of shop mechanics and using gauges, meters, hand tools, and power tools. Teaches laboratory sessions in absence of teaching assistant.

Knowledge: Administration and Management; Economics and Accounting; Computers and Electronics; Engineering and Technology; Mathematics; Physics; Chemistry; Biology; Education and Training; English Language

Abilities: Speech Recognition

Excavation and Loading Machine Operators

- ▲ Growth: 11%
- ▲ Annual Job Openings: 4,626
- ▲ Yearly Earnings $28,558
- ▲ Education Required: Moderate-term O-J-T
- ▲ Self-employed: 18%
- ▲ Part-time: 4%

Excavating and Loading Machine Operators

Operate machinery equipped with scoops, shovels, or buckets to excavate and load loose materials. Operates power machinery, such as power shovel, stripping shovel, scraper loader (mucking machine), or backhoe (trench-excavating machine), to excavate and load material. Observes hand signals, grade stakes, and other markings when operating machines. Receives written or oral instructions to move or excavate material. Measures and verifies levels of rock or gravel, base, and other excavated material. Lubricates and repairs machinery and replaces parts, such as gears, bearings, and bucket teeth. Directs ground workers engaged in activities, such as moving stakes or markers.

Knowledge: Mechanical

Abilities: Spatial Orientation; Multilimb Coordination; Reaction Time; Trunk Strength; Gross Body Coordination; Gross Body Equilibrium; Depth Perception

Extruding and Forming Machine Operators

- ▲ Growth: 10%
- ▲ Annual Job Openings: 3,021
- ▲ Yearly Earnings $24,252
- ▲ Education Required: Moderate-term O-J-T
- ▲ Self-employed: 0%
- ▲ Part-time: 5%

Extruding and Forming Machine Operators and Tenders, Synthetic or Glass Fibers

Operate or tend machines that extrude and form continuous filaments from synthetic materials, such as liquid polymer, rayon, and fiberglass, preparatory to further processing. Operates or tends machines that extrude and form filaments from synthetic materials. Loads and adjusts materials into extruding and forming machines, using hand tools. Moves controls to activate and adjust extruding and forming machines. Presses buttons to stop machine when process is completed or malfunction detected. Observes machine operation, control board, and gauges to detect malfunctions. Removes excess or completed filament from machine, using hand tools. Notifies workers of defects and to adjust extruding and forming machines. Cleans and maintains extruding and forming machines, using hand tools. Records operational data on tag and attaches to machine.

Knowledge: None above average

Abilities: Perceptual Speed; Control Precision

Farm and Home Management Advisors

▲ Growth: -38%
▲ Annual Job Openings: 3,078
▲ Yearly Earnings $48,505
▲ Education Required: Bachelor's degree
▲ Self-employed: 9%
▲ Part-time: 42%

Farm and Home Management Advisors

Advise, instruct, and assist individuals and families engaged in agriculture, agricultural-related processes, or home economics activities. Demonstrate procedures and apply research findings to solve problems; instruct and train in product development, sales, and the utilization of machinery and equipment to promote general welfare. Include county agricultural agents, feed and farm management advisers, home economists, and extension service advisers. Advises farmers in matters such as feeding and health maintenance of livestock, cultivation, growing and harvesting practices, and budgeting. Advises individuals and families on home management practices, such as budget planning, meal preparation, energy conservation, clothing, and home furnishings. Conducts classes to educate others in subjects such as nutrition, home management, home furnishing, child care, and farming techniques. Plans, develops, organizes, and evaluates training programs in subjects such as home management, horticulture, and consumer information. Collects and evaluates data to ascertain needs and develop programs beneficial to community. Delivers lectures to organizations or talks over radio and television to disseminate information and promote objectives of program. Organizes, advises, and participates in community activities and organizations, such as county and state fair events and 4-H clubs. Prepares leaflets, pamphlets, and other material, such as visual aids for educational and informational purposes.

Knowledge: Administration and Management; Economics and Accounting; Sales and Marketing; Personnel and Human Resources; Food Production; Computers and Electronics; Mathematics; Chemistry; Biology; Education and Training; Communications and Media; Transportation

Abilities: Oral Expression; Originality; Mathematical Reasoning; Number Facility; Near Vision; Far Vision; Speech Recognition; Speech Clarity

Farm Workers

▲ Growth: -9%

▲ Annual Job Openings: 217,762

▲ Yearly Earnings $14,248

▲ Education Required: Short-term O-J-T

▲ Self-employed: 4%

▲ Part-time: 21%

Farm Equipment Operators

Drive and control farm equipment to till soil and to plant, cultivate, and harvest crops. Drives tractor with implements to plow, plant, cultivate, or harvest crops and to move trailers for crop harvest. Manipulates controls to set, activate, and regulate mechanisms on machinery such as self-propelled machines, conveyors, separators, cleaners, and dryers. Drives truck to haul harvested crops, supplies, tools, or farm workers. Drives truck, or tractor with trailer attached, alongside crew loading crop or adjacent to harvesting machine. Sprays fertilizer or pesticide solutions, using hand sprayer, to control insects, fungus and weed growth, and diseases. Observes and listens to machinery operation to detect equipment malfunction, and removes obstruction to avoid damage to product or machinery. Attaches farm implements, such as plow, disc, sprayer, or harvester, to tractor, using bolts and mechanic's hand tools. Drives horses or mules to tow farm equipment and plant, cultivate, or harvest crops. Discards diseased or rotting product, and guides product on conveyor to regulate flow through machine. Positions boxes or attaches bags at discharge end of machinery to catch products, places lids on boxes, and closes sacks. Thins, hoes, weeds, or prunes row crops, fruit trees, or vines, using hand implements. Loads hoppers, containers, or conveyors to feed machine with products, using suction gates, shovel, or pitchfork. Adjusts, repairs, lubricates, and services farm machinery, and notifies supervisor or appropriate personnel when machinery malfunctions. Walks beside or rides on planting machine while inserting plants in planter mechanism at specified intervals. Irrigates soil, using portable pipe or ditch system, and maintains ditch or pipe and pumps. Mixes specified materials or chemicals and dumps solutions, powders, or seeds into planter or sprayer machinery. Loads and unloads crops or containers of materials, manually or using conveyors, handtruck, forklift, or transfer auger. Weighs crop-filled containers and records weights and other identifying information. Hand-picks fruit, such as apples, oranges, or strawberries. Oversees work crew engaged in planting, weeding, or harvesting activities.

Knowledge: Food Production; Mechanical; Chemistry; Foreign Language; Transportation

Abilities: Information Ordering; Spatial Orientation; Time Sharing; Manual Dexterity; Finger

Dexterity; Control Precision; Multilimb Coordination; Response Orientation; Rate Control; Reaction Time; Speed of Limb Movement; Static Strength; Explosive Strength; Dynamic Strength; Trunk Strength; Stamina; Extent Flexibility; Dynamic Flexibility; Gross Body Equilibrium; Far Vision; Night Vision; Peripheral Vision; Hearing Sensitivity; Sound Localization

General Farmworkers

Apply pesticides, herbicides, and fertilizer to crops and livestock; plant, maintain, and harvest food crops; and tend livestock and poultry. Repair farm buildings and fences. Duties may include operating milking machines and other dairy processing equipment, supervising seasonal help, irrigating crops, and hauling livestock products to market. Operates tractors, tractor-drawn machinery, and self-propelled machinery to plow, harrow, and fertilize soil and plant, cultivate, spray, and harvest crops. Feeds, waters, grooms, and otherwise cares for livestock and poultry. Harvests fruits and vegetables by hand. Digs and transplants seedlings by hand. Repairs farm buildings, fences, and other structures. Sets up and operates irrigation equipment. Clears and maintains irrigation ditches. Operates truck to haul livestock and products to market. Loads agricultural products into trucks for transport. Cleans barns, stables, pens, and kennels. Administers simple medications to animals and fowls. Repairs and maintains farm vehicles, implements, and mechanical equipment. Oversees casual and seasonal help during planting and harvesting.

Knowledge: Food Production; Building and Construction; Mechanical; Chemistry; Biology; Foreign Language; Transportation

Abilities: Spatial Orientation; Manual Dexterity; Control Precision; Multilimb Coordination; Response Orientation; Rate Control; Reaction Time; Wrist-Finger Speed; Speed of Limb Movement; Static Strength; Explosive Strength; Dynamic Strength; Trunk Strength; Stamina; Extent Flexibility; Dynamic Flexibility; Gross Body Coordination; Gross Body Equilibrium; Night Vision; Peripheral Vision; Depth Perception; Glare Sensitivity; Hearing Sensitivity; Auditory Attention; Sound Localization

Farmworkers, Food and Fiber Crops

Plant, cultivate, and harvest food and fiber products, such as grains, vegetables, fruits, nuts, and field crops (e.g., cotton, mint, hops, and tobacco). Use hand tools, such as shovels, trowels, hoes, tampers, pruning hooks, shears, and knives. Duties may include tilling soil and applying fertilizers; transplanting, weeding, thinning, or pruning crops; applying fungicides, herbicides, or pesticides; and packing and loading harvested products. May construct trellises, repair fences and farm building, or participate in irrigation activities. Include workers involved in expediting pollination and those who cut seed tuber crops into sections for planting. Plants seeds or digs up and transplants seedlings and sets, using hand tools such as hoes. Pulls, cuts, or chops out weeds and surplus seedlings. Cuts and trims away leaves, plant tops, and unwanted branches from plants to promote growth of produce. Grooves dirt along row to facilitate irrigation, and mounds dirt around plant to protect roots. Cuts or pulls tops and other foliage from harvested crops. Loads produce in containers or onto trucks or field conveyors, or lays bunches of produce along row for collection. Sprays plants with prescribed herbicides, fungicides, and pesticides to control diseases and insects. Repairs fences and buildings, using carpenter's tools. Sets up poles and strings wire or twine to build trellises or fences for vines or running plants. Picks produce from plant, pulls produce from soil, cuts produce from stem or root, or shakes produce from vine or tree. Ties harvested produce in bundles, using twine, wire, or rubber bands. Moves supplies, equipment, seedlings, and harvested crops from one place to another, and loads and unloads trucks. Carries and positions irrigation pipes and clears irrigation ditches, using shovel. Picks out debris, such as vines and culls, to clean harvested crops, and cleans up area around harvesting machines. Cleans, lubricates, sharpens, or otherwise maintains farm machines and equipment.

Knowledge: Food Production

Abilities: Manual Dexterity; Wrist-Finger Speed; Static Strength; Explosive Strength; Dynamic Strength; Trunk Strength; Stamina; Dynamic Flexibility; Gross Body Coordination; Gross Body Equilibrium; Glare Sensitivity

Farmworkers, Farm and Ranch Animals

Attend to live farm or ranch animals, including cattle, sheep, swine, goats, and poultry produced for animal products, such as meat, fur, skins, feathers, milk, and eggs. Duties may include feeding, watering, herding, grazing, castrating, branding, debeaking, weighing, catching, and loading animals. May maintain records on animals, examine animals to detect diseases and injuries, assist in birth deliveries, and administer medications, vaccinations, or insecticides as appropriate. May clean and maintain animal housing areas. Include workers who tend dairy milking machines, shear wool from sheep, collect eggs in hatcheries, place shoes on animals' hooves, and tend bee colonies. Waters livestock. Herds livestock to pasture for grazing or to scales, trucks, or other enclosures. Examines animals to detect disease and injuries. Applies or administers medications and vaccinates animals. Sprays livestock with disinfectants and insecticides. Cleans stalls, pens, and equipment, using disinfectant solutions, brushes, shovels and water hoses. Castrates or docks ears and tails of animals. Marks livestock to identify ownership and grade, using brands, tags, paint, or tattoos. Assists with birthing of animals. Debeaks and trims wings of poultry. Fills feed troughs with feed. Milks farm animals, such as cows and goats, by hand or using milking machine. Collects, inspects, packs, or places eggs in incubator. Mixes feed, additives, and medicines in prescribed portions. Maintains growth, feeding, production, and cost records. Inspects and repairs fences, stalls, and pens. Moves equipment, poultry, or livestock manually from one location to another using truck or cart. Grooms, clips, and trims animals. Segregates animals according to weight, age, color, and physical condition. Maintains equipment and machinery.

Knowledge: Food Production; Biology

Abilities: Manual Dexterity; Multilimb Coordination; Rate Control; Reaction Time; Speed of Limb Movement; Static Strength; Explosive Strength; Dynamic Strength; Trunk Strength; Stamina; Dynamic Flexibility; Gross Body Coordination; Gross Body Equilibrium

Irrigation Workers

Irrigate crops, using sprinklers or gravity flow system. Operates gates, checks, turnouts, and wasteways to regulate water flow into canals and laterals. Removes plugs from portholes to release water, and replugs when area is filled with water. Starts motor that pumps water through system, and opens valves to direct water. Observes rate of flow, and adjusts valves to ensure uniform distribution of water. Disassembles portable system, and moves to next location after specified time interval. Lays out pipe along designated settings, and attaches sprinkler heads at specified points. Connects pipe to gate or pipe system, using hand tools. Measures or estimates quantity of water required and delivered and duration of delivery. Shovels and packs dirt in low spots of embankment, or cuts trenches in high areas to direct water flow. Patrols area to detect leaks, breaks, weak areas, or obstructions and damage to irrigation system. Writes reports and keeps records of deliveries, users, quantity of water used, condition of system and equipment, or repairs needed. Lubricates, adjusts, and repairs or replaces parts to maintain system, using hand tools.

Knowledge: Food Production; Building and Construction

Abilities: Dynamic Strength; Trunk Strength; Gross Body Equilibrium

Financial Managers

- ▲ Growth: 18%
- ▲ Annual Job Openings: 74,297
- ▲ Yearly Earnings $54,392
- ▲ Education Required: Work experience, plus degree
- ▲ Self-employed: 1%
- ▲ Part-time: 2%

Treasurers, Controllers, and Chief Financial Officers

Plan, direct, and coordinate the financial activities of an organization at the highest level of management. Include financial reserve officers. Directs financial planning, procurement, and investment of funds for organization. Directs preparation of budgets. Prepares reports or directs preparation of reports summarizing organization's current and forecasted financial position, business activity, and reports required by regulatory agencies. Prepares financial reports or directs preparation of reports. Recommends to management major economic objectives and policies. Delegates authority for receipt, disbursement, banking, protection, and custody of funds, securities, and financial instruments. Analyzes past, present, and expected operations. Plans and implements new operating procedures to improve efficiency and reduce costs. Ensures that institution reserves meet legal requirements. Coordinates activities of assigned program and interprets policies and practices. Arranges audits of company accounts. Advises management on investments and loans for short- and long-range financial plans. Manages accounting department. Evaluates need for procurement of funds and investment of surplus. Determines methods and procedures for carrying out assigned program. Develops policies and procedures for account collections and extension of credit to customers.

Knowledge: Administration and Management; Economics and Accounting; Sales and Marketing; Personnel and Human Resources; Mathematics; Psychology; English Language; History and Archeology; Philosophy and Theology; Law, Government, and Jurisprudence; Communications and Media

Abilities: Oral Comprehension; Written Comprehension; Oral Expression; Written Expression; Fluency of Ideas; Originality; Problem Sensitivity; Deductive Reasoning; Inductive Reasoning; Information Ordering; Category Flexibility; Mathematical Reasoning; Number Facility; Memorization; Speed of Closure; Perceptual Speed; Selective Attention; Near Vision; Speech Recognition; Speech Clarity

Financial Managers, Branch or Department

Direct and coordinate financial activities of workers in a branch, office, or department of an establishment, such as branch bank, brokerage firm, risk and insurance department, or credit department. Directs and coordinates activities of workers engaged in conducting credit investigations and collecting delinquent accounts of customers. Plans, directs, and coordinates risk and insurance programs of establishment to control risks and losses. Manages branch or office of financial institution. Directs and coordinates activities to implement institution policies, procedures, and practices concerning granting or extending lines of credit and loans. Prepares financial and regulatory reports required by law, regulations, and board of directors. Analyzes and classifies risks as to frequency and financial impact of risk on company. Selects appropriate technique to minimize loss, such as avoidance and loss prevention and reduction. Prepares operational and risk reports for management analysis. Directs floor operations of brokerage firm engaged in buying and selling securities at exchange. Establishes procedures for custody and control of assets, records, loan collateral, and securities to ensure safekeeping. Evaluates effectiveness of current collection policies and procedures. Directs insurance negotiations, selects insurance brokers and carriers, and places insurance. Evaluates data pertaining to costs to plan budget. Reviews collection reports to ascertain status of collections and balances outstanding. Monitors order flow and transactions that brokerage firm executes on floor of exchange. Reviews reports of securities transactions and price lists to analyze market conditions. Establishes credit limitations on customer account. Examines, evaluates, and processes loan applications. Submits delinquent accounts to attorney or outside agency for collection.

Knowledge: Administration and Management; Economics and Accounting; Sales and Marketing; Personnel and Human Resources; Mathematics; Psychology; English Language; History and Archeology; Law, Government, and Jurisprudence

Abilities: Oral Comprehension; Written Comprehension; Oral Expression; Written Expression; Fluency of Ideas; Originality; Problem Sensitivity; Deductive Reasoning; Inductive Reasoning; Information Ordering; Category Flexibility; Mathematical Reasoning; Number Facility; Memorization; Speed of Closure; Selective Attention; Time Sharing; Near Vision; Far Vision; Speech Recognition; Speech Clarity

Fire Fighting and Prevention Supervisors

▲ Growth: 1%
▲ Annual Job Openings: 470
▲ Yearly Earnings $40,981
▲ Education Required: Work experience in a related occupation
▲ Self-employed: 0%
▲ Part-time: 2%

Municipal Fire Fighting and Prevention Supervisors

Supervise fire fighters who control and extinguish municipal fires, protect life and property, and conduct rescue efforts. Coordinates and supervises fire-fighting and rescue activities, and reports events to supervisor, using two-way radio. Assesses nature and extent of fire, condition of building, danger to adjacent buildings, and water supply to determine crew or company requirements. Evaluates efficiency and performance of employees, and recommends awards for service. Directs investigation of cases of suspected arson, hazards, and false alarms. Trains subordinates in use of equipment, methods of extinguishing fires, and rescue operations. Directs building inspections to ensure compliance with fire and safety regulations. Inspects fire stations, equipment, and records to ensure efficiency and enforcement of departmental regulations. Keeps equipment and personnel records. Confers with civic representatives, and plans talks and demonstrations of fire safety to direct fire prevention information program. Oversees review of new building plans to ensure compliance with laws, ordinances, and administrative rules for public fire safety. Orders and directs fire drills for occupants of buildings. Writes and submits proposals for new equipment or modification of existing equipment. Studies and interprets fire safety codes to establish procedures for issuing permits regulating storage or use of hazardous or flammable substances. Compiles report of fire call, listing location, type, probable cause, estimated damage, and disposition.

Knowledge: Administration and Management; Personnel and Human Resources; Building and Construction; Geography; Medicine and Dentistry; Education and Training; Public Safety and Security; Telecommunications

Abilities: Oral Expression; Fluency of Ideas; Originality; Problem Sensitivity; Deductive Reasoning; Inductive Reasoning; Information Ordering; Speed of Closure; Flexibility of Closure; Spatial Orientation; Selective Attention; Time Sharing; Multilimb Coordination; Response Orientation; Rate Control; Reaction Time; Speed of Limb Movement; Static Strength; Explosive Strength; Dynamic Strength; Trunk Strength; Stamina; Dynamic Flexibility; Gross Body Coordination; Gross Body Equilibrium; Near Vision; Far Vision; Night Vision; Peripheral Vision; Depth Perception; Glare Sensitivity; Hearing Sensitivity; Auditory Attention; Sound Localization; Speech Recognition; Speech Clarity

Forest Fire Fighting and Prevention Supervisors

Supervise fire fighters who control and suppress fires in forests or on vacant public land. Dispatches crews according to reported size, location, and condition of forest fires. Directs loading of fire-suppression equipment into aircraft and parachuting of equipment to crews on ground. Observes fire and crews from air to determine force requirements and note changing conditions. Maintains radio communication with crews at fire scene to inform crews and base of changing conditions and learn of casualties. Parachutes to major fire locations and directs fire containment and suppression activities. Trains workers in parachute jumping, fire suppression, aerial observation, and radio communication.

Knowledge: Administration and Management; Chemistry; Geography; Education and Training; Public Safety and Security; Transportation

Abilities: Oral Expression; Fluency of Ideas; Problem Sensitivity; Speed of Closure; Flexibility of Closure; Spatial Orientation; Selective Attention; Time Sharing; Response Orientation; Rate Control; Reaction Time; Speed of Limb Movement; Static Strength; Explosive Strength; Dynamic Strength; Trunk Strength; Stamina; Dynamic Flexibility; Gross Body Coordination; Gross Body Equilibrium; Far Vision; Night Vision; Peripheral Vision; Depth Perception; Glare Sensitivity; Hearing Sensitivity; Auditory Attention; Sound Localization; Speech Recognition; Speech Clarity

Flight Attendants

Growth: 35%
Annual Job Openings: 9,844
Yearly Earnings $36,441
Education Required: Long-term O-J-T
Self-employed: 0%
Part-time: 45%

Flight Attendants

Provide personal services to ensure the safety and comfort of airline passengers during flight. Greet passengers, verify tickets, record destinations, and assign seats. Explain use of safety equipment. Serve meals and beverages. Greets passengers, verifies tickets, records destinations, and directs passengers to assigned seats. Explains use of safety equipment to passengers. Serves prepared meals and beverages. Assists passengers to store carry-on luggage in overhead, garment, or under-seat storage. Walks aisle of plane to verify that passengers have complied with federal regulations prior to take off. Administers first aid to passengers in distress, when needed. Collects money for meals and beverages. Prepares reports showing place of departure and destination, passenger ticket numbers, meal and beverages inventories, and lost and found articles.

Knowledge: Customer and Personal Service; Psychology; Geography; Medicine and Dentistry; Therapy and Counseling; Public Safety and Security; Transportation

Abilities: Reaction Time; Gross Body Equilibrium; Speech Recognition

Food and Beverage Production Workers

▲ Growth: 29%
▲ Annual Job Openings: 6,257
▲ Yearly Earnings $22,214
▲ Education Required: Long-term O-J-T
▲ Self-employed: 2%
▲ Part-time: 14%

Food Batchmakers

Set up and operate equipment that mixes, blends, or cooks ingredients used in the manufacturing of food products, according to formulas or recipes. May modify or reformulate recipes to produce products of specific flavor, texture, and color. This occupation requires at least 1 year (and often more) of training or experience. Include candy makers, almond paste mixers, cheesemakers, flavorings compounders, and

honey graders and blenders. Calculates ingredient amounts to formulate or modify recipes to produce food product of specific flavor, texture, clarity, bouquet, and color. Fills processing or cooking container, such as water-cooled kettle, steam-jacketed rotating cooker, pressure cooker, or vat, with ingredients, following recipe. Mixes or blends ingredients, according to recipe, using paddle or agitator. Determines mixing sequence, based on knowledge of temperature effects and solubility and miscibility properties of specific ingredients. Stirs and cooks ingredients at specified temperatures. Operates refining machine to reduce size of cooked batch. Measures and weighs ingredients, using English or metric measures and balance scales. Separates, spreads, kneads, spins, casts, cuts, or rolls food product by hand or using machine. Homogenizes or pasteurizes material to prevent separation of substances or to obtain prescribed butterfat content. Examines, feels, and tastes product to evaluate color, texture, flavor, and bouquet. Tests food product sample for moisture content, acidity level, or butter-fat content. Cools food product batch on slabs or in water-cooled kettle. Grades food product according to government regulations or according to type, color, bouquet, and moisture content. Records amounts of ingredients used, test results, and time cycles. Gives directions to other workers who are assisting in batchmaking process.

Knowledge: Food Production

Abilities: Information Ordering; Memorization

Food Counter and Fountain Workers

▲ Growth: 14%
▲ Annual Job Openings: 727,389
▲ Yearly Earnings $12,292
▲ Education Required: Short-term O-J-T
▲ Self-employed: 0%
▲ Part-time: 62%

Counter Attendants—Lunchroom, Coffee Shop, or Cafeteria

Serve food to diners at counter or from a steamtable. Exclude counter attendants who also wait tables. Serves food, beverages, or desserts to customers in variety of settings, such as take-out counter of restaurant or lunchroom. Serves salads, vegetables, meat, breads, and cocktails; ladles soups and sauces; portions desserts; and fills beverage cups and glasses. Calls order to kitchen and picks up and serves order when it is ready. Writes items ordered on tickets, totals orders, passes orders to cook, and gives ticket stubs to customers to identify filled orders. Serves sandwiches, salads, beverages, desserts, and candies to employees in industrial establishment. Replenishes foods at serving stations. Prepares and serves soft drinks and ice cream dishes, such as sundaes, using memorized formulas and methods of following directions. Brews coffee and tea and fills containers with requested beverages. Wraps menu items, such as sandwiches, hot entrees, and desserts. Accepts payment for food, using cash register or adding machine to total check. Prepares sandwiches, salads, and other short-order items. Carves meat. Serves employees from mobile canteen. Adds relishes and garnishes according to instructions. Scrubs and polishes counters, steamtables, and other equipment; cleans glasses, dishes, and fountain equipment; and polishes metalwork on fountain. Sells cigars and cigarettes. Orders items to replace stocks.

Knowledge: Sales and Marketing; Customer and Personal Service

Abilities: None above average

Food Preparation Workers

▲ Growth: 19%
▲ Annual Job Openings: 573,079
▲ Yearly Earnings $13,769
▲ Education Required: Short-term O-J-T
▲ Self-employed: 0%
▲ Part-time: 57%

Food Preparation Workers

Perform a variety of food preparation duties other than cooking, such as preparing cold foods and shellfish, slicing meat, and brewing coffee or tea. Cleans and portions, and cuts or peels various foods to prepare for cooking or serving. Prepares variety of foods according to customers' orders or instructions of superior, following approved procedures. Portions and arranges food on serving dishes, trays, carts, or conveyor belts. Cleans, cuts, slices, or disjoints meats and poultry to prepare for cooking. Prepares and serves variety of beverages, such as coffee, tea, and soft drinks. Carries food supplies, equipment, and utensils to and from storage and work areas. Stores food in designated containers and storage areas to prevent spoilage. Distributes food to waiters and waitresses to serve to customers. Cleans and maintains work areas, equipment, and utensils. Requisitions, stores, and distributes food supplies, equipment, and utensils. Butchers and cleans fowl, fish, poultry, and shellfish to prepare for cooking or serving. Serves food to customers.

Knowledge: Customer and Personal Service; Food Production

Abilities: Manual Dexterity; Reaction Time; Wrist-Finger Speed; Trunk Strength; Extent Flexibility; Gross Body Equilibrium; Hearing Sensitivity

Kitchen Helpers

Maintain and clean kitchen work areas, equipment, and utensils. Cleans and maintains work areas, equipment, and utensils. Removes garbage and trash and places refuse in designated pick-up area. Carries or transfers by handtruck supplies and equipment between storage and work areas. Stocks serving stations with food and utensils. Prepares and packages individual place settings. Loads or unloads trucks used in delivering or picking up food and supplies. Cleans and prepares various foods for cooking or serving. Sets up banquet tables.

Knowledge: Food Production

Abilities: Wrist-Finger Speed; Dynamic Strength; Trunk Strength; Extent Flexibility; Dynamic Flexibility; Gross Body Equilibrium; Peripheral Vision

Combined Food Preparation and Service Workers

Perform duties which combine both food preparation and food service. Workers who spend more than 80 percent of their time in one job are classified in that occupation. Selects food items from serving or storage areas and places food and beverage items on serving tray or in take-out bag. Makes and serves hot and cold beverages or desserts. Cooks or reheats food items, such as french fries. Requests and records customer order and computes bill. Notifies kitchen personnel of shortages or special orders. Receives payment.

Knowledge: Sales and Marketing; Customer and Personal Service; Food Production

Abilities: Reaction Time; Wrist-Finger Speed; Gross Body Equilibrium

Food Service and Lodging Managers

- ▲ Growth: 29%
- ▲ Annual Job Openings: 68,207
- ▲ Yearly Earnings $26,561
- ▲ Education Required: Work experience in a related occupation
- ▲ Self-employed: 35%
- ▲ Part-time: 8%

Lodging Managers

Plan, direct, and coordinate activities of an organization or department that provides lodging and other accommodations. Exclude food-service managers in lodging establishments. Coordinates front-office activities of hotel or motel and resolves problems. Manages and maintains temporary or permanent lodging facilities. Answers inquiries pertaining to hotel policies and services and resolves occupants' complaints. Confers and cooperates with other department heads to ensure coordination of hotel activities. Interviews and hires applicants. Assigns duties and shifts to workers and observes performances to ensure operating procedures. Purchases supplies and arranges for outside services, such as fuel delivery, laundry, maintenance and repair, and trash collection. Receives and processes advance registration payments, sends out letters of confirmation, and returns checks when registration cannot be accepted. Shows and rents or assigns accommodations. Arranges for medical aid for park patrons. Collects rent and records data pertaining to rent funds and expenditures. Patrols facilities and grounds and investigates disturbances. Greets and registers guests. Arranges telephone answering service, delivers mail and packages, and answers questions regarding locations for eating and entertainment. Makes minor electrical, plumbing, and structural repairs. Rents equipment, such as rowboats, water skis, and fishing tackle, and coordinates intramural activities of patrons of park. Mows and waters lawns, and cultivates flower beds and shrubbery. Cleans accommodations after guests' departure. Cleans public areas, such as entrances, halls, and laundry rooms, and fires boilers. Sells light lunches, candy, tobacco, and other sundry items.

Knowledge: Administration and Management; Clerical; Economics and Accounting; Sales and Marketing; Customer and Personal Service; Personnel and Human Resources; Food Production; Building and Construction; Psychology; Sociology and Anthropology; Geography; Medicine and Dentistry; Foreign Language; History and Archeology; Philosophy and Theology; Public Safety and Security; Law, Government, and Jurisprudence; Telecommunications

Abilities: Problem Sensitivity; Category Flexibility; Mathematical Reasoning; Number Facility; Memorization; Flexibility of Closure; Perceptual Speed; Spatial Orientation; Time Sharing; Response Orientation; Dynamic Strength; Stamina; Gross Body Equilibrium; Near Vision; Far Vision; Night Vision; Peripheral Vision; Glare Sensitivity; Hearing Sensitivity; Sound Localization; Speech Recognition; Speech Clarity

Food-Service Managers

Plan, direct, and coordinate activities of an organization or department that serves food and beverages. Monitors compliance with health and fire regulations regarding food preparation and serving and building maintenance in lodging and dining facility. Plans menus and food utilization based on anticipated number of guests, nutritional value, palatability, popularity, and costs. Organizes and directs worker-training programs, resolves personnel problems, hires new staff, and evaluates employee performance in dining and lodging facilities. Coordinates assignments of cooking personnel to ensure economical use of food and timely preparation. Estimates food, liquor, wine, and other beverage consumption to anticipate amount to be purchased or requisitioned. Monitors food preparation and methods, size of portions, and garnishing and presentation of food to ensure food is prepared and presented in accepted manner. Monitors budget and payroll records, and reviews financial transactions to ensure expenditures are authorized and budgeted. Investigates and resolves complaints regarding food quality and service or accommodations. Reviews menus and analyzes recipes to determine labor and overhead costs, and assigns prices to menu items. Establishes and enforces nutrition standards for dining establishment based on accepted industry standards. Keeps records required by government agencies regarding sanitation and food subsidies, where indicated. Tests cooked food by tasting and smelling to ensure palatability and flavor conformity. Coordinates activities of residential camp workers, including assignment of living quarters. Assists underage workers to obtain work permits and health and birth certificates, and arranges for medical care for sick or injured workers. Creates specialty dishes and develops recipes to be used in dining facility.

Knowledge: Administration and Management; Clerical; Economics and Accounting; Sales and Marketing; Customer and Personal Service; Personnel and Human Resources; Production and Processing; Food Production; Psychology; Medicine and Dentistry; Therapy and Counseling; Education and Training; Public Safety and Security; Law, Government, and Jurisprudence

Abilities: Oral Expression; Fluency of Ideas; Originality; Problem Sensitivity; Deductive Reasoning; Category Flexibility; Mathematical Reasoning; Number Facility; Memorization; Time Sharing; Gross Body Equilibrium; Far Vision; Visual Color Discrimination; Night Vision; Peripheral Vision; Auditory Attention; Speech Recognition; Speech Clarity

Chefs and Head Cooks

Direct preparation, seasoning, and cooking of salads, soups, fish, meats, vegetables, desserts, or other foods. May plan and price menu items, order supplies, and keep records and accounts. May participate in cooking. Supervises and coordinates activities of cooks and workers engaged in food preparation. Observes workers and work procedures to ensure compliance with established standards. Trains and otherwise instructs cooks and workers in proper food preparation procedures. Helps cooks and workers cook and prepare food on demand. Estimates amounts and costs, and requisitions supplies and equipment to ensure efficient operation. Determines production schedules and worker-time requirements to ensure timely delivery of services. Collaborates with specified personnel, and plans and develops recipes and menus. Inspects supplies, equipment, and work areas to ensure conformance to established standards. Records production and operational data on specified forms. Evaluates and solves procedural problems to ensure safe and efficient operations.

Knowledge: Administration and Management; Economics and Accounting; Personnel and Human Resources; Food Production; Education and Training

Abilities: Originality; Perceptual Speed; Time Sharing; Manual Dexterity; Finger Dexterity; Wrist-Finger Speed

First-Line Supervisors/Managers of Food Preparation and Serving Workers

Supervise workers engaged in serving and preparing food. Supervises and coordinates activities of workers engaged in preparing and serving food and other related duties. Observes and evaluates workers and work procedures to ensure quality standards and service. Assigns duties, responsibilities, and work stations to employees, following work requirements. Collaborates with specified personnel to plan menus, serving arrangements, and other related details. Specifies food portions and courses, production and time sequences, and work station and equipment arrangements. Inspects supplies, equipment, and work areas to ensure efficient service and conformance to standards. Trains workers in proper food preparation and service procedures. Recommends measures to improve work procedures and worker performance, to increase quality of services and job safety. Records production and operational data on specified forms. Purchases or requisitions supplies and equipment to ensure quality and timely delivery of services. Resolves customer complaints regarding food service. Initiates personnel actions, such as hires and discharges, to ensure proper staffing. Receives, issues, and takes inventory of supplies and equipment, and reports shortages to designated personnel. Analyzes operational problems, such as theft and wastage, and establishes controls. Schedules parties and reservations, and greets and escorts guests to seating arrangements.

Knowledge: Administration and Management; Customer and Personal Service; Personnel and Human Resources; Production and Processing; Food Production

Abilities: Originality; Deductive Reasoning; Time Sharing; Auditory Attention; Speech Recognition; Speech Clarity

First-Line Supervisors/Hospitality and Personal Service Workers

Supervise workers engaged in providing hospitality and personal services. Supervises and coordinates activities of workers engaged in lodging and personal services. Observes and evaluates workers' appearance and performance to ensure quality service and compliance with specifications. Assigns work schedules, following work requirements, to ensure quality and timely delivery of services. Trains workers in proper operational procedures and functions, and explains company policy. Resolves customer complaints regarding worker performance and services rendered. Collaborates with personnel to plan and develop programs of events, schedules of activities, and menus. Analyzes and records personnel and operational data and writes activity reports. Inspects work areas and operating equipment to ensure conformance to established standards. Requisitions supplies, equipment, and designated services, to ensure quality and timely service and efficient operations. Informs workers about interests of specific groups. Furnishes customers with information on events and activities.

Knowledge: Administration and Management; Customer and Personal Service; Personnel and Human Resources; Psychology; Education and Training

Abilities: Time Sharing

Foresters and Conservation Scientists

▲ Growth: 17%
▲ Annual Job Openings: 3,200
▲ Yearly Earnings $36,649
▲ Education Required: Bachelor's degree
▲ Self-employed: 4%
▲ Part-time: 6%

Environmental Scientists

Conduct research to develop methods of abating, controlling, or remediating sources of environmental pollutants, utilizing knowledge of various scientific disciplines. Identify and analyze sources of pollution to determine their effects. Collect and synthesize data derived from pollution-emission measurements, atmospheric monitoring, meteorological and mineralogical information, or soil and water samples. Exclude wildlife conservationists and natural resource scientists. Plans and develops research models using knowledge of mathematical and statistical concepts. Collects, identifies, and analyzes data to assess sources of pollution, determine their effects, and establish standards. Determines data collection methods to be employed in research projects and surveys. Prepares graphs or charts from data samples, and advises enforcement personnel on proper standards and regulations.

Knowledge: Mathematics; Physics; Chemistry; Biology

Abilities: Deductive Reasoning; Mathematical Reasoning; Number Facility

Foresters

Plan, develop, and control environmental factors affecting forests and their resources for economic and recreation purposes. Plans and directs forestation and reforestation projects. Investigates adaptability of different tree species to new environmental conditions, such as soil type, climate, and altitude. Determines methods of cutting and removing timber with minimum waste and environmental damage. Plans cutting programs to assure continuous production or to assist timber companies to achieve production goals. Researches forest propagation and culture affecting tree growth rates, yield, and duration and seed production, growth viability, and germination of different species. Analyzes forest conditions to determine reason for prevalence of different variety of trees. Studies classification, life history, light and soil requirements, and resistance to disease and insects of different tree species. Maps forest areas and estimates standing timber and future growth. Manages tree nurseries and thins forest to encourage natural growth of sprouts or seedlings of desired varieties. Participates in environmental studies and prepares environmental reports. Assists in planning and implementing projects for control of floods, soil erosion, tree diseases, infestation, and forest fires. Plans and directs construction and maintenance of recreation facilities, fire towers, trails, roads, and fire breaks. Develops techniques for measuring and identifying trees. Patrols forests and enforces laws. Directs suppression of forest fires and fights forest fires. Advises landowners on forestry management techniques. Conducts public educational programs on forest care and conservation. Suggests methods of processing wood for various uses. Manages timber sales for government agency or landowner, and administers budgets. Supervises activities of other forestry workers.

Knowledge: Administration and Management; Economics and Accounting; Sales and Marketing; Personnel and Human Resources; Production and Processing; Engineering and Technology; Design; Building and Construction; Mathematics; Physics; Chemistry; Biology; Sociology and Anthropology; Geography; Education and Training; English Language; History and Archeology; Philosophy and Theology; Public Safety and Security; Law, Government, and Jurisprudence; Telecommunications; Communications and Media; Transportation

Abilities: Written Comprehension; Written Expression; Fluency of Ideas; Originality; Problem Sensitivity; Deductive Reasoning; Inductive Reasoning; Category Flexibility; Memorization; Speed of Closure; Flexibility of Closure; Spatial Orientation; Visualization; Time Sharing; Stamina; Far Vision; Night Vision; Speech Clarity

Soil Conservationists

Plan and develop coordinated practices for soil erosion control, soil and water conservation, and sound land use. Plans soil management practices, such as crop rotation, reforestation, permanent vegetation, contour plowing, or terracing, to maintain soil and conserve water. Develops plans for conservation, such as conservation cropping systems, woodlands management, pasture planning, and engineering systems. Analyzes results of investigations to determine measures needed to maintain or restore proper soil management. Conducts surveys and investigations of various land uses, such as rural or urban, agriculture, construction, forestry, or mining. Computes design specification for implementation of conservation practices, using survey and field information technical guides, engineering manuals, and calculator. Develops or participates in environmental studies. Monitors projects during and after construction to ensure projects conform to design specifications. Computes cost estimates of different conservation practices based on needs of land users, maintenance requirements, and life expectancy of practices. Surveys property to mark locations and measurements, using surveying instruments. Discusses conservation plans, problems, and alternative solutions with land users, applying knowledge of agronomy, soil science, forestry, or agricultural sciences. Revisits land users to view implemented land use practices and plans.

Knowledge: Administration and Management; Economics and Accounting; Food Production; Engineering and Technology; Design; Building and Construction; Mathematics; Physics; Chemistry; Biology; Geography; Education and Training; English Language; History and Archeology; Philosophy and Theology

Abilities: Oral Expression; Written Expression; Fluency of Ideas; Originality; Problem Sensitivity; Deductive Reasoning; Inductive Reasoning; Information Ordering; Number Facility; Memorization; Speed of Closure; Flexibility of Closure; Spatial Orientation; Far Vision; Depth Perception

Wood Technologists

Conduct research to determine composition, properties, behavior, utilization, development, treatments, and processing methods of wood and wood products. Studies methods of curing wood to determine best and most economical procedure. Investigates processes for converting wood into commodities such as alcohol, veneer, plywood, wood plastics, and other uses. Investigates methods of turning waste wood materials into useful products. Analyzes physical, chemical, and biological properties of wood. Develops and improves methods of preserving and treating wood with substances to increase resistance to wear, fire, fungi, and infestation. Conducts test to determine stability, strength, hardness, and crystallinity of wood under variety of conditions. Determines best types of wood for specific applications. Conducts tests to determine ability of wood adhesives to withstand water, oil penetration, and temperature extremes. Evaluates and improves effectiveness of industrial equipment and production processes for wood.

Knowledge: Production and Processing; Engineering and Technology; Building and Construction; Mathematics; Physics; Chemistry; Biology; Geography; English Language

Abilities: Fluency of Ideas; Originality; Inductive Reasoning; Information Ordering; Category Flexibility; Speed of Closure

Range Managers

Research or study rangeland management practices to provide sustained production of forage, livestock, and wildlife. Studies rangelands to determine best grazing seasons. Studies rangelands to determine number and kind of livestock that can be most profitably grazed. Studies forage plants and their growth requirements to determine varieties best suited to particular range. Develops improved practices for range reseeding. Develops methods for controlling poisonous plants in rangelands. Develops methods for protecting range from fire and rodent damage. Plans and directs maintenance of range improvements. Plans and directs construction of range improvements, such as fencing, corrals, stock-watering reservoirs and soil-erosion control structures.

Knowledge: Administration and Management; Economics and Accounting; Food Production; Building and Construction; Biology; Geography; Law, Government, and Jurisprudence

Abilities: Spatial Orientation

Park Naturalists

Plan, develop, and conduct programs to inform public of historical, natural, and scientific features of national, state, or local park. Conducts field trips to point out scientific, historic, and natural features of park. Plans and develops audio-visual devices for public programs. Interviews specialists in desired fields to obtain and develop data for park information programs. Confers with park staff to determine subjects to be presented to public. Prepares and presents illustrated lectures of park features. Constructs historical, scientific, and nature visitor-center displays. Takes photographs and motion pictures to illustrate lectures and publications and to develop displays. Surveys park to determine forest conditions. Surveys park to determine distribution and abundance of fauna and flora. Plans and organizes activities of seasonal staff members. Maintains official park photographic and information files. Performs emergency duties to protect human life, government property, and natural features of park.

Knowledge: Administration and Management; Biology; Geography; Education and Training; English Language; Fine Arts; History and Archeology; Communications and Media

Abilities: Spatial Orientation; Time Sharing; Stamina; Gross Body Equilibrium

Freight, Stock, and Material Movers

- ▲ Growth: 5%
- ▲ Annual Job Openings: 232,034
- ▲ Yearly Earnings $19,302
- ▲ Education Required: Short-term O-J-T
- ▲ Self-employed: 1%
- ▲ Part-time: 38%

Freight, Stock, and Material Movers—Hand

Load, unload and move materials at plant, yard, or other worksite. Loads and unloads materials to and from designated storage areas, such as racks and shelves, or vehicles, such as trucks. Transports receptacles to and from designated areas, by hand or using dollies, handtrucks, and wheelbarrows. Secures lifting attachments to materials and conveys load to destination, using crane or hoist. Directs spouts and positions receptacles, such as bins, carts, and containers, to receive loads. Stacks or piles materials, such as lumber, boards, or pallets. Shovels materials—such as gravel, ice or spilled concrete—into containers and bins or onto conveyors. Bundles and bands material, such as fodder and tobacco leaves, using banding machines. Reads work orders or receives and listens to oral instructions to determine work assignment. Sorts and stores items according to specifications. Installs protective devices, such as bracing, padding, or strapping, to prevent shifting or damage to items being transported. Cleans work area, using brooms, rags, and cleaning compounds. Attaches identifying tags or marks information on containers. Records number of units handled and moved, using daily production sheet or work tickets. Adjusts or replaces equipment parts, such as rollers, belts, plugs, and caps, using hand tools. Assembles product containers and crates, using hand tools and precut lumber.

Knowledge: Production and Processing

Abilities: Multilimb Coordination; Static Strength; Trunk Strength; Stamina; Extent Flexibility; Gross Body Coordination; Gross Body Equilibrium

Furniture Finishers

▲ Growth: 12%

▲ Annual Job Openings: 7,479

▲ Yearly Earnings $19,635

▲ Education Required: Long-term O-J-T

▲ Self-employed: 20%

▲ Part-time: 9%

Furniture Finishers

Shape, finish, and refinish damaged, worn, or used furniture or new high-grade furniture to specified color or finish, utilizing knowledge of wood properties, finishes, and furniture style. Disassembles items, masks areas adjacent to those items being refinished, and removes accessories, using hand tools, to prepare for finishing. Removes old finish and damaged or deteriorated parts, using hand tools, abrasives, or solvents. Fills cracks, blemishes, or depressions and repairs broken parts, using plastic or wood putty, glue, nails, or screws. Treats warped or stained surfaces to restore original contour and color. Smooths and shapes surfaces with sandpaper, pumice stone, steel wool, or chisel. Washes or bleaches surface to return to natural color or prepare for application of finish. Brushes, sprays, or hand rubs finishing ingredients onto and into grain of wood. Finishes surfaces of new furniture pieces to replicate antiques by distressing surfaces with abrasives before staining. Examines furniture to determine extent of damage or deterioration, and determines method of repair or restoration. Selects appropriate finishing ingredients, such as paint, stain, lacquer, shellac, or varnish, for wood surface. Mixes finish ingredients to obtain desired color or shade of existing finish. Stencils, gilds, embosses, or paints designs or borders on restored pieces to reproduce original appearance. Polishes, sprays, or waxes finished pieces to match surrounding finish. Replaces and refurbishes upholstery of item, using tacks, adhesives, softeners, solvents, stains, or polish. Spreads graining ink over metal portions of furniture to simulate wood-grain finish.

Knowledge: Building and Construction; Chemistry; Fine Arts

Abilities: Speed of Limb Movement; Dynamic Flexibility; Visual Color Discrimination

Gardeners and Groundskeepers

▲ Growth: 0%
▲ Annual Job Openings: 188,023
▲ Yearly Earnings $18,491
▲ Education Required: Short-term O-J-T
▲ Self-employed: 0%
▲ Part-time: 28%

Gardeners and Groundskeepers

Mow, water, and fertilize grass and shrubs; prune trees and hedges; and remove debris, litter, or snow, using hand and power tools or equipment to maintain grounds of private or public property. Plants grass, flowers, trees, and shrubs, using gardening tools. Prunes and trims trees, shrubs, and hedges, using shears, pruners, or chainsaw. Mows grass or turf, using hand or power mower. Mixes and sprays or spreads fertilizer, herbicides, or insecticides onto grass, shrubs, and trees, using hand or automatic sprayer or spreader. Repairs and maintains walks, fences, benches, burial sites, buildings, and tools and equipment, using hand tools and power tools. Waters grass, shrubs, or trees, using hose or by activating fixed or portable sprinkler system. Weeds and grubs around trees, bushes, and flower beds. Conditions and prepares soil for planting, using gardening tools. Removes leaves and other debris or litter from grounds, using rake, broom, or leaf blower. Shovels snow and spreads salt on walks and driveways. Cultivates grass or lawn, using power aerator and thatcher. Operates tractor or backhoe, using attachments, to till, dig, cultivate, grade, spray fertilizer or herbicide, mow, or remove snow. Records lawn-care services rendered, materials used, and charges assessed on appropriate forms.

Knowledge: Chemistry

Abilities: Static Strength; Explosive Strength; Dynamic Strength; Trunk Strength; Stamina; Extent Flexibility; Dynamic Flexibility; Gross Body Coordination; Gross Body Equilibrium

Yard Workers, Private Household

Maintain and keep grounds of private residence in neat and orderly condition. Plants, transplants, fertilizes, sprays with pesticides, prunes, cultivates, and waters flowers, shrubbery, and trees. Seeds and mows lawns, rakes leaves, and keeps ground free of debris. Cleans patio furniture and garage, and shovels snow from walks. Whitewashes or paints fences. Washes and polishes automobiles.

Knowledge: None above average

Abilities: Static Strength; Dynamic Strength; Trunk Strength; Stamina; Dynamic Flexibility

General Managers and Top Executives

▲ Growth: 15%

▲ Annual Job Openings: 288,825

▲ Yearly Earnings $58,344

▲ Education Required: Work experience, plus degree

▲ Self-employed: 0%

▲ Part-time: 6%

Mining Superintendents and Supervisors

Plan, direct, and coordinate mining operations to extract mineral ore or aggregate from underground or surface mines, quarries, or pits. Confers with engineering, supervisory, and maintenance personnel to plan and coordinate mine development and operations. Directs opening or closing of mine sections, pits, or other work areas, and installation or removal of equipment. Studies land contours and rock formations to specify locations for mine shafts, pillars, and timbers and to determine equipment needs. Directs and coordinates enforcement of mining laws and safety regulations and reports violations. Studies maps and blueprints to determine prospective locations for mine haulage ways, access roads, rail tracks, and conveyor systems. Reviews, consolidates, and oversees updating of mine records, such as geological and survey reports, air quality, safety reports, and production logs. Inspects mine to detect production, equipment, safety, and personnel problems, and recommends steps to improve conditions and increase production. Calculates mining and quarrying operational costs and potential income, and determines activities to maximize income. Negotiates with workers, supervisors, union personnel, and other parties to resolve grievances or settle complaints.

Knowledge: Administration and Management; Economics and Accounting; Personnel and Human Resources; Production and Processing; Design; Building and Construction; Geography; Public Safety and Security

Abilities: Oral Comprehension; Mathematical Reasoning; Spatial Orientation

Oil and Gas Drilling and Production Superintendents

Plan, direct, and coordinate activities required to erect, install, and maintain equipment for exploratory or production drilling of oil and gas. May direct technical processes and analyses to resolve drilling problems and to monitor and control operating costs and production efficiency. Plans and directs erection of drilling rigs and installation and maintenance of equipment, such as pumping units and compressor stations. Determines procedures to resolve drilling problems, service well equipment, clean wells, and dismantle and store derricks and drill equipment. Directs technical processes related to drilling, such as treatment of oil and gas, sediment analysis, well logging, and formation testing. Analyzes production reports and formulates drilling and production procedures to control well production in accordance with proration regulations. Directs petroleum exploration parties engaged in drilling for samples of subsurface stratigraphy and in seismic prospecting.

Knowledge: Administration and Management; Production and Processing; Engineering and Technology; Building and Construction; Physics

Abilities: Fluency of Ideas; Deductive Reasoning; Inductive Reasoning; Information Ordering; Category Flexibility; Memorization; Speed of Closure; Flexibility of Closure; Perceptual Speed; Spatial Orientation; Visualization; Selective Attention; Time Sharing; Response Orientation; Gross Body Equilibrium; Far Vision; Peripheral Vision

Private Sector Executives

Determine and formulate policies and business strategies, and provide overall direction of private sector organizations. Plan, direct, and coordinate operational activities at the highest level of management, with the help of subordinate managers. Directs, plans, and implements policies and objectives of organization or business in accordance with charter and board of directors. Directs activities of organization to plan procedures, establish responsibilities, and coordinate functions among departments and sites. Confers with board members, organization officials, and staff members to establish policies and formulate plans. Analyzes operations to evaluate performance of company and staff and to determine areas of cost reduction and program improvement. Reviews financial statements and sales and activity reports to ensure that organization's objectives are achieved. Directs and coordinates organization's financial and budget activities to fund operations, maximize investments, and increase efficiency. Assigns or delegates responsibilities to subordinates. Directs and coordinates activities of business or department concerned with production, pricing, sales, and/or distribution of products. Directs and coordinates activities of business involved with buying and selling investment products and financial services. Directs nonmerchandising departments of business, such as advertising, purchasing, credit, and accounting. Establishes internal control procedures. Prepares reports and budgets. Presides over or serves on board of directors, management committees, or other governing boards. Negotiates or approves contracts with suppliers and distributors, and with maintenance, janitorial, and security providers. Promotes objectives of institution or business before associations, public, government agencies, or community groups. Screens, selects, hires, transfers, and discharges employees. Administers program for selection of sites, construction of buildings, and provision of equipment and supplies. Directs in-service training of staff.

Knowledge: Administration and Management; Economics and Accounting; Sales and Marketing; Customer and Personal Service; Personnel and Human Resources; Production and Processing; Food Production; Engineering and Technology; Building and Construction; Mathematics; Psychology; Sociology and Anthropology; Geography; Therapy and Counseling; Education and Training; English Language; Foreign Language; History and Archeology;

Philosophy and Theology; Public Safety and Security; Law, Government, and Jurisprudence; Communications and Media; Transportation

Abilities: Oral Comprehension; Written Comprehension; Oral Expression; Written Expression; Fluency of Ideas; Originality; Problem Sensitivity; Deductive Reasoning; Inductive Reasoning; Information Ordering; Category Flexibility; Mathematical Reasoning; Number Facility; Memorization; Speed of Closure; Perceptual Speed; Selective Attention; Time Sharing; Near Vision; Auditory Attention; Speech Recognition; Speech Clarity

General Office Clerks

▲ Growth: 7%

▲ Annual Job Openings: 661,333

▲ Yearly Earnings $19,281

▲ Education Required: Short-term O-J-T

▲ Self-employed: 0%

▲ Part-time: 30%

General Office Clerks

Perform duties too varied and diverse to be classified in any specific office clerical occupation. Clerical duties may be assigned in accordance with the office procedures of individual establishments and may include a combination of bookkeeping, typing, stenography, office machine operation, and filing. Compiles, copies, sorts, and files records of office activities, business transactions, and other activities. Computes, records, and proofreads data and other information, such as records or reports. Operates office machines, such as photocopier, telecopier, and personal computer. Completes and mails bills, contracts, policies, invoices, or checks. Stuffs envelopes and addresses, stamps, sorts, and distributes mail, packages, and other materials. Transcribes dictation and composes and types letters and other correspondence, using typewriter or computer. Orders materials, supplies, and services, and completes records and reports. Answers telephone, responds to requests, delivers messages, and runs errands. Reviews files, records, and other documents to obtain information to respond to requests. Completes work schedules and arranges appointments for staff and students. Collects, counts, and disburses money, completes banking transactions, and processes payroll. Communicates with customers, employees, and other individuals to disseminate or explain information.

Knowledge: Clerical; Economics and Accounting; Customer and Personal Service; Telecommunications

Abilities: Number Facility; Perceptual Speed; Wrist-Finger Speed; Near Vision; Speech Recognition

General Utility Maintenance Repairers

▲ Growth: 18%
▲ Annual Job Openings: 192,097
▲ Yearly Earnings $23,233
▲ Education Required: Long-term O-J-T
▲ Self-employed: 3%
▲ Part-time: 9%

Maintenance Repairers, General Utility

Perform work involving two or more maintenance skills to keep machines, mechanical equipment, or structure of an establishment in repair. Duties may involve pipefitting, boilermaking, insulating, welding, machining, machine and equipment repairing, carpentry, and electrical work. May also include planning and laying out of work relating to repairs; repairing electrical or mechanical equipment; installing, aligning, and balancing new equipment; and repairing buildings, floors, or stairs. This occupation is generally found in small establishments, where specialization in maintenance work is impractical. Inspects and tests machinery and equipment to diagnose machine malfunctions. Dismantles and reassembles defective machines and equipment. Installs new or repaired parts. Cleans and lubricates shafts, bearings, gears, and other parts of machinery. Installs or repairs wiring and electrical and electronic components. Assembles, installs, or repairs pipe systems and hydraulic and pneumatic equipment. Installs machinery and equipment. Assembles, installs, or repairs plumbing. Paints and repairs woodwork and plaster. Lays brick to repair and maintain physical structure of establishment. Sets up and operates machine tools to repair or fabricate machine parts, jigs and fixtures, and tools. Operates cutting torch or welding equipment to cut or join metal parts. Fabricates and repairs counters, benches, partitions, and other wooden structures, such as sheds and outbuildings. Records repairs made and costs. Estimates costs of repairs.

Knowledge: Engineering and Technology; Design; Building and Construction; Mechanical; Public Safety and Security

Abilities: Problem Sensitivity; Information Ordering; Category Flexibility; Memorization; Speed of Closure; Flexibility of Closure; Perceptual Speed; Spatial Orientation; Visualization; Selective Attention; Arm-Hand Steadiness; Manual Dexterity; Finger Dexterity; Control Precision; Multilimb Coordination; Response Orientation; Reaction Time; Wrist-Finger Speed; Speed of Limb Movement; Static Strength; Explosive Strength; Dynamic Strength; Trunk Strength; Stamina; Extent Flexibility; Dynamic Flexibility; Gross Body Coordination; Gross Body Equilibrium; Far Vision; Visual Color Discrimination; Night Vision; Peripheral Vision; Depth Perception; Glare Sensitivity; Hearing Sensitivity; Auditory Attention; Sound Localization

Geologists, Geophysicists, and Oceanographers

- ▲ Growth: 15%
- ▲ Annual Job Openings: 1,687
- ▲ Yearly Earnings $52,083
- ▲ Education Required: Bachelor's degree
- ▲ Self-employed: 15%
- ▲ Part-time: 6%

Geologists

Study composition, structure, and history of the earth's crust; examine rocks, minerals, and fossil remains to identify and determine the sequence of processes affecting the development of the earth; apply knowledge of chemistry, physics, biology, and mathematics to explain these phenomena and to help locate mineral and petroleum deposits and underground water resources; prepare geologic reports and maps; and interpret research data to recommend further action for study. Studies, examines, measures, and classifies composition, structure, and history of earth's crust, including rocks, minerals, fossils, soil, and ocean floor. Identifies and determines sequence of processes affecting development of earth. Locates and estimates probable gas and oil deposits, using aerial photographs, charts, and research and survey results. Prepares geological reports, maps, charts, and diagrams. Interprets research data, and recommends further study or action. Analyzes engineering problems at construction projects, such as dams, tunnels, and large buildings, applying geological knowledge. Tests industrial diamonds and abrasives, soil, or rocks to determine geological characteristics, using optical, X ray, heat, acid, and precision instruments. Inspects proposed construction site and sets up test equipment and drilling machinery. Measures characteristics of earth, using seismograph, gravimeter, torsion balance, magnetometer, pendulum devices, and electrical resistivity apparatus. Directs field crews drilling exploratory wells and boreholes or collecting samples of rocks and soil. Recommends and prepares reports on foundation design, acquisition, retention, or release of property leases, or areas of further research. Develops instruments for geological work, such as diamond tools and dies, jeweled bearings, and grinding laps and wheels. Repairs diamond and abrasive tools.

Knowledge: Administration and Management; Engineering and Technology; Design; Mechanical; Mathematics; Physics; Chemistry; Biology; Psychology; Sociology and Anthropology; Geography; English Language; History and Archeology; Communications and Media

Abilities: Oral Comprehension; Written Comprehension; Written Expression; Deductive Reasoning; Inductive Reasoning; Category Flexibility; Mathematical Reasoning; Number Facility; Memorization; Flexibility of Closure

Geophysicists

Study physical aspects of the earth, including the atmosphere and hydrosphere. Investigate and measure seismic, gravitational, electrical, thermal, and magnetic forces affecting the earth, utilizing principles of physics, mathematics, and chemistry. Studies and analyzes physical aspects of the earth, including atmosphere and hydrosphere, and interior structure. Studies, measures, and interprets seismic, gravitational, electrical, thermal, and magnetic forces and data affecting the earth. Studies, maps, and charts distribution, disposition, and development of waters of land areas, including form and intensity of precipitation. Studies waters of land areas to determine modes of return to ocean and atmosphere. Investigates origin and activity of glaciers, volcanoes, and earthquakes. Compiles and evaluates data to prepare navigational charts and maps, predict atmospheric conditions, and prepare environmental reports. Evaluates data in reference to project planning, such as flood and drought control, water power and supply, drainage, irrigation, and inland navigation. Prepares and issues maps and reports indicating areas of seismic risk to existing or proposed construction or development.

Knowledge: Mathematics; Physics; Chemistry; Geography; English Language; History and Archeology; Communications and Media

Abilities: Oral Comprehension; Written Comprehension; Written Expression; Fluency of Ideas; Deductive Reasoning; Inductive Reasoning; Category Flexibility; Mathematical Reasoning; Number Facility; Flexibility of Closure

Guards

- ▲ Growth: 23%
- ▲ Annual Job Openings: 283,077
- ▲ Yearly Earnings $16,640
- ▲ Education Required: Short-term O-J-T
- ▲ Self-employed: 0%
- ▲ Part-time: 19%

Guards and Watch Guards

Stand guard at entrance gate or walk about premises of business or industrial establishment to prevent theft, violence, or infractions of rules. Guard property against fire, theft, vandalism, and illegal entry. Direct patrons or employees and answer questions relative to services of establishment. Control traffic to and from buildings and grounds. Include workers who perform these functions using a car patrol. Patrols industrial and commercial premises to prevent and detect signs of intrusion and ensure security of doors, windows, and gates. Monitors and authorizes entrance and departure of employees, visitors, and other persons to guard against theft and to maintain security of premises. Warns persons of rule infractions or violations, and apprehends or evicts violators from premises, using force when necessary. Answers alarms and investigates disturbances. Circulates among visitors, patrons, and employees to preserve order and protect property. Calls police or fire departments in cases of emergency, such as fire or presence of unauthorized persons. Inspects and adjusts security systems, equipment, and machinery to ensure operational use and to detect evidence of tampering. Operates detecting devices to screen individuals and prevent passage of prohibited articles into restricted areas. Drives and guards armored vehicle to transport money and valuables to prevent theft and ensure safe delivery. Answers telephone calls to take messages, answer questions, and provide information during nonbusiness hours or when switchboard is closed. Writes reports of daily activities and irregularities, such as equipment or property damage, theft, presence of unauthorized persons, or unusual occurrences. Escorts or drives motor vehicle to transport individuals to specified locations and to provide personal protection. Monitors and adjusts controls that regulate building systems, such as air-conditioning, furnace, or boiler. Picks up and removes garbage, mows lawns, and sweeps gate areas to maintain grounds and premises.

Knowledge: Customer and Personal Service; Psychology; Geography; Public Safety and Security; Law, Government, and Jurisprudence; Telecommunications; Transportation

Abilities: Memorization; Flexibility of Closure; Perceptual Speed; Spatial Orientation; Selective Attention; Time Sharing; Multilimb Coordination; Response Orientation; Rate Control; Reaction Time; Speed of Limb Movement; Static Strength; Explosive Strength; Dynamic Strength; Trunk Strength; Stamina; Gross Body Coordination; Gross Body Equilibrium; Far Vision; Night Vision; Peripheral Vision; Depth Perception; Glare Sensitivity; Hearing Sensitivity; Auditory Attention; Sound Localization; Speech Recognition

Hairdressers, Hairstylists, and Cosmetologists

▲ Growth: 10%

▲ Annual Job Openings: 90,496

▲ Yearly Earnings $16,744

▲ Education Required: Postsecondary vocational training

▲ Self-employed: 42%

▲ Part-time: 36%

Hairdressers, Hairstylists, and Cosmetologists

Provide beauty services, such as shampooing, cutting, coloring, and styling hair, and massaging and treating scalp. May also apply make-up, dress wigs, perform hair removal, and provide nail and skin care services. Cuts, trims, and shapes hair or hair pieces, using clippers, scissors, trimmers, and razors. Shampoos, rinses, and dries hair and scalp orhair pieces with water, liquid soap, or other solutions. Bleaches, dyes, or tints hair, using applicator or brush. Applies water, setting, or waving solutions to hair and winds hair on curlers or rollers. Combs, brushes, and sprays hair or wigs to set style. Attaches wig or hairpiece to model head and dresses wigs and hairpieces according to instructions, samples, sketches, or photographs. Analyzes patron's hair and other physical features or reads make-up instructions to determine and recommend beauty treatment. Massages and treats scalp for hygienic and remedial purposes, using hands, fingers, or vibrating equipment. Administers therapeutic medication and advises patron to seek medical treatment for chronic or contagious scalp conditions. Recommends and applies cosmetics, lotions, and creams to patron to soften and lubricate skin and enhance and restore natural appearance. Shapes and colors eyebrows or eyelashes and removes facial hair, using depilatory cream and tweezers. Cleans, shapes, and polishes fingernails and toenails, using files and nail polish. Updates and maintains customer information records, such as beauty services provided or personal effects of deceased patron.

Knowledge: Customer and Personal Service

Abilities: Originality; Arm-Hand Steadiness; Manual Dexterity; Finger Dexterity; Dynamic Flexibility; Gross Body Equilibrium; Visual Color Discrimination

Make-Up Artists, Theatrical and Performance

Apply make-up to performers to reflect period, setting, and situation of their role. Applies make-up to performers to alter their appearance to accord with their roles. Selects desired makeup shades from stock, or mixes oil, grease, and coloring to achieve special color effects. Attaches prostheses to performer and applies make-up to change physical features and depict desired character. Designs rubber or plastic prostheses and requisitions materials, such as wigs, beards, and special cosmetics. Studies production information, such as character, period settings, and situations to determine make-up requirements. Confers with stage or motion picture officials and performers to determine dress or make-up alterations. Examines sketches, photographs, and plaster models to obtain desired character image depiction. Creates character drawings or models, based upon independent research to augment period production files.

Knowledge: Sociology and Anthropology; Fine Arts; History and Archeology

Abilities: Originality; Visualization; Arm-Hand Steadiness; Manual Dexterity; Finger Dexterity; Visual Color Discrimination

Electrologists

Remove unwanted hair from patrons for cosmetic purposes using electrolysis equipment. Swabs skin area with antiseptic solution and inserts needle into hair follicle and papilla. Presses switch and adjusts timing and controls of equipment to regulate flow of electricity through needles to decompose papilla cells. Removes needle or needles and pulls hair from follicle, using tweezers. Positions sterile bulbous or round-tipped needles into electrodes of galvanic or short-wave electrical equipment. Places secondary electrode in patron's hand to complete circuit and stabilize amount of electricity during equipment operation.

Knowledge: Customer and Personal Service

Abilities: Arm-Hand Steadiness; Manual Dexterity; Finger Dexterity; Control Precision; Wrist-Finger Speed; Near Vision

Hand Packers and Packagers

▲ Growth: 23%
▲ Annual Job Openings: 271,086
▲ Yearly Earnings $14,560
▲ Education Required: Short-term O-J-T
▲ Self-employed: 0%
▲ Part-time: 16%

Packers and Packagers—Hand

Pack or package by hand a wide variety of products and materials. Fastens and wraps products and materials, using hand tools. Seals containers or materials, using glues, fasteners, and hand tools. Assembles and lines cartons, crates, and containers, using hand tools. Places or pours products or materials into containers, using hand tools and equipment. Obtains and sorts products, materials, and orders, using hand tools. Marks and labels containers or products, using marking instruments. Examines and inspects containers, materials, and products to ensure packaging process meets specifications. Loads materials and products into package processing equipment. Records product and packaging information on specified forms and records. Measures, weighs, and counts products and materials, using equipment. Removes and places completed or defective product or materials on moving equipment or specified area. Tends packing machines and equipment that prepare and package materials and products. Cleans containers, materials, or work area, using cleaning solutions and hand tools.

Knowledge: None above average

Abilities: Manual Dexterity; Dynamic Flexibility

Hand Workers

▲ Growth: 1%
▲ Annual Job Openings: 267,301
▲ Yearly Earnings $17,825
▲ Education Required: Short-term O-J-T
▲ Self-employed: 3%
▲ Part-time: 8%

Pantograph Engravers

Affix identifying information onto a variety of materials and products, using engraving machines or equipment. Starts machine and guides stylus over template, causing cutting tool to simultaneously duplicate design or letters on workpiece. Adjusts depth and size of cut by adjusting height of work table or by adjusting gauge on machine arms. Sets stylus at beginning of pattern. Selects and inserts letter or design template beneath stylus attached to machine cutting tool or router, according to work order. Positions and secures workpiece—such as nameplate, stamp, seal, badge, trophy, or bowling ball—in holding fixture, using measuring instruments. Sets reduction scale to obtain required reproduction ratio on workpiece. Inserts cutting tool or bit into machine and secures with wrench. Observes action of cutting tool through microscope, and adjusts movement of stylus to ensure accurate reproduction. Brushes acid over designated engraving to darken or highlight inscription. Verifies conformance to specifications, using micrometers and calipers. Examines engraving for quality of cut, burrs, rough spots, and irregular or incomplete engraving. Sharpens cutting tools on cutter grinder.

Knowledge: None above average

Abilities: Arm-Hand Steadiness; Manual Dexterity; Control Precision; Rate Control; Wrist-Finger Speed; Near Vision; Depth Perception

Etchers, Hand

Etch patterns, designs, lettering, or figures onto a variety of materials and products. Exposes workpiece to acid to develop etch pattern, such as designs, lettering, or figures. Fills etched characters with opaque paste to improve readability. Prepares workpiece for etching by cutting, sanding, cleaning, or treating with wax, acid resist, lime, etching powder, or light-sensitive enamel. Transfers image to workpiece, using contact printer, pantograph stylus, silkscreen printing device, or stamp pad. Neutralizes workpiece to remove acid, wax, or enamel, using water or solvents. Measures and marks workpiece, such as plastic, fiberglass, epoxy board, metal, or glass, using measuring and calibrating equipment. Prepares etching solution according to formula. Inspects etched work for uniformity, using calibrated microscope and gauge. Positions and secures workpiece to be etched on set-up board. Compares workpiece design—such as lettering, trademark, numerals, or lines—to sample to verify development of pattern. Reduces artwork, using reduction camera.

Knowledge: Production and Processing; Design; Fine Arts

Abilities: Arm-Hand Steadiness; Manual Dexterity; Finger Dexterity

Printers, Hand

Print patterns, designs, and lettering by hand onto a variety of materials and products. Applies ink, paint, color paste, metallic foil, or carbon tissue to workpiece or printing mechanism. Reads blueprints, work orders, or specifications to determine design or letters to be imprinted and location of imprint on workpiece. Lays out and marks workpiece, using measuring and drawing equipment. Prepares surface of workpiece, using solvents, pumice, photo resist solution, or lacquer. Aligns, positions, and secures workpiece in holding fixture or on work table. Sets guides and positions design template, transfer, screen, stamp, type bar, frame, or heated imprint bar over workpiece in printing mechanism. Operates printing equipment such as screen printer, silk screen press, stamp, or heat imprints, to imprint design on workpiece. Inspects workpiece for defects and uniformity of depth, and to ensure quality of printing. Mixes chemicals, inks, or paints, according to standard formula. Cleans equipment, using spatula, water, or solvent. Fabricates silk screen stencils or prepares photomasks for reticle-making process, using photographic equipment. Affixes gummed labels or decals to workpiece, using automatic equipment or roller.

Knowledge: Production and Processing; Fine Arts

Abilities: Arm-Hand Steadiness; Finger Dexterity; Rate Control; Visual Color Discrimination

Engravers, Hand

Engrave designs and identifying information onto rollers or plates used in printing. Cuts grooves of specified depth and uniformity into printing roller, following lines of design impression. Cuts around drawn pattern leaving raised design or letters, using cutting tools. Presses sketch on copper printing roller to produce impression of design. Traces pattern of design and letters in reverse on linoleum or on two- or three-ply rubber, using ruler, pencil, drawing instruments, or cutting tools. Cuts strip of engraving gum (two- or three-ply rubber, cemented to cloth backing), using knife. Prepares additional rubber plates for jobs requiring colors by omitting different portions of design or lettering on each plate. Refers to sketch to ensure that lines of only one printing color are engraved into each roller. Glues rubber or linoleum pattern to wood block. Punches holes in plate to fasten plate to press, using hand tools. Inspects designs for defective engraving and re-engraves to meet specifications.

Knowledge: Production and Processing; Design; Fine Arts

Abilities: Arm-Hand Steadiness; Manual Dexterity; Finger Dexterity; Visual Color Discrimination; Depth Perception

Assemblers and Fabricators— Except Machine, Electrical, Electronic, and Precision

Assemble or fit together parts to form complete units or subassemblies at a bench or conveyor line, or on the floor. Work may involve the use of hand tools, power tools, and special equipment in order to carry out fitting and assembly operations. Include assemblers whose duties are of a nonprecision nature. Exclude electrical, electronic, machine, and precision assemblers, and workers who perform specialized operations exclusively as part of assembly operations, such as riveting, welding, soldering, machining, or sawing. Bolts, clips, nails, rivets, screws, welds, or otherwise fastens component parts of assembly together, using hand tools, power tools, or bench machines. Sews, staples, or tacks material together, using sewing machine, staple gun, or hand tools. Positions, fits, or aligns parts on workbench, floor, or machine, following blueprints, diagrams, guides, holes, reference marks, or work orders. Drills, taps, or reams holes to prepare parts for assembly, using arbor or drill press or other bench-mounted drills. Files, grinds, planes, sands, or buffs parts to remove burrs, alter shape, improve fit, or smooth finish, using hand tools or power tools. Applies adhesive, bonding agent, sealant, or paint to surface of material by brushing, spraying, dipping, or rolling. Bends, crimps, or presses materials to specified shape or curvature, using hand tools, bending machine, or pressing machine. Holds parts during assembly, using hands, clamps, pneumatic screw presses, or other work aids. Pours, stuffs, or otherwise fills products or containers with specified amount of material. Measures and marks reference lines and points on parts, according to specifications, using template, rule, or other marking device. Cuts materials, such as fabric, metal, paper, or wood, into specified dimensions or shapes, using cutting machine, scissors, or knife. Reads process charts, work orders, blueprints, or other specifications to determine assembly sequence, machine and tooling requirements, measurements, and tolerances. Inspects, tests, and verifies accuracy of assembled article for conformance to standards, using measuring or testing equipment or by visual examination. Adjusts, repairs, or replaces defective product parts, using hand tools. Cleans dust, dirt, oil, and other foreign matter from material or machine surfaces, using cleaning solution, rags, or air hose. Records production data on paper or in computer. Lifts, loads, sorts, and moves materials, supplies, and finished products between storage and work areas, using pushcart, hoist, or dolly. Packages product in containers for shipment or ties into bundles. Stamps, labels, or otherwise marks product or packages with identifying data.

Knowledge: Production and Processing; Building and Construction

Abilities: Visualization; Arm-Hand Steadiness; Manual Dexterity; Finger Dexterity; Control Precision; Multilimb Coordination; Wrist-Finger Speed; Speed of Limb Movement

H

Intermediate Hand Workers

Workers who manually perform handwork that usually requires three months to two years to obtain proficiency. Performs the same or similar process for multiple items or the same items. (Note: Workers do not perform all tasks; job activity is represented by one or two task statements.) Cleans, presses, or dyes articles, such as clothing, rugs, or furnishings, to improve appearance, using hand tools or hand-operated equipment. Assembles parts and materials of metal, wood, and plastic, according to specifications, using hand tools. Shapes material by cumulative addition of material to build up original mass, and presses material into shape. Sorts, weighs, or packages materials. Embroiders or hand-sews designs over stamped or stenciled patterns on fabric. Stretches, bends, straightens, shapes, pounds, or presses metal or plastic, according to specifications, using hand tools. Joins parts together and fastens with sticky substances, such as cement, glue, paste, gum, or other adhesives, or caulks seams. Threads or pulls cables or lines through ducts or fabric seams. Folds fabrics to make pleats or to pack parachutes. Punches symbols in perforated tape or notches in negative film, using electric tape puncher, film footage counter, and hand holder. Smooths and finishes materials such as leather or bisque ware. Stacks or arranges products, such as blocks, bricks, pipe, and roofing tile, in specified patterns. Positions and aligns materials and parts in preparation for assembly or other production processes such as grinding. Mixes or blends materials in solid, fluid, semi-fluid, and gaseous states, according to formula. Determines style and size of standard patterns, and gathers and assembles specified materials and accessories in preparation for next procedure. Sharpens objects, such as buhrstones in grain grinding mills, using sharpening tools. Fills containers, such as thermostat bellows or illuminated sign tubing, with gas or liquid. Converts fiber raw stock into yarn and thread, or interlaces and works yarns to form woven, nonwoven, knitted, and tufted fabrics. Removes metals, such gold, platinum, and palladium, from objects such as dentures and extracted teeth, using furnace, retort, and laboratory equipment. Prepares products for use, such as burning interior of barrel to be used for aging whiskey.

Knowledge: Production and Processing; Building and Construction

Abilities: Perceptual Speed; Selective Attention; Arm-Hand Steadiness; Finger Dexterity; Speed of Limb Movement; Dynamic Flexibility; Gross Body Equilibrium; Visual Color Discrimination; Depth Perception; Hearing Sensitivity

Elemental Hand Workers

Workers who perform handwork that requires less than three months to obtain proficiency. (Note: Workers do not perform all tasks; job activity is represented by one or two task statements.) Cleans, blocks, dyes, presses, brushes, or treats articles such as shoes, furniture, drapes, leather goods, or ophthalmic or optical elements. Mixes or blends materials in solid, fluid, semi-fluid, and gaseous states, such as chemicals or food products, according to formula. Converts fiber stock into yarn and thread, or braids, interlaces, or works materials to form fabric, decorative designs, or rugs by hand. Fills molds or ladles with molten metal, hot material, or other substances to produce products, and removes products from molds. Stretches, bends, straightens, forms, shapes, pounds, wraps, or folds materials, according to specifications, using hand tools. Assembles or disassembles parts and materials, according to standard patterns, using hand tools. Splices and joins parts together with adhesives, caulks or seals seams, or binds materials, using binding, strapping, crimping, or soldering tools. Smooths, trims, and finishes materials, parts, and products, using sanding or buffing tools, according to specifications. Repairs, replaces, or adjusts parts, either fabric, paper, or metal, according to instructions or specifications, using hand tools. Cuts, saws, splits, or drills material or products in preparation for further processing, according to specifications, using hand tools. Threads materials, such as cable, rope, string, or yarn, through openings to thread machines, wire, or assemble clothes or jewelry. Loads, sorts, weighs, stacks, arranges, or packages materials, parts, or products, according to instructions. Applies coating to material, such as paint, oil, lacquer, chemical(s), or powder, using sprayer, squeeze bottle, brush, or dipping method. Stamps, marks, or traces patterns on products, parts, or materials, using pencil, hand-transfer press, or perforating tool. Screws or hammers nails or pegs into products, using hammer or screwdriver, according to instructions. Repairs, cuts, or softens glass, using torch, hot wire, or furnace, according to instructions. Charges, positions covers, and seals storage batteries. Skims or siphons materials, such as slag or plasma, preparatory to further processing. Combs, brushes, ties, sorts, or cuts human or doll hair or material nap, according to specifications. Positions, aligns, and secures molds, materials, parts, or products in preparation for assembly or other production processes.

Knowledge: None above average

Abilities: Manual Dexterity; Finger Dexterity; Wrist-Finger Speed; Speed of Limb Movement

Health Care Support Specialists

▲ Growth: 24%

▲ Annual Job Openings: 45,719

▲ Yearly Earnings $31,054

▲ Education Required: Associate degree

▲ Self-employed: 3%

▲ Part-time: 22%

Dietetic Technicians

Provide service in assigned areas of food service management. Teach principles of food and nutrition and provide dietary counseling under direction of dietitians. Guides individuals and families in food selection, preparation, and menu planning, based upon nutritional needs. Plans menus based on established guidelines. Obtains and evaluates dietary histories of individuals to plan nutritional programs. Selects, schedules, and conducts orientation and in-service education programs. Standardizes recipes and tests new products for use in facility. Supervises food production and service. Assists in referrals for continuity of patient care. Assists in implementing established cost control procedures. Develops job specifications, job descriptions, and work schedules.

Knowledge: Administration and Management; Economics and Accounting; Customer and Personal Service; Personnel and Human Resources; Food Production; Chemistry; Biology; Psychology; Sociology and Anthropology; Medicine and Dentistry; Education and Training

Abilities: Fluency of Ideas; Originality; Speech Clarity

Health Service Coordinators

Conduct or coordinate health programs or services in hospitals, private homes, businesses, or other institutions. Monitors medical records to schedule services or to determine patient review dates according to established criteria. Analyzes utilization of health care program and legitimacy of admission and treatment to ensure quality or compliance with reimbursement policies. Formulates and negotiates health program contracts between insurance companies and health care providers, utilizing standard agreement procedures and insurance company policies. Presents health care program to participating parties and discusses program modifications or health and nutritional issues. Interviews individuals to obtain participant medical histories and maintains health records. Evaluates services and prepares reports. Investigates and resolves claims reimbursement and program procedural problems. Reviews application for patient admission, according to insurance and governmental standards, and approves admission or refers for review. Abstracts or compiles information and data and maintains statistics. Oversees and coordinates activities of staff or in hospital services. Conducts information and training workshops on resolving claim processing errors. Participates in health advisory committee or quality assurance reviews.

Knowledge: Administration and Management; Clerical; Customer and Personal Service; Personnel and Human Resources; Medicine and Dentistry; Therapy and Counseling; Education and Training

Abilities: Oral Comprehension; Written Comprehension; Oral Expression; Written Expression; Problem Sensitivity; Deductive Reasoning; Inductive Reasoning; Mathematical Reasoning; Number Facility; Memorization; Perceptual Speed; Time Sharing

Transplant Coordinators

Plan and coordinate organ and tissue services and solicit medical and community groups for organ and tissue donors. Assists medical team in retrieval of organs for transplantation, using medical instruments. Solicits medical and community groups for organ donors. Coordinates in-hospital services. Communicates with donors, patients, and health team members to ensure comprehensive documentation. Analyzes medical data of organ donors and recipients from medical and social records, physical examination, and consultation with health team. Compares collected data to normal values and correlates. Correlates and summarizes laboratory reports, X rays, and office test to assist physician to determine medical suitability for procedure. Schedules recipient and donor laboratory tests to determine histocompatibility of blood or tissue of recipient donor. Counsels recipient and donor to alleviate anxieties and assists recipient and donor throughout procedure. Assesses progress of patient and offers advice and assistance to patient following transplant. Advises post-operative patients on therapies for managing health after transplant and serves as team member monitor.

Knowledge: Administration and Management; Clerical; Customer and Personal Service; Mathematics; Biology; Psychology; Medicine and Dentistry; Therapy and Counseling

Abilities: Oral Comprehension; Written Comprehension; Oral Expression; Written Expression; Problem Sensitivity; Inductive Reasoning; Information Ordering; Memorization; Speed of Closure; Flexibility of Closure; Perceptual Speed; Time Sharing; Arm-Hand Steadiness; Manual Dexterity; Finger Dexterity; Response Orientation; Reaction Time; Wrist-Finger Speed; Near Vision; Depth Perception; Speech Recognition; Speech Clarity

Occupational Health and Safety Specialists

Review, evaluate, and analyze work environments and design programs and procedures to control, eliminate, and prevent disease or injury caused by chemical, physical, and biological agents or ergonomic factors. Investigates adequacy of ventilation, exhaust equipment, lighting, and other conditions which may affect employee health, comfort, or efficiency. Conducts evaluations of exposure to ionizing and nonionizing radiation and to noise. Collects samples of dust, gases, vapors, and other potentially toxic materials for analysis. Recommends measures to ensure maximum employee protection. Collaborates with engineers and physicians to institute control and remedial measures for hazardous and potentially hazardous conditions of equipment. Participates in educational meetings to instruct employees in matters pertaining to occupational health and prevention of accidents. Prepares reports, including observations, analysis of contaminants, and recommendation for control and correction of hazards. Reviews physicians' reports and conducts worker studies to determine if diseases or illnesses are job-related. Prepares and calibrates equipment used to collect and analyze samples. Prepares documents to be used in legal proceedings and gives testimony in court proceedings. Uses cost-benefit analysis to justify money spent.

Knowledge: Economics and Accounting; Physics; Chemistry; Biology; Medicine and Dentistry; Education and Training; Public Safety and Security; Law, Government, and Jurisprudence

Abilities: Written Comprehension; Oral Expression; Written Expression; Originality; Problem Sensitivity; Deductive Reasoning; Inductive Reasoning; Mathematical Reasoning; Number Facility; Memorization; Speed of Closure; Flexibility of Closure

Orthotists and Prosthetists

Fabricate and fit orthopedic braces or prostheses to assist patients with disabling conditions of limbs and spine, or with partial or total absence of limb. Fits patients for device, using static and dynamic alignments. Assists physician in formulating specifications and prescription for orthopedic and/or prosthetic devices. Designs orthopedic and prosthetic devices, according to physician's prescription. Selects materials and components, and makes cast measurements, model modifications, and layouts, using measuring equipment. Evaluates device on patient and makes adjustments to assure fit, function, comfort, and quality. Instructs patients in use of orthopedic or prosthetic devices. Examines, measures, and evaluates patients' needs in relation to disease and functional loss. Maintains patients' records. Repairs and maintains orthopedic prosthetic devices, using hand tools. Supervises laboratory activities or activities of prosthetic assistants and support staff relating to development of orthopedic or prosthetic devices. Lectures and demonstrates to colleagues and other professionals concerned with orthopedics or prosthetics. Participates in research to modify design, fit, and function of orthopedic or prosthetic devices.

Knowledge: Customer and Personal Service; Engineering and Technology; Design; Building and Construction; Psychology; Medicine and Dentistry; Therapy and Counseling; Education and Training

Abilities: Oral Comprehension; Written Comprehension; Oral Expression; Fluency of Ideas; Originality; Problem Sensitivity; Deductive Reasoning; Inductive Reasoning; Category Flexibility; Speed of Closure; Visualization; Time Sharing; Arm-Hand Steadiness; Finger Dexterity; Control Precision; Near Vision; Speech Clarity

Pheresis Technicians

Collect blood components and provide therapeutic treatment, such as replacement of plasma or removal of white blood cells or platelets, using blood cell separator equipment. Punctures vein of donor/patient with needle to connect donor or patient to tubing of equipment in preparation for procedure. Adjusts equipment settings for blood collection or replacement. Monitors equipment and observes warning lights indicating equipment problems. Connects and installs tubing, fluid containers, and other components to set up equipment. Compiles and evaluates donor/patient information, such as blood pressure and weight, to ensure that screening criteria are met. Explains procedures to patient to reduce anxieties and obtain cooperation. Talks to and observes patient for distress or side effects, such as nausea or fainting, during procedure. Records information such as flow rate, anticoagulant rate, temperature, and blood pressure following blood collection or treatment. Forwards collection bag to laboratory for testing or further processing.

Knowledge: Biology; Psychology; Medicine and Dentistry; Therapy and Counseling

Abilities: Perceptual Speed; Arm-Hand Steadiness; Manual Dexterity; Finger Dexterity; Control Precision; Response Orientation; Reaction Time; Wrist-Finger Speed; Near Vision

Optometric and Ophthalmic Technicians

Test and measure eye function to assist with diagnosis and treatment of disease. Tests and measures patient's acuity, peripheral vision, depth perception, focus, ocular movement and color, as requested by physician. Measures intraocular pressure of eyes, using glaucoma test. Measures axial length of eye, using ultrasound equipment. Examines eye for abnormalities of cornea and anterior or posterior chambers, using slit lamp. Applies drops to anesthetize, dilate, or medicate eyes. Instructs patient in eye care and use of glasses or contact lenses. Instructs patient in vision therapy, using eye exercises. Obtains and records patient's preliminary case history. Adjusts and repairs glasses, using screwdrivers and pliers. Assists patient in frame selection. Assists in fabrication of eye glasses or contact lenses. Develops visual skills, near-visual discrimination, and depth perception, using developmental glasses. Maintains records, schedules appointments, and performs bookkeeping, correspondence, and filing. Maintains inventory of materials and cleans instruments.

Knowledge: Customer and Personal Service; Biology; Medicine and Dentistry; Therapy and Counseling

Abilities: Near Vision; Peripheral Vision; Depth Perception

Audiometrists

Administer audiometric screening and threshold tests under supervision of audiologist or otolaryngologist and refer individual to audiologist or other health professional for test interpretation or further examination. Fits earphones on individuals and provides instruction on procedures to be followed. Adjusts audiometer to control sound emitted and records subjects' responses. Refers individuals to audiologist for interpretation of test results and more definitive hearing examination, or to physician for medical examination.

Knowledge: None above average

Abilities: None above average

Dialysis Technicians

Set up and operate hemodialysis machine to provide dialysis treatment for patients with kidney failure. Starts blood flow at prescribed rate. Inspects equipment settings, including pressure, conductivity, and temperature, to ensure conformance to safety standards. Attaches tubing to assemble machine for use. Mixes solution according to formula and primes equipment. Calculates fluid removal or replacement to be achieved during dialysis procedure. Monitors patient for adverse reaction and machine malfunction. Cleans area of access with antiseptic solution. Connects patient to machine, using needle or catheter. Records patient's predialysis and postdialysis weight, temperature, and blood pressure. Explains procedures and operation of equipment to patient. Transports patient to and from treatment room.

Knowledge: Customer and Personal Service; Chemistry; Biology; Medicine and Dentistry; Therapy and Counseling

Abilities: Information Ordering

Heat, Air Conditioning, and Refrigeration Mechanics and Installers

- ▲ Growth: 17%
- ▲ Annual Job Openings: 22,587
- ▲ Yearly Earnings $29,161
- ▲ Education Required: Long-term O-J-T
- ▲ Self-employed: 14%
- ▲ Part-time: 4%

Heating and Air-Conditioning Mechanics

Install, service, and repair heating and air-conditioning systems in residences and commercial establishments. Installs, connects, and adjusts thermostats, humidistats, and timers, using hand tools. Repairs or replaces defective equipment, components, or wiring. Joins pipes or tubing to equipment and to fuel, water, or refrigerant source, to form complete circuit. Fabricates, assembles, and installs duct work and chassis parts, using portable metal-working tools and welding equipment. Tests electrical circuits and components for continuity, using electrical test equipment. Disassembles system and cleans and oils parts. Assembles, positions, and mounts heating or cooling equipment, following blueprints. Tests pipe or tubing joints and connections for leaks, using pressure gauge or soap-and-water solution. Installs auxiliary components to heating-cooling equipment, such as expansion and discharge valves, air ducts, pipes, blowers, dampers, flues, and stokers, following blueprints. Adjusts system controls to setting recommended by manufacturer to balance system, using hand tools. Inspects and tests system to verify system compliance with plans and specifications and to detect malfunctions. Discusses heating-cooling system malfunctions with users to isolate problems or to verify malfunctions have been corrected. Inspects inoperative equipment to locate source of trouble. Studies blueprints to determine configuration of heating or cooling equipment components. Wraps pipes in insulation and secures it in place with cement or wire bands. Lays out and connects electrical wiring between controls and equipment according to wiring diagram, using electrician's hand tools. Reassembles equipment and starts unit to test operation. Measures, cuts, threads, and bends pipe or tubing, using pipefitter's tools. Cuts and drills holes in floors, walls, and roof to install equipment, using power saws and drills.

Knowledge: Engineering and Technology; Design; Building and Construction; Mechanical

Abilities: Arm-Hand Steadiness; Manual Dexterity; Finger Dexterity; Multilimb Coordination; Extent Flexibility; Gross Body Equilibrium

Refrigeration Mechanics

Install and repair industrial and commercial refrigerating systems. Mounts compressor, condenser, and other components in specified location on frame, using hand tools and acetylene welding equipment. Assembles structural and functional components, such as controls, switches, gauges, wiring harnesses, valves, pumps, compressors, condensers, cores, and pipes. Installs expansion and control valves, using acetylene torch and wrenches. Replaces or adjusts defective or worn parts to repair system, and reassembles system. Cuts, bends, threads, and connects pipe to functional components and water, power, or refrigeration system. Brazes or solders parts to repair defective joints and leaks. Fabricates and assembles components and structural portions of refrigeration system, using hand tools, power tools, and welding equipment. Drills holes and installs mounting brackets and hangers into floor and walls of building. Lifts and aligns components into position, using hoist or block and tackle. Adjusts valves according to specifications, and charges system with specified type of refrigerant. Observes system operation, using gauges and instruments, and adjusts or replaces mechanisms and parts, according to specifications. Dismantles malfunctioning systems and tests components, using electrical, mechanical, and pneumatic testing equipment. Lays out reference points for installation of structural and functional components, using measuring instruments. Tests lines, components, and connections for leaks. Reads blueprints to determine location, size, capacity, and type of components needed to build refrigeration system. Keeps records of repairs and replacements made and causes of malfunctions.

Knowledge: Engineering and Technology; Design; Building and Construction; Mechanical

Abilities: Static Strength; Explosive Strength; Extent Flexibility; Gross Body Equilibrium

Helpers and Laborers

- ▲ Growth: 16%
- ▲ Annual Job Openings: 586,697
- ▲ Yearly Earnings $19,177
- ▲ Education Required: Short-term O-J-T
- ▲ Self-employed: 1%
- ▲ Part-time: 16%

Helpers—Mechanics and Repairers

Help mechanics and repairers in maintenance, parts replacement, and repair of vehicles, industrial machinery, and electrical and electronic equipment. Perform duties such as furnishing tools, materials, and supplies to other workers; cleaning work area, machines, and tools; and holding materials or tools for other workers. Helps mechanics and repairers maintain and repair vehicles, industrial machinery, and electrical and electronic equipment. Furnishes tools, parts, equipment, and supplies to other workers. Cleans or lubricates vehicles, machinery, equipment, instruments, tools, work areas, and other objects, using hand tools, power tools, and cleaning equipment. Transfers equipment, tools, parts, and other objects to and from work stations and other areas, using hand tools, power tools, and moving equipment. Assembles and disassembles machinery, equipment, components, and other parts, using hand tools and power tools. Installs or replaces machinery, equipment, and new or replacement parts and instruments, using hand tools or power tools. Adjusts and connects or disconnects wiring, piping, tubing, and other parts, using hand tools or power tools. Applies protective materials to equipment, components, and parts to prevent defects and corrosion. Tends and observes equipment and machinery to verify efficient and safe operation. Positions vehicles, machinery, equipment, physical structures, and other objects for assembly or installation, using hand tools, power tools, and moving equipment. Examines and tests machinery, equipment, components, and parts for defects and to ensure proper functioning. Builds or erects and maintains physical structures, using hand tools or power tools.

Knowledge: Building and Construction; Mechanical

Abilities: Speed of Limb Movement; Static Strength; Explosive Strength; Dynamic Strength; Trunk Strength; Stamina; Extent Flexibility; Dynamic Flexibility; Gross Body Coordination; Gross Body Equilibrium; Visual Color Discrimination; Hearing Sensitivity; Auditory Attention; Sound Localization

Helpers—Extractive Workers

Help extractive craft workers—such as earth drillers, blasters and explosives workers, derrick operators, and mining machine operators—by performing duties of lesser skill. Duties include supplyingequipment or cleaning work area. Exclude apprentice workers (which are reported with the appropriate construction or maintenance trade occupation). Exclude laborers who do not primarily assist extractive craft workers. Assists workers to extract geological materials, using hand tools and equipment. Drives moving equipment to transport materials and parts to excavation site. Unloads materials, devices, and machine parts, using hand tools. Sets up and adjusts equipment used to excavate geological materials. Loads materials into gas or well hole or equipment, using hand tools. Organizes materials and prepares site for excavation or boring, using hand tools. Dismantles extracting and boring equipment used for excavation, using hand tools. Observes and monitors equipment operation during extraction process. Repairs and maintains automotive and drilling equipment, using hand tools. Signals workers to start extraction or boring process of geological materials. Examines and collects geological matter, using hand tools and testing devices.

Knowledge: Mechanical; Physics; Transportation

Abilities: Rate Control; Speed of Limb Movement; Static Strength; Explosive Strength; Dynamic Strength; Stamina; Dynamic Flexibility; Gross Body Coordination; Gross Body Equilibrium

Stevedores, Except Equipment Operators

Manually load and unload ship cargo. Stack cargo in transit shed or in hold of ship using pallet or cargo board. Attach and move slings to lift cargo. Guide load lift. Exclude workers who primarily load and unload ship cargo using power equipment, such as power winches, cranes, and lift trucks. Carries or moves cargo by handtruck to wharf, and stacks cargo on pallets to facilitate transfer to and from ship. Stacks cargo in transit shed or in hold of ship as directed. Attaches and moves slings used to lift cargo. Guides load being lifted to prevent swinging. Shores cargo in ship's hold to prevent shifting during voyage.

Knowledge: Transportation

Abilities: Speed of Limb Movement; Static Strength; Explosive Strength; Dynamic Strength; Trunk Strength; Stamina; Extent Flexibility; Dynamic Flexibility; Gross Body Coordination; Gross Body Equilibrium; Peripheral Vision; Depth Perception; Glare Sensitivity

Grips and Set-Up Workers—Motion Picture Sets, Studios, and Stages

Arrange equipment; raise and lower scenery; move dollies, cranes, and booms; and perform other duties for motion picture, recording, or television industry. Arranges equipment preparatory to sessions and performances following work order specifications and handles props during performances. Rigs and dismantles stage or set equipment, such as frames, scaffolding, platforms, or backdrops, using carpenter's hand tools. Adjusts controls to raise and lower scenery and stage curtain during performance, following cues. Adjusts controls to guide, position, and move equipment, such as cranes, booms, and cameras. Erects canvas covers to protect equipment from weather. Reads work orders and follows oral instructions to determine specified material and equipment to be moved and its relocation. Connects electrical equipment to power source and tests equipment before performance. Orders equipment and maintains equipment storage areas. Sews and repairs items, using materials and hand tools such as canvas and sewing machines. Produces special lighting and sound effects during performances, using various machines and devices.

Knowledge: Building and Construction

Abilities: Spatial Orientation; Visualization; Static Strength; Trunk Strength; Extent Flexibility; Gross Body Equilibrium; Depth Perception

Production Laborers

Perform variety of routine tasks to assist in production activities. Carries or handtrucks supplies to work stations. Loads and unloads items from machines, conveyors, and conveyance. Lifts raw materials, final products, and items packed for shipment, manually or using hoist. Breaks up defective products for reprocessing. Attaches slings, ropes, cables, or identification tags to objects, such as pipes, hoses, and bundles. Weighs raw materials for distribution. Ties product in bundles for further processing or shipment, following prescribed procedure. Threads ends of items such as thread, cloth, and lace through needles, rollers, and around take-up tube. Positions spout or chute of storage bin to fill containers during processing. Places product in equipment or on work surface for further processing, inspecting, or wrapping. Cuts or breaks flashing from materials or products. Separates product according to weight, grade, size, and composition of material used to produce product. Folds parts of product and final product during processing. Washes machines, equipment, vehicles, and products, such as prints, rugs, and table linens. Counts finished product to determine completion of production order. Inserts parts into partial assembly, during various stages of assembly to complete product. Feeds items into processing machine. Mixes ingredients, according to formulae. Examines product to verify conformance to company standards. Records information, such as number of product tested, meter readings, and date and time product was placed in oven.

Knowledge: Production and Processing

Abilities: Arm-Hand Steadiness; Manual Dexterity; Multilimb Coordination; Rate Control; Speed of Limb Movement; Static Strength; Explosive Strength; Dynamic Strength; Trunk Strength; Stamina; Extent Flexibility; Dynamic Flexibility; Gross Body Coordination; Gross Body Equilibrium

Production Helpers

Perform variety of tasks requiring limited knowledge of production processes in support of skilled production workers. Cleans and lubricates equipment. Dumps materials into machine hopper prior to mixing. Loads and unloads processing equipment or conveyance used to receive raw materials or to ship finished products. Marks or tags identification on parts. Observes operation and notifies equipment operator of malfunctions. Places or positions equipment or partially assembled product for further processing, manually or using hoist. Reads gauges and charts, and records data. Removes product, machine attachments, and waste material from machine. Starts machines or equipment to begin process. Turns valves to regulate flow of liquids or air, to reverse machine, to start pump, and to regulate equipment. Mixes ingredients, according to procedure. Tends equipment to facilitate process. Replaces damaged or worn equipment parts. Measures amount of ingredients, length of extruded article, or work to ensure conformance to specifications. Signals coworkers to facilitate moving product during processing.

Knowledge: Production and Processing; Mechanical

Abilities: Reaction Time; Speed of Limb Movement; Static Strength; Stamina; Dynamic Flexibility; Gross Body Equilibrium; Auditory Attention

Home Health Aides

- ▲ Growth: 77%
- ▲ Annual Job Openings: 156,127
- ▲ Yearly Earnings $16,286
- ▲ Education Required: Short-term O-J-T
- ▲ Self-employed: 4%
- ▲ Part-time: 26%

Home Health Aides

Care for elderly, convalescent, or handicapped person in home of patient. Perform duties for patient such as changing bed linen; preparing meals; assisting in and out of bed; bathing, dressing, and grooming; and administering oral medications under doctors' orders or direction of nurse. Exclude nursing aides and homemakers. Changes bed linens, washes and irons patient's laundry, and cleans patient's quarters. Assists patients into and out of bed, automobile, or wheelchair, to lavatory, and up and down stairs. Administers prescribed oral medication under written direction of physician or as directed by home care nurse and aide. Purchases, prepares, and serves food for patient and other members of family, following special prescribed diets. Massages patient and applies preparations and treatment, such as liniment or alcohol rubs and heat-lamp stimulation. Visits several households to provide daily health care to patients. Maintains records of services performed and of apparent condition of patient. Entertains patient, reads aloud, and plays cards and other games with patient. Performs variety of miscellaneous duties as requested, such as obtaining household supplies and running errands.

Knowledge: Customer and Personal Service; Psychology; Medicine and Dentistry; Therapy and Counseling

Abilities: Static Strength

Hotel Desk Clerks

- ▲ Growth: 21%
- ▲ Annual Job Openings: 51,216
- ▲ Yearly Earnings $14,643
- ▲ Education Required: Short-term O-J-T
- ▲ Self-employed: 0%
- ▲ Part-time: 25%

Hotel Desk Clerks

Accommodate hotel patrons by registering and assigning rooms to guests, issuing room keys, transmitting and receiving messages, keeping records of occupied rooms

and guests' accounts, making and confirming reservations, and presenting statements to and collecting payments from departing guests. Greets, registers, and assigns rooms to guests of hotel or motel. Keeps records of room availability and guests' accounts, manually or using computer. Computes bill, collects payment, and makes change for guests. Makes and confirms reservations. Posts charges, such as room, food, liquor, or telephone, to ledger, manually or using computer. Transmits and receives messages, using telephone or telephone switchboard. Issues room key and escort instructions to bellhop. Date-stamps, sorts, and racks incoming mail and messages. Answers inquiries pertaining to hotel services; registration of guests; and shopping, dining, entertainment, and travel directions. Makes restaurant, transportation, or entertainment reservations, and arranges for tours. Deposits guests' valuables in hotel safe or safe-deposit box. Orders complimentary flowers or champagne for guests.

Knowledge: Clerical; Customer and Personal Service; Transportation

Abilities: None above average

Human Services Workers

▲ Growth: 55%
▲ Annual Job Openings: 42,907
▲ Yearly Earnings $21,112
▲ Education Required: Moderate-term O-J-T
▲ Self-employed: 0%
▲ Part-time: 42%

Human Services Workers

Assist social group workers and caseworkers with developing, organizing, and conducting programs to prevent and resolve problems relevant to substance abuse and human relationships. Aid families and clients in obtaining information on the use of social and community services. May recommend additional services. Exclude residential counselors and psychiatric technicians. Visits individuals in homes or attends group meetings to provide information on agency services, requirements, and procedures. Advises clients regarding food stamps, child care, food, money management, sanitation, and housekeeping. Interviews individuals and family members to compile information on social, educational, criminal, institutional, or drug history. Provides information on and refers individuals to public or private agencies and community services for assistance. Assists clients with preparation of forms, such as tax or rent forms. Assists in locating housing for displaced individuals. Assists in planning of food budget, utilizing charts and sample budgets. Monitors free, supplementary meal program to ensure cleanliness of facility and that eligibility guidelines are met for persons receiving meals. Meets with youth groups to acquaint them with consequences of delinquent acts. Observes clients' food selections, and recommends alternate economical and nutritional food choices. Observes and discusses meal preparation, and suggests alternate methods of food preparation. Consults with supervisor concerning programs for individual families. Oversees day-to-day group activities of residents in institution. Transports and accompanies clients to shopping area and to appointments, using automobile. Explains rules established by owner or management, such as sanitation and maintenance requirements, and parking regulations. Demonstrates use and care of equipment for tenant use. Informs tenants of facilities, such as laundries and playgrounds. Submits to and reviews reports and problems with superior. Keeps records and prepares reports for owner or management concerning visits with clients. Cares for children in client's home during client's appointments.

Knowledge: Administration and Management; Clerical; Customer and Personal Service; Food Production; Psychology; Sociology and Anthropology; Therapy and Counseling; Education and Training; Philosophy and Theology; Transportation

Abilities: Oral Expression; Time Sharing

Industrial Engineers

- ▲ Growth: 14%
- ▲ Annual Job Openings: 3,554
- ▲ Yearly Earnings $51,064
- ▲ Education Required: Bachelor's Degree
- ▲ Self-employed: 3%
- ▲ Part-time: 2%

Industrial Engineers, Except Safety

Perform engineering duties in planning and overseeing the utilization of production facilities and personnel in department or other subdivision of industrial establishment. Plan equipment layout, work flow, and accident prevention measures to maintain efficient and safe utilization of plant facilities. Plan and oversee work, study, and training programs to promote efficient worker utilization. Develop and oversee quality control, inventory control, and production record systems. Exclude industrial product safety engineers. Analyzes statistical data and product specifications to determine standards and establish quality and reliability objectives of finished product. Develops manufacturing methods, labor utilization standards, and cost analysis systems to promote efficient staff and facility utilization. Drafts and designs layout of equipment, materials, and workspace to illustrate maximum efficiency, using drafting tools and computer. Plans and establishes sequence of operations to fabricate and assemble parts or products and to promote efficient utilization of resources. Reviews production schedules, engineering specifications, orders, and related information to obtain knowledge of manufacturing methods, procedures, and activities. Studies operations sequence, material flow, functional statements, organization charts, and project information to determine worker functions and responsibilities. Formulates sampling procedures and designs and develops forms and instructions for recording, evaluating, and reporting quality and reliability data. Applies statistical methods and performs mathematical calculations to determine manufacturing processes, staff requirements, and production standards. Coordinates quality control objectives and activities to resolve production problems, maximize product reliability, and minimize cost. Communicates with management and user personnel to develop production and design standards. Recommends methods for improving utilization of personnel, material, and utilities. Estimates production cost and effect of product design changes for management review, action, and control. Completes production reports, purchase orders, and material, tool, and equipment lists. Directs workers engaged in product measurement, inspection, and testing activities to ensure quality control and reliability. Records or oversees recording of information to ensure currency of engineering drawings and documentation of production problems. Regulates and alters workflow schedules, according to established manufacturing sequences and lead times, to expedite production operations. Implements methods and procedures for disposition of discrepant material and defective or damaged parts, and assesses cost and responsibility. Evaluates precision and accuracy of production and testing equipment and engineering drawings to formulate corrective action plan. Confers with vendors, staff, and management personnel regarding purchases, procedures, product specifications, manufacturing capabilities, and project status. Schedules deliveries based on production forecasts, material substitutions, storage and handling facilities, and maintenance requirements.

Knowledge: Administration and Management; Clerical; Economics and Accounting; Personnel and Human Resources; Production and Processing; Engineering and Technology; Design; Mathematics; Physics; Psychology; Education and Training; Public Safety and Security

Abilities: Oral Comprehension; Written Comprehension; Oral Expression; Written Expression; Fluency of Ideas; Originality; Deductive Reasoning; Inductive Reasoning; Information Ordering; Category Flexibility; Mathematical Reasoning; Number Facility; Visualization; Speech Recognition

Industrial Production Managers

- ▲ Growth: -3%
- ▲ Annual Job Openings: 14,917
- ▲ Yearly Earnings $50,710
- ▲ Education Required: Bachelor's degree
- ▲ Self-employed: 0%
- ▲ Part-time: 6%

Industrial Production Managers

Plan, organize, direct, control, and coordinate the work activities and resources necessary for manufacturing products in accordance with cost, quality, and quantity specifications. Directs and coordinates production, processing, distribution, and marketing activities of industrial organization. Reviews processing schedules and production orders to determine staffing requirements, work procedures, and duty assignments. Reviews plans and confers with research and support staff to develop new products and processes or the quality of existing products. Initiates and coordinates inventory and cost control programs. Analyzes production, quality control, maintenance, and other operational reports to detect production problems. Reviews operations and confers with technical or administrative staff to resolve production or processing problems. Negotiates material prices with suppliers. Develops budgets and approves expenditures for supplies, materials, and human resources. Coordinates and recommends procedures for facility and equipment maintenance or modification. Examines samples of raw products or directs testing during processing to ensure finished products conform to prescribed quality standards. Prepares and maintains production reports and personnel records. Hires, trains, evaluates, and discharges staff. Resolves personnel grievances. Plans and develops sales or promotional programs for products in new and existing markets.

Knowledge: Administration and Management; Economics and Accounting; Sales and Marketing; Customer and Personal Service; Personnel and Human Resources; Production and Processing; Food Production; Chemistry; Psychology; Sociology and Anthropology; Education and Training; Law, Government, and Jurisprudence; Communications and Media; Transportation

Abilities: Oral Comprehension; Written Comprehension; Oral Expression; Written Expression; Fluency of Ideas; Originality; Problem Sensitivity; Deductive Reasoning; Inductive Reasoning; Information Ordering; Category Flexibility; Mathematical Reasoning; Number Facility; Memorization; Speed of Closure; Flexibility of Closure; Perceptual Speed; Near Vision; Visual Color Discrimination; Speech Recognition; Speech Clarity

Industrial Truck and Tractor Operators

▲ Growth: 12%
▲ Annual Job Openings: 74,968
▲ Yearly Earnings $24,564
▲ Education Required: Short-term O-J-T
▲ Self-employed: 0%
▲ Part-time: 3%

Industrial Truck and Tractor Operators

Operate gasoline- or electric-powered industrial trucks or tractors equipped with forklift, elevated platform, or trailer hitch to move materials around a warehouse, storage yard, factory, construction site, or similar location. Exclude logging tractor operators. Moves controls to drive gasoline- or electric-powered trucks, cars, or tractors and to transport materials between loading, processing, and storage areas. Moves levers and controls to operate lifting devices—such as forklifts, lift beams and swivel-hooks, hoists, and elevating platforms—to load, unload, transport, and stack material. Positions lifting device under, over, or around loaded pallets, skids, and boxes, and secures material or products for transport to designated areas. Hooks tow trucks to trailer hitches and fastens attachments—such as graders, plows, rollers, and winch cables—to tractor, using hitchpins. Turns valves and opens chutes to dump, spray, or release materials from dumpcars or storage bins into hoppers. Performs routine maintenance on vehicles and auxiliary equipment, such as cleaning, lubricating, recharging batteries, fueling, or replacing liquefied-gas tank. Manually loads or unloads materials onto or off pallets, skids, platforms, cars, or lifting devices. Operates or tends automatic stacking, loading, packaging, or cutting machines. Weighs materials or products and records weight and other production data on tags or labels. Signals workers to discharge, dump, or level materials. Operates coke ovens, driers, or other receptacles to process material or products. Inventories, issues, and maintains records of supplies and materials.

Knowledge: Mechanical; Transportation

Abilities: Spatial Orientation; Control Precision; Multilimb Coordination; Response Orientation; Speed of Limb Movement; Static Strength; Trunk Strength; Extent Flexibility; Dynamic Flexibility; Gross Body Equilibrium; Peripheral Vision; Depth Perception

Institution or Cafeteria Cooks

▲ Growth: 5%
▲ Annual Job Openings: 120,220
▲ Yearly Earnings $16,078
▲ Education Required: Long-term O-J-T
▲ Self-employed: 0%
▲ Part-time: 38%

Cooks, Institution or Cafeteria

Prepare and cook family-style meals for institutions such as schools, hospitals, or cafeterias. Usually prepare meals in large quantities rather than to individual order. May cook for employees in office building or other large facility. Cooks foodstuffs according to menu, special dietary or nutritional restrictions, and number of persons to be served. Prepares and cooks vegetables, salads, dressings, and desserts. Cleans, cuts, and cooks meat, fish, and poultry. Bakes breads, rolls, and other pastries. Plans menus, taking advantage of foods in season and local availability. Requisitions food supplies, kitchen equipment and appliances, and other supplies, and receives deliveries. Cleans and inspects galley equipment, kitchen appliances, and work areas for cleanliness and functional operation. Apportions and serves food to residents, employees, or patrons. Compiles and maintains food cost records and accounts. Washes pots, pans, dishes, utensils, and other cooking equipment. Directs activities of one or more workers who assist in preparing and serving meals.

Knowledge: Administration and Management; Economics and Accounting; Customer and Personal Service; Food Production

Abilities: None above average

Cooks, Short Order

Prepare and cook to order a variety of foods that require only a short preparation time. May take orders from customers and serve patrons at counters or tables. Exclude cooks, specialty fast foods. Takes order from customer and cooks foods requiring short preparation time, according to customer requirements. Completes order from steamtable and serves customer at table or counter. Carves meats, makes sandwiches, and brews coffee. Cleans food preparation equipment, work area, and counter or tables. Accepts payment and makes change, or writes charge slip.

Knowledge: Customer and Personal Service; Food Production

Abilities: None above average

Insulation Workers

▲ Growth: 19%
▲ Annual Job Openings: 22,457
▲ Yearly Earnings $27,372
▲ Education Required: Moderate-term O-J-T
▲ Self-employed: 1%
▲ Part-time: 4%

Insulation Workers

Cover and line structures with asbestos, cork, canvas, tar paper, magnesia, and related materials, using saws, knives, rasps, trowels, and other tools and implements. May also specialize in providing blown-in insulation. Fits, wraps, or attaches insulating materials to structures of surfaces, using hand tools or wires, following blueprint specifications. Evenly distributes insulating materials into small spaces within floors, ceilings, or walls, using blower and hose attachments or cement mortar. Covers, seals or finishes insulated surfaces or access holes with plastic covers, canvas ships, sealant, tape, cement, or asphalt mastic. Prepares surfaces for insulation application by brushing or spreading on adhesives, cement, or asphalt or by attaching metal pins to surfaces. Reads blueprints and selects appropriate insulation, based on the heat-retaining or excluding characteristics of the material. Measures and cuts insulation for covering surfaces, using tape measure, handsaw, knife, or scissors. Moves controls, buttons, or levers to start blower and regulate flow of materials through nozzle. Fills blower hopper with insulating materials.

Knowledge: Building and Construction

Abilities: None above average

Insurance Adjusters, Examiners, and Investigators

▲ Growth: 23%

▲ Annual Job Openings: 21,662

▲ Yearly Earnings $38,230

▲ Education Required: Long-term O-J-T

▲ Self-employed: 5%

▲ Part-time: 7%

Insurance Adjusters, Examiners, and Investigators

Investigate, analyze, and determine the extent of insurance company's liability concerning personal, casualty, or property loss or damages, and attempt to effect settlement with claimants. Correspond with or interview medical specialists, agents, witnesses, or claimants to compile information. Calculate benefit payments and approve payment of claims within a certain monetary limit. Exclude insurance sales agents, insurance policy processing clerks, and claims clerks. Investigates and assesses damage to property. Interviews or corresponds with claimant and witnesses, consults police and hospital records, and inspects property damage to determine extent of liability. Interviews or corresponds with agents and claimants to correct errors or omissions and to investigate questionable entries. Analyzes information gathered by investigation and reports findings and recommendations. Negotiates claim settlements and recommends litigation when settlement cannot be negotiated. Examines titles to property to determine validity and acts as company agent in transactions with property owners. Examines claims form and other records to determine insurance coverage. Collects evidence to support contested claims in court. Prepares report of findings of investigation. Communicates with former associates to verify employment record and to obtain background information regarding persons or businesses applying for credit. Refers questionable claims to investigator or claims adjuster for investigation or settlement. Obtains credit information from banks and other credit services.

Knowledge: Economics and Accounting; Personnel and Human Resources; Public Safety and Security; Law, Government, and Jurisprudence

Abilities: Written Comprehension; Oral Expression; Written Expression; Inductive Reasoning; Mathematical Reasoning; Number Facility; Near Vision

Insurance Appraisers, Auto Damage

Appraise automobile or other vehicle damage to determine cost of repair for insurance claim settlement and seek agreement with automotive repair shop on cost of repair. Prepare insurance forms to indicate repair cost or cost estimates and recommenda-

tions. Estimates parts and labor to repair damage, using standard automotive labor and parts-cost manuals and knowledge of automotive repair. Reviews repair-cost estimates with automobile-repair shop to secure agreement on cost of repairs. Examines damaged vehicle to determine extent of structural, body, mechanical, electrical, or interior damage. Prepares insurance forms to indicate repair-cost estimates and recommendations. Evaluates practicality of repair as opposed to payment of market value of vehicle before accident. Determines salvage value on total-loss vehicle. Arranges to have damage appraised by another appraiser to resolve disagreement with shop on repair cost.

Knowledge: Economics and Accounting

Abilities: Mathematical Reasoning; Number Facility

Insurance Claims Clerks

- ▲ Growth: 26%
- ▲ Annual Job Openings: 15,014
- ▲ Yearly Earnings $23,795
- ▲ Education Required: Moderate-term O-J-T
- ▲ Self-employed: 0%
- ▲ Part-time: 7%

Insurance Claims Clerks

Obtain information from insured or designated persons for purpose of settling claim with insurance carrier. Contacts insured or other involved persons for missing information. Prepares and reviews insurance-claim forms and related documents for completeness. Reviews insurance policy to determine coverage. Posts or attaches information to claim file. Transmits claims for payment or further investigation. Calculates amount of claim.

Knowledge: Clerical; Economics and Accounting; Law, Government, and Jurisprudence

Abilities: Number Facility; Near Vision; Speech Recognition

Insurance Policy Processing Clerks

Process applications for, changes to, reinstatement of, and cancellation of insurance policies. Duties include reviewing insurance applications to ensure that all questions have been answered, compiling data on insurance policy changes, changing policy records to conform to insured party's specifications, compiling data on lapsed insurance policies to determine automatic reinstatement according to company policies, canceling insurance policies as requested by agents, and verifying the accuracy of insurance company records. Exclude insurance claims clerks and banking insurance clerks. Reviews and verifies data, such as age, name, address, and principal sum and value of property on insurance applications and policies. Compares information from application to criteria for policy reinstatement, and approves reinstatement when criteria are met. Examines letters from policy holders or agents, original insurance applications, and other company documents to determine changes are needed and effects of changes. Computes refund and prepares and mails cancellation letter with canceled policy to policy holder. Checks computations of interest accrued, premiums due, and settlement surrender on loan values. Calculates premiums, commissions, adjustments, and new reserve requirements, using insurance rate standards. Corresponds with insured or agent to obtain information or inform them of status or changes to application of account. Notifies insurance agent and accounting department of policy cancellation. Receives computer printout of policy cancellations or obtains cancellation card from file. Transcribes data to worksheets and enters data into computer for use in preparing documents and adjusting accounts. Collects initial premiums, issues receipts, and compiles periodic reports for management.

Knowledge: Clerical

Abilities: Mathematical Reasoning; Number Facility; Speech Clarity

Claims Takers, Unemployment Benefits

Interview unemployed workers and compile data to determine eligibility for unemployment benefits. Interviews claimants returning at specified intervals to certify claimants for continuing benefits. Reviews data on job applications or claim forms to ensure completeness. Assists applicants completing application forms for job referrals or unemployment compensation claims. Answers questions concerning registration for jobs or application for unemployment benefits. Assists applicants in filling out forms, using knowledge of information required or native language of applicant. Schedules unemployment insurance claimants for adjudication interview when question of eligibility arises. Refers applicants to job opening or interview with other staff, in accordance with administrative guidelines or office procedure.

Knowledge: Clerical; Customer and Personal Service; Personnel and Human Resources; Therapy and Counseling; Foreign Language

Abilities: None above average

Insurance Claims Examiners

▲ Growth: 22%

▲ Annual Job Openings: 7,281

▲ Yearly Earnings $41,142

▲ Education Required: Bachelor's degree

▲ Self-employed: 0%

▲ Part-time: 7%

Claims Examiners, Property and Casualty Insurance

Review settled insurance claims to determine that payments and settlements have been made in accordance with company practices and procedures, ensuring that adjusters have followed proper methods. Report overpayments, underpayments, and other irregularities. Confer with legal counsel on claims requiring litigation. Analyzes data used in settling claim to determine its validity in payment of claims. Reports overpayments, underpayments, and other irregularities. Confers with legal counsel on claims requiring litigation.

Knowledge: Law, Government, and Jurisprudence

Abilities: Number Facility

Interior Designers

▲ Growth: 28%

▲ Annual Job Openings: 9,238

▲ Yearly Earnings $32,094

▲ Education Required: Bachelor's degree

▲ Self-employed: 41%

▲ Part-time: 20%

Interior Designers

Plan, design, and furnish interiors of residential, commercial, or industrial buildings. Formulate design which is practical, aesthetic, and conducive to intended purposes, such as raising productivity, selling merchandise, or improving lifestyle. May specialize in a particular field, style, or phase of interior design. Exclude merchandise display designers. Formulates environmental plan to be practical, aesthetic, and conducive to intended purposes, such as raising productivity or selling merchandise. Selects or designs and purchases furnishings, artworks, and accessories. Confers with client to determine factors affecting planning interior environments, such as budget, architectural preferences, and purpose and function. Plans and designs interior environments for boats, planes, buses, trains, and other enclosed spaces. Advises client on interior design factors, such as space planning, layout and utilization of furnishings and equipment, and color coordination. Renders design ideas in form of paste-ups or drawings. Estimates material requirements and costs, and presents design to client for approval. Subcontracts fabrication, installation, and arrangement of carpeting, fixtures, accessories, draperies, paint and wall coverings, artwork, furniture, and related items.

Knowledge: Administration and Management; Sales and Marketing; Customer and Personal Service; Design; Fine Arts

Abilities: Fluency of Ideas; Originality; Visualization; Visual Color Discrimination

Interviewing Clerks

- ▲ Growth: 18%
- ▲ Annual Job Openings: 19,262
- ▲ Yearly Earnings: $18,075
- ▲ Education Required: Short-term O-J-T
- ▲ Self-employed: 1%
- ▲ Part-time: 32%

Interviewing Clerks, Except Personnel and Social Welfare

Interview public to obtain information. Contact persons by telephone, mail, or in person for the purpose of completing forms, applications, or questionnaires. Ask specific questions, record answers, and assist persons with completing forms. May sort, classify, and file forms. Exclude workers whose primary duty is processing applications. Contacts persons at home, place of business, or field location, by telephone, mail, or in person. Asks questions to obtain various specified information, such as person's name, address, age, religion, and state of residency. Records results and data from interview or survey, using computer or specified form. Assists person in filling out application or questionnaire. Compiles and sorts data from interview, and reviews to correct errors. Explains reason for questioning, and other specified information.

Knowledge: Clerical; Personnel and Human Resources

Abilities: None above average

Janitors, Cleaners, and Maids

▲ Growth: 4%

▲ Annual Job Openings: 818,941

▲ Yearly Earnings $16,432

▲ Education Required: Short-term O-J-T

▲ Self-employed: 4%

▲ Part-time: 32%

Maids and Housekeeping Cleaners

Perform any combination of tasks to maintain private households or commercial establishments, such as hotels, restaurants, and hospitals, in a clean and orderly manner. Duties include making beds, replenishing linens, cleaning rooms and halls, and arranging furniture. Cleans rooms, hallways, lobbies, lounges, restrooms, corridors, elevators, stairways, locker rooms, and other work areas. Cleans rugs, carpets, upholstered furniture, and draperies, using vacuum cleaner. Dusts furniture and equipment. Empties wastebaskets, and empties and cleans ashtrays. Sweeps, scrubs, waxes, and polishes floors, using brooms, mops, and powered scrubbing and waxing machines. Collects soiled linens for laundering, and receives and stores linen supplies in linen closet. Polishes metalwork, such as fixtures and fittings. Washes walls, ceiling, and woodwork. Washes windows, door panels, and sills. Transports trash and waste to disposal area. Replenishes supplies, such as drinking glasses, writing supplies, and bathroom items. Moves and arranges furniture, turns mattresses, hangs draperies, dusts venetian blinds, and polishes metalwork to ready hotel facilities for occupancy. Washes beds and mattresses, and remakes beds after dismissal of hospital patients. Replaces light bulbs. Arranges decorations, apparatus, or furniture for banquets and social functions. Cleans and removes debris from driveway and garage areas. Prepares sample rooms for sales meetings. Delivers television sets, ironing boards, baby cribs, and rollaway beds to guests rooms. Cleans swimming pool with vacuum.

Knowledge: Customer and Personal Service

Abilities: None above average

Janitors and Cleaners, Except Maids and Housekeeping Cleaners

Keep building in clean and orderly condition. Perform heavy cleaning duties, such as operating motor-driven cleaning equipment, mopping floors, washing walls and glass, and removing rubbish. Duties may include tending furnace and boiler, performing routine maintenance activities, notifying management of need for repairs and additions, and cleaning snow or debris from sidewalk. Sweeps, mops, scrubs, and vacuums floors of buildings, using cleaning solutions, tools, and equipment. Cleans or polishes walls, ceilings, windows, plant equipment,and building fixtures, using-steam cleaning equipment, scrapers, brooms, and variety of hand and power tools. Applies waxes or sealers to wood or concrete floors. Gathers and empties trash. Tends, cleans, adjusts, and services furnaces, air-conditioners, boilers, and other building heating and cooling systems. Notifies management personnel concerning need for major repairs or additions to building operating systems. Removes snow from sidewalks, driveways, and parking areas, using snowplow, snowblower, and snow shovel, and spreads snow-melting chemicals. Dusts furniture, walls, machines, and equipment. Services and repairs cleaning and maintenance equipment and machinery and performs minor routine painting, plumbing, electrical, and related activities. Cleans and restores building interiors damaged by fire, smoke, or water, using commercial cleaning equipment. Cleans chimneys, flues, and connecting pipes, using power and hand tools. Drives vehicles, such as vans, industrial trucks, or industrial vacuum cleaners. Mixes water and detergents or acids in container to prepare cleaning solutions, according to specifications. Mows and trims lawns and shrubbery, using mowers and hand and power trimmers, and clears debris from grounds. Cleans laboratory equipment, such as glassware and metal instruments, using solvents, brushes, rags, and power cleaning equipment. Sprays insecticides and fumigants to prevent insect and rodent infestation. Requisitions supplies and equipment used in cleaning and maintenance duties. Sets up, arranges, and removes decorations, tables, chairs, ladders, and scaffolding for events such as banquets and social functions. Moves items between departments, manually or using handtruck.

Knowledge: Building and Construction; Mechanical; Chemistry; Transportation

Abilities: Information Ordering; Spatial Orientation; Manual Dexterity; Multilimb Coordination; Response Orientation; Rate Control; Reaction Time; Wrist-Finger Speed; Speed of Limb Movement; Static Strength; Explosive Strength; Dynamic Strength; Trunk Strength; Stamina; Extent Flexibility; Dynamic Flexibility; Gross Body Coordination; Gross Body Equilibrium; Night Vision; Depth Perception; Glare Sensitivity; Hearing Sensitivity; Sound Localization

Judges and Magistrates

- ▲ Growth: 2%
- ▲ Annual Job Openings: 3,558
- ▲ Yearly Earnings $51,667
- ▲ Education Required: Work experience, plus degree
- ▲ Self-employed: 0%
- ▲ Part-time: 7%

Judges and Magistrates

Judges arbitrate, advise, and administer justice in a court of law. Sentence defendant in criminal cases according to statutes of state or federal government. May determine liability of defendant in civil cases. Magistrates adjudicate criminal cases not involving

penitentiary sentences and civil cases concerning damages below a sum specified by state law. May issue marriage licenses and perform wedding ceremonies. Listens to presentation of case, rules on admissibility of evidence and methods of conducting testimony, and settles disputes between opposing attorneys. Instructs jury on applicable law, and directs jury to deduce facts from evidence presented. Sentences defendant in criminal cases, on conviction by jury, according to statutes of state or federal government. Adjudicates cases involving motor vehicle laws. Establishes rules of procedure on questions for which standard procedures have not been established by law or by superior court. Conducts preliminary hearings in felony cases to determine reasonable and probable cause to hold defendant for further proceedings or trial. Reads or listens to allegations made by plaintiff in civil suits to determine their sufficiency. Awards judicial relief to litigants in civil cases in relation to findings by jury or by court. Examines evidence in criminal cases to determine if evidence will support charges. Performs wedding ceremonies.

Knowledge: Economics and Accounting; Personnel and Human Resources; Psychology; Sociology and Anthropology; Geography; English Language; History and Archeology; Philosophy and Theology; Public Safety and Security; Law, Government, and Jurisprudence; Communications and Media

Abilities: Oral Comprehension; Written Comprehension; Oral Expression; Originality; Problem Sensitivity; Deductive Reasoning; Inductive Reasoning; Information Ordering; Memorization; Speed of Closure; Flexibility of Closure; Selective Attention; Time Sharing; Speech Clarity

Adjudicators, Hearings Officers, and Judicial Reviewers

Conduct hearings to review and decide claims filed by the government against individuals or organizations, or individual eligibility issues concerning social programs, disability, or unemployment benefits. Determine the existence and the amount of liability; recommend the acceptance or rejection of claims; or compromise settlements according to laws, regulations, policies, and precedent decisions. Confer with persons or organizations involved, and prepare written decisions. Arranges and conducts hearings to obtain information and evidence relative to disposition of claim. Determines existence and amount of liability, according to law, administrative and judicial precedents, and evidence. Counsels parties, and recommends acceptance or rejection of compromise settlement offers. Prepares written opinions and decisions. Analyzes evidence and applicable law, regulations, policy, and precedent decisions to determine conclusions. Interviews or corresponds with claimants or agents to elicit information. Questions witnesses to obtain information. Reviews and evaluates data on documents, such as claim applications, birth or death certificates, and physician or employer records. Rules on exceptions, motions, and admissibility of evidence. Researches laws, regulations, policies, and precedent decisions to prepare for hearings. Participates in court proceedings. Issues subpoenas and administers oaths to prepare for formal hearing. Obtains additional information to clarify evidence. Authorizes payment of valid claims. Notifies claimant of denied claim and appeal rights. Conducts studies of appeals procedures in field agencies to ensure adherence to legal requirements and to facilitate determination of cases.

Knowledge: Administration and Management; Psychology; Sociology and Anthropology; Therapy and Counseling; English Language; History and Archeology; Philosophy and Theology; Law, Government, and Jurisprudence

Abilities: Oral Comprehension; Written Comprehension; Written Expression; Deductive Reasoning; Inductive Reasoning; Memorization; Speech Clarity

Landscape Architects

▲ Growth: 21%
▲ Annual Job Openings: 1,593
▲ Yearly Earnings $38,875
▲ Education Required: Bachelor's degree
▲ Self-employed: 30%
▲ Part-time: 8%

Landscape Architects

Plan and design land areas for such projects as parks and other recreational facilities, airports, highways, hospitals, schools, land subdivisions, and commercial, industrial, and residential sites. Prepares site plans, specifications, and cost estimates for land development, coordinating arrangement of existing and proposed land features and structures. Compiles and analyzes data on conditions, such as location, drainage, and location of structures, for environmental reports and landscaping plans. Inspects landscape work to ensure compliance with specifications, approves quality of materials and work, and advises client and construction personnel. Confers with clients, engineering personnel, and architects on overall program.

Knowledge: Administration and Management; Economics and Accounting; Customer and Personal Service; Engineering and Technology; Design; Building and Construction; Mathematics; Physics; Biology; Geography; English Language; Fine Arts; History and Archeology; Public Safety and Security; Law, Government, and Jurisprudence

Abilities: Written Comprehension; Fluency of Ideas; Originality; Information Ordering; Spatial Orientation; Visualization; Far Vision

Laundry and Drycleaning Machine Operators

- ▲ Growth: 22%
- ▲ Annual Job Openings: 30,822
- ▲ Yearly Earnings $14,580
- ▲ Education Required: Moderate-term O-J-T
- ▲ Self-employed: 11%
- ▲ Part-time: 26%

Spotters, Dry Cleaning

Identify stains in wool, synthetic, and silk garments and household fabrics and apply chemical solutions to remove stain. Determine spotting procedures on basis of type of fabric and nature of stain. Inspects spots to ascertain composition and select solvent. Sprinkles chemical solvents over stain and pats area with brush or sponge until stain is removed. Applies bleaching powder to spot, and sprays with steam to remove stains from certain fabrics which do not respond to other cleaning solvents. Applies chemicals to neutralize effect of solvents. Sprays steam, water, or air over spot to flush out chemicals, dry material, raise nap, or brighten color. Cleans fabric using vacuum or airhose. Mixes bleaching agent with hot water in vats and soaks material until it is bleached. Spreads article on worktable and positions stain over vacuum head or on marble slab. Operates drycleaning machine.

Knowledge: Chemistry

Abilities: Visual Color Discrimination

Laundry and Dry-cleaning Machine Operators and Tenders, Except Pressing

Operate or tend washing or dry-cleaning machines to wash or dry-clean commercial, industrial, or household articles, such as cloth garments, suede, leather, furs, blankets, draperies, fine linens, rugs, and carpets. Starts washer, dry-cleaner, drier, or extractor, and turns valves or levers to regulate and monitor cleaning or drying operations. Loads or directs other workers to load articles into washer or dry-cleaning machine. Mixes and adds detergents, dyes, bleach, starch, and other solutions and chemicals to clean, color, dry, or stiffen articles. Starts pumps to operate distilling system that drains and reclaims dry-cleaning solvents. Tends variety of automatic machines that comb and polish furs; clean, sterilize, and fluff feathers and blankets; and roll and package towels. Adjusts switches to tend and regulate equipment that fumigates and removes foreign matter from furs. Removes or directs other workers to remove items from washer or dry-cleaning machine and into extractor or tumbler. Cleans machine filters and lubricates equipment. Washes, dry-cleans, or glazes delicate articles or fur garment linings by hand, using mild detergent or dry-cleaning solutions. Presoaks, sterilizes, scrubs, spot-cleans, and dries contaminated or stained articles, using neutralizer solutions and portable machines. Examines and sorts articles to be cleaned into lots, according to color, fabric, dirt content, and cleaning technique required. Sorts and counts articles removed from dryer and folds, wraps, or hangs items for airing out, pick-up, or delivery. Receives and marks articles for laundry or-dry cleaning with identifying code number or name, using hand or machine marker. Irons or presses articles, fabrics, and furs, using hand iron or pressing machine. Hangs curtains, drapes, blankets, pants, and other garments on stretch frames to dry, and transports items between specified locations. Mends and sews articles, using hand stitching, adhesive patch, or power sewing machine.

Knowledge: None above average

Abilities: Speed of Limb Movement; Dynamic Strength; Trunk Strength; Stamina; Dynamic Flexibility; Gross Body Coordination; Gross Body Equilibrium

Law Clerks

▲ Growth: 12%
▲ Annual Job Openings: 8,181
▲ Yearly Earnings $26,748
▲ Education Required: Associate degree
▲ Self-employed: 2%
▲ Part-time: 9%

Law Clerks

Research legal data for brief or argument based on statutory law or decisions. Search for and study legal records and documents to obtain data applicable to case under consideration. Prepare rough drafts of briefs or arguments. File pleadings for firm with court clerk. Serve copies of pleading on opposing counsel. Prepare affidavits of documents and keep document file and correspondence of cases. Researches and analyzes law sources to prepare legal documents for review, approval, and use by attorney. Files pleadings with court clerk. Prepares affidavits of documents, and maintains document file. Investigates facts and law of case to determine causes of action and to prepare case accordingly. Delivers or directs delivery of subpoenas to witness and parties to action. Searches patent files to ascertain originality of parent application. Stores, catalogs, and maintains currency of legal volumes. Appraises and inventories real and personal property for estate planning. Directs and coordinates activities of law office employees. Prepares real estate closing statement, and assists in closing process. Communicates and arbitrates disputes between disputing parties. Prepares office accounts and tax returns.

Knowledge: Administration and Management; Clerical; Economics and Accounting; Personnel and Human Resources; English Language; Law, Government, and Jurisprudence; Communications and Media

Abilities: Written Comprehension; Number Facility; Near Vision; Speech Recognition; Speech Clarity

Lawn Service Managers

▲ Growth: 22%
▲ Annual Job Openings: 4,637
▲ Yearly Earnings $25,916
▲ Education Required: Work experience in a related occupation
▲ Self-employed: 64%
▲ Part-time: 24%

Lawn Service Managers

Plan, organize, direct, control, and coordinate activities of workers engaged in pruning trees and shrubs, cultivating lawns, and applying pesticides and other chemicals, according to service contract specifications. Work may involve reviewing contracts to ascertain service, machine, and workforce requirements; answering inquiries from potential customers regarding methods, material, and price ranges; and preparing service estimates according to labor, material, and machine costs. Supervises workers who provide groundskeeping services on a contract basis. Reviews contracts to ascertain service, machine, and workforce requirements for job. Answers customers' questions about groundskeeping care requirements. Prepares service cost estimates for customers. Schedules work for crew according to weather conditions, availability of equipment, and seasonal limitations. Investigates customer complaints. Spot-checks completed work to improve quality of service and to ensure contract compliance. Suggests changes in work procedures and orders corrective work done. Prepares work activity and personnel reports.

Knowledge: Administration and Management; Economics and Accounting; Sales and Marketing; Customer and Personal Service; Personnel and Human Resources

Abilities: None above average

Lawyers

▲ Growth: 19%
▲ Annual Job Openings: 45,929
▲ Yearly Earnings $70,116
▲ Education Required: First professional degree
▲ Self-employed: 31%
▲ Part-time: 7%

Lawyers

Conduct criminal and civil lawsuits, draw up legal documents, advise clients as to legal rights, and practice other phases of law. May represent client in court or before

quasi-judicial or administrative agencies of government. May specialize in a single area of law, such as patent law, corporate law, or criminal law. Conducts case, examining and cross-examining witnesses, and summarizes case to judge or jury. Represents client in court or before government agency, or prosecutes or defends defendant in civil or criminal litigation. Advises client concerning business transactions, claim liability, advisability of prosecuting or defending law suits, or legal rights and obligations. Interviews client and witnesses to ascertain facts of case. Gathers evidence to formulate defense or to initiate legal actions. Examines legal data to determine advisability of defending or prosecuting lawsuit. Evaluates findings and develops strategy and arguments in preparation for presentation of case. Studies Constitution, statutes, decisions, regulations, and ordinances of quasi-judicial bodies. Confers with colleagues with specialty in area of legal issue to establish and verify basis for legal proceeding. Interprets laws, rulings, and regulations for individuals and business. Prepares and files legal briefs. Presents evidence to grand jury for indictment or release of accused. Prepares and drafts legal documents, such as wills, deeds, patent applications, mortgages, leases, and contracts. Prepares opinions on legal issues. Probates wills and represents and advises executors and administrators of estates. Acts as agent, trustee, guardian, or executor for business or individual. Searches for and examines public and other legal records to write opinions or establish ownership.

Knowledge: Administration and Management; Clerical; Computers and Electronics; Psychology; Sociology and Anthropology; Therapy and Counseling; Education and Training; English Language; Public Safety and Security; Law, Government, and Jurisprudence

Abilities: Oral Comprehension; Written Comprehension; Oral Expression; Written Expression; Originality; Deductive Reasoning; Inductive Reasoning; Time Sharing; Speech Clarity

Legal Secretaries

- ▲ Growth: 13%
- ▲ Annual Job Openings: 49,667
- ▲ Yearly Earnings $29,348
- ▲ Education Required: Postsecondary vocational training
- ▲ Self-employed: 0%
- ▲ Part-time: 19%

Legal Secretaries

Prepare legal papers and correspondence, such as summonses, complaints, motions, and subpoenas. May review law journals and other legal publications to identify court decisions pertinent to pending cases and submit articles to company officials. Must be familiar with legal terminology, procedures, and documents, as well as legal research. Prepares and processes legal documents and papers, such as summonses, subpoenas, complaints, appeals, motions, and pretrial agreements. Reviews legal publications and performs database searches to identify laws and court decisions relevant to pending cases. Submits articles and information from searches to attorneys for review and approval for use. Assists attorneys in collecting information such as employment, medical, and other records. Organizes and maintains law libraries and document and case files. Completes various forms, such as accident reports, trial and courtroom requests, and applications for clients. Mails, faxes, or arranges for delivery of legal correspondence to clients, witnesses, and court officials. Attends legal meetings, such as client interviews, hearings, or depositions, and takes notes. Drafts and types office memos. Receives and places telephone calls. Schedules and makes appointments. Makes photocopies of correspondence, documents, and other printed matter.

Knowledge: Clerical; Economics and Accounting; Computers and Electronics; Law, Government, and Jurisprudence

Abilities: Written Comprehension; Time Sharing; Wrist-Finger Speed; Near Vision; Speech Recognition

Library Assistants and Bookmobile Drivers

- ▲ Growth: 15%
- ▲ Annual Job Openings: 32,759
- ▲ Yearly Earnings $17,472
- ▲ Education Required: Short-term O-J-T
- ▲ Self-employed: 0%
- ▲ Part-time: 61%

Library Assistants and Bookmobile Drivers

Library assistants compile records; sort and shelve books; issue and receive library materials, such as pictures, cards, slides, phonograph records, and microfilm; and handle tape decks. Locate library materials for loan, and replace materials in shelving area (stacks) or files according to identification number and title. Register patrons to permit them to borrow books, periodicals, and other library materials. Bookmobile drivers operate a bookmobile or light truck that pulls a book trailer to specific locations on a predetermined schedule and assist with providing services in mobile library. Issues borrower's identification card according to established procedures. Drives bookmobile to specified locations following library services schedule and to garage for preventive maintenance and repairs. Issues books to patrons and records information on borrower's card, by hand or using photographic equipment. Sorts books, publications, and other items according to procedure and returns them to shelves, files, or other designated storage area. Locates library materials for patrons, such as books, periodicals, tape cassettes, Braille volumes, and pictures. Classifies and catalogs items according to contents and purpose, and prepares index cards for file reference. Maintains records of items received, stored, issued, and returned and files catalog cards according to system used. Answers routine inquiries and refers patrons who need professional assistance to librarian. Delivers and retrieves items to and from departments by hand or pushcart. Prepares, stores, and retrieves classification and catalog information, lecture notes, or other documents related to document stored, using computer. Reviews records, such as microfilm and issue cards, to determine title of overdue materials and to identify borrower. Inspects returned books for damage, verifies due-date, and computes and receives overdue fines. Selects substitute titles, following criteria such as age, education, and interest, when requested materials are unavailable. Places books in mailing container, affixes address label, and secures container with straps for mailing to blind library patrons. Operates and maintains audio-visual equipment and explains use of reference equipment to patrons. Prepares address labels for books to be mailed, overdue notices, and duty schedules, using computer or typewriter. Repairs books, using mending tape and paste and brush, and places plastic covers on new books.

Knowledge: Clerical; Customer and Personal Service; History and Archeology

Abilities: Category Flexibility; Memorization; Time Sharing, Reaction Time; Wrist-Finger Speed

Library Technical Assistants

▲ Growth: 28%
▲ Annual Job Openings: 10,919
▲ Yearly Earnings: $20,945
▲ Education Required: Short-term O-J-T
▲ Self-employed: 0%
▲ Part-time: 11%

Technical Assistants, Library

Assist librarians by furnishing information on library sciences, facilities, and rules; by assisting readers in the use of card catalogs and indexes to locate books and other materials; and by answering questions that require only brief consultation of standard reference. May catalog books or train and supervise clerical staff. Assists patrons in operating equipment, and obtaining library materials and services, and explains use of reference tools. Reviews subject matter of materials to be classified and selects classification numbers and headings according to Dewey Decimal, Library of Congress, or other classification systems. Processes print and nonprint library materials, and classifies and catalogs materials. Files catalog cards according to system used. Verifies bibliographical data, including author, title, publisher, publication date, and edition, on computer terminal. Issues identification card to borrowers and checks materials in and out. Directs activities of library clerks and aides. Compiles and maintains records relating to circulation, materials, and equipment. Prepares order slips for materials, follows up on orders, and compiles lists of materials acquired or withdrawn. Composes explanatory summaries of contents of books or other reference materials. Designs posters and special displays to promote use of library facilities or specific reading program at library.

Knowledge: Clerical; Customer and Personal Service; English Language; Communications and Media

Abilities: Category Flexibility; Perceptual Speed

Audio-Visual Specialists

Plan and prepare audio-visual teaching aids and methods for use in school system.
Plans and develops preproduction ideas into outlines, scripts, continuity, story boards, and graphics, or directs assistants to develop ideas. Sets up, adjusts, and operates equipment such as cameras, sound mixers, and recorders during production. Constructs and positions properties, sets, lighting equipment, and other equipment. Determines format, approach, content, level, and medium to meet objectives most effectively within budgetary constraints, utilizing research, knowledge, and training. Locates and secures settings, properties, effects, and other production necessities. Develops production ideas based on assignment or generates own ideas based on objectives and interest. Develops manuals, texts, workbooks, or related materials for use in conjunction with production materials. Executes, or directs assistants to execute, rough and finished graphics and graphic designs. Performs narration or presents announcements. Reviews, evaluates, and directs modifications to material produced independently by other personnel. Directs and coordinates activities of assistants and other personnel during production. Conducts training sessions on selection, use, and design of audio-visual materials, and operation of presentation equipment.

Knowledge: Administration and Management; Economics and Accounting; Personnel and Human Resources; Computers and Electronics; Building and Construction; Psychology; Education and Training; English Language; Fine Arts; History and Archeology; Telecommunications; Communications and Media

Abilities: Written Expression; Fluency of Ideas; Originality; Information Ordering; Category Flexibility; Memorization; Visualization; Selective Attention; Time Sharing; Rate Control; Gross Body Equilibrium; Night Vision; Peripheral Vision; Depth Perception; Glare Sensitivity; Hearing Sensitivity; Sound Localization; Speech Recognition; Speech Clarity

Licensed Practical Nurses

▲ Growth: 21%
▲ Annual Job Openings: 81,622
▲ Yearly Earnings $26,020
▲ Education Required: Postsecondary vocational training
▲ Self-employed: 0%
▲ Part-time: 22%

Licensed Practical Nurses

Care for ill, injured, convalescent, and handicapped persons in hospitals, clinics, private homes, sanitariums, and similar institutions. Administers specified medication, orally or by subcutaneous or intramuscular injection, and notes time and amount on patients' charts. Provides medical treatment and personal care to patients in private home settings. Takes and records patients' vital signs. Dresses wounds and gives enemas, douches, alcohol rubs, and massages. Applies compresses, ice bags, and hot water bottles. Observes patients and reports adverse reactions to medication or treatment to medical personnel in charge. Bathes, dresses, and assists patients in walking and turning. Assembles and uses such equipment as catheters, tracheotomy tubes, and oxygen suppliers. Collects samples, such as urine, blood, and sputum, from patients for testing, and performs routine laboratory tests on samples. Sterilizes equipment and supplies, using germicides, sterilizer, or autoclave. Records food and fluid intake and output. Prepares or examines food trays for prescribed diet and feeds patients. Assists in delivery, care, and feeding of infants. Cleans rooms, makes beds, and answers patients' calls. Washes and dresses bodies of deceased persons. Inventories and requisitions supplies.

Knowledge: Customer and Personal Service; Chemistry; Biology; Psychology; Sociology and Anthropology; Medicine and Dentistry; Therapy and Counseling

Abilities: Reaction Time

Life Scientists

▲ Growth: -3%
▲ Annual Job Openings: 53
▲ Yearly Earnings $44,137
▲ Education Required: Doctor's degree
▲ Self-employed: 0%
▲ Part-time: 6%

No job descriptions available from the Department of Labor.

Loan and Credit Clerks

▲ Growth: 10%
▲ Annual Job Openings: 34,251
▲ Yearly Earnings $22,089
▲ Education Required: Short-term O-J-T
▲ Self-employed: 0%
▲ Part-time: 15%

Loan and Credit Clerks

Assemble documents, prepare papers, process applications, and complete transactions of individuals applying for loans and credit. Loan clerks review loan papers to ensure completeness; operate typewriters to prepare correspondence, reports, and loan documents from draft; and complete transactions between loan establishment, borrowers, and sellers upon approval of loan. Credit clerks interview applicants to obtain personal and financial data; determine credit worthiness; process applications; and notify customer of acceptance or rejection of credit. Exclude loan interviewers. Verifies and examines information and accuracy of loan application and closing documents. Prepares and types loan applications, closing documents, legal documents, letters, forms, government notices, and checks, using computer. Interviews loan applicant to obtain personal and financial data and to assist in filling out application. Assembles and compiles documents for closing, such as title abstract, insurance form, loan form, and tax receipt. Records applications for loan and credit, loan information, and disbursement of funds, using computer. Submits loan application with recommendation for underwriting approval. Contacts customer by mail, telephone, or in person concerning acceptance or rejection of application. Contacts credit bureaus, employers, and other sources to check applicant credit and personal references. Checks value of customer collateral to be held as loan security. Calculates, reviews, and corrects errors on interest, principal, payment, and closing costs, using computer or calculator. Answers questions and advises customer regarding loans and transactions. Schedules and conducts closing of mortgage transaction. Presents loan and repayment schedule to customer. Establishes credit limit and grants extension of credit on overdue accounts. Files and maintains loan records. Orders property insurance or mortgage insurance policies to ensure protection against loss on mortgaged property. Accepts payment on accounts. Reviews customer accounts to determine whether payments are made on time and that other loan terms are being followed.

Knowledge: Clerical; Economics and Accounting; Customer and Personal Service; Law, Government, and Jurisprudence

Abilities: Mathematical Reasoning; Number Facility; Perceptual Speed; Wrist-Finger Speed; Near Vision; Speech Recognition

Loan Officers and Counselors

▲ Growth: 28%
▲ Annual Job Openings: 29,989
▲ Yearly Earnings $37,419
▲ Education Required: Bachelor's degree
▲ Self-employed: 0%
▲ Part-time: 7%

Loan Officers and Counselors

Evaluate, authorize, or recommend approval of commercial, real estate, or credit loans. Advise borrowers on financial status and methods of payments. Include mortgage loan officers or agents, collection analysts, and loan servicing officers. Analyzes applicant financial status, credit, and property evaluation to determine feasibility of granting loan. Approves loan within specified limits. Refers loan to loan committee for approval. Evaluates acceptability of loan to corporations that buy real estate loans on secondary mortgage markets. Interviews applicant and requests specified information for loan application. Contacts applicant or creditors to resolve questions regarding application information. Ensures loan agreements are complete and accurate according to policy. Computes payment schedule. Submits application to credit analyst for verification and recommendation. Petitions court to transfer title and deeds of collateral to bank. Confers with underwriters to aid in resolving mortgage application problems. Analyzes potential loan markets to develop prospects for loans. Arranges for maintenance and liquidation of delinquent property. Contacts customers to arrange payment of delinquent loan balances. Supervises loan personnel.

Knowledge: Clerical; Economics and Accounting; Sales and Marketing; Customer and Personal Service; Personnel and Human Resources; Mathematics; Law, Government, and Jurisprudence; Communications and Media

Abilities: Oral Comprehension; Written Comprehension; Oral Expression; Written Expression; Problem Sensitivity; Deductive Reasoning; Inductive Reasoning; Information Ordering; Category Flexibility; Mathematical Reasoning; Number Facility; Memorization; Near Vision; Speech Recognition; Speech Clarity

Locksmiths and Safe Repairers

▲ Growth: 15%

▲ Annual Job Openings: 2,054

▲ Yearly Earnings $26,270

▲ Education Required: Moderate-term O-J-T

▲ Self-employed: 39%

▲ Part-time: 7%

Locksmiths and Safe Repairers

Repair and open locks, make keys, and change locks and safe combinations. May install and repair safes. Disassembles mechanical or electrical locking devices and repairs or replaces worn tumblers, springs, and other parts, using hand tools. Inserts new or repaired tumblers into lock to change combination. Repairs and adjusts safes, vault doors, and vault components, using hand tools, lathe, drill press, and welding and acetylene cutting apparatus. Cuts new or duplicate keys, using key-cutting machine. Installs safes, vault doors, and deposit boxes according to blueprints, using equipment such as power drill, tap, die, truck crane, and dolly. Opens safe locks by drilling. Moves picklock in cylinder to open door locks without keys. Removes interior and exterior finishes on safes and vaults and sprays on new finishes. Keeps record of company locks and keys.

Knowledge: Mechanical

Abilities: Arm-Hand Steadiness; Finger Dexterity

Machine Operators, Tenders, Setters, and Set-up Operators

▲ Growth: 11%

▲ Annual Job Openings: 55,263

▲ Yearly Earnings $24,731

▲ Education Required: Moderate-term O-J-T

▲ Self-employed: 2%

▲ Part-time: 4%

Cooling and Freezing Equipment Operators and Tenders

Operate or tend equipment—such as cooling and freezing units, refrigerators, batch freezers, and freezing tunnels—to cool or freeze products such as ice cream, meat, blood plasma, and chemicals, preparatory to storage, shipment, or further processing. Starts pumps, agitators, and conveyors, and turns valves to admit or transfer product, refrigerant, or mix. Adjusts machine or freezer speed and air intake to obtain desired consistency and amount of product. Starts equipment to blend contents or mix with air to prevent sticking to vat. Monitors pressure gauges, flowmeters, thermometers, or product, and adjusts controls to maintain specified conditions. Positions molds on conveyor, and measures and adjusts level of fill, using depth gauge. Places or positions containers into equipment and removes containers after cooling or freezing process. Measures or weighs specified amounts of ingredients or material, and adds into tanks, vats, or equipment. Assembles or attaches pipes, fittings, or valves, using hand tools. Inserts forming fixture, and starts machine that cuts frozen product into measured portions or specified shapes. Stirs material with spoon or paddle to mix ingredients or allow even cooling and to prevent coagulation. Draws sample of product and tests for specific gravity, acidity, or sugar content, using hydrometer, pH meter, or refractometer. Flushes lines with solutions or steam to clean and sterilize equipment. Scrapes, dislodges, or breaks excess frost or ice from equipment. Cleans, maintains, and repairs machines. Loads and positions wrapping paper, sticks, bags, or cartons into dispensing machines, and removes jammed sticks, using pliers or picks. Records temperatures, amount of materials processed, or test results on report form.

Knowledge: Food Production; Chemistry

Abilities: Perceptual Speed; Manual Dexterity; Finger Dexterity; Reaction Time; Wrist-Finger Speed; Speed of Limb Movement; Stamina; Extent Flexibility; Dynamic Flexibility; Gross Body Coordination; Gross Body Equilibrium

Fiber Product Machine Cutters

Set up and operate machine to cut or slice fiber material, such as paper, wallboard, and insulation material. Adjusts machine controls to position and align and to regulate speed and pressure of components. Activates machine to cut, slice, slit, perforate, or score fiber products, such as paperboard sheets, rubber shoe soles, or plaster wallboard. Selects and installs machine components, such as cutting blades, rollers, and templates, according to specifications, using hand tools. Monitors operation of cutting or slicing machine to detect malfunctions, removes defective or substandard materials, and readjusts machine components to conform to standards. Reviews work orders, blueprints, specifications, or job samples to determine components, settings, and adjustments for cutting and slicing machines. Positions materials, such as rubber, paper, or leather, on feeding mechanism of cutting or slicing machine. Examines, measures, and weighs materials or products to verify conformance to specifications, using measuring devices, such as ruler, micrometer, or scale. Replaces worn or broken parts, and cleans and lubricates cutting or slicing machine to maintain equipment in working order. Removes completed materials or products from cutting or slicing machine and stacks or stores for additional processing. Maintains production records, such as quantity, type, and dimensions of materials produced.

Knowledge: Production and Processing

Abilities: Perceptual Speed; Manual Dexterity; Control Precision; Rate Control; Reaction Time; Static Strength; Explosive Strength; Dynamic Flexibility; Gross Body Equilibrium

Stone Sawyers

Set up and operate gang saws, reciprocating saws, circular saws, or wire saws to cut blocks of stone into specified dimensions. Starts saw and moves blade across surface of material, such as stone, concrete slabs, and asbestos-cement sheets and pipes, to saw. Adjusts blade pressure against stone, using ammeter, and lowers blade in stone as cut depth increases. Starts pump to circulate water and abrasive onto blade or cable during cutting. Changes or replaces saw blades, cables, and grinding wheels, using wrench. Turns crank or presses button to move car under sawing cable or saw frame. Aligns cable or blades with marks on stone, and presses button or turns lever to lower sawing cable or blades to stone. Observes operation to detect uneven sawing and exhausted abrasive supply, and tightens pulleys or adds abrasive to maintain cutting speed. Marks dimensions or traces on stone according to diagram, using chisel and hammer, straightedge, rule, and chalked string. Builds bed of timbers on car, and aligns and levels stone on bed, using crowbar, sledgehammer, wedges, blocks, rule, and spirit level. Washes stone, using water hose, and verifies width or thickness of cut stone, using rule. Operates crane or signals crane operator to position or remove stone from car or saw bed.

Knowledge: Building and Construction; Mechanical

Abilities: Manual Dexterity; Control Precision; Multilimb Coordination; Rate Control; Reaction Time; Speed of Limb Movement; Static Strength; Explosive Strength; Dynamic Strength; Trunk Strength; Stamina; Dynamic Flexibility; Gross Body Coordination; Gross Body Equilibrium; Peripheral Vision; Depth Perception

Glass Machine Cutters

Set up and operate machines to cut glass. Operates single-cut machine to cut glass. Starts machine to verify set-up and makes adjustments. Adjusts position, height, and stroke of cutting bridges, manually or by turning controls, to score glass to specific dimensions. Adjusts timing mechanism to synchronize breaker bar to snap glass at score. Removes and replaces worn cutter heads, using hand tools. Starts vacuum-cupped crane, to lift and transfer glass. Measures glass with tape to verify dimensions and observes glass to detect defects. Reviews work orders and maintains record of production, using counter. Directs workers on cutting team.

Knowledge: Production and Processing

Abilities: Arm-Hand Steadiness; Manual Dexterity; Control Precision; Rate Control; Dynamic Flexibility; Depth Perception

Cleaning, Washing, and Pickling Equipment Operators and Tenders

Operate or tend machines to wash or clean items—such as barrels or kegs, glass products, tin plate surfaces, dried fruit, pulp, animal stock, coal, manufactured articles,

plastic, or rubber—to remove impurities preparatory to further processing. Observes machine operation, gauges, or thermometer, and adjusts controls to maintain operation, according to specifications. Sets controls to regulate temperature and length of cycle and starts conveyors, pumps, agitators, and machines. Adds specified amounts of chemicals into equipment at required time to maintain level and concentration of solution. Drains, cleans, and refills machine or tank at designated intervals with cleaning solution or water. Loads and unloads objects to and from machine, conveyor, or rack. Examines and inspects machine for malfunctions, and product for conformance to processing specifications. Draws samples for laboratory analysis or tests solutions for conformance to specifications, such as acidity or specific gravity. Measures, weighs, or mixes specified quantity of cleaning solutions, using measuring tank, calibrated rod, or suction tube. Adjusts, cleans, and lubricates mechanical parts of machine, using hand tools and grease gun. Records gauge readings, materials used, processing time, or test results in production log.

Knowledge: None above average

Abilities: Rate Control

Portable Machine Cutters

Use portable electric cutter to cut multiple layers of fabric into parts for articles, such as awnings, fitted sheets, garments, hats, stuffed toys, and upholstered furniture. Cuts multiple layers of fabrics into parts for articles, such as canvas goods, garments, and upholstered furniture. Spreads fabric on table in single or multiple layers and guides layers around cutter blade. Drills holes through layers of fabric or cuts notches in edges of parts to mark parts for assembly. Sharpens or changes cutter blades when quality of cut indicates blade is dull. Positions pattern over fabric and traces outline of pattern, using chalk or crayon. Separates cutting waste according to material.

Knowledge: Production and Processing

Abilities: Arm-Hand Steadiness; Manual Dexterity

Management Analysts

▲ Growth: 21%
▲ Annual Job Openings: 46,026
▲ Yearly Earnings $48,193
▲ Education Required: Master's degree
▲ Self-employed: 45%
▲ Part-time: 19%

Management Analysts

Review, analyze, and suggest improvements to business and organizational systems to assist management in operating more efficiently and effectively. Conduct organizational studies and evaluations, design systems and procedures, conduct work simplification and measurement studies, and prepare operations and procedures manuals. Exclude computer systems analysts. Reviews forms and reports, and confers with management and users about format, distribution, and purpose to identify problems and improvements. Develops and implements records management program for filing, protection, and retrieval of records, and assures compliance with program. Reviews records retention schedules and recordkeeping requirements to plan transfer of active records to inactive or archival storage or destruction. Reports findings and prepares recommendations for new systems, procedures, or organizational changes. Interviews personnel and conducts on-site observation to ascertain unit functions, work performed, and methods, equipment, and personnel used. Prepares manuals and trains workers in use of new forms, reports, procedures, or equipment, according to organizational policy. Designs, evaluates, recommends, and approves changes of forms and reports. Implements new systems, trains personnel in use, and reviews operations to ensure that systems are applied and functioning as designed. Recommends purchase of storage equipment, and designs area layout to locate equipment in space available. Directs records management personnel and supporting technical, micrographics, and printing workers.

Knowledge: Administration and Management; Clerical; Economics and Accounting; Personnel and Human Resources; Production and Processing; Mathematics; Psychology; Education and Training; English Language; Law, Government, and Jurisprudence

Abilities: Oral Comprehension; Written Expression; Fluency of Ideas; Originality; Problem Sensitivity; Category Flexibility; Speed of Closure; Visualization; Speech Clarity

Management Support Specialists

▲ Growth: 20%
▲ Annual Job Openings: 124,342
▲ Yearly Earnings $38,251
▲ Education Required: Bachelor's degree
▲ Self-employed: 6%
▲ Part-time: 7%

Purchasing Agents and Buyers, Farm Products

Arrange or contract for the purchase of farm products for further processing or resale. Negotiates contracts with farmers for production or purchase of agricultural products such as milk, grains, and Christmas trees. Arranges sales, loans, or financing for supplies, such as equipment, seed, feed, fertilizer, and chemicals. Reviews orders and determines product types and quantities required to meet demand. Plans and arranges for transportation for crops, milk, or other products to dairy or processing facility. Inspects and tests crops or other farm products to determine quality and to detect evidence of disease or insect damage. Estimates production possibilities by surveying property and studying factors such as history of crop rotation, soil fertility, and irrigation facilities. Maintains records of business transactions. Advises farm groups and growers on land preparation and livestock care to maximize quantity and quality of production. Coordinates and directs activities of workers engaged in cutting, transporting, storing, or milling products, and in maintaining records. Writes articles for publication.

Knowledge: Administration and Management; Clerical; Economics and Accounting; Sales and Marketing; Production and Processing; Food Production; Mathematics; Biology; English Language; Communications and Media; Transportation

Abilities: Written Expression; Category Flexibility; Mathematical Reasoning; Number Facility; Memorization; Gross Body Equilibrium; Speech Clarity

Legislative Assistants

Perform research into governmental laws and procedures to resolve problems or complaints of constituents or to assist legislator in preparation of proposed legislation. Conducts research in such areas as laws, procedures, and systems of government and subject matter of proposed legislation. Analyzes voting records, existing and pending legislation, political activity, or constituent problems to determine action to take. Confers with personnel, such as constituents, representatives of federal agencies, and members of press to gather and provide information. Attends committee meetings to obtain information on proposed legislation. Briefs legislator on issues and recommends action to be taken. Prepares correspondence, reports, and preliminary drafts of bills and speeches. Assists in campaign activities.

Knowledge: English Language; Law, Government, and Jurisprudence

Abilities: Oral Comprehension; Written Comprehension; Oral Expression; Written Expression; Fluency of Ideas; Originality; Deductive Reasoning; Inductive Reasoning; Speed of Closure; Gross Body Equilibrium; Far Vision

Executive Secretaries and Administrative Assistants

Aid executive by coordinating office services, such as personnel, budget preparation and control, housekeeping, records control, and special management studies. Coordinates and directs office services, such as records and budget preparation, personnel, and housekeeping, to aid executives. Prepares records and reports, such as recommendations for solutions of administrative problems and annual reports. Files and retrieves corporation documents, records, and reports. Analyzes operating practices and procedures to create new or to revise existing methods. Interprets administrative and operating policies and procedures for employees. Studies management methods to improve workflow, simplify reporting procedures, or implement cost reductions. Plans conferences. Reads and answers correspondence.

Knowledge: Administration and Management; Clerical; Economics and Accounting

Abilities: Wrist-Finger Speed; Near Vision

Land Leasing and Permit Agents

Arrange for property leases or permits for special use, such as mineral prospecting or movie production. Negotiates agreements, such as leases, options, and royalty payments, with property representatives. Draws up agreements according to negotiated terms, applying knowledge of company policies and local, state, and federal laws. Confers with others regarding characteristics of location desired and lease and use of property. Obtains signatures on documents from company and property representatives. Seeks new locations for prospecting or production activities. Consults with authorities and landowners, and researches company policies and local, state, and Federal laws to obtain regulatory information. Searches public records to determine legal ownership of land and mineral rights for property. Writes purchase orders and bank checks as specified by leases, agreements, and contracts. Draws sketches of locations and terrain to be traversed. Posts markers on property to indicate locations.

Knowledge: Economics and Accounting; Geography; Law, Government, and Jurisprudence

Abilities: Written Comprehension; Written Expression; Perceptual Speed

Meeting and Convention Planners

Coordinate activities of staff and convention personnel to make arrangements for group meetings and conventions. Directs and coordinates activities of staff and convention personnel to make arrangements, prepare facilities, and provide services for events. Consults with customer to determine objectives and requirements for events, such as meetings, conferences, and conventions. Plans and develops programs, budgets, and services, such as lodging, catering, and entertainment, according to customer requirements. Evaluates and selects providers of services, such as meeting facilities, speakers, and transportation, according to customer requirements. Negotiates contracts with such providers as hotels, convention centers, and speakers. Inspects rooms and displays for conformance to customer requirements, and conducts post-meeting evaluations to improve future events. Speaks with attendees and resolves complaints to maintain goodwill. Obtains permits from fire and health departments to erect displays and exhibits and to serve food at events. Reviews bills for accuracy and approves payment. Maintains records of events. Reads trade publications, attends seminars, and consults with other meeting professionals to keep abreast of meeting management standards and trends.

Knowledge: Administration and Management, Economics and Accounting; Sales and Marketing; Customer and Personal Service; Sociology and Anthropology; Foreign Language; Public Safety and Security; Law, Government, and Jurisprudence; Telecommunications; Communications and Media

Abilities: Oral Comprehension; Category Flexibility

Customs Brokers

Prepare and compile documents required by federal government for discharge of foreign cargo at domestic port to serve as intermediary between importers, merchant shipping companies, airlines, railroads, trucking companies, pipeline operators, and the United States Customs Service. Completes entry papers from shipper's invoice, in accordance with federal regulations, for discharge of foreign cargo at domestic port. Submits entry papers to U.S. Customs Service, according to federal regulations. Prepares papers for shipper to appeal duty charges imposed by Customs Service. Quotes duty rates on goods to be imported, based on knowledge of federal tariffs and excise taxes. Arranges for payment of duties as specified by law. Registers foreign ships with U.S. Coast Guard. Provides storage and transportation of imported goods from port to final destination.

Knowledge: Economics and Accounting; Geography; Foreign Language; Law, Government, and Jurisprudence; Transportation

Abilities: None above average

Management Support Workers

▲ Growth: 26%
▲ Annual Job Openings: 154,129
▲ Yearly Earnings $35,339
▲ Education Required: Bachelor's degree
▲ Self-employed: 2%
▲ Part-time: 20%

Interpreters and Translators

Translate and interpret written or spoken communications from one language to another or from spoken to manual sign language used by hearing-impaired. Translates approximate or exact message of speaker into specified language, orally or by using hand signs for hearing-impaired. Translates responses from second language to first. Reads written material, such as legal documents, scientific works, or news reports, and rewrites material into specified language, according to established rules of grammar. Listens to statements of speaker to ascertain meaning and to remember what is said, using electronic audio system. Receives information on subject to be discussed prior to interpreting session.

Knowledge: Sociology and Anthropology; English Language; Foreign Language; History and Archeology; Communications and Media

Abilities: Oral Comprehension; Written Comprehension; Oral Expression; Written Expression; Memorization; Selective Attention; Auditory Attention; Speech Recognition; Speech Clarity

City Planning Aides

Compile data from various sources, such as maps, reports, and field and file investigations, for use by city planner in making planning studies. Summarizes information from maps, reports, investigations, and books. Prepares reports, using statistics, charts, and graphs, to illustrate planning studies in areas such as population, land use, or zoning. Prepares and updates files and records. Conducts interviews and surveys and observes conditions which affect land usage. Answers public inquiries.

Knowledge: Clerical; Mathematics; Geography

Abilities: None of the above

Manicurists

- ▲ Growth: 45%
- ▲ Annual Job Openings: 8,973
- ▲ Yearly Earnings $15,392
- ▲ Education Required: Postsecondary vocational training
- ▲ Self-employed: 43%
- ▲ Part-time: 36%

Manicurists

Clean, shape, and polish customers' fingernails and toenails. Removes previously applied nail polish, using liquid remover and swabs. Shapes and smooths ends of nails, using scissors, files, and emery boards. Cleans customers' nails in soapy water, using swabs, files, and orange sticks. Applies clear or colored liquid polish onto nails with brush. Forms artificial fingernails on customer's fingers. Roughens surfaces of fingernails, using abrasive wheel. Polishes nails, using powdered polish and buffer. Brushes additional powder and solvent onto new growth between cuticles and nails to maintain nail appearance. Attaches paper forms to tips of customer's fingers to support and shape artificial nails. Brushes coats of powder and solvent onto nails and paper forms with handbrush to extend nails to desired length. Softens nail cuticles with water and oil, pushes back cuticles, using cuticle knife, and trims cuticles, using scissors or nippers. Removes paper forms and shapes and smooths edges of nails, using rotary abrasive wheel. Whitens underside of nails with white paste or pencil.

Knowledge: Customer and Personal Service

Abilities: Arm-Hand Steadiness; Finger Dexterity; Visual Color Discrimination; Glare Sensitivity

Marketing and Sales Worker Supervisors

▲ Growth: 11%

▲ Annual Job Openings: 305,545

▲ Yearly Earnings $32,718

▲ Education Required: Work experience in a related occupation

▲ Self-employed: 34%

▲ Part-time: 8%

First-Line Supervisors and Manager/ Supervisors—Sales and Related Workers

Directly supervise and coordinate activities of marketing, sales, and related workers. May perform management functions, such as budgeting, accounting, marketing, and personnel work, in addition to their supervisory duties. Directs and supervises employees engaged in sales, inventory-taking, reconciling cash receipts, or performing specific service such as pumping gasoline for customers. Plans and prepares work schedules and assigns employees to specific duties. Hires, trains, and evaluates personnel in sales or marketing establishment. Coordinates sales promotion activities and prepares merchandise displays and advertising copy. Confers with company officials to develop methods and procedures to increase sales, expand markets, and promote business. Keeps records of employees' work schedules and time cards. Prepares sales and inventory reports for management and budget departments. Assists sales staff in completing complicated and difficult sales. Listens to and resolves customer complaints regarding service, product, or personnel. Keeps records pertaining to purchases, sales, and requisitions. Examines merchandise to ensure that it is correctly priced and displayed and functions as advertised. Formulates pricing policies on merchandise according to requirements for profitability of store operations. Analyzes customers' wants and needs by observing which items sell most rapidly. Inventories stock and reorders when inventories drop to specified level. Prepares rental or lease agreement, specifying charges and payment procedures, for use of machinery, tools, or other such items. Examines products purchased for resale or received for storage to determine condition of product or item.

Knowledge: Administration and Management; Economics and Accounting; Sales and Marketing; Customer and Personal Service; Personnel and Human Resources; Mathematics; Psychology; Education and Training; Communications and Media

Abilities: Fluency of Ideas; Originality; Number Facility; Time Sharing

Marketing, Advertising, and Public Relations Managers

▲ Growth: 29%
▲ Annual Job Openings: 54,600
▲ Yearly Earnings $53,601
▲ Education Required: Work experience, plus degree
▲ Self-employed: 2%
▲ Part-time: 2%

M

Advertising and Promotions Managers

Plan and direct advertising policies and programs or produce collateral materials, such as posters, contests, coupons, or giveaways, to create extra interest in the purchase of a product or service for a department, an entire organization, or on an account basis. Directs activities of workers engaged in developing and producing advertisements. Plans and executes advertising policies of organization. Plans and prepares advertising and promotional material. Confers with department heads and/or staff to discuss topics such as contracts, selection of advertising media, or product to be advertised. Formulates plans to extend business with established accounts and transacts business as agent for advertising accounts. Coordinates activities of departments, such as sales, graphic arts, media, finance, and research. Confers with clients to provide marketing or technical advice. Monitors and analyzes sales promotion results to determine cost effectiveness of promotion campaign. Inspects layouts and advertising copy and edits scripts, audio and video tapes, and other promotional material for adherence to specifications. Supervises and trains service representatives. Reads trade journals and professional literature to stay informed on trends, innovations, and changes that affect media planning. Consults publications to learn about conventions and social functions, and organizes prospect files for promotional purposes. Represents company at trade association meetings to promote products. Directs product research and development. Contacts organizations to explain services and facilities offered or to secure props, audio-visual materials, and sound effects. Adjusts broadcasting schedules due to program cancellation. Directs conversion of products from USA to foreign standards. Inspects premises of assigned stores for adequate security and compliance with safety codes and ordinances.

Knowledge: Administration and Management; Economics and Accounting; Sales and Marketing; Customer and Personal Service; Personnel and Human Resources; Mathematics; Psychology; Sociology and Anthropology; Geography; Education and Training; English Language; Foreign Language; Fine Arts; History and Archeology; Philosophy and Theology; Public Safety and Security; Law, Government, and Jurisprudence; Telecommunications; Communications and Media

Abilities: Oral Comprehension; Written Comprehension; Oral Expression; Written Expression; Fluency of Ideas; Originality; Problem Sensitivity; Deductive Reasoning; Inductive

Reasoning; Category Flexibility; Mathematical Reasoning; Number Facility; Memorization; Speed of Closure; Visualization; Selective Attention; Time Sharing; Near Vision; Far Vision; Visual Color Discrimination; Speech Recognition; Speech Clarity

Sales Managers

Direct the actual distribution or movement of a product or service to customers. Coordinate sales distribution by establishing sales territories, quotas, and goals, and establish training programs for sales representatives. Analyze sales statistics gathered by staff to determine sales potential and inventory requirements, and monitor the preferences of customers. Directs and coordinates activities involving sales of manufactured goods, service outlets, technical services, operating retail chain, and advertising services for publication. Plans and directs staffing, training, and performance evaluations to develop and control sales and service programs. Directs, coordinates, and reviews activities in sales and service accounting and recordkeeping, and receiving and shipping operations. Analyzes marketing potential of new and existing store locations, sales statistics, and expenditures to formulate policy. Confers or consults with department heads to plan advertising services, secure information on appliances and equipment, and customer-required specifications. Reviews operational records and reports to project sales and determine profitability. Advises dealers and distributors on policies and operating procedures to ensure functional effectiveness of business. Directs foreign sales and service outlets of organization. Visits franchised dealers to stimulate interest in establishment or expansion of leasing programs. Directs clerical staff to maintain export correspondence, bid requests, and credit collections, and current information on tariffs, licenses, and restrictions. Confers with potential customers regarding equipment needs and advises customers on types of equipment to purchase. Resolves customer complaints regarding sales and service. Represents company at trade association meetings to promote products. Directs product research and development. Inspects premises of assigned stores for adequate security exits and compliance with safety codes and ordinances. Direct conversion of products from USA to foreign standards.

Knowledge: Administration and Management; Clerical; Economics and Accounting; Sales and Marketing; Customer and Personal Service; Personnel and Human Resources; Mathematics; Psychology; Sociology and Anthropology; Geography; Education and Training; English Language; Foreign Language; History and Archeology; Philosophy and Theology; Public Safety and Security; Law, Government, and Jurisprudence; Communications and Media; Transportation

Abilities: Oral Comprehension; Written Comprehension; Oral Expression; Written Expression; Fluency of Ideas; Originality; Problem Sensitivity; Deductive Reasoning; Inductive Reasoning; Category Flexibility; Mathematical Reasoning; Number Facility; Memorization; Selective Attention; Time Sharing; Near Vision; Far Vision; Speech Recognition; Speech Clarity

Marketing Managers

Determine the demand for products and services offered by a firm and its competitors and identify potential customers. Develop pricing strategies with the goal of maximizing the firm's profits or share of the market while ensuring the firm's customers are satisfied. Oversee product development or monitor trends that indicate the need for new products and services. Plans and administers marketing and distribution of broadcasting television programs and negotiates agreements for ancillary properties. Develops marketing strategy, based on knowledge of establishment policy, nature of market, and cost and mark-up factors. Coordinates and publicizes product marketing activities. Directs activities of world trade department in chamber of commerce to assist business concerns in developing and utilizing foreign markets. Conducts economic and commercial surveys in foreign countries to locate markets for products and services. Analyzes foreign business developments and fashion and trade journals regarding fashion trends and opportunities for selling and buying products. Promotes new fashions and coordinates promotional activities, such as fashion shows, to induce consumer acceptance. Reviews inventory of television programs and films produced and distribution rights to determine potential markets for broadcasting station. Consults with buying personnel to gain advice regarding type of fashions store will purchase and feature for season. Advises exporters and importers on documentation procedures and certifies commercial documents that are required by foreign countries. Confers with legal staff to resolve problems, such as copyrights and royalty sharing with outside producers and distributors. Advises business and other groups on local, national, and international legislation affecting world trade. Negotiates with media agents to secure agreements for translation of materials into other media. Entertains foreign governmental officials and business representatives to promote trade relations. Prepare report of marketing activities for state and federal agencies. Contracts with models, musicians, caterers, and other personnel to manage staging of fashion shows. Selects garments and accessories to be shown at fashion shows. Arranges for reproduction of visual materials and edits materials according to specific market or customer requirements. Promotes travel to other countries. Compiles catalog of audio-visual offerings and sets prices and rental fees. Provides information on current fashion, style trends, and use of accessories.

Knowledge: Administration and Management; Economics and Accounting; Sales and Marketing; Customer and Personal Service; Personnel and Human Resources; Mathematics; Psychology; Sociology and Anthropology; Geography; Education and Training; English Language; Foreign Language; Fine Arts; History and Archeology; Philosophy and Theology; Law, Government, and Jurisprudence; Communications and Media; Transportation

Abilities: Oral Comprehension; Written Comprehension; Oral Expression; Written Expression; Fluency of Ideas; Originality; Problem Sensitivity; Deductive Reasoning; Inductive Reasoning; Information Ordering; Category Flexibility; Mathematical Reasoning; Number Facility; Memorization; Visualization; Selective Attention; Time Sharing; Near Vision; Visual Color Discrimination; Auditory Attention; Speech Recognition; Speech Clarity

Fundraising Directors

Plan and direct activities to solicit and maintain funds for special projects and non-profit organizations, such as charities, universities, museums, and other organizations dependent upon voluntary financial contributions. Plan and directs solicitation of funds for broadcasting stations and institutions such as zoos and museums. Establishes fundraising goals. Assigns responsibilities for personal solicitation efforts. Plans and coordinates benefit events. Develops schedule for disbursing solicited funds. Develops public relations materials to enhance institution image and promote fundraising program. Organizes direct mail campaign to reach potential contributors. Researches public and private grant agencies and foundations to identify sources of funding. Supervises and coordinates activities of workers engaged in maintaining records of contributors and grants and preparing letters of appreciation. Purchases mailing list of potential donors or negotiates agreements with other organizations for exchange of mailing lists. Specializes in solicitation of funding from government, foundation, or corporation sources. Serves as liaison between broadcast departmental staff and funding establishment personnel to provide project information and to solve problems.

Knowledge: Administration and Management; Economics and Accounting; Sales and Marketing; Psychology; Sociology and Anthropology; Geography; English Language; Foreign Language; Fine Arts; Philosophy and Theology; Law, Government, and Jurisprudence; Telecommunications; Communications and Media

Abilities: Oral Comprehension; Written Comprehension; Oral Expression; Written Expression; Fluency of Ideas; Originality; Inductive Reasoning; Mathematical Reasoning; Number Facility; Memorization; Time Sharing; Far Vision; Speech Recognition; Speech Clarity

Grant Coordinators

Research, develop, and coordinate development of proposals for funding and funding sources to establish or maintain grant-funded programs in public or private organizations. Prepares proposal narrative justifying budgetary expenditures for approval by organization officials. Writes and submits grant proposal application to funding agency or foundation. Directs and coordinates evaluation and monitoring of grant-funded programs. Consults with personnel to determine goals, objectives, and budgetary requirements of organizations, such as nonprofit agencies, institutions, or school systems. Researches availability of grant funds from public and private agencies to determine feasibility of developing programs to supplement budget allocations. Completes reports as specified by grant. Confers with representatives of funding sources to complete details of proposal. Maintains files on grants.

Knowledge: Administration and Management; Economics and Accounting; English Language; Law, Government, and Jurisprudence

Abilities: Oral Comprehension; Written Comprehension; Oral Expression; Written Expression; Fluency of Ideas; Perceptual Speed; Selective Attention

Agents and Business Managers of Artists, Performers, and Athletes

Represent and promote artists, performers, and athletes to prospective employers. May handle contract negotiations and other business matters for clients. Negotiates with management, promoters, union officials, and other persons, to obtain contracts for clients such as entertainers, artists, and athletes. Manages business affairs for clients, such as obtaining travel and lodging accommodations, selling tickets, marketing and advertising, and paying expenses. Schedules promotional or performance engagements for clients. Advises clients on financial and legal matters, such as investments and taxes. Collects fees, commission, or other payment, according to contract terms. Obtains information and inspects facilities, equipment, and accommodations of potential performance venue. Hires trainer or coach to advise client on performance matters, such as training techniques or presentation of act. Prepares periodic accounting statements for clients concerning financial affairs. Conducts auditions or interviews new clients.

Knowledge: Administration and Management; Economics and Accounting; Sales and Marketing; Personnel and Human Resources; Fine Arts; Law, Government, and Jurisprudence

Abilities: Speech Recognition; Speech Clarity

Materials Engineers

▲ Growth: 7%
▲ Annual Job Openings: 933
▲ Yearly Earnings $49,566
▲ Education Required: Bachelor's degree
▲ Self-employed: 0%
▲ Part-time: 3%

Ceramic Engineers

Conduct research, design machinery, and develop processing techniques related to the manufacturing of ceramic products. Conducts research into methods of processing, forming, and firing of clays to develop new ceramic products. Designs machinery, equipment, and apparatus for forming, firing, and handling products. Develops processing techniques and directs technical work concerned with manufacture of ceramic products. Directs testing of physical, chemical, and heat-resisting properties of materials. Analyzes results of tests to determine combinations of materials which will improve quality of products. Coordinates testing activities of finished products for such characteristics as texture, color, durability, glazing, and refractory properties. Directs and coordinates manufacturing of prototype ceramic product. Designs and directs others in fabrication of testing and test-control apparatus and equipment. Directs and coordinates activities concerned with development, procurement, installation, and calibration of test and recording instruments, equipment, and control devices. Prepares or directs preparation of product layout and detailed drawings. Prepares technical reports for use by engineering and management personnel.

Knowledge: Administration and Management; Production and Processing; Computers and Electronics; Engineering and Technology; Design; Mathematics; Physics; Chemistry; English Language

Abilities: Written Expression; Originality; Deductive Reasoning; Number Facility; Visualization; Visual Color Discrimination; Speech Clarity

Metallurgists

Investigate properties of metals and develop methods to produce new alloys, applications, and processes of extracting metals from their ores, and to commercially fabricate products from metals. Conducts microscopic and macroscopic studies of metals and alloys to determine their physical characteristics, properties, and reactions to processing techniques. Tests and investigates alloys to develop new or improved grades or production methods, and to determine compliance with manufacturing standards. Develops and improves processes for melting, hot-working, cold-working, heat-treating, molding, and pouring metals. Originates, controls, and develops processes used in extracting metals from their ores. Studies ore reduction problems to determine most efficient methods of producing metals commercially. Consults with engineers to develop methods of manufacturing alloys at minimum costs. Interprets findings and prepares drawings, charts, and graphs for reference or instructional purposes. Makes experimental sand molds, and tests sand for permeability, strength, and chemical composition. Writes reports referencing findings, conclusions, and recommendations. Directs laboratory personnel in preparing samples, and designates area of samples for microscopic or macroscopic examinations. Controls temperature adjustments, charge mixtures, and other variables on blast and steel-melting furnaces.

Knowledge: Administration and Management; Production and Processing; Engineering and Technology; Design; Physics; Chemistry; Geography; English Language

Abilities: Oral Comprehension; Written Comprehension; Written Expression; Originality; Deductive Reasoning; Inductive Reasoning; Category Flexibility; Mathematical Reasoning; Number Facility; Memorization; Near Vision

Welding Engineers

Develop welding techniques, procedures, and applications of welding equipment to problems involving fabrication of metals. Conducts research and development investigations to improve existing or to develop new welding equipment. Conducts research and development investigations to develop new or to modify current welding techniques and procedures. Conducts research and development investigations to develop and test new fabrication processes and procedures. Establishes welding procedures for production and welding personnel, to ensure compliance with specifications, processes, and heating requirements. Evaluates new equipment, techniques, and materials in welding field for possible application to current welding problems or production processes. Prepares technical reports identifying results of research and development and preventive maintenance investigations. Directs and coordinates technical inspections to ensure compliance with established welding procedures and standards. Contacts other agencies, engineering personnel, or clients to exchange ideas, information, or technical advice.

Knowledge: Engineering and Technology; Design; Building and Construction; Mathematics; Physics

Abilities: Written Expression; Fluency of Ideas; Originality; Problem Sensitivity; Inductive Reasoning; Flexibility of Closure

Materials Engineers

Evaluate materials and develop machinery and processes to manufacture materials for use in products that must meet specialized design and performance specifications. Develop new uses for known materials. Include those working with composite materials or specializing in one type of material, such as graphite, metal and metal alloys, ceramics and glass, plastics and polymers, and naturally occurring materials. Include metallurgists and metallurgical engineers, ceramic engineers, and welding engineers. Reviews new product plans and makes recommendations for material selection based on design objectives and cost. Plans and implements laboratory operations to develop material and fabrication procedures that maintain cost and performance standards. Evaluates technical and economic factors relating to process or product design objectives. Reviews product failure data and interprets laboratory test results to determine material or process causes. Confers with producers of material during investigation and evaluation of material for product applications.

Knowledge: Economics and Accounting; Production and Processing; Engineering and Technology; Design; Mathematics; Physics; Chemistry; English Language

Abilities: Written Comprehension; Written Expression; Fluency of Ideas; Originality; Problem Sensitivity; Deductive Reasoning; Inductive Reasoning; Mathematical Reasoning; Number Facility; Flexibility of Closure; Perceptual Speed; Visualization; Selective Attention

Mathematicians

▲ Growth: 9%

▲ Annual Job Openings: 960

▲ Yearly Earnings $46,342

▲ Education Required: Doctor's degree

▲ Self-employed: 8%

▲ Part-time: 5%

Mathematicians

Conduct research in fundamental mathematics or in application of mathematical techniques to science, management, and other fields. Solve or direct solutions to problems in various fields by mathematical methods. Conducts research in fundamental mathematics and in application of mathematical techniques to science, management, and other fields. Conceives or directs ideas for application of mathematics to wide variety of fields, including science, engineering, military planning, electronic data processing, and management. Conducts research in such branches of mathematics as algebra, geometry, number theory, logic, and topology. Performs computations and applies methods of numerical analysis. Studies and tests hypotheses and alternative theories. Applies mathematics or mathematical methods of numerical analysis, and operates or directs operation of desk calculators and mechanical and other functional areas. Utilizes knowledge of such subjects or fields as physics, engineering, astronomy, biology, economics, business and industrial management, or cryptography. Operates or directs operation of desk calculators and mechanical and electronic computation machines, analyzers, and plotters in solving problem support of mathematical, scientific, or industrial research. Acts as advisor or consultant to research personnel concerning mathematical methods and applications.

Knowledge: Administration and Management; Economics and Accounting; Computers and Electronics; Engineering and Technology; Mathematics; Physics

Abilities: Oral Comprehension; Written Expression; Fluency of Ideas; Originality; Deductive Reasoning; Inductive Reasoning; Information Ordering; Mathematical Reasoning; Number Facility; Memorization

Weight Analysts

Analyze and calculate weight data of structural assemblies, components, and loads for purposes of weight, balance, loading, and operational functions of ships, aircraft, space vehicles, missiles, research instrumentation, and commercial and industrial products and systems. Studies weight factors involved in new designs or modifications, utilizing computer techniques for analysis and simulation. Analyzes data and prepares reports of weight distribution estimates for use in design studies. Weighs parts, assemblies, or completed products; estimates weight of parts from engineering drawings; and calculates weight distribution to determine balance. Confers with design engineering personnel to ensure coordination of weight, balance, and load specification with other phases of product development. May analyze various systems, structures, and support equipment designs to obtain information on most efficient compromise between weight, operations, and cost. May prepare cargo and equipment loading sequences to maintain balance of aircraft or space vehicle within specified load limits. Prepares reports or graphic data for designers when weight and balance require engineering changes. Prepares technical reports on inertia, static and dynamic balance, dead weight distribution, cargo and fuselage compartments, and fuel center of gravity travel. May conduct research and analysis to develop new techniques for weight-estimating criteria.

Knowledge: Production and Processing; Computers and Electronics; Engineering and Technology; Design; Mathematics; Physics; Transportation

Abilities: Oral Comprehension; Written Expression; Deductive Reasoning; Inductive Reasoning; Mathematical Reasoning; Number Facility

Meat, Poultry, and Fish Cutters and Trimmers

- ▲ Growth: 23%
- ▲ Annual Job Openings: 26,398
- ▲ Yearly Earnings $15,308
- ▲ Education Required: Short-term O-J-T
- ▲ Self-employed: 0%
- ▲ Part-time: 8%

Meat, Poultry, and Fish Cutters and Trimmers—Hand

Use hand tools to perform a wide variety of food cutting and trimming tasks that require skills less than that of the precision level. Include meat boners, carcass splitters, poultry eviscerators, fish cleaners and butchers, skinners, and stickers. Trims, slices, and sections carcasses for future processing. Cuts and trims meat to prepare for packing. Removes parts such as skin, feathers, scales, or bones from carcass. Inspects meat products for defects or blemishes. Cleans carcasses and removes waste products or defective portions. Separates meats and byproducts into specified containers. Slaughters live animals. Weighs meats and tags containers for weight and contents. Obtains and distributes specified meat or carcass. Seals containers of meat.

Knowledge: Food Production; Biology

Abilities: Manual Dexterity; Wrist-Finger Speed; Speed of Limb Movement; Static Strength; Dynamic Strength; Trunk Strength; Extent Flexibility; Dynamic Flexibility; Gross Body Equilibrium

Mechanical Engineers

▲ Growth: 16%

▲ Annual Job Openings: 14,290

▲ Yearly Earnings $48,900

▲ Education Required: Bachelor's degree

▲ Self-employed: 1%

▲ Part-time: 2%

Mechanical Engineers

Perform engineering duties in planning and designing tools, engines, machines, and other mechanically functioning equipment. Oversee installation, operation, maintenance, and repair of such equipment as centralized heat, gas, water, and steam systems. Designs products and systems to meet process requirements, applying knowledge of engineering principles. Oversees installation to ensure machines and equipment are installed and functioning according to specifications. Coordinates building, fabrication, and installation of product design and operation, maintenance, and repair activities to utilize machines and equipment. Specifies system components or directs modification of products to ensure conformance with engineering design and performance specifications. Inspects, evaluates, and arranges field installations, and recommends design modifications to eliminate machine or system malfunctions. Alters or modifies design to obtain specified functional and operational performance. Investigates equipment failures and difficulties, diagnoses faulty operation, and makes recommendations to maintenance crew. Examines gas-powered equipment after installation to ensure proper functioning, and solves problems concerned with equipment. Studies industrial processes to determine where and how application of gas fuel-consuming equipment can be made. Researches and analyzes data, such as customer design proposal, specifications, and manuals, to determine feasibility of design or application. Plans and directs engineering personnel in fabrication of test control apparatus and equipment, and develops procedures for testing products. Confers with establishment personnel and engineers to implement operating procedures and resolve system malfunctions, and to provide technical information. Develops models of alternate processing methods to test feasibility or new applications of system components, and recommends implementation of procedures. Tests ability of machines, such as robot, to perform tasks, using teach pendant and precision measuring instruments and following specifications. Selects or designs robot tools to meet specifications, using robot manuals and either drafting tools or computer and software programs. Assists drafter in developing structural design of product, using drafting tools or computer-assisted design/drafting equipment and software. Conducts experiments to test and analyze existing designs and equipment to obtain data on performance of product, and prepares reports. Determines parts supply, maintenance tasks, safety procedures, and service schedules required to maintain machines and equipment in prescribed condition. Writes operating programs, using existing computer program, or writes own computer programs, applying knowledge of programming language and computer. Participates in meetings, seminars, and training sessions to stay apprised of new developments in field.

Knowledge: Production and Processing; Computers and Electronics; Engineering and Technology; Design; Building and Construction; Mechanical; Mathematics; Physics

Abilities: Oral Comprehension; Written Comprehension; Oral Expression; Written Expression; Fluency of Ideas; Originality; Problem Sensitivity; Deductive Reasoning; Inductive Reasoning; Information Ordering; Category Flexibility; Mathematical Reasoning; Number Facility; Memorization; Speed of Closure; Flexibility of Closure; Perceptual Speed; Visualization; Selective Attention; Time Sharing; Near Vision; Visual Color Discrimination; Hearing Sensitivity; Sound Localization; Speech Recognition

Medical Assistants

▲ Growth: 74%
▲ Annual Job Openings: 34,511
▲ Yearly Earnings $19,864
▲ Education Required: Moderate-term O-J-T
▲ Self-employed: 0%
▲ Part-time: 22%

Medical Assistants

Perform various duties under the direction of physician in examination and treatment of patients. Prepare treatment room, inventory supplies and instruments, and set up patient for attention of physician. Hand instruments and materials to physician as directed. Schedule appointments, keep medical records, and perform secretarial duties. Prepares treatment rooms for examination of patients. Hands instruments and materials to physician. Schedules appointments. Maintains medical records. Interviews patients; measures vital signs, weight, and height; and records information. Inventories and orders medical supplies and materials. Cleans and sterilizes instruments. Contacts medical facility or department to schedule patients for tests. Computes and mails monthly statements to patients and records transactions. Lifts and turns patients. Completes insurance forms. Gives physiotherapy treatments, such as diathermy, galvanics, and hydrotherapy. Operates X ray, electrocardiograph (EKG), and other equipment to administer routine diagnostic tests. Receives payment for bills. Gives injections or treatments to patients. Performs routine laboratory tests.

Knowledge: Clerical; Economics and Accounting; Customer and Personal Service; Chemistry; Biology; Psychology; Medicine and Dentistry; Therapy and Counseling; English Language; Foreign Language; Public Safety and Security; Law, Government, and Jurisprudence

Abilities: Problem Sensitivity; Information Ordering; Category Flexibility; Number Facility; Memorization; Speed of Closure; Flexibility of Closure; Selective Attention; Arm-Hand Steadiness; Finger Dexterity; Control Precision; Response Orientation; Reaction Time; Near Vision; Visual Color Discrimination; Night Vision; Peripheral Vision; Hearing Sensitivity; Auditory Attention; Sound Localization; Speech Recognition

Morgue Attendants

Assist pathologist by preparing bodies and organ specimens for postmortem examinations. May maintain morgue room, laboratory supplies, instruments, and equipment. Lays out surgical instruments and laboratory supplies for postmortem examination by pathologist. Washes table, storage trays, and instruments, sharpens knives, and replaces soiled linens. Places body on autopsy table or in refrigerated compartment, using portable hoist and stretcher. Mixes preserving fluids according to formulas, preserves specimens, and stains slides. Closes postmortem incisions, using surgical needle and thread, and fills cranium with plaster. Records identifying information for morgue file. Photographs specimens, using camera. Releases body to authorized person, according to established procedure. Waters, feeds, and cleans quarters for animals used in medical research.

Knowledge: Chemistry; Biology

Abilities: Selective Attention; Depth Perception

Phlebotomists

Draw blood from patients or donors in hospital, blood bank, or similar facility for analysis or other medical purposes. Assembles equipment for drawing blood, such as needles, tourniquet, gauze, blood collection devices, cotton, and alcohol, according to test or procedure requirements. Applies tourniquet, inserts needle into vein or pricks finger, draws blood into collection bag or tube, and applies treatment to puncture site. Labels and stores blood containers. Examines patients to take vital signs. Conducts medical testing procedures to screen blood samples. Conducts interviews to gather and record patient information, such as medical and personal history. Converses with patient or donor to explain and allay fears of procedure.

Knowledge: Medicine and Dentistry

Abilities: Selective Attention; Arm-Hand Steadiness; Response Orientation; Visual Color Discrimination; Hearing Sensitivity; Auditory Attention; Sound Localization

Medical Records Technicians

▲ Growth: 51%
▲ Annual Job Openings: 13,258
▲ Yearly Earnings $20,488
▲ Education Required: Associate degree
▲ Self-employed: 0%
▲ Part-time: 22%

Medical Records Technicians

Compile and maintain medical records of hospital and clinic patients. Compiles and maintains medical records of patients to document condition and treatment and to provide data for research studies. Compiles medical care and census data for statistical reports on diseases treated, surgery performed, and use of hospital beds. Maintains variety of health record indexes and storage and retrieval systems. Reviews records for completeness and to abstract and code data, using standard classification systems, and to identify and compile patient data. Enters data such as demographic characteristics, history and extent of disease, diagnostic procedures, and treatment into computer. Contacts discharge patients, their families, and physicians to maintain registry with follow-up information, such as quality of life and length of survival of cancer patients. Prepares statistical reports, narrative reports, and graphic presentations of tumor registry data for use by hospital staff, researchers, and other users. Assists in special studies or research, as needed.

Knowledge: Clerical; Computers and Electronics; Mathematics; Medicine and Dentistry

Abilities: Wrist-Finger Speed

Medical Scientists

▲ Growth: 25%
▲ Annual Job Openings: 3,333
▲ Yearly Earnings $56,659
▲ Education Required: Doctor's degree
▲ Self-employed: 1%
▲ Part-time: 6%

Medical Scientists

Conduct research dealing with the understanding of human diseases and the improvement of human health. Engage in clinical investigation or other research, production, technical writing, or related activities. Include medical scientists such as physicians, dentists, public health specialists, pharmacologists, and medical pathologists. Exclude practitioners who provide medical care or dispense drugs. Plans and directs studies to investigate human or animal disease, preventive methods, and treatments for disease. Analyzes data, applying statistical techniques and scientific knowledge, prepares reports, and presents findings. Investigates cause, progress, life cycle, or mode of transmission of diseases or parasites. Studies effects of drugs, gases, pesticides, parasites, or micro-organisms, or health and physiological processes of animals and humans. Conducts research to develop methodologies, instrumentation, or identification, diagnosing, and treatment procedures for medical application. Plans methodological design of research study and arranges for data collection. Examines organs, tissues, cell structures, or micro-organisms by systematic observation or using microscope. Consults with and advises physicians, educators, researchers, and others regarding medical applications of sciences, such as physics, biology, and chemistry. Prepares and analyzes samples for toxicity, bacteria, or micro-organisms or to study cell structure and properties. Confers with health department, industry personnel, physicians, and others to develop health safety standards and programs to improve public health. Standardizes drug dosages, methods of immunization, and procedures for manufacture of drugs and medicinal compounds. Teaches principles of medicine and medical and laboratory procedures to physicians, residents, students, and technicians. Supervises activities of clerical and statistical or laboratory personnel.

Knowledge: Food Production; Mathematics; Physics; Chemistry; Biology; Psychology; Medicine and Dentistry; Therapy and Counseling; Education and Training; Foreign Language; History and Archeology; Public Safety and Security; Law, Government, and Jurisprudence; Telecommunications; Communications and Media; Transportation

Abilities: Oral Comprehension; Written Comprehension; Oral Expression; Written Expression; Fluency of Ideas; Originality; Problem Sensitivity; Deductive Reasoning; Inductive Reasoning; Information Ordering; Category Flexibility; Mathematical Reasoning; Number Facility; Speed of Closure; Flexibility of Closure; Perceptual Speed; Time Sharing; Arm-Hand Steadiness; Finger Dexterity; Near Vision; Night Vision; Speech Clarity

Medical Secretaries

- ▲ Growth: 32%
- ▲ Annual Job Openings: 39,871
- ▲ Yearly Earnings $21,756
- ▲ Education Required: Postsecondary vocational training
- ▲ Self-employed: 0%
- ▲ Part-time: 19%

Medical Secretaries

Perform secretarial duties utilizing specific knowledge of medical terminology and hospital, clinic, or laboratory procedures. Duties include taking dictation and compiling and recording medical charts, reports, and correspondence, using a typewriter or

computer. Duties also may include preparing and sending bills to patients or recording appointments. Compiles and records medical charts, reports, and correspondence, using typewriter, personal computer, or word processor. Performs secretarial duties, utilizing knowledge of medical terminology and hospital, clinic, or laboratory procedures. Takes dictation, using shorthand or dictaphone. Answers telephone, schedules appointments, and greets and directs visitors. Maintains files.

Knowledge: Clerical; Computers and Electronics

Abilities: Wrist-Finger Speed

Messengers

▲ Growth: 11%
▲ Annual Job Openings: 25,352
▲ Yearly Earnings $17,118
▲ Education Required: Short-term O-J-T
▲ Self-employed: 7%
▲ Part-time: 34%

Couriers and Messengers

Pick up and carry messages, documents, packages, and other items between offices or departments within an establishment or to other business concerns, traveling by foot, bicycle, motorcycle, automobile, or public conveyance. Delivers messages and items, such as documents, packages, and food, between establishment departments and to other establishments and private homes. Receives message or materials to be delivered, and information on recipient, such as name, address, and telephone number. Walks, rides bicycle, drives vehicle, or uses public conveyance to reach destination to deliver message or materials in person. Calls by telephone to deliver verbal messages. Records information, such as items received and delivered and recipient's reply to message. Obtains signature, receipt, or payment from recipient for articles delivered. Monitors fluid levels and replenishes fuel to maintain delivery vehicle.

Knowledge: None above average

Abilities: Spatial Orientation; Response Orientation; Rate Control; Reaction Time; Speed of Limb Movement; Stamina; Gross Body Coordination; Gross Body Equilibrium; Far Vision; Night Vision; Glare Sensitivity; Speech Recognition

Metal and Plastic Machine Setters and Operators

▲ Growth: 16%
▲ Annual Job Openings: 20,091
▲ Yearly Earnings $24,107
▲ Education Required: Moderate-term O-J-T
▲ Self-employed: 0%
▲ Part-time: 1%

Nonelectrolytic Plating and Coating Machine Setters and Set-Up Operators, Metal and Plastic

Set up or set up and operate nonelectrolytic plating or coating machines, such as hot-dip lines and metal-spraying machines, to coat metal or plastic products or parts with metal. Measures and sets stops, rolls, brushes, and guides on automatic feeder and conveying equipment or coating machines, using micrometer, rule, and hand tools. Adjusts controls to set temperatures of coating substance, and adjusts speeds of machines and equipment. Attaches nozzle, positions gun, connects hoses, and threads wire to set up metal-spraying machine. Ignites gun and adjusts controls to regulate wire feed, air pressure, and flow of oxygen and fuel to operate metal-spraying machine. Installs gears and holding devices on conveyor equipment. Reads production schedule to determine set-up of equipment and machines. Mixes alodize solution in tank of machine, according to formula, and verifies solution concentration, using gauge. Positions workpieces, starts operation of machines and conveyors, and feeds workpieces into machines to be coated. Adjusts controls to synchronize equipment speed with speed of coating or spraying machine. Operates hoist to place workpieces onto machine feed carriage or spindle. Inspects coated products for defects and specified color and coverage. Operates sandblasting equipment to roughen and clean surface of workpieces. Preheats workpieces in oven.

Knowledge: Production and Processing

Abilities: Control Precision; Rate Control; Visual Color Discrimination

Nonelectrolytic Plating and Coating Machine Operators and Tenders, Metal and Plastic

Operate or tend nonelectrolytic plating or coating machines, such as metal-spraying machines and vacuum-metalizing machines, to coat metal or plastic products or parts with metal. Observes gauges and adjusts controls of machine to regulate functions, such as speed and temperature, according to specifications. Sprays coating in specified pattern according to instructions, and inspects area for defects, such as air bubbles or uneven coverage. Presses or turns controls to activate and set equipment operation according to specifications. Positions and feeds materials on plate into machine, manually or automatically, for processing. Fills machine receptacle with coating material or solution. Immerses workpieces in coating solution for specified time. Mixes coating material or solution according to formula, or uses premixed solutions. Places materials on racks and transfers to oven to dry for a specified period of time. Removes excess material or impurities from objects, using air hose or grinding machine. Cuts metal or other materials, using shears or band saw. Measures or weighs materials, using ruler, calculator, and scale. Positions containers to receive parts, and loads or unloads materials in containers, using dolly or handtruck. Cleans and maintains equipment, using water hose and scraper. Solders equipment and visually examines for completeness. Cleans workpieces, using wire brush. Maintains production records. Replaces worn parts and adjusts equipment components, using hand tools.

Knowledge: Production and Processing; Chemistry

Abilities: None above average

Metal Fabricators

▲ Growth: 11%
▲ Annual Job Openings: 5,701
▲ Yearly Earnings $23,379
▲ Education Required: Moderate-term O-J-T
▲ Self-employed: 0%
▲ Part-time: 2%

Metal Fabricators, Structural Metal Products

Fabricate and assemble structural metal products, such as frameworks or shells for machinery, ovens, tanks, and stacks, and metal parts for buildings and bridges, according to job order or blueprints. Develops layout and plans sequence of operations for fabricating and assembling structural metal products, applying trigonometry and knowledge of metal. Locates and marks bending and cutting lines onto workpiece, allowing for stock thickness and machine and welding shrinkage. Sets up and operates fabricating machines, such as brakes, rolls, shears, flame cutters, and drill presses. Hammers, chips, and grinds workpiece to cut, bend, and straighten metal. Positions, aligns, fits, and welds together parts, using jigs, welding torch, and hand tools. Preheats workpieces to render them malleable, using hand torch or furnace. Verifies conformance of workpiece to specifications, using square, ruler, and measuring tape. Sets up and operates machine tools associated with fabricating shops, such as radial drill, end mill, and edge planer. Designs and constructs templates and fixtures, using hand tools.

Knowledge: Production and Processing; Engineering and Technology; Design; Building and Construction; Mechanical

Abilities: Control Precision; Static Strength; Explosive Strength; Extent Flexibility

Meteorologists

▲ Growth: 8%
▲ Annual Job Openings: 421
▲ Yearly Earnings $47,673
▲ Education Required: Bachelor's degree
▲ Self-employed: 0%
▲ Part-time: 6%

Atmospheric and Space Scientists

Investigate atmospheric phenomena and interpret meteorological data gathered by surface and air stations, satellites, and radar, to prepare reports and forecasts for public and other uses. Include weather analysts and forecasters who work for radio and TV stations and whose functions require the detailed knowledge of a meteorologist. Analyzes and interprets meteorological data gathered by surface and upper air stations, satellites, and radar, to prepare reports and forecasts. Studies and interprets synoptic reports, maps, photographs, and prognostic charts to predict long- and short-range weather conditions. Prepares special forecasts and briefings for air and sea transportation, agriculture, fire prevention, air-pollution control, and school groups. Operates computer graphic equipment to produce weather reports and maps for analysis, distribution, or use in televised weather broadcast. Conducts basic or applied research in meteorology. Issues hurricane and other severe weather warnings. Broadcasts weather forecasts over television or radio. Directs forecasting services at weather station or at radio or television broadcasting facility. Establishes and staffs weather observation stations.

Knowledge: Administration and Management; Clerical; Personnel and Human Resources; Computers and Electronics; Mathematics; Physics; Sociology and Anthropology; Geography; Education and Training; English Language; Foreign Language; Telecommunications; Communications and Media

Abilities: Written Expression; Originality; Problem Sensitivity; Deductive Reasoning; Inductive Reasoning; Memorization; Speed of Closure; Flexibility of Closure; Perceptual Speed; Spatial Orientation; Selective Attention; Time Sharing; Glare Sensitivity; Speech Clarity

 Best Jobs for the 21st Century™ © 1999, JIST Works, Inc., Indianapolis, IN

Mineral Extraction Workers

▲ Growth: 12%

▲ Annual Job Openings: 27,481

▲ Yearly Earnings $27,081

▲ Education Required: Moderate-term O-J-T

▲ Self-employed: 2%

▲ Part-time: 2%

Continuous Mining Machine Operators

Operate self-propelled mining machines that rip coal, metal and nonmetal ores, rock, stone, or sand from the face and load it onto conveyors or into shuttle cars in a continuous operation. Moves levers to sump (advance) ripper bar or boring head into face of coal seam. Starts machine to gather coal and convey it to floor or shuttle car. Moves lever to raise and lower hydraulic safety bar that supports roof above machine until other workers complete their framing. Drives machine into position at working face. Repairs, oils, and adjusts machine and changes cutting teeth, using wrench.

Knowledge: Mechanical

Abilities: Multilimb Coordination; Night Vision; Peripheral Vision; Depth Perception

Derrick Operators, Oil and Gas Extraction

Rig derrick equipment and operate pumps to circulate mud through drill hole. Starts pumps that circulate mud through drill pipe and borehole to cool drill bit and flush out drill-cuttings. Sets and bolts crown block to posts at top of derrick. Strings cables through pulleys and blocks. Clamps holding fixture on end of hoisting cable. Mixes drilling mud, using portable power mixer. Weighs clay. Cleans and oils pulleys, blocks, and cables. Repairs pumps.

Knowledge: Mechanical; Physics

Abilities: Static Strength; Extent Flexibility: Gross Body Equilibrium

Roustabouts

Assemble or repair oil field equipment using hand and power tools. Perform other tasks as needed. Bolts or nails together wood or steel framework to erect derrick. Dismantles and assembles boilers and steam engine parts, using hand tools and power tools. Connects tanks and flow lines, using wrenches. Bolts together pump and engine parts. Unscrews or tightens pipe, casing, tubing, and pump rods, using hand and power wrenches and tongs. Digs holes, sets forms, and mixes and pours concrete into forms to make foundations for wood or steel derricks.

Knowledge: Engineering and Technology; Building and Construction; Mechanical

Abilities: Static Strength; Explosive Strength; Dynamic Strength; Trunk Strength; Stamina; Dynamic Flexibility; Gross Body Equilibrium

Miners and Petroleum and Gas Extractive Workers

Perform a variety of duties, such as erecting and repairing shaft supports, operating mining machines, and setting explosives, to extract minerals or oil and gas from the earth. Operates cutting or drilling machine, uses pick, or sets off explosives to mine ore, coal, or rock in underground mine. Connects and disconnects rod and tubing sections as they move to and from wellhole, using hand wrenches and power tongs. Mines precious metals from sand and gravel, using inclined trough with riffles or cleats at bottom. Inserts and places waterproof sealer, bullet, igniting charge, and fuse in gun port and assembles cylinders. Dumps sand and cement over shot of nitroglycerin in oil or gas well, using special bailer and hoist. Advances coal conveyors and jack units forward to facilitate making new cuts in coal strata, using horizontal jacks. Tightens or unscrews wellhead connections, using pipe wrench, and replaces or removes dumping unit head. Guides tubing sections being moved to and from wellhole to derrick or ground rack, using tubing lifting clamp. Operates pneumatic jack in coordination with other jacks to raise or lower offshore oil drilling barge. Pulls lever to position jacks, and fastens or unfastens guy lines to support and level derrick and pulling machine. Loads sand, tamping materials, and cement into bailer, lowers bailer and tools into borehole, and dumps cement, using hoist. Performs mine development, such as opening new passageways, air vents, auxiliary tunnels and rooms to facilitate mining operations.

Knowledge: Production and Processing; Engineering and Technology; Building and Construction; Mechanical Physics; Public Safety and Security; Law, Government, and Jurisprudence

Abilities: Perceptual Speed; Spatial Orientation; Arm-Hand Steadiness; Manual Dexterity; Control Precision; Multilimb Coordination; Rate Control; Speed of Limb Movement: Static Strength; Trunk Strength; Stamina; Extent Flexibility; Dynamic Flexibility; Gross Body Coordination; Gross Body Equilibrium; Night Vision; Peripheral Vision; Depth Perception; Glare Sensitivity

Mining Engineers

▲ Growth: -13%
▲ Annual Job Openings: 130
▲ Yearly Earnings $49,836
▲ Education Required: Bachelor's degree
▲ Self-employed: 0%
▲ Part-time: 3%

M

Mining Engineers, Including Mine Safety

Determine the location and plan the extraction of coal, metallic ores, nonmetallic minerals, and building materials, such as stone and gravel. Work involves conducting preliminary surveys of deposits or undeveloped mines and planning their development; examining deposits or mines to determine whether they can be worked at a profit; making geological and topographical surveys; evolving methods of mining best suited to character, type, and size of deposits; and supervising mining operations. Lays out and directs mine construction operations. Plans and coordinates mining processes and labor utilization. Plans, conducts, or directs others in performing mining experiments to test or prove research findings. Evaluates data to develop new mining products, equipment, or processes. Devises methods to solve environmental problems and reclaim mine sites. Analyzes labor requirements, equipment needs, and operational costs to prepare budget. Plans and supervises construction of access roads, power supplies, and water, communication, ventilation, and drainage systems. Directs and coordinates manufacturing or building of prototype mining product or system. Inspects mining areas for unsafe equipment and working conditions, tests air, and recommends installation or alteration of air-circulation equipment. Prepares technical reports for use by mining, engineering, and management personnel. Prepares or directs preparation of product or system layout and detailed drawings and schematics. Determines conditions under which tests are to be conducted and sequences and phases of test operations. Designs and maintains protective and rescue equipment and safety devices. Instructs mine personnel in safe working practices, first aid, and compliance with mining laws and practices, and promotes safety. Leads rescue activities, investigates accidents, reports causes, and recommends remedial actions. Confers with others to clarify or resolve problems. Designs and directs other personnel in fabrication of testing and test-control apparatus and equipment. Directs and coordinates activities concerned with development, procurement, installation, and calibration of test and recording instruments, equipment, and control devices.

Knowledge: Administration and Management; Economics and Accounting; Personnel and Human Resources; Production and Processing; Engineering and Technology; Design; Building and Construction; Mechanical; Mathematics; Physics; Chemistry; Geography; Education and Training; English Language; Public Safety and Security; Law, Government, and Jurisprudence; Transportation

Abilities: Oral Comprehension; Written Comprehension; Oral Expression; Written Expression; Fluency of Ideas; Originality; Problem Sensitivity; Deductive Reasoning; Inductive Reasoning; Information Ordering; Number Facility; Speed of Closure; Flexibility of Closure; Visualization; Gross Body Equilibrium; Far Vision; Night Vision

Musicians

▲ Growth: 33%

▲ Annual Job Openings: 49,350

▲ Yearly Earnings $30,888

▲ Education Required: Long-term O-J-T

▲ Self-employed: 26%

▲ Part-time: 53%

Music Directors

Direct and conduct instrumental or vocal performances by musical groups, such as orchestras or choirs. Directs group at rehearsals and live or recorded performances to achieve desired effects, such as tonal and harmonic balance dynamics, rhythm, and tempo. Selects vocal, instrumental, and recorded music suitable to type of performance requirements to accommodate ability of group. Issues assignments and reviews work of staff in such areas as scoring, arranging, and copying music, lyric, and vocal coaching. Positions members within group to obtain balance among instrumental sections. Auditions and selects vocal and instrumental groups for musical presentations. Transcribes musical compositions and melodic lines to adapt them to or create particular style for group. Engages services of composer to write score of motion picture television program. Schedules tours and performances and arranges for transportation and lodging. Evaluates subordinates' job performance and initiates and recommends personnel actions.

Knowledge: Administration and Management; Personnel and Human Resources; Foreign Language; Fine Arts

Abilities: Oral Comprehension; Oral Expression; Fluency of Ideas; Originality; Flexibility of Closure; Hearing Sensitivity; Auditory Attention; Sound Localization; Speech Recognition

Music Arrangers and Orchestrators

Write and transcribe musical scores. Composes musical scores for orchestra, band, choral group, or individual instrumentalist or vocalist, using knowledge of music theory and instrumental and vocal capabilities. Transposes music from one voice or instrument to another to accommodate particular musician in musical group. Adapts musical composition for orchestra, band, choral group, or individual to style for which it was not originally written. Transcribes musical parts from score written by arranger or orchestrator for each instrument or voice, using knowledge of music composition. Copies parts from score for individual performers. Determines voice, instrument, harmonic structure, rhythm, tempo, and tone balance to achieve desired effect.

Knowledge: Foreign Language; Fine Arts

Abilities: Fluency of Ideas; Originality; Hearing Sensitivity; Auditory Attention; Sound Localization

Singers

Sing songs on stage, radio, television, or motion pictures. Sings before audience or recipient of message as soloist, or in group, as member of vocal ensemble. Sings a cappella or with musical accompaniment. Memorizes musical selections and routines, or sings following printed text, musical notation, or customer instructions. Interprets or modifies music, applying knowledge of harmony, melody, rhythm, and voice production, to individualize presentation and maintain audience interest. Observes choral leader or prompter for cues or directions in vocal presentation. Practices songs and routines to maintain and improve vocal skills.

Knowledge: Foreign Language; Fine Arts

Abilities: Originality; Memorization, Hearing Sensitivity; Auditory Attention; Sound Localization; Speech Clarity

Composers

Compose music for orchestra, choral group, or band. Creates original musical form or writes within circumscribed musical form, such as sonata, symphony, or opera. Creates musical and tonal structure, applying elements of music theory, such as instrumental and vocal capabilities. Develops pattern of harmony, applying knowledge of music theory. Synthesizes ideas for melody of musical scores for choral group or band. Determines basic pattern of melody, applying knowledge of music theory. Transcribes or records musical ideas into notes on scored music paper.

Knowledge: Fine Arts; History and Archeology

Abilities: Fluency of Ideas; Originality; Flexibility of Closure; Hearing Sensitivity; Auditory Attention; Sound Localization

Prompters

Prompt performers in stage productions. Speaks or signs in language required by opera to prompt performers. Marks copy of vocal score to note cues. Observes orchestra conductor and follows vocal score to time cues accurately.

Knowledge: Foreign Language; Fine Arts

Abilities: Hearing Sensitivity; Auditory Attention; Sound Localization

Musicians, Instrumental

Play one or more musical instruments in recital, in accompaniment, or as members of an orchestra, band, or other musical group. Plays musical instrument as soloist or as member of musical group, such as orchestra or band, to entertain audience. Plays from memory or by following score. Studies and rehearses music to learn and interpret score. Improvises music during performance. Practices performance on musical instrument to maintain and improve skills. Memorizes musical scores. Transposes music to play in alternate key or to fit individual style or purposes. Composes new musical scores. Teaches music for specific instruments. Directs band or orchestra.

Knowledge: Psychology; Education and Training; Fine Arts; History and Archeology

Abilities: Oral Comprehension; Oral Expression; Fluency of Ideas; Originality; Category Flexibility; Memorization; Speed of Closure; Flexibility of Closure; Perceptual Speed; Selective Attention; Time Sharing; Manual Dexterity; Finger Dexterity; Multilimb Coordination; Response Orientation; Reaction Time; Wrist-Finger Speed; Speed of Limb Movement; Near Vision; Far Vision; Night Vision; Peripheral Vision; Glare Sensitivity; Hearing Sensitivity; Auditory Attention; Sound Localization; Speech Recognition; Speech Clarity

Nuclear Engineers

▲ Growth: 5%
▲ Annual Job Openings: 715
▲ Yearly Earnings $57,740
▲ Education Required: Bachelor's degree
▲ Self-employed: 0%
▲ Part-time: 3%

Nuclear Engineers

Conduct research on nuclear engineering problems. or apply principles and theory of nuclear science to problems concerned with release, control, and utilization of nuclear energy. Determines potential hazard and accident conditions which may exist in fuel handling and storage and recommends preventive measures. Performs experiments to determine acceptable methods of nuclear material usage, nuclear fuel reclamation, and waste disposal. Formulates equations that describe phenomena occurring during fission of nuclear fuels, and develops analytical models for research. Analyzes available data and consults with other scientists to determine parameters of experimentation and suitability of analytical models. Plans and designs nuclear research to discover facts or to test, prove, or modify known nuclear theories. Conducts tests to research nuclear fuel behavior and nuclear machinery and equipment performance. Examines accidents and obtains data to formulate preventive measures. Evaluates research findings to develop new concepts of thermonuclear analysis and new uses of radioactive models. Synthesizes analyses of tests results and prepares technical reports of findings and recommendations. Inspects nuclear fuels, waste, equipment, test-reactor vessel and related systems, and control instrumentation to identify potential problems or hazards. Monitors nuclear operations to identify potential or inherent design, construction, or operational problems to ensure safe operations. Designs and develops nuclear machinery and equipment, such as reactor cores, radiation shielding, and associated instrumentation and control mechanisms. Designs and oversees construction and operation of nuclear fuels reprocessing systems and reclamation systems. Computes cost estimates of construction projects, prepares project proposals, and discusses projects with vendors, contractors, and nuclear facility's review board. Formulates and initiates corrective actions and orders plant shutdown in emergency situations. Maintains reports to summarize work and document plant operations. Writes operational instructions relative to nuclear plant operation and nuclear fuel and waste handling and disposal. Directs operating and maintenance activities of operational nuclear facility.

Knowledge: Administration and Management; Economics and Accounting; Computers and Electronics; Engineering and Technology; Design; Building and Construction; Mathematics; Physics; Chemistry; Education and Training; English Language; Public Safety and Security

Abilities: Oral Comprehension; Written Comprehension; Oral Expression; Written Expression; Fluency of Ideas; Originality; Problem Sensitivity; Deductive Reasoning; Inductive Reasoning; Information Ordering; Mathematical Reasoning; Number Facility; Speed of Closure; Flexibility of Closure; Perceptual Speed; Visualization; Selective Attention; Time Sharing; Control Precision; Response Orientation; Rate Control; Reaction Time; Hearing Sensitivity; Auditory Attention; Speech Recognition; Speech Clarity

Nuclear Medicine Technologists

▲ Growth: 13%
▲ Annual Job Openings: 866
▲ Yearly Earnings $38,604
▲ Education Required: Associate degree
▲ Self-employed: 0%
▲ Part-time: 17%

Nuclear Medicine Technologists

Prepare, administer, and measure radioactive isotopes in therapeutic, diagnostic, and tracer studies utilizing a variety of radioisotope equipment. Prepare stock solutions of radioactive materials and calculate doses to be administered by radiologist. Subject patients to radiation. Execute blood volume, red cell survival, and fat absorption studies following standard laboratory techniques. Administers radiopharmaceuticals or radiation to patient to detect or treat diseases, using radioisotope equipment, under direction of physician. Calculates, measures, prepares, and records radiation dosage or radiopharmaceuticals, using computer and following physician's prescription and X rays. Measures glandular activity, blood volume, red cell survival, and radioactivity of patient, using scanners, Geiger counters, scintillometers, and other laboratory equipment. Positions radiation fields, radiation beams, and patient to develop most effective treatment of patient's disease, using computer. Maintains and calibrates radioisotope and laboratory equipment. Develops computer protocols and treatment procedures for nuclear medicine studies and treatment programs. Disposes of radioactive materials and stores radiopharmaceuticals, following radiation safety procedures. Trains, coordinates, and monitors nuclear medicine technologists' activities to ensure accuracy and safety.

Knowledge: Clerical; Computers and Electronics; Physics; Chemistry; Biology; Medicine and Dentistry; Therapy and Counseling

Abilities: Oral Comprehension; Written Comprehension; Problem Sensitivity; Deductive Reasoning; Information Ordering

Numerical Control Machine Tool Operators and Tenders

▲ Growth: 27%

▲ Annual Job Openings: 12,786

▲ Yearly Earnings $26,644

▲ Education Required: Moderate-term O-J-T

▲ Self-employed: 0%

▲ Part-time: 2%

Numerical Control Machine Tool Operators and Tenders, Metal and Plastic

Set up and operate numerical control (magnetic- or punched-tape-controlled) machine tools that automatically mill, drill, broach, and ream metal and plastic parts. May adjust machine feed and speed, change cutting tools, or adjust machine controls when automatic programming is faulty or if machine malfunctions. Selects, measures, assembles, and sets machine tools, such as drill bits and milling or cutting tools, using precision gauges and instruments. Mounts, installs, aligns, and secures tools, attachments, fixtures, and workpiece on machine, using hand tools and precision measuring instruments. Loads control media, such as tape, card, or disk, in machine controller, or enters commands to retrieve programmed instructions. Determines specifications or procedures for tooling set-up, machine operation, workpiece dimensions, or numerical control sequences, using blueprints, instructions, and machine knowledge. Positions and secures workpiece on machine bed, indexing table, fixture, or dispensing or holding device. Lays out and marks areas of part to be shot-peened, and fills hopper with shot. Calculates and sets machine controls to position tools, synchronize tape and tool, or regulate cutting depth, speed, feed, or coolant flow. Starts automatic operation of numerical control machine to machine parts or test set-up, workpiece dimensions, or programming. Monitors machine operation and control panel displays to detect malfunctions and compare readings to specifications. Stops machine to remove finished workpiece or change tooling, set-up, or workpiece placement, according to required machining sequence. Enters commands or manually adjusts machine controls to correct malfunctions or tolerances. Lifts workpiece to machine manually, with hoist or crane, or with tweezers. Measures dimensions of finished workpiece to ensure conformance to specifications, using precision measuring instruments, templates, and fixtures. Operates lathe, drill-press, jig-boring machine, or other machines manually or semiautomatically. Examines electronic components for defects and completeness of laser-beam trimming, using microscope. Maintains machines and removes and replaces broken or worn machine tools, using hand tools. Confers with supervisor or programmer to resolve machine malfunctions and production errors, and obtains approval to continue production. Cleans machine, tooling, and parts, using solvent or solution and rag.

Knowledge: Production and Processing; Engineering and Technology; Design

Abilities: Rate Control; Reaction Time; Wrist-Finger Speed; Dynamic Strength; Dynamic Flexibility

Nursery and Greenhouse Managers

- ▲ Growth: 19%
- ▲ Annual Job Openings: 2,575
- ▲ Yearly Earnings $26,104
- ▲ Education Required: Work experience in a related occupation
- ▲ Self-employed: 73%
- ▲ Part-time: 24%

Nursery and Greenhouse Managers

Plan, organize, direct, control, and coordinate activities of workers engaged in propagating, cultivating, and harvesting horticultural specialties, such as trees, shrubs, flowers, mushrooms, and other plants. Work may involve training new employees in gardening techniques, inspecting facilities for signs of disrepair, and delegating repair duties to staff. Manages nursery to grow horticultural plants for sale to trade or retail customers, for display or exhibition, or for research. Hires workers and directs supervisors and workers planting seeds, controlling plant growth and disease, and potting or cutting plants for marketing. Determines type and quantity of horticultural plants to be grown, such as trees, shrubs, flowers, ornamental plants, or vegetables, based on budget, projected sales volume, or executive directive. Grows horticultural plants under controlled conditions hydroponically. Considers such factors as whether plants need hothouse/greenhouse or natural weather growing conditions. Selects and purchases seed, plant nutrients, and disease-control chemicals. Tours work areas to observe work being done, to inspect crops, and to evaluate plant and soil conditions. Confers with horticultural personnel in planning facility renovations or additions. Coordinates clerical, recordkeeping, inventory, requisition, and marketing activities. Sells gardening accessories, such as sprays, garden implements, and plant nutrients. Negotiates contracts for lease of lands or trucks or for purchase of trees. Represents establishment and provides horticultural information to public through radio, television, or newspaper media. Designs floral exhibits and prepares scale drawings of exhibits.

Knowledge: Administration and Management; Clerical; Economics and Accounting; Sales and Marketing; Customer and Personal Service; Personnel and Human Resources; Production and Processing; Food Production; Design; Chemistry; Biology; Education and Training; Communications and Media

Abilities: Originality; Category Flexibility; Number Facility

Nursing Aides, Orderlies, and Attendants

- ▲ Growth: 25%
- ▲ Annual Job Openings: 304,868
- ▲ Yearly Earnings $16,120
- ▲ Education Required: Short-term O-J-T
- ▲ Self-employed: 2%
- ▲ Part-time: 26%

Nursing Aides, Orderlies, and Attendants

Work under the direction of nursing or medical staff to provide auxiliary services in the care of patients. Perform duties such as answering patient's call bell, serving and collecting food trays, and feeding patients. Orderlies are primarily concerned with setting up equipment and relieving nurses of heavier work. Exclude psychiatric aides and home health aides. Feeds patients unable to feed themselves. Sets up equipment, such as oxygen tents, portable x-ray machines, and overhead irrigation bottles. Prepares food trays. Bathes, grooms, and dresses patients. Assists patient to walk. Turns and repositions bedfast patients, alone or with assistance, to prevent bedsores. Transports patient to areas, such as operating and X ray rooms. Measures and records food and liquid intake and output. Administers massages and alcohol rubs. Measures and records vital signs. Sterilizes equipment and supplies. Administers medication as directed by physician or nurse. Administers catheterizations, bladder irrigations, enemas, and douches. Cleans room and changes linen. Stores, prepares, and issues dressing packs, treatment trays, and other supplies.

Knowledge: Customer and Personal Service; Chemistry; Psychology; Medicine and Dentistry; Therapy and Counseling; Foreign Language; Philosophy and Theology

Abilities: Memorization; Perceptual Speed; Spatial Orientation; Selective Attention; Arm-Hand Steadiness; Manual Dexterity; Multilimb Coordination; Response Orientation; Reaction Time; Static Strength; Dynamic Strength; Trunk Strength; Extent Flexibility; Dynamic Flexibility; Gross Body Equilibrium; Visual Color Discrimination; Night Vision; Peripheral Vision; Hearing Sensitivity; Sound Localization; Speech Recognition

Patient Transporters

Transport medical patients in bed, wheeled cart, or wheelchair to designated areas within medical facility during patient stay, or assist ambulatory patients in walking to prevent falling accidents. Directs or escorts patient from admitting office or reception desk to designated area of hospital or medical facility. Assists patient in walking to destination to prevent accidents by falling. Transports nonambulatory patient in wheelchair, bed, or gurney to designated area within hospital or medical facility. Reads or listens to instructions to determine patient name, destination, mode of travel, time, and other data. Carries patient's personal belongings to destination. Delivers mail, messages, medical records, or other items within facility.

Knowledge: Customer and Personal Service

Abilities: Stamina

Occupational Therapists

- ▲ Growth: 66%
- ▲ Annual Job Openings: 9,543
- ▲ Yearly Earnings $46,779
- ▲ Education Required: Bachelor's degree
- ▲ Self-employed: 4%
- ▲ Part-time: 20%

Occupational Therapists

Plan, organize, and participate in medically-oriented occupational programs in hospital or similar institution to rehabilitate patients who are physically or mentally ill. Plans, organizes, and conducts occupational therapy program in hospital, institutional, or community setting. Plans programs and social activities to help patients learn work skills and adjust to handicaps. Selects activities which will help individual learn work skills within limits of individual's mental and physical capabilities. Teaches individual skills and techniques required for participation in activities, and evaluates individual's progress. Recommends changes in individual's work or living environment, consistent with needs and capabilities. Consults with rehabilitation team to select activity programs and coordinate occupational therapy with other therapeutic activities. Arranges salaried employment for mentally ill patients within hospital environment. Lays out materials for individual's use, and cleans and repairs tools after therapy sessions. Requisitions supplies and equipment, and designs and constructs special equipment, such as splints and braces. Trains nurses and other medical staff in therapy techniques and objectives. Processes payroll, distributes salaries, and completes and maintains necessary records.

Knowledge: Administration and Management; Clerical; Economics and Accounting; Customer and Personal Service; Personnel and Human Resources; Biology; Psychology;

Sociology and Anthropology; Medicine and Dentistry; Therapy and Counseling; Education and Training; Foreign Language

Abilities: None above average

Manual Arts Therapists

Instruct patients in prescribed manual arts activities, such as woodworking, photography, or graphic arts, to prevent anatomical and physiological deconditioning and to assist in maintaining, improving, or developing work skills. Teaches patient manual arts activities, such as woodworking, graphic arts, or photography. Observes and interacts with patient to evaluate progress of patient in meeting physical and mental demands of employment. Confers with other rehabilitation team members to develop treatment plan to prevent physical deconditioning and enhance work skills of patient. Plans and organizes work activities according to patient's capabilities and disabilities. Prepares reports showing development of patient's work tolerance and emotional and social adjustment.

Knowledge: Customer and Personal Service; Psychology; Therapy and Counseling; Education and Training; Fine Arts

Abilities: Oral Comprehension; Written Expression; Originality; Problem Sensitivity; Time Sharing; Arm-Hand Steadiness; Multilimb Coordination

Occupational Therapy Assistants and Aides

- ▲ Growth: 69%
- ▲ Annual Job Openings: 3,684
- ▲ Yearly Earnings $28,683
- ▲ Education Required: Moderate-term O-J-T
- ▲ Self-employed: 0%
- ▲ Part-time: 24%

Occupational Therapy Assistants and Aides

Assist occupational therapists in administering medically-oriented occupational programs to assist in rehabilitating patients in hospitals and similar institutions. Assists occupational therapist to plan, implement, and administer educational, vocational, and recreational activities to restore, reinforce, and enhance task performances. Assists in evaluation of physically, developmentally, mentally retarded, or emotionally disabled client's daily living skills and capacities. Instructs or assists in instructing patient and family in home programs and basic living skills as well as care and use of adaptive equipment. Reports information and observations to supervisor verbally. Helps professional staff demonstrate therapy techniques, such as manual and creative arts and games. Transports patient to and from occupational therapy work area. Designs and adapts equipment and working-living environment. Maintains observed information in client records and prepares written reports. Assists educational specialist or clinical psychologist in administering situational or diagnostic tests to measure client's abilities or progress. Fabricates splints and other assistant devices. Prepares work material, assembles and maintains equipment, and orders supplies.

Knowledge: Clerical; Customer and Personal Service; Biology; Psychology; Medicine and Dentistry; Therapy and Counseling; Education and Training; Foreign Language

Abilities: Gross Body Coordination; Gross Body Equilibrium

Office Machine and Cash Register Servicers

▲ Growth: 18%

▲ Annual Job Openings: 1,267

▲ Yearly Earnings $24,897

▲ Education Required: Long-term O-J-T

▲ Self-employed: 4%

▲ Part-time: 1%

Office Machine and Cash Register Servicers

Repair and service office machines, such as adding, accounting, calculating, duplicating, and typewriting machines. Include worker s who repair manual, electrical, and electronic office machines. Exclude those who repair computerized systems and word processing systems. Tests machine to locate cause of electrical problems, using testing devices such as voltmeter, ohmmeter, and circuit test equipment. Disassembles machine and examines parts, such as wires, gears, and bearings, for wear and defects, using hand tools, power tools, and measuring devices. Repairs, adjusts, or replaces electrical and mechanical components and parts, using hand tools, power tools, and soldering or welding equipment. Operates machine, such as typewriter, cash register, or adding machine, to test functioning of parts and mechanisms. Reads specifications, such as blueprints, charts, and schematics, to determine machine settings and adjustments. Cleans and oils mechanical parts to maintain machine. Assembles and installs machine according to specifications, using hand tools, power tools, and measuring devices. Fabricates and reshapes parts, such as shims or bolts, on bench lathe or grinder. Instructs operators and servicers in operation, maintenance, assembly, and repair of machine.

Knowledge: Computers and Electronics; Engineering and Technology; Design; Mechanical; Education and Training; Foreign Language; Telecommunications

Abilities: Visualization; Arm-Hand Steadiness; Finger Dexterity; Visual Color Discrimination; Speech Clarity

Operating Engineers

▲ Growth: 14%
▲ Annual Job Openings: 12,085
▲ Yearly Earnings $35,027
▲ Education Required: Moderate-term O-J-T
▲ Self-employed: 8%
▲ Part-time: 2%

Operating Engineers

Operate several types of power construction equipment—such as compressors, pumps, hoists, derricks, cranes, shovels, tractors, scrapers, or motor graders—that excavates, moves and grades earth, erects structures, or pours concrete or other hard surface pavement. May repair and maintain equipment in addition to other duties. Exclude workers who specialize in operation of a single type of heavy equipment, such as a bulldozer or crane. Adjusts handwheels and depresses pedals to drive machines and control attachments, such as blades, buckets, scrapers, and swing booms. Turns valves to control air and water output of compressors and pumps. Repairs and maintains equipment. Operates machinery on sales lot or customer's property to demonstrate salable features of construction equipment.

Knowledge: Sales and Marketing; Building and Construction; Mechanical

Abilities: Multilimb Coordination

Operations Research Analysts

▲ Growth: 8%
▲ Annual Job Openings: 5,316
▲ Yearly Earnings $45,760
▲ Education Required: Master's degree
▲ Self-employed: 3%
▲ Part-time: 2%

Operations and Systems Researchers and Analysts, Except Computer

Conduct analyses of management and operational problems in terms of management information and concepts. Formulate mathematical or simulation models of the problem for solution by computer or other method. May develop and supply time and cost networks, such as program evaluation and review techniques. Analyzes problem in terms of management information, and conceptualizes and defines problem. Prepares model of problem in form of one or several equations that relate constants and variables, restrictions, alternatives, conflicting objectives, and their numerical parameters. Specifies manipulative or computational methods to be applied to model. Performs validation and testing of model to ensure adequacy, or determines need for reformulation. Evaluates implementation and effectiveness of research. Designs, conducts, and evaluates experimental operational models where insufficient data exists to formulate model. Develops and applies time and cost networks to plan and control large projects. Defines data requirements and gathers and validates information, applying judgment and statistical tests. Studies information and selects plan from competitive proposals that afford maximum probability of profit or effectiveness relating to cost or risk. Prepares for management reports defining problem, evaluation, and possible solution.

Knowledge: Administration and Management; Clerical; Economics and Accounting; Sales and Marketing; Personnel and Human Resources; Production and Processing; Computers and Electronics; Mathematics; Communications and Media

Abilities: Oral Comprehension; Written Comprehension; Oral Expression; Written Expression; Fluency of Ideas; Deductive Reasoning; Mathematical Reasoning; Number Facility

Optometrists

▲ Growth: 12%
▲ Annual Job Openings: 1,630
▲ Yearly Earnings $64,209
▲ Education Required: First professional degree
▲ Self-employed: 38%
▲ Part-time: 10%

Optometrists

Diagnose, manage, and treat conditions and diseases of the human eye and visual system. Examine eyes to determine visual efficiency and performance by use of instruments and observation. Prescribe corrective procedures. Prescribes eyeglasses, contact lenses, and other vision aids or therapeutic procedures to correct or conserve vision. Examines eyes to determine visual acuity and perception and to diagnose diseases and other abnormalities, such as glaucoma and color blindness. Consults with and refers patients to ophthalmologist or other health care practitioner if additional medical treatment is determined necessary. Prescribes medications to treat eye diseases if state laws permit. Conducts research, instructs in college or university, acts as consultant, or works in public health field.

Knowledge: Chemistry; Biology; Medicine and Dentistry; Therapy and Counseling; Education and Training; Foreign Language

Abilities: Oral Comprehension; Written Comprehension; Oral Expression; Written Expression; Problem Sensitivity; Deductive Reasoning; Inductive Reasoning; Flexibility of Closure; Near Vision

Packaging and Filling Machine Operators

▲ Growth: 16%
▲ Annual Job Openings: 74,811
▲ Yearly Earnings $19,697
▲ Education Required: Moderate-term O-J-T
▲ Self-employed: 0%
▲ Part-time: 7%

Packaging and Filling Machine Operators and Tenders

Operate or tend machines—such as filling machines, casing-running machines, ham-rolling machines, preservative filling machines, baling machines, wrapping machines, and stuffing machines—to prepare industrial or consumer products—such as gas cylinders, meat and other food products, tobacco, insulation, ammunition, stuffed toys, and athletic equipment—for storage or shipment. Tends or operates machine that packages product. Operates mechanism to cut filler product or packaging material. Regulates machine flow, speed, and temperature. Starts machine by engaging controls. Stops or resets machine when malfunction occurs, and clears machine jams. Adjusts machine tension and pressure and machine components according to size or processing angle of product. Observes machine operations to ensure quality and conformity of filled or packaged products to standards. Removes finished packaged items from machine, and separates rejected items. Inspects and removes defective product and packaging material. Stocks product for packaging or filling machine operation. Stocks packaging material for machine processing. Tests and evaluates product, and verifies product weight or measurement to ensure quality standards. Secures finished packaged items by hand-tying, sewing, or attaching fastener. Cleans, oils, and makes minor repairs to machinery and equipment. Counts and records finished and rejected packaged items. Stacks finished packaged items or packs items in cartons or containers. Attaches identification labels to finished packaged items.

Knowledge: Production and Processing; Food Production

Abilities: Perceptual Speed; Manual Dexterity; Finger Dexterity; Control Precision; Response Orientation; Rate Control; Reaction Time; Speed of Limb Movement; Static Strength; Trunk Strength; Extent Flexibility; Dynamic Flexibility; Gross Body Equilibrium; Peripheral Vision; Hearing Sensitivity; Sound Localization

Painters and Paperhangers

▲ Growth: 15%
▲ Annual Job Openings: 71,544
▲ Yearly Earnings $26,062
▲ Education Required: Moderate-term O-J-T
▲ Self-employed: 41%
▲ Part-time: 9%

Painters, Construction and Maintenance

Paint walls, equipment, buildings, bridges, and other structural surfaces, using brushes, rollers, and spray guns. May remove old paint to prepare surface prior to painting. May mix colors or oils to obtain desired color or consistency. Exclude workers who specialize in hanging wallpaper. Paints surfaces, using brushes, spray gun, or rollers. Applies paint to simulate wood grain, marble, brick, or stonework. Bakes finish on painted and enameled articles in baking oven. Sands surfaces between coats, and polishes final coat to specified finish. Cuts stencils, and brushes and sprays lettering and decorations on surfaces. Washes and treats surfaces with oil, turpentine, mildew remover, or other preparations. Smooths surfaces, using sandpaper, scrapers, brushes, steel wool, or sanding machine. Mixes and matches colors of paint, stain, or varnish. Sprays or brushes hot plastics or pitch onto surfaces. Fills cracks, holes, and joints with caulk putty, plaster, or other filler, using caulking gun or putty knife. Removes fixtures, such as pictures and electric switch covers, from walls prior to painting. Burns off old paint, using blowtorch. Covers surfaces with drop cloths or masking tape and paper to protect surface during painting. Erects scaffolding or sets up ladders to work above ground level. Reads work order or receives instructions from supervisor or homeowner. Cuts glass and installs window and door panes.

Knowledge: Building and Construction

Abilities: Wrist-Finger Speed; Dynamic Strength; Stamina; Gross Body Equilibrium; Visual Color Discrimination

Paperhangers

Cover interior walls and ceilings of rooms with decorative wallpaper or fabric, or attach advertising posters on surfaces, such as walls and billboards. Duties include removing old materials from surface to be papered. Applies thinned glue to waterproof, porous surfaces, using brush, roller, or pasting machine. Measures and cuts strips from roll of wallpaper or fabric, using shears or razor. Mixes paste, using paste-powder and water, and brushes paste onto surface. Trims rough edges from strips, using straightedge and trimming knife. Aligns and places strips or poster sections of billboard on surface to match adjacent edges. Smooths strips or poster sections with brush or roller to remove wrinkles and bubbles and to smooth joints. Trims excess material at ceiling or baseboard, using knife. Marks vertical guideline on wall to align first strip, using plumb bob and chalkline. Applies acetic acid to damp plaster to prevent lime from bleeding through paper. Staples or tacks advertising posters onto fences, walls, or poles. Measures walls and ceiling to compute number and length of strips required to cover surface. Smooths rough spots on walls and ceilings, using sandpaper. Fills holes and cracks with plaster, using trowel. Removes old paper, using water, steam machine, or chemical remover and scraper. Removes paint, varnish, and grease from surfaces, using paint remover and water soda solution. Erects and works from scaffold.

Knowledge: Building and Construction

Abilities: Stamina; Extent Flexibility; Gross Body Equilibrium

Painting, Coating, and Decorating Workers

▲ Growth: 10%

▲ Annual Job Openings: 5,584

▲ Yearly Earnings $18,928

▲ Education Required: Short-term O-J-T

▲ Self-employed: 8%

▲ Part-time: 8%

Hand Painting, Coating, or Decorating Workers

Paint, coat, or decorate, using hand tools or power tools, a wide variety of manufactured items. Applies coating, such as paint, ink, or lacquer, to protect or decorate workpiece surface, using spray gun, pen, or brush. Immerses workpiece into coating material for specified time. Positions and glues decorative pieces in cutout section, following pattern. Reads job order and inspects workpiece to determine work procedure and materials required. Conceals blemishes in workpiece, such as nicks and dents, using filler, such as putty. Rinses coated workpiece to remove excess coating material or to facilitate setting of finish coat on workpiece. Drains or wipes workpiece to remove excess coating material or to facilitate setting of finish coat on workpiece. Examines finished surface of workpiece to verify conformance to specifications, and retouches defective areas of surface. Cleans surface of workpiece in preparation for coating, using cleaning fluid, solvent, brushes, scraper, steam, sandpaper, or cloth. Cuts out sections in surface of material to be inlaid with decorative pieces, using pattern and knife or scissors. Places coated workpiece in oven or dryer for specified time to dry or harden finish. Melts or heats coating material to specified temperature. Selects and mixes ingredients to prepare coating substance, according to specifications, using paddle or mechanical mixer. Cleans and maintains tools and equipment, using solvent, brushes, and rags.

Knowledge: None above average

Abilities: Wrist-Finger Speed; Visual Color Discrimination

Paralegals

▲ Growth: 68%
▲ Annual Job Openings: 21,705
▲ Yearly Earnings $32,032
▲ Education Required: Associate degree
▲ Self-employed: 2%
▲ Part-time: 12%

Paralegals and Legal Assistants

Assist lawyers by researching legal precedent, investigating facts, or preparing legal documents. Conduct research to support a legal proceeding, to formulate a defense, or to initiate legal action. Gathers and analyzes research data, such as statutes, decisions, and legal articles, codes, and documents. Prepares legal documents, including briefs, pleadings, appeals, wills, and contracts. Investigates facts and law of cases to determine causes of action and to prepare cases. Prepares affidavits or other documents, maintains document file, and files pleadings with court clerk. Appraises and inventories real and personal property for estate planning. Arbitrates disputes between parties, and assists in real estate closing process. Calls upon witnesses to testify at hearing. Answers questions regarding legal issues pertaining to civil service hearings. Directs and coordinates law office activity, including delivery of subpoenas. Completes office accounts, tax returns, and real estate closing statements. Keeps and monitors legal volumes to ensure that law library is up-to-date. Presents arguments and evidence to support appeal at appeal hearing.

Knowledge: Administration and Management; Clerical; Economics and Accounting; Personnel and Human Resources; Computers and Electronics; Sociology and Anthropology; English Language; Law, Government, and Jurisprudence

Abilities: Oral Comprehension; Written Comprehension; Oral Expression; Written Expression; Deductive Reasoning

Parking Lot Attendants

▲ Growth: 26%
▲ Annual Job Openings: 12,214
▲ Yearly Earnings $14,352
▲ Education Required: Short-term O-J-T
▲ Self-employed: 0%
▲ Part-time: 15%

Parking Lot Attendants

Park autos or issue tickets for customers in a parking lot or garage. Parks automobiles in parking lot, storage garage, or new car lot. Places numbered tag on windshield of automobile to be parked, and hands customer similar tag to be used in locating parked automobile. Collects parking fee from customer, based on charges for time automobile is parked. Takes numbered tag from customer, locates car, and delivers it to customer, or directs customer to parked car. Patrols area to prevent thefts of parked automobiles or items in automobiles. Assigns stock control numbers to vehicles, and catalogs and stores keys. Compares serial numbers of incoming vehicles against invoice. Signals or directs vehicle drivers with hands or flashlight to parking area. Keeps new car lot in order and maximizes use of space. Lifts, positions, and removes barricades to open or close parking areas. Inspects vehicles to detect damage and to verify presence of accessories listed on invoice. Records description of damages and lists missing items on delivery receipt. Services vehicles with gas, oil, and water. Services cars in storage to protect tires, battery, and finish against deterioration.

Knowledge: None above average

Abilities: None above average

Paving and Surfacing Equipment Operators

▲ Growth: 30%
▲ Annual Job Openings: 13,012
▲ Yearly Earnings $25,334
▲ Education Required: Moderate-term O-J-T
▲ Self-employed: 1%
▲ Part-time: 8%

Paving, Surfacing, and Tamping Equipment Operators

Operate equipment used for applying concrete, asphalt, or other materials to roadbeds, parking lots, or airport runways and taxiways, or equipment used for tamping gravel, dirt, or other materials. Include concrete and asphalt paving machine operators, form tampers, tamping machine operators, and stone spreader operators. Operates machine or manually rolls surfaces to compact earth fills, foundation forms, and finished road materials, according to grade specifications. Operates machine to spread, smooth, or steel-reinforce stone, concrete, or asphalt. Operates machine to mix and spray binding, waterproofing, and curing compounds. Operates machine to clean or cut expansion joints in concrete or asphalt and to rout out cracks in pavement. Drives and operates curbing machine to extrude concrete or asphalt curbing. Starts machine, engages clutch, pushes and moves levers, and turns wheels to control and guide machine along forms or guidelines. Monitors machine operation and observes distribution of paving material to adjust machine settings or material flow. Lights burner or starts heating unit of machine and regulates temperature. Drives machine onto truck trailer and drives truck to transport machine to and from job site. Installs dies, cutters, and extensions to screed onto machine, using hand tools. Fills tank, hopper, or machine with paving materials. Cleans, maintains, and repairs equipment, according to specifications, using mechanic's hand tools, or reports malfunction to supervisor. Sets up forms and lays out guidelines for curbs, according to written specifications, using string, spray paint, and concrete/water mix.

Knowledge: Mechanical; Transportation

Abilities: Manual Dexterity; Control Precision; Multilimb Coordination; Response Orientation; Rate Control; Reaction Time; Speed of Limb Movement; Static Strength; Explosive Strength; Dynamic Strength; Trunk Strength; Stamina; Dynamic Flexibility; Gross Body Coordination; Gross Body Equilibrium; Far Vision; Peripheral Vision; Depth Perception; Glare Sensitivity

Personal and Home Care Aides

▲ Growth: 85%
▲ Annual Job Openings: 58,134
▲ Yearly Earnings $13,832
▲ Education Required: Short-term O-J-T
▲ Self-employed: 0%
▲ Part-time: 42%

Personal and Home Care Aides

Perform a variety of tasks at places of residence. Duties include keeping house and advising families having problems with such things as nutrition, cleanliness, and household utilities. Exclude nursing aides and home health aides. Advises and assists family members in planning nutritious meals, purchasing and preparing foods, and utilizing commodities from surplus food programs. Explains fundamental hygiene principles. Evaluates needs of individuals served and plans for continuing services. Assists in training children. Prepares and maintains records of assistance rendered. Gives bedside care to incapacitated individuals and trains family members to provide bedside care. Assists client with dressing, undressing, and toilet activities. Assigns housekeeping duties according to children's capabilities. Assists parents in establishing good study habits for children. Obtains information for clients, for personal and business purposes. Drives motor vehicle to transport clients to specified locations. Types correspondence and reports.

Knowledge: Clerical; Customer and Personal Service; Food Production; Psychology; Sociology and Anthropology; Medicine and Dentistry; Therapy and Counseling; Education and Training; Transportation

Abilities: None above average

Personal Service Workers

▲ Growth: 31%

▲ Annual Job Openings: 279,051

▲ Yearly Earnings $17,201

▲ Education Required: Work experience in a related occupation

▲ Self-employed: 9%

▲ Part-time: 40%

Funeral Attendants

Perform variety of tasks during funeral, such as placing casket in parlor or chapel prior to service, arranging floral offerings or lights around casket, directing or escorting mourners, closing casket, and issuing and storing funeral equipment. Places casket in parlor or chapel prior to wake or funeral. Arranges floral offerings or lights around casket. Directs or escorts mourners to parlor or chapel in which wake or funeral is being held. Assists in closing casket. Issues and stores funeral equipment. Carries flowers to hearse or limousine for transportation to place of interment. Assists mourners in and out of limousines. Assists in carrying casket.

Knowledge: Customer and Personal Service; Psychology; Sociology and Anthropology

Abilities: Static Strength; Gross Body Equilibrium

Passenger Service Representatives

Render specialized personal service such as assisting elderly persons, unaccompanied children, distinguished persons and other special passengers to facilitate movement of passengers through terminal and to create goodwill. Greets passengers and guests and answers questions concerning flight schedules, terminal facilities, seat selection, fares, travel itineraries, and accommodations. Directs or escorts passengers to lounge, departure gates, and other terminal facilities. Transports special passengers, such as unaccompanied children, injured persons, and elderly people, to boarding area, using electric cart. Contacts other stations to reserve special services for arriving passengers. Arranges for air and ground transportation. Assembles and forwards luggage to departing aircraft. Verifies passenger reservations. Admits members and guests to airline lounge, and serves refreshments, such as cocktails, coffee, and snacks, using serving tray. Provides first aid to ill or injured passengers and obtains medical help. Removes trash and dishes from lounge area.

Knowledge: Customer and Personal Service; Medicine and Dentistry; Foreign Language; Transportation

Abilities: Spatial Orientation; Gross Body Equilibrium; Auditory Attention; Sound Localization; Speech Recognition; Speech Clarity

Personal Attendants

Perform a variety of personal services such as arranging for or providing valet services, issuing locker room supplies, or checking hats and coats for customers in club, restaurant, recreational facility, hotel, or other hospitality establishment. Explains nature and cost of services and facilities available, demonstrates use of equipment, and answers customer inquiries. Interviews, evaluates, and advises client to develop personal improvement plan, such as weight loss, using scales, measures, and recommended guidelines. Conducts body-conditioning therapy, such as steam or electric shock, using physical or visual stimuli. Assists customers in tub or steam room, bathes or massages them, using water, brush, mitt, sponge, and towel, to clean skin. Packs equipment and uniforms and attends to needs of individual athletes in clubhouse. Arranges, supervises, and provides valet services such as clothes pressing, shoe shining, sending and receiving mail, and car parking. Cleans and polishes footwear, using brush, sponge, cleaning fluid, polish, wax, liquid or sole dressing, and dauber. Schedules appointments for client sessions, registers guests, and assigns accommodations. Issues keys, athletic equipment, or supplies, such as soap, towels, and weight loss aids. Stores personal possessions for patrons, issues a claim check for articles stored, and returns articles on receipt of check. Assists persons in establishments such as apartments, hotels, or hospitals, by opening doors, carrying bags, and performing related services. Transports customers and baggage, using motor vehicle. Records and reviews client's activities to assure program is followed. Sells service-related products and collects fees for services, rent, products, or supplies. Secures boat to dock, using mooring lines, connects utility lines to boat, and pumps water from boat for patrons. Performs general cleaning and maintenance of facilities and equipment, using mop, broom, lawn mower, and other cleaning aids. Inspects building and grounds, and reports or removes unauthorized or undesirable persons.

Knowledge: Sales and Marketing; Customer and Personal Service; Transportation

Abilities: Gross Body Equilibrium; Night Vision; Glare Sensitivity; Auditory Attention; Speech Recognition

Social Escorts

Attend functions as a social partner to enable accompanied individual to attend and engage in social functions requiring a partner, or to provide companionship while visiting public establishments. Accompanies persons to public establishments and social functions to provide companionship, partner, or protection. Suggests places of entertainment and arranges for transportation and tickets. Introduces unaccompanied persons to hosts or hostesses to distribute patrons among them. Explains procedure for engaging social partner to unaccompanied persons at establishment. Collects tickets or fees for time spent with person. Counts tickets collected from patrons and submits tickets to management at end of shift. Inspects clothing of hosts or hostesses to ensure clean, pleasing personal appearance.

P

Knowledge: Sales and Marketing; Customer and Personal Service

Abilities: Auditory Attention; Sound Localization; Speech Recognition

Personnel, Training, and Labor Relations Managers

▲ Growth: 18%

▲ Annual Job Openings: 20,995

▲ Yearly Earnings $45,988

▲ Education Required: Work experience, plus degree

▲ Self-employed: 0%

▲ Part-time: 3%

Human Resources Managers

Plan, direct, and coordinate human resource management activities of an organization to maximize the strategic use of human resources, and maintain functions such as employee compensation, recruitment, personnel policies, and regulatory compliance. Formulates policies and procedures for recruitment, testing, placement, classification, orientation, benefits, and labor and industrial relations. Plans, directs, supervises, and coordinates work activities of subordinates and staff relating to employment, compensation, labor relations, and employee relations. Directs preparation and distribution of written and verbal information to inform employees of benefits, compensation, and personnel policies. Evaluates and modifies benefits policies to establish competitive programs and to ensure compliance with legal requirements. Analyzes compensation policies, government regulations, and prevailing wage rates to develop competitive compensation plan. Develops methods to improve employment policies, processes, and practices, and recommends changes to management. Prepares personnel forecast to project employment needs. Prepares budget for personnel operations. Prepares and delivers presentations and reports to corporate officers or other management regarding human resource management policies and practices and recommendations for change. Negotiates bargaining agreements and resolves labor disputes. Meets with shop stewards and supervisors to resolve grievances. Conducts exit interviews to identify reasons for employee termination and writes separation notices. Plans and conducts new employee orientation to foster positive attitude toward organizational objectives. Writes directives advising department managers of organization policy in personnel matters such as equal employment opportunity, sexual harassment, and discrimination. Studies legislation, arbitration decisions, and collective bargaining contracts to assess industry trends. Maintains records and compiles statistical reports concerning personnel-related data such as hires, transfers, performance appraisals, and absenteeism rates. Analyzes statistical data and reports to identify and determine causes of personnel problems and develop recommendations for improvement of organization's personnel policies and practices. Represents organization at personnel-related hearings and investigations. Contracts with vendors to provide employee services, such as canteen, transportation, or relocation service. Investigates industrial accidents and prepares reports for insurance carrier.

Knowledge: Administration and Management; Economics and Accounting; Personnel and Human Resources; Mathematics; Psychology; Education and Training; English Language; Law, Government, and Jurisprudence

Abilities: Oral Comprehension; Written Comprehension; Oral Expression; Written Expression; Fluency of Ideas; Originality; Problem Sensitivity; Deductive Reasoning; Inductive Reasoning; Information Ordering; Category Flexibility; Mathematical Reasoning; Number Facility; Memorization; Speed of Closure; Flexibility of Closure; Perceptual Speed; Selective Attention; Time Sharing; Gross Body Equilibrium; Far Vision

Training and Development Managers

Plan, direct, and coordinate the training activities of an organization. Analyzes training needs to develop new training programs or to modify and improve existing programs. Plans and develops training procedures utilizing knowledge of relative effectiveness of individual training, classroom training, demonstrations, on-the-job training, meetings, conferences, and workshops. Formulates training policies and schedules, utilizing knowledge of identified training needs. Evaluates effectiveness of training programs and instructor performance. Develops and organizes training manuals, multimedia visual aids, and other educational materials. Coordinates established courses with technical and professional courses provided by community schools, and designates training procedures. Develops testing and evaluation procedures. Confers with management and supervisory personnel to identify training needs based on projected production processes, changes, and other factors. Reviews and evaluates training and apprenticeship programs for compliance with government standards. Prepares training budget for department or organization. Trains instructors and supervisors in effective training techniques. Interprets and clarifies regulatory policies governing apprenticeship training programs, and provides information and assistance to trainees and labor and management representatives.

Knowledge: Administration and Management; Personnel and Human Resources; Psychology; Education and Training; Law, Government, and Jurisprudence

Abilities: Oral Comprehension; Written Comprehension; Oral Expression; Written Expression; Fluency of Ideas; Originality; Problem Sensitivity; Deductive Reasoning; Inductive Reasoning; Category Flexibility; Mathematical Reasoning; Number Facility; Memorization; Speed of Closure; Flexibility of Closure; Perceptual Speed; Selective Attention; Time Sharing; Far Vision

Labor Relations Managers

Plan, direct, and coordinate the labor relations program of an organization. Analyze and interpret collective bargaining agreements and advise management and union officials in development, application, and interpretation of labor relations policies and practices. Represents management in labor contract negotiations to reconcile opposing claims and recommend concessions, or proposes adoption of new procedures. Analyzes collective bargaining agreements to interpret intent, spirit, and terms of contract. Compiles information on disagreement and determines points of issue, according to knowledge of labor, business, and government responsibilities under law. Advises management and union officials on development, application, and interpretation of company labor relations policies and practices. Arranges and schedules meetings between parties in labor dispute to investigate and resolve grievances. Monitors implementation of policies concerning wages, hours, and working conditions to ensure compliance to labor contract terms. Supervises work activities of employees involved in labor relations functions of organization. Completes statistical reports on cases, findings, and resolved issues.

Knowledge: Administration and Management; Personnel and Human Resources; Mathematics; English Language; Law, Government, and Jurisprudence

Abilities: Oral Comprehension; Written Comprehension; Oral Expression; Written Expression; Fluency of Ideas; Originality; Problem Sensitivity; Inductive Reasoning; Information Ordering; Memorization; Speech Clarity

Personnel, Training, and Labor Relations Specialists

- ▲ Growth: 18%
- ▲ Annual Job Openings: 36,049
- ▲ Yearly Earnings $36,566
- ▲ Education Required: Bachelor's degree
- ▲ Self-employed: 4%
- ▲ Part-time: 6%

Employee Assistance Specialists

Coordinate activities of employers to set up and operate programs to help employees overcome behavioral or medical problems, such as substance abuse, that affect job performance. Develops or leads group to develop employee assistance programs, policies, and procedures. Plans and conducts training sessions for company officials to develop skills to identify and assist with resolving employee behavioral problems. Consults with employer to establish referral network for group or individual counseling of troubled employees. Consults with staff of employee assistance program to monitor progress of program. Consults with employer representatives to develop education and prevention program. Analyzes character and type of business establishments, and compiles list of prospective employers to implement assistance programs. Contacts prospective employers to explain program advantages and fees, and negotiates participation agreement with interested employers. Writes announcements and advertisements for newspapers and other publications to promote employee assistance program within business community.

Knowledge: Administration and Management; Sales and Marketing; Customer and Personal Service; Personnel and Human Resources; Psychology; Sociology and Anthropology;

Therapy and Counseling; Education and Training

Abilities: Oral Comprehension; Written Comprehension; Oral Expression; Written Expression; Originality; Problem Sensitivity; Deductive Reasoning; Inductive Reasoning; Information Ordering; Near Vision; Speech Clarity

Job and Occupational Analysts

Collect, analyze, and classify occupational data to develop job or occupational descriptions or profiles to facilitate personnel management decision making and to develop career information. Analyzes organizational, occupational, and industrial data to facilitate organizational functions and provide technical information to business, industry, and government. Researches job and worker requirements, structural and functional relationships among jobs and occupations, and occupational trends. Observes and interviews employees to collect job, organizational, and occupational information. Prepares reports, such as job descriptions, organization and flow charts, and career path reports, to summarize job analysis information. Consults with business, industry, government, and union officials to arrange for, plan, and design occupational studies and surveys. Prepares research results for publication in form of journals, books, manuals, and film. Determines need for and develops job analysis instruments and materials. Evaluates and improves methods and techniques for selecting, promoting, evaluating, and training workers. Plans and develops curricula and materials for training programs and conducts training.

Knowledge: Administration and Management; Clerical; Personnel and Human Resources; Food Production; Computers and Electronics; Mathematics; Psychology; Education and Training; English Language; History and Archeology; Philosophy and Theology; Communications and Media

Abilities: Oral Comprehension; Oral Expression; Written Expression; Originality; Deductive Reasoning; Number Facility; Time Sharing; Near Vision; Night Vision; Auditory Attention; Speech Clarity

Employer Relations and Placement Specialists

Develop relationships with employers to facilitate placement of job applicants or students in employment opportunities. Establishes and maintains relationships with employers to determine personnel needs, promote use of service, and monitor progress of placed individuals. Confers with employers to resolve problems relating to employment service effectiveness, employer compliance, and employer recruitment activities. Arranges job interviews for applicants. Receives and records information from employers regarding employment opportunities. Directs and coordinates job placement programs and job analysis services. Conducts surveys of local labor market, and assists employers in revising organizational policies such as job standards and compensation. Promotes, develops, and terminates on-the-job and auxiliary training programs and assists in writing contracts. Instructs applicants in resume writing, job search, and interviewing skills, and conducts in-service training for personnel of placement service. Interviews applicants to determine interests, qualifications, and employment eligibility, and assists in developing employment and curriculum plans. Collects, organizes, and analyzes occupational, educational, and economic information for placement services and to maintain occupational library. Develops placement office procedures, establishes work loads, assigns tasks, and reviews activity reports.

Knowledge: Administration and Management; Clerical; Sales and Marketing; Customer and Personal Service; Personnel and Human Resources; Computers and Electronics; Psychology; Sociology and Anthropology; Geography; Therapy and Counseling; Education and Training

Abilities: Oral Expression; Written Expression; Fluency of Ideas; Originality; Deductive Reasoning; Near Vision; Speech Recognition; Speech Clarity

Employee Relations Specialists

Perform a variety of duties to promote employee welfare, such as resolving human relations problems and promoting employee health and well-being. Interviews workers and discusses with personnel human relations, and work-related problems that adversely affect morale, health, and productivity. Evaluates and resolves human relations, labor relations, and work-related problems, and meets with management to determine appropriate action. Explains and provides advice to workers about company and governmental rules, regulations, and procedures, and need for compliance. Counsels employees regarding work, family, or personal problems. Explains company compensation and benefit programs, such as medical, insurance, retirement, and savings plans, and enrolls workers in specified programs. Arranges for employee library, lunchroom, recreational facilities, and activities. Develops, schedules, and conducts technical, management, and interpersonal skills training to improve employee performance. Prepares newsletter and other reports to communicate information about employee concerns and comments and organizational actions taken. Attends conferences and meetings, as employee-management liaison, to facilitate communication between parties. Prepares reports and enters and updates medical, insurance, retirement, and other personnel forms and records, using computer. Audits benefit accounts and examines records to ensure compliance with standards and regulations. Arranges for employee physical examinations, first aid, and other medical attention. Inspects facilities to determine if lighting, sanitation, and security are adequate and to ensure compliance to standards. Supervises clerical or administrative personnel.

Knowledge: Administration and Management; Clerical; Economics and Accounting; Customer and Personal Service; Personnel and Human Resources; Computers and Electronics; Psychology; Sociology and Anthropology; Therapy and Counseling; Education and Training; Law, Government, and Jurisprudence; Communications and Media

Abilities: Oral Expression; Fluency of Ideas; Originality; Near Vision; Auditory Attention; Speech Clarity

Employee Training Specialists

Coordinate and conduct employee training programs to train new and existing employees how to perform required work, improve work methods, or comply with policies, procedures, or regulations. Develops and conducts orientation and training for employees or customers of industrial or commercial establishment. Confers with managers, instructors, or customer representatives of industrial or commercial establishment to determine training needs. Evaluates training materials, such as outlines, text, and handouts, prepared by instructors. Assigns instructors to conduct training and assists them in obtaining required training materials. Schedules classes based on availability of classrooms, equipment, and instructors. Coordinates recruitment and placement of participants in skill training. Organizes and develops training procedure manuals and guides. Attends meetings and seminars to obtain information useful to train staff and to inform management of training programs and goals. Maintains records and writes reports to monitor and evaluate training activities and program effectiveness. Supervises instructors, monitors and evaluates instructor performance, and refers instructors to classes for skill development. Monitors training costs to ensure budget is not exceeded, and prepares budget report to justify expenditures. Refers trainees with social problems to appropriate service agency. Screens, hires, and assigns workers to positions based on qualifications.

Knowledge: Administration and Management; Clerical; Economics and Accounting; Sales and Marketing; Customer and Personal Service; Personnel and Human Resources; Psychology; Sociology and Anthropology; Therapy and Counseling; Education and Training; Foreign Language; Communications and Media

Abilities: Oral Expression; Written Expression; Fluency of Ideas; Originality; Mathematical Reasoning; Selective Attention; Wrist-Finger Speed; Near Vision; Far Vision; Night Vision; Speech Recognition; Speech Clarity

Personnel Recruiters

Seek out, interview, and screen applicants to fill existing and future job openings and promote career opportunities within organization. Interviews applicants to obtain work history, training, education, job skills, and other background information. Provides potential applicants with information regarding facilities, operations, benefits, and job or career opportunities in organization. Conducts reference and background checks on applicants. Contacts college representatives to arrange for and schedule on-campus interviews with students. Reviews and evaluates applicant qualifications or eligibility for specified licensing, according to established guidelines and designated licensing codes. Notifies applicants by mail or telephone to inform them of employment possibilities, consideration, and selection. Hires or refers applicants to other hiring personnel in organization. Arranges for interviews and travel and lodging for selected applicants at company expense. Evaluates recruitment and selection criteria to ensure conformance to professional, statistical, and testing standards, and recommends revision as needed. Assists and advises establishment management in organizing, preparing, and implementing recruiting and retention programs. Speaks to

P

civic, social, and other groups to provide information concerning job possibilities and career opportunities. Prepares and maintains employment records and authorizes paperwork assigning applicant to positions. Corrects and scores portions of examinations used to screen and select applicants. Projects yearly recruitment expenditures for budgetary consideration and control.

Knowledge: Administration and Management; Clerical; Sales and Marketing; Personnel and Human Resources; Computers and Electronics; Psychology; Philosophy and Theology; Law, Government, and Jurisprudence

Abilities: Originality; Mathematical Reasoning; Number Facility; Time Sharing; Auditory Attention; Speech Recognition; Speech Clarity

Labor Relations Specialists

Mediate, arbitrate, and conciliate disputes over negotiations of labor agreements or labor relations disputes. Conducts arbitration hearings concerning disputes over negotiations of labor contracts and agreements between labor and management. Mediates and assists disagreeing parties to compromise or otherwise negotiate on agreement regarding dispute. Renders decision to settle dispute, protect public interests, prevent employee wage loss, and minimize business interruptions, and issues report concerning settlement. Interrogates parties and clarifies problems to focus discussion on crucial points of disagreement. Investigates labor disputes upon request of bona fide party, following labor laws, industry practices, and labor relations social policies. Analyzes information to evaluate contentions of parties regarding disputed contract provisions. Promotes use of fact-finding, mediation, conciliation, and advisory services to prevent or resolve labor disputes and maintain labor relations. Prepares and issues reports regarding results of arbitration, decisions reached, or outcomes of negotiations. Conducts representation elections and oversees balloting procedures according to written consent agreement of concerned parties in labor dispute.

Knowledge: Administration and Management; Customer and Personal Service; Personnel and Human Resources; Psychology; Law, Government, and Jurisprudence

Abilities: Oral Comprehension; Written Comprehension; Oral Expression; Written Expression; Fluency of Ideas; Originality; Problem Sensitivity; Deductive Reasoning; Inductive Reasoning; Speed of Closure; Selective Attention; Near Vision; Auditory Attention; Speech Recognition; Speech Clarity

Pest Controllers and Assistants

▲ Growth: 22%
▲ Annual Job Openings: 16,835
▲ Yearly Earnings $21,507
▲ Education Required: Moderate-term O-J-T
▲ Self-employed: 9%
▲ Part-time: 30%

Pest Controllers and Assistants

Spray or release chemical solutions or toxic gases and set mechanical traps to kill pests and vermin such as mice, termites, and roaches that infest buildings and surrounding areas. Sprays or dusts chemical solutions, powders, or gases into rooms; onto clothing, furnishings or wood; and over marshlands, ditches, and catch-basins. Sets mechanical traps and places poisonous paste or bait in sewers, burrows, and ditches. Inspects premises to identify infestation source and extent of damage to property, wall, and roof porosity, and access to infested locations. Cuts or bores openings in building or surrounding concrete, accesses infested areas, inserts nozzle, and injects pesticide to impregnate ground. Studies preliminary reports and diagrams of infested area, and determines treatment type required to eliminate and prevent recurrence of infestation. Directs and/or assists other workers in treatment and extermination processes to eliminate and control rodents, insects, and weeds. Measures area dimensions requiring treatment, using rule, calculates fumigant requirements, and estimates cost for service. Cleans and removes blockages from infested areas to facilitate spraying procedure and provide drainage, using broom, mop, shovel, and rake. Positions and fastens edges of tarpaulins over building and tapes vents to ensure air-tight environment. Holds halide lamp near tarpaulin seams and building vents to detect leaking fumigant. Posts warning signs and locks building doors to secure area to be fumigated. Drives truck equipped with power spraying equipment. Records work activities performed. Cleans worksite after completion of job. Digs up and burns or sprays weeds with herbicides.

Knowledge: Chemistry

Abilities: Gross Body Equilibrium

P

Petroleum Engineers

▲ Growth: -14%
▲ Annual Job Openings: 549
▲ Yearly Earnings $68,224
▲ Education Required: Bachelor's degree
▲ Self-employed: 5%
▲ Part-time: 3%

Petroleum Engineers

Devise methods to improve oil and gas well production and determine the need for new or modified tool designs. Oversee drilling and offer technical advice to achieve economical and satisfactory progress. Designs or modifies mining and oil field machinery and tools, applying engineering principles. Conducts engineering research experiments to improve or modify mining and oil machinery and operations. Develops plans for oil and gas field drilling, and for product recovery and treatment. Confers with scientific, engineering, and technical personnel to resolve design, research, and testing problems. Evaluates findings to develop, design, or test equipment or processes. Monitors production rates, and plans rework processes to improve production. Analyzes data to recommend placement of wells and supplementary processes to enhance production. Assists engineering and other personnel to solve operating problems. Coordinates activities of workers engaged in research, planning, and development. Inspects oil and gas wells to determine that installations are completed. Assigns work to staff to obtain maximum utilization of personnel. Interprets drilling and testing information for personnel. Tests machinery and equipment to ensure conformance to performance specifications and to ensure safety. Writes technical reports for engineering and management personnel.

Knowledge: Administration and Management; Personnel and Human Resources; Production and Processing; Engineering and Technology; Design; Mechanical; Mathematics; Physics; English Language

Abilities: Oral Comprehension; Written Comprehension; Oral Expression; Written Expression; Fluency of Ideas; Originality; Problem Sensitivity; Deductive Reasoning; Inductive Reasoning; Information Ordering; Category Flexibility; Mathematical Reasoning; Number Facility; Memorization; Speed of Closure; Flexibility of Closure; Perceptual Speed; Spatial Orientation; Visualization; Time Sharing; Response Orientation; Rate Control; Gross Body Equilibrium; Peripheral Vision; Depth Perception; Glare Sensitivity; Hearing Sensitivity; Auditory Attention; Sound Localization

Pharmacists

- ▲ Growth: 13%
- ▲ Annual Job Openings: 13,826
- ▲ Yearly Earnings $55,328
- ▲ Education Required: Bachelor's degree
- ▲ Self-employed: 4%
- ▲ Part-time: 24%

Pharmacists

Compound and dispense medications following prescriptions issued by physicians, dentists, or other authorized medical practitioners. Compounds medications, using standard formulas and processes, such as weighing, measuring, and mixing ingredients. Compounds radioactive substances and reagents to prepare radiopharmaceuticals, following radiopharmacy laboratory procedures. Plans and implements procedures in pharmacy, such as mixing, packaging, and labeling pharmaceuticals according to policies and legal requirements. Reviews prescription to assure accuracy and determine ingredients needed and suitability of radiopharmaceutical prescriptions. Answers questions and provides information to pharmacy customers on drug interactions, side effects, dosage, and storage of pharmaceuticals. Assays prepared radiopharmaceutical, using instruments and equipment to verify rate of drug disintegration and to ensure patient receives required dose. Calculates volume of radioactive pharmaceutical required to provide patient with desired level of radioactivity at prescribed time. Consults medical staff to advise on drug applications and characteristics and to review and evaluate quality and effectiveness of radiopharmaceuticals. Maintains established procedures concerning quality assurance, security of controlled substances, and disposal of hazardous waste. Maintains records, such as pharmacy files, charge system, inventory, and control records for radioactive nuclei. Oversees preparation and dispensation of experimental drugs. Verifies that specified radioactive substance and reagent will give desired results in examination or treatment procedures. Analyzes records to indicate prescribing trends and excessive usage. Directs and coordinates, through subordinate supervisory personnel, activities and functions of pharmacy. Directs pharmacy personnel programs, such as hiring, training, and intern programs. Prepares pharmacy budget. Observes pharmacy personnel at work to develop quality assurance techniques to ensure safe, legal, and ethical practices. Participates in development of computer programs for pharmacy information-management systems, patient and department charge systems, and inventory control. Conducts research to develop or improve radiopharmaceuticals. Instructs students, interns, and other medical personnel on matters pertaining to pharmacy or concerning radiopharmacy use, characteristics, and compounding procedures.

Knowledge: Administration and Management; Clerical; Economics and Accounting; Personnel and Human Resources; Computers and Electronics; Chemistry; Biology; Medicine and Dentistry; Therapy and Counseling; Education and Training; English Language; Foreign Language; Law, Government, and Jurisprudence

Abilities: Oral Comprehension; Written Comprehension; Oral Expression; Information Ordering; Mathematical Reasoning

Pharmacy Technicians

▲ Growth: 11%

▲ Annual Job Openings: 9,841

▲ Yearly Earnings $31,054

▲ Education Required: Moderate-term O-J-T

▲ Self-employed: 0%

▲ Part-time: 22%

Pharmacy Technicians

Fill orders for unit doses and prepackaged pharmaceuticals and perform other related duties under the supervision and direction of a pharmacy supervisor or staff pharmacist. Duties include keeping records of drugs delivered to the pharmacy, storing incoming merchandise in proper locations, and informing the supervisor of stock needs and shortages. May clean equipment used in the performance of duties and assist in the care and maintenance of equipment and supplies. Assists pharmacist to prepare and dispense medication. Mixes pharmaceutical preparations, fills bottles with prescribed tablets and capsules, and types labels for bottles. Processes records of medication and equipment dispensed to hospital patient, computes charges, and enters data in computer. Receives and stores incoming supplies. Counts stock and enters data in computer to maintain inventory records. Prepares intravenous (IV) packs, using sterile technique, under supervision of hospital pharmacist. Cleans equipment and sterilizes glassware according to prescribed methods.

Knowledge: Clerical; Chemistry; Medicine and Dentistry

Abilities: None above average

Photographers

▲ Growth: 17%
▲ Annual Job Openings: 20,243
▲ Yearly Earnings $23,379
▲ Education Required: Moderate-term O-J-T
▲ Self-employed: 46%
▲ Part-time: 23%

Professional Photographers

Photograph subjects or newsworthy events, using still cameras, color or black-and-white film, and variety of photographic accessories. Exclude scientific photographers. Photographs subjects or newsworthy events, using still cameras, to produce pictures, related to an area of interest. Sights camera and takes pictures of subjects or newsworthy events. Adjusts camera based on lighting, subject material, distance, and film speed. Estimates or measures light level, distance, and number of exposures needed, using measuring devices and formulas. Selects and assembles equipment and required background properties, according to subject, materials, and conditions. Observes and arranges subject material in desired position. Confers with personnel to discuss subject material or newsworthy events and conditions of shoot. Removes and develops exposed film, using chemicals, touch-up tools, and equipment. Travels to assigned location to set up equipment and take photograph. Directs activities of workers in setting up equipment used to photograph subjects or newsworthy events.

Knowledge: Chemistry; Geography; Fine Arts; History and Archeology; Communications and Media

Abilities: Fluency of Ideas; Originality; Information Ordering; Category Flexibility; Memorization; Flexibility of Closure; Perceptual Speed; Spatial Orientation; Visualization; Selective Attention; Time Sharing; Arm-Hand Steadiness; Finger Dexterity; Control Precision; Response Orientation; Rate Control; Reaction Time; Wrist-Finger Speed; Gross Body Equilibrium; Near Vision; Far Vision; Visual Color Discrimination; Night Vision; Peripheral Vision; Depth Perception; Glare Sensitivity

Photographers, Scientific

Photograph variety of subject materials to illustrate or record scientific/medical data or phenomena, utilizing knowledge of scientific procedures and photographic technology and techniques. Photographs variety of subject materials to illustrate or record scientific or medical data or phenomena, related to an area of interest. Sights and focuses camera to take picture of subject material to illustrate or record scientific or medical data or phenomena. Plans methods and procedures for photographing subject material, and sets up required equipment. Observes and arranges subject material to desired position. Removes exposed film and develops film, using chemicals, touch-up tools, and equipment. Engages in research to develop new photographic procedure, materials, and scientific data.

Knowledge: Engineering and Technology; Physics; Chemistry; Medicine and Dentistry; Fine Arts; Communications and Media

Abilities: Fluency of Ideas; Originality; Information Ordering; Category Flexibility; Memorization; Speed of Closure; Flexibility of Closure; Perceptual Speed; Spatial Orientation; Time Sharing; Response Orientation; Rate Control; Reaction Time; Gross Body Equilibrium; Near Vision; Far Vision; Visual Color Discrimination; Night Vision; Peripheral Vision; Depth Perception; Glare Sensitivity

Physical and Corrective Therapy Assistants

▲ Growth: 79%

▲ Annual Job Openings: 26,479

▲ Yearly Earnings $23,587

▲ Education Required: Moderate-term O-J-T

▲ Self-employed: 0%

▲ Part-time: 34%

Physical and Corrective Therapy Assistants and Aides

Prepare patient and/or administer physical therapy treatment, such as massages, traction, and heat, light, and sound treatment. Instruct, motivate, and assist patients with learning and improving functional activities. Normally work under the direction of a physical or corrective therapist. Administers active and passive manual therapeutic exercises; therapeutic massage; and heat, light, sound, water, and electrical modality treatments, such as ultrasound. Instructs, motivates, and assists patients to learn and improve functional activities, such as perambulation, transfer, ambulation, and daily-living activities. Safeguards, motivates, and assists patients practicing exercises and functional activities under direction of professional staff. Administers traction to relieve neck and back pain, using intermittent and static traction equipment. Trains patients in use and care of orthopedic braces, prostheses, and supportive devices, such as crutches. Provides routine treatments, such as hydrotherapy, hot and cold packs, and paraffin bath. Adjusts fit of supportive devices for patients, as instructed. Observes patients during treatments, compiles and evaluates data on patients' responses to treatments and progress, and reports to physical therapist. Secures patients into or onto therapy equipment. Confers with physical therapy staff and others to discuss and evaluate patient information for planning, modifying, and coordinating treatment. Measures patient's range-of-joint motion, body parts, and vital signs to determine effects of treatments or for patient evaluations. Assists patients to dress, undress, and put on and remove supportive devices, such as braces, splints, and slings. Records treatment given and equipment used. Fits patients for orthopedic braces, prostheses, and supportive devices, such as crutches. Monitors treatments administered by physical therapy aides. Transports patients to and from treatment area. Gives orientation to new physical therapist assistants and directs and gives instruction to physical therapy aides. Cleans work area and equipment after treatment. Performs clerical duties, such as taking inventory, ordering supplies, answering telephone, taking messages, and filling out forms.

Knowledge: Clerical; Customer and Personal Service; Biology; Psychology; Medicine and Dentistry; Therapy and Counseling; Education and Training

Abilities: None above average

Physical Scientists

- ▲ Growth: 28%
- ▲ Annual Job Openings: 4,131
- ▲ Yearly Earnings $47,632
- ▲ Education Required: Bachelor's degree
- ▲ Self-employed: 7%
- ▲ Part-time: 6%

Geographer

Study nature and use of areas of earth's surface, relating and interpreting interactions of physical and cultural phenomena. Conduct research on physical aspects of a region, including land forms, climates, soils, plants and animals, and conduct research on the spatial implications of human activities within a given area, including social characteristics, economic activities, and political organization, as well as researching interdependence between regions at scales ranging from local to global. Collects data on physical characteristics of specified area, such as geological formation, climate, and vegetation, using surveying or meteorological equipment. Studies population characteristics within area, such as ethnic distribution and economic activity. Constructs and interprets maps, graphs, and diagrams. Uses surveying equipment to assess geology, physics, and biology within given area. Prepares environmental impact reports based on results of study. Advises governments and organizations on ethnic and natural boundaries between nation or administrative areas.

Knowledge: Physics; Biology; Sociology and Anthropology; Geography; Foreign Language; History and Archeology

Abilities: Written Expression; Flexibility of Discourse; Spatial Orientation; Far Vision; Visual Color Discrimination; Night Vision; Depth Perception

Materials Scientists

Research and study the structures and chemical properties of various natural and manmade materials, including metals, alloys, rubber, ceramics, semiconductors, poly-

mers, and glass. **Determine ways to strengthen or combine materials, or develop new materials with new or specific properties for use in a variety of products and applications. Include glass scientists, ceramic scientists, metallurgical scientists, and polymer scientists.** Plans laboratory experiments to confirm feasibility of processes and techniques to produce materials having special characteristics. Studies structures and properties of materials, such as metals, alloys, polymers, and ceramics, to obtain research data. Reports materials study findings for other scientists and requesters. Guides technical staff engaged in developing materials for specific use in projected product or device.

Knowledge: Administration and Management; Engineering and Technology; Mathematics; Physics; Chemistry; English Language; Foreign Language; Communications and Media

Abilities: Oral Comprehension; Written Comprehension; Oral Expression; Written Expression; Fluency of Ideas; Originality; Deductive Reasoning; Mathematical Reasoning; Number Facility; Speed of Closure

Physical Therapists

▲ Growth: 71%

▲ Annual Job Openings: 19,122

▲ Yearly Earnings $52,811

▲ Education Required: Bachelor's degree

▲ Self-employed: 6%

▲ Part-time: 20%

Physical Therapists

Apply techniques and treatments that help relieve pain, increase the patient's strength, and decrease or prevent deformity and crippling. Administers manual exercises to improve and maintain function. Administers treatment involving application of physical agents, using equipment, moist packs, ultraviolet and infrared lamps, and ultrasound machines. Administers massage, applying knowledge of massage techniques and body physiology. Administers traction to relieve pain, using traction equipment. Instructs, motivates, and assists patient to perform various physical activities and use supportive devices, such as crutches, canes, and prostheses. Evaluates effects of treatment at various stages and adjusts treatment to achieve maximum benefit. Tests and measures patient's strength, motor development, sensory perception, functional capacity, and respiratory and circulatory efficiency, and records data. Reviews physician's referral and patient's condition and medical records to determine physical therapy treatment required. Plans and prepares written treatment program based on evaluation of patient data. Instructs patient and family in treatment procedures to be continued at home. Evaluates, fits, and adjusts prosthetic and orthotic devices and recommends modification to orthotist. Confers with medical practitioners to obtain additional information, suggest revisions in treatment, and integrate physical therapy into patient's care. Records treatment, response, and progress in patient's chart, or enters information into computer. Plans, directs, and coordinates physical therapy program. Orients, instructs, and directs work activities of assistants, aides, and students. Plans and develops physical therapy research programs and participates in conducting research. Writes technical articles and reports for publications. Plans and conducts lectures and training programs on physical therapy and related topics for medical staff, students, and community groups.

Knowledge: Administration and Management; Customer and Personal Service; Biology; Psychology; Medicine and Dentistry; Therapy and Counseling; Education and Training; English Language

Abilities: Speech Clarity

Corrective Therapists

Apply techniques and treatments designed to prevent muscular deconditioning resulting from long convalescence or inactivity due to chronic illness. Applies skin lubricant and massages client's body to relax muscles, stimulate nerves, promote range of motion, and release tissue. Plans and organizes program treatment procedures with client, or in collaboration with others on rehabilitation team. Demonstrates and directs client to participate in body movements designed to improve muscular function and flexibility and to reduce tension. Teaches client spatial and body awareness, new movement skills, and effective and expressive body habits. Instructs patient in use of prostheses, devices such as canes, crutches, and braces, and walking skills for sightless patients. Observes and/or photographs client's arm and leg movements, posture, and flexibility to evaluate client in relation to established norms. Observes and evaluates client's progress during treatment program and modifies treatment as required. Teaches client stress management, relaxation, and hygiene techniques to compensate for disabilities. Interviews patient or consults client's questionnaire to determine client's medical history and physical condition. Prepares reports describing client's treatment, progress, emotional reactions, and response to treatment. Consults with client to establish rapport, discuss program goals, and motivate patient.

Knowledge: Customer and Personal Service; Biology; Psychology; Medicine and Dentistry; Therapy and Counseling; Education and Training; Communications and Media

Abilities: Fluency of Ideas; Originality; Problem Sensitivity; Deductive Reasoning; Inductive Reasoning; Memorization; Arm-Hand Steadiness; Finger Dexterity; Multilimb Coordination; Wrist-Finger Speed; Speed of Limb Movement; Dynamic Strength; Trunk Strength; Stamina; Dynamic Flexibility; Gross Body Coordination; Gross Body Equilibrium

P

Physician Assistants

▲ Growth: 47%
▲ Annual Job Openings: 5,090
▲ Yearly Earnings $40,414
▲ Education Required: Bachelor's degree
▲ Self-employed: 1%
▲ Part-time: 24%

Physician Assistants

Provide patient services under direct supervision and responsibility of doctor of medicine or osteopathy. Elicit detailed patient histories and make complete physical examinations. Reach tentative diagnosis and order appropriate laboratory tests. Require substantial educational preparation, usually at junior or 4-year colleges. Most physician's assistants complete 2 years of formal training, but training may vary from 1 to 5 years depending on the nature of the training and previous education and experience. May require certification. Exclude nurses and ambulance attendants, whose training is limited to the application of first aid. Examines patient. Administers or orders diagnostic tests, such as x-ray, electrocardiogram, and laboratory tests. Compiles patient medical data, including health history and results of physical examination. Interprets diagnostic test results for deviations from normal. Performs therapeutic procedures, such as injections, immunizations, suturing and wound care, and managing infection. Counsels patients regarding prescribed therapeutic regimens, normal growth and development, family planning, emotional problems of daily living, and health maintenance. Develops and implements patient management plans, records progress notes, and assists in provision of continuity of care.

Knowledge: Chemistry; Biology; Psychology; Medicine and Dentistry; Therapy and Counseling

Abilities: Problem Sensitivity; Inductive Reasoning; Information Ordering; Speed of Closure; Arm-Hand Steadiness

Physicians

▲ Growth: 21%
▲ Annual Job Openings: 29,681
▲ Yearly Earnings $96,636
▲ Education Required: First professional degree
▲ Self-employed: 16%
▲ Part-time: 7%

Doctors of Medicine (MD)

Diagnose illness and prescribe and administer treatment for injury and disease. Exclude doctors of osteopathy, psychiatrists, anesthesiologists, surgeons, and pathologists. Examines or conducts tests on patient to provide information on medical condition. Analyzes records, reports, test results, or examination information to diagnose medical condition of patient. Prescribes or administers treatment, therapy, medication, vaccination, and other specialized medical care to treat or prevent illness, disease, or injury. Monitors patient's condition and progress and reevaluates treatments as necessary. Explains procedures and discusses test results on prescribed treatments with patients. Operates on patients to remove, repair, or improve functioning of diseased or injured body parts and systems, and delivers babies. Collects, records, and maintains patient information, such as medical history, reports, and examination results. Refers patients to medical specialist or other practitioner when necessary. Advises patients and community concerning diet, activity, hygiene, and disease prevention. Plans, implements, or administers health programs or standards in hospital, business, or community for information, prevention, or treatment of injury or illness. Directs and coordinates activities of nurses, students, assistants, specialists, therapists, and other medical staff. Prepares reports for government or management of birth, death, and disease statistics, workforce evaluations, or medical status of individuals. Conducts research to study anatomy and develop or test medications, treatments, or procedures to prevent or control disease or injury.

Knowledge: Administration and Management; Personnel and Human Resources; Mathematics; Physics; Chemistry; Biology; Psychology; Sociology and Anthropology; Medicine and Dentistry; Therapy and Counseling; Education and Training; English Language; Foreign Language; Law, Government, and Jurisprudence

Abilities: Oral Comprehension; Written Comprehension; Oral Expression; Written Expression; Fluency of Ideas; Problem Sensitivity; Deductive Reasoning; Inductive Reasoning; Information Ordering; Mathematical Reasoning; Number Facility; Speed of Closure; Flexibility of Closure; Perceptual Speed; Selective Attention; Time Sharing; Arm-Hand Steadiness; Manual Dexterity; Finger Dexterity; Control Precision; Multilimb Coordination; Response Orientation; Reaction Time; Wrist-Finger Speed; Near Vision; Visual Color Discrimination; Hearing Sensitivity; Auditory Attention; Speech Clarity

Doctors of Osteopathy (DO)

Diagnose illness and prescribe and administer treatment for injury and disease with emphasis on body's musculoskeletal system. Prescribes and administers medical, surgical, or manipulative therapy treatments to correct disorders or injuries of bones, muscles, or nerves. Examines or conducts test on patient to provide information on musculoskeletal system, using diagnostic images, drugs, and other aids. Analyzes reports and test or examination findings to diagnose musculoskeletal system impairment. Operates on patient to repair injuries or improve functions of musculoskeletal system. Advises patient and community of prevention and treatment of injury of musculoskeletal system. Conducts research to develop and test medications or medical techniques to cure or control disease or injury of musculoskeletal system. Directs and coordinates activities of nurses, assistants, and other medical staff.

Knowledge: Customer and Personal Service; Mathematics; Chemistry; Biology; Psychology; Sociology and Anthropology; Medicine and Dentistry; Therapy and Counseling; English Language

Abilities: Oral Comprehension; Written Comprehension; Oral Expression; Written Expression; Problem Sensitivity; Deductive Reasoning; Inductive Reasoning; Information Ordering; Memorization; Speed of Closure; Flexibility of Closure; Selective Attention; Time Sharing; Arm-Hand Steadiness; Manual Dexterity; Finger Dexterity; Reaction Time; Wrist-Finger Speed; Near Vision; Speech Clarity

Psychiatrists

Diagnose mental, emotional, and behavioral disorders and prescribe medication or administer psychotherapeutic treatments to treat disorders. Analyzes and evaluates patient data and test or examination findings to diagnose nature and extent of mental disorder. Prescribes, directs, and administers psychotherapeutic treatments or medications to treat mental, emotional, or behavioral disorders. Examines or conducts laboratory or diagnostic tests on patient to provide information on general physical condition and mental disorder. Gathers and maintains patient information and records, including social and medical history obtained from patient, relatives, and other professionals. Reviews and evaluates treatment procedures and outcomes of other psychiatrists and medical professionals. Advises and informs guardians, relatives, and significant others of patient's condition and treatment. Prepares case reports and summaries for government agencies. Teaches, conducts research, and publishes findings to increase understanding of mental, emotional, and behavioral states and disorders.

Knowledge: Customer and Personal Service; Chemistry; Biology; Psychology; Sociology and Anthropology; Medicine and Dentistry; Therapy and Counseling; Education and Training; English Language; Philosophy and Theology; Law, Government, and Jurisprudence; Communications and Media

Abilities: Oral Comprehension; Written Comprehension; Oral Expression; Written Expression; Problem Sensitivity; Deductive Reasoning; Inductive Reasoning; Information Ordering; Memorization; Speed of Closure; Selective Attention; Speech Recognition; Speech Clarity

Anesthesiologists

Administer anesthetic during surgery or other medical procedures. Administers anesthetic or sedation during medical procedures, using local, intravenous, spinal, or caudal methods. Monitors patient before, during, and after anesthesia and counteracts adverse reactions or complications. Examines patient to determine risk during surgical, obstetrical, and other medical procedures. Confers with medical professional to determine type and method of anesthetic or sedation to render patient insensible to pain. Records type and amount of anesthesia and patient condition throughout procedure. Positions patient on operating table to maximize patient comfort and surgical accessibility. Informs students and staff of types and methods of anesthesia administration, signs of complications, and emergency methods to counteract reactions.

Knowledge: Chemistry; Biology; Medicine and Dentistry; English Language

Abilities: Problem Sensitivity; Time Sharing; Control Precision; Speech Clarity

Surgeons

Perform surgery to repair injuries; remove or repair diseased organs, bones, or tissue; correct deformities, or improve function in patients. Operates on patient to correct deformities, repair injuries, prevent diseases, or improve or restore patient's functions. Analyzes patient's medical history, medication allergies, physical condition, and examination results to verify operation's necessity and to determine best procedure. Examines patient to provide information on medical condition and patient's surgical risk. Refers patient to medical specialist or other practitioners when necessary. Conducts research to develop and test surgical techniques to improve operating procedures and outcomes. Examines instruments, equipment, and operating room to ensure sterility. Directs and coordinates activities of nurses, assistants, specialists, and other medical staff.

Knowledge: Administration and Management; Physics; Chemistry; Biology; Psychology; Medicine and Dentistry; Therapy and Counseling; English Language

Abilities: Written Comprehension; Oral Expression; Written Expression; Fluency of Ideas; Originality; Problem Sensitivity; Deductive Reasoning; Inductive Reasoning; Information Ordering; Category Flexibility; Mathematical Reasoning; Number Facility; Memorization; Speed of Closure; Flexibility of Closure; Perceptual Speed; Spatial Orientation; Visualization; Selective Attention; Time Sharing; Arm-Hand Steadiness; Manual Dexterity; Finger Dexterity; Control Precision; Multilimb Coordination; Response Orientation; Rate Control; Reaction Time; Wrist-Finger Speed; Speed of Limb Movement; Explosive Strength; Dynamic Strength; Trunk Strength; Stamina; Gross Body Equilibrium; Near Vision; Depth Perception; Sound Localization; Speech Clarity

Pathologists

Research or study the nature, cause, effects, and development of diseases; and determine presence and extent of disease in body tissue, fluids, secretions, and other specimens. Conducts research to gain knowledge of nature, cause, and development of diseases, and resulting structural and functional body changes. Examines, collects tissue or fluid samples, and conducts tests on patient to provide information on patient's disease. Diagnoses nature, cause, and development of disease and resulting changes of patient's body, using results of sample analyses and tests. Performs autopsies to determine nature and extent of disease, cause of death, and effects of treatment. Advises other medical practitioners on nature, cause, and development of diseases. Directs and coordinates activities of nurses, students, and other staff in medical school, hospital, medical examiner's office, or research institute.

Knowledge: Administration and Management; Mathematics; Chemistry; Biology; Medicine and Dentistry; Therapy and Counseling; Education and Training; English Language

Abilities: Oral Comprehension; Written Comprehension; Oral Expression; Written Expression; Fluency of Ideas; Originality; Problem Sensitivity; Deductive Reasoning; Inductive Reasoning; Information Ordering; Category Flexibility; Mathematical Reasoning; Memorization; Speed of Closure; Flexibility of Closure; Perceptual Speed; Arm-Hand Steadiness; Manual Dexterity; Finger Dexterity; Control Precision; Multilimb Coordination; Wrist-Finger Speed; Speed of Limb Movement; Near Vision; Visual Color Discrimination

Physicists and Astronomers

- ▲ Growth: -2%
- ▲ Annual Job Openings: 1,073
- ▲ Yearly Earnings $62,774
- ▲ Education Required: Doctor's degree
- ▲ Self-employed: 0%
- ▲ Part-time: 6%

Physicists

Conduct research into the phases of physical phenomena, develop theories and laws on the basis of observation and experiments, and devise methods to apply laws and theories to industry and other fields. Observes structure and properties of matter and transformation and propagation of energy, using masers, lasers, telescopes, and other equipment. Analyzes results of experiments designed to detect and measure previously unobserved physical phenomena. Conducts instrumental analyses to determine physical properties of materials. Describes and expresses observations and conclusions in mathematical terms. Conducts application analysis to determine commercial, industrial, scientific, medical, military, or other uses for electro-optical devices. Assists in developing standards of permissible concentrations of radioisotopes in liquids and gases. Designs electronic circuitry and optical components with scientific characteristics to fit within specified mechanical limits and perform according to specifications. Assists with development of manufacturing, assembly, and fabrication processes of lasers, masers, infrared, and other light-emitting and light-sensitive devices. Conducts research pertaining to potential environmental impact of proposed atomic energy-related industrial development to determine qualifications for licensing. Directs testing and monitoring of contamination of radioactive equipment and recording of personnel and plant area radiation exposure data. Consults other scientists regarding innovations to ensure equipment or plant design conforms to health physics standards for protection of personnel. Incorporates methods for maintenance and repair of components and designs, and develops test instrumentation and test procedures. Advises authorities in procedures to be followed in radiation incidents or hazards, and assists in civil defense planning. Supervises subordinate personnel, including graduate students, in scientific activities or research. Writes for or serves as consultant for professional journals or other media. Trains technicians to assist in scientific experimentation and research.

Knowledge: Personnel and Human Resources; Production and Processing; Computers and Electronics; Engineering and Technology; Design; Mathematics; Physics; Chemistry; Education and Training; English Language; Foreign Language; History and Archeology; Communications and Media

Abilities: Oral Comprehension; Written Comprehension; Oral Expression; Written Expression; Fluency of Ideas; Originality; Problem Sensitivity; Deductive Reasoning; Inductive Reasoning; Information Ordering; Category Flexibility; Mathematical Reasoning; Number Facility; Memorization; Speed of Closure; Speech Recognition; Speech Clarity

Astronomers

Observe, research, and interpret celestial and astronomical phenomena to increase basic knowledge; and apply such information to practical problems. Studies celestial phenomena from ground or above atmosphere, using various optical devices such as telescopes situated on ground or attached to satellites. Studies history, structure, extent, and evolution of stars, stellar systems, and universe. Calculates orbits and determines sizes, shapes, brightness, and motions of different celestial bodies. Computes positions of sun, moon, planets, stars, nebulae, and galaxies. Determines exact time by celestial observations, and conducts research into relationships between time and space. Analyzes wave lengths of radiation from celestial bodies, as observed in all ranges of spectrum. Develops mathematical tables giving positions of sun, moon, planets, and stars at given times for use by air and sea navigators. Designs optical, mechanical, and electronic instruments for astronomical research.

Knowledge: Computers and Electronics; Engineering and Technology; Design; Mathematics; Physics; Geography; English Language; History and Archeology

Abilities: Written Comprehension; Written Expression; Fluency of Ideas; Deductive Reasoning; Inductive Reasoning; Category Flexibility; Mathematical Reasoning; Number Facility; Far Vision; Night Vision; Peripheral Vision; Depth Perception; Glare Sensitivity

Plant and System Operators

- ▲ Growth: 15%
- ▲ Annual Job Openings: 4,753
- ▲ Yearly Earnings $23,566
- ▲ Education Required: Long-term O-J-T
- ▲ Self-employed: 0%
- ▲ Part-time: 1%

Chemical Plant and Systems Operators

Control or operate an entire chemical process or system of machines, such as reduction pots and heated air towers, through the use of panelboards, control boards, or semi-automatic equipment. Turns valves to regulate flow of product or byproducts through agitator tanks, storage drums, or neutralizer tanks, according to process. Starts pumps to wash and rinse reactor vessels, to exhaust gases and vapors, and to mix product with water. Moves control settings to make control adjustments on equipment units affecting speed of chemical reactions and quality and yield. Monitors recording instruments, flowmeters, panel lights, and other indicators, and listens for warning signals to verify conformity of process conditions. Interprets chemical reactions visible through sight glasses or on television monitor and reviews laboratory test reports for process adjustments. Adjusts feed valves to regulate flow of liquor and steam to stills and of water to condensers and dephlegmator. Admits natural gas under pressure to exhaust naphtha from reactors. Manually regulates or shuts down equipment during emergency situations, as directed by supervisory personnel. Produces concentrated ammonia liquor by condensing vapors in water-cooled condensers. Records operating data, such as process conditions, test results, and instruments readings, calculating material requirements or yield according to formulas. Determines amount of ammonia in waste liquor and water, using titration test, and adjusts temperatures and pressures to reduce loss. Defrosts frozen valves, using steam hose.

Knowledge: Production and Processing; Chemistry; Public Safety and Security

Abilities: Information Ordering; Control Precision; Reaction Time

Petroleum Pump Systems Operators

Control or operate manifold and pumping systems to circulate liquids through a petroleum refinery. Exclude workers who do not operate entire manifold or pumping systems. Starts battery of pumps, observes pressure meters and flowmeters, and turns valves to regulate pumping speeds according to schedules. Turns handwheels to open line valves and direct flow of product. Synchronizes activities with other pumphouses to ensure continuous flow of products and minimum of contamination between products. Plans movement of products through lines to processing, storage, and shipping units, utilizing knowledge of interconnections and capacities system. Reads operating schedules or instructions from dispatcher. Blends oils and gasolines. Signals other workers by telephone or radio to operate pumps, open and close valves, and check temperatures. Repairs pumps, lines, and auxiliary equipment. Records operating data, such as products and quantities pumped, stocks used, gauging results, and operating time.

Knowledge: Mechanical; Chemistry

Abilities: Rate Control

Power Reactor Operators

Control nuclear reactor that produces steam for generation of electric power. Coordinate operation of auxiliary equipment. Adjusts controls to start and shut down reactor and to regulate factors that affect reactor power level, following standard practices. Dispatches orders and instructions to personnel through radiotelephone or intercommunication system to coordinate operation of auxiliary equipment. Controls dual purpose reactors that produce plutonium and steam. Controls operation of auxiliary equipment, such as turbines and generators. Assists in preparing, transferring, loading, and unloading nuclear fuel elements.

Knowledge: Engineering and Technology; Physics; Chemistry; Telecommunications

Abilities: None above average

Stationary Engineers

Operate and maintain stationary engines and mechanical equipment to provide utilities for buildings or industrial processes. Operate equipment such as steam engines, generators, motors, turbines, and steam boilers. Adjusts controls and valves on equipment to provide power and regulate and set operations of system and industrial processes. Inspects equipment to determine need for repair, lubrication, or adjustment. Lights burners and opens valves on equipment, such as condensers, pumps, and compressors, to prepare system for operation. Reads dials of temperature, pressure, and ampere gauges and meters to detect malfunctions and ensure specified operation of equipment. Lubricates, maintains, and repairs equipment, using hand tools and power tools. Adds chemicals or tends equipment to maintain temperature of fluids or atmosphere or to prevent scale buildup. Tests electrical system to determine voltage, using voltage meter. Records temperature, pressure, water levels, fuel consumption, and other data at specified intervals in logbook. Cleans equipment, using airhose, brushes, and rags, and drains water from pipes and air reservoir. Measures and tests moisture content of air, density of brine, or other operating indicators, using hydrometer and other instruments.

Knowledge: Computers and Electronics; Engineering and Technology; Mechanical; Physics

Abilities: None above average

Plasterers

▲ Growth: 13%

▲ Annual Job Openings: 4,579

▲ Yearly Earnings $29,806

▲ Education Required: Long-term O-J-T

▲ Self-employed: 21%

▲ Part-time: 8%

Plasterers and Stucco Masons

Apply coats of plaster onto interior or exterior walls, ceilings, or partitions of buildings to produce finished surface according to blueprints, architect's drawings, or oral instructions. Applies coats of plaster or stucco to walls, ceilings, or partitions of buildings. Creates decorative textures in finish coat, using sand, pebbles, or stones. Mixes mortar to desired consistency and puts up scaffolds. Installs guidewires on exterior surface of buildings to indicate thickness of plaster or stucco. Applies weatherproof, decorative covering to exterior surfaces of building. Molds and installs ornamental plaster pieces, panels, and trim. Directs workers to mix plaster to desired consistency and to erect scaffolds.

Knowledge: Building and Construction

Abilities: Dynamic Strength; Dynamic Flexibility; Gross Body Equilibrium; Glare Sensitivity

Plastic Molding Machine Operators and Setters

▲ Growth: 18%

▲ Annual Job Openings: 15,111

▲ Yearly Earnings $19,760

▲ Education Required: Moderate-term O-J-T

▲ Self-employed: 0%

▲ Part-time: 2%

Plastic Molding and Casting Machine Setters and Set-Up Operators

Set up or set up and operate plastic molding machines, such as compression or injection molding machines, to mold, form, or cast thermoplastic materials to specified shape. Positions, aligns, and secures assembled mold, mold components, and machine accessories onto machine press bed, and attaches connecting lines. Installs dies onto machine or press and coats dies with parting agent, according to work order specifications. Sets machine controls to regulate molding temperature, volume, pressure, and time, according to knowledge of plastics and molding procedures. Presses button or pulls lever to activate machine to inject dies and compress compounds to form and cure specified products. Reads specifications to determine set-up and prescribed temperature and time settings to mold, form, or cast plastic materials. Weighs premixed compounds and dumps compound into die well, or fills hoppers of machines that automatically supply compound to die. Observes and adjusts machine set-up and operations to eliminate production of defective parts and products. Mixes catalysts, thermoplastic materials, and coloring pigments according to formula, using paddle and mixing machine. Measures and visually inspects products for surface and dimension defects, using precision measuring instruments, to ensure conformance to specifications. Removes finished or cured product from dies or mold, using hand tools and airhose. Trims excess material from part, using knife, and grinds scrap plastic into powder for reuse. Repairs and maintains machines and auxiliary equipment, using hand tools and power tools.

Knowledge: Production and Processing; Mechanical

Abilities: Control Precision; Wrist-Finger Speed; Explosive Strength; Dynamic Flexibility

Plastic Molding and Casting Machine Operators and Tenders

Operate or tend plastic molding machines, such as compression or injection molding machines, to mold, form, or cast thermoplastic materials to specified shape. Starts machine that automatically liquefies plastic material in heating chamber, injects liquefied material into mold, and ejects molded product. Turns valves and dials of machines to regulate pressure and temperature, to set press-cycle time, and to close press. Observes meters and gauges to verify specified temperatures, pressures, and press-cycle times. Observes continuous operation of automatic machine and width and alignment of plastic sheeting to ensure side flanges. Dumps plastic powder, preformed plastic pellets, or preformed rubber slugs into hopper of molding machine. Pulls level and toggle latches to fill mold and regulate tension on sheeting and to release mold covers. Mixes and pours liquid plastic into rotating drum of machine that spreads, hardens, and shapes mixture. Fills tubs, molds, or cavities of machine with plastic material in solid or liquid form prior to activating machine. Examines molded product for surface defects, such as dents, bubbles, thin areas, and cracks. Positions mold frame to correct alignment and tubs containing mixture on top of mold to facilitate loading of molds. Removes product from mold or conveyor, and cleans and reloads mold. Weighs prescribed amounts of material for molded part and finished product to ensure specifications are maintained. Heats plastic material prior to forming product, or cools product after processing to prevent distortion. Breaks seals that hold plastic product in molds, using hand tool, and removes product from mold. Feels stiffness and consistency of molded sheeting to detect machinery malfunction. Stacks molded parts in boxes or on conveyor for subsequent processing, or leaves parts in mold to cool. Reports defect in molds to supervisor. Throws flash and rejected parts into grinder machine to be recycled. Signals co-worker to synchronize feed of materials into molding process. Trims flashing from product.

Knowledge: Production and Processing; Mechanical

Abilities: Perceptual Speed; Control Precision; Rate Control; Reaction Time; Speed of Limb Movement; Static Strength; Dynamic Strength; Trunk Strength; Stamina; Dynamic Flexibility; Gross Body Coordination; Gross Body Equilibrium

Podiatrists

▲ Growth: 10%

▲ Annual Job Openings: 616

▲ Yearly Earnings $85,134

▲ Education Required: First professional degree

▲ Self-employed: 33%

▲ Part-time: 10%

Podiatrists

Diagnose and treat diseases and deformities of the human foot. Diagnoses ailments, such as tumors, ulcers, fractures, skin or nail diseases, and deformities, utilizing urinalysis, blood tests, and X rays. Treats conditions such as corns, calluses, ingrown nails, tumors, shortened tendons, bunions, cysts, and abscesses by surgical methods. Corrects deformities by means of plaster casts and strapping. Treats bone, muscle, and joint disorders. Treats deformities by mechanical and electrical methods, such as whirlpool or paraffin baths and short-wave and low-voltage currents. Prescribes corrective footwear. Prescribes drugs. Makes and fits prosthetic appliances. Performs surgery. Treats children's foot diseases. Advises patients concerning continued treatment of disorders and foot care to prevent recurrence of disorders. Refers patients to physician when symptoms indicative of systemic disorders, such as arthritis or diabetes, are observed in feet and legs.

Knowledge: Customer and Personal Service; Physics; Chemistry; Biology; Psychology; Sociology and Anthropology; Medicine and Dentistry; Therapy and Counseling; English Language; Philosophy and Theology

Abilities: Fluency of Ideas; Problem Sensitivity; Deductive Reasoning; Inductive Reasoning; Memorization; Speed of Closure; Flexibility of Closure; Perceptual Speed; Selective Attention; Time Sharing; Arm-Hand Steadiness; Manual Dexterity; Finger Dexterity; Control Precision; Response Orientation; Reaction Time; Wrist-Finger Speed; Speed of Limb Movement; Near Vision; Night Vision; Depth Perception; Glare Sensitivity

Police and Detective Supervisors

▲ Growth: -1%

▲ Annual Job Openings: 1,203

▲ Yearly Earnings $44,928

▲ Education Required: Work experience in a related occupation

▲ Self-employed: 0%

▲ Part-time: 0%

Police and Detective Supervisors

Supervise and coordinate activities of members of police force. Prepares work schedules, assigns duties, and develops and revises departmental procedures. Supervises and coordinates investigation of criminal cases. Monitors and evaluates job performance of subordinates. Disciplines staff for violation of department rules and regulations. Directs collection, preparation, and handling of evidence and personal property of prisoners. Assists subordinates in performing job duties. Investigates and resolves personnel problems within organization. Investigates charges of misconduct against staff. Prepares reports and directs preparation, handling, and maintenance of departmental records. Trains staff. Prepares budgets and manages expenditures of department funds. Inspects facilities, supplies, vehicles, and equipment to ensure conformance to standards. Requisitions and issues department equipment and supplies. Directs release or transfer of prisoners. Reviews contents of written orders to ensure adherence to legal requirements. Prepares news releases and responds to police correspondence. Cooperates with court personnel and officials from other law enforcement agencies, and testifies in court. Conducts raids and orders detention of witnesses and suspects for questioning. Meets with civic, educational, and community groups to develop community programs and events, and addresses groups concerning law enforcement subjects.

Knowledge: Administration and Management; Clerical; Economics and Accounting; Sales and Marketing; Customer and Personal Service; Personnel and Human Resources; Psychology; Sociology and Anthropology; Geography; Medicine and Dentistry; Therapy and Counseling; Education and Training; English Language; Foreign Language; Philosophy and Theology; Public Safety and Security; Law, Government, and Jurisprudence; Telecommunications; Communications and Media; Transportation

Abilities: Oral Comprehension; Written Comprehension; Oral Expression; Written Expression; Fluency of Ideas; Originality; Problem Sensitivity; Deductive Reasoning; Inductive Reasoning; Information Ordering; Category Flexibility; Mathematical Reasoning; Number Facility; Memorization; Speed of Closure; Flexibility of Closure; Spatial Orientation; Visualization; Selective Attention; Time Sharing; Multilimb Coordination; Response Orientation; Rate Control; Reaction Time; Wrist-Finger Speed; Speed of Limb Movement; Static Strength; Explosive Strength; Dynamic Strength; Trunk Strength; Stamina; Extent

Flexibility; Gross Body Coordination; Gross Body Equilibrium; Near Vision; Far Vision; Night Vision; Peripheral Vision; Depth Perception; Hearing Sensitivity; Auditory Attention; Sound Localization; Speech Recognition; Speech Clarity

Police Detectives

▲ Growth: 8%

▲ Annual Job Openings: 3,216

▲ Yearly Earnings $41,267

▲ Education Required: Work experience in a related occupation

▲ Self-employed: 0%

▲ Part-time: 1%

Polygraph Examiners

Interrogate and screen individuals to detect deception, using polygraph equipment. Interrogates individual and interprets, diagnoses, and evaluates individual's emotional responses and other reactions to questions posed. Attaches apparatus to individual's skin to measure and record changes in respiration, blood pressure, and perspiration. Prepares reports and keeps records of examinations. Conducts investigation, when assigned to criminal case, to gather information for use in interrogation. Testifies in court on matters relating to polygraph examinations. Teaches classes on interrogation techniques, methods, and uses.

Knowledge: Biology; Psychology; Education and Training; Law, Government, and Jurisprudence

Abilities: Oral Expression; Inductive Reasoning; Speed of Closure; Flexibility of Closure

Police Detectives

Conduct investigations to prevent crimes or to solve criminal cases. Examines scene of crime to obtain clues and gather evidence. Interviews complainant, witnesses, and accused persons to obtain facts or statements; and records interviews, using recording device. Investigates establishments or persons to establish facts supporting complainant or accused, using supportive information from witnesses or tangible evidence. Maintains surveillance of establishments to attain identifying information on suspects. Arrests or assists in arrest of criminals or suspects. Records progress of investigation, maintains informational files on suspects, and submits reports to commanding officer or magistrate to authorize warrants. Observes and photographs narcotics purchase transaction to compile evidence and protect undercover investigators. Reviews governmental agency files to obtain identifying data pertaining to suspects or establishments suspected of violating anti-vice laws. Prepares assigned cases for court and charges or responses to charges, according to formalized procedures. Compiles identifying information on suspects charged with selling narcotics. Examines prescriptions in pharmacies and physicians' records to ascertain legality of sale and distribution of narcotics, and determines drug stock. Testifies before court and grand jury and appears in court as witness. Schedules polygraph test for consenting parties, and records results of test interpretations for presentation with findings. Selects undercover officer best suited to contact suspect and purchase narcotics. Obtains police funds required to make purchase.

Knowledge: Clerical; Psychology; Sociology and Anthropology; Geography; Foreign Language; Public Safety and Security; Law, Government, and Jurisprudence; Telecommunications

Abilities: Oral Comprehension; Deductive Reasoning; Inductive Reasoning; Speed of Closure; Flexibility of Closure; Selective Attention; Reaction Time; Explosive Strength; Gross Body Coordination; Gross Body Equilibrium; Night Vision; Peripheral Vision; Glare Sensitivity; Auditory Attention; Sound Localization

Police Identification and Records Officers

Collect evidence at crime scene, classify and identify fingerprints, and photograph evidence for use in criminal and civil cases. Dusts selected areas of crime scene to locate and reveal latent fingerprints. Lifts prints from crime site, using special tape. Photographs crime or accident scene to obtain record of evidence. Photographs, records physical description, and fingerprints homicide victims and suspects for identification. Classifies and files fingerprints. Develops film and prints, using photographic developing equipment. Submits evidence to supervisor.

Knowledge: Clerical; Chemistry; Public Safety and Security; Law, Government, and Jurisprudence

Abilities: Category Flexibility

Criminal Investigators and Special Agents

Investigate alleged or suspected criminal violations of federal, state, or local laws to determine if evidence is sufficient to recommend prosecution. Obtains and verifies evidence or establishes facts by interviewing, observing, and interrogating suspects and witnesses and analyzing records. Analyzes charge, complaint, or allegation of law violation to identify issues involved and types of evidence needed. Assists in determining scope, timing, and direction of investigation. Examines records to detect links in chain of evidence or information. Searches for evidence, dusts surfaces to reveal latent fingerprints, and records evidence and documents, using cameras and investigative equipment. Obtains and uses search and arrest warrants. Vacuums site to collect physical evidence, and submits evidence to supervisor for verification. Compares crime scene fingerprints with those of suspect or with fingerprint files to identify perpetrator, using computer. Develops and uses informants to get leads to information. Maintains surveillance and performs undercover assignments. Lifts print on tape and transfers print to permanent record card. Presents findings in reports. Reports critical information to and coordinates activities with other offices or agencies when applicable. Prepares and photographs plastic moulage of footprints and tire tracks. Photographs, fingerprints, and measures height and weight of arrested suspect, noting physical characteristics, and posts data on record for filing. Manipulates mask mirror on specialized equipment to prepare montage of suspect according to description from witnesses. Serves subpoenas or other official papers. Testifies before grand juries. Fingerprints applicant for employment or federal clearance, and forwards prints to other law enforcement agencies.

Knowledge: Psychology; Sociology and Anthropology; Geography; Philosophy and Theology; Public Safety and Security; Law, Government, and Jurisprudence; Telecommunications

Abilities: Oral Expression; Written Expression; Fluency of Ideas; Inductive Reasoning; Memorization; Flexibility of Closure; Perceptual Speed; Selective Attention; Near Vision; Far Vision; Night Vision; Peripheral Vision; Glare Sensitivity; Sound Localization; Speech Recognition; Speech Clarity

Police Patrol Officers

▲ Growth: 18%

▲ Annual Job Openings: 22,701

▲ Yearly Earnings $35,484

▲ Education Required: Long-term O-J-T

▲ Self-employed: 0%

▲ Part-time: 1%

Police Investigators—Patrollers

Patrol assigned area to enforce laws and ordinances, regulate traffic, control crowds, prevent crime, and arrest violators. Patrols specific area on foot, horseback, or motorized conveyance. Maintains order, responds to emergencies, protects people and property, and enforces motor vehicle and criminal laws. Arrests perpetrators of criminal acts or submits citations or warnings to violators of motor vehicle ordinances. Monitors traffic to ensure motorists observe traffic regulations and exhibit safe driving procedures. Directs traffic flow and reroutes traffic in case of emergencies. Reviews facts to determine if criminal act or statute violation is involved. Evaluates complaint and emergency-request information to determine response requirements. Investigates traffic accidents and other accidents to determine causes and to determine if crime has been committed. Provides road information to assist motorists. Relays complaint and emergency-request information to appropriate agency dispatcher. Records facts, photographs and diagrams crime or accident scene, and interviews principal and eye witnesses. Expedites processing of prisoners, and prepares and maintains records of prisoner bookings and prisoner status during booking and pretrial process. Testifies in court to present evidence or to act as witness in traffic and criminal cases. Prepares reports to document activities. Renders aid to accident victims and other persons requiring first aid for physical injuries.

Knowledge: Clerical; Customer and Personal Service; Psychology; Sociology and Anthropology; Geography; Medicine and Dentistry; Therapy and Counseling; Foreign Language; Philosophy and Theology; Public Safety and Security; Law, Government, and Jurisprudence; Telecommunications; Transportation

Abilities: Oral Comprehension; Oral Expression; Written Expression; Fluency of Ideas; Originality; Problem Sensitivity; Deductive Reasoning; Inductive Reasoning; Memorization; Speed of Closure; Flexibility of Closure; Perceptual Speed; Spatial Orientation; Selective Attention; Time Sharing; Multilimb Coordination; Response Orientation; Rate Control; Reaction Time; Speed of Limb Movement; Static Strength; Explosive Strength; Dynamic Strength; Stamina; Dynamic Flexibility; Gross Body Coordination; Gross Body Equilibrium; Far Vision; Visual Color Discrimination; Night Vision; Peripheral Vision; Depth Perception; Glare Sensitivity; Hearing Sensitivity; Sound Localization; Speech Recognition; Speech Clarity

Highway Patrol Pilots

Pilot aircraft to patrol highway and enforce traffic laws. Pilots airplane to maintain order, respond to emergencies, enforce traffic and criminal laws, and apprehend criminals. Informs ground personnel of traffic congestion or unsafe driving conditions to ensure traffic flow and reduce incidence of accidents. Informs ground personnel where to reroute traffic in case of emergencies. Arrests perpetrator of criminal act or submits citation or warning to violator of motor vehicle ordinance. Investigates traffic accidents and other accidents to determine causes and to determine if crime was committed. Reviews facts to determine if criminal act or statute violation is involved. Records facts, photographs and diagrams crime or accident scene, and interviews witnesses to gather information for possible use in legal action or safety programs. Testifies in court to present evidence or to act as witness in traffic and criminal cases. Renders aid to accident victims and other persons requiring first aid for physical injuries. Evaluates complaint and emergency-request information to determine response requirements. Relays complaint and emergency-request information to appropriate agency dispatcher. Prepares reports to document activities. Expedites processing of prisoners, prepares and maintains records of prisoner bookings, and maintains record of prisoner status during booking and pretrial process. Contacts health and social agencies to refer persons for assistance.

Knowledge: Customer and Personal Service; Psychology; Sociology and Anthropology; Geography; Medicine and Dentistry; Therapy and Counseling; Foreign Language; Philosophy and Theology; Public Safety and Security; Law, Government, and Jurisprudence; Telecommunications; Transportation

Abilities: Oral Expression; Fluency of Ideas; Problem Sensitivity; Deductive Reasoning; Inductive Reasoning; Information Ordering; Category Flexibility; Memorization; Speed of Closure; Flexibility of Closure; Perceptual Speed; Spatial Orientation; Selective Attention; Time Sharing; Control Precision; Multilimb Coordination; Response Orientation; Rate Control; Reaction Time; Wrist-Finger Speed; Speed of Limb Movement; Static Strength; Explosive Strength; Dynamic Strength; Trunk Strength; Extent Flexibility; Dynamic Flexibility; Gross

Body Coordination; Gross Body Equilibrium; Near Vision; Far Vision; Night Vision; Peripheral Vision; Depth Perception; Glare Sensitivity; Hearing Sensitivity; Auditory Attention; Sound Localization; Speech Recognition; Speech Clarity

Postal Mail Carriers

- ▲ Growth: 11%
- ▲ Annual Job Openings: 6,160
- ▲ Yearly Earnings $28,371
- ▲ Education Required: Short-term O-J-T
- ▲ Self-employed: 0%
- ▲ Part-time: 8%

Postal Mail Carriers

Sort mail for delivery. Deliver mail on established route by vehicle or on foot. Inserts mail into slots of mail rack to sort mail for delivery. Delivers mail to residences and business establishments along route. Drives vehicle over established route. Completes delivery forms, collects charges, and obtains signatures on receipts for delivery of specified types of mail. Enters changes of address in route book and readdresses mail to be forwarded. Picks up outgoing mail. Sells stamps and issues money orders.

Knowledge: Geography; Transportation

Abilities: Spatial Orientation

Power Distributors and Dispatchers

- ▲ Growth: -4%
- ▲ Annual Job Openings: 756
- ▲ Yearly Earnings $45,905
- ▲ Education Required: Long-term O-J-T
- ▲ Self-employed: 0%
- ▲ Part-time: 1%

Power Distributors and Dispatchers

Coordinate, regulate, or distribute electricity or steam in generating stations and substations, and over electric power lines. May work for utility company or in a large industrial establishment. May spend some time generating power. Controls and operates equipment to regulate or distribute electricity or steam, according to data provided by recording or indicating instruments or computers. Adjusts controls to regulate the flow of power between generating stations, substations, and distribution lines. Turns and moves controls to adjust and activate power distribution equipment and machines. Calculates and

Best Jobs for the 21st Century™ © 1999, JIST Works, Inc., Indianapolis, IN

determines load estimates or equipment requirements to control electrical distribution equipment or stations. Monitors switchboard and control board to ensure equipment operation and electrical and steam distribution. Directs activities of personnel engaged in the controlling and operating of electrical distribution equipment and machinery. Compiles and records operational data, such as chart and meter readings, power demands, and usage and operating times. Tends auxiliary equipment used in the power distribution process. Notifies workers or utilities of electrical and steam distribution process changes. Inspects equipment to ensure specifications are met and to detect defects. Repairs, maintains, and cleans equipment and machines, using hand tools.

Knowledge: Mechanical; Physics

Abilities: Perceptual Speed; Selective Attention; Time Sharing; Response Orientation; Reaction Time; Gross Body Equilibrium; Far Vision; Hearing Sensitivity; Auditory Attention; Sound Localization

Preschool and Kindergarten Teachers

- ▲ Growth: 20%
- ▲ Annual Job Openings: 77,151
- ▲ Yearly Earnings $30,180
- ▲ Education Required: Bachelor's degree
- ▲ Self-employed: 1%
- ▲ Part-time: 32%

Teachers—Preschool

Instruct children (normally up to 5 years of age) in activities designed to promote social, physical, and intellectual growth needed for primary school in preschool, daycare center, or other child development facility. May be required to hold state certification. Instructs children in activities designed to promote social, physical, and intellectual growth in a facility such as preschool or daycare center. Plans individual and group activities for children, such as learning to listen to instructions, playing with others, and using play equipment. Demonstrates activity. Structures play activities to instill concepts of respect and concern for others. Monitors individual and/or group activities to prevent accidents and promote social skills. Reads books to entire class or to small groups. Confers with parents to explain preschool program and to discuss ways they can develop their child's interest. Plans instructional activities for teacher aide. Administers tests to determine each child's level of development according to design of test. Attends staff meetings.

Knowledge: Customer and Personal Service; Psychology; Sociology and Anthropology; Therapy and Counseling; Education and Training; Foreign Language; Fine Arts; History and Archeology; Philosophy and Theology

Abilities: Fluency of Ideas; Originality; Memorization; Time Sharing; Far Vision; Peripheral Vision; Speech Recognition

Teachers—Kindergarten

Teach elemental natural and social science, personal hygiene, music, art, and literature to children from 4 to 6 years old. Promote physical, mental, and social development. May be required to hold state certification. Teaches elemental science, personal hygiene, and humanities to children to promote physical, mental, and social development. Supervises student activities, such as field visits, to stimulate student interest and broaden understanding of physical and social environment. Organizes and conducts games and group projects to develop cooperative behavior and assist children in forming satisfying relationships. Encourages students in activities, such as singing, dancing, and rhythmic activities, to promote self- expression and appreciation of aesthetic experience. Instructs children in practices of personal cleanliness and self-care. Observes children to detect signs of ill health or emotional disturbance, and to evaluate progress. Discusses student problems and progress with parents. Alternates periods of strenuous activity with periods of rest or light activity to avoid overstimulation and fatigue.

Knowledge: Customer and Personal Service; Psychology; Sociology and Anthropology; Geography; Medicine and Dentistry; Therapy and Counseling; Education and Training; English Language; Foreign Language; Fine Arts; History and Archeology; Philosophy and Theology; Law, Government, and Jurisprudence; Communications and Media

Abilities: Fluency of Ideas; Originality; Problem Sensitivity; Deductive Reasoning; Category Flexibility; Memorization; Speed of Closure; Flexibility of Closure; Spatial Orientation; Selective Attention; Time Sharing; Far Vision; Night Vision; Peripheral Vision; Hearing Sensitivity; Auditory Attention; Sound Localization; Speech Recognition; Speech Clarity

Printing Related Setters and Operators

▲ Growth: 14%

▲ Annual Job Openings: 1,499

▲ Yearly Earnings $25,313

▲ Education Required: Moderate-term O-J-T

▲ Self-employed: 0%

▲ Part-time: 3%

Offset Lithographic Press Setters and Set-up Operators

Set up or set up and operate offset printing press, either sheet or web fed, to print single and multicolor copy from lithographic plates. Examine job order to determine press operating time, quantity to be printed, and stock specifications. Examines job order to determine quantity to be printed, stock specifications, colors, and special printing instructions. Starts press and examines printed copy for ink density, position on paper, and registration. Makes adjustments to press throughout production run to maintain specific registration and color density. Installs and locks plate into position, using hand tools, to achieve pressure required for printing. Measures paper thickness and adjusts space between blanket and impression cylinders according to thickness of paper stock. Measures plate thickness and inserts packing sheets on plate cylinder to build up plate to printing height. Washes plate to remove protective gum coating. Fills ink and dampening solution fountains, and adjusts controls to regulate flow of ink and dampening solution to plate cylinder. Applies packing sheets to blanket cylinder to build up blanket thickness to diameter of plate cylinder. Loads paper into feeder or installs rolls of paper, adjusts feeder and delivery mechanisms, and unloads printed material from delivery mechanism. Removes and cleans plate and cylinders.

Knowledge: Production and Processing; Mechanical

Abilities: None above average

Letterpress Setters and Set-up Operators

Set up or set up and operate direct relief letterpresses, either sheet or roll (web) fed, to produce single or multicolor printed material, such as newspapers, books, and periodicals. Moves controls to set or adjust ink flow, tension rollers, paper guides, and feed controls. Positions and installs printing plates, cylinder packing, die, and type forms in press, according to specifications, using hand tools. Loads, positions, and adjusts unprinted materials on holding fixtures or in feeding mechanism of press. Pushes buttons or moves controls to start printing press and control operation. Monitors feeding and printing operations to maintain specified operating levels and detect malfunctions. Mixes colors or inks and fills reservoirs. Dismantles and reassembles printing unit or parts, using hand tools, to repair, clean, maintain, or adjust press. Operates specially-equipped presses and auxiliary equipment, such as cutting, folding, numbering, and pasting devices. Reads work orders and job specifications to select ink and paper stock. Inspects printed materials for irregularities such as off-level areas, variations in ink volume, register slippage, and poor color register. Record and maintain production logsheet. Directs and monitors activities of apprentices and feeding or stacking workers.

Knowledge: None above average

Abilities: Perceptual Speed; Visual Color Discrimination

Screen Printing Machine Setters and Set-up Operators

Set up or set up and operate screen printing machines to print designs onto articles and materials, such as glass or plasticware, cloth, and paper. Sets and adjusts screws, belts, drive assemblies, pneumatic lifting mechanisms, and bolts on screen printing machine to specifications. Starts dyeing oven and sets thermostat to temperature specified for printing run. Reviews print order to determine settings and adjustments required to set up manually controlled or automatic screen printing machine or decorating equipment. Measures, aligns and positions screen and squeegee attachment, using gauge and hand tools. Determines from orders type and color of designs to print. Mixes paints according to formula, using bench mixer. Examines product for paint smears, position of design, or other defects and adjusts equipment. Compares ink or paint prepared for printing run with master color swatch to confirm accuracy of match. Inspects printing equipment and replaces damaged or defective parts, such as switches, pulleys, fixtures, screws, and bolts. Patrols printing area to monitor production activities and to detect problems, such as mechanical breakdowns or malfunctions. Counts and records quantities printed in production log. Trains workers in use of printing equipment and in quality standards.

Knowledge: Production and Processing; Mechanical; Education and Training; Fine Arts

Abilities: None above average

Embossing Machine Set-Up Operators

Set up and operate embossing machines. Sets guides to hold cover in position and adjusts table height to obtain correct depth of impression. Starts machine to lower ram and impress cardboard. Stamps embossing design on workpiece, using heated work tools. Positions, installs, and locks embossed plate in chase and locks chase in bed of press. Makes impression of embossing to desired depth in composition on platen, trims off excess, and allows composition to harden. Sets sheets singly in gauge pins and starts press. Mixes embossing composition to putty-like consistency, spreads glue on platen, and applies thin pad of composition over glue. Scrapes high spots on counter die to prevent from puncturing paper. Cuts surface of cardboard leaving design or letters, using hand tools. Removes and stacks embossed covers.

Knowledge: Production and Processing

Abilities: None above average

Casting Machine Set-Up Operators

Set up and operate machines to cast and assemble printing type. Sets up matrices in assembly stick by hand according to specifications. Starts machine and monitors operation for proper functioning. Stops machine when galley is full or when strip is completed. Positions composing stick to length of line specified in casting instructions. Inserts and locks galley or matrix case into place on machine. Places reel of controller paper on holder, threads around reels, and attaches to winding roll. Removes and stores assembly stick, controller reel, and matrix case. Forwards galley to appropriate personnel for proofing.

Knowledge: None above average

Abilities: Manual Dexterity

Plate Finishers

Set up and operate equipment to trim and mount electrotype or stereotype plates. Selects cutting position and sets controls of saws, milling machines, and routers following specifications. Operates cutting tools to shave and smooth plates to specified thickness. Operates plate-curving machine to cut plates to fit printing press. Mounts finished plates on wood or metal blocks, using hammer and nails or thermoplastic adhesive and heat press. Operates press to print proof of plate, observing printing quality. Rubs surface with finishing material to reveal unevenness. Taps plate with hammer and block to flatten until even. Examines plates with magnifier or microscope to detect flaws, using engraver's tools.

Knowledge: Production and Processing

Abilities: Rate Control; Reaction Time; Explosive Strength; Dynamic Strength

Private Detectives

- ▲ Growth: 19%
- ▲ Annual Job Openings: 17,441
- ▲ Yearly Earnings $24,648
- ▲ Education Required: Moderate-term O-J-T
- ▲ Self-employed: 17%
- ▲ Part-time: 19%

Detectives and Investigators, Except Public

Protect property, merchandise, and money of store or similar establishment by detecting theft, shoplifting, or other unlawful practices by public or employees. Perform necessary action to preserve order and enforce standards of decorum established by management. Include investigators who conduct private investigations, such as obtaining confidential information, seeking missing persons, or investigating crimes and thefts. Enforces conformance to establishment rules and protects persons or property. Observes employees or customers and patrols premises to detect violations and obtain evidence, using binoculars, cameras, and television. Questions persons to obtain evidence for cases of divorce, child custody, or missing persons, or individuals' character or financial status. Examines crime scene for clues or fingerprints, and submits evidence to laboratory for analysis. Warns and ejects troublemakers from premises, and apprehends and releases suspects to authorities or security personnel. Obtains and analyzes information on suspects, crimes, and disturbances to solve cases, identify criminal activity, and maintain public peace and order. Counts cash and reviews transactions, sales checks, and register tapes to verify amount of cash and shortages. Confers with establishment officials, security department, police, or postal officials to identify problems, provide information, and receive instructions. Alerts staff and superiors of presence of suspect in establishment. Writes reports and case summaries to document investigations or inform supervisors. Testifies at hearings and court trials to present evidence. Locates persons using phone or mail directories to collect money owed or to serve legal papers. Evaluates performance and honesty of employees by posing as customer or employee and comparing employee to standards. Assists victims, police, fire department, and others during emergencies.

Knowledge: Psychology; Therapy and Counseling; Public Safety and Security; Law, Government, and Jurisprudence; Telecommunications

Abilities: Fluency of Ideas; Originality; Inductive Reasoning; Speed of Closure; Flexibility of Closure; Selective Attention; Time Sharing; Response Orientation; Rate Control; Reaction Time; Speed of Limb Movement; Explosive Strength; Stamina; Gross Body Coordination; Gross Body Equilibrium; Far Vision; Night Vision; Peripheral Vision; Auditory Attention; Sound Localization; Speech Recognition

Private Household Child Care Workers

- ▲ Growth: -9%
- ▲ Annual Job Openings: 146,546
- ▲ Yearly Earnings $13,998
- ▲ Education Required: Short-term O-J-T
- ▲ Self-employed: 0%
- ▲ Part-time: 51%

Child Monitors, Private Household

Attend to and care for children in private home. Observes and monitors play activities of children. Prepares and serves meals or formulas. Dresses or assists children to dress and bathe. Entertains children by reading to or playing games with them. Accompanies children on walks and other outings. Keeps children's quarters clean and washes clothing.

Knowledge: Customer and Personal Service; Psychology

Abilities: None above average

Producers, Directors, Actors, and Entertainers

▲ Growth: 24%
▲ Annual Job Openings: 17,112
▲ Yearly Earnings $35,339
▲ Education Required: Long-term O-J-T
▲ Self-employed: 27%
▲ Part-time: 25%

Announcers, Except Radio and Television

Announce information to patrons of sporting and other entertainment events using public address system. Announces program and substitutions or other changes to patrons. Informs patrons of coming events or emergency calls. Observes event to provide running commentary of activities, such as play-by-play description, or explanation of official decisions. Speaks extemporaneously to audience on items of interest, such as background and history of event or past record of participants. Reads prepared script to describe acts or tricks during performance. Furnishes information concerning play to scoreboard operator. Provides information about event to cue operation of scoreboard or control board.

Knowledge: Communications and Media

Abilities: Selective Attention; Time Sharing; Far Vision; Night Vision; Peripheral Vision; Glare Sensitivity; Auditory Attention; Speech Recognition; Speech Clarity

Film Editors

Edit motion picture film and sound tracks. Edits film and video tape to insert music, dialogue, and sound effects, and to correct errors, using editing equipment. Trims film segments to specified lengths and reassembles segments in sequence that presents story with maximum effect. Reviews assembled film or edited video tape on screen or monitor and makes corrections. Evaluates and selects scenes in terms of dramatic and entertainment value and story continuity. Studies script and confers with producers and directors concerning layout or editing to increase dramatic or entertainment value of production. Supervises and coordinates activities of workers engaged in editing and assembling filmed scenes photographed by others. Operates studio or portable, shoulder-mounted camera.

Knowledge: Computers and Electronics; English Language; Fine Arts; Telecommunications; Communications and Media

Abilities: Fluency of Ideas; Originality; Information Ordering; Category Flexibility; Speed of Closure; Perceptual Speed; Visualization; Time Sharing; Rate Control; Gross Body Equilibrium; Far Vision; Visual Color Discrimination; Night Vision; Peripheral Vision; Glare Sensitivity; Hearing Sensitivity; Auditory Attention; Sound Localization; Speech Recognition

P

Actors and Performers

Perform dramatic roles, comedic routines, or tricks of illusion to entertain audiences.
Portrays and interprets role, using speech, gestures, and body movements, to entertain radio, film, television, or live audience. Performs original and stock tricks of illusion to entertain and mystify audience, occasionally including audience members as participants. Tells jokes, performs comic dances and songs, impersonates mannerisms and voices of others, contorts face, and uses other devices to amuse audience. Performs humorous and serious interpretations of emotions, actions, and situations, using only body movements, facial expressions, and gestures. Reads and rehearses role from script to learn lines, stunts, and cues as directed. Reads from script or book to narrate action, inform, or entertain audience, utilizing few or no stage props. Dresses in comical clown costume and make-up and performs comedy routines to entertain audience. Prepares for and performs action stunts for motion picture, television, or stage production. Sings or dances during dramatic or comedy performance. Manipulates string, wire, rod, or fingers to animate puppet or dummy in synchronization to talking, singing, or recorded program. Signals start and introduces performers to stimulate excitement and to coordinate smooth transition of acts during circus performance. Writes original or adapted material for drama, comedy, puppet show, narration, or other performance. Constructs puppets and ventriloquist dummies, and sews accessory clothing, using hand tools and machines. Designs, builds, and repairs equipment for stunts.

Knowledge: Fine Arts; Communications and Media

Abilities: Originality; Memorization; Spatial Orientation; Reaction Time; Speed of Limb Movement; Dynamic Flexibility; Gross Body Coordination; Gross Body Equilibrium; Near Vision; Speech Clarity

Extras/Stand-Ins

Perform as nonspeaking member of scene in stage, motion picture, or television productions. Performs as nonspeaking member of scene in stage, motion picture, or television production. Portrays image and imitates gestures and mannerisms of star performer in motion picture or television performance. Parades across stage to display costumes and provide background for chorus line in stage or film production. Substitutes for star performer to determine desired angle, lighting effects, and background prior to actual filming. Dresses in costume of star performer to perform roles or act as photographic double. Performs activities that require special skills, such as dancing, swimming, skating, handling livestock, or riding. Rehearses and performs pantomime, portraying points essential in staging of scenes.

Knowledge: Fine Arts

Abilities: Speed of Limb Movement; Explosive Strength; Dynamic Flexibility; Gross Body Coordination; Gross Body Equilibrium

Amusement Entertainers

Entertain audiences by exhibiting special skills, such as juggling, diving, swimming, acrobatics, or by performing daredevil feats. Performs daredevil feats, such as being shot from cannon, parachuting from airplane, or diving from platform, at carnivals, fairs, and circuses. Juggles and balances objects, such as balls, knives, plates, tenpins, and hats, to entertain audience. Performs synchronized swimming, water-ballet, and underwater swimming routines to entertain audience. Performs specialty act, such as fire eating, sword swallowing, or snake charming, in sideshow or amusement park. Hypnotizes others to entertain audience at nightclub, live variety show, television, or other venue. Dives to bottom of fish tank in diving suit to feed, describe, and identify fish to inform and entertain audience. Sells tickets or performs other duties when not performing for audience. Cleans fish tank bottom and windows, using suction hose and scrubbing brush. Observes, reports, and treats diseased fish in tank during underwater activity.

Knowledge: None above average

Abilities. Spatial Orientation; Multilimb Coordination; Rate Control; Wrist-Finger Speed; Speed of Limb Movement; Explosive Strength; Dynamic Strength; Trunk Strength; Stamina; Extent Flexibility; Dynamic Flexibility; Gross Body Coordination; Gross Body Equilibrium; Peripheral Vision; Depth Perception

Equestrian Performers

Ride horses at circus, carnival, exhibition, or rodeo, performing feats of equestrian skills and daring to entertain audiences. Performs acrobatic stunts on horseback to entertain audience at circus, exhibition, or horse show. Demonstrates skill in bronco riding, calf roping, steer wrestling, or other rodeo events to entertain and compete for prize money. Rides bareback to perform feats of skill and daring. Rides or leads horse at horse show to display best points of animal before judges and audience.

Knowledge: None above average

Abilities: Spatial Orientation; Multilimb Coordination; Response Orientation; Rate Control; Reaction Time; Speed of Limb Movement; Static Strength; Explosive Strength; Dynamic Strength; Trunk Strength; Stamina; Extent Flexibility; Dynamic Flexibility; Gross Body Coordination; Gross Body Equilibrium; Peripheral Vision; Depth Perception

Producers

Plan and coordinate various aspects of radio, television, stage, or motion picture production, such as selecting script, coordinating writing, directing, and editing; and arranging financing. Coordinates various aspects of production, such as audio and camera work, music, timing, writing, and staging. Conducts meetings with staff to discuss production progress and to ensure production objectives are attained. Selects and hires cast and staff members and arbitrates personnel disputes. Directs activities of one or more departments of motion picture studio and prepares rehearsal call sheets and reports of activities and operating costs. Reviews film, recordings, or rehearsals to ensure conformance to production and broadcast standards. Produces shows for special occasions, such as holiday or testimonial. Composes and edits script, or outlines story for screenwriter to write script. Obtains and distributes costumes, props, music, and studio equipment to complete production. Establishes management policies, production schedules, and operating budgets for production. Distributes rehearsal call sheets and copies of script, arranges for rehearsal quarters, and contacts cast members to verify readiness for rehearsal. Times scene and calculates program timing. Reads manuscript and selects play for stage performance. Selects scenes from taped program to be used for promotional purposes. Represents network or company in negotiations with independent producers.

Knowledge: Administration and Management; Economics and Accounting; Personnel and Human Resources; English Language; Fine Arts; Communications and Media

Abilities: Oral Comprehension; Written Comprehension; Oral Expression; Written Expression; Fluency of Ideas; Originality; Problem Sensitivity; Information Ordering; Memorization; Time Sharing; Speech Recognition; Speech Clarity

Directors—Stage, Motion Picture, Television, and Radio

Interpret script, conduct rehearsals, and direct activities of cast and technical crew for stage, motion picture, television, or radio programs. Reads and rehearses cast to develop performance based on script interpretations. Directs cast, crew, and technicians during production or recording and filming in studio or on location. Directs live broadcasts, films and recordings, or nonbroadcast programming for public entertainment or education. Confers with technical directors, managers, and writers to discuss details of production, such as photography, script, music, sets, and costumes. Establishes pace of program and sequences of scenes according to time requirements and cast and set accessibility. Coaches performers in acting techniques to develop and improve performance and image. Approves equipment and elements required for production, such as scenery, lights, props, costumes, choreography, and music. Interprets stage-set diagrams to determine stage layout, and supervises placement of equipment and scenery. Auditions and selects cast and technical staff. Compiles cue words and phrases and cues announcers, cast members, and technicians during performances. Cuts and edits film or tape to integrate component parts of film into desired sequence. Writes and compiles letters, memos, notes, scripts, and other program material, using computer. Reviews educational material to gather information for scripts. Coordinates animal performances at amusement park to educate visitors.

Knowledge: Administration and Management; Fine Arts; Communications and Media

Abilities: Oral Expression; Fluency of Ideas; Originality; Category Flexibility; Memorization; Speed of Closure; Visualization; Selective Attention; Time Sharing; Gross Body Equilibrium; Far Vision; Auditory Attention; Sound Localization; Speech Clarity

Program Directors

Direct and coordinate activities of personnel engaged in preparation of radio or television station program schedules and programs, such as sports or news. Directs and coordinates activities of personnel engaged in broadcast news, sports, or programming. Plans and schedules programming and event coverage based on length of broadcast and available station or network time. Evaluates length, content, and suitability of programs for broadcast. Reviews, corrects, and advises member stations concerning programs and schedules. Coordinates activities between departments, such as news and programming. Confers with directors and production staff to discuss issues, such as production and casting problems, budget, policy, and news coverage. Directs set-up of remote facilities and installs or cancels programs at remote stations. Establishes work schedules and hires, assigns, and evaluates staff. Monitors and reviews news and programming copy and film, using audio or video equipment. Originates feature ideas and researches program topics for implementation. Examines expenditures to ensure programming and broadcasting activities are within budget. Writes news copy, notes, letters, and memos, using computer. Arranges for office space and equipment.

Knowledge: Administration and Management; Economics and Accounting; Personnel and Human Resources; Communications and Media

Abilities: Oral Comprehension; Oral Expression; Written Expression; Fluency of Ideas; Originality; Deductive Reasoning; Memorization; Perceptual Speed; Near Vision

Talent Directors

Audition and interview performers to select most appropriate talent for parts in stage, television, radio, or motion picture productions. Auditions and interviews performers to identify most suitable talent for broadcasting, stage, or musical production. Selects performer or submits list of suitable performers to producer or director for final selection. Arranges for screen tests or auditions for new performers. Maintains talent file, including information about personalities, such as specialties, past performances, and availability. Negotiates contract agreements with performers. Directs recording sessions for musical artists. Promotes record sales by personal appearances and contacts with broadcasting personalities.

Knowledge: Administration and Management; Sales and Marketing; Personnel and Human Resources; Fine Arts; Communications and Media

Abilities: Memorization; Hearing Sensitivity

Technical Directors/Managers

Coordinate activities of technical departments, such as taping, editing, engineering, and maintenance, to produce radio or television programs. Coordinates activities of radio or television studio and control-room personnel to ensure technical quality of programs. Supervises and assigns duties to workers engaged in technical control and production of radio and television programs. Observes picture through monitor and directs camera and video staff concerning shading and composition. Coordinates elements of program, such as audio, camera, special effects, timing, and script, to ensure production objectives are met. Schedules use of studio and editing facilities for producers and engineering and maintenance staff. Monitors broadcast to ensure that programs conform with station or network policies and regulations. Directs personnel in auditioning talent and programs. Trains workers in use of equipment, such as switcher, camera, monitor, microphones, and lights. Operates equipment to produce programs or broadcast live programs from remote locations.

Knowledge: Administration and Management; Personnel and Human Resources; Education and Training; Fine Arts; Telecommunications; Communications and Media

Abilities: Memorization; Speed of Closure; Perceptual Speed; Selective Attention; Time Sharing; Reaction Time; Gross Body Equilibrium; Near Vision; Far Vision; Visual Color Discrimination; Hearing Sensitivity; Auditory Attention; Sound Localization

Studio, Stage, and Special Effects Technicians

Install, operate, and maintain special equipment used in stage, television, or motion picture production. Modifies lighting and sound equipment and adjusts controls to achieve desired effects, according to specifications, using hand tools. Installs special effects properties, lighting fixtures, and sound equipment in specified locations in theater, using hand tools and power tools. Connects wiring for light and sound equipment to power source and control panel, using hand tools and power tools. Repairs and maintains equipment, using hand tools and precision instruments, according to preventive maintenance schedule and knowledge of electronics. Constructs and assembles special effects properties, using hand tools, power tools, and materials such as wood, metal, or plastic. Studies blueprint or layout of stage to determine type and placement of equipment needed for specified event. Reads script and confers with production personnel to determine specified effects. Selects and synchronizes music with visual display and other recorded commentary. Directs crew in setting up, arranging, and operating equipment for use in theater.

Knowledge: Computers and Electronics; Design; Building and Construction; Physics; Fine Arts

Abilities: Fluency of Ideas; Originality; Finger Dexterity; Gross Body Equilibrium

Models

Model for photographers or artists, or display merchandise or depict characters. Poses as subject for paintings, sculptures, and other types of art for translation into plastic or pictorial values. Poses as directed or strikes suitable interpretive poses for promoting and selling merchandise or fashions during photo session. Wears character costumes and impersonates characters portrayed to amuse children and adults. Impersonates holiday or storybook characters to promote sales or to entertain at conventions and in stores, hospitals, parks, and private homes. Stands, turns, and walks to demonstrate features of garment to observers at fashion shows, private showings, and retail establishments. Hands out samples or presents, demonstrates toys, and converses with children and adults while dressed in costume. Dresses in sample or completed garments and selects own accessories. Appears in costume parade. Applies make-up to face and styles hair to enhance appearance, considering such factors as color, camera techniques, and facial features. Informs prospective purchasers as to model, number, and price of garments and department where garment can be purchased. Solicits donations on street for charitable purposes.

Knowledge: Sales and Marketing; Sociology and Anthropology; Fine Arts; Communications and Media

Abilities: Gross Body Coordination; Gross Body Equilibrium; Glare Sensitivity

Production Engineers

- ▲ Growth: 14%
- ▲ Annual Job Openings: 19,706
- ▲ Yearly Earnings $54,329
- ▲ Education Required: Bachelor's degree
- ▲ Self-employed: 3%
- ▲ Part-time: 4%

Agricultural Engineers

Apply knowledge of engineering technology and biological science to agricultural problems concerned with power and machinery, electrification, structures, soil and water conservation, and processing of agricultural products. Designs and directs manufacture of equipment for land tillage and fertilization, plant and animal disease and insect control, and for harvesting or moving commodities. Designs and supervises erection of crop storage, animal shelter, and residential structures and heating, lighting, cooling, plumbing, and waste disposal systems. Designs and supervises installation of equipment and instruments used to evaluate and process farm products, and to automate agricultural operations. Develops criteria for design, manufacture, or construction of equipment, structures, and facilities. Plans and directs construction of rural electric-power distribution systems, and irrigation, drainage, and flood control systems for soil and water conservation. Designs sensing, measuring, and recording devices and instrumentation used to study plant or animal life. Studies such problems as effect of temperature, humidity, and light on plants and animals and effectiveness of different insecticides. Conducts research to develop agricultural machinery and equipment. Designs agricultural machinery and equipment. Conducts tests on agricultural machinery and equipment. Conducts radio and television educational programs to provide assistance to farmers, local groups, and related farm cooperatives.

Knowledge: Administration and Management; Economics and Accounting; Production and Processing; Food Production; Computers and Electronics; Engineering and Technology; Design; Building and Construction; Mechanical; Mathematics; Physics; Chemistry; Biology; Sociology and Anthropology; Geography; Education and Training; English Language; Philosophy and Theology; Law, Government, and Jurisprudence; Communications and Media; Transportation

Abilities: Oral Comprehension; Written Comprehension; Written Expression; Fluency of Ideas; Originality; Problem Sensitivity; Deductive Reasoning; Inductive Reasoning; Information Ordering; Category Flexibility; Mathematical Reasoning; Number Facility; Memorization; Speed of Closure; Flexibility of Closure; Visualization; Selective Attention; Time Sharing; Speech Clarity

Industrial Safety and Health Engineers

Plan, implement, and coordinate safety programs to prevent or correct unsafe environmental working conditions. Devises and implements safety or industrial health program to prevent, correct, or control unsafe environmental conditions. Examines plans and specifications for new machinery or equipment to determine if all safety requirements have been included. Conducts or coordinates training of workers concerning safety laws and regulations; use of safety equipment, devices, and clothing; and first aid. Inspects facilities, machinery, and safety equipment to identify and correct potential hazards, and to ensure compliance with safety regulations. Conducts or directs testing of air quality, noise, temperature, or radiation to verify compliance with health and safety regulations. Provides technical guidance to organizations regarding how to handle health-related problems, such as water and air pollution. Compiles, analyzes, and interprets statistical data related to exposure factors concerning occupational illnesses and accidents. Installs or directs installation of safety devices on machinery. Investigates causes of industrial accidents or injuries to develop solutions to minimize or prevent recurrence. Conducts plant or area surveys to determine safety levels for exposure to materials and conditions. Checks floors of plant to ensure they are strong enough to support heavy machinery. Designs and builds safety devices for machinery or safety clothing. Prepares reports of findings from investigation of accidents, inspection of facilities, or testing of environment. Maintains liaison with outside organizations, such as fire departments, mutual aid societies, and rescue teams.

Knowledge: Administration and Management; Engineering and Technology; Design; Building and Construction; Mathematics; Physics; Chemistry; Biology; Education and Training; Public Safety and Security; Law, Government, and Jurisprudence

Abilities: Oral Comprehension; Written Expression; Fluency of Ideas; Problem Sensitivity; Deductive Reasoning; Inductive Reasoning; Category Flexibility; Mathematical Reasoning; Number Facility; Flexibility of Closure

Fire-Prevention and Protection Engineers

Research causes of fires; determine fire protection methods; and design or recommend materials or equipment, such as structural components or fire-detection equipment, to assist organizations in safeguarding life and property against fire, explosion, and related hazards. Determines fire causes and methods of fire prevention. Studies properties concerning fire prevention factors, such as fire-resistance of construction, contents, water supply and delivery, and exits. Recommends and advises on use of fire-detection equipment, extinguishing devices, or methods to alleviate conditions conducive to fire. Conducts research on fire retardants and fire safety of materials and devices to determine cause and methods of fire prevention. Advises and plans for prevention of destruction by fire, wind, water, or other causes of damage. Evaluates fire departments and laws and regulations affecting fire prevention or fire safety. Organizes and trains personnel to carry out fire-protection programs. Designs fire-detection equipment, alarm systems, fire-extinguishing devices and systems, or structural components protection. Teaches courses on fire prevention and protection.

Knowledge: Sales and Marketing; Engineering and Technology; Design; Building and Construction; Physics; Chemistry; Geography; Education and Training; Public Safety and Security; Law, Government, and Jurisprudence; Telecommunications; Communications and Media

Abilities: Deductive Reasoning; Inductive Reasoning; Category Flexibility

Product Safety Engineers

Develop and conduct tests to evaluate product safety levels, and recommend measures to reduce or eliminate hazards. Conducts research to evaluate safety levels for products. Evaluates potential health hazards or damage which could occur from misuse of product, and engineers solutions to improve safety. Investigates causes of accidents, injuries, or illnesses from product usage to develop solutions to minimize or prevent recurrence. Advises and recommends procedures for detection, prevention, and elimination of physical, chemical, or other product hazards. Participates in preparation of product usage and precautionary label instructions. Prepares reports of findings from investigation of accidents.

Knowledge: Production and Processing; Engineering and Technology; Physics; Chemistry; Biology; English Language; Public Safety and Security

Abilities: Written Expression; Fluency of Ideas; Problem Sensitivity; Deductive Reasoning; Inductive Reasoning; Category Flexibility

Marine Engineers

Design, develop, and take responsibility for the installation of ship machinery and related equipment, including propulsion machines and power supply systems. Exclude marine architects. Designs and oversees testing, installation, and repair of marine apparatus and equipment. Conducts analytical, environmental, operational, or performance studies to develop design for products, such as marine engines, equipment, and structures. Prepares or directs preparation of product or system layout and detailed drawings and schematics. Evaluates operation of marine equipment during acceptance testing and shakedown cruises. Analyzes data to determine feasibility of product proposal. Directs and coordinates manufacturing or building of prototype marine product or system. Confers with research personnel to clarify or resolve problems and develop or modify design. Investigates and observes tests on machinery and equipment for compliance with standards. Conducts environmental, operational, or performance tests on marine machinery and equipment. Plans, conducts, or directs personnel in performing engineering experiments to test or prove theories and principles. Determines conditions under which tests are to be conducted and sequences and phases of test operations. Maintains and coordinates repair of marine machinery and equipment for installation on vessels. Inspects marine equipment and machinery to draw up work requests and job specifications. Reviews work requests and compares them with previous work completed on ship to ensure costs are economically sound. Prepares technical reports on types of testing conducted, completed repairs, and cost of repairs for engineering, management, or sales personnel. Prepares technical reports for use by engineering, management, or sales personnel. Maintains contact and formulates reports for contractors and clients to ensure completion of work at minimum cost. Coordinates activities with those of regulatory bodies to ensure repairs and alterations are at minimum cost, consistent with safety. Obtains readings on tail shaft and tail shaft bearings, using measuring devices. Procures materials needed to repair marine equipment and machinery.

Knowledge: Administration and Management; Economics and Accounting; Engineering and Technology; Design; Building and Construction; Mechanical; Mathematics; Physics; Chemistry; Geography; English Language; Public Safety and Security; Law, Government, and Jurisprudence; Transportation

Abilities: Written Comprehension; Written Expression; Fluency of Ideas; Originality; Problem Sensitivity; Deductive Reasoning; Inductive Reasoning; Information Ordering; Number Facility; Memorization; Speed of Closure; Perceptual Speed; Visualization; Selective Attention; Gross Body Equilibrium

Production Engineers

Develop, advance, and improve products, processes, or materials, and build or supervise the building of prototypes. May operate machinery, equipment, or hand tools to produce their prototypes. Conducts research and analytical studies to develop design or specifications for products. Directs and coordinates manufacturing of building of prototype or system. Confers with research and other engineering personnel to clarify and resolve problems, and prepares design modifications as needed. Prepares or directs preparation of product or system layout and detailed drawings and schematics. Analyzes data to determine feasibility of product proposal. Plans and develops experimental test programs. Analyzes test data and reports to determine if design meets functional and performance specifications. Evaluates engineering test results for possible application to development of systems or other uses.

Knowledge: Administration and Management; Production and Processing; Computers and Electronics; Engineering and Technology; Design; Mechanical; Mathematics; Physics; English Language

Abilities: Fluency of Ideas; Originality; Problem Sensitivity; Information Ordering; Mathematical Reasoning; Visualization; Speech Clarity

Property and Real Estate Managers

- ▲ Growth: 16%
- ▲ Annual Job Openings: 29,483
- ▲ Yearly Earnings $33,113
- ▲ Education Required: Bachelor's degree
- ▲ Self-employed: 41%
- ▲ Part-time: 21%

Land Leasing and Development Managers

Plan, direct, and coordinate the acquisition or disposition of land, rights-of-way, or property rights for development, mineral, oil, or gas rights, or other special use through options, purchase, or lease agreements. Makes final decisions regarding sales, leases, and purchases of real property based on evaluation of costs, available resources, and organizational interests. Negotiates terms and conditions of agreements with property owners, public officials, and community representatives, and signs contracts to finalize transactions. Directs and coordinates collection and auditing of funds from sales, purchases, and leases. Directs staff activities, such as preparing appraisal reports and feasibility studies, identifying availability and quality of land, and ascertaining ownership. Administers and interprets general policies made by company officials and ensures conformance to established standards. Studies financial transactions of competing companies or brokers to determine expenditure necessary to obtain leases and other contracts. Prepares statistical abstracts to reveal trends in tax rates and proportion of workforce having specified skills in a given community. Evaluates and promotes industrial-development potential of company properties. Plans and directs field staff activities such as mineral sampling, surveying, and water testing to determine optimal land usage. Coordinates research activities with public utilities, universities, and other groups. Authorizes or requests authorization for maintenance of noncontrolled company properties such as dwellings, hotels, or commissaries. Determines roads, bridges, and utility systems that must be maintained during construction. Settles claims for property or crop damage.

Knowledge: Administration and Management; Economics and Accounting; Sales and Marketing; Mathematics; Geography; English Language; Law, Government, and Jurisprudence

Abilities: Mathematical Reasoning; Number Facility; Speech Clarity

Property, Real Estate, and Community Association Managers

Plan, direct, and coordinate selling, buying, leasing, or governance activities of commercial, industrial, or residential real estate properties. Include managers of homeowner and condominium associations, rented or leased housing units, buildings, or land (including rights-of-way). Exclude workers whose duties are not primarily managerial. Workers who are engaged primarily in direct buying, selling, or renting of real estate are reported as sales workers. Manages and oversees operations, maintenance, and administrative functions for commercial, industrial, or residential properties. Directs collection of monthly assessments, rental fees and deposits, and payment of insurance premiums, mortgage, taxes, and incurred operating expenses. Meets with clients to negotiate management and service contracts, determine priorities, and discuss financial and operational status of property. Plans, schedules, and coordinates general maintenance, major repairs, and remodeling or construction projects for commercial or residential property. Investigates complaints, disturbances, and violations, and resolves problems following management rules and regulations. Recruits, hires, and trains managerial, clerical, and maintenance staff, or contracts with vendors for security, maintenance, extermination, or groundskeeping personnel. Directs and coordinates the activities of staff and contract personnel and evaluates performance. Maintains records of sales, rental or usage activity, special permits issued, maintenance and operating costs, or property availability. Purchases building and maintenance supplies, equipment, or furniture. Develops and administers annual operating budget. Negotiates for sale, lease, or development of property, and completes or reviews appropriate documents and forms. Inspects facilities and equipment, and inventories building contents to document damage and determine repair needs. Assembles and analyzes construction and vendor service contract bids. Confers with legal authority to ensure transactions and terminations of contracts and agreements are in accordance with court orders, laws, and regulations. Maintains contact with insurance carrier, fire and police departments, and other agencies to ensure protection and compliance with codes and regulations. Prepares reports summarizing financial and operational status of property or facility. Meets with prospective leasers to show property, explain terms of occupancy, and provide information about local area.

Knowledge: Administration and Management; Economics and Accounting; Sales and Marketing; Personnel and Human Resources; Building and Construction; Law, Government, and Jurisprudence

Abilities: Written Expression; Mathematical Reasoning; Number Facility; Speech Recognition

Property Records Managers

Direct and coordinate activities in an organization relating to searching, examining, and recording information for property-related documents to determine status of property titles or property rights. Directs and coordinates researching and recordkeeping activities concerning ownership, contractual terms and conditions, and expiration dates of land documents. Prepares work schedules, and assigns projects to prioritize activities for title search staff. Monitors status of pending research assignments, and confers with staff to resolve production and quality problems. Confers with employees and other managers to establish and modify policies and procedures. Conducts performance appraisals and makes recommendations for personnel actions such as promotions, remedial training, transfers, and terminations. Authorizes royalty payments, bonuses, and other compensation as specified by terms and conditions of legal documents. Oversees the signing of real estate closing documents to verify transfer of title and proper disbursement of documents and escrow funds. Develops and conducts training programs for new hires, and provides continuing in-service training for current employees. Oversees preparation of timesheets, and reviews payroll information. Recruits, interviews, and hires title department personnel. Performs difficult and involved title searches. Reviews accuracy and completeness of legal documents, such as title reports, deeds, affidavits, and other data, to ensure the legality of business transactions. Discusses search delays and title defects, such as outstanding liens or judgments, with legal counsel. Prepares reports to summarize terms and conditions of existing contracts, leases, and agreements, and to provide information for renegotiations. Completes purchase orders for equipment and supplies.

Knowledge: Administration and Management; Economics and Accounting; Personnel and Human Resources; Education and Training; English Language; Law, Government, and Jurioprudonoo

Abilities: Written Comprehension; Written Expression; Speech Clarity

Pruners

- ▲ Growth: 16%
- ▲ Annual Job Openings: 9,030
- ▲ Yearly Earnings $22,880
- ▲ Education Required: Short-term O-J-T
- ▲ Self-employed: 0%
- ▲ Part-time: 25%

Pruners

Prune and treat ornamental and shade trees and shrubs in yards and parks to improve their appearance, health, and value. Cut away dead and excess branches from trees, using handsaws, pruning hooks, sheers, and clippers. May use truck-mounted hydraulic lifts and power pruners. May scrape decayed matter from cavities in trees and fill holes with cement to promote healing and prevent further deterioration. Exclude workers who also perform duties of sprayers/applicators or lawn maintenance workers. Cuts away dead and excess branches from trees, using handsaws, pruning hooks, sheers, and clippers. Uses truck-mounted hydraulic lifts and pruners and power pruners. Scrapes decayed matter from cavities in trees, and fills holes with cement to promote healing and to prevent further deterioration. Applies tar or other protective substances to cut surfaces to seal surfaces against insects. Prunes, cuts down, fertilizes, and sprays trees, as directed by tree surgeon. Climbs trees, using climbing hooks and belts, or climbs ladders to gain access to work area.

Knowledge: Chemistry; Biology

Abilities: Multilimb Coordination; Speed of Limb Movement; Explosive Strength; Dynamic Strength; Stamina; Extent Flexibility; Dynamic Flexibility; Gross Body Coordination; Gross Body Equilibrium

Psychologists

▲ Growth: 8%
▲ Annual Job Openings: 10,914
▲ Yearly Earnings $48,089
▲ Education Required: Master's degree
▲ Self-employed: 40%
▲ Part-time: 23%

Developmental Psychologists

Study and research the emotional, mental, physical, and social growth and development of individuals, from birth to death, to increase understanding of human behavior and processes of human growth and decline. Formulates hypothesis or researches problem regarding growth, development, and decline of emotional, mental, physical, and social processes in individuals. Selects or develops method of investigation to test hypothesis. Studies behavior of children to analyze processes of learning, language development, and parental influence on children's behavior. Analyzes growth or change of social values and attitudes, using information obtained from observation, questionnaires, and interviews. Administers intelligence and performance tests to establish and measure human patterns of intellectual and psychological growth, development, and decline. Observes and records behavior of infants to establish patterns of social, motor, and sensory development. Formulates theories based on research findings for application in such fields as juvenile delinquency, education, parenting, and gerontology. Experiments with animals to conduct cross-species comparative studies to contribute to understanding of human behavior.

Knowledge: Mathematics; Biology; Psychology; Sociology and Anthropology; Therapy and Counseling; Education and Training; English Language; Philosophy and Theology

Abilities: Oral Comprehension; Written Comprehension; Written Expression; Fluency of Ideas; Originality; Problem Sensitivity; Deductive Reasoning; Inductive Reasoning; Information Ordering; Category Flexibility; Mathematical Reasoning; Number Facility; Memorization; Speed of Closure; Flexibility of Closure; Perceptual Speed; Selective Attention; Speech Recognition; Speech Clarity

Experimental Psychologists

Plan, design, and conduct, laboratory experiments to investigate animal or human physiology, perception, memory, learning, personality, and cognitive processes. Conduct interdisciplinary studies with scientists in such fields as physiology, biology, and sociology. Formulates hypotheses and experimental designs to investigate problems of perception, memory, learning, personality, and cognitive processes. Selects, controls, and modifies variables in human or animal laboratory experiments, and observes and records behavior in relation to variables. Analyzes test results, using statistical techniques, and evaluates significance of data in relation to original hypotheses. Conducts research in areas such as aesthetics, learning, emotion, motivation, electroencephalography, motor skills, autonomic functions, and the relationship of behavior to physiology. Designs and constructs equipment and apparatus for laboratory study. Writes scientific papers describing experiments and interpreting research results for publication or presentation. Studies animal behavior to develop theories on comparison of animal and human behavior. Collaborates with scientists in such fields as physiology, biology, and sociology to conduct interdisciplinary studies and formulate theories of behavior.

Knowledge: Mathematics; Biology; Psychology; Sociology and Anthropology; English Language

Abilities: Oral Comprehension; Written Comprehension; Oral Expression; Written Expression; Fluency of Ideas; Originality; Deductive Reasoning; Inductive Reasoning; Information Ordering; Category Flexibility; Mathematical Reasoning; Number Facility; Memorization; Speed of Closure; Speech Clarity

Educational Psychologists

Investigate processes of learning and teaching, and develop psychological principles and techniques applicable to educational problems. Conducts experiments to study educational problems, such as motivation, adjustment, teacher training, and individual differences in mental abilities. Conducts research to aid introduction of programs in schools to meet current psychological, educational, and sociological needs of children. Investigates traits, attitudes, and feelings of teachers to predict conditions that affect teachers' mental health and success with students. Formulates achievement, diagnostic, and predictive tests to aid teachers in planning methods and content of instruction. Interprets and explains test results—in terms of norms, reliability, and validity—to teachers, counselors, students, and other entitled parties. Plans remedial classes and testing programs designed to meet needs of special students. Advises teachers and other school personnel on methods to enhance school and classroom atmosphere to maximize student learning and motivation. Analyzes characteristics and adjustment needs of students having various mental abilities, and recommends educational program to promote maximum adjustment. Evaluates needs, limitations, and potentials of child, through observation, review of school records, and consultation with parents and school personnel. Administers standardized tests to evaluate intelligence, achievement, and personality, and to diagnose disabilities and difficulties among students.

Collaborates with education specialists in developing curriculum content and methods of organizing and conducting classroom work. Recommends placement of students in classes and treatment programs based on individual needs. Counsels pupils individually and in groups, to assist pupils to achieve personal, social, and emotional adjustment. Advises school board, superintendent, administrative committees, and parent-teacher groups regarding provision of psychological services within educational system or school. Refers individuals to community agencies to obtain medical, vocational, or social services for child or family.

Knowledge: Administration and Management; Mathematics; Psychology; Sociology and Anthropology; Therapy and Counseling; Education and Training; English Language

Abilities: Oral Comprehension; Written Comprehension; Oral Expression; Written Expression; Fluency of Ideas; Originality; Problem Sensitivity; Deductive Reasoning; Inductive Reasoning; Information Ordering; Category Flexibility; Mathematical Reasoning; Number Facility; Memorization; Speed of Closure; Flexibility of Closure; Perceptual Speed; Auditory Attention

Social Psychologists

Investigate psychological aspects of human interrelationships to gain understanding of individual and group thought, feeling, and behavior. Conduct research to analyze attitude, motivation, opinion, and group behavior, using behavioral observation, experimentation, or survey techniques. Observes and analyzes individual relationships, behavior, and attitudes within and toward religious, racial, political, occupational, and other groups. Researches variables, such as prejudice, values transmission, motivation, morals, leadership, and the contribution of social factors to behavior. Conducts surveys and polls, using statistical sampling techniques, to measure and analyze attitudes and opinions. Utilizes research findings to predict economic, political, and other behavior of groups. Develops techniques, such as rating scales and sampling methods, to collect and measure behavioral data. Prepares reports documenting research methods and findings.

Knowledge: Administration and Management; Mathematics; Psychology; Sociology and Anthropology; English Language; Philosophy and Theology

Abilities: Oral Comprehension; Written Comprehension; Oral Expression; Written Expression; Fluency of Ideas; Originality; Problem Sensitivity; Deductive Reasoning; Inductive Reasoning; Information Ordering; Mathematical Reasoning; Memorization; Speed of Closure; Flexibility of Closure; Speech Clarity

Clinical Psychologists

Diagnose or evaluate mental and emotional disorders of individuals through observation, interview, and psychological tests; formulate and administer programs of treatment. Observes individual at play, in group interactions, or other situations to detect indications of mental deficiency, abnormal behavior, or maladjustment. Develops treatment plan, including type, frequency, intensity, and duration of therapy, in collaboration with psychiatrists and other specialists. Analyzes information to assess client problems, determine advisability of counseling, and refer client to other specialists, institutions, or support services. Conducts individual and group counseling sessions regarding psychological or emotional problems, such as stress, substance abuse, and family situations. Responds to client reactions, evaluates effectiveness of counseling or treatment, and modifies plan as needed. Interviews individuals, couples, or families, and reviews records to obtain information on medical, psychological, emotional, relationship, or other problems. Selects, administers, scores, and interprets psychological tests to obtain information on individual's intelligence, achievement, interest, and personality. Utilizes treatment methods, such as psychotherapy, hypnosis, behavior modification, stress reduction therapy, psychodrama, and play therapy. Plans and develops accredited psychological service programs in psychiatric center or hospital, in collaboration with psychiatrists and other professional staff. Consults reference material, such as textbooks, manuals, and journals, to identify symptoms, make diagnoses, and develop approach to treatment. Assists clients to gain insight, define goals, and plan action to achieve effective personal, social, educational, and vocational development and adjustment. Provides occupational, educational, and other information to enable individual to formulate realistic educational and vocational plans. Plans, supervises, and conducts psychological research in fields such as personality development and diagnosis, treatment, and prevention of mental disorders. Directs, coordinates, and evaluates activities of psychological staff and student interns engaged in patient evaluation and treatment in psychiatric facility. Provides psychological services and advice to private firms and community agencies on individual cases or mental health programs. Develops, directs, and participates in staff training programs.

Knowledge: Administration and Management; Customer and Personal Service; Personnel and Human Resources; Biology; Psychology; Sociology and Anthropology; Medicine and Dentistry; Therapy and Counseling; Education and Training; English Language

Abilities: Oral Comprehension; Written Comprehension; Oral Expression; Written Expression; Fluency of Ideas; Originality; Problem Sensitivity; Deductive Reasoning; Inductive Reasoning; Information Ordering; Category Flexibility; Memorization; Speed of Closure; Flexibility of Closure; Near Vision; Speech Recognition; Speech Clarity

Counseling Psychologists

Assess and evaluate individuals' problems through the use of case histories, interviews, and observation, and provide individual or group counseling services to assist individuals in achieving more effective personal, social, educational, and vocational development and adjustment. Counsels clients to assist them in understanding personal or interactive problems, defining goals, and developing realistic action plans. Collects information about individuals or clients, using interviews, case histories, observational techniques, and other assessment methods. Develops therapeutic and treatment plans based on individual interests, abilities, or needs of clients. Selects, administers, or interprets psychological tests to assess intelligence, aptitude, ability, or interests. Advises clients on the potential benefits of counseling, or makes referrals to specialists or other institutions for noncounseling problems. Analyzes data, such as interview notes, test results, and reference manuals and texts to identify symptoms and diagnose the nature of client's problems. Evaluates results of counseling methods to determine the reliability and validity of treatments. Consults with other professionals to discuss therapy or treatment, counseling resources or techniques, and to share occupational information. Conducts research to develop or improve diagnostic or therapeutic counseling techniques.

Knowledge: Psychology; Sociology and Anthropology; Therapy and Counseling; Education and Training; Philosophy and Theology

Abilities: Oral Comprehension; Written Comprehension; Oral Expression; Written Expression; Originality; Problem Sensitivity; Deductive Reasoning; Inductive Reasoning; Memorization; Speed of Closure; Speech Recognition; Speech Clarity

Industrial-Organizational Psychologists

Apply principles of psychology and human behavior to personnel, administration, management, sales, and marketing problems. Develop personnel policies, instruments, and programs for the selection, placement, training and development, and evaluation of employees. Conduct organizational analysis and programs for organizational development. Conduct research studies of leadership, supervision, morale, motivation, and worker productivity. Develops interview techniques, rating scales, and psychological tests to assess skills, abilities, and interests as aids in selection, placement, and promotion. Conducts research studies of physical work environments, organizational structure, communication systems, group interaction, morale, and motivation to assess organizational functioning. Analyzes data, using statistical methods and applications, to evaluate and measure the effectiveness of program implementation or training. Advises management in strategic changes to personnel, managerial, and marketing policies and practices to improve organizational effectiveness and efficiency. Studies consumer reaction to new products and package designs, using surveys and tests, and measures the effectiveness of advertising media. Plans, develops, and organizes training programs, applying principles of learning and individual differences. Analyzes job requirements to establish criteria for classification, selection, training, and other related personnel functions. Observes and interviews workers to identify the physical, mutual, and educational requirements of job.

Knowledge: Administration and Management; Sales and Marketing; Personnel and Human Resources; Mathematics; Psychology; Sociology and Anthropology; Therapy and Counseling; Education and Training; Philosophy and Theology

Abilities: Oral Comprehension; Written Comprehension; Oral Expression; Written Expression; Fluency of Ideas; Originality; Problem Sensitivity; Inductive Reasoning; Mathematical Reasoning; Speech Clarity

Public Relations Specialists and Publicity Writers

▲ Growth: 27%
▲ Annual Job Openings: 17,954
▲ Yearly Earnings $33,862
▲ Education Required: Bachelor's degree
▲ Self-employed: 4%
▲ Part-time: 25%

Public Relations Specialists and Publicity Writers

Engage in promoting or creating goodwill for individuals, groups, or organizations by writing or selecting favorable publicity material and releasing it through various communications media. Prepare and arrange displays, make speeches, and perform related publicity efforts. Plans and directs development and communication of informational programs designed to keep public informed of client's products, accomplishments, or agenda. Prepares and distributes fact sheets, news releases, photographs, scripts, motion pictures, or tape recordings to media representatives and others. Promotes sales and/or creates goodwill for client's products, services, or persona by coordinating exhibits, lectures, contests, or public appearances. Prepares or edits organizational publications, such as newsletters to employees or public or stockholders' reports, to favorably present client's viewpoint. Studies needs, objectives, and policies of organization or individual seeking to influence public opinion or promote specific products. Conducts market and public opinion research to introduce or test specific products or measure public opinion. Counsels clients in effective ways of communicating with public. Consults with advertising agencies or staff to arrange promotional campaigns in all types of media for products, organizations, or individuals. Purchases advertising space and time as required to promote client's product or agenda. Arranges for and conducts public-contact programs designed to meet client's objectives. Confers with production and support personnel to coordinate production of advertisements and promotions. Represents client during community projects and at public, social, and business gatherings.

Knowledge: Clerical; Sales and Marketing; Personnel and Human Resources; Computers and Electronics; Psychology; Sociology and Anthropology; Therapy and Counseling; Education and Training; Communications and Media

Abilities: Oral Expression; Written Expression; Fluency of Ideas; Originality; Deductive Reasoning; Mathematical Reasoning; Number Facility; Speed of Closure; Near Vision; Auditory Attention; Speech Recognition; Speech Clarity

Purchasing Managers

▲ Growth: 8%

▲ Annual Job Openings: 10,746

▲ Yearly Earnings $40,934

▲ Education Required: Work experience, plus degree

▲ Self-employed: 0%

▲ Part-time: 2%

Purchasing Managers

Plan, direct, and coordinate the activities of buyers, purchasing officers, and related workers involved in purchasing materials, products, or services. Include wholesale or retail trade merchandising managers. Directs and coordinates activities of personnel engaged in buying, selling, and distributing materials, equipment, machinery, and supplies. Develops and implements office, operations, and systems instructions, policies, and procedures. Conducts inventory and directs buyers in purchase of products, materials, and supplies. Determines merchandise costs and formulates and coordinates merchandising policies and activities to ensure profit. Represents company in formulating policies and negotiating contracts with suppliers and unions. Prepares, reviews, and processes requisitions and purchase orders for supplies and equipment. Analyzes market and delivery systems to determine present and future material availability. Prepares report regarding market conditions and merchandise costs. Consults with department personnel to develop and plan sales promotion programs. Studies work flow, sequence of operations, and office arrangement to determine need for new or improved office machines.

Knowledge: Administration and Management; Economics and Accounting; Sales and Marketing; Personnel and Human Resources; Production and Processing; Mathematics; Sociology and Anthropology

Abilities: Fluency of Ideas; Originality; Category Flexibility; Mathematical Reasoning; Number Facility; Speech Clarity

Radiologic Technologists

▲ Growth: 29%
▲ Annual Job Openings: 12,865
▲ Yearly Earnings $31,969
▲ Education Required: Associate degree
▲ Self-employed: 0%
▲ Part-time: 17%

Radiation Therapists

Provide radiation therapy to patients as prescribed by a radiologist, according to established practices and standards. Duties may include reviewing prescription and diagnosis; acting as liaison with physician and supportive care personnel; preparing equipment, such as immobilization, treatment, and protection devices; and maintaining records, reports, and files. May assist in dosimetry procedures and tumor localization. Reviews prescription, diagnosis, patient chart, and identification. Acts as liaison with physician and supportive care personnel. Maintains records, reports, and files as required. Prepares equipment, such as immobilization, treatment, and protection devices, and positions patient according to prescription. Enters data into computer and sets controls to operate and adjust equipment and regulate dosage. Follows principles of radiation protection for patient, self, and others. Observes and reassures patient during treatment and reports unusual reactions to physician. Photographs treated area of patient and processes film.

Knowledge: Clerical; Customer and Personal Service; Computers and Electronics; Biology; Medicine and Dentistry; Therapy and Counseling

Abilities: Category Flexibility; Speed of Closure; Flexibility of Closure; Selective Attention; Response Orientation; Gross Body Equilibrium; Speech Clarity

Radiologic Technologists

Take X rays and CAT scans or administer nonradioactive materials into patient's blood stream for diagnostic purposes. Include technologists who specialize in other modalities, such as computed tomography, ultrasound, and magnetic resonance. Include workers whose primary duties are to demonstrate portions of the human body on X ray film or fluoroscopic screen. Operates or oversees operation of radiologic and magnetic imaging equipment to produce photographs of the body for diagnostic purposes. Administers oral or injected contrast media to patients. Operates fluoroscope to aid physician to view and guide wire or catheter through blood vessels to area of interest. Positions imaging equipment and adjusts controls to set exposure time and distance, according to specification of examination. Keys commands and data into computer to document and specify scan sequences, adjust transmitters and receivers, or photograph certain images. Monitors video display of area being, scanned and adjusts density or contrast to improve picture quality. Monitors use of radiation safety measures to comply with government regulations and to ensure safety of patients and staff. Positions and immobilizes patient on examining table. Reviews and evaluates developed X rays, videotape, or computer-generated information for technical quality. Explains procedures and observes patients to ensure safety and comfort during scan. Demonstrates new equipment, procedures, and techniques, and provides technical assistance to staff. Assigns duties to radiologic staff to maintain patient flows and achieve production goals. Develops departmental operating budget and coordinates purchase of supplies and equipment. Evaluates radiologic staff and recommends or implements personnel actions, such as promotions or disciplinary procedures.

Knowledge: Computers and Electronics; Chemistry; Biology; Psychology; Medicine and Dentistry

Abilities: None above average

Radiologic Technicians

Maintain and use equipment and supplies necessary to demonstrate portions of the human body on X ray film or fluoroscopic screen for diagnostic purposes. Uses beam-restrictive devices and patient-shielding skills to minimize radiation exposure to patient and staff. Moves X ray equipment into position and adjusts controls to set exposure factors, such as time and distance. Operates mobile X ray equipment in operating room, emergency room, or at patient's bedside. Positions patient on examining table and adjusts equipment to obtain optimum view of specific body area requested by physician. Explains procedures to patient to reduce anxieties and obtain patient cooperation.

Knowledge: Customer and Personal Service; Biology; Medicine and Dentistry

Abilities: Gross Body Coordination

Real Estate Agents

▲ Growth: 6%

▲ Annual Job Openings: 41,554

▲ Yearly Earnings $45,219

▲ Education Required: Postsecondary vocational training

▲ Self-employed: 71%

▲ Part-time: 16%

Sales Agents, Real Estate

Rent, buy, and sell property to clients. Perform duties such as studying property listings, interviewing prospective clients, accompanying clients to property site, discussing conditions of sale, and drawing up real estate contracts. Displays and explains features of property to client, and discusses conditions of sale or terms of lease. Answers client's questions regarding work under construction, financing, maintenance, repairs, and appraisals. Interviews prospective tenants and records information to ascertain needs and qualifications. Solicits and compiles listings of available rental property. Prepares real estate contracts, such as closing statements, deeds, leases, and mortgages, and negotiates loans on property. Reviews plans and recommends to client construction features. Enumerates options on new home sales. Oversees signing of real estate documents, disburses funds, and coordinates closing activities. Collects rental deposit. Locates and appraises undeveloped areas for building sites, based on evaluation of area market conditions. Appraises client's unimproved property to determine loan value. Plans and organizes sales promotion programs and materials, including newspaper advertisements and real estate promotional booklets. Investigates client's financial and credit status to determine eligibility for financing. Searches public records to ascertain that client has clear title to property. Reviews trade journals and relevant literature and attends staff and association meetings to remain knowledgeable about real estate market. Inspects condition of premises and arranges for or notifies owner of necessary maintenance. Secures construction financing with own firm or mortgage company. Contacts utility companies for service hook-up to client's property. Conducts seminars and training sessions for sales agents to improve sales techniques.

Knowledge: Economics and Accounting; Sales and Marketing; Mathematics; Sociology and Anthropology; Geography; Law, Government, and Jurisprudence; Communications and Media

Abilities: Number Facility; Spatial Orientation; Speech Recognition

Real Estate Appraisers

- ▲ Growth: 12%
- ▲ Annual Job Openings: 7,984
- ▲ Yearly Earnings $38,334
- ▲ Education Required: Work experience in a related occupation
- ▲ Self-employed: 23%
- ▲ Part-time: 16%

Assessors

Appraise real and personal property to determine its fair value. May assess taxes in accordance with prescribed schedules. Appraises real and personal property, such as aircraft, marine craft, buildings, and land, to determine fair value. Inspects property, considering factors such as market value, location, and building or replacement costs, to determine appraisal value. Assesses and computes taxes according to prescribed tax tables and schedules. Writes and submits appraisal and tax reports for public record. Interprets property laws, formulates operational policies, and directs assessment office activities.

Knowledge: Economics and Accounting; Mathematics; Geography; Law, Government, and Jurisprudence

Abilities: Inductive Reasoning; Mathematical Reasoning; Number Facility; Gross Body Equilibrium

Appraisers, Real Estate

Appraise real property to determine its value for purchase, sales, investment, mortgage, or loan purposes. Considers such factors as depreciation, value comparison of similar property, and income potential, when computing final estimation of property value. Inspects property for construction, condition, and functional design and takes property measurements. Considers location and trends or impending changes that could influence future value of property. Interviews persons familiar with property and immediate surroundings, such as contractors, home owners, and other realtors to obtain pertinent information. Prepares written report, utilizing data collected, and submits report to corroborate value established. Searches public records for transactions, such as sales, leases, and assessments. Photographs interiors and exteriors of property to assist in estimating property value, to substantiate finding, and to complete appraisal report.

Knowledge: Administration and Management; Clerical; Economics and Accounting; Personnel and Human Resources; Building and Construction; Geography; Public Safety and Security; Law, Government, and Jurisprudence; Communications and Media

Abilities: Deductive Reasoning; Number Facility

Receptionists and Information Clerks

- ▲ Growth: 30%
- ▲ Annual Job Openings: 336,852
- ▲ Yearly Earnings $18,075
- ▲ Education Required: Short-term O-J-T
- ▲ Self-employed: 1%
- ▲ Part-time: 35%

Receptionists and Information Clerks

Answer inquiries and obtain information for general public (e.g., customers, visitors, and other interested parties). Provide information regarding activities conducted at establishment; location of departments, offices, and employees within organization; or services in a hotel. May perform other clerical duties as assigned. Exclude receptionists who operate switchboards. Greets persons entering establishment, determines nature and purpose of visit, and directs visitor to specific destination, or answers questions and provides information. Provides information to public regarding tours, classes, workshops, and other programs. Answers telephone to schedule future appointments, provide information, or forward call. Provides information to public concerning available land leases, land classification, or mineral resources. Registers visitors of public facility, such as national park or military base, collects fees, explains regulations, and assigns sites. Transmits information or documents to customer, using computer, mail, or facsimile. Analyzes data to determine answer to customer or public inquiry. Records, compiles, enters, and retrieves information, by hand or using computer. Collects and distributes messages for employees of organization. Calculates and quotes rates for tours, stocks, insurance policies, and other products and services. Types memos, correspondence, travel vouchers, or other documents. Enrolls individuals to participate in programs, prepares lists, notifies individuals of acceptance in programs, and arranges and schedules space and equipment for participants. Files and maintains records. Hears and resolves complaints from customers and public. Conducts tours or delivers talks describing features of public facility, such as historic site or national park. Receives payment and records receipts for services. Examines, completes, and processes land use documents, and collects fees. Monitors public facilities, such as campgrounds, to ensure compliance with regulations. Participates in activities at national park or other public facility, such as first-aid treatment, fire suppression, conservation, or restoration of buildings. Performs duties such as taking care of plants and straightening magazines to maintain lobby or reception area. Operates telephone switchboard to receive incoming calls.

Knowledge: Clerical; Customer and Personal Service; Geography; Foreign Language; History and Archeology; Telecommunications

Abilities: Memorization; Spatial Orientation; Wrist-Finger Speed; Speech Recognition; Speech Clarity

Recreation Workers

▲ Growth: 22%

▲ Annual Job Openings: 29,880

▲ Yearly Earnings $17,139

▲ Education Required: Bachelor's degree

▲ Self-employed: 0%

▲ Part-time: 14%

Recreation Workers

Conduct recreation activities with groups in public, private, or volunteer agencies or recreation facilities. Organize and promote activities such as arts and crafts, sports, games, music, dramatics, social recreation, camping, and hobbies, taking into account needs and interests of individual members. Organizes, leads, and promotes interest in facility activities, such as arts, crafts, sports, games, camping, and hobbies. Conducts recreational activities and instructs participants to develop skills in provided activities. Arranges for activity requirements, such as entertainment and setting up equipment and decorations. Schedules facility activities and maintains record of programs. Explains principles, techniques, and safety procedures of facility activities to participants, and demonstrates use of material and equipment. Ascertains and interprets group interests, evaluates equipment and facilities, and adapts activities to meet participant needs. Meets and collaborates with agency personnel, community organizations, and other professional personnel to plan balanced recreational programs for participants. Enforces rules and regulations of facility, maintains discipline, and ensures safety. Greets and introduces new arrivals to other guests, acquaints arrivals with facilities, and encourages group participation. Tests and documents content of swimming pool water, and schedules maintenance and use of facilities. Supervises and coordinates work activities of personnel, trains staff, and assigns duties. Schedules maintenance and use of facilities. Evaluates staff performance and records reflective information on performance evaluation forms. Completes and maintains time and attendance forms and inventory lists. Meets with staff to discuss rules, regulations, and work-related problems. Administers first aid, according to prescribed procedures, or notifies emergency medical personnel when necessary. Assists management to resolve complaints.

Knowledge: Administration and Management; Customer and Personal Service; Personnel and Human Resources; Psychology; Sociology and Anthropology; Medicine and Dentistry; Therapy and Counseling; Education and Training; Foreign Language; Fine Arts; Public Safety and Security; Law, Government, and Jurisprudence; Communications and Media

Abilities: Oral Expression; Fluency of Ideas; Originality; Category Flexibility; Memorization; Spatial Orientation; Time Sharing; Gross Body Coordination; Gross Body Equilibrium; Far Vision; Night Vision; Speech Recognition; Speech Clarity

Recreational Therapists

▲ Growth: 21%
▲ Annual Job Openings: 3,414
▲ Yearly Earnings $26,769
▲ Education Required: Bachelor's degree
▲ Self-employed: 26%
▲ Part-time: 20%

Recreational Therapists

Plan, organize, and direct medically-approved recreation programs for patients in hospitals, nursing homes, or other institutions. Activities include sports, trips, dramatics, social activities, and arts and crafts. Organizes and participates in activities to assist patient in developing needed skills and to make patient aware of available recreational resources. Instructs patient in activities and techniques, such as sports, dance, gardening, music, or art, designed to meet specific physical or psychological needs. Observes and confers with patient to assess patient's needs, capabilities, and interests and to devise treatment plan. Develops treatment plan to meet needs of patient, based on needs assessment and objectives of therapy. Analyzes patient's reactions to treatment experiences to assess progress and effectiveness of treatment plan. Modifies content of patient's treatment program based on observation and evaluation of progress. Confers with members of treatment team to determine patient's needs, capabilities, and interests, and to determine objectives of therapy. Counsels and encourages patient to develop leisure activities. Prepares and submits reports and charts to treatment team to reflect patients' reactions and evidence of progress or regression. Attends and participates in professional conferences and workshops to enhance efficiency and knowledge. Maintains and repairs art materials and equipment.

Knowledge: Administration and Management; Customer and Personal Service; Biology; Psychology; Sociology and Anthropology; Medicine and Dentistry; Therapy and Counseling; Education and Training; English Language; Philosophy and Theology

Abilities: Originality; Memorization; Time Sharing; Gross Body Equilibrium; Night Vision; Peripheral Vision; Speech Clarity

Registered Nurses

▲ Growth: 21%
▲ Annual Job Openings: 165,362
▲ Yearly Earnings $40,310
▲ Education Required: Associate degree
▲ Self-employed: 0%
▲ Part time: 26%

Registered Nurses

Administer nursing care to ill or injured persons. Licensing or registration required. Include administrative, public health, industrial, private duty, and surgical nurses. Provides health care, first aid, and immunization in facilities such as schools, hospitals, and industry. Observes patient's skin color, dilation of pupils, and computerized equipment to monitor vital signs. Records patient's medical information and vital signs. Administers local, inhalation, intravenous, and other anesthetics. Prepares patients for and assists with examinations. Orders, interprets, and evaluates diagnostic tests to identify and assess patient's condition. Prepares rooms, sterile instruments, equipment, and supplies, and hands items to surgeon. Prescribes or recommends drugs or other forms of treatment, such as physical therapy, inhalation therapy, or related therapeutic procedures. Contracts independently to render nursing care, usually to one patient, in hospital or private home. Provides prenatal and postnatal care to obstetrical patients under supervision of obstetrician. Discusses cases with physician or obstetrician. Informs physician of patient's condition during anesthesia. Administers stipulated emergency measures, and contacts obstetrician when deviations from standard are encountered during pregnancy or delivery. Advises and consults with specified personnel concerning necessary precautions to be taken to prevent possible contamination or infection. Instructs on topics, such as health education, disease prevention, childbirth, and home nursing, and develops health improvement programs. Delivers infants and performs postpartum examinations and treatment. Refers students or patients to community agencies furnishing assistance, and cooperates with agencies. Conducts specified laboratory tests. Maintains stock of supplies. Directs and coordinates infection-control program in hospital.

Knowledge: Administration and Management; Clerical; Customer and Personal Service; Personnel and Human Resources; Chemistry; Biology; Psychology; Sociology and Anthropology; Medicine and Dentistry; Therapy and Counseling; Education and Training; English Language; Foreign Language; Philosophy and Theology; Public Safety and Security; Law, Government, and Jurisprudence; Communications and Media

Abilities: Oral Comprehension; Written Comprehension; Oral Expression; Written Expression; Fluency of Ideas; Originality; Problem Sensitivity; Deductive Reasoning; Inductive Reasoning; Information Ordering; Category Flexibility; Mathematical Reasoning; Memorization; Speed of Closure; Perceptual Speed; Spatial Orientation; Selective Attention; Time Sharing; Arm-Hand Steadiness; Manual Dexterity; Finger Dexterity; Response Orientation; Reaction Time; Wrist-Finger Speed; Static Strength; Gross Body Equilibrium; Near Vision; Visual Color Discrimination; Night Vision; Peripheral Vision; Hearing Sensitivity; Auditory Attention; Sound Localization; Speech Recognition; Speech Clarity

Residential Counselors

▲ Growth: 41%

▲ Annual Job Openings: 38,516

▲ Yearly Earnings $19,260

▲ Education Required: Bachelor's degree

▲ Self-employed: 0%

▲ Part-time: 18%

Residential Counselors

Coordinate activities for residents of care and treatment institutions, boarding schools, college fraternities or sororities, children's homes, or similar establishments. Work includes developing or assisting in the development of program plans for individuals, maintaining household records, and assigning rooms. Counsel residents in identifying and resolving social or other problems. Order supplies and determine need for maintenance, repairs, and furnishings. Assigns room, assists in planning recreational activities, and supervises work and study programs. Counsels residents in identifying and resolving social and other problems. Orders supplies and determines need for maintenance, repairs, and furnishings. Compiles records of daily activities of residents. Ascertains need for and secures service of physician. Escorts individuals on trips outside establishment for shopping or to obtain medical or dental services. Chaperons group-sponsored trips and social functions. Hires and supervises activities of housekeeping personnel. Plans menus of meals for residents of establishment. Answers telephone. Sorts and distributes mail.

Knowledge: Administration and Management; Customer and Personal Service; Personnel and Human Resources; Psychology; Sociology and Anthropology; Medicine and Dentistry; Therapy and Counseling; Philosophy and Theology; Transportation

Abilities: Originality; Night Vision

Respiratory Therapists

▲ Growth: 46%

▲ Annual Job Openings: 9,453

▲ Yearly Earnings $32,780

▲ Education Required: Associate degree

▲ Self-employed: 0%

▲ Part-time: 20%

Respiratory Therapists

Set up and operate various types of equipment, such as ventilators, oxygen tents, resuscitators, and incubators, to administer oxygen and other gases to patients. Sets up and operates devices, such as mechanical ventilators, therapeutic gas administration apparatus, environmental control systems, and aerosol generators. Operates equipment to administer medicinal gases and aerosol drugs to patients following specified parameters of treatment. Reads prescription, measures arterial blood gases, and reviews patient information to assess patient condition. Monitors patient's physiological responses to therapy, such as vital signs, arterial blood gases, and blood chemistry changes. Performs pulmonary function and adjusts equipment to obtain optimum results to therapy. Inspects and tests respiratory therapy equipment to ensure equipment is functioning safely and efficiently. Determines requirements for treatment, such as type and duration of therapy, and medication and dosages. Determines most suitable method of administering inhalants, precautions to be observed, and potential modifications needed, compatible with physician's orders. Performs bronchopulmonary drainage and assists patient in performing breathing exercises. Consults with physician in event of adverse reactions. Maintains patient's chart which contains pertinent identification and therapy information. Orders repairs when necessary. Demonstrates respiratory care procedures to trainees and other health care personnel.

Knowledge: Chemistry; Biology; Psychology; Medicine and Dentistry; Therapy and Counseling; Education and Training

Abilities: None above average

Restaurant Cooks

▲ Growth: 15%
▲ Annual Job Openings: 224,725
▲ Yearly Earnings $16,182
▲ Education Required: Long-term O-J-T
▲ Self-employed: 3%
▲ Part-time: 38%

Cooks, Restaurant

Prepare, season, and cook soups, meats, vegetables, desserts, and other foodstuffs in restaurants. May order supplies, keep records and accounts, price items on menu, or plan menu. Weighs, measures, and mixes ingredients according to recipe or personal judgment, using various kitchen utensils and equipment. Bakes, roasts, broils, and steams meats, fish, vegetables, and other foods. Observes and tests food to determine that it is cooked, by tasting, smelling, or piercing, and turns or stirs food if necessary. Seasons and cooks food according to recipes or personal judgment and experience. Regulates temperature of ovens, broilers, grills, and roasters. Prepares, seasons, and barbecues pork, beef, chicken, and other types of meat. Bakes bread, rolls, cakes, and pastry. Inspects food preparation and serving areas to ensure observance of safe, sanitary food-handling practices. Washes, peels, cuts, and seeds fruits and vegetables to prepare fruits and vegetables for use. Portions, arranges, and garnishes food, and serves food to waiter or patron. Prepares dishes, such as meat loaves, casseroles, and salads. Prepares appetizers, sauces, dressings, relishes, and hors d'oeuvres. Prepares sandwiches. Prepares frozen dessert items. Plans items on menu. Carves and trims meats, such as beef, veal, ham, pork, and lamb, for hot or cold service or for sandwiches. Butchers and dresses animals, fowl, or shellfish, or cuts and bones meat prior to cooking. Estimates food consumption and requisitions or purchases supplies, or procures food from storage. Designs and prepares decorated foods and artistic food arrangements. Hires, trains, and supervises other cooks and kitchen staff. Carves decorations out of ice, using chisels and ice picks. Participates in or attends culinary exhibitions and conferences.

Knowledge: Administration and Management; Sales and Marketing; Customer and Personal Service; Personnel and Human Resources; Food Production; Education and Training; Foreign Language; Fine Arts; Public Safety and Security; Law, Government, and Jurisprudence

Abilities: Fluency of Ideas; Originality; Deductive Reasoning; Information Ordering; Category Flexibility; Memorization; Perceptual Speed; Time Sharing; Response Orientation; Wrist-Finger Speed; Gross Body Equilibrium; Visual Color Discrimination; Night Vision; Peripheral Vision

Retail Salespersons

▲ Growth: 10%
▲ Annual Job Openings: 1236,273
▲ Yearly Earnings $17,180
▲ Education Required: Short-term O-J-T
▲ Self-employed: 4%
▲ Part-time: 40%

Salespersons, Retail

Sell to the public any of a wide variety of merchandise, such as furniture, motor vehicles, appliances, or apparel. Include workers who sell less expensive merchandise, where a knowledge of the item sold is not a primary requirement. Exclude cashiers. Prepares sales slip or sales contract. Computes sale price of merchandise. Describes merchandise and explains use, operation, and care of merchandise to customers. Sells or arranges for delivery, insurance, financing, or service contracts for merchandise. Totals purchases, receives payment, makes change, or processes credit transaction. Recommends, selects, and obtains merchandise based on customer needs and desires. Demonstrates use or operation of merchandise. Greets customer. Fits or assists customers in trying on merchandise. Estimates quantity and cost of merchandise required, such as paint or floor covering. Tickets, arranges, and displays merchandise to promote sales. Maintains records related to sales. Estimates and quotes trade-in allowances. Estimates cost of repair or alteration of merchandise. Wraps merchandise. Rents merchandise to customers. Inventories stock. Requisitions new stock. Cleans shelves, counters, and tables. Repairs or alters merchandise.

Knowledge: Economics and Accounting; Sales and Marketing; Customer and Personal Service

Abilities: Memorization; Gross Body Equilibrium; Visual Color Discrimination; Speech Recognition

Salespersons, Parts

Sell spare and replaceable parts and equipment from behind counter in agency, repair shop, or parts store. Determine make, year, and type of part needed by observing damaged part or listening to a description of malfunction. Read catalog to find stock number, price, etc., and fill customer's order from stock. Exclude workers whose primary responsibilities are to receive, store, and issue materials, equipment, and other items from stockroom. Determines replacement part required, according to inspection of old part, customer request, or customer description of malfunction. Reads catalog, microfiche viewer, or computer display to determine replacement part stock number and price. Fills customer orders from stock. Advises customer on substitution or modification of part when identical replacement is not available. Examines returned part for defects, and exchanges defective part or refunds money. Prepares sales slip or sales contract. Receives payment or obtains credit authorization. Receives and fills telephone orders for parts. Demonstrates equipment to customer and explains functioning of equipment. Discusses use and features of various parts, based on knowledge of machine or equipment. Measures parts, using precision measuring instruments to determine whether similar parts may be machined to required size. Places new merchandise on display. Marks and stores parts in stockroom according to prearranged system. Takes inventory of stock. Repairs parts or equipment.

Knowledge: Sales and Marketing; Customer and Personal Service; Mechanical; Telecommunications

Abilities: Memorization; Visualization; Gross Body Equilibrium; Visual Color Discrimination; Auditory Attention; Speech Recognition

Telemarketers, Door-to-Door Sales Workers, News and Street Vendors, and Other Related Workers

Solicit orders for goods or services over the telephone; sell goods or services door-to-door or on the street. Contacts customers by phone, mail, or in person to offer or persuade them to purchase merchandise or services. Explains products or services and prices and demonstrates use of products. Writes orders for merchandise or enters orders into computer. Circulates among potential customers or travels by foot, truck, automobile, or bicycle to deliver or sell merchandise or services. Arranges buying party and solicits sponsorship of parties to sell merchandise. Delivers merchandise, serves customer, collects money, and makes change. Distributes product samples or literature that details products or services. Maintains records of accounts and orders and develops prospect lists. Orders or purchases supplies and stocks cart or stand. Sets up and displays sample merchandise at parties or stands.

Knowledge: Sales and Marketing; Customer and Personal Service

Abilities: None above average

Demonstrators and Promoters

Demonstrate merchandise and answer questions for the purpose of creating public interest in buying the products. Demonstrates and explains products, methods, or services to persuade customers to purchase products or utilize services available, and answers questions. Visits homes, community organizations, stores, and schools to demonstrate products or services. Attends trade, traveling, promotional, educational, or amusement exhibits to answer visitors' questions and to protect exhibit against theft or damage. Sets up and arranges display to attract attention of prospective customers. Suggests product improvements to employer and product to purchase to customer. Gives product samples or token gifts to customers, and distributes handbills, brochures, or gift certificates to passersby. Answers telephone and written requests from customers for information about product use, and writes articles and pamphlets on product. Lectures and shows slides to users of company product. Advises customers on homemaking problems related to products or services offered by company. Wears costume or sign boards and walks in public to attract attention to advertise merchandise, services, or belief. Contacts businesses and civic establishments and arranges to exhibit and sell merchandise made by disadvantaged persons. Instructs customers in alteration of products. Represents utility company as guest on radio or television programs to discuss proper use and conservation of company's product. Develops list of prospective clients from sources, such as newspaper items, company records, local merchants, and customers. Solicits new organization membership. Trains demonstrators to present company's products or services. Conducts guided tours of plant where product is made. Prepares reports of services rendered and visits made for parent organization and member firms. Drives truck and trailer to transport exhibit. Collects fees or accepts donations.

Knowledge: Clerical; Sales and Marketing; Customer and Personal Service; Sociology and Anthropology; Education and Training; English Language; Communications and Media

Abilities: Oral Expression; Written Expression; Fluency of Ideas; Originality; Memorization; Response Orientation; Night Vision; Speech Clarity

Sales Specialists and Support Workers

▲ Growth: 23%
▲ Annual Job Openings: 765,025
▲ Yearly Earnings $24,502
▲ Education Required: Moderate-term O-J-T
▲ Self-employed: 9%
▲ Part-time: 22%

Sales Agents, Selected Business Services

Sell selected services, such as building maintenance, credit reporting, bookkeeping, security, printing, and storage space, to businesses. Exclude advertising, insurance, financial, and real estate sales agents. Personally visits, telephones, or writes prospective and current customers to explain benefits of service or expanded service. Consults with customers concerning needs; inspects buildings and equipment; and reviews building plans to determine services to be offered. Writes orders or service contracts for new and current customers, and schedules initiation or discontinuance of services. Analyzes information obtained from prospective client and writes prospectus or recommendations for service. Computes and quotes prices, fares, and rates and explains details such as routes, regulations, and schedules to customer. Explains methods for using service or equipment to customer, or assists customer in developing operating procedures for use with service. Develops prospective customer list from business and telephone directories, telephone inquiries received, and business associates, and by observing business establishments. Reviews past orders and current accounts to generate ideas on expanding services to customers. Consults with technical staff to obtain information on special problems or current price quotes. Confers with customers to verify service satisfaction or investigate and resolve customer complaints and other problems. Writes and distributes sales pamphlets, promotional letters or materials, and other advertising aids. Collects payments on account and records or directs staff to record customer payments received. Speaks to individuals or groups on behalf of customer to stimulate interest in or use of customer services or products. Reviews customer accounts and prepares written reports of services rendered, including problems encountered. Reviews customer inventory records to determine charges for replacement of damaged rental articles, and recommends discontinuance of service when necessary. Serves as advertiser or coordinator during hotel function, such as convention or meeting.

Knowledge: Administration and Management; Clerical; Economics and Accounting; Sales and Marketing; Customer and Personal Service; English Language; Communications and Media

Abilities: Written Comprehension; Oral Expression; Written Expression; Fluency of Ideas; Originality; Memorization

Site Leasing and Promotion Agents

Promote products by obtaining leases for outdoor advertising sites or permission to display product promotional items in establishments. Persuades property owners to lease sites for erection of billboard signs used in outdoor advertising. Visits retail establishments and clubs to persuade customers to use display items to promote sale of company products. Arranges price and draws up lease. Arranges display of items in customer's establishment. Locates potential billboard sites, using automobile to travel through assigned district. Searches legal records for land ownership. Delivers promotion items, such as posters, glasses, napkins, and samples of product. Takes sales order from customer.

Knowledge: Sales and Marketing; Psychology; Geography; Law, Government, and Jurisprudence; Communications and Media

Abilities: None above average

Sales Agents, Advertising

Sell or solicit advertising, such as graphic art, advertising space in publications, custom-made signs, and air time on TV and radio. Advises customer on advantages of various types of programming and methods of composing layouts and designs for signs and displays. Exhibits prepared layouts with mats and copy with headings. Visits advertisers to point out advantages of publication. Draws up contract covering arrangements for designing, fabricating, erecting, and maintaining sign or display. Sells signs to be made according to customers' specifications, utilizing knowledge of lettering, color harmony, and sign-making processes. Calls on prospects and presents outlines of various programs or commercial announcements. Informs customer of types of artwork available by providing samples. Prepares list of prospects for classified and display space for publication from leads in other papers and from old accounts. Obtains pertinent information concerning prospect's past and current advertising for use in sales presentation. Calls on advertisers and sales promotion people to obtain information concerning prospects for current advertising and sales promotion. Prepares promotional plans, sales literature, and sales contracts, using computer. Plans and sketches layouts to meet customer needs. Computes job costs. Writes copy as part of layout. Collects payments due. Delivers advertising or illustration proofs to customer for approval. Arranges for and accompanies prospect to commercial taping sessions.

Knowledge: Sales and Marketing; Psychology; English Language; Fine Arts; Communications and Media

Abilities: Oral Expression; Originality; Speech Recognition

Sales Representatives, Service

Contact prospective customers to sell services, such as educational courses, dance instructions, cable television, furniture repair, auto leasing, and burial needs. Interviews customer to ascertain and evaluate needs and wishes of customer. Explains advantages and features of service being rented or sold to stimulate customer's interest. Answers customer's questions pertaining to service being offered. Advises customer on variables and options to assist customer in making decision. Computes estimate or final cost of sale and presents information to customer. Compiles list of prospective customers for use as sales leads, using newspapers, directories and other sources. Confers with other company personnel to convey customer's needs and to plan program to meet customer's needs. Compiles and records sales and lease information and records of expenses incurred. Prepares and sends leasing contract to leasing agency. Evaluates advertising campaigns and administrative procedures to increase sales and efficiency. Receives payments. Purchases items and prices items for profitable resale.

Knowledge: Administration and Management; Economics and Accounting; Sales and Marketing; Customer and Personal Service

Abilities: Oral Expression; Mathematical Reasoning; Speech Recognition

Fund Raisers and Solicitors

Solicit contributions to support nonprofit organization, such as charity or university. May encourage individuals to join or participate in activities of organization. Writes, visits, or telephones potential blood donors, contributors, and members to explain blood program or to solicit contributions or membership in organization. Collects pledges, funds, or gifts-in-kind from contributors, or membership dues or payments for publications. Compiles and analyzes information about potential contributors to develop mailing or contact lists and to prepare promotional campaign. Prepares brochures for mail-solicitation programs. Schedules appointments for blood donations or for pick-up of gifts-in-kind. Sells emblems or other tokens of organization represented. Plans social functions to generate interest and enthusiasm for activity being promoted. Records and maintains records of activities, such as members enrolled, funds pledged or collected, expenses incurred, and donors enlisted. Writes letter to express appreciation for donation. Trains volunteers to perform certain duties to assist fund raising. Consults blood bank records to answer questions, monitor activity, or resolve problems of blood donor group.

Knowledge: Administration and Management; Clerical; Economics and Accounting; Sales and Marketing; Psychology; Sociology and Anthropology; Education and Training; Communications and Media

Abilities: None above average

Sales Engineers

Sell business goods or services that require a technical background equivalent to a baccalaureate degree in engineering. Exclude engineers whose primary function is not marketing or sales. Calls on management representatives at commercial, industrial, and other establishments to convince prospective clients to buy products or services offered. Assists sales force in sale of company products. Demonstrates and explains product or service to customer representatives, such as engineers, architects, and other professionals. Draws up sales or service contract for products or services. Provides technical services to clients relating to use, operation, and maintenance of equipment. Arranges for trial installations of equipment. Designs draft variations of standard products in order to meet customer needs. Reviews customer documents to develop and prepare cost estimates or projected production increases from use of proposed equipment or services. Draws up or proposes changes in equipment, processes, materials, or services resulting in cost reduction or improvement in customer operations. Assists in development of custom-made machinery. Diagnoses problems with equipment installed. Provides technical training to employees of client.

Knowledge: Economics and Accounting; Sales and Marketing; Customer and Personal Service; Production and Processing; Computers and Electronics; Engineering and Technology; Design; Mechanical; Mathematics; Physics; Psychology; Education and Training; English Language; History and Archeology; Telecommunications

Abilities: Oral Comprehension; Written Comprehension; Oral Expression; Written Expression; Fluency of Ideas; Originality; Problem Sensitivity; Deductive Reasoning; Inductive Reasoning; Information Ordering; Category Flexibility; Mathematical Reasoning; Number Facility; Memorization; Speed of Closure; Visualization; Selective Attention; Time Sharing; Response Orientation; Rate Control; Reaction Time; Extent Flexibility; Gross Body Equilibrium; Near Vision; Far Vision; Visual Color Discrimination; Night Vision; Peripheral Vision; Hearing Sensitivity; Auditory Attention; Sound Localization; Speech Recognition; Speech Clarity

Sales Representatives, Agricultural

Sell agricultural products and services, such as animal feeds, farm and garden equipment, and dairy, poultry, and veterinarian supplies. Solicits orders from customers in person or by phone. Displays or shows customer agricultural-related products. Quotes prices and credit terms. Compiles lists of prospective customers for use as sales leads. Prepares sales contracts for orders obtained. Consults with customer regarding installation, set-up, or layout of agricultural equipment and machines. Informs customer of estimated delivery schedule, service contracts, warranty, or other information pertaining to purchased products. Demonstrates use of agricultural equipment or machines. Prepares reports of business transactions. Recommends changes in customer use of agricultural products to improve production.

Knowledge: Economics and Accounting; Sales and Marketing; Customer and Personal Service; Food Production

Abilities: Speech Recognition

Sales Representatives, Chemical and Pharmaceutical

Sell chemical or pharmaceutical products or services, such as acids, industrial chemicals, agricultural chemicals, medicines, drugs, and water treatment supplies. Promotes and sells pharmaceutical and chemical products to potential customers. Explains water treatment package benefits to customer, and sells chemicals to treat and resolve water process problems. Distributes drug samples to customer and takes orders for pharmaceutical supply items from customer. Discusses characteristics and clinical studies pertaining to pharmaceutical products with physicians, dentists, hospitals, and retail/wholesale establishments. Estimates and advises customer of service costs to correct water-treatment process problems. Inspects, tests, and observes chemical changes in water system equipment, utilizing test kit, reference manual, and knowledge of chemical treatment.

Knowledge: Sales and Marketing; Chemistry

Abilities: Oral Expression

Sales Representatives, Electrical/Electronic

Sell electrical, electronic, or related products or services, such as communication equipment, radiographic-inspection equipment and services, ultrasonic equipment, electronics parts, computers, and EDP systems. Analyzes communication needs of customer and consults with staff engineers regarding technical problems. Recommends equipment to meet customer requirements, considering salable features, such as flexibility, cost, capacity, and economy of operation. Sells electrical or electronic equipment, such as computers and data-processing and radiographic equipment to businesses and industrial establishments. Negotiates terms of sale and services with customer. Trains establishment personnel in equipment use, utilizing knowledge of electronics and product sold.

Knowledge: Economics and Accounting; Sales and Marketing; Computers and Electronics; Psychology; Education and Training; Telecommunications

Abilities: None of the above

Sales Representatives, Mechanical Equipment and Supplies

Sell mechanical equipment, machinery, materials, and supplies, such as aircraft and railroad equipment and parts, construction machinery, material-handling equipment, industrial machinery, and welding equipment. Recommends and sells textile, industrial, construction, railroad, and oilfield machinery, equipment, materials, and supplies, and services utilizing knowledge of machine operations. Contacts current and potential customers, visits establishments to evaluate needs, and promotes sale of products and services. Computes installation or production costs, estimates savings, and prepares and submits bid specifications to customer for review and approval. Submits orders for product and follows up on order to verify material list accuracy and that delivery schedule meets project deadline. Arranges for installation and test-operation of machinery and recommends solutions to product-related problems. Appraises equipment and verifies customer credit rating to establish trade-in value and contract terms. Demonstrates and explains use of installed equipment and production processes. Reviews existing machinery/equipment placement and diagrams proposal to illustrate efficient space utilization, using standard measuring devices and templates. Inspects establishment premises to verify installation feasibility, and obtains building blueprints and elevator specifications to submit to engineering department for bid. Attends sales and trade meetings and reads related publications to obtain current market condition information, business trends, and industry developments.

Knowledge: Economics and Accounting; Sales and Marketing; Customer and Personal Service; Mathematics

Abilities: Oral Expression; Problem Sensitivity; Memorization; Speech Recognition; Speech Clarity

Sales Representatives, Medical

Sell medical equipment, products, and services. Does not include pharmaceutical sales representatives. Promotes sale of medical and dental equipment, supplies, and services to doctors, dentists, hospitals, medical schools, and retail establishments. Selects surgical appliances from stock, and fits and sells appliances to customer. Studies data describing new products to accurately recommend purchase of equipment and supplies. Writes specifications to order custom-made surgical appliances, using customer measurements and physician prescriptions. Advises customer regarding office layout, legal and insurance regulations, cost analysis, and collection methods. Designs and fabricates custom-made medical appliances.

Knowledge: Economics and Accounting; Sales and Marketing; Design; Mathematics; Medicine and Dentistry

Abilities: Speech Recognition

Sales Representatives, Instruments

Sell precision instruments, such as dynamometers and spring scales, and laboratory, navigation, and surveying instruments. Assists customer with product selection, utilizing knowledge of engineering specifications and catalog resources. Sells weighing and other precision instruments, such as spring scales and dynamometers, and laboratory, navigational, and surveying instruments to customer. Evaluates customer needs and emphasizes product features based on technical knowledge of product capabilities and limitations.

Knowledge: Sales and Marketing

Abilities: None above average

Sales Representatives, Except Retail and Scientific and Related Products and Services

Sell goods or services for wholesalers or manufacturers to businesses or groups of individuals. Solicit orders from established clients or secure new customers. Work requires substantial knowledge of items sold. Contacts regular and prospective customers to solicit orders. Recommends products to customers, based on customers' specific needs and interests. Answers questions about products, prices, durability, and credit terms. Meets with customers to demonstrate and explain features of products. Prepares lists of prospective customers. Reviews sales records and current market information to determine value or sales potential of product. Estimates delivery dates and arranges delivery schedules. Completes sales contracts or forms to record sales information. Instructs customers in use of products. Assists and advises retail dealers in use of sales promotion techniques. Investigates and resolves customer complaints. Forwards orders to manufacturer. Assembles and stocks product displays in retail stores. Writes reports on sales and products. Prepares drawings, estimates, and bids to meet specific needs of customer. Obtains credit information on prospective customers. Oversees delivery or installation of products or equipment.

Knowledge: Economics and Accounting; Sales and Marketing; Customer and Personal Service; Mathematics; Psychology; Sociology and Anthropology; Education and Training; Foreign Language; Philosophy and Theology; Communications and Media; Transportation

Abilities: Fluency of Ideas; Originality; Category Flexibility; Mathematical Reasoning; Number Facility; Memorization; Response Orientation; Speech Recognition; Speech Clarity

Merchandise Appraisers and Auctioneers

Appraise and estimate value of items, such as paintings, antiques, jewelry, cameras, musical instruments, machinery, and fixtures for loan, insurance, or sale purposes. May sell merchandise at auction. Examines items and estimates values, based on knowledge of specific article, current market values, and economic trends. Examines and assigns value to item based on knowledge of values or accepted listing of wholesale prices. Tests art works and antiques, using X rays and chemicals, to detect forgery or to otherwise authenticate item. Weighs gold or silver articles on coin scales or employs acid tests to determine carat content and purity to verify value of articles. Inspects diamonds and other gems for flaws and color, using loupe (magnifying glass). Prepares and submits reports of estimates to clients, such as insurance firms, lending agencies, government offices, creditors, courts, or attorneys. Illuminates artworks, using quartz light, to examine color quality, brushstroke style, and other characteristics to identify artist or period. Selects item and describes and provides information about merchandise to be auctioned, such as history and ownership, to encourage bidding. Continues to ask for bids, attempting to stimulate buying desire of bidders, and closes sale to highest bidder. Issues pawn or pledge tickets, keeps record of loans, and computes interest when pledges are redeemed or extended.

Knowledge: Economics and Accounting; Sales and Marketing; Fine Arts; History and Archeology; Law, Government, and Jurisprudence

Abilities: Number Facility; Memorization; Near Vision; Visual Color Discrimination; Speech Clarity

Home Furnishings Estimators

Measure dimensions and estimate price of making and installing household accessories. Measures windows for draperies and shades, furniture for upholstery, and window and door frames for doors, windows, and screen. Computes cost of fabric and hardware, according to measurements, work specifications, and type of fabric to be used, using calculator and price listings. Itemizes labor in fabrication and installation of goods and records total price on sales check or contract. Discusses selection of fabric and other materials with customer, using material samples. Draws sketches to scale of work to be done. Confers with architects and interior decorators to obtain additional information when computing cost estimates on commercial orders.

Knowledge: Sales and Marketing; Customer and Personal Service; Design; Building and Construction

Abilities: Gross Body Equilibrium; Visual Color Discrimination

Sales Consultants

Select, recommend, or purchase merchandise or services for customers shopping either in person or by telephone at department or specialty stores. Include personal shoppers and wedding consultants. Accompanies customer when shopping or shops for customer to purchase specific merchandise. Recommends, displays, and sells trousseau for bride, and attire for attendants, and advises on selection of tableware, stationery, flowers, and caterers. Provides customers with catalogs, promotional material and information, price of merchandise, shipping time and costs, and store services. Takes orders and prepares special order worksheet for such items as decorated cakes, cut flowers, personalized stationery, and merchandise rentals. Answers customers' telephone, mail, and in-person inquiries and directs customers to appropriate sales area. Resolves customer complaints and requests for refunds, exchanges, repairs, replacements, and adjustments. Issues temporary customer identification cards in group buying stores, such as military shops and special discount stores. Arranges for gift wrapping, monogramming, printing, and fabrication of such items as desk nameplates or rubber stamps. Approves customers' checks and provides checking service according to exchange policy. Keeps record of services in progress, notifies customer when service is completed, and accepts payment for services. Arranges for photographers to take pictures, and attends rehearsals to advise wedding party regarding etiquette. Keeps records of items in layaway, receives and posts customer payments, and prepares and forwards delinquent notices.

Knowledge: Sales and Marketing; Customer and Personal Service

Abilities: Visual Color Discrimination; Speech Recognition

Science and Mathematics Technicians

▲ Growth: 13%
▲ Annual Job Openings: 23,270
▲ Yearly Earnings $34,465
▲ Education Required: Associate degree
▲ Self-employed: 0%
▲ Part-time: 11%

Biological and Agricultural Technologists

Study and apply biological and agricultural principles to experiment, test, and develop new and improved methods in production, preservation, and processing of plant and animal life. Applies scientific principles to devise new or improved methods of production, preservation, and processing of plant and animal life. Develops improved manufacturing methods for natural and synthetic fibers. Analyses the nature and use of animal, plant, and synthetic fibers. Tests the quality control of plant, animal, and synthetic products. Experiments with methods of handling, processing, and packaging dairy products.

Knowledge: Production and Processing; Food Production; Mathematics; Chemistry; Biology

Abilities: Originality; Deductive Reasoning; Inductive Reasoning; Mathematical Reasoning; Memorization

Artificial Breeding Technicians

Collect, inject, measure, or test animal semen to breed livestock or to develop improved artificial insemination methods. Attaches vial or sheath to genitals of animal to collect semen sample. Examines semen sample to determine its quality, using microscope and other devices. Measures and transfers semen into insemination containers. Injects semen samples into animals, using syringe. Adds chemicals to semen, and refrigerates semen samples to preserve them. Experiments with tests to improve sample purity and preservation. Records information on semen collection and artificial insemination. Observes animals to determine best times for artificial insemination. Cleans and sterilizes laboratory equipment.

Knowledge: Food Production; Chemistry; Biology; Medicine and Dentistry

Abilities: None above average

Biological and Agricultural Technicians

Set up and maintain laboratory, and collect and record data to assist scientists in biology, plant pathology, and related agricultural science experiments. Sets up laboratory and field equipment to assist research workers. Cleans and maintains laboratory and field equipment and work areas. Plants seeds in specified area, and counts plants that grow, to determine germination rate of seeds. Examines animals and specimens to determine presence of disease or other problems. Pricks animals, and collects blood samples for testing, using hand-held devices. Waters and feeds rations to livestock and laboratory animals. Records production and test data for evaluation by personnel. Adjusts testing equipment and prepares culture media, following standard procedures. Measures or weighs ingredients used in testing or as animal feed.

Knowledge: Food Production; Biology

Abilities: None above average

Biology Specimen Technicians

Prepare biological specimens of plant and animal life for use as instructional aids in schools, museums, and other institutions. Dissects, trims, and stains section of plant or animal to display desired features. Selects specimens of plant or animal life to prepare as instructional aids. Assembles and positions components of specimen in mold, using pins and holding devices. Embeds biological specimens of plant and animal life in plastic, using molding techniques. Arranges specimens between sheets of paper to protect them and to stack them in pressing frame. Mounts dried specimens on heavy paper, using glue or other materials. Mixes one of various types of plastic to embed specimen in mold. Records information to identify specimens and method of preservation, and to maintain specimen file. Tightens frame section with screws to compress stacks and to press dry specimens into desired configuration. Turns valves to release fumes that fumigate plant specimens.

Knowledge: Chemistry; Biology

Abilities: Category Flexibility; Finger Dexterity

Chemical Technicians and Technologists

Conduct chemical and physical laboratory tests to assist scientists in making qualitative and quantitative analyses of solids, liquids, and gaseous materials. Tests and analyzes chemical and physical properties of liquids, solids, gases, radioactive and biological materials, and products such as perfumes. Prepares chemical solutions for products and processes, following standardized formulas, or creates experimental formulas. Sets up and calibrates laboratory equipment and instruments used for testing, process control, product development, and research. Cleans and sterilizes laboratory equipment. Documents results of tests and analyses, and writes technical reports or prepares graphs and charts. Reviews process paperwork for products to ensure compliance to standards and specifications. Directs other workers in compounding and distilling chemicals.

Knowledge: Mathematics; Chemistry; Biology; English Language

Abilities: Written Comprehension; Written Expression; Deductive Reasoning; Information Ordering; Category Flexibility; Mathematical Reasoning; Number Facility; Memorization; Perceptual Speed; Arm-Hand Steadiness; Control Precision; Visual Color Discrimination

Food Science Technicians and Technologists

Perform standardized qualitative and quantitative tests to determine physical or chemical properties of food or beverage products. Conducts standardized tests on food, beverages, additives, and preservatives to ensure compliance to standards, for factors such as color, texture, nutrients, and coloring. Tastes or smells food or beverages to ensure flavor meets specifications or to select samples with specific characteristics. Analyzes test results to classify product, or compares results with standard tables. Computes moisture or salt content, percentage of ingredients, formulas, or other product factors, using mathematical and chemical procedures. Examines chemical and biological samples to identify cell structure, bacteria, or extraneous material, using microscope. Mixes, blends, or cultivates ingredients to make reagents or to manufacture food or beverage products. Records and compiles test results, and prepares graphs, charts, and reports. Prepares slides and incubates slides with cell cultures. Measures, tests, and weighs bottles, cans, and other containers to ensure that hardness, strength, and dimensions meet specifications. Orders supplies to maintain inventory in laboratory or in storage facility of food or beverage processing plant. Cleans and sterilizes laboratory equipment.

Knowledge: Production and Processing; Food Production; Mathematics; Chemistry; Biology; English Language

Abilities: Information Ordering; Category Flexibility; Mathematical Reasoning; Number Facility; Visual Color Discrimination

Assayers

Test ores and minerals and analyze results to determine value and properties. Performs dry-method processes, such as applying heat in furnace to form slags of lead, borax, or other impurities, to test ores and minerals. Analyzes test results to determine value and properties of ores and minerals, using spectroscope and other instruments and laboratory equipment. Separates metals from dross materials by liquid processes, such as flotation or solution, to test ores and minerals. Weighs ore residues to determine proportion of gold, silver, platinum, or other metals, using balance scale.

Knowledge: History and Archeology

Abilities: Category Flexibility; Flexibility of Closure; Near Vision; Visual Color Discrimination

Textile Science Technicians and Technologists

Conduct tests to determine characteristics of textile products, fibers, and related materials and adherence to specifications. May develop and test color formulas. Performs standardized tests to determine chemical characteristics of fiber, such as shrinkage, absorbency, color value, fading, or fire retardancy. Measures physical characteristics of fiber, such as tensile and tear strength, using testing equipment. Photographs, develops, and prints samples of fibers, using microphotographic and photographic equipment. Examines photographs or fiber and cloth samples under microscope to determine characteristics, such as fiber type, weave, structure, or threads per inch. Prepares fiber or cloth samples for microscopic or photographic analysis and chemical and physical testing. Compares printed cloth specimen with customer sample or with test results. Inspects finished material for conformance to plant and customer specifications. Classifies textiles and fibers according to quality. Tests related textile items, such as buckles, buttons, bindings, laces, or oil and soap products. Prepares reports of test findings or file folders containing color formulas. Selects dyes and develops color formulas and color charts to match textile product to customer specifications. Mixes colors for dyes or chemicals for use in removing stains. Inventories and requisitions supplies. Coordinates activities of department with other departments.

Knowledge: Production and Processing; Chemistry; Fine Arts

Abilities: Category Flexibility; Perceptual Speed; Near Vision; Visual Color Discrimination

Environmental Science Technicians

Perform laboratory and field tests to monitor environmental resources and determine sources of pollution, under direction of environmental scientist. Collect samples of gases, soil, water, and other materials for testing. May recommend remediation treatment to resolve pollution problems. Collects samples of gases, soils, water, industrial wastewater, and asbestos products to conduct tests on pollutant levels. Performs chemical and physical laboratory and field tests on collected samples to assess compliance with pollution standards, using test instruments. Conducts standardized tests to ensure materials and supplies used throughout power-supply system meet processing and safety specifications. Examines and analyzes material for presence and concentration of contaminants such as asbestos in environment, using variety of microscopes. Weighs, analyzes, and measures collected sample particles, such as lead, coal dust, or rock, to determine concentration of pollutants. Calculates amount of pollutant in samples or computes air pollution or gas flow in industrial processes, using chemical and mathematical formulas. Prepares samples or photomicrographs for testing and analysis. Determines amounts and kinds of chemicals to use in destroying harmful organisms and removing impurities from purification systems. Sets up equipment or station to monitor and collect pollutants from sites, such as smoke stacks, manufacturing plants, or mechanical equipment. Records test data and prepares reports, summaries, and charts that interpret test results and recommend changes. Develops procedures and directs activities of workers in laboratory. Calibrates microscopes and test instruments. Discusses test results and analyses with customers.

Knowledge: Mathematics; Physics; Chemistry; Biology; English Language; Public Safety and Security; Communications and Media

Abilities: Oral Comprehension; Written Comprehension; Oral Expression; Written Expression; Problem Sensitivity; Deductive Reasoning; Inductive Reasoning; Information Ordering; Category Flexibility; Mathematical Reasoning; Number Facility; Memorization; Speed of Closure; Flexibility of Closure; Perceptual Speed; Arm-Hand Steadiness; Finger Dexterity; Control Precision; Gross Body Equilibrium; Near Vision; Far Vision

Nuclear Equipment Operation Technicians

Operate equipment used for the release, control, and utilization of nuclear energy to assist scientists in laboratory and production activities. Sets control panel switches and activates equipment, such as nuclear reactor, particle accelerator, or gamma radiation equipment, according to specifications. Calculates equipment operating factors, such as radiation time, dosage, temperature, and pressure, using standard formulas and conversion tables. Monitors instruments, gauges, and recording devices in control room during operation of equipment, under direction of nuclear experimenter. Adjusts controls of equipment to control particle beam, chain reaction, or radiation, according to specifications. Reviews experiment schedule to determine specifications, such as subatomic particle parameters, radiation time, dosage, and gamma intensity. Installs instrumentation leads in reactor core to measure operating temperature and pressure according to mockups, blueprints, and diagrams. Positions fuel elements in reactor or environmental chamber, according to specified configuration, using slave manipulators or extension tools. Controls laboratory compounding equipment enclosed in protective hot cell to prepare radioisotopes and other radioactive materials. Transfers experimental materials to and from specified containers and to tube, chamber, or tunnel, using slave manipulators or extension tools. Sets up and operates machines to saw fuel elements to size or to cut and polish test pieces, following blueprints and other specifications. Withdraws radioactive sample for analysis, fills container with prescribed quantity of material for shipment, or removes spent fuel elements. Tests physical, chemical, or metallurgical properties of experimental materials, according to standardized procedures, using test equipment and measuring instruments. Communicates with maintenance personnel to ensure readiness of support systems and to warn of radiation hazards. Writes summary of activities or records experiment data in log for further analysis by engineers, scientists, or customers, or for future reference. Disassembles, cleans, and decontaminates hot cells and reactor parts during maintenance shutdown, using slave manipulators, crane, and hand tools. Modifies, devises, and maintains equipment used in operations.

Knowledge: Production and Processing; Engineering and Technology; Design; Mathematics; Physics; Chemistry; Public Safety and Security

Abilities: Problem Sensitivity; Information Ordering; Mathematical Reasoning; Number Facility; Memorization; Perceptual Speed; Time Sharing; Arm-Hand Steadiness; Manual Dexterity; Finger Dexterity; Control Precision; Response Orientation; Rate Control; Reaction Time

Nuclear Monitoring Technicians

Collect and test samples to monitor results of nuclear experiments and contamination of humans, facilities, and environment. Measures intensity and identifies type of radiation in work areas, equipment, and materials, using radiation detectors and other instruments. Collects samples of air, water, gases, and solids to determine radioactivity levels of contamination. Assists in setting up equipment that automatically detects area radiation deviations, and tests detection equipment to ensure accuracy. Calculates safe radiation exposure time for personnel, using plant contamination readings and prescribed safe levels of radiation. Observes projected photographs to locate particle tracks and events, and compiles lists of events from particle detectors. Scans photographic emulsions exposed to direct radiation to compute track properties from standard formulas, using microscope with scales and protractors. Monitors personnel for length and intensity of exposure to radiation for health and safety purposes. Calibrates and maintains chemical instrumentation sensing elements and sampling system equipment, using calibration instruments and hand tools. Informs supervisors to take action when individual exposures or area radiation levels approach maximum permissible limits. Prepares reports on contamination tests, material and equipment decontaminated, and methods used in decontamination process. Confers with scientist directing project to determine significant events to watch for during test. Instructs personnel in radiation safety procedures, and demonstrates use of protective clothing and equipment. Determines or recommends radioactive decontamination procedures, according to size and nature of equipment and degree of contamination. Weighs and mixes decontamination chemical solutions in tank, and immerses objects in solution for specified time, using hoist. Enters data into computer to record characteristics of nuclear events and locating coordinates of particles. Decontaminates objects by cleaning with soap or solvents or by abrading, using wire brush, buffing wheel, or sandblasting machine. Places radioactive waste, such as sweepings and broken sample bottles, into containers for disposal.

Knowledge: Computers and Electronics; Engineering and Technology; Mathematics; Physics; Chemistry; Biology; Medicine and Dentistry; Education and Training; English Language; Public Safety and Security; Communications and Media

Abilities: Oral Comprehension; Written Comprehension; Oral Expression; Problem Sensitivity; Deductive Reasoning; Inductive Reasoning; Information Ordering; Category Flexibility; Mathematical Reasoning; Number Facility; Speed of Closure; Selective Attention; Manual Dexterity; Finger Dexterity; Control Precision; Dynamic Flexibility; Gross Body Equilibrium; Near Vision; Speech Clarity

Geological Data Technicians

Measure, record, and evaluate geological data, such as core samples and cuttings, used in prospecting for oil or gas. Measures geological characteristics used in prospecting for oil or gas, using measuring instruments. Records readings to obtain data used in prospecting for oil or gas. Evaluates and interprets core samples and cuttings, and other geological data used in prospecting for oil or gas. Operates and adjusts equipment and apparatus to obtain geological data. Reads and studies reports to compile information and data for geological and geophysical prospecting. Sets up, or directs set-up, of instruments used to collect geological data. Collects samples and cuttings, using equipment and hand tools. Interviews individuals and researches public databases to obtain information Assembles, maintains, and distributes information for library or record system. Plans and directs activities of workers who operate equipment to collect data, or operates equipment. Develops and prints photographic recordings of information, using equipment. Diagnoses and repairs malfunctioning instruments and equipment, using manufacturers' manuals and hand tools. Develops and designs packing materials and handling procedures for shipping of objects. Prepares and attaches packing instructions to shipping container.

Knowledge: Administration and Management; Clerical; Production and Processing; Engineering and Technology; Physics

Abilities: Written Comprehension; Fluency of Ideas; Deductive Reasoning; Information Ordering; Mathematical Reasoning; Number Facility; Speed of Closure; Flexibility of Closure; Time Sharing; Control Precision; Gross Body Equilibrium; Far Vision; Visual Color Discrimination; Speech Clarity

Geological Sample Test Technicians

Test and analyze geological samples, crude oil, or petroleum products to detect presence of petroleum, gas, or mineral deposits indicating potential for exploration and production, or to determine physical and chemical properties to ensure that products meet quality standards. Tests samples for content and characteristics, using laboratory apparatus and testing equipment. Analyzes samples to determine presence, quantity, and quality of products, such as oil or gases. Records testing and operational data for review and further analysis. Collects solid and fluid samples from oil or gas bearing formations for analysis. Assembles and disassembles testing, measuring, and mechanical equipment and devices. Adjusts and repairs testing, electrical, and mechanical equipment and devices. Inspects engines for wear and defective parts, using equipment and measuring devices. Supervises and coordinates activities of workers, including initiating and recommending personnel actions.

Knowledge: Personnel and Human Resources; Mechanical; Physics; Chemistry

Abilities: Inductive Reasoning; Information Ordering; Mathematical Reasoning; Number Facility; Flexibility of Closure; Wrist-Finger Speed; Visual Color Discrimination

Meteorological Technicians

Analyze and record oceanographic and meteorological data to forecast changes in weather or sea conditions, and to determine trends in movement and utilization of water. Analyzes oceanographic and meteorological data to forecast changes in water, weather, and sea conditions. Observes general weather conditions and visibility, and reads test or measuring instruments to collect meteorological and oceanographic data. Prepares maps, charts, graphs, and technical reports describing surface weather, upper air, and sea conditions. Recommends or positions equipment and instruments used to test, manipulate, or adjust for environmental conditions. Prepares warnings or briefings regarding current or predicted environmental conditions, using teletype machine. Pilots and controls submersible craft to conduct research, salvage, or rescue operations, in accordance with plans. Plans and develops operational procedures or techniques to conduct underwater research. Installs, maintains, and conducts operational tests of watercraft, equipment, and facilities.

Knowledge: Computers and Electronics; Design; Mathematics; Physics; Geography; English Language; Communications and Media; Transportation

Abilities: Written Comprehension; Written Expression; Problem Sensitivity; Deductive Reasoning; Inductive Reasoning; Information Ordering; Category Flexibility; Number Facility; Memorization; Speed of Closure; Flexibility of Closure; Perceptual Speed; Spatial Orientation; Selective Attention; Time Sharing; Response Orientation; Rate Control; Wrist-Finger Speed; Gross Body Equilibrium; Near Vision; Far Vision; Night Vision; Depth Perception; Glare Sensitivity

Criminalists and Ballistics Experts

Examine, identify, classify, and analyze evidence related to criminology. Examines, tests, and analyzes tissue samples, chemical substances, physical materials, and ballistics evidence, using recording, measuring, and testing equipment. Interprets laboratory findings and test results to identify and classify substances, materials, and other evidence collected at crime scene. Collects and preserves criminal evidence used to solve cases. Confers with ballistics, fingerprinting, handwriting, documents, electronics, medical, chemical, or metallurgical experts concerning evidence and its interpretation. Reconstructs crime scene to determine relationships among pieces of evidence. Prepares reports or presentations of findings, investigative methods, or laboratory techniques. Testifies as expert witness on evidence or laboratory techniques in trials or hearings.

Knowledge: Computers and Electronics; Chemistry; Biology; Medicine and Dentistry; English Language; Public Safety and Security; Law, Government, and Jurisprudence

Abilities: Oral Expression; Written Expression; Fluency of Ideas; Originality; Inductive Reasoning; Information Ordering; Category Flexibility; Number Facility; Memorization; Speed of Closure; Flexibility of Closure; Spatial Orientation; Visualization; Near Vision; Visual Color Discrimination; Night Vision; Peripheral Vision; Depth Perception; Glare Sensitivity; Speech Clarity

Scientific Helpers

Assist supervising scientists to research problems and conduct experiments and tests. Prepares and tests mineralogical or geophysical samples for analysis or examination. Compiles and records mineralogical or geophysical sample data specifications. Joins scientists on mineralogical or geophysical expeditions to collect samples. Packs and labels mineralogical or geophysical specimens.

Knowledge: Production and Processing; Physics; Geography; History and Archeology

Abilities: Information Ordering; Category Flexibility; Memorization; Flexibility of Closure; Manual Dexterity; Stamina; Gross Body Coordination; Gross Body Equilibrium; Visual Color Discrimination

Mathematical Technicians

Apply standardized mathematical formulas, principles, and methodologies to technical problems in engineering and physical science in relation to specific industrial and research objectives, processes, equipment, and products. Selects most feasible combination and sequence of computational methods to reduce raw data to meaningful and manageable terms. Analyzes raw data from computer or recorded on photographic film or other media. Selects most economical and reliable combination of manual, mechanical, or data processing methods and equipment consistent with data reduction requirements. Calculates data for analysis, using computer or calculator. Translates data into numerical values, equations, flowcharts, graphs, or other media. Modifies standard formulas to conform to data processing method selected. Analyzes processed data to detect errors. Confers with professional, scientific, and engineering personnel to plan project.

Knowledge: Computers and Electronics; Engineering and Technology; Mathematics; English Language

Abilities: Oral Comprehension; Fluency of Ideas; Deductive Reasoning; Mathematical Reasoning; Number Facility

Taxidermists

Prepare, stuff, and mount skins of birds, fish, or mammals in lifelike form. Removes skin from animal, using knives, scissors, and pliers, and rubs preservative solutions into skin. Constructs wire foundation or plaster mold, and forms body, using papier-mache and tape, to display lifelike from. Covers foundation with skin, using adhesive or modeling clay. Affixes eyes, teeth, and claws to specimen, using adhesive. Dresses feathers and brushes fur to enhance lifelike appearance. Mounts specimen in case to present animal in its natural environment. Prepares animal carcasses for scientific or exhibition purposes.

Knowledge: Biology

Abilities: Visualization; Arm-Hand Steadiness

Secondary School Teachers

▲ Growth: 22%
▲ Annual Job Openings: 168,392
▲ Yearly Earnings $36,784
▲ Education Required: Bachelor's degree
▲ Self-employed: 0%
▲ Part-time: 10%

Teachers—Secondary School

Instruct students in public or private schools in one or more subjects, such as English, mathematics, or social studies. May be designated according to subject matter specialty, such as typing instructors, commercial teachers, or English teachers. Include vocational high school teachers. Instructs students, using various teaching methods, such as lecture and demonstration. Assigns lessons and corrects homework. Develops and administers tests. Prepares course outlines and objectives according to curriculum guidelines or state and local requirements. Uses audio-visual aids and other materials to supplement presentations. Evaluates, records, and reports student progress. Confers with students, parents, and school counselors to resolve behavioral and academic problems. Maintains discipline in classroom. Participates in faculty and professional meetings, educational conferences, and teacher training workshops. Selects, stores, orders, issues, and inventories classroom equipment, materials, and supplies. Keeps attendance records. Performs advisory duties, such as sponsoring student organizations or clubs, helping students select courses, and counseling students with problems.

Knowledge: Administration and Management; Clerical; Psychology; Sociology and Anthropology; Geography; Therapy and Counseling; Education and Training; English Language; Foreign Language; History and Archeology; Philosophy and Theology

Abilities: Oral Comprehension; Written Comprehension; Oral Expression; Written Expression; Originality; Memorization; Time Sharing; Speech Recognition; Speech Clarity

Secretaries

▲ Growth: 0%
▲ Annual Job Openings: 433,901
▲ Yearly Earnings $23,129
▲ Education Required: Postsecondary vocational training
▲ Self-employed: 0%
▲ Part-time: 19%

Secretaries, Except Legal and Medical

Relieve officials of clerical work and minor administrative and business details by scheduling appointments, giving information to callers, taking dictation, composing and typing routine correspondence (using typewriter or computer), reading and routing incoming mail, filing correspondence and other records, and other assigned clerical duties. Exclude executive secretaries. Answers telephone and gives information to callers, takes messages, or transfers calls to appropriate individuals. Opens incoming mail and routes mail to appropriate individuals. Answers routine correspondence. Composes and distributes meeting notes, correspondence, and reports. Schedules appointments. Maintains calendar and coordinates conferences and meetings. Takes dictation, in shorthand or by machine, and transcribes information. Locates and attaches appropriate file to incoming correspondence requiring reply. Files correspondence and other records. Makes copies of correspondence and other printed matter. Arranges travel schedules and reservations. Greets and welcomes visitors, determines nature of business, and conducts visitors to employer or appropriate person. Compiles and maintains lists and records, using typewriter or computer. Records and types minutes of meetings, using typewriter or computer. Compiles and types statistical reports, using typewriter or computer. Mails newsletters, promotional material, and other information. Orders and dispenses supplies. Prepares and mails checks. Collects and disburses funds from cash account and keeps records. Provides customer services such as order placement and account information.

Knowledge: Clerical; Economics and Accounting; Customer and Personal Service; Computers and Electronics; Geography; English Language; Communications and Media; Transportation

Abilities: Category Flexibility; Memorization; Speed of Closure; Perceptual Speed; Finger Dexterity; Wrist-Finger Speed; Near Vision; Speech Recognition

Securities and Financial Services Sales Workers

▲ Growth: 38%

▲ Annual Job Openings: 40,568

▲ Yearly Earnings $59,633

▲ Education Required: Long-term O-J-T

▲ Self-employed: 24%

▲ Part-time: 8%

Sales Agents, Securities and Commodities

Buy and sell securities in investment and trading firms and develop and implement financial plans for individuals, businesses, and organizations. Develops financial plan based on analysis of client's financial status, and discusses financial options with client. Contacts exchange or brokerage firm to execute order or buys and sells securities based on market quotation and competition in market. Records transactions accurately and keeps client informed about transactions. Analyzes market conditions to determine optimum time to execute securities transactions. Keeps informed about political and economic trends that influence stock prices. Reads corporate reports and calculates ratios to determine best prospects for profit on stock purchase and to monitor client account. Interviews client to determine client's assets, liabilities, cash flow, insurance coverage, tax status, and financial objectives. Reviews all securities transactions to ensure accuracy of information and that trades conform to regulations of governing agencies. Prepares documents to implement plan selected by client. Completes sales order tickets and submits for processing of client-requested transaction. Informs and advises concerned parties regarding fluctuations and securities transactions affecting plan or account. Prepares financial reports to monitor client or corporate finances. Identifies potential clients, using advertising campaigns, mailing lists, and personal contacts, and solicits business.

Knowledge: Economics and Accounting; Sales and Marketing; Customer and Personal Service; Personnel and Human Resources; Computers and Electronics; Mathematics

Abilities: Written Comprehension; Written Expression; Fluency of Ideas; Deductive Reasoning; Mathematical Reasoning; Number Facility; Speed of Closure; Near Vision; Speech Recognition; Speech Clarity

Sales Agents, Financial Services

Sell financial services, such as loan, tax, and securities counseling, to customers of financial institutions and business establishments. Sells services and equipment, such as trust, investment, and check processing services. Develops prospects from current commercial customers, referral leads, and sales and trade meetings. Contacts prospective customers to present information and explain available services. Determines customers' financial services needs and prepares proposals to sell services. Reviews business trends and advises customers regarding expected fluctuations. Makes presentations on financial services to groups to attract new clients. Prepares forms or agreement to complete sale. Evaluates costs and revenue of agreements to determine continued profitability.

Knowledge: Economics and Accounting; Sales and Marketing; Customer and Personal Service; Computers and Electronics; Law, Government, and Jurisprudence

Abilities: Written Comprehension; Deductive Reasoning; Mathematical Reasoning; Number Facility; Near Vision; Speech Recognition; Speech Clarity

Service Managers

- ▲ Growth: 21%
- ▲ Annual Job Openings: 171,229
- ▲ Yearly Earnings $48,339
- ▲ Education Required: Work experience, plus degree
- ▲ Self-employed: 52%
- ▲ Part-time: 7%

Nursing Directors

Plan, direct, and coordinate facilities or programs providing nursing care. Include directors of schools of nursing. Plans curricula and schedules health education instruction training and counseling for nursing school, in-service, and community programs. Plans, directs, and administers nursing services or educational programs in health care facilities. Establishes and revises policies and procedures, such as selection, performance, and compensation standards, organizational objectives, and medical and maintenance procedures. Prepares budget and administers health care programs and services within budgetary limitations. Recruits, interviews, selects, and assigns nursing and health services staff, faculty, and students. Conducts studies and site visits to assess program needs and evaluate the cost-effectiveness and efficiency of existing services. Prepares, maintains, and updates nursing policy and procedure manuals. Establishes records of management systems for health services, patients, staff, and nursing students. Consults with legal counsel, community groups, medical staff, and administrators regarding the application of nursing principles to industrial and social welfare problems. Directs collection, analysis, and interpretation of health service and utilization statistics. Acts as liaison between health care institution or facility and community to promote cooperative relationships and plan integrated programming.

Knowledge: Administration and Management; Clerical; Economics and Accounting; Sales and Marketing; Customer and Personal Service; Personnel and Human Resources; Mathematics; Biology; Psychology; Sociology and Anthropology; Medicine and Dentistry; Therapy and Counseling; Education and Training

Abilities: Oral Comprehension; Written Comprehension; Oral Expression; Written Expression; Originality; Speech Clarity

Medical and Health Services Managers

Plan, direct, and coordinate medicine and health services in hospitals, clinics, managed care organizations, public health agencies, or similar organizations. Include hospital administrators, long-term care administrators, and other health care facility administrators. Administers fiscal operations, such as planning budgets, authorizing expenditures, and coordinating financial reporting. Directs and coordinates activities of medical, nursing, technical, clerical, service, and maintenance personnel of health care facility or mobile unit. Develops or expands medical programs or health services for research, rehabilitation, and community health promotion. Develops organizational policies and procedures, and establishes evaluative or operational criteria for facility or medical unit. Implements and administers programs and services for health care or medical facility. Establishes work schedules and assignments for staff, according to workload, space, and equipment availability. Prepares activity reports to inform management of the status and implementation plans of programs, services, and quality initiatives. Recruits, hires, and evaluates the performance of medical staff and auxiliary personnel. Reviews and analyzes facility activities and data to aid planning and cash- and risk-management and to improve service utilization. Consults with medical, business, and community groups to discuss service problems, coordinate activities and plans, and promote health programs. Develops instructional materials and conducts in-service and community-based educational programs. Inspects facilities for emergency readiness and compliance of access, safety, and sanitation regulations, and recommends building or equipment modifications. Develops and maintains computerized records management system to store or process personnel or activity data.

Knowledge: Administration and Management; Clerical; Economics and Accounting; Sales and Marketing; Customer and Personal Service; Personnel and Human Resources; Mathematics; Psychology; Medicine and Dentistry; Therapy and Counseling; Education and Training; Public Safety and Security; Communications and Media

Abilities: Written Comprehension; Oral Expression; Written Expression; Fluency of Ideas; Originality; Information Ordering; Mathematical Reasoning; Time Sharing; Speech Recognition; Speech Clarity

Amusement and Recreation Establishment Managers

Plan, direct, and coordinate the activities of organizations that provide amusement or recreational facilities or services to the public. Plans, organizes, and coordinates programs of recreational activities, entertainment, or instructional classes. Formulates and establishes operational policies, such as hours of operation, fee amounts, and accounting procedures. Determines work activities necessary to operate facility, and assigns duties to staff accordingly. Prepares, compiles, and maintains budgets, schedules of activities or personnel, and inventory or accounting records. Hires, promotes, and discharges workers. Enforces laws, safety regulations, and establishment rules concerning personnel or patron behavior. Purchases or orders supplies and equipment. Confers with patrons or employees to resolve grievances or work problems. Trains staff or instructs patrons in recreational activities, such as swimming, skating, dancing, riding animals, or shooting firearms. Inspects facilities for cleanliness, maintenance needs, or compliance with health and safety regulations. Plans and initiates promotional projects and writes materials to publicize and advertise recreational facilities and activities. Advises patrons of available facilities and activities and registers them for rental of facility or equipment, or for particular activity. Collects fees and issues receipts to patrons for use of facilities or participation in activities. Sells recreational supplies and equipment or lessons to patrons.

Knowledge: Administration and Management; Economics and Accounting; Sales and Marketing; Customer and Personal Service; Personnel and Human Resources; Education and Training; Public Safety and Security; Law, Government, and Jurisprudence

Abilities: Fluency of Ideas; Originality; Number Facility; Perceptual Speed; Gross Body Equilibrium; Far Vision

Social and Community Service Managers

Plan, organize, and coordinate the activities of a social service program or community outreach organization. Oversee the program or organization's budget and policies regarding participant involvement, program requirements, and benefits. Work may involve directing social workers, counselors, or probation officers. Confers and consults with individuals, groups, and committees to determine needs and to plan, implement, and extend organization's programs and services. Determines organizational policies and defines scope of services offered and administration of procedures. Establishes and maintains relationships with other agencies and organizations in community to meet and not duplicate community needs and services. Assigns duties to staff or volunteers. Plans, directs, and prepares fundraising activities and public relations materials. Researches and analyzes member or community needs as basis for community development. Participates in program activities to serve clients of agency. Prepares, distributes, and maintains records and reports, such as budgets, personnel records, or training manuals. Coordinates volunteer service programs, such as Red Cross, hospital volunteers, or vocational training for disabled individuals. Speaks to community groups to explain and interpret agency purpose, programs, and policies. Advises volunteers and volunteer leaders to ensure quality of programs and effective use of resources. Instructs and trains agency staff or volunteers in skills required to provide services. Interviews, recruits, or hires volunteers and staff. Observes workers to evaluate performance and ensure that work meets established standards.

Knowledge: Administration and Management; Economics and Accounting; Customer and Personal Service; Personnel and Human Resources; Sociology and Anthropology; Education and Training; English Language; Communications and Media

Abilities: Written Comprehension; Written Expression; Fluency of Ideas; Originality; Category Flexibility; Mathematical Reasoning; Perceptual Speed; Selective Attention; Speech Clarity

Association Managers and Administrators

Direct and coordinate activities of professional, trade, or business associations to achieve goals, objectives, and standards of association. Coordinates committees or board of directors of association to evaluate services, recommend new programs, or promote association. Plans, directs, or participates in preparation and presentation of educational material to membership or public using various media. Plans, develops, and implements new programs and ideas based on evaluation of current programs. Directs and coordinates association functions, such as conventions, exhibits, and local or regional workshops or meetings. Directs surveys and compilation of membership data, such as average income, benefits, standards, or common problems. Advises chapters, members, or businesses of association regarding financial, organizational, growth, or membership problems. Analyzes factors affecting association, members, or member organizations, such as legislation and taxation or economic conditions and trends. Prepares monthly or annual budget reports and oversees finances of association. Represents association at public, social, or business receptions, or in negotiations with representatives of government, business, or labor organizations. Visits members or chapters of association to ensure association standards are being met and to promote goodwill.

Knowledge: Administration and Management; Economics and Accounting; Mathematics; Education and Training

Abilities: Oral Comprehension; Written Comprehension; Oral Expression; Written Expression; Originality; Deductive Reasoning; Inductive Reasoning; Information Ordering; Category Flexibility; Mathematical Reasoning; Number Facility; Memorization; Near Vision; Speech Recognition; Speech Clarity

Service Establishment Managers

Manage service establishment or direct and coordinate service activities within an establishment. Plan, direct, and coordinate service operations within an organization, or the activities of organizations that provide services. Directs worker activities in service establishments, such as travel agencies, health clubs, or beauty salons, or in customer service departments. Plans and adjusts work schedule and assigns duties to meet customer demands. Coordinates sales promotion activities and sells services to clients. Communicates with customer to ascertain needs, advise on services, adjust complaints, or negotiate contracts. Keeps records of work hours, labor costs, expenditures, receipts, and materials used, to analyze and prepare operation reports or budget. Observes worker performance and reviews employees' work to ensure accuracy or quality of work. Interviews and hires personnel. Orients and trains new personnel in job duties, safety and health rules, company policies, and performance requirements. Confers with employees to give performance feedback, assist with providing services, and solve problems. Transfers or discharges employees, according to work performance. Requisitions or purchases equipment or supplies to enable establishment to provide services.

Knowledge: Administration and Management; Economics and Accounting; Sales and Marketing; Customer and Personal Service; Personnel and Human Resources; Education and Training

Abilities: Number Facility; Perceptual Speed; Time Sharing; Far Vision; Sound Localization

Gambling Establishment Managers

Plan, direct, and coordinate the activities of organizations or establishments, such as casinos, cardrooms, and racetracks, that provide gambling or games-of-chance activities to the public. Review operational expenses, budget estimates, betting accounts, and collection reports for accuracy. Observes and supervises operation to ensure that employees render prompt and courteous service to patrons. Establishes policies on types of gambling offered, odds, extension of credit, and serving food and beverages. Directs workers compiling summary sheets for each race or event to show amount wagered and amount to be paid to winners. Prepares work schedules, assigns work stations, and keeps attendance records. Resolves customer complaints regarding service. Interviews and hires workers. Trains new workers and evaluates their performance. Explains and interprets house rules, such as game rules and betting limits, to patrons. Records, issues receipts for, and pays off bets.

Knowledge: Administration and Management; Economics and Accounting; Customer and Personal Service; Personnel and Human Resources; Mathematics

Abilities: Mathematical Reasoning; Number Facility; Time Sharing

Security Managers

Plan, direct, and coordinate implementation of security procedures, systems, and personnel to protect private or public property and personnel from theft, fire, and personal injury. Inspects premises to determine security needs, test alarm systems and safety equipment, or detect safety hazards. Analyzes security needs; plans and directs implementation of security measures, such as security or safety systems; and estimates costs of operation. Develops and establishes security procedures for establishment or for protection of individual, group, or property. Confers with management to determine need for programs and to formulate and coordinate security programs with establishment activities. Directs activities of personnel in developing, revising, or updating company security measures, to comply with federal regulations. Confers with client regarding security needs, evaluation of services, or problems with security systems. Assigns workers to shifts, posts, or patrol, according to protection requirements or size and nature of establishment. Interviews and hires security workers. Observes workers' performance of duties to evaluate efficiency and to detect and correct inefficient or improper work practices. Trains workers in security operations, such as first aid, fire safety, and detecting and apprehending intruders or shoplifters. Conducts background investigations of job applicants or employees to obtain information such as personal histories, character references, or wage garnishments. Monitors or supervises monitoring of alarm system controls and investigation of alarm signals. Conducts or directs surveillance of premises or suspects. Interprets company policies and procedures for workers. Studies federal security regulations, and consults with federal representatives for interpretation or application of particular regulations to company operations. Responds to calls from subordinates to direct activities during fires, storms, riots, and other emergencies. Prepares reports concerning investigations, security needs and recommendations, or security manual of procedures. Investigates crimes committed against client or establishment, such as fraud, robbery, arson, or patent infringement. Confers and cooperates with police, fire, and civil defense authorities to coordinate activities during emergency. Contacts business establishments to promote sales of security services.

Knowledge: Administration and Management; Sales and Marketing; Customer and Personal Service; Personnel and Human Resources; Education and Training; Public Safety and Security; Law, Government, and Jurisprudence

Abilities: Written Comprehension; Fluency of Ideas; Deductive Reasoning; Inductive Reasoning; Speed of Closure; Flexibility of Closure; Perceptual Speed; Spatial Orientation; Selective Attention; Time Sharing; Response Orientation; Rate Control; Reaction Time; Gross Body Equilibrium; Near Vision; Far Vision; Night Vision; Peripheral Vision; Hearing Sensitivity; Auditory Attention; Sound Localization

Ship Captains and Pilots

- ▲ Growth: -2%
- ▲ Annual Job Openings: 1,049
- ▲ Yearly Earnings $40,809
- ▲ Education Required: Work experience in a related occupation
- ▲ Self-employed: 10%
- ▲ Part-time: 3%

Ship and Boat Captains

Command vessels in oceans, bays, lakes, rivers, and coastal waters. Commands water vessels, such as passenger and freight vessels, fishing vessels, yachts, tugboats, barges, deep submergence vehicles, and ferryboats. Directs and coordinates activities of crew or workers, such as loading and unloading, operating signal devices, fishing, and repairing defective equipment. Steers and operates vessel or orders helmsperson to steer vessel, using radio, depth finder, radar, lights, buoys, and lighthouses. Computes position, sets course, and determines speed, using charts, area plotting sheets, compass, sextant, and knowledge of local conditions. Inspects vessel to ensure safety of crew and passengers, efficient and safe operation of vessel and equipment, and conformance to regulations. Signals crew or deckhands to rig tow lines, open or close gates and ramps, and pull guard chains across entry. Monitors sonar and navigational aids and reads gauges to verify sufficient levels of hydraulic fluid, air pressure, and oxygen. Calculates sighting of land, using electronic sounding devices and following contour lines on chart. Maintains records of daily activities, movements, and ports-of-call, and prepares progress and personnel reports. Interviews, hires, and instructs crew, and assigns watches and living quarters. Tows and maneuvers barge or signals tugboat to tow barge to destination. Signals passing vessels, using whistle, flashing lights, flags, and radio. Purchases supplies and equipment, contacts buyers to sell fish, and resolves questions or problems with customs officials. Collects fares from customers or signals ferryboat helper to collect fares.

Knowledge: Administration and Management; Personnel and Human Resources; Computers and Electronics; Mathematics; Physics; Geography; Foreign Language; Public Safety and Security; Law, Government, and Jurisprudence; Telecommunications; Transportation

Abilities: Spatial Orientation; Selective Attention; Time Sharing; Control Precision; Multilimb Coordination; Response Orientation; Rate Control; Reaction Time; Speed of Limb Movement; Gross Body Equilibrium; Far Vision; Night Vision; Peripheral Vision; Depth Perception; Glare Sensitivity; Hearing Sensitivity; Auditory Attention; Sound Localization; Speech Recognition; Speech Clarity

Pilots, Ship

Command ships to steer them into and out of harbors, estuaries, straits, and sounds, and on rivers, lakes, and bays. Must be licensed by U.S. Coast Guard with limitations indicating class and tonnage of vessels for which license is valid and route and waters that may be piloted. Directs course and speed of ship on basis of specialized knowledge of local winds, weather, tides, and current. Orders worker at helm to steer ship. Navigates ship to avoid reefs, outlying shoals, and other hazards, utilizing aids to navigation, such as lighthouses and buoys. Signals tugboat captain to berth and unberth ship.

Knowledge: Physics; Geography; Public Safety and Security; Law, Government, and Jurisprudence; Transportation

Abilities: Memorization; Flexibility of Closure; Spatial Orientation; Selective Attention; Time Sharing; Control Precision; Response Orientation; Rate Control; Reaction Time; Speed of Limb Movement; Gross Body Equilibrium; Far Vision; Night Vision; Peripheral Vision; Depth Perception; Glare Sensitivity; Auditory Attention; Sound Localization

Short Order and Fast Food Cooks

▲ Growth: 22%
▲ Annual Job Openings: 237,301
▲ Yearly Earnings $14,414
▲ Education Required: Short-term O-J-T
▲ Self-employed: 1%
▲ Part-time: 38%

Cooks, Specialty Fast Food

Prepare and cook food in a fast-food restaurant with a limited menu. Duties of the cooks are limited to one or two basic items, such as hamburgers, chicken, pizza, tacos, or fish and chips, and normally involve operating large-volume single-purpose cooking equipment. Prepares specialty foods, such as pizzas, fish and chips, sandwiches, and tacos, following specific methods, usually requiring short preparation time. Reads food order slip or receives verbal instructions as to food required by patron, and prepares and cooks food according to instructions. Measures required ingredients needed for specific food item being prepared. Slices meats, cheeses, and vegetables, using knives and food-slicing machines. Prepares dough, following recipe. Cleans work area and food preparation equipment. Prepares and serves beverage, such as coffee and fountain drinks. Serves orders to customers at window or counter.

Knowledge: Customer and Personal Service

Abilities: None above average

Ski Patrol Workers and Life Guards

▲ Growth: 17%
▲ Annual Job Openings: 53,969
▲ Yearly Earnings $18,678
▲ Education Required: Short-term O-J-T
▲ Self-employed: 0%
▲ Part-time: 51%

Protective Service Workers, Recreational

Monitor recreational areas, such as pools, beaches, or ski slopes, to provide assistance and protection to participants. Patrols or monitors recreational areas, such as trails, slopes, and swimming areas, on foot, in vehicle, or from tower. Cautions recreational participant regarding inclement weather, unsafe areas, or illegal conduct. Rescues distressed persons, using rescue techniques and equipment. Observes activities in assigned area with binoculars to detect hazards, disturbances, or safety infractions. Contacts emergency medical services in case of serious injury. Examines injured persons and administers first aid or cardiopulmonary resuscitation, utilizing training and medical supplies and equipment. Inspects facilities for cleanliness and maintains order in recreational areas. Inspects recreational equipment, such as rope tows, T-bar, J-bar, and chairlifts, for safety hazards and damage or wear. Maintains information on emergency medical treatment and weather and beach conditions, using report forms. Instructs participants in skiing, swimming, or other recreational activity. Participates in recreational demonstrations to entertain resort guests.

Knowledge: Medicine and Dentistry; Public Safety and Security

Abilities: Flexibility of Closure; Spatial Orientation; Selective Attention; Time Sharing; Multilimb Coordination; Response Orientation; Reaction Time; Speed of Limb Movement; Static Strength; Explosive Strength; Dynamic Strength; Trunk Strength; Stamina; Extent Flexibility; Dynamic Flexibility; Gross Body Coordination; Gross Body Equilibrium; Far Vision; Night Vision; Peripheral Vision; Depth Perception; Glare Sensitivity; Hearing Sensitivity; Auditory Attention; Sound Localization; Speech Clarity

Social Workers

▲ Growth: 32%

▲ Annual Job Openings: 75,554

▲ Yearly Earnings $31,220

▲ Education Required: Bachelor's degree

▲ Self-employed: 2%

▲ Part-time: 11%

Community Organization Social Workers

Plan, organize, and work with community groups to help solve social problems and deliver specialized social services. Organizes projects, such as discussion groups, and conducts consumer problem surveys to stimulate civic responsibility and promote group work concepts. Investigates problems of assigned community and individuals disadvantaged because of income, age, or economic or personal handicaps, to determine needs. Develops, organizes, and directs customized programs, such as physical, educational, recreational, or cultural activities, for individuals and groups. Reviews and evaluates available resources and services from local agencies to provide social assistance for clients. Secures and coordinates community social service assistance, such as health, welfare, and education for individuals and families. Assists communities in establishing new local affiliates or programs. Initiates and maintains liaison between housing authority and local agencies to promote development and management of public housing. Speaks before groups to explain supportive services and resources available to persons needing special assistance. Facilitates establishment of constructive relationships between tenants and housing management, and among tenants. Interprets standards and program goals of national or state agencies to assist local organizations in establishing goals and standards. Coordinates work activities of individuals to improve vocational skills. Writes proposals to obtain government or private funding for projects designed to meet needs of community. Maintains records and prepares reports on community topics, such as work activities, local conditions, and developing trends. Assesses complexity level of individual's capacity to perform work activities. Identifies individual's behavior deviations and assists individual to resolve work-related difficulties. Demonstrates and instructs participants in activities, such as sports, dances, games, arts, crafts, and dramatics. Demonstrates job duties to individuals, oversees and monitors work performance, and examines workpiece to verify adherence to specifications. Recruits, trains, and supervises paid staff and volunteers in specific assignments. Prepares and presents budgets.

Knowledge: Administration and Management; Sales and Marketing; Customer and Personal Service; Personnel and Human Resources; Psychology; Sociology and Anthropology; Therapy and Counseling; Education and Training; English Language; Communications and Media

Abilities: Time Sharing; Speech Recognition

Social Workers

Counsel and aid individuals and families with problems relating to personal and family adjustments, finances, employment, food, clothing, housing, or other human needs and conditions. Counsels individuals or family members regarding behavior modifications, rehabilitation, social adjustments, financial assistance, vocational training, child care, or medical care. Counsels parents with child-rearing problems and children and youth with difficulties in social adjustments. Interviews individuals to assess social and emotional capabilities, physical and mental impairments, and financial needs. Refers client to community resources for needed assistance. Arranges for daycare, homemaker service, prenatal care, and child planning programs for clients in need of such services. Leads group counseling sessions to provide support in such areas as grief, stress, or chemical dependency. Counsels students whose behavior, school progress, or mental or physical impairment indicates need for assistance. Arranges for medical, psychiatric, and other tests that may disclose cause of difficulties and indicate remedial measures. Consults with parents, teachers, and other school personnel to determine causes of problems and effect solutions. Serves as liaison between student, home, school, family service agencies, child guidance clinics, courts, protective services, doctors, and clergy members. Investigates home conditions to determine suitability of foster or adoptive home, or to protect children from harmful environment. Develops program content and organizes and leads activities planned to enhance social development of individual members and accomplishment of group goals. Determines client's eligibility for financial assistance. Reviews service plan and performs follow-up to determine quantity and quality of service provided to client. Places children in foster or adoptive homes, institutions, or medical treatment centers. Evaluates personal characteristics of foster home or adoption applicants. Maintains case history records and prepares reports. Collects supplementary information, such as employment, medical records, or school reports. Assists travelers, including runaways, migrants, transients, refugees, repatriated Americans, and problem families.

Knowledge: Administration and Management; Clerical; Customer and Personal Service; Psychology; Sociology and Anthropology; Therapy and Counseling; Foreign Language; Philosophy and Theology; Law, Government, and Jurisprudence

Abilities: Oral Comprehension; Oral Expression

Probation and Correctional Treatment Specialists

Provide social services to assist in rehabilitation of law offenders in custody or on probation. Include probation and parole officers. Counsels offender and refers offender to social resources of community for assistance. Provides guidance to inmates or offenders, such as development of vocational and educational plans and available social services. Formulates rehabilitation plan for each assigned offender or inmate. Interviews offender or inmate to determine social progress and individual problems, needs, interests, and attitude. Consults with attorneys, judges, and institution personnel to evaluate inmate's social progress. Conducts follow-up interview with offender or inmate to ascertain progress made. Determines nature and extent of inmate's or offender's criminal record and current and prospective social problems. Reviews and evaluates legal and social history and progress of offender or inmate. Informs offender or inmate of requirements of conditional release, such as office visits, restitution payments, or educational and employment stipulations. Confers with inmate's or offender's family to identify needs and problems, and to ensure that family and business are attended to. Makes recommendations concerning conditional release or institutionalization of offender or inmate. Assists offender or inmate with matters concerning detainers, sentences in other jurisdictions, writs, and applications for social assistance. Develops and prepares informational packets of social agencies and assistance organizations and programs for inmate or offender. Prepares and maintains case folder for each assigned inmate or offender. Conducts prehearing or presentencing investigations, and testifies in court.

Knowledge: Psychology; Sociology and Anthropology; Therapy and Counseling; Public Safety and Security; Law, Government, and Jurisprudence

Abilities: None above average

Solderers and Brazers

- ▲ Growth: 21%
- ▲ Annual Job Openings: 4,882
- ▲ Yearly Earnings $16,910
- ▲ Education Required: Short-term O-J-T
- ▲ Self-employed: 0%
- ▲ Part-time: 8%

Solderers

Solder together components to assemble fabricated metal products, using soldering iron. Melts and applies solder along adjoining edges of workpieces to solder joints, using soldering iron, gas torch, or electric-ultrasonic equipment. Melts and applies solder to fill holes, indentations, and seams of fabricated metal products, using soldering equipment. Heats soldering iron or workpiece to specified temperature for soldering, using gas flame or electric current. Dips workpieces into molten solder or places solder strip between seams and heats seam with iron to band items together. Aligns and clamps workpieces together, using rule, square, or hand tools, or positions items in fixtures, jigs, or vise. Applies flux to workpiece surfaces in preparation for soldering. Grinds, cuts, buffs, or bends edges of workpieces to be joined to ensure snug fit, using power grinder and hand tools. Melts and separates soldered joints to repair misaligned or damaged assemblies, using soldering equipment. Removes workpieces from molten solder and holds parts together until color indicates that solder has set. Cleans tip of soldering iron, using chemical solution or cleaning compound. Cleans workpieces, using chemical solution, file, wire brush, or grinder.

Knowledge: None above average

Abilities: Arm-Hand Steadiness; Manual Dexterity; Finger Dexterity; Wrist-Finger Speed; Speed of Limb Movement

Brazers

Braze together components to assemble fabricated metal parts, using torch or welding machine and flux. Guides torch and rod along joint of workpieces to heat to brazing temperature, melt braze alloy, and bond workpieces together. Adjusts electric current and timing cycle of resistance welding machine to heat metal to bonding temperature. Selects torch tip, flux, and brazing alloy from data charts or work order. Connects hoses from torch to regulator valves and cylinders of oxygen and specified fuel gas, acetylene or natural. Turns valves to start flow of gases, lights flame, and adjusts valves to obtain desired color and size of flame. Brushes flux onto joint of workpiece, or dips braze rod into flux to prevent oxidation of metal. Melts and separates brazed joints to remove and straighten damaged or misaligned components, using hand torch or furnace. Aligns and secures workpieces in fixtures, jigs, or vise, using rule, square, or template. Examines seam and rebrazes defective joints or broken parts. Cleans joints of workpieces, using wire brush or by dipping them into cleaning solution. Removes workpiece from fixture, using tongs, and cools workpiece, using air or water. Cuts carbon electrodes to specified size and shape, using cutoff saw.

Knowledge: None above average

Abilities: Glare Sensitivity

Special Education Teachers

- ▲ Growth: 59%
- ▲ Annual Job Openings: 49,029
- ▲ Yearly Earnings $37,104
- ▲ Education Required: Bachelor's degree
- ▲ Self-employed: 0%
- ▲ Part-time: 12%

Special Education Vocational Training Teachers

Plan and conduct special education work and study programs or teach vocational skills to handicapped students. Counsels and instructs students in matters such as vocational choices, job readiness, and job retention skills and behaviors. Instructs students in areas such as personal-social skills and work-related attitudes and behaviors. Confers with students, parents, school personnel, and other individuals to plan vocational training that meet needs, interests, and abilities of students. Develops work opportunities that allow students to experience success in performing tasks of increasing difficulty and that teach work values. Confers with potential employers to obtain cooperation, adapting work situations to special needs of students. Confers with employers and visits worksite to monitor progress of students. Establishes contacts with employers and employment agencies and surveys newspapers and other sources to locate work opportunities for students. Evaluates and selects program participants according to specified criteria. Determines support needed to meet employer requirements and fulfill program goals. Assists students in applying for jobs and accompanies students to employment interviews. Conducts field trips to enable students to learn about job activities and to explore work environments.

Knowledge: Administration and Management; Sales and Marketing; Customer and Personal Service; Personnel and Human Resources; Psychology; Sociology and Anthropology; Therapy and Counseling; Education and Training; Philosophy and Theology

Abilities: Written Comprehension; Oral Expression

Teachers—Emotionally Impaired, Mentally Impaired, and Learning Disabled

Teach basic academic and living skills to students with emotional or mental impairments or learning disabilities. Teaches socially acceptable behavior, employing techniques such as behavior modification and positive reinforcement. Instructs students, using special educational strategies and techniques to improve sensory-motor and perceptual-motor development, memory, language, and cognition. Instructs students in academic subjects, utilizing various teaching techniques, such as phonetics, multisensory learning, and repetition, to reinforce learning. Instructs students in daily living skills required for independent maintenance and economic self-sufficiency, such as hygiene, safety, and food preparation. Plans curriculum and other instructional materials to meet student's needs, considering such factors as physical, emotional, and educational abilities. Selects and teaches reading material and math problems related to everyday life of individual student. Administers and interprets results of ability and achievement tests. Confers with parents, administrators, testing specialists, social workers, and others to develop individual educational plan for student. Confers with other staff members to plan programs designed to promote educational, physical, and social development of students. Works with students to increase motivation. Provides consistent reinforcement to learning, and continuous feedback to students. Observes, evaluates, and prepares reports on progress of students. Meets with parents to provide support, guidance in using community resources, and skills in dealing with students' learning impairments.

Knowledge: Customer and Personal Service; Psychology; Sociology and Anthropology; Medicine and Dentistry; Therapy and Counseling; Education and Training; English Language; Foreign Language

Abilities: Written Comprehension; Oral Expression; Written Expression; Speech Clarity

Teachers—Physically, Visually, and Hearing Impaired

Teach elementary and secondary school subjects to physically, visually, and hearing impaired students. Teaches academic subjects, daily living skills, and vocational skills to students, adapting teaching techniques to meet individual needs of students. Plans curriculum and prepares lessons and other materials, considering such factors as individual needs and learning levels and physical limitations of students. Instructs students in various forms of communication, such as gestures, sign language, finger spelling, and cues. Instructs students in reading and writing, using magnification equipment and large-print material or Braille system. Confers with parents, administrators, testing specialists, social workers, and others to develop individual educational program. Encourages students' participation in verbal and sensory classroom experiences to ensure comprehension of subject matter and development of social and communication skills. Attends and interprets lectures and instructions for students enrolled in regular classes, using sign language. Transcribes lessons and other materials into Braille for blind students or large print for low-vision students. Arranges for and conducts field trips designed to promote experiential learning. Discusses with parents how parents can encourage students' independence and well-being and to provide guidance in using community resources. Tests students' hearing aids to ensure hearing aids are functioning. Arranges and adjusts tools, work aids, and equipment utilized by students in classroom, such as specially equipped work tables, computers, and typewriters. Devises special teaching tools, techniques, and equipment.

Knowledge: Administration and Management; Clerical; Customer and Personal Service; Biology; Psychology; Sociology and Anthropology; Therapy and Counseling; Education and Training; English Language; Foreign Language; History and Archeology; Philosophy and Theology

Abilities: Oral Comprehension; Written Comprehension; Oral Expression; Originality; Auditory Attention; Speech Recognition; Speech Clarity

Special Education Evaluators

Assess type and degree of disability of handicapped children to aid in determining special programs and services required to meet educational needs. Observes student behavior and rates strength and weakness of factors, such as motivation, cooperativeness, aggression, and task completion. Tests children to detect learning limitations, and recommends follow-up activities, consultation, or services. Selects, administers, and scores tests to measure individual's aptitudes, educational achievements, perceptual motor skills, vision, and hearing. Evaluates student's readiness to transfer from special classes to regular classroom. Determines evaluation procedures for children having or suspected of having learning disabilities, mental retardation, behavior disorders, or physical handicaps. Confers with school or other personnel and studies records to obtain additional information on nature and severity of disability. Administers work-related tests and reviews records and other data to assess student vocational interests and abilities. Reports findings for staff consideration in placement of children in educational programs. Provides supportive services to regular classroom teacher.

Knowledge: Customer and Personal Service; Psychology; Sociology and Anthropology; Therapy and Counseling; Education and Training

Abilities: Oral Comprehension; Written Comprehension; Oral Expression; Written Expression

Parent Instructors—Child Development and Rehabilitation

Instruct parents of mentally and physically handicapped children in therapy techniques and behavior modification. Instructs parents in behavior modification, physical development, language development, and conceptual learning exercises and activities. Develops individual teaching plan covering self-help, motor, social, cognitive, and language skills development for parents to implement in home. Evaluates child's responses to determine level of physical and mental development. Determines parent's ability to comprehend and apply therapeutic and behavior modification techniques. Revises teaching plan to correspond with child's rate of development. Counsels parents and organizes groups of parents in similar situations to provide social and emotional support to parents. Consults and coordinates plans with other professionals. Teaches preschool subjects, such as limited-vocabulary sign language and color recognition, to children capable of learning such subjects. Refers parents and children to social services agencies for additional services and financial assistance.

Knowledge: Customer and Personal Service; Psychology; Sociology and Anthropology; Medicine and Dentistry; Therapy and Counseling; Education and Training

Abilities: Oral Comprehension; Fluency of Ideas; Speech Clarity

Specialty Food Workers

▲ Growth: 27%
▲ Annual Job Openings: 82,637
▲ Yearly Earnings $15,038
▲ Education Required: Short-term O-J-T
▲ Self-employed: 1%
▲ Part-time: 58%

Food Servers, Outside

Serve food to patrons outside of a restaurant environment, such as in hotels, hospital rooms, or cars. Exclude food vendors. Serves food and refreshments to patrons in automobiles and rooms. Prepares and delivers food trays. Places filled order on tray and fastens tray to car door, and removes equipment from room or automobile. Apportions and places food servings on plates and trays according to diet list on menu card. Examines filled tray for completeness and places on cart, dumbwaiter, or conveyor belt. Takes order and relays order to kitchen or serving counter to be filled. Carries silverware, linen, and food on tray or uses cart. Pushes carts to halls or ward kitchen, and serves trays to patients. Removes tray and stacks dishes for return to kitchen. Reads production orders on color-coded menu cards on trays to determine items to place on food tray. Prepares food items, such as sandwiches, salads, soups, and beverages, and places items, such as eating utensils, napkins, and condiments, on trays. Prepares fountain drinks, such as sodas, milkshakes, and malted milks. Records amount and types of special food items served to customers. Places servings in blender to make foods for soft or liquid diets. Totals and presents check to customer and accepts payment for service. Restocks service counter with items, such as ice, napkins, and straws. Washes dishes and cleans work area, tables, cabinets, and ovens. Sweeps service area with broom.

Knowledge: None above average

Abilities: None above average

Food Order Expediters

Expedite food preparation by calling out customers' orders to cooks and food preparation workers. Inspect portions and presentation of prepared orders, and notify wait staff when orders are ready to be served. Calls out and verifies food orders to cooks and kitchen workers. Notifies serving personnel when order is ready. Reviews orders for accuracy and tabulates check. Examines portioning and garnishing of completed food orders. Assists in preparation and cooking of food that can be completed in a short period of time. Records supplies used to accumulate food control data.

Knowledge: Food Production

Abilities: Memorization; Perceptual Speed

Specialty Mechanics, Installers, and Repairers

▲ Growth: 18%

▲ Annual Job Openings: 34,082

▲ Yearly Earnings $28,080

▲ Education Required: Long-term O-J-T

▲ Self-employed: 1%

▲ Part-time: 5%

Railcar Repairers

Repair and rebuild railroad rolling stock, mine cars, and trolley or subway cars, according to federal and company regulations and specifications. Exclude engine specialists. Repairs, reassembles, and replaces defective parts following diagrams. Repairs structural metal sections, such as panels, underframing, and piping, using torch, wrench, hand tools, power tools, and welding equipment. Examines car roof for wear and damage and repairs defective sections, using roofing material, cement, nails, and waterproof paint. Installs and repairs interior flooring, walls, plumbing, steps, and platforms. Inspects components such as bearings, seals, gaskets, wheels, truck and brake assemblies, air cylinder reservoirs, valves, and coupler assemblies. Aligns car sides for installation of car ends and crossties, using width gauge, turnbuckle, and wrench. Repairs signage, using hand tools. Replaces defective wiring and insulation, and tightens electrical connections, using hand tools. Disassembles units, such as water pump, control valve, governor, distributor, windshield wiper motor, compressor and roller bearings. Tests units before and after repairs for operability. Adjusts repaired or replaced units as needed, following diagrams. Repairs window sash frames, attaches weather stripping and channels to frame, and replaces window glass, using hand tools. Measures sections and drills holes to prepare replacement sections for reassembly. Measures diameter of axle wheel seats, using micrometer, and marks dimension on axle for boring of wheels to specified dimensions. Tests electric systems of cars, using ammeter and by operating light and signal switches. Fabricates and installs interior fixtures, such as cabinets and other wood fixtures, using carpentry tools. Removes locomotive, car mechanical unit, or other component, using pneumatic hoist and jack, pinch bar, hand tools, and cutting torch. Records condition of cars, repairs made, and other repair work to be performed. Cleans units and components, using compressed air blower.

Knowledge: Engineering and Technology; Building and Construction; Mechanical; Transportation

Abilities: Multilimb Coordination; Static Strength; Explosive Strength; Extent Flexibility; Gross Body Equilibrium; Night Vision; Peripheral Vision; Depth Perception; Glare Sensitivity

Installers and Repairers—Manufactured Buildings, Mobile Homes, and Travel Trailers

Install, repair, and maintain units and systems in mobile homes, prefabricated buildings, or travel trailers, using hand tools or power tools. Locates and repairs frayed wiring, broken connections, or incorrect wiring, using ohmmeter, soldering iron, tape, and hand tools. Repairs plumbing and propane gas lines, using caulking compounds and plastic or copper pipe. Inspects, examines, and tests operation of parts or systems to be repaired and to verify completeness of work performed. Removes damaged exterior panels, repairs and replaces structural frame members, and seals leaks, using hand tools. Repairs leaks with caulking compound or replaces pipes, using pipe wrench. Connects electrical system to outside power source and activates switches to test operation of appliances and light fixtures. Connects water hose to inlet pipe of plumbing system and tests operation of toilets and sinks. Confers with customer or reads work order to determine nature and extent of damage to unit. Lists parts needed, estimates costs, and plans work procedure, using parts list, technical manuals, and diagrams. Opens and closes doors, windows, and drawers to test their operation and trims edges to fit, using jack plane or drawknife. Refinishes wood surfaces on cabinets, doors, moldings, and floors, using power sander, putty, spray equipment, brush, paints, or varnishes. Resets hardware, using chisel, mallet, and screwdriver. Seals open side of modular units to prepare them for shipment, using polyethylene sheets, nails, and hammer.

Knowledge: Building and Construction; Mechanical

Abilities: Control Precision; Trunk Strength; Extent Flexibility; Gross Body Equilibrium

Product Repairers

Repair, mend, or install a wide variety of nonelectrical, manufactured products. May use hand tools and machines. Replaces or repairs worn, damaged, or defective parts according to specifications or customer needs. Disassembles and inspects item to remove or adjust parts. Attaches or installs new section or part, using hand or power tools and following prescribed procedure. Fills and patches cracks, holes, and chips to repair product surface. Smooths repaired section and paints, stains, shellacs, or oils surfaces of item to restore original appearance. Tests item before and after repairs, to verify conformance to specifications. Examines product to determine damage or defects and needed repairs. Reviews customer or manufacturer specifications to determine method of repairing item. Makes parts from materials, such as wood, metal, rubber, leather, fabric, or plastic. Places item being repaired in jigs or heat device to facilitate repairs. Cleans and polishes item, using power tools such as buffing machine and sandblasting equipment. Measures item and verifies shape to facilitate repairs. Wipes, washes, or cleans product, using cloth and cleaning solution. Reweighs item to achieve specified weight. Stamps identifying information on repaired item. Stacks or packages repaired items for shipment or storage. Keeps and maintains records of inventory and customer data. Sells items.

Knowledge: Sales and Marketing; Production and Processing; Engineering and Technology; Building and Construction; Mechanical

Abilities: Visualization; Arm-Hand Steadiness; Finger Dexterity; Visual Color Discrimination

Blacksmiths

Forge and repair metal products, according to work order, diagram, or sample, using furnace or forge and hand tools. Heats metal stock or parts in furnace or forge, and tempers forged articles. Hammers stock into specified size and shape, using hammer and anvil or power hammer. Repairs metal articles and farm machinery, such as tongs, hooks, or chains, according to work orders, diagrams, or sample parts. Designs jigs and fixtures, and forges tools and tool parts, such as hammers, chisels, or angle heads. Repairs castings and forgings, using special cold process that requires no welding. Cuts, assembles, and welds metal parts, using welding equipment. Calculates extent of fracture and tensile strength and distribution of strain in material for use in cold repair process. Inserts holding and locking devices in casting and smooths finish using air-powered tools, punches, and strippers. Records repair or fabrication of tools or machine parts.

Knowledge: Production and Processing; Building and Construction

Abilities: Arm-Hand Steadiness; Wrist-Finger Speed; Speed of Limb Movement; Static Strength; Explosive Strength; Dynamic Strength; Trunk Strength; Stamina; Extent Flexibility; Dynamic Flexibility; Gross Body Coordination; Gross Body Equilibrium

Gunsmiths

Repair and modify firearms to blueprint and customer specifications, using hand tools and machines, such as grinders, planers, and millers. Operates metal-working machines to enlarge caliber of bore, cut rifling in barrel, and grind and polish metal parts of firearms. Installs and aligns parts of gun, such as action sights, barrel, or choke device, using screws and hand tools. Refinishes wooden stocks for guns, using sanding and rubbing tools, finishing oil, and lacquer. Immerses metal parts in bluing salt bath to rust-proof surface and impart blue color to metal. Fires gun to determine strength characteristics, correct alignment, and assembly of piece. Designs and fabricates tools, testing equipment, and parts for guns according to blueprint or customer specifications, using hand tools and machines. Develops plans and calculates details—such as bullet-flight arcs, projectile velocity, and sight positions—to design new gun.

Knowledge: Design; Physics

Abilities: Originality; Visualization; Arm-Hand Steadiness; Manual Dexterity; Finger Dexterity; Wrist-Finger Speed; Speed of Limb Movement; Explosive Strength; Dynamic Strength

Automobile Wreckers

Salvage usable parts from wrecked vehicles, using hand tools and cutting torch. Dismantles wrecked vehicles, using hand tools, bolt cutters, and welding torch, and removes usable parts. Cleans salvaged parts, using solvents and brush, or vapor-degreasing machine. Stores parts in bins according to condition and part number. Sorts, piles, and loads scrap onto railroad cars or trucks. Drives tow truck. Sells usable parts, such as automobile glass and tires.

Knowledge: Sales and Marketing

Abilities: Arm-Hand Steadiness; Manual Dexterity; Multilimb Coordination; Rate Control; Reaction Time; Speed of Limb Movement; Static Strength; Explosive Strength; Dynamic Strength; Trunk Strength; Stamina; Extent Flexibility; Dynamic Flexibility; Gross Body Coordination; Gross Body Equilibrium

Specialty Records Clerks

▲ Growth: 10%

▲ Annual Job Openings: 34,193

▲ Yearly Earnings $22,568

▲ Education Required: Short-term O-J-T

▲ Self-employed: 0%

▲ Part-time: 16%

Transportation Agents

Expedite movement of freight, mail, baggage, and passengers through airline terminals. Route inbound and outbound air freight shipments. May prepare airway bill of lading on freight and record baggage, mail, freight, weights, and number of passengers on airplane. Prepares airway bill of lading on freight from consignors, and routes freight on first available flight. Prepares manifest showing baggage, mail, freight weights, and number of passengers on airplane, and teletypes data to destination. Obtains flight number, airplane number, and names of crew members from dispatcher and records data on flight papers of airplane. Oversees or participates in loading cargo to ensure completeness of load and even distribution of weight. Verifies passengers' tickets as they board plane. Unloads inbound freight and baggage and notifies consignees of arrival of shipments. Positions ramp for loading of airplane. Arranges for delivery of freight and baggage to consignees. Removes ramp and signals pilot that personnel and equipment are clear of plane. Forces conditioned air into interior of plane for passenger comfort prior to departure, using mobile aircraft-air-conditioning unit.

Knowledge: Clerical; Customer and Personal Service; Geography; Telecommunications; Transportation

Abilities: Static Strength

Marking Clerks

Print and attach price tickets to articles of merchandise using one of several methods, such as marking price on tickets by hand or using ticket-printing machine. Marks selling price by hand on boxes containing merchandise or on price tickets. Presses lever or plunger of mechanism that pins, pastes, ties, or staples ticket to article. Prints information on tickets, using ticket-printing machine. Records price, buyer, and grade of tobacco on tickets attached to piles or baskets of tobacco as tobacco is auctioned. Pastes, staples, sews, or otherwise fastens tickets, tags, labels, or shipping documents to cloth or carpeting. Attaches price ticket to each article, and signals purchaser to raise bids that are below government support price. Indicates price, size, style, color, and inspection results on tags, tickets, and labels, using rubber stamp or writing instrument. Compares printed price tickets with entries on purchase order to verify accuracy, and notifies supervisor of discrepancies.

Records number and types of articles marked and packs articles in boxes. Performs other clerical tasks during periods between auction sales. Computes number of rolls of cloth to be produced from each lot to determine required number of tags or labels. Trims excess threads from selvage (finished edge) of cloth, using scissors or shears. Keeps records of production, returned goods, and personnel transactions.

Knowledge: Clerical

Abilities: None above average

Engineering Clerks

Compile, maintain, check, release, and distribute engineering control records, such as blueprints, drawings, engineering documents, parts listings, and catalogs. Releases data and documentation to authorized departments and organizations. Prepares or maintains manual or computerized record systems. Examines engineering drawings, blueprints, orders, and other documentation for completeness and accuracy. Confers with document originators or engineering liaison personnel to resolve discrepancies and update documents. Reviews engineering data and compiles list of materials, parts, and equipment required for manufacturing product. Determines material requirements for fabricating parts, considering size, cutting, and forming involved. Operates reproduction equipment. Prepares reports and memorandums. Assists in determining spare parts inventory requirements for customers.

Knowledge: Clerical

Abilities: Near Vision

Transportation Maintenance Clerks

Compile and record information, such as amount of equipment usage, time between inspections, repairs made, materials used, and hours of work expended, to document maintenance of transportation equipment. Compiles data from flight schedules to compute usage of airplanes, gasoline, and individual parts. Compiles and records information regarding track and right-of-way repair and maintenance by railroad section crews. Maintains file for individual parts with notations of time used and inspection results. Records work notations onto inspection report forms. Notifies inspection department when parts and airplanes approach date for inspection, including accumulated time and routing schedule. Prepares reports for Federal Aviation Administration on schedule delays caused by mechanical difficulties. Requisitions needed materials. Keeps employee time records.

Knowledge: Clerical; Transportation

Abilities: None above average

Speech-Language Pathologists and Audiologists

▲ Growth: 51%
▲ Annual Job Openings: 12,202
▲ Yearly Earnings $42,702
▲ Education Required: Master's degree
▲ Self-employed: 6%
▲ Part-time: 20%

Speech-Language Pathologists and Audiologists

Examine and provide remedial services for persons with speech and hearing disorders. Perform research related to speech and language problems. Administers hearing or speech/language evaluations, tests, or examinations to patients to collect information on type and degree of impairment. Conducts or directs research and reports findings on speech or hearing topics to develop procedures, technology, or treatments. Evaluates hearing and speech/language test results and medical or background information to determine hearing or speech impairment and treatment. Counsels and instructs clients in techniques to improve speech or hearing impairment, including sign language or lip-reading. Plans and conducts prevention and treatment programs for clients' hearing or speech problems. Records and maintains reports of speech or hearing research or treatments. Refers clients to additional medical or educational services if needed. Advises educators or other medical staff on speech or hearing topics. Participates in conferences or training to update or share knowledge of new hearing or speech disorder treatment methods or technology. Teaches staff or students about hearing or speech disorders, including explaining new treatments or equipment. Directs and coordinates staff activities of speech or hearing clinic, and hires, trains, and evaluates personnel. Prepares budget requesting funding for specific projects, including equipment, supplies, and staff.

Knowledge: Administration and Management; Economics and Accounting; Customer and Personal Service; Personnel and Human Resources; Biology; Psychology; Medicine and Dentistry; Therapy and Counseling; Education and Training; English Language; Foreign Language; Telecommunications

Abilities: Oral Comprehension; Written Comprehension; Oral Expression; Written Expression; Hearing Sensitivity; Auditory Attention; Sound Localization; Speech Recognition; Speech Clarity

Sports Instructors and Coaches

▲ Growth: 41%
▲ Annual Job Openings: 82,035
▲ Yearly Earnings $22,900
▲ Education Required: Moderate-term O-J-T
▲ Self-employed: 0%
▲ Part-time: 42%

Instructors and Coaches, Sports and Physical Training

Instruct or coach groups or individuals in the fundamentals of sports. Demonstrate techniques and methods of participation. Observe and inform participants of corrective measures necessary to improve their skills. Those required to hold teaching degrees are included in the appropriate teaching category. Teaches individual and team sports to participants, utilizing knowledge of sports techniques and of physical capabilities of participants. Organizes, leads, instructs, and referees indoor and outdoor games, such as volleyball, baseball, and basketball. Plans physical education program to promote development of participant physical attributes and social skills. Explains and enforces safety rules and regulations. Teaches and demonstrates use of gymnastic and training apparatus, such as trampolines and weights. Organizes and conducts competitions and tournaments. Selects, stores, orders, issues, and inventories equipment, materials, and supplies. Advises participants in use of heat or ultraviolet treatments and hot baths.

Knowledge: Customer and Personal Service; Psychology; Sociology and Anthropology; Medicine and Dentistry; Therapy and Counseling; Education and Training; History and Archeology

Abilities: Oral Comprehension; Oral Expression; Fluency of Ideas; Memorization; Spatial Orientation; Visualization; Selective Attention; Time Sharing; Manual Dexterity; Multilimb Coordination; Response Orientation; Rate Control; Reaction Time; Speed of Limb Movement; Static Strength; Explosive Strength; Dynamic Strength; Trunk Strength; Stamina; Extent Flexibility; Dynamic Flexibility; Gross Body Coordination; Gross Body Equilibrium; Far Vision; Night Vision; Peripheral Vision; Depth Perception; Glare Sensitivity; Auditory Attention; Sound Localization; Speech Recognition; Speech Clarity

Sprayers Applicators

▲ Growth: 21%
▲ Annual Job Openings: 5,889
▲ Yearly Earnings $20,508
▲ Education Required: Moderate-term O-J-T
▲ Self-employed: 0%
▲ Part-time: 28%

Sprayers/Applicators

Spray herbicides, pesticides, and fungicides on trees, shrubs, and lawns, using hoses and truck-mounted tank. Fill sprayer tank with water and chemicals, according to prescribed formula. May use portable spray equipment. Exclude workers who also perform duties of lawn maintenance workers or pruners. Lifts, pushes, and swings nozzle, hose, and tube to direct spray over designated area. Covers area to specified depth, applying knowledge of weather conditions, droplet size, elevation-to-distance ratio, and obstructions. Fills sprayer tank with water and chemicals, according to formula. Connects hoses and nozzles, selected according to terrain, distribution pattern requirements, type of infestation, and velocity. Starts motor and engages machinery, such as sprayer agitator and pump. Gives driving instructions to truck driver, using hand and horn signals, to ensure complete coverage of designated area. Cleans and services machinery to ensure operating efficiency, using water, gasoline, lubricants, and hand tools. Sprays livestock with pesticides. Plants grass with seed spreader and operates straw blower to cover seeded area with asphalt and straw mixture.

Knowledge: Food Production; Chemistry

Abilities: Explosive Strength; Dynamic Strength; Stamina; Dynamic Flexibility

Statisticians

▲ Growth: 1%
▲ Annual Job Openings: 937
▲ Yearly Earnings $47,507
▲ Education Required: Bachelor's degree
▲ Self-employed: 0%
▲ Part-time: 5%

Statisticians

Plan surveys and collect, organize, interpret, summarize, and analyze numerical data, applying statistical theory and methods to provide usable information in scientific, business, economic, and other fields. Data derived from surveys may represent either

complete enumeration or statistical samples. Include mathematical statisticians who are engaged in the development of mathematical theory associated with the application of statistical techniques. Conducts research into mathematical theories and proofs that form basis of science of statistics. Plans data collection, and analyzes and interprets numerical data from experiments, studies, surveys, and other sources. Applies statistical methodology to provide information for scientific research and statistical analysis. Plans methods to collect information and develops questionnaire techniques according to survey design. Conducts surveys utilizing sampling techniques or complete enumeration bases. Analyzes and interprets statistics to point up significant differences in relationships among sources of information, and prepares conclusions and forecasts. Develops and tests experimental designs, sampling techniques, and analytical methods, and prepares recommendations concerning their use. Investigates, evaluates, and reports on applicability, efficiency, and accuracy of statistical methods used to obtain and evaluate data. Evaluates reliability of source information, adjusts and weighs raw data, and organizes results into form compatible with analysis by computers or other methods. Develops statistical methodology. Examines theories, such as those of probability and inference, to discover mathematical bases for new or improved methods of obtaining and evaluating numerical data. Presents numerical information by computer readouts, graphs, charts, tables, written reports, or other methods. Describes sources of information, and limitations on reliability and usability.

Knowledge: Administration and Management; Economics and Accounting; Computers and Electronics; Mathematics; English Language; Philosophy and Theology

Abilities: Written Comprehension; Written Expression; Fluency of Ideas; Originality; Deductive Reasoning; Inductive Reasoning; Information Ordering; Category Flexibility; Mathematical Reasoning; Number Facility; Memorization; Speed of Closure; Flexibility of Closure; Perceptual Speed; Finger Dexterity

Financial Analysts, Statistical

Conduct statistical analyses of information affecting investment programs of public or private institutions and private individuals. Analyzes financial information to forecast business, industry, and economic conditions, for use in making investment decisions. Interprets data concerning price, yield, stability, and future trends in investment risks and economic influences pertinent to investments. Gathers information such as industry, regulatory, and economic information, company financial statements, financial periodicals, and newspapers. Recommends investment timing and buy-and-orders to company or to staff of investment establishment of advising clients. Draws charts and graphs to illustrate reports, using computer. Calls brokers and purchases investments for company, according to company policy.

Knowledge: Economics and Accounting; Sales and Marketing; Computers and Electronics; Mathematics; Foreign Language; History and Archeology; Law, Government, and Jurisprudence

Abilities: Oral Comprehension; Written Comprehension; Oral Expression; Written Expression; Fluency of Ideas; Originality; Deductive Reasoning; Inductive Reasoning; Category Flexibility; Mathematical Reasoning; Number Facility; Memorization; Speed of Closure; Selective Attention; Near Vision; Speech Recognition

Stock Clerks

▲ Growth: 3%

▲ Annual Job Openings: 346,772

▲ Yearly Earnings $19,344

▲ Education Required: Short-term O-J-T

▲ Self-employed: 0%

▲ Part-time: 13%

Stock Clerks, Sales Floor

Receive, store, and issue sales floor merchandise. Stock shelves, racks, cases, bins, and tables with merchandise, and arrange merchandise displays to attract customers. May periodically take physical count of stock or check and mark merchandise. Receives, opens, and unpacks cartons or crates of merchandise and checks invoice against items received. Stocks storage areas and displays with new or transferred merchandise. Sets up advertising signs and displays merchandise on shelves, counters, or tables to attract customers and promote sales. Takes inventory or examines merchandise to identify items to be reordered or replenished. Stamps, attaches, or changes price tags on merchandise, referring to price list. Requisitions merchandise from supplier based on available space, merchandise on hand, customer demand, or advertised specials. Cleans display cases, shelves, and aisles. Itemizes and totals customer merchandise selection at check-out counter, using cash register, and accepts cash or charge card for purchases. Answers questions and advises customer in selection of merchandise. Cuts lumber, screening, glass, and related materials to size requested by customer. Packs customer purchases in bags or cartons. Transports packages to customer vehicle.

Knowledge: Clerical; Sales and Marketing

Abilities: Category Flexibility; Memorization; Perceptual Speed; Spatial Orientation; Visualization; Manual Dexterity; Multilimb Coordination; Speed of Limb Movement; Static Strength; Dynamic Strength; Trunk Strength; Extent Flexibility; Dynamic Flexibility; Gross Body Equilibrium; Far Vision; Speech Recognition

Stock Clerks—Stockroom, Warehouse, or Storage Yard

Receive, store, and issue materials, equipment, and other items from stockroom, warehouse, or storage yard. Keep records and compile stock reports. Exclude stockroom la-

borers and workers whose primary duties involve shipping, weighing, and checking.
Receives, counts, and stores stock items and records data, manually or using computer.
Records nature, quantity, value, or location of material, supplies, or equipment received,
shipped, used, or issued to workers. Compares office inventory records with sales orders, invoices, or requisitions to verify accuracy and receipt of items. Locates and selects material,
supplies, tools, equipment, or other articles from stock, or issues stock item to workers.
Compiles, reviews, and maintains data from contracts, purchase orders, requisitions, and
other documents to determine supply needs. Packs, unpacks, and marks stock items, using
identification tag, stamp, electric marking tool, or other labeling equipment. Determines
method of storage, identification, and stock location based on turnover, environmental factors, and physical capacity of facility. Delivers products, supplies, and equipment to designated area, and determines sequence and release of back orders according to stock
availability. Verifies computations against physical count of stock, adjusts for errors, or in
vestigates discrepancies. Prepares documents, such as inventory balance, price lists, shortages, expenditures, and periodic reports, using computer, typewriter, or calculator. Receives
and fills orders or sells supplies, materials, and products to customers. Purchases or prepares
documents to purchase new or additional stock and recommends disposal of excess, defective, or obsolete stock. Confers with engineering and purchasing personnel and vendors regarding procurement and stock availability. Examines and inspects stock items for wear or
defects, reports damage to supervisor, and disposes of or returns items to vendor. Adjusts,
repairs, assembles, or prepares products, supplies, equipment, or other items, according to
specifications or customer requirements. Assists or directs other stockroom, warehouse, or
storage yard workers. Cleans and maintains supplies, tools, equipment, instruments, and
storage areas to ensure compliance to safety regulations. Drives truck to pick up incoming
stock or deliver parts to designated locations.

Knowledge: Clerical; Computers and Electronics

Abilities: Category Flexibility; Spatial Orientation; Trunk Strength; Extent Flexibility; Dynamic
Flexibility; Gross Body Coordination; Gross Body Equilibrium

Order Fillers, Wholesale and Retail Sales

**Fill customers' mail and telephone orders from stored merchandise in accordance with
specifications on sales slips or order forms. Duties include computing prices of items,
completing order receipts, keeping records of outgoing orders, and requisitioning additional materials, supplies, and equipment. Exclude laborers, stock clerks, and workers whose primary duties involve weighing and checking.** Computes price of each group
of items. Reads order to ascertain catalog number, size, color, and quantity of merchandise.
Obtains merchandise from bins or shelves. Places merchandise on conveyor leading to
wrapping area.

Knowledge: None above average

Abilities: None above average

Surgical Technologists

▲ Growth: 32%

▲ Annual Job Openings: 6,642

▲ Yearly Earnings $25,001

▲ Education Required: Postsecondary vocational training

▲ Self-employed: 0%

▲ Part-time: 22%

Surgical Technologists and Technicians

Perform any combination of the following tasks, either before, during, or after an operation: prepare patient by washing, shaving, etc.; place equipment and supplies in operating room according to surgeon's instructions; arrange instruments under direction of nurse; maintain specified supply of fluids for use during operation; adjust lights and equipment as directed; hand instruments and supplies to surgeon, hold retractors, and cut sutures as directed; count sponges, needles, and instruments used during operation; and clean operating room. Places equipment and supplies in operating room and arranges instruments, according to instruction. Maintains supply of fluids, such as plasma, saline, blood, and glucose, for use during operation. Hands instruments and supplies to surgeon, holds retractors and cuts sutures, and performs other tasks as directed by surgeon during operation. Cleans operating room. Counts sponges, needles, and instruments before and after operation. Washes and sterilizes equipment, using germicides and sterilizers. Assists team members to place and position patient on table. Puts dressings on patient following surgery. Scrubs arms and hands and dons gown and gloves. Aids team to don gowns and gloves.

Knowledge: Biology; Medicine and Dentistry

Abilities: None above average

Systems Analysts

▲ Growth: 103%
▲ Annual Job Openings: 87,318
▲ Yearly Earnings $48,360
▲ Education Required: Bachelor's degree
▲ Self-employed: 7%
▲ Part-time: 5%

Computer Security Specialists

Plan, coordinate, and implement security measures for information systems to regulate access to computer data files and prevent unauthorized modification, destruction, or disclosure of information. Develops plans to safeguard computer files against accidental or unauthorized modification, destruction, or disclosure and to meet emergency data processing needs. Coordinates implementation of computer system plan with establishment personnel and outside vendors. Tests data processing system to ensure functioning of data processing activities and security measures. Modifies computer security files to incorporate new software, correct errors, or change individual access status. Confers with personnel to discuss issues such as computer data access needs, security violations, and programming changes. Monitors use of data files and regulates access to safeguard information in computer files. Writes reports to document computer security and emergency measures policies, procedures, and test results.

Knowledge: Administration and Management; Computers and Electronics; Philosophy and Theology; Public Safety and Security

Abilities: Oral Comprehension; Written Comprehension; Fluency of Ideas; Deductive Reasoning; Inductive Reasoning; Information Ordering; Speed of Closure; Flexibility of Closure; Visualization

Systems Analysts, Electronic Data Processing

Analyze business, scientific, and technical problems for application to electronic data processing systems. Exclude persons working primarily as engineers, mathematicians, or scientists. Analyzes, plans, and tests computer programs, using programming and system techniques. Consults with staff and users to identify operating procedure problems. Formulates and reviews plans outlining steps required to develop programs to meet staff and user requirements. Devises flowcharts and diagrams to illustrate steps and to describe logical operational steps of program. Writes documentation to describe and develop installation and operating procedures of programs. Coordinates installation of computer programs and operating systems, and tests, maintains, and monitors computer system. Reads manuals, periodicals, and technical reports to learn how to develop programs to meet staff and user requirements. Sets up computer test to find and correct program or system errors. Writes and revises quality standards and test procedures, and modifies existing procedures for program and system design for evaluation. Reviews and analyzes computer printouts and performance indications to locate code problems. Modifies program to correct errors by correcting computer codes. Enters instructions into computer to test program or system for conformance to standards. Assists staff and users to solve computer-related problems, such as malfunctions and program problems. Trains staff and users to use computer system and its programs.

Knowledge: Clerical; Customer and Personal Service; Computers and Electronics; Mathematics; Education and Training; English Language; Telecommunications; Communications and Media

Abilities: Oral Comprehension; Written Comprehension; Oral Expression; Written Expression; Fluency of Ideas; Originality; Problem Sensitivity; Deductive Reasoning; Inductive Reasoning; Information Ordering; Category Flexibility; Mathematical Reasoning; Number Facility; Memorization; Speed of Closure; Flexibility of Closure; Perceptual Speed; Visualization; Selective Attention; Wrist-Finger Speed; Near Vision; Visual Color Discrimination; Speech Recognition; Speech Clarity

Geographic Information System Specialists

Design and coordinate development of integrated geographical information system database of spatial and nonspatial data; develop analyses and presentation of this data, applying knowledge of geographic information system. Designs database and coordinates physical changes to database, applying additional knowledge of spatial feature representations. Chooses and applies analysis procedures for spatial and nonspatial data. Determines how to analyze spatial relationships, including adjacency, containment, and proximity. Decides effective presentation of information, and selects cartographic and additional elements. Determines information to be queried, such as location, characteristics of location, trend, pattern, routing, and modeling various series of events. Meets with users to develop system or project requirements. Creates maps and graphs, using computer and geographic information system software and related equipment. Reviews existing and incoming data for currency, accuracy, usefulness, quality, and documentation. Selects or verifies designations of cartographic symbols. Presents information to users and answers questions. Oversees entry of data into database, including applications, keyboard entry, manual digitizing, scanning, and automatic conversion. Recommends procedures to increase data accessibility and ease of use. Discusses problems in development of transportation planning and modeling, marketing and demographic mapping, or assessment of geologic and environmental factors.

Knowledge: Administration and Management; Sales and Marketing; Computers and Electronics; Design; Mathematics; Physics; Sociology and Anthropology; Geography; English Language; Transportation

Abilities: Written Expression; Fluency of Ideas; Originality; Inductive Reasoning; Information Ordering; Category Flexibility; Mathematical Reasoning; Number Facility; Perceptual Speed; Spatial Orientation; Visualization; Selective Attention; Speech Clarity

Data Communications Analysts

Research, test, evaluate, and recommend data communications hardware and software. Analyzes test data and recommends hardware or software for purchase. Identifies areas of operation which need upgraded equipment, such as modems, fiber optic cables, and telephone wires. Tests and evaluates hardware and software to determine efficiency, reliability, and compatibility with existing system. Reads technical manuals and brochures to determine equipment which meets establishment requirements. Monitors system performance. Conducts survey to determine user needs. Develops and writes procedures for installation, use, and solving problems of communications hardware and software. Visits vendors to learn about available products or services. Assists users to identify and solve data communication problems. Trains users in use of equipment.

Knowledge: Sales and Marketing; Customer and Personal Service; Computers and Electronics; Mathematics; Psychology; Education and Training; Telecommunications; Communications and Media

Abilities: Oral Comprehension; Written Comprehension; Oral Expression; Written Expression; Fluency of Ideas; Originality; Deductive Reasoning; Inductive Reasoning; Mathematical Reasoning; Number Facility; Selective Attention; Near Vision; Speech Clarity

Teacher Aides and Educational Assistants

▲ Growth: 38%
▲ Annual Job Openings: 353,119
▲ Yearly Earnings: $15,974
▲ Education Required: Short-term O-J-T
▲ Self-employed: 0%
▲ Part-time: 46%

Teacher Aides, Paraprofessional

Perform duties that are instructional in nature, or deliver direct services to students and/or parents. Serve in a position for which a teacher or another professional has ultimate responsibility for the design and implementation of educational programs and services. Presents subject matter to students, using lecture, discussion, or supervised role-playing methods. Helps students, individually or in groups, with lesson assignments to present or reinforce learning concepts. Prepares lesson outline and plan in assigned area and submits outline to teacher for review. Plans, prepares, and develops various teaching aids, such as bibliographies, charts, and graphs. Discusses assigned teaching area with classroom teacher to coordinate instructional efforts. Prepares, administers, and grades examinations. Confers with parents on progress of students.

Knowledge: Psychology; Sociology and Anthropology; Education and Training; English Language; History and Archeology; Philosophy and Theology

Abilities: None above average

Teacher Aides and Educational Assistants, Clerical

Arrange work materials, supervise students at play, and operate audio-visual equipment under guidance of a teacher. Distributes teaching materials to students, such as textbooks, workbooks, or paper and pencils. Operates learning aids, such as film and slide projectors and tape recorders. Activates audio-visual receiver and monitors classroom viewing of live or recorded courses transmitted by communication satellite. Maintains order within school and school grounds. Takes class attendance and maintains class attendance records. Types material and operates duplicating equipment to reproduce instructional materials. Grades homework and tests and computes and records results, using answer sheets or electronic marking devices. Requisitions teaching materials and stockroom supplies. Collects completed assignments and tests and mails to training center or institute of higher learning. Stimulates classroom discussion following broadcast of seminar, and consolidates and transmits students' questions for direct response via satellite.

Knowledge: Clerical; Customer and Personal Service; Psychology; Sociology and Anthropology; Therapy and Counseling; Education and Training; English Language; Foreign Language; History and Archeology; Telecommunications; Communications and Media

Abilities: Category Flexibility; Memorization; Speed of Closure; Time Sharing; Response Orientation; Reaction Time; Far Vision; Peripheral Vision; Auditory Attention; Sound Localization; Speech Recognition; Speech Clarity

Telephone and Cable TV Line Installers and Repairers

▲ Growth: 21%
▲ Annual Job Openings: 465
▲ Yearly Earnings $31,532
▲ Education Required: Long-term O-J-T
▲ Self-employed: 0%
▲ Part-time: 0%

Telephone and Cable Television Line Installers and Repairers

String and repair telephone and television cable and other equipment for transmitting messages or TV programming. Duties include locating and repairing defects in existing systems; placing, rearranging, and removing underground or aerial cables; installing supports, insulation, or guy wire systems; and other auxiliary tasks necessary to maintain lines and cables. Installs terminal boxes and strings lead-in wires, using electrician's tools. Repairs cable system, defective lines, and auxiliary equipment. Ascends poles or enters tunnels and sewers to string lines and install terminal boxes, auxiliary equipment, and appliances, according to diagrams. Pulls lines through ducts by hand or with use of winch. Computes impedance of wire from pole to house to determine additional resistance needed for reducing signal to desired level. Connects television set to cable system, evaluates incoming signal, and adjusts system to ensure optimum reception. Measures television signal strength at utility pole, using electronic test equipment. Installs and removes plant equipment, such as call boxes and clocks. Digs holes, using power auger or shovel, and hoists poles upright into holes, using truck-mounted winch. Fills and tamps holes, using cement, earth, and tamping device. Cleans and maintains tools and test equipment. Communicates with supervisor to receive instructions and technical advice and to report problems. Explains cable service to subscriber. Collects installation fees.

Knowledge: Computers and Electronics; Telecommunications

Abilities: Manual Dexterity; Gross Body Coordination; Gross Body Equilibrium

Television and Movie Camera Operators

▲ Growth: 15%
▲ Annual Job Openings: 2,440
▲ Yearly Earnings $25,792
▲ Education Required: Moderate-term O-J-T
▲ Self-employed: 7%
▲ Part-time: 23%

Camera Operators, Television and Motion Picture

Operate television or motion picture camera to photograph scenes for TV broadcasts, advertising, or motion pictures. Sets up cameras, optical printers and related equipment to produce photographs and special effects. Adjusts position and controls of camera, printer, and related equipment to produce desired effects, using precision measuring instruments. Selects cameras, accessories, equipment, and film stock to use during filming, using knowledge of filming techniques, requirements, and computations. Observes set or location for potential problems and to determine filming and lighting requirements. Views film to resolve problems of exposure control, subject and camera movement, changes in subject distance, and related variables. Reads work order to determine specifications and location of subject material. Analyzes specifications to determine work procedures, sequence of operations, and machine set-up. Confers with director and electrician regarding interpretation of scene, desired effects, and filming and lighting requirements. Reads charts and computes ratios to determine variables, such as lighting, shutter angles, filter factors, and camera distance. Exposes frames of film in sequential order and regulates exposures and aperture to obtain special effects. Instructs camera operators regarding camera set-up, angles, distances, movement, and other variables and cues for starting and stopping filming.

Knowledge: Physics; Fine Arts; Telecommunications; Communications and Media

Abilities: Flexibility of Closure; Spatial Orientation; Visualization; Selective Attention; Time Sharing; Arm-Hand Steadiness; Rate Control; Far Vision; Visual Color Discrimination; Peripheral Vision; Depth Perception

Textile Bleaching and Dyeing Machine Operators

▲ Growth: 10%
▲ Annual Job Openings: 3,881
▲ Yearly Earnings $18,886
▲ Education Required: Moderate-term O-J-T
▲ Self-employed: 0%
▲ Part-time: 5%

Textile Bleaching and Dyeing Machine Operators and Tenders

Operate or tend machines, such as padding machines, treating tanks, dye jigs, and vats—to bleach, shrink, wash, dye, and finish textiles—such as cloth, yarn, greige cloth, and fiberglass sliver—preparatory to further processing. Starts machines and equipment to process and finish textile goods prior to further processing, following instructions. Observes display screen, control panel and equipment, and cloth entering or exiting process to determine whether to adjust equipment controls. Presses, pushes, or turns controls to initiate or adjust steps in process. Mixes or adds dyes, water, detergents, or chemicals to tanks to dilute or strengthen solutions as indicated by tests. Mounts roll of cloth on machine, using hoist, or places textile goods in machines or pieces of equipment. Threads ends of cloth or twine through specified sections of equipment prior to processing. Removes items, such as dyed articles, cloth, cones, and bobbins, from tanks and machines for drying and further processing. Creels machine with bobbins or twine. Keys in processing instructions to program electronic equipment. Soaks specified textile products for designated time. Tests solutions used to process textile goods to detect variations from standards, using standard procedures. Weighs ingredient to be mixed together to process textiles. Examines and feels products to determine variation from processing standards. Sews ends of cloth together by hand or using machine to form endless length of cloth to facilitate processing. Positions cloth truck to facilitate processing cloth. Records information, such as fabric yardage processed, temperature readings, fabric tensions, machine speeds, and delays caused by range malfunctions. Notifies supervisor of equipment malfunctions and coworkers to initiate steps in processing of textile goods. Confers with coworkers to ascertain information regarding customer orders, process steps to be completed during shift, or reason for delays. Ravels seams connecting cloth ends after processing is completed. Cleans machines and equipment.

Knowledge: Production and Processing; Chemistry

Abilities: Arm-Hand Steadiness; Manual Dexterity; Control Precision; Rate Control; Wrist-Finger Speed; Speed of Limb Movement; Static Strength; Dynamic Strength; Trunk Strength; Stamina; Dynamic Flexibility; Gross Body Coordination; Gross Body Equilibrium; Visual Color Discrimination

Therapeutic Services and Adminstration

▲ Growth: 67%
▲ Annual Job Openings: 4,767
▲ Yearly Earnings $31,865
▲ Education Required: Bachelor's degree
▲ Self-employed: 3%
▲ Part-time: 20%

Social Workers, Medical and Psychiatric

Counsel and aid individuals and families with problems that may arise during or following the recovery from physical or mental illness, by providing supportive services designed to help the persons understand, accept, and follow medical recommendations. Include chemical dependency counselors. Counsels clients and patients, individually and in group sessions, to assist in overcoming dependencies, adjusting to life, and making changes. Counsels family members to assist in understanding, dealing with, and supporting client or patient. Interviews client, reviews records, and confers with other professionals to evaluate mental or physical condition of client or patient. Formulates or coordinates program plan for treatment, care, and rehabilitation of client or patient, based on social work experience and knowledge. Monitors, evaluates, and records client progress according to measurable goals described in treatment and care plan. Modifies treatment plan to comply with changes in client's status. Refers patient, client, or family to community resources to assist in recovery from mental or physical illness. Intervenes as advocate for client or patient to resolve emergency problems in crisis situation. Plans and conducts programs to prevent substance abuse or improve health and counseling services in community. Develops and monitors budgetary expenditures for program. Supervises and directs other workers providing services to client or patient.

Knowledge: Customer and Personal Service; Personnel and Human Resources; Psychology; Sociology and Anthropology; Medicine and Dentistry; Therapy and Counseling; Education and Training; Philosophy and Theology; Communications and Media

Abilities: Oral Expression; Fluency of Ideas; Originality; Problem Sensitivity; Time Sharing; Speech Recognition; Speech Clarity

Exercise Physiologists

Develop, implement, and coordinate exercise programs and administer medical tests, under physician's supervision, to program participants to promote physical fitness. Records heart activity, using electrocardiograph (EKG) machine, while participant undergoes stress test on treadmill, under physician's supervision. Measures oxygen consumption and lung functioning, using spirometer. Measures amount of fat in body, using hydrostatic scale, skinfold calipers, and tape measure to assess body composition. Performs routine laboratory tests of blood samples for cholesterol level and glucose tolerance. Conducts individual and group aerobic, strength, and flexibility exercises. Writes initial and follow-up exercise prescriptions for participants, following physician's recommendation, specifying equipment, such as treadmill, track, or bike. Demonstrates correct use of exercise equipment and exercise routines. Interprets test results. Observes participants during exercise for signs of stress. Teaches behavior modification classes, such as stress management, weight control, and related subjects. Interviews participants to obtain vital statistics and medical history and records information. Explains program and test procedures to participants. Schedules other examinations and tests, such as physical examination, chest X ray, and urinalysis. Records test data in participant's record. Orders material and supplies. Adjusts and calibrates exercise equipment, using hand tools.

Knowledge: Customer and Personal Service; Chemistry; Biology; Psychology; Medicine and Dentistry; Therapy and Counseling; Education and Training; Foreign Language

Abilities: Written Comprehension; Multilimb Coordination; Stamina; Dynamic Flexibility; Gross Body Coordination; Gross Body Equilibrium

Orientation and Mobility Therapists

Train blind and visually impaired clients in the techniques of daily living to maximize independence and personal adjustment. Trains clients in awareness of physical environment through sense of smell, hearing, and touch. Teaches clients personal skills, such as eating, grooming, dressing, and use of bathroom facilities. Teaches clients home management skills, such as cooking and coin and money identification. Teaches clients communication skills, such as use of telephone. Teaches clients to protect body, using hands and arms to detect obstacles. Teaches clients to read and write Braille. Trains clients to travel alone, with or without cane, through use of variety of actual or simulated travel situations and exercises. Instructs clients in use of reading machines and common electrical devices, and in development of effective listening techniques. Administers assessment tests to clients to determine present and required or desired orientation and mobility skills. Instructs clients in arts, crafts, and recreational skills, such as macrame, leatherworking, sewing, ceramics, and piano playing. Interviews clients to obtain information concerning medical history, lifestyle, or other pertinent information. Instructs clients in group activities, such as swimming, dancing, or playing modified sports activities. Prepares progress report for use of rehabilitation team to evaluate clients' ability to perform varied activities essential to daily living.

Knowledge: Customer and Personal Service; Psychology; Medicine and Dentistry; Therapy and Counseling; Education and Training; Foreign Language; Fine Arts; Telecommunications

Abilities: None above average

Title Examiners and Searchers

▲ Growth: 13%

▲ Annual Job Openings: 3,107

▲ Yearly Earnings $26,000

▲ Education Required: Moderate-term O-J-T

▲ Self-employed: 18%

▲ Part-time: 12%

Title Searchers

Compile list of mortgages, deeds, contracts, judgments, and other instruments pertaining to title, by searching public and private records of real estate or title insurance company. Searches lot books, geographic and general indices, and assessor's rolls to compile lists of transactions pertaining to property. Reads search request to ascertain type of title evidence required, and to obtain description of property and names of involved parties. Compares legal description of property with legal description contained in records and indices, to verify such factors as deed ownership. Compiles information and documents required for title binder. Requisitions maps or drawings delineating property from company title plant, county surveyor, or assessor's office. Examines title to determine if there are restrictions limiting use of property, lists restrictions, and indicates action needed for clear title. Uses computerized system to retrieve additional documentation needed to complete real estate transaction. Confers with realtors, lending institution personnel, buyers, sellers, contractors, surveyors, and courthouse personnel to obtain additional information. Retrieves and examines closing files for accuracy and to ensure that information included is recorded and executed according to regulations. Prepares title commitment and final policy of title insurance based on information compiled from title search. Prepares closing statement, utilizing knowledge and expertise in real estate procedures.

Knowledge: Clerical; Economics and Accounting; Computers and Electronics; Sociology and Anthropology; Geography; English Language; History and Archeology; Law, Government, and Jurisprudence

Abilities: Written Comprehension; Written Expression

Title Examiners and Abstractors

Title examiners search public records and examine titles to determine legal condition of property title. Copy or summarize (abstract) recorded documents which affect condition of title to property (e.g., mortgages, trust deeds, and contracts). May prepare and issue policy that guarantees legality of title. Abstractors summarize pertinent legal or insurance details or sections of statutes or case law from reference books for purpose of examination, proof, or ready reference. Search out titles to determine if title deed is correct. Copies or summarizes recorded documents, such as mortgages, trust deeds, and contracts, affecting title to property. Examines mortgages, liens, judgments, easements, vital statistics, plat books, and maps to verify property legal description, ownership, and restrictions. Analyzes encumbrances to title, statutes and case law, and prepares report outlining encumbrances and actions required to clear title. Prepares and issues title insurance policy. Searches records to determine if delinquent taxes are due. Prepares correspondence and other records. Confers with interested parties to resolve problems and impart information. Directs activities of workers searching records and examining titles to real property. Verifies computations of fees, rentals, bonuses, commissions, and other expenses.

Knowledge: Administration and Management; Clerical; Economics and Accounting; Geography; English Language; Law, Government, and Jurisprudence

Abilities: Written Comprehension; Written Expression; Near Vision

Traffic, Shipping, and Receiving Clerks

▲ Growth: 9%
▲ Annual Job Openings: 163,214
▲ Yearly Earnings $21,881
▲ Education Required: Short-term O-J-T
▲ Self-employed: 0%
▲ Part-time: 9%

Shipping, Receiving, and Traffic Clerks

Verify and keep records on incoming and outgoing shipments. Prepare items for shipment. Duties include assembling, addressing, stamping, and shipping merchandise or material; receiving, unpacking, verifying, and recording incoming merchandise or material; and arranging for the transportation of products. Exclude laborers, stock clerks, and workers whose primary duties involve weighing and checking. Examines contents and compares with records, such as manifests, invoices, or orders, to verify accuracy of incoming or outgoing shipment. Records shipment data, such as weight, charges, space availability, damages, and discrepancies, for reporting, accounting, and recordkeeping purposes. Determines shipping method for materials, using knowledge of shipping procedures, routes, and rates. Contacts carrier representative to make arrangements and to issue instructions for shipping and delivery of materials. Packs, seals, labels, and affixes postage to prepare materials for shipping, using work devices such as hand tools, power tools, and postage meter. Prepares documents, such as work orders, bills of lading, and shipping orders to route materials. Computes amounts, such as space available and shipping, storage, and demurrage charges, using calculator or price list. Confers and corresponds with establishment representatives to rectify problems such as damages, shortages, and nonconformance to specifications. Delivers or routes materials to departments, using work devices such as handtruck, conveyor, or sorting bins. Requisitions and stores shipping materials and supplies to maintain inventory of stock.

Knowledge: Clerical; Economics and Accounting; Philosophy and Theology; Transportation

Abilities: Stamina; Gross Body Equilibrium; Speech Recognition

Transportation and Material Moving Operators

▲ Growth: 15%

▲ Annual Job Openings: 22,268

▲ Yearly Earnings $24,793

▲ Education Required: Moderate-term O-J-T

▲ Self-employed: 0%

▲ Part-time: 12%

Aerial Tram Tenders

Tend aerial tramways to convey refuse, coal, ore, or other materials from plant or mine. Controls movement of tram buckets along cable, using control buttons. Monitors tramway control panel for signal indicating malfunction of equipment. Loads and unloads buckets, using levers and control buttons. Repairs and maintains tram buckets, overhead cables, and pulleys.

Knowledge: None above average

Abilities: Rate Control; Glare Sensitivity

Dragline Operators

Operate power-driven crane equipment with dragline bucket to excavate or move sand, gravel, mud, or other materials. Moves controls to position boom, lower and drag bucket through material, and release material at unloading point. Directs workers engaged in placing blocks and outriggers to prevent capsizing of machine when lifting heavy loads. Drives machine to worksite.

Knowledge: Building and Construction; Transportation

Abilities: Control Precision; Multilimb Coordination; Response Orientation; Rate Control; Far Vision; Peripheral Vision; Depth Perception

Dredge Operators

Operate power-driven dredges to mine sand, gravel, or other materials from lakes, rivers, or streams, and to excavate and maintain navigable channels in waterways. Starts and stops engines to operate equipment. Moves levers to position dredge for excavation, engage hydraulic pump, raise and lower suction boom, and control rotation of cutter head. Starts power winch that draws in or lets out cable to change position of dredge, or pulls in and lets out cable manually. Lowers anchor pole to verify depth of excavation, using winch, or scans depth gauge to determine depth of excavation. Directs workers placing shore anchors and cables, laying additional pipes from dredge to shore, and pumping water from pontoons.

Knowledge: Engineering and Technology; Geography; Transportation

Abilities: Static Strength; Gross Body Equilibrium; Peripheral Vision; Depth Perception; Glare Sensitivity; Sound Localization

Loading Machine Operators, Underground Mining

Operate underground loading machines to load coal, ore, or rock into shuttle or mine cars or onto conveyors. Loading equipment may include power shovels, hoisting engines equipped with cable-drawn scraper or scoop, or machines equipped with gathering arms and conveyor. Moves levers to start, raise, and position conveyor boom and gathering arms; force shovel into pile; and move and dump material. Advances machine to gather material and convey it into car at rear. Stops gathering arms when car is full. Drives machine into pile of material blasted from working face. Pries off loose material from roof and moves it into path of machine with crowbar. Moves trailing electrical cable clear of obstructions, using rubber safety gloves. Replaces hydraulic hoses, headlight bulbs, and gathering-arm teeth.

Knowledge: Mechanical

Abilities: Spatial Orientation; Gross Body Equilibrium; Night Vision; Peripheral Vision; Depth Perception; Sound Localization

Shuttle Car Operators

Operate diesel- or electric-powered shuttle cars in underground mine, to transport materials from working face to mine cars or to conveyor. Positions shuttle car under discharge conveyor of loading machine and observes that materials are loaded according to specifications. Controls conveyor, which runs entire length of shuttle car, to apportion load as loading progresses. Drives loaded shuttle car to ramp and moves controls to discharge load into mine car or onto conveyor. Maneuvers shuttle car to keep its nose under discharge conveyor. Moves mine cars into position to be loaded from shuttle car. Charges batteries when operating battery-powered vehicle.

Knowledge: Transportation

Abilities: Multilimb Coordination; Rate Control; Night Vision; Peripheral Vision; Depth Perception

Conveyor Operators and Tenders

Control or tend conveyors or conveyor systems that move materials or products to and from stockpiles, processing stations, departments, vehicles, and underground worksites. May control speed and routing of materials or products. Manipulates controls, levers, and valves to start pumps, auxiliary equipment, or conveyors and to adjust equipment positions, speed, timing, and material flow. Observes conveyor operations and monitors lights, dials, and gauges to maintain specified operating levels and to detect equipment malfunctions. Stops equipment or machinery and clears jams, using poles, bars, and hand tools, or removes damaged materials from conveyors. Reads production and delivery schedules, and confers with supervisor to determine processing procedures. Loads, unloads, or adjusts materials or products on conveyors by hand or using lifts and hoists. Inspects equipment and machinery to prevent loss of materials or products during transit. Signals workers in other departments to move materials, products, or machinery, or notifies work stations of shipments enroute and estimated delivery times. Moves, assembles, and connects hoses or nozzles to material hoppers, storage tanks, conveyor sections or chutes, and pumps. Repairs or replaces equipment components or parts such as blades, rolls, and pumps. Cleans, sterilizes, and maintains equipment, machinery, and work stations, using hand tools, shovels, brooms, chemicals, hoses, and lubricants. Repairs or replaces equipment components or parts such as blades, rolls, and pumps. Weighs or measures materials and products, using scales or other measuring instruments, to verify specified tonnage and prevent overloads. Collects samples of materials or products for laboratory analysis and ensures conformance to specifications. Affixes identifying information to materials or products, using hand tools. Records production data, such as weight, type, quantity, and storage locations of materials, and documents equipment downtime. Distributes materials, supplies, and equipment to work stations, using lifts and trucks.

Knowledge: Production and Processing

Abilities: Perceptual Speed; Multilimb Coordination; Rate Control; Trunk Strength

Pump Operators

Tend, control, or operate power-driven, stationary, or portable pumps and manifold systems, to transfer gases, liquids, slurries, or powdered materials to and from various vessels and processes. Operates or tends power-driven, stationary, or portable pumps to transfer substances such as gases, liquids, slurries, or powdered materials. Turns valves and starts pump to commence or regulate flow of substances. Tends vessels that store substances such as gases, liquids, slurries, or powdered materials. Connects hoses and pipes to pumps and vessels, using hand tools. Observes gauges and flowmeter to ascertain that specifications are met, such as tank level, chemical amounts, and pressure. Adds chemicals and solutions to tank to ensure specifications are met. Tends auxiliary equipment such as water treatment and refrigeration units and heat exchanges. Communicates with workers to start flow of materials or substance. Cleans and maintains pumps and vessels, using hand tools and equipment. Collects and delivers sample solutions for laboratory analysis. Tests materials and solutions, using testing equipment. Transfers materials to and from vessels, using moving equipment. Inspects and reports vessel and pump abnormalities such as leaks and pressure and temperature fluctuations. Records information such as type and quantity of material, and operating data.

Knowledge: Production and Processing; Mechanical; Physics; Chemistry

Abilities: Control Precision; Rate Control; Speed of Limb Movement; Trunk Strength; Stamina; Dynamic Flexibility; Gross Body Coordination; Gross Body Equilibrium

Transportation Equipment Painters

▲ Growth: 19%

▲ Annual Job Openings: 7,029

▲ Yearly Earnings $30,180

▲ Education Required: Moderate-term O-J-T

▲ Self-employed: 18%

▲ Part time: 5%

Painters, Transportation Equipment

Operate or tend painting machines to paint surfaces of transportation equipment, such as automobiles, buses, trucks, boats, and airplanes. Pours paint into spray gun and sprays specified amount of primer, decorative, or finish coatings onto prepared surfaces. Paints areas inaccessible to spray gun, or retouches painted surface, using brush. Paints designs, lettering, or other identifying information on vehicles, using paint brush or paint sprayer. Mixes, stirs, and thins paint or other coatings, using spatula or power mixing equipment. Selects paint according to company requirements and matches colors of paint following specified color charts. Disassembles sprayer and power equipment, such as sandblaster, and cleans equipment and hand tools, using solvents, wire brushes, and cloths. Regulates controls on portable ventilators and exhaust units to cure and dry paint or other coatings. Lays out logos, symbols, or designs on painted surfaces, according to blueprint specifications, using measuring instruments, stencils, and patterns. Strips grease, dirt, paint, and rust from vehicle surface, using abrasives, solvents, brushes, blowtorch, or sandblaster. Sets up portable ventilators, exhaust units, ladders, and scaffolding. Removes accessories from vehicles, such as chrome or mirrors, and masks other surfaces with tape or paper. Operates lifting and moving devices to move equipment or materials to access areas to be painted.

Knowledge: None above average

Abilities: Dynamic Flexibility; Gross Body Equilibrium; Visual Color Discrimination

Travel Agents

▲ Growth: 24%

▲ Annual Job Openings: 38,234

▲ Yearly Earnings $21,964

▲ Education Required: Postsecondary vocational training

▲ Self-employed: 15%

▲ Part-time: 31%

Travel Agents

Plan trips for travel agency customers. Duties include determining destination, modes of transportation, travel dates, costs, and accommodations required; and planning, describing, or selling itinerary package tours. May specialize in foreign or domestic service, individual or group travel, specific geographical area, airplane charters, or package tours. Plans, describes, arranges, and sells itinerary tour packages and promotional travel incentives offered by various travel carriers. Converses with customer to determine destination, mode of transportation, travel dates, financial considerations, and accommodations required. Computes cost of travel and accommodations, using calculator, computer, carrier tariff books, and hotel rate books, or quotes package tour's costs. Books transportation and hotel reservations, using computer terminal or telephone. Provides customer with brochures and publications containing travel information, such as local customs, points of interest, or foreign country regulations. Prints or requests transportation carrier tickets, using computer printer system or system link to travel carrier. Collects payment for transportation and accommodations from customer.

Knowledge: Clerical; Sales and Marketing; Customer and Personal Service; Sociology and Anthropology; Geography; Foreign Language; Transportation

Abilities: None above average

Travel Guides

Plan, organize, and conduct cruises, tours, and expeditions for individuals and groups. Plans tour itinerary, applying knowledge of travel routes and destination sites. Arranges for transportation, accommodations, activity equipment, and services of medical personnel. Selects activity tour sites, and leads individuals or groups to location, and describes points of interest. Verifies quantity and quality of equipment to ensure that prerequisite needs for expeditions and tours have been met. Instructs novices in climbing techniques, mountaineering, and wilderness survival, and demonstrates use of hunting, fishing, and climbing equipment. Obtains or assists tourists to obtain permits and documents, such as visas, passports, and health certificates, and to convert currency. Pitches camp and prepares meals for tour group members. Explains hunting and fishing laws to group to ensure compliance. Pilots airplane or drives land and water vehicles to transport tourists to activity/tour site. Administers first aid to injured group participants. Sells or rents equipment, clothing, and supplies.

Knowledge: Administration and Management; Sales and Marketing; Customer and Personal Service; Sociology and Anthropology; Geography; Medicine and Dentistry; Foreign Language; History and Archeology; Public Safety and Security; Law, Government, and Jurisprudence; Communications and Media; Transportation

Abilities: Memorization; Spatial Orientation; Time Sharing; Multilimb Coordination; Response Orientation; Rate Control; Reaction Time; Dynamic Strength; Trunk Strength; Stamina; Gross Body Coordination; Gross Body Equilibrium; Night Vision; Peripheral Vision; Depth Perception; Glare Sensitivity; Auditory Attention; Sound Localization; Speech Recognition; Speech Clarity

Truck Drivers Light and Heavy

- ▲ Growth: 15%
- ▲ Annual Job Openings: 346,612
- ▲ Yearly Earnings $24,273
- ▲ Education Required: Short-term O-J-T
- ▲ Self-employed: 10%
- ▲ Part-time: 9%

Truck Drivers, Heavy

Drive trucks with capacity of more than three tons to transport materials to specified destinations. Drives truck with capacity of more than three tons to transport and deliver cargo, materials, or damaged vehicles. Maintains radio or telephone contact with base or supervisor to receive instructions or to be dispatched to a new location. Maintains truck log according to state and federal regulations. Keeps record of materials and products transported. Positions blocks and ties rope around items to secure cargo for transport. Cleans, inspects, and services vehicle. Operates equipment on vehicle to load, unload, or disperse cargo or materials. Obtains customer signature or collects payment for goods delivered and delivery charges. Assists in loading and unloading truck manually.

Knowledge: Geography; Public Safety and Security; Law, Government, and Jurisprudence; Telecommunications; Transportation

Abilities: Spatial Orientation; Time Sharing; Control Precision; Multilimb Coordination; Response Orientation; Rate Control; Reaction Time; Wrist-Finger Speed; Speed of Limb Movement; Static Strength; Explosive Strength; Dynamic Strength; Trunk Strength; Stamina; Extent Flexibility; Dynamic Flexibility; Gross Body Coordination; Gross Body Equilibrium; Far Vision; Night Vision; Peripheral Vision; Depth Perception; Glare Sensitivity; Hearing Sensitivity; Auditory Attention; Sound Localization

Tractor-Trailer Truck Drivers

Drive tractor-trailer trucks to transport products, livestock, or materials to specified destinations. Drives tractor-trailer combination, applying knowledge of commercial driving regulations, to transport and deliver products, livestock, or materials, usually over long distances. Maneuvers truck into loading or unloading position, following signals from loading crew as needed. Drives truck to weigh station before and after loading and along route, to document weight and conform to state regulations. Maintains driver log according to I.C.C. regulations. Inspects truck before and after trips and submits report indicating truck condition. Reads bill of lading to determine assignment. Fastens chains or binders to secure load on trailer during transit. Loads or unloads, or assists in loading and unloading truck. Works as member of two-person team driving tractor with sleeper bunk behind cab. Services truck with oil, fuel, and radiator fluid to maintain tractor-trailer. Obtains customer's signature or collects payment for services. Inventories and inspects goods to be moved. Wraps goods using pads, packing paper, and containers, and secures load to trailer wall using straps. Gives directions to helper in packing and moving goods to trailer.

Knowledge: Geography; Public Safety and Security; Law, Government, and Jurisprudence; Transportation

Abilities: Spatial Orientation; Visualization; Time Sharing; Manual Dexterity; Multilimb Coordination; Response Orientation; Rate Control; Reaction Time; Wrist-Finger Speed; Speed of Limb Movement; Static Strength; Explosive Strength; Dynamic Strength; Trunk Strength; Stamina; Extent Flexibility; Dynamic Flexibility; Gross Body Coordination; Gross Body Equilibrium; Far Vision; Night Vision; Peripheral Vision; Depth Perception; Glare Sensitivity; Hearing Sensitivity; Auditory Attention

Truck Drivers, Light—Including Delivery and Route Workers

Drive a truck, van, or automobile with a capacity under three tons. May drive light truck to deliver or pick up merchandise. May load and unload truck. Drives truck, van, or automobile with capacity under three tons to transport materials, products, or people. Loads and unloads truck, van, or automobile. Communicates with base or other vehicles using telephone or radio. Maintains records such as vehicle log, record of cargo, or billing statements in accordance with regulations. Inspects and maintains vehicle equipment and supplies. Presents billing invoice and collects receipt or payment. Assists passengers into and out of vehicle. Performs emergency roadside repairs.

Knowledge: Geography; Law, Government, and Jurisprudence; Telecommunications; Transportation

Abilities: Spatial Orientation; Time Sharing; Control Precision; Multilimb Coordination; Response Orientation; Rate Control; Reaction Time; Static Strength; Explosive Strength; Dynamic Strength; Trunk Strength; Stamina; Extent Flexibility; Dynamic Flexibility; Gross

Body Coordination; Gross Body Equilibrium; Far Vision; Night Vision; Peripheral Vision; Depth Perception; Glare Sensitivity; Hearing Sensitivity; Auditory Attention; Sound Localization; Speech Recognition

Tutors and Instructors

▲ Growth: 15%
▲ Annual Job Openings: 149,064
▲ Yearly Earnings $26,000
▲ Education Required: Bachelor's degree
▲ Self-employed: 10%
▲ Part-time: 39%

Public Health Educators

Plan, organize, and direct health education programs for group and community needs. Plans and provides educational opportunities for health personnel. Collaborates with health specialists and civic groups to ascertain community health needs, determine availability of services, and develop goals. Promotes health discussions in schools, industry, and community agencies. Conducts community surveys to ascertain health needs, develop desirable health goals, and determine availability of professional health services. Prepares and disseminates educational and informational materials. Develops and maintains cooperation between public, civic, professional, and voluntary agencies.

Knowledge: Administration and Management; Sales and Marketing; Customer and Personal Service; Biology; Psychology; Sociology and Anthropology; Medicine and Dentistry; Therapy and Counseling; Education and Training; English Language; Philosophy and Theology; Communications and Media

Abilities: Oral Expression; Originality; Inductive Reasoning; Speech Clarity

Typists and Word Processors

▲ Growth: 0%
▲ Annual Job Openings: 120,405
▲ Yearly Earnings $21,403
▲ Education Required: Moderate-term O-J-T
▲ Self-employed: 0%
▲ Part-time: 28%

Typists, Including Word Processing

Use typewriter or computer to type letters, reports, forms, or other straight copy material from rough draft, corrected copy, or voice recording. May perform other clerical duties as assigned. Exclude keypunchers, secretaries, and stenographers. Types from rough draft, corrected copy, or previous version displayed on screen, using computer or typewriter. Types from recorded dictation. Addresses envelopes or prepares envelope labels, using typewriter or computer. Gathers and arranges material to be typed, following instructions. Adjusts settings for format, page layout, line spacing, and other style requirements. Checks completed work for spelling, grammar, punctuation, and format. Stores completed documents on computer hard drive or data storage medium, such as disk. Transcribes stenotyped notes of court proceedings. Prints and makes copy of work. Files and stores completed documents. Collates pages of reports and other documents prepared. Sorts and distributes mail. Answers telephone. Operates duplicating machine. Transmits work electronically to other locations. Computes and verifies totals on report forms, requisitions, or bills, using adding machine or calculator. Keeps records of work performed. Uses data entry device, such as optical scanner, to input data into computer for revision or editing.

Knowledge: Clerical; Computers and Electronics; English Language

Abilities: Category Flexibility; Perceptual Speed; Wrist-Finger Speed; Near Vision; Auditory Attention; Speech Recognition

Urban and Regional Planners

- ▲ Growth: 5%
- ▲ Annual Job Openings: 3,856
- ▲ Yearly Earnings $40,934
- ▲ Education Required: Master's degree
- ▲ Self-employed: 3%
- ▲ Part-time: 18%

Urban and Regional Planners

Develop comprehensive plans and programs for use of land and physical facilities of cities, counties, and metropolitan areas. Develops alternative plans with recommendations for program or project. Compiles, organizes, and analyzes data on economic, social, and physical factors affecting land use, using statistical methods. Reviews and evaluates environmental impact reports applying to specific private and public planning projects and programs. Evaluates information to determine feasibility of proposals or to identify factors requiring amendment. Recommends governmental measures affecting land use, public utilities, community facilities, housing, and transportation. Discusses purpose of land use projects, such as transportation, conservation, residential, commercial, industrial, and community use, with planning officials. Prepares or requisitions graphic and narrative report on land use data. Determines regulatory limitations on project. Conducts field investigations, economic or public opinion surveys, demographic studies, or other research to gather required information. Advises planning officials on feasibility, cost effectiveness, regulatory conformance, and alternative recommendations for project. Maintains collection of socio-economic, environmental, and regulatory data related to land use for governmental and private sectors.

Knowledge: Administration and Management; Clerical; Economics and Accounting; Sales and Marketing; Computers and Electronics; Engineering and Technology; Design; Building and Construction; Mathematics; Biology; Sociology and Anthropology; Geography; Education and Training; English Language; History and Archeology; Philosophy and Theology; Public Safety and Security; Law, Government, and Jurisprudence; Communications and Media; Transportation

Abilities: Oral Comprehension; Written Comprehension; Oral Expression; Written Expression; Fluency of Ideas; Originality; Problem Sensitivity; Deductive Reasoning; Inductive Reasoning; Category Flexibility; Mathematical Reasoning; Number Facility; Speed of Closure; Speech Clarity

Ushers, Lobby Attendants, and Ticket Takers

- ▲ Growth: 28%
- ▲ Annual Job Openings: 25,394
- ▲ Yearly Earnings $12,230
- ▲ Education Required: Short-term O-J-T
- ▲ Self-employed: 0%
- ▲ Part-time: 48%

Tour Guides and Escorts

Escort individuals or groups on sightseeing tours or through places of interest, such as industrial establishments, public buildings, and art galleries. Escorts group on city and establishment tours, describes points of interest, and responds to questions. Drives motor vehicle to transport visitors to establishments and tour site locations. Provides directions and other pertinent information to visitors. Distributes brochures, conveys background information, and explains establishment processes and operations at tour site. Monitors visitors' activities and cautions visitors not complying with establishment regulations. Greets and registers visitors and issues identification badges and safety devices. Assumes responsibility for safety of group. Plans rest stops and refreshment items. Speaks foreign language to communicate with foreign visitors. Solicits tour patronage and collects fees and tickets from group members. Carries equipment, luggage, or sample cases for visitors and provides errand service. Performs clerical duties, such as filing, typing, operating switchboard, and delivering and collection of mail and messages. Monitors facilities and notifies establishment personnel of need for maintenance.

Knowledge: Sales and Marketing; Customer and Personal Service; Geography; Foreign Language; Fine Arts; History and Archeology; Communications and Media; Transportation

Abilities: Memorization; Spatial Orientation; Time Sharing; Rate Control; Reaction Time; Night Vision; Speech Recognition; Speech Clarity

Ushers, Lobby Attendants, and Ticket Takers

Assist patrons at entertainment events, such as sporting events, motion pictures, or theater performances. Collect admission tickets and passes from patrons. May assist in finding seats, searching for lost articles, and locating such facilities as restrooms and telephones. Collects admission tickets and passes from patrons at entertainment events. Assists patrons to find seats, search for lost articles, and locate facilities, such as restrooms and telephones. Verifies credentials of patrons desiring entrance into press-box, and permits only authorized persons to enter. Examines ticket or pass to verify authenticity, using criteria such as color and date issued. Refuses admittance to patrons without ticket or pass, or those who are undesirable for reasons such as intoxication or improper attire. Distributes programs to patrons, or door checks to patrons temporarily leaving establishment. Greets patrons desiring to attend entertainment events. Counts and records number of tickets collected. Monitors patrons' activities to prevent disorderly conduct and rowdiness and to detect infractions of rules. Serves patrons at refreshment stand during intermission. Runs errand for patrons of press-box, such as obtaining refreshments and carrying news releases. Parks car or directs patron to parking space at drive-in theater, indicating available space with flashlight. Attaches loudspeaker to automobile door and turns controls to adjust volume. Assists other workers to change advertising display.

Knowledge: Customer and Personal Service; Foreign Language

Abilities: None above average

Locker Room, Coatroom, and Dressing Room Attendants

Provide personal items to patrons or customers in locker rooms, dressing rooms, or coatrooms. Seats patrons, massages body or gives baths, and furnishes towel or dries patron. Selects and fits clothing or costume for patrons. Issues or distributes clothing articles and assists patron to dress. Procures beverage, food, and other items as requested. Turns controls to regulate temperature or room environment. Examines dress, accessories, or equipment to ensure conformance with specifications. Collects and organizes clothing, accessories, or linens. Maintains and cleans dressing and bathing areas or lavatories. Alters, mends, presses, and spot-cleans costumes, clothing, or wardrobe accessories. Sends out clothing articles for major repair or cleaning.

Knowledge: Customer and Personal Service

Abilities: None above average

Vehicle Washers and Equipment Cleaners

▲ Growth: 25%
▲ Annual Job Openings: 103,946
▲ Yearly Earnings $14,684
▲ Education Required: Short-term O-J-T
▲ Self-employed: 6%
▲ Part-time: 22%

Vehicle Washers and Equipment Cleaners

Wash or otherwise clean vehicles, machinery, and other equipment. Use such materials as water, cleaning agents, brushes, cloths, and hoses. Exclude janitors and building cleaners. Scrubs, scrapes, or sprays machine parts, equipment, or vehicles, using scrapers, brushes, cleaners, disinfectants, insecticides, acid, and abrasives. Presoaks or rinses machine parts, equipment, or vehicles by immersing objects in cleaning solutions or water, manually or using hoists. Presses buttons to activate cleaning equipment or machines. Turns valves or handles on equipment to regulate pressure and flow of water, air, steam, or abrasives from sprayer nozzles. Turns valves or disconnects hoses to eliminate water, cleaning solutions, or vapors from machinery or tanks. Sweeps, shovels, or vacuums loose debris and salvageable scrap into containers, and removes from work area. Mixes cleaning solutions and abrasive compositions and other compounds according to formula. Monitors operation of cleaning machines, and stops machine or notifies supervisor when malfunctions occur. Connects hoses and lines to pumps and other equipment. Disassembles and reassembles machines or equipment, or removes and reattaches vehicle parts and trim, using hand tools. Places objects on drying racks or dyes surfaces, using cloth, squeegees, or air compressors. Examines and inspects parts, equipment, and vehicles for cleanliness, damage, and compliance with standards or regulations. Applies paints, dyes, polishes, reconditioners, and masking materials to vehicles to preserve, protect, or restore color and condition. Lubricates machinery, vehicles, and equipment, and performs minor repairs and adjustments, using hand tools. Transports materials, equipment, or supplies to and from work area, using carts or hoists. Collects and tests samples of cleaning solutions and vapors. Records production and operational data on specified forms. Maintains inventories of supplies.

Knowledge: None above average

Abilities: Speed of Limb Movement; Trunk Strength; Stamina; Extent Flexibility; Dynamic Flexibility; Gross Body Equilibrium

Veterinarians and Veterinary Inspectors

▲ Growth: 23%

▲ Annual Job Openings: 2,381

▲ Yearly Earnings $52,936

▲ Education Required: First professional degree

▲ Self-employed: 35%

▲ Part-time: 10%

Veterinary Pathologists

Study nature, cause, and development of animal diseases; form and structure of animals; or drugs related to veterinary medicine. Performs biopsies, and tests and analyzes body tissue and fluids to diagnose presence, source, and stage of disease in animals. Investigates efficiency of vaccines, antigens, antibiotics, and other materials in prevention, diagnosis, and cure of animal diseases. Studies drugs, including material medical and therapeutics, as related to veterinary medicine. Conducts research on animal parasites in domestic animals to determine control and preventive measures, utilizing chemicals, heat, electricity, and methods. Studies factors influencing existence and spread of diseases among humans and animals, particularly those diseases transmissible from animals to humans. Conducts further research to expand scope of findings, or recommends treatment to consulting veterinary personnel. Identifies laboratory cultures of micro-organisms taken from diseased animals by microscopic examination and bacteriological tests. Tests virulence of pathogenic organisms by observing effects of inoculations on laboratory and other animals. Studies form and structure of animals, both gross and microscopic. Studies function and mechanism of systems and organs in healthy and diseased animals. Prepares laboratory cultures of micro-organisms taken from body fluids and tissues of diseased animals for additional study. Directs activities of veterinary pathology department in educational institution or industrial establishment.

Knowledge: Administration and Management; Food Production; Mathematics; Chemistry; Biology; Medicine and Dentistry; Therapy and Counseling; Education and Training; English Language; Philosophy and Theology; Public Safety and Security

Abilities: Oral Comprehension; Written Comprehension; Oral Expression; Written Expression; Fluency of Ideas; Originality; Problem Sensitivity; Deductive Reasoning; Inductive Reasoning; Information Ordering; Category Flexibility; Memorization; Speed of Closure; Flexibility of Closure; Perceptual Speed; Finger Dexterity; Control Precision; Near Vision

Veterinarians

Diagnose and treat medical problems in animals. Exclude veterinary inspectors and veterinary pathologists. Examines animal to determine nature of disease or injury, and treats animal surgically or medically. Inspects and tests horses, sheep, poultry flocks, and other animals for diseases, and inoculates animals against various diseases, including rabies. Examines laboratory animals to detect indications of disease or injury, and treats animals to prevent spread of disease. Conducts postmortem studies and analyzes results to determine cause of death. Establishes and conducts quarantine and testing procedures for incoming animals to prevent spread of disease and compliance with governmental regulations. Inspects housing and advises animal owners regarding sanitary measures, feeding, and general care to promote health of animals. Consults with veterinarians in general practice seeking advice in treatment of exotic animals. Participates in research projects, plans procedures, and selects animals for scientific research based on knowledge of species and research principles. Ensures compliance with regulations governing humane and ethical treatment of animals used in scientific research. Oversees activities concerned with feeding, care, and maintenance of animal quarters to ensure compliance with laboratory regulations. Participates in planning and executing nutrition and reproduction programs for animals, particularly animals on endangered species list. Trains zoo personnel in handling and care of animals. Exchanges information with zoos and aquariums concerning care, transfer, sale, or trade of animals to maintain all-species nationwide inventory. Teaches or conducts research in universities or in commercial setting.

Knowledge: Mathematics; Chemistry; Biology; Psychology; Medicine and Dentistry; Therapy and Counseling; Education and Training; English Language; Philosophy and Theology; Public Safety and Security

Abilities: Oral Comprehension; Written Comprehension; Oral Expression; Written Expression; Fluency of Ideas; Originality; Problem Sensitivity; Deductive Reasoning; Inductive Reasoning; Information Ordering; Category Flexibility; Memorization; Speed of Closure; Flexibility of Closure; Perceptual Speed; Selective Attention; Time Sharing; Arm-Hand Steadiness; Manual Dexterity; Finger Dexterity; Control Precision; Multilimb Coordination; Response Orientation; Rate Control; Wrist-Finger Speed; Speed of Limb Movement; Near Vision; Visual Color Discrimination; Glare Sensitivity; Hearing Sensitivity; Speech Clarity

Veterinary Inspectors

Inspect animals for presence of disease in facilities such as laboratories, livestock sites, and livestock slaughter or meat-processing facilities. Examines animals used in production process to determine presence of disease. Examines animal and carcass before and after slaughtering to detect evidence of disease or other abnormal conditions. Tests animals and submits specimens of tissue and other parts for laboratory analysis. Inspects processing areas where livestock and poultry are slaughtered and processed to ensure compliance with governmental standards. Reports existence of disease conditions to state and federal authorities. Inspects facilities engaged in processing milk and milk products to ensure compliance with governmental standards. Inspects facilities where serums and other products used in treatment of animals are manufactured to ensure governmental standards are maintained. Institutes and enforces quarantine or other regulations governing import, export, and interstate movement of livestock. Determines that ingredients used in processing and marketing meat and meat products comply with governmental standards of purity and grading. Advises live-stock owners of economic aspects of disease eradication. Advises consumers and public health officials of implications of diseases transmissible from animals to humans.

Knowledge: Economics and Accounting; Production and Processing; Food Production; Chemistry; Biology; Geography; Medicine and Dentistry; English Language; Philosophy and Theology; Public Safety and Security; Law, Government, and Jurisprudence

Abilities: Problem Sensitivity; Inductive Reasoning; Speed of Closure; Flexibility of Closure; Perceptual Speed; Visual Color Discrimination; Auditory Attention

Veterinary Assistants

- ▲ Growth: 28%
- ▲ Annual Job Openings: 7,248
- ▲ Yearly Earnings $15,787
- ▲ Education Required: Short-term O-J-T
- ▲ Self-employed: 0%
- ▲ Part-time: 38%

Veterinary Assistants

Examine animals for veterinarian, prepare animals for surgery, perform post-operational medical treatment as needed, and give medications to animals. Usually work directly under veterinarian. Receive extensive training on the job and may also have some postsecondary education, such as trade school or junior college. Assists veterinarian in variety of animal health care duties, including injections, venipunctures, and wound dressings. Prepares examination or treatment room, and holds or restrains animal during procedures. Prepares patient, medications, equipment, and instruments for surgical procedures, using specialized knowledge. Assists veterinarian during surgical procedures, passing instruments and materials in accordance with oral instructions. Completes routine laboratory tests and cares for and feeds laboratory animals. Assists professional personnel with research projects in commercial, public health, or research laboratories. Inspects products or carcasses to ensure compliance with health standards, when employed in food processing plant.

Knowledge: Food Production; Biology; Medicine and Dentistry; Therapy and Counseling

Abilities: Oral Comprehension; Speed of Closure; Flexibility of Closure; Perceptual Speed; Selective Attention; Arm-Hand Steadiness; Finger Dexterity; Response Orientation; Speed of Limb Movement; Gross Body Equilibrium; Visual Color Discrimination; Peripheral Vision

Vocational Education and Training Instructors

▲ Growth: 23%
▲ Annual Job Openings: 82,354
▲ Yearly Earnings $33,800
▲ Education Required: Work experience in a related occupation
▲ Self-employed: 0%
▲ Part-time: 42%

Teachers and Instructors—Vocational Education and Training

Teach or instruct vocational and/or occupational subjects at the postsecondary level (but at less than the baccalaureate) to students who have graduated or left high school. Subjects include business, secretarial science, data processing, trades, and practical nursing. Include correspondence school instructors; industrial, commercial, and government training instructors; and adult education teachers and instructors who prepare persons to operate industrial machinery and equipment and transportation and communications equipment. Teaching may take place in public or private schools whose primary business is education or in a school associated with an organization whose primary business is other than education. Conducts on-the-job training, classes, or training sessions to teach and demonstrate principles, techniques, procedures, or methods of designated subjects. Presents lectures and conducts discussions to increase students' knowledge and competence, using visual aids, such as graphs, charts, videotapes, and slides. Observes and evaluates students' work to determine progress, provide feedback, and make suggestions for improvement. Develops training programs, teaching aids, and study materials for instruction in vocational or occupational subjects. Plans course content and method of instruction. Prepares outline of instructional program and training schedule, and establishes course goals. Selects and assembles books, materials, supplies, and equipment for training, courses, or projects. Administers oral, written, or performance tests to measure progress and to evaluate effectiveness of training. Determines training needs of students or workers. Corrects, grades, and comments on lesson assignments. Develops instructional software, multimedia visual aids, and computer tutorials. Prepares reports and maintains records, such as student grades, attendance, training activities, production records, and supply or equipment inventories. Reviews enrollment applications and corresponds with applicants. Arranges for lectures by subject matter experts in designated fields. Recommends advancement, transfer, or termination of student or trainee based on mastery of subject. Participates in meetings, seminars, and training sessions, and integrates relevant information into training program. Solves operational problems and provides technical assistance with equipment and process techniques.

Knowledge: Sociology and Anthropology; Education and Training; English Language; History and Archeology; Philosophy and Theology

Abilities: Oral Expression; Fluency of Ideas; Originality; Speech Clarity

Waiters and Waitresses

▲ Growth: 11%

▲ Annual Job Openings: 714,482

▲ Yearly Earnings $11,689

▲ Education Required: Short-term O-J-T

▲ Self-employed: 0%

▲ Part-time: 57%

Waiters/Waitresses

Take food orders and serve food and beverages to patrons in dining establishments.
Takes order from patron for food or beverage, writing order down or memorizing it. Relays order to kitchen, or enters order into computer. Serves meals or beverages to patrons. Observes patrons to respond to additional requests and to determine when meal has been completed or beverage consumed. Presents menu to patron, suggests food or beverage selections, and answers questions regarding preparation and service. Obtains and replenishes supplies of food, tableware, and linen. Serves, or assists patrons to serve themselves at buffet or smorgasbord table. Computes cost of meal or beverage. Accepts payment and returns change, or refers patron to cashier. Removes dishes and glasses from table or counter and takes them to kitchen for cleaning. Prepares hot, cold, and mixed drinks for patrons, and chills bottles of wine. Garnishes and decorates dishes preparatory to serving. Cleans and arranges assigned station, including side stands, chairs, and table pieces, such as linen, silverware, and glassware. Carves meats, bones fish and fowl, and prepares special dishes and desserts at work station or patron's table. Prepares salads, appetizers, and cold dishes, portions desserts, brews coffee, and performs other services as determined by establishment's size and practices. Fills salt, pepper, sugar, cream, condiment, and napkin containers. Washes glassware and silverware. Delivers messages to patrons.

Knowledge: Sales and Marketing; Customer and Personal Service; Food Production; Foreign Language

Abilities: Memorization; Response Orientation; Reaction Time; Wrist-Finger Speed; Speed of Limb Movement; Trunk Strength; Stamina; Dynamic Flexibility; Gross Body Coordination; Gross Body Equilibrium; Night Vision; Peripheral Vision; Auditory Attention; Speech Recognition

Wine Stewards/Stewardesses

Select, requisition, store, and serve wines in restaurant. Assist patrons making wine selections to accompany meals. Replenish stock and maintain storage conditions for wine inventory. Discusses wines with patrons and assists patrons to make wine selection, applying knowledge of wines. Serves wines to patrons. Maintains inventory of wine in stock. Selects and orders wine to replenish stock. Stores wine on racks or shelves. Tastes wine prior to serving.

Knowledge: Sales and Marketing; Customer and Personal Service; Food Production; Geography; Foreign Language

Abilities: Category Flexibility; Memorization; Night Vision; Speech Recognition

Water and Liquid Waste Treatment Plant and System Operators

▲ Growth: 23%
▲ Annual Job Openings: 5,419
▲ Yearly Earnings $28,766
▲ Education Required: Long-term O-J-T
▲ Self-employed: 0%
▲ Part-time: 1%

Water Treatment Plant and System Operators

Operate and control pollution treatment equipment to clean, purify, and neutralize water for human consumption. Operate and control equipment to remove harmful domestic and industrial pollution from wastewater in sewage treatment plants. Operates and adjusts controls on equipment to purify and clarify water, process or dispose of sewage, and generate power. Inspects equipment and monitors operating conditions, meters, and gauges to determine load requirements and detect malfunctions. Adds chemicals, such as ammonia, chlorine, and lime, to disinfect and deodorize water and other liquids. Collects and tests water and sewage samples, using test equipment and color analysis standards. Records operational data, personnel attendance, and meter and gauge readings on specified forms. Cleans and maintains tanks and filter beds, using hand tools and power tools. Maintains, repairs, and lubricates equipment, using hand tools and power tools. Directs and coordinates plant workers engaged in routine operations and maintenance activities.

Knowledge: Production and Processing; Mechanical; Chemistry; Public Safety and Security

Abilities: Information Ordering; Perceptual Speed; Selective Attention; Time Sharing; Control Precision; Rate Control; Dynamic Flexibility; Gross Body Coordination; Gross Body Equilibrium

Water Treatment Plant Attendants

Tend pumps, conveyors, blowers, chlorinators, vacuum filters, and other equipment used to decontaminate sewage. Operates and tends equipment—such as pumps, conveyors, blowers, and vacuum filters—that decontaminates wastewater. Adjusts pipe valves to regulate flow velocity to separate sludge by sedimentation. Turns valves to aerate sewage outflow and to control temperatures in tanks. Reads charts, flow meters, and gauges to monitor plant operations and detect equipment malfunctions. Collects samples to test water quality or purity.

Knowledge: Production and Processing

Abilities: Control Precision; Gross Body Equilibrium

Wholesale and Retail Sales Order Fillers

- ▲ Growth: 12%
- ▲ Annual Job Openings: 38,294
- ▲ Yearly Earnings $18,886
- ▲ Education Required: Short-term O-J-T
- ▲ Self-employed: 0%
- ▲ Part-time: 12%

Wood Machinists

- ▲ Growth: 14%
- ▲ Annual Job Openings: 2,342
- ▲ Yearly Earnings $19,718
- ▲ Education Required: Long-term O-J-T
- ▲ Self-employed: 0%
- ▲ Part-time: 5%

Pattern Makers, Wood

Plan, lay out, and construct wooden unit or sectional patterns used in forming sand molds for castings, according to blueprint specifications. Plans, lays out, and draws outline of unit, sectional patterns, or full-scale mock-up of products. Fits, fastens, and assembles wood parts together to form pattern, model, or section, using glue, nails, dowels, bolts, and screws. Sets up, operates, and adjusts variety of woodworking machines to cut and shape sections, parts, and patterns, according to specifications. Trims, smooths and shapes surfaces, and planes, shaves, files, scrapes, and sands models to attain specified shapes, using hand tools. Constructs wooden models, templates, full-scale mock-up, and molds for parts of products. Reads blueprints, drawing, or written specifications to determine size and shape of pattern and required machine set-up. Trims, smoothes and shapes surfaces, and planes, shaves, files, scrapes, and sands models to attain specified shapes, using hand tools. Shellacs, lacquers, or waxes finished pattern or model. Marks identifying information, such as colors or codes, on patterns, parts, and templates to indicate assembly method. Issues patterns to designated machine operators, and maintains pattern record for reference.

Knowledge: Design; Building and Construction

Abilities: None above average

Jig Builders

Build jigs used as guides for assembling wooden containers. Assembles jigs to be used as guides for assembling barrels or boxes. Measures and marks positions of stops on work table, following blueprints. Nails stops to work table as indicated on blueprint. Reads blueprints to determine size and shape of wooden container.

Knowledge: Building and Construction

Abilities: None above average

Woodworking Layout Workers

Lay out outline of frames and furniture parts on woodstock to guide machine operators working from blueprints, job orders, or models. Measures and marks with rule, square, and pencil or crayon, outlines of cuts to be made by various machine operators. Traces outlines from blueprints for decorative or irregular cutting on bandsaw. Traces around patterns to indicate cutting lines. Calibrates and records machining dimensions on stock or pattern for use in production as guide for machining parts. Studies architectural drawing or blueprint of part or full assembly to be made. Selects stock lumber of necessary size.

Knowledge: Design; Building and Construction

Abilities: None above average

Wood Machinists

Set up and operate a variety of woodworking machines to surface, cut, and shape lumber, and to fabricate parts for wood products, such as door and window frames, furniture, and sashes, according to specifications. Exclude workers primarily concerned with one or a limited number of machine phases and include them with their specialty. Operates variety of machines to saw, smooth, shape, bore holes in, and cut slots, grooves, and designs in woodstock. Selects, installs, and adjusts saw blades, cutter heads, boring bits, and sanding belts in respective machines, using hand tools and rule. Starts machine and makes trial cut. Periodically verifies dimensions of parts for adherence to specifications, using gauges and templates. Assembles fabricated parts to make millwork products, such as doors, sashes, and door and window frames.

Knowledge: Production and Processing; Building and Construction

Abilities: None above average

Writers and Editors

▲ Growth: 21%
▲ Annual Job Openings: 41,449
▲ Yearly Earnings $38,355
▲ Education Required: Bachelor's degree
▲ Self-employed: 31%
▲ Part-time: 18%

Columnists, Critics, and Commentators

Write commentaries or critical reviews based on analysis of news items or literary, musical, or artistic works and performances. Analyzes and interprets news, current issues, and personal experiences to formulate ideas and other materials for column or commentary. Analyzes factors such as theme, expression, and technique, and forms critical opinions of literary, musical, dramatic, or visual art works and performances. Writes column, editorial, commentary, or review to stimulate or influence public opinion. Gathers information and develops perspective through research, interview, experience, and attendance at political, news, sports, artistic, social, and other functions. Revises text to meet editorial approval or to fit time or space requirements. Selects and organizes material pertinent to presentation into appropriate media form and format. Enters information into computer to prepare commentary or review. Discusses issues with editor of publication or broadcast facility editorial board to establish priorities and positions. Presents commentary live or in recorded form when working in broadcast medium.

Knowledge: Computers and Electronics; English Language; Fine Arts; Communications and Media

Abilities: Written Expression; Fluency of Ideas; Originality; Category Flexibility; Speed of Closure; Perceptual Speed

Poets and Lyricists

Write poetry or song lyrics for publication or performance. Writes words to fit musical compositions, including lyrics for operas, musical plays, and choral works. Writes narrative, dramatic, lyric, or other types of poetry for publication. Adapts text to accommodate musical requirements of composer and singer. Chooses subject matter and suitable form to express personal feeling and experience or ideas or to narrate story or event.

Knowledge: English Language; Fine Arts; Communications and Media

Abilities: Written Expression; Fluency of Ideas; Originality; Hearing Sensitivity

Creative Writers

Create original written works, such as plays or prose, for publication or performance. Writes fiction or nonfiction prose work, such as short story, novel, biography, article, descriptive or critical analysis, or essay. Writes play or script for moving pictures or television, based on original ideas or adapted from fictional, historical, or narrative sources. Writes humorous material for publication or performance, such as comedy routines, gags, comedy shows, or scripts for entertainers. Organizes material for project, plans arrangement or outline, and writes synopsis. Develops factors, such as theme, plot, characterization, psychological analysis, historical environment, action, and dialogue, to create material. Selects subject or theme for writing project based on personal interest and writing specialty, or on assignment from publisher, client, producer, or director. Reviews, submits for approval, and revises written material to meet personal standards and satisfy needs of client, publisher, director, or producer. Conducts research to obtain factual information and authentic detail, utilizing sources such as newspaper accounts, diaries, and interviews. Confers with client, publisher, or producer to discuss development changes or revisions. Collaborates with other writers on specific projects.

Knowledge: Sociology and Anthropology; English Language; Fine Arts; Communications and Media

Abilities: Oral Comprehension; Written Comprehension; Written Expression; Fluency of Ideas; Originality; Inductive Reasoning; Near Vision

Editors

Perform variety of editorial duties, such as laying out, indexing, and revising content of written materials in preparation for final publication. Exclude managing editors, programming and script editors, book editors, and film editors. Plans and prepares page layouts to position and space articles and photographs or illustrations. Reads and evaluates manuscripts or other materials submitted for publication, and confers with authors regarding changes or publication. Writes and rewrites headlines, captions, columns, articles, and stories to conform to publication's style, editorial policy, and publishing requirements. Determines placement of stories based on relative significance, available space, and knowledge of layout principles. Confers with management and editorial staff members regarding placement of developing news stories. Reads copy or proof to detect and correct errors in spelling, punctuation, and syntax, and indicates corrections, using standard proofreading and typesetting symbols. Selects and crops photographs and illustrative materials to conform to space and subject matter requirements. Reviews and approves proofs submitted by composing room. Reads material to determine items to be included in index of book or other publication. Arranges topical or alphabetical list of index items, according to page or chapter, indicating location of item in text. Verifies facts, dates, and statistics, using standard reference sources. Compiles index cross-references and related items, such as glossaries, bibliographies, and footnotes. Selects local, state, national, and international news items received by wire from press associations.

Knowledge: English Language; Communications and Media

Abilities: Written Comprehension; Written Expression; Originality; Problem Sensitivity; Deductive Reasoning; Information Ordering; Memorization; Flexibility of Closure; Visualization; Near Vision

Managing Editors

Direct and coordinate editorial operations of newspaper, newspaper department, or magazine. Include workers who formulate editorial policy. Formulates editorial and publication policies in consultation and negotiation with owner's representative, executives, editorial policy committee, and department heads. Directs and coordinates editorial departments and activities of personnel engaged in selecting, gathering, and editing news and photography for radio, television station, or print. Assigns research, writing, and editorial duties to staff members and reviews work products. Confers with management and staff to relay information, develop operating procedures and schedules, allocate space or time, and solve problems. Originates or approves story ideas or themes, sets priorities, and assigns coverage to members of reporting and photography staff. Directs page make-up of publication, organizes material, plans page layouts, and selects type. Edits copy or reviews edited copy to ensure that writing meets establishment standards and slanderous, libelous, and profane statements are avoided. Reviews final proofs, approves or makes changes, and performs other editorial duties. Coordinates and tracks assignments, using computer and two-way radio. Writes leading or policy editorials, headlines, articles, and other materials. Reads and selects submitted material, such as letters and articles, for publication. Secures graphic material from picture sources and assigns artists and photographers to produce pictures, illustrations, and cartoons. Interviews individuals and attends gatherings to obtain items for publication, verify facts, and clarify information. Represents organization at professional and community functions and maintains contact with outside agencies. Performs personnel-related activities, such as hiring, reviewing work, and terminating employment.

Knowledge: Administration and Management; Personnel and Human Resources; Computers and Electronics; English Language; Communications and Media

Abilities: Oral Comprehension; Written Comprehension; Oral Expression; Written Expression; Fluency of Ideas; Originality; Deductive Reasoning; Category Flexibility; Memorization; Speed of Closure; Flexibility of Closure; Perceptual Speed; Selective Attention; Time Sharing

Programming and Script Editors and Coordinators

Direct and coordinate activities of workers who prepare scripts for radio, television, or motion picture productions. Include workers who develop, write, and edit proposals for new radio or television programs. Reviews writers' work and gives instruction and direction regarding changes, additions, and corrections. Hires, assigns work to, and supervises staff and freelance writers or other employees. Writes or edits proposals for original program concepts, and submits proposals for review by programming, financial, and other departmental personnel. Evaluates stories, proposals, or other materials to determine potential and feasibility of development into scripts or programs. Reads and evaluates written material to select writers and stories for radio, television, or motion picture production. Edits material to ensure conformance with company policy and standards, copyright laws, and federal regulations. Rewrites, combines, and polishes draft scripts, as necessary, to prepare scripts for production. Participates in selection of researchers, consultants, producers, and on-air personalities to facilitate development of program ideas. Maintains liaison between program production department and proposal originators to ensure timely exchange of information regarding project. Recommends purchasing material for use in developing scripts, in consultation with production head. Authorizes budget preparation for final proposals.

Knowledge: Administration and Management; Economics and Accounting; Personnel and Human Resources; English Language; Fine Arts; Communications and Media

Abilities: Oral Comprehension; Written Comprehension; Written Expression; Fluency of Ideas; Originality; Inductive Reasoning

Book Editors

Secure, select, and coordinate publication of manuscripts in book form. Confers with author and publisher to arrange purchase and details such as publication date, royalties, and quantity to be printed. Coordinates book design and production activities. Makes recommendations regarding procurement and revision of manuscript. Contracts design and production or personally designs and produces book. Reviews submitted book manuscript and determines market demand based on consumer trends and personal knowledge. Assigns and supervises editorial staff work activities.

Knowledge: Administration and Management; Sales and Marketing; English Language; Communications and Media

Abilities: Written Comprehension; Fluency of Ideas; Originality; Category Flexibility; Speed of Closure; Flexibility of Closure; Selective Attention

Readers

Read books, plays, or scripts to prepare synopses for review by editorial staff or to recommend content revisions. Reads novels, stories, and plays and prepares synopses for review by editorial department or film, radio, or television producer. Recommends revisions to or disallows broadcast of materials violating federal regulations or station standards. Reads and listens to material to be broadcast on radio or television to detect vulgar, libelous, or misleading statements. Prepares recommended editorial revisions in script, using computer or typewriter. Suggests possible treatment of selected materials in film or program. Confers with sales or advertising agency personnel to report on revised or disallowed commercials.

Knowledge: English Language; Communications and Media

Abilities: Written Comprehension; Written Expression; Originality; Flexibility of Closure; Wrist-Finger Speed; Near Vision

Caption Writers

Write caption phrases of dialogue for hearing-impaired and foreign language-speaking viewers of movie or television productions. Writes captions to describe music and background noises. Watches production and reviews captions simultaneously to determine which caption phrases require editing. Translates foreign-language dialogue into English-language captions or English dialogue into foreign-language captions. Enters commands to synchronize captions with dialogue and place on the screen. Operates computerized captioning system for movies or television productions for hearing-impaired and foreign-language speaking viewers. Edits translations for correctness of grammar, punctuation, and clarity of expression. Oversees encoding of captions to master tape of television production. Discusses captions with directors or producers of movie and television productions.

Knowledge: Computers and Electronics; English Language; Foreign Language; Communications and Media

Abilities: Wrist-Finger Speed; Near Vision

Copy Writers

Write advertising copy for use by publication or broadcast media to promote sale of goods and services. Writes advertising copy for use by publication or broadcast media and revises copy according to supervisor's instructions. Writes articles, bulletins, sales letters, speeches, and other related informative and promotional material. Prepares advertising copy, using computer. Consults with sales media and marketing representatives to obtain information on product or service and discuss style and length of advertising copy. Obtains additional background and current development information through research and interviews. Reviews advertising trends, consumer surveys, and other data regarding marketing of goods and services to formulate approach.

Knowledge: Sales and Marketing; Computers and Electronics; English Language; Communications and Media

Abilities: Oral Comprehension; Written Comprehension; Written Expression; Fluency of Ideas; Originality; Wrist-Finger Speed; Near Vision

Dictionary Editors

Research information about words, and write and review definitions for publication in dictionary. Conducts or directs research to discover origin, spelling, syllabication, pronunciation, meaning, and usage of words. Organizes research material and writes definitions for general or specialized dictionary. Studies frequency of use for specific words and other factors to select words for inclusion in dictionary. Edits and reviews definitions written by other staff prior to publication. Selects drawings or other graphic material to illustrate word meaning.

Knowledge: English Language

Abilities: Written Expression; Category Flexibility; Speed of Closure; Perceptual Speed; Selective Attention

Technical Writers

Write or edit technical materials, such as equipment manuals, appendices, and operating and maintenance instructions. May oversee preparation of illustrations, photographs, diagrams, and charts; and assist in layout work. Organizes material and completes writing assignment according to set standards regarding order, clarity, conciseness, style, and terminology. Writes speeches, articles, and public or employee relations releases. Studies drawings, specifications, mock ups, and product samples to integrate and delineate technology, operating procedure, and production sequence and detail. Reviews published materials and recommends revisions or changes in scope, format, content, and methods of reproduction and binding. Assists in laying out material for publication. Interviews production and engineering personnel and reads journals and other material to become familiar with product technologies and production methods. Reviews manufacturer's and trade catalogs, drawings, and other data relative to operation, maintenance, and service of equipment. Edits, standardizes, or makes changes to material prepared by other writers or establishment personnel. Analyzes developments in specific field to determine need for revisions in previously published materials and development of new material. Observes production, developmental, and experimental activities to determine operating procedure and detail. Selects photographs, drawings, sketches, diagrams, and charts to illustrate material. Maintains records and files of work and revisions. Draws sketches to illustrate specified materials or assembly sequence. Arranges for typing, duplication, and distribution of material. Assigns work to other writers and oversees and edits their work.

Knowledge: Administration and Management; Clerical; Computers and Electronics; Engineering and Technology; Design; Sociology and Anthropology; Education and Training; English Language; Telecommunications; Communications and Media

Abilities: Oral Comprehension; Written Comprehension; Written Expression; Fluency of Ideas; Originality; Inductive Reasoning; Information Ordering; Speed of Closure; Perceptual Speed

Bibliography

Best Career Resources, Including Internet Sites

Compiled by Mike Farr

> This annotated bibliography was developed by Mike Farr for use in various books he has written, including *America's Fastest Growing Jobs*, *America's Top Jobs for People Without a Four-Year Degree, Fourth Edition*, and others. It is used here with permission.

This is not a conventional bibliography. My comments are informal and admittedly biased, and I include only materials I like in some way. I developed this bibliography for a book I wrote titled *The Very Quick Job Search*. Because the bibliography was so well received there, I made a few changes and include it here for your information.

I've been looking at career materials for over 20 years, and it still amazes me how much junk is out there. A good example are resume books that still suggest that sending out many good-looking resumes is the way to get a job. While the advice on creating a resume may be good, the advice on *using* it is—too often—not. I tried to sort the wheat from the chaff, so materials that I do not consider good or useful are not listed.

I emphasize books you are most likely to find in a bookstore or good library. Materials published or distributed by JIST are among those listed, as are some that I have written. Of course, I tend to be enthusiastic about materials I have been involved in, although I try to be objective.

I organize the materials into categories and provide comments on many titles. Within categories, books are not presented in a particular order, although titles published by JIST are listed first. For brevity, I only mention a publisher if it is JIST. I don't provide publication dates, because materials are often updated regularly.

A good bookstore or library should be able to locate a book by its title and author. Most bookstores have a computer that allows them to find any book you want. Ask them to look up a desired title in *Books in Print*. Some materials are rather obscure and not easy to obtain. Others are out of print (it's difficult to keep up with all this), although you may find them though an inter-library loan program. Ask your librarian to help you locate something you *really* want.

So browse the descriptions that follow. Remember that this an informal list rather than a formal bibliography, but I hope you find it helpful.

General Advice on Finding Career and Job Search Information

As mentioned, many resource materials I mention in this bibliography can be found in a good library. Libraries have more information than I can list, including journals, newspapers, books, CD-ROM databases, access to the Internet, and other resources. So here are some tips for using the library as your job search friend.

The librarian: Your friendly librarian can be one of your best sources of specific information during your job search. If you can ask the question, he or she can probably give you some ideas on where to find an answer.

Finding Facts Fast: Todd. Perhaps the best book on finding out about anything at the library or elsewhere. Great research aid.

Trade magazines and journals: Most libraries will have one or more professional journals related to a variety of major career areas. Staying current on the publications in your field will help you in the interviewing process. These publications sometimes have job listings.

You Can Get Anything You Want: Dawson.

Develop a Network of Contacts, Including Networking With Members of Professional and Trade Associations

You already know hundreds of people, and networking to meet more is covered in many job search books I recommend. Consider joining professional associations related to the job you want. Your membership gives you access to meetings, newsletters, and other information sources. But the biggest benefit is that other members are an excellent source of networking opportunities.

They often hire or supervise people with similar skills—or know those who do. You can get access to membership lists and use the contact information to call members in your area or in any part of the country. Make lots of phone contacts, send JIST Cards, resumes, and thank-you notes—and get lots of interviews!

Directories

People who work in the careers that interest you can tell you which organizations to join. A good library will often have one or more helpful directories including the following:

Career Guide to Professional Associations: Garrett Park Press. Describes more than 2,500 professional associations. The information is more oriented to the job seeker than is the *Encyclopedia of Associations,* but some information may not be current.

Encyclopedia of Associations: Gale Research Company. A listing of more than 22,000 professional, trade, and other nonprofit organizations in the United States, representing more issues than you can imagine. It cross-references them in various helpful ways.

Encyclopedia of Associations—International Organizations: Gale Research. A listing of more than 11,000 organizations in 180 countries. Includes trade, business, and commercial associations, and associations of labor unions.

Professional & Trade Association Job Finder: By career category, details over 1,000 sources of information, referrals and more.

Newspapers and Professional Journals

While the want ads in newspapers represent relatively few of the available job openings—and allow almost everyone to apply for them—some people do get jobs from want ads. Newspapers also contain other useful employment information. Look for tips on new or expanding businesses and leads for unadvertised job openings. Articles about new or expanding companies can be valuable leads for new job possibilities.

If relocating is a possibility, look at newspapers from other areas. They can serve as a source of job leads as well as indicate some idea of the job market. The major out-of-town newspapers are sold in most large cities and are available in many public libraries.

Some newspapers such as *The New York Times*, *The Chicago Tribune*, and *The Financial Times* are national in scope. *The National Business Employment Weekly*, published by *The Wall Street Journal*, contains much information of interest to professional job seekers. But remember that competition for jobs advertised in these sources is fierce and don't rely on them too heavily.

Review these sources for articles mentioning your target companies. Look for information on new products, expansions, consolidations, relocations, promotions, articles by executives in the companies, annual company earnings, and current problems.

Check back issues of newspapers for old want ads. They can provide important information on job duties, salary, and benefits. There may even be a want ad for a job in which you are interested. Perhaps the job was never filled or the person previously hired has already moved on.

Specialty newspapers such as *The National Business Employment Weekly* have a compilation of the previous week's want ads from the regional editions of *The Wall Street Journal*, plus its own want ads. *National Ad Search* is a weekly tabloid that has a compilation of want ads from 75 key newspapers across the U.S. Expect major competition for jobs listed this widely.

Back issues of major newspapers can be accessed on the Internet, allowing you to sort by key words or for specific geographic areas.

Business Newsbank, Newsbank, Inc.: This service provides the narrative of articles from newspapers and business journals from 400 cities. It cross-references information by company name, individual's name, industry, or product category.

New York Times Index: A thorough index of all stories that appear in the *Times*.

Wall Street Journal Index: This is an important source of information on larger business and business trends.

Where the Jobs Are: 1200 Journals with Job/Career Openings: Feingold and Winkler. A unique resource providing tips on responding to journal ads and a cross-reference to specific journals by job type.

Where to Find Business Information: Brownstone and Curruth. Lists and describes the many newsletters, journals, computer databases, books, and other sources of business information.

I provide additional details on using the newspapers in the section titled "Getting Information on Specific Employers."

Job Search and Career Planning Books by Yours Truly

I've worked on many job search, career planning, and occupational information books, assessment tests, videos, and software over the years. Some are readily available in bookstores and libraries, while others are used by schools, institutions, and instructors. Most of my materials are published by JIST and many are included in the various sections of this bibliography, along with brief descriptions.

I feel strongly that only two main issues in the career planning and job search field really matter. The first is that it is essential to select a career that will satisfy you. This involves knowing yourself well enough to select *the* job rather than *a* job. The second issue is, if you need to find a job, you might as well find a good one and do it in as little time as possible. All of my books incorporate these simple principles and tend to be practical and results-oriented. Here is a partial list, should this be of interest to you:

Books You Are Most Likely to Find in Bookstores and Libraries

The Very Quick Job Search—Get a Good Job in Less Time

How to Get a Job Now!—Six Easy Steps to Getting a Better Job

The Quick Resume and Cover Letter Book

The Quick Interview and Salary Negotiation Book

America's Top Resumes for America's Top Jobs

America's Fastest Growing Jobs

America's Top Jobs for College Graduates

America's Top Jobs for People Without a Four-Year Degree

America's Top Medical, Education, and Human Services Jobs

America's Top Office, Management, Sales, & Professional Jobs

Best Jobs for the 21st Century (coauthored with LaVerne Ludden)

Occupational Reference Books

My name appears on several occupational reference books that can be found in libraries. These books are mostly based on information obtained from government sources. I was part of a team that made the information useful. Calling anyone an author of these books is a bit of a stretch, although I spent many hours working on them. These titles include the following:

*The O*NET Dictionary of Occupational Titles*

The Enhanced Occupational Outlook Handbook

The Complete Guide to Occupational Exploration

Materials Used in Schools and Other Programs

One of my life's missions has been to improve the information and training that students and job seekers receive in career and job search programs. Here are some materials I have authored for this use —most are *not* available in bookstores but can be obtained from JIST.

The Quick Job Search: A 36-page book covering the essentials needed for a successful job search. Very short but covers the basics.

The JIST Career Planning and Job Search Course: For instructors, a complete curriculum I wrote to support the use of *The Very Quick Job Search*. It includes lesson plans, over 50 overhead transparencies, and reproducible handout masters.

The JIST Course: The Young Person's Guide to Getting and Keeping a Good Job: Coauthored by Marie Pavlicko for use by high school students. It was field tested with thousands of students. Good graphics and easy-to-follow narrative. Accompanying instructor's guide and transparency set.

The Right Job for You: A thorough career planning book that includes lots of information and worksheets.

The Guide for Occupational Exploration Inventory: This is an interest "test" to help with career exploration.

The Work Book: Getting the Job You Want: This is my first job search book. Originally published in 1981, it has been revised several times and has sold over 300,000 copies. It remains popular in post-secondary schools and programs. An instructor's guide is available. Published by McGraw-Hill, Glencoe Division.

Job Finding Fast: A thorough book that includes sections on career decision making as well as job seeking. It was written to support a full course or program at the post-secondary or college level. An instructor's guide is available. Also published by McGraw-Hill, Glencoe Division.

Videos and software: I've written content scripts for numerous job search and career-related videos and have worked on a variety of career-related software.

Etcetera: I've worked on many workbooks and other projects over the years, including several series for youth coauthored with Susan Christophersen (The Living Skills Series and The Career and Life Skills Series). I have edited or helped to develop many others. It's been work and it's been fun.

Career Materials Published by JIST

I formerly listed career-related books published by JIST in a separate section, but the list became too long. Besides, I only included those JIST books that were likely to be found in a bookstore

or library and excluded many videos, assessment tests, instructional materials, and books used in schools and institutions. The JIST books you are most likely to find in a bookstore or library are now included in the various subsections of this bibliography. If you want a more thorough list, contact JIST for a catalog. JIST's Internet site (www.JIST.com) provides free chapters of many books and links to other career-related sites.

Information on Occupations and Industries

Hundreds of books provide information on jobs, and most libraries have a basic selection. I suggest you begin with the general career references, and then look for more specific information on jobs that interest you most.

While most people focus their career-planning time on choosing an occupation, I suggest you also consider the industry where you want to work. For example, if you have experience in accounting (a career) and an interest in airplanes (an industry), perhaps accounting-oriented jobs in a flight-related industry such as airports, airplane manufacturing, or air-transportation regulation would be your best fit. I include industry references for this reason and recommend you browse some of them.

Best Sources of Information on Industries

Career Guide to America's Top Industries: Based on information from the U. S. Department of Labor, provides details on over 40 major industries. Easy-to-read and loaded with helpful information, it was written specifically to assist in career planning and job seeking. If you are going to use one book on industries, this is the one I recommend. JIST.

U.S. Industrial Outlook: Based on information

from the U.S. Department of Commerce, it provides business forecasts for over 300 industries. Good source of information to review prior to interviews.

Standard Industrial Classification Manual (SIC): A standard reference developed by the U.S. Department of Commerce that lists all industries in an organized way. Accountants, banks, the IRS, and many others use it as a way to codify business. While I would not recommend this as light reading, it is useful for identifying more specialized industries for a job search or career exploration. Available from JIST.

North American Industrial Classification System (NAICS): A new system to replace the SIC Manual was introduced in 1998 and will be used in Mexico, the United States, and Canada. This book has similar uses to the older SIC manual. Available from JIST.

Best Sources of Information on Occupations

The Occupational Outlook Handbook: Highly recommended. Published by the U.S. Department of Labor and updated every other year, provides descriptions for 250 major jobs covering 87 percent of the workforce. The descriptions are well written and provide information on pay, working conditions, related jobs, projected growth, and more. A very helpful book for exploring career options or for job seeking. Available from JIST.

America's Top 300 Jobs: This is a "bookstore" version of the ***Occupational Outlook Handbook*** that includes descriptions for all 250 jobs plus additional information. JIST.

The Enhanced Occupational Outlook Handbook: Includes all the descriptions in the ***Occupational Outlook Handbook*** plus 3,000 descriptions of more specialized jobs and 5,000 additional titles. Easy to use. JIST.

The O*NET Dictionary of Occupational Titles: This is the first book to provide information on the new O*NET jobs. A new database of occupations called the Occupational Information Network (O*NET) will replace the ***Dictionary of Occupational Titles.*** This new book provides descriptions for the approximately 1,200 new O*NET jobs plus details on related skills, earnings, abilities, education and other requirements for each. JIST.

America's Top Jobs Series. Each book in this series includes about 100 job descriptions plus a review of job market trends, career planning and job search advice, summary information on hundreds of additional jobs and useful appendices. The job descriptions are based on those used in the ***Occupational Outlook Handbook*** and include details on pay, education required, working conditions, and more. All are published by JIST.

America's Fastest Growing Jobs: J. Michael Farr.

America's Top Jobs for College Graduates: J. Michael Farr.

America's Top Jobs for People Without a Four-Year Degree: J. Michael Farr.

America's Top Medical, Education, and Human Services Jobs: J. Michael Farr.

America's Top Office, Management, Sales, & Professional Jobs: J. Michael Farr.

America's Federal Jobs

America's Top Military Careers

Best Jobs for the 21st Century: J. Michael Farr and LaVerne Ludden. Lists of jobs for best paying, highest earning at different education levels and other criteria plus hundreds of job descriptions. JIST.

Complete Guide For Occupational Exploration: The U.S. Department of Labor developed the GOE to help people explore careers based on interests. The CGOE narrows broad interests to the many specific jobs within each major category. It lists over 12,000 jobs by occupational cluster, interests, abilities, and traits required for successful performance. You can look up jobs by industry, types of skills or abilities required, values, related home/leisure activities, military experience, education required, or related jobs you have had. JIST.

Enhanced Guide For Occupational Exploration: Similar to the CGOE, but also provides descriptions for 2,500 jobs. These jobs cover 95 percent of the workforce and few people will miss those that are not listed. JIST.

Dictionary Of Occupational Titles: Published by the U.S. Department of Labor, the DOT provides brief descriptions for 12,741 jobs — more than any other reference. It is a large book, over 1,400 pages, and not particularly easy-to-use. But is a standard reference that many other books cross-reference. Available from JIST.

More Career Information Books

Hundreds of books provide information on specific careers. I've selected representative titles but you will find many others in a good library.

American Almanac of Jobs and Salaries: Wright. Useful data on pay and opportunities for hundreds of jobs.

Career Connection for College Education—A Guide to College Education and related Career Opportunities, revised edition: Fred Rowe. Provides information on over 100 college majors and 1,000 occupations that are related to them. Includes information on salaries, course require-

ments, related high school courses and other details useful in planning a college major. JIST.

Career Connection for Technical Education—A Guide to Technical Training and Related Career Opportunities: Fred Rowe. Similar to the above but providing information on 70 technical training majors and 450 related occupations. JIST

Career Finder—Pathways to Over 1,500 Entry-Level Jobs: Schwartz and Breckner.

Careers without College Series: A series of 11 books for those not planning on a four-year college degree. Topics on health care, fashion, cars, office, sports, and others.

Choosing an Airline Career: March.

Discover the Best Jobs for You!: Krannich and Krannich. Explores skills and interests and explores specific jobs.

Encyclopedia of Careers: Ferguson Publishing. A series of books providing useful information on all major occupations.

Great Careers: The 4th of July Guide to Careers, Internships, and Volunteer Opportunities in the Non-Profit Sector: An enormous reference of books and programs covering jobs with a social cause.

High Paying Jobs in 6 Months or Less: For jobs requiring brief training.

High Tech Jobs for Non High Tech Grads: O'Brien. Good ideas for those without technical training.

Jobs Rated Almanac: Krantz. Ranks 250 jobs by pay, benefits, stress, and other criteria.

Occu-facts: Provides one page descriptions for over 500 jobs in an easy-to-read format. Jobs are arranged into groups of similar occupations, which encourages its use as a career exploration tool.

Opportunities in... Series: A series books published by VGM Career Horizons. Each covers related jobs in that field, skills required, working conditions, pay, education required, jargon. Some of the careers covered are Secretarial; Health and Medical Careers; Office Occupations; Data Processing; Computer Science; Travel Careers; Hotel and Motel Management; Cable Television; Accounting.

Outdoor Careers: Shenk.

Peterson's Engineering, Science and Computer Jobs: An annual update of 900 employers, types of jobs, more.

Professional Careers Series: Another series of books on a variety of professional jobs including finance, medicine, law, computers, accounting, business, and others.

Real Estate Careers: Jamic and Rejnis.

Revised Handbook for Analyzing Jobs: A technical book describing various coding systems used to quantify and categorize jobs. Available from JIST.

Worker Trait Data Book: Donald Mayall. A technical book that provides coded information on over 12,000 jobs in the Dictionary of Occupational Titles. Much of this information is not available elsewhere. JIST.

Worker Trait Group Guide: A simpler version of the **Guide for Occupational Exploration** providing information on clusters of similar jobs. Available from JIST.

Career Planning and Job Search Books

There are innumerable job search and career planning books and more are published all the time. Most are written by corporate recruiters, headhunters, social workers, academics, and personnel experts who are well intentioned but have little practical experience in determining whether the job search methods they recommend actually work. Many books provide advice that would, if followed, actually slow down the job search process.

Generally, I discard books that suggest sending out resumes or answering want ads as good job search methods—or that do not include methods appropriate for approaching smaller businesses. The research clearly indicates the importance of these issues, and anyone who is not aware of this should not be considered an expert. So, in my humble opinion, here are some of the better books.

Highly Recommended Career Planning and Job Search Books

This is a short list that includes a few of my own books, a few books published by JIST, and a few books published by others that I like and are widely regarded as among the best books on their topics.

The Very Quick Job Search—Get a Good Job in Less Time: J. Michael Farr. This is my most thorough job search book, and it includes lots of information on career planning and, of course, job seeking. This is the book I would recommend to a friend who was out of work, if I had to recommend just one book. While written as a "bookstore" book, it is widely used in schools and colleges. There is an accompanying activities book, curriculum, and transparency set. This book has won a variety of awards including best career book of the year. JIST.

How to Get a Job Now!—Six Easy Steps for Getting a Better Job: J. Michael Farr. This is a short book that covers the basics in an interactive format. I included those things I believe most important to know if you want to get a better job in less time. JIST.

Using the Internet and the World Wide Web in Your Job Search: Fred Jandt and Mary Nemnich. For new or more experienced Internet users, it is full of information on getting career information, finding job listings, creating electronic resumes, networking with user groups, and other interesting techniques. Reviews all major career sites. JIST.

The PIE Method for Career Success—A New Job Search Strategy: Daniel Porot. The PIE method (Pleasure, Information, and Employment)uses a visual and creative format to present career planning and job search techniques. The author is one of Europe's major career consultants and this book presents his powerful career planning and job seeking concepts in a memorable way. JIST.

Inside Secrets of Finding a Teaching Job: Jack and Diane Warner and Clyde Bryan. Practical advice for new and experienced teachers looking for a new job. JIST.

What Color Is Your Parachute?: Richard N. Bolles. This is the best selling career-changing book ever. Well written and entertaining, it is updated each year and includes a useful self assessment section, "The Quick Job Hunting Map." Bolles is fun to read and the book is highly recommended.

The Complete Job Search Handbook: All the Skills You Need to Get Any Job, and Have a Good Time Doing It: Howard Figler. A solid book with lots of exercises to assess skills, values, and needs. Procedures for exploring careers and developing a job objective. An excellent book that is loaded with innovative ideas.

Other Career and Job Search Books for a General Audience

Getting the Job You Really Want: J. Michael Farr. Covers career planning and job seeking topics in a workbook format with lots of activities. Very popular in schools and job search programs and available in bookstores. An instructor's guide is also available. JIST.

Job Search 101—Getting Started on Your Career Path: Pat Morton and Marcia Fox. For college seniors and recent graduates seeking entry-level jobs. JIST.

Job Finding Fast: J. Michael Farr. A thorough career planning and job search workbook used in colleges. An instructor's guide is available. Available from JIST.

Job Strategies for Professionals: Based on advice provided by the U.S. Department of Labor, it provides job search advice for professionals and managers who have lost their jobs. JIST.

Job Rights and Survival Strategies—A Handbook for Terminated Employees: Paul Tobias and Susan Sauter. Covers the legal rights and benefits as well as how to handle these traumatic situations with dignity. Distributed by JIST.

900,000 Plus Jobs Annually: Feingold and Winkler. Reviews 900+ periodicals that list openings and positions wanted in hundreds of fields.

Big Splash in a Small Pond—Finding a Great Job in a Small Company: Resnick and Pechter.

Change Your Job, Change Your Life: Krannich. Reviews jobs trends and job search methods.

Do What You Are—Discover the Perfect Career for You Through the Secrets of Personality Type: Tieger and Barron-Tieger.

Go Hire Yourself An Employer: Richard Irish. Lots of good stuff in this new revision. Covers skills identification, job search, resumes, interviews, the unemployment "blahs," succeeding on the next job, and other topics.

Guerrilla Tactics in the New Job Market: Tom Jackson.

Professional Careers Sourcebook, an Informational Guide for Career Planning: K. Savage and C. Dorgan

Hardball Job Hunting Tactics: Dick Wright. From a trainer with lots of experience with the hard to employ. Excellent sections on completing applications (a topic not often covered well) and resumes. Brief but good section on job search. Tips for people with various "problems" on how to overcome them.

How to Get Interviews from Classified Job Ads: Elderkin.

Information Interviewing: What It Is and How to Use It in Your Career: Martha Stoodley.

Job & Career Building: Richard Germann and Peter Arnold. A good choice for laid off professionals, managers, and others with more experience and training.

Job Hunters Sourcebook: Where to Find Employment Leads and Other Job Search Sources: Michelle LeCompte.

Marketing Yourself: The Ultimate Job Seeker's Guide: Dorothy Leeds.

New Network Your Way to Job and Career Success: Ron and Carol Krannich.

Re-Careering in Turbulent Times: Ronald Krannich. Lots of good material including employment trends, selecting a career, getting training and education, communication skills, sources of job leads, interviewing, resumes, relocation, public employment opportunities, and career advancement.

Robert Half On Hiring: Robert Half. Written to help employers select better employees. Most of the advice is based on a series of employer surveys providing unique insight into how employers make hiring decisions.

Selling On The Phone: Porterfield. Self-teaching guide for telemarketing and other sales approaches. Good ideas for reinforcing effective phone skills in the job search.

Starting Over: You in the New Workplace: Jo Danna.

The Complete Job Search Book: Richard Beatty.

The Job Bank Guide to Employment Services: Bob Adams.

The Only Job Hunting Guide You'll Ever Need: Kathryn Ross Petras.

Three Boxes Life and How to Get Out of Them: Richard Bolles. Introduces the concepts of "life/work planning." Very thorough.

Where Do I Go From Here With the Rest of My Life?: John Crystal and Richard Bolles. John Crystal has died, but his techniques and insights into the career planning process helped to start an important movement that came to be called "Life/Work Planning."

Who's Hiring Who: Richard Lathrop. Solid, practical information for job seekers. Good self-assessment sections and excellent resume advice (he calls them "qualifications briefs"). I particularly like this book and respect Lathrop's work.

Specialized Career and Job Search Books

Many books have been written on specialized career and job search topics. For example, there are books to help various segments of our population gain a competitive edge; books on specialized job search methods (such as using the telephone);

and books on getting certain types of jobs (such as those with small business or overseas jobs). Some of these materials are not easily categorized into one group, so look through the entire list for things related to your situation— there is probably something in here that "fits."

Internet Job Search Books

The Internet is a growing source of information on all topics, but you can also waste a lot of time there unless you know where to look. Here are a few helpful guides to get you started.

Using the Internet and the World Wide Web in Your Job Search: Fred Jandt and Mary Nemnich. A good book for both new and more experienced Internet users. Lists all major career sites and, more importantly, tells you how to use the Internet in effective ways. JIST.

The Quick Internet Guide to Career and College Information: Anne Wolfinger. A time-saving and brief guide for educators, counselors, and employment professionals to the best sites and how to use them. JIST.

Electronic Job Search Revolution: Kennedy and Morrow. Tips on using your computer and online services to get jobs.

Resources for Youth and Parents

An enormous number of materials are available for young people to help them explore career alternatives. I present only a few here. Most are not available in bookstores and are available only from the publishers. If you help youth I suggest you contact JIST and ask for their institutional catalog; it presents materials from a variety of publishers. I also include a few good books for parents to help their kids in their quest for a career (and, of course, to get them out of the house).

Helping Your Child Choose a Career: Luthor Otto. One of the most helpful books available on the topic for parents, teachers, and even kids. Comprehensive and sensible advice. JIST.

Young Person's OOH: For grades 6-10. Provides information on 250 jobs listed in the *Occupational Outlook Handbook* plus career exploration advice. JIST.

Young Person's Guide to Getting & Keeping a Good Job: J. Michael Farr and Marie Pavilicko. A practical workbook for high school students. A separate instructor's guide and overhead transparencies are also available. JIST.

Creating Your Life's Work Portfolio for High School Students: Good activities and content. JIST.

Career and Life Skills Series: J. Michael Farr and Susan Christophersen. Four books for grades 7-12 on career preparation. JIST.

HIRE Learning Series: Patricia Duffy and T. Walter Wannie. Three books for high school students on career planning, job seeking, and job success. JIST.

Dream Catchers: Norene Lindsay. A career exploration workbook for grades 5 to 8. JIST.

Pathfinder—Exploring Career and Educational Paths: Norene Lindsay. A workbook for high school students with a separate instructor's guide. JIST.

Secrets to Getting Better Grades: Brian Marshall and Wendy Ford. Teaches students to study smart, with lots of practical tips for notes, tests, papers, memory, and other techniques. JIST.

Exploring Careers—A Young Person's Guide to Over 300 Careers, revised edition: A revision of the original, published by the U.S. Department of Labor. An excellent resource for young people, providing details on over 300 jobs in an interesting format. JIST.

Career Coaching Your Kids: Montross et al. Tips on helping your children explore career options.

Career Discovery Encyclopedia: This is a six-volume set for grades 4 and up with reading level at about the 7th grade, appropriate through high school. Excellent, with over 1,000 pages and helpful ways to look up jobs. A school or other good library may have them. Excellent.

Children's Dictionary of Occupations. For elementary and middle school students, covers 300 occupations.

Directory of American Youth Organizations: Erickson. Lists more than 500 organizations.

Job Power: The Young People's Job Finding Guide: Haldane and Martin. One of our favorite books for group process ideas on skills identification and selecting a job objective. Simple, direct, useful for any age.

Joyce Lain Kennedy's Career Book: Kennedy and Laramore. A very thorough book, covering just about everything that a young person (or parent) would need to know about career and life decisions. Highly recommended.

Parents With Careers Workbook: Good worksheets and advice on getting organized, child care, home management, single parents, dual careers, time use, and so on.

Summer Jobs for Students: Reviews sources for 20,000 summer jobs and explains how to use the Internet for additional information.

Books for Working Parents and Couples

Home But Not Alone—The Parents' Work-at-Home Handbook: Katherine Murray. A very good book that won an award for being one of the top three business books of the year. Lots of solid tips. JIST.

The Working Parents' Handbook—How to Succeed at Work, Raise Your Kids, Maintain a Home, and Still Have Time for You: Katherine Murray. An entertaining and helpful book providing advice on handling the multiple roles of working parents. Excellent. JIST.

Surviving Your Partner's Job Loss: Jukes and Rosenberg.

The Three Career Couple: Byalick and Saslow. On handling two jobs plus a family.

Books to Help Get Jobs in the Government, Education, and Nonprofit Sector

The Unauthorized Teacher's Survival Guide: Jack Warner, Clyde Bryan with Diane Warner. Great advice for new and experienced teachers telling you the things you do not learn in teacher's college. JIST.

Inside Secrets of Finding a Teaching Job: Jack Warner, Clyde Bryan with Diane Warner. Helpful techniques for finding a job in teaching, based on years of experience and interviews with many educators. JIST.

Alternative Careers for Teachers: Pollack and Beard. Good ideas on getting a job in another field using transferable skills.

Careers in Local and State Government: Zehring. Where they are, how to apply, take tests, internships, and summer jobs. Job search tips.

Complete Guide to Public Employment: Krannich. Reviews opportunities with federal and local governments, associations, nonprofits, foundations, research, international, and many other institutions. Well done.

Doing Well by Doing Good—The First Complete Guide to Careers in the Non-Profit Sector: McAdam.

Moving Out Of Education: A Guide To Career Management & Change: Krannich and Banis. Good tips for this special situation from an ex-educator who moved out.

Take Charge of Your Own Career—A Guide to Federal Employment: Moore and Vanderwey.

Minorities and Immigrants

Best Companies for Minorities: Graham. Profiles of 85 companies.

Career Opportunities for Bilinguals and Multiculturals —A Directory of Resources in Education, Employment and Business: Wertsman. Over 3,500 listings.

Directory of Special Programs for Minority Group Members: Willis L. Johnson. Over 2,800 sources of training, jobs, scholarships, programs.

Finding a Job in the United States: Friedenberg and Bradley.

Minority Career Guide: Kastre, Kastre, and Edwards.

Minority Organizations—The Directory of Special Programs for Minority Group Members: Oakes. The largest source of information available covering over 5,800 professional organizations and resources.

Stepping Up: Placing Minority Women Into Managerial and Professional Jobs: Tips to replicate results of a program that increased the pay, advancement, and retention of minority women.

The Big Book of Minority Opportunities—Directory of   Special Programs for Minority Group Members: Oakes. 4,000 source of scholarships, financial aid, and special programs.

The Black Woman's Career Guide: Nivens. Good advice on over 50 good jobs, dress and grooming, skills ID, job search, and more.

The Colorblind Career: Stenson. Tips for African-American, Hispanic, and Asian-Americans to succeed.

Workers Over 40, Displaced Workers, Retirement Issues

Arthur Young's Pre-Retirement Planning Book: Very well done book. Lots of worksheets.

Cracking the Over 50 Job Market: Conner. Good job search advice.

Getting a Job After 50: John S. Morgan.

Getting a Job After 50: Morgan. Age discrimination is real and people over 50 need better than average job seeking skills to overcome this.

Helping the Dislocated Worker: Ashley and Zahniser. Reviews suggested services and programs—helpful for program planners.

Job Hunting After 50: Strategies for Success: Samuel Ray.

Job Hunting for the 40+ Executive: Birsner. Good advice on the personal and job search needs of middle-aged executives.

Mid Career Job Hunting: Official Handbook of the 40+ Club: E. Patricia Birsner. Solid advice on getting back on track and getting a job.

Retirement Careers: Marsh.

Second Careers—New Ways to Work After 50: Bird. Analyzes career changes of over 6,000 people and how it worked out.

The Over 40 Job Guide: Petras.

People with Disabilities, Disadvantaged Groups, The Homeless

Know-How is the Key: Dixie Lee Wright. A job search program (student workbook and instructor's guide) for high school through young adult "special needs" students with learning and other disabilities. JIST.

Americans with Disabilities Handbook—and Technical Assistance Manual: Government publication providing comprehensive information on the Americans With Disabilities Act (ADA)and how it is interpreted. Available from JIST.

A Helping Hand, A Guide to Customized Support Services for Special Populations: Thorough guide for program operators who emphasize employment—JTPA, older workers, ex-offenders, others.

Bouncing Back from Injury: How to Take Charge of Your Recuperation: Karen Klein and Carla Derrick Hope.

Career Success for People with Physical Disabilities: Kissane. Good advice for job seekers. Lots of exercises.

Complete Guide to Employing Persons with Disabilities: Henry McCarthy. From the National Rehabilitation Information Center; phone (800) 346-2742.

Job Hunting for the Disabled: Adele Lewis and Edith Marks. Interest surveys, programs, job descriptions, and job search tips.

Job Strategies for People With Disabilities: Witt. Good advice as well as lists of resource materials and programs.

Job-Hunting Tips for the So-Called Handicapped or People Who Have Disabilities: Richard N. Bolles.

No One is Unemployable: Angel and Harney. A good resource for welfare-to-work, ex-offender programs, and other "difficult" populations.

Recovery from Alcohol and Substance Abuse, Coping with Job Loss

Career Knockouts: How to Battle Back: Joyce Lain Kennedy. Avoiding, learning and even benefiting from job failures.

Clean, Sober and Unemployed: Elliot. Good advice for recovering substance abusers.

Coping with Unemployment: Jud. Dealing with long-term unemployment.

Sacked! Why Good People Get Fired and How to Avoid It: Gould.

Termination Trap: Best Strategies for a Job Going Sour: Cohen. Excellent insights on avoiding or dealing with job loss.

The Career Seekers: Tannenbaum. For anyone recovering from codependency or in a recovery program.

People with Four-Year College, Advanced Degrees, and Technical Training

Finding a Job in Your Field: A Handbook for Ph.D.'s & M.A.'s

Jobs for English Majors and Other Smart People: Good tips for liberal arts grads.

The MBA's Guide to Career Planning: Ed Holton

The High-Tech Career Book: Collard.

Job Search for the Technical Professional: Moore. For programmers and engineers.

Military/Veterans

Many good materials are available to help vets transition to "civilian" employment. Following are some of the specific ones, but many of the career and job search books (such as *America's Top Resumes*) include veterans among their examples.

America's Top Military Careers: Based on Dept. of Defense information, provides details on 200 enlisted and officer occupations including civilian counterparts. JIST.

Complete Guide for Occupational Exploration: Among other things, this comprehensive career reference book cross references military occupations to over 12,000 civilian job titles. JIST.

Jobs and the Military Spouse—Married, Mobile, and Motivated for the New Job Market: Farley.

Resume and Job Hunting Guide for Present and Future Veterans: DePrez. Helpful book with some good techniques.

Veteran's Survival Guide to Good Jobs in Bad Times: Grant's Guides.

You and the Armed Forces: Marrs. Better understand career options and what to expect from military life.

Young Person's Guide to Military Service: Bradley. Covers pros and cons of going into the services. Good sections for minorities and women.

Your Career in the Military: Gordan. Reviews advantages of education and money. Enlistment options and procedures.

Women

More women are in the workforce more than ever, and they tend to be better educated than average. But women without advanced educations and who are single heads of households are not doing as well. Special advice and resources are clearly needed; here are just a few.

Congratulations! You've Been Fired: Sound Advice for Women Who've Been Terminated, Pink

Slipped, Downsized or Otherwise Unemployed: Emily Koltnow and Lynne S. Dumas.

Developing New Horizons for Women: Ruth Helm Osborn. Very good text to improve self-esteem, identify strengths, and develop long-range life and career plans.

Directory of Special Opportunities for Women: Over 1,000 resources for women entering and re-entering the workforce. Recommended.

Good Enough for Mothers: Marshall. Balancing work and family.

Homemaker's Complete Guide to Entering the Job Market: Lussier. Useful techniques to transfer homemaking skills to work world and find a job.

Resume Guide for Women of the '90s: *Marino.*

The Extra Edge: Mitchell. Success strategies for women, based on data from women grads of Harvard Business School.

The Woman's Job Search Handbook: Bloomburg and Holden. Well done career planning and job search techniques.

Time for a Change: A Woman's Guide to Non-Traditional Occupations: For women considering non-traditional jobs: exercises and narrative, plus a review of 10 growth-oriented jobs.

Winning the Salary Game: Salary Negotiations for Women: Sherry Chastain.

Yes to Career Success!: Hennekins.

International Jobs

If you want to work in another country, you had better do your homework in advance. For example, you should carefully consider personal and family issues that might impede a full adjustment to your host country. Here are some resources to help you consider this option.

Directory of European Industrial and Trade Associations: CBD Research, Kent, England. Lists the industrial and trade associations of Europe.

Directory of European Professional and Learned Societies: CBD Research, Kent, England. Similar in format but deals strictly with learned and professional societies.

Foreign Jobs: The Most Popular Countries: Casewit. Profiles desirable countries and how to get jobs there.

How to Get a Job in Europe—The Insider's Guide: Surrey Books. Gives country-by-country listings of newspapers, business directories, regulations, organizations and other useful information.

How to Get a Job in the Pacific Rim: Surrey Books. Information similar to above, but for countries bordering the Pacific Ocean.

International Agencies: These agencies maintain lists of people available to work as consultants, and you might want to register with one or more: World Bank; U.S. Aid for International Development (USAID); United Nations Development Program; United National Industrial Development Organization.

International Careers: Bob Adams, Inc. Information on finding government, corporate, and nonprofit jobs.

International Employment Hotline: Names and addresses of government and non-government hiring organizations.

International Jobs: Where They Are, How to Get Them: A Handbook for Over 500 Career Opportunities Around the World: Kocher.

Key British Enterprises: Dun and Bradstreet. Detailed information on the 50,000 British companies that together employ more than a third of the British workforce.

Passport to Overseas Employment—100,000 Job Opportunities Abroad: Information on overseas careers, study, and volunteer programs.

Principal International Businesses: Dun and Bradstreet. While not aimed at the job seeker, it provides details on more than 55,000 companies in 143 countries.

Teaching English Abroad: Griffith.

The Complete Guide to International Jobs and Careers: Your Passport to a World of Exciting and Exotic Employment: Ron and Carol Krannich

The Peace Corps: Wages are low and living conditions basic, but if you are interested in helping people, the Peace Corps is a possibility.

The U.S. government: Don't overlook government jobs; there are many foreign assignments. A larger library may have the publications ***Federal Career Opportunities*** or the ***Federal News Digest,*** which list openings. Federal jobs are listed on the Internet and available through most state employment service offices.

Books on Interviewing and Salary Negotiations

The two most important parts of a job search are getting interviews and doing well in them. I suggest that *the* most important interview question to answer well is "Why should I hire you over someone else?" It takes considerable self-analysis to answer this well. Curling up with a good job search book will help you know that you *do* have good things to say about yourself. Then there is the interview issue of pay, which is where many people lose more money in 30 seconds than at any other time in their lives. Or, worse, they get a job they hate. So here are some good resources on interviewing and salary negotiations, in hopes that they are of help to you.

The Quick Interview and Salary Negotiation Book—Dramatically Improve Your Interviewing Skills and Pay in a Matter of Hours: Mike Farr. A substantial book, but I arranged it so that you can read the first section and do better in interviews later that day. Also covers career planning, job seeking, resumes, pay rates, and other topics of importance for a job seeker. JIST.

101 Dynamite Questions to Ask at Your Job Interview: Fein.

50 Winning Answers to Interview Questions: Albrecht.

American Almanac of Jobs and Salaries: Wright. Covers hundreds of careers in the public and private sector.

American Salaries and Wages Survey: Gale Research. Detailed information on salaries and wages for thousands of jobs, by region. Also gives cost-of-living data, which is helpful in determining what the salary differences really mean.

AMS Office, Professional and Data Processing Salaries Report: Administrative Management Society. Salary distributions for 40 occupations by company size, type of business, and geographic region.

Dynamite Answers to Interview Questions: Ron and Carol Krannich.

Getting To Yes: Negotiating Agreements Without Giving In: Fisher and Ury. Good negotiating tips for anything.

How To Have A Winning Job Interview: Bloch. Good advice in a readable format, with lots of activities.

How to Make $1000 a Minute—Negotiating Your Salaries and Raises: Jack Chapman. Tips on getting more money and benefits during the critical part of a job offer.

Interviewing for Success: Ron and Carol Krannich.

Interviews That Get Results: Vik. Good tips for job seekers.

Knock'em Dead: With Great Answers to Tough Interview Questions: Martin John Yate.

Make Your Job Interview A Success: Biegeleisen. Good checklists, interview answers, grooming tips, and other content.

Out Interviewing the Interviewer: Merman and McLaughlin. Good exercises, case studies and tips for experienced and not-so-experienced job seekers.

Perks and Parachutes: Tarrant.

Power Interviewing: Job Winning Tactics from Fortune 500 Recruiters: Yeager and Hough.

Ready, Aim, You're Hired!: How to Job-Interview Successfully Anytime, Anywhere with Anyone: Hellman.

State and Metropolitan Area Data Book: Helpful details from the U.S. Department of Commerce providing unemployment rates, average income, employment and population growth, and other details for all major regions—important for those considering a move.

Sweaty Palms—The Neglected Art of Being Interviewed: Anthony Medley. Fun factual tips on illegal questions, problem interviews, appropriate dress and behaviors.

The Evaluation Interview: Richard Fear. Considered a classic for anyone who is, or wants to be, a professional interviewer.

The Five Minute Interview: Richard H. Beatty.

The Ultimate Interview: How to Get It, Get Ready, and Get the Job You Want: Caple.

When Do I Start?: Clearly written, good content.

White Collar Pay: Private Goods-Producing Industries: U.S. Department of Labor's Bureau of Labor Statistics. Good source of salary information for white collar jobs.

Winning The Salary Game: Salary Negotiations for Women: Chastain. Good Strategies for men, too.

Books on Resumes and Cover Letters

There are hundreds (thousands?) of resume books and most offer bad advice. They often suggest that a good/better/best/perfect resume, sent out to lots of people, will get interviews, but the research clearly indicates that this is not the case. In addition to bad job search advice, many resume books offer unnecessarily rigid advice about the resume itself (that their way is the one enlightened way to do a resume).

In contrast, I believe that resumes are an important tool in the job search but that active job search methods (such as contacting employers by phone) are more effective than passive ones (like sending unsolicited resumes). And I do not believe that one formula exists for a good resume. Like people, resumes can be different. Of course, JIST's resume books are included here; I think they are among the best available.

America's Top Resumes for America's Top Jobs: J. Michael Farr. This is a big book, with 381 sample resumes covering over 200 major jobs. Resumes were selected from submissions by professional resume writers from all over North America. I took this approach to provide a rich array of writing styles, designs, and approaches to solving resume problems. From entry-level to very experienced, there are good examples here for everyone. JIST.

The Quick Resume and Cover Letter Book—Write and Use an Effective Resume in Only One Day: J. Michael Farr. Starting with an "instant" resume worksheet and basic formats you can complete in an hour or so, this book then takes you on a tour of everything you need to know about resumes and, more importantly, how to use them in your job search. Lots of good examples plus advice on cover letters, the job search and related matters. JIST.

The Resume Solution—How to Write (and Use) a Resume That Gets Results: David Swanson. Lots of good advice and examples for creating superior resumes. Very strong on resume design and layout and provides a step-by-step approach that is very easy to follow. JIST.

Gallery of Best Resumes: David Noble. Advice and over 200 examples from professional resume writers. Lots of variety in content and design; an excellent resource. I consider it to be the best resume library, because the resumes are organized into useful categories and are all different. JIST.

The Edge Resume & Job Search Strategy: Bill Corbin and Shelbi Wright. The only book I know of that includes sample resumes using special papers and die-cut shapes. Unique. Distributed by JIST.

Gallery of Best Resumes for Two-Year Degree Graduates: David Noble. An excellent selection of over 200 sample resumes submitted by professional resume writers. Good advice and lots of excellent samples. A very good resource book that organizes resumes by occupational category. JIST.

Professional Resumes for Executives, Managers, and Other Administrators: A New Gallery of Best Resumes by Professional Resume Writers: David Noble. Includes more than 200 resumes, organized by occupation. JIST.

The Federal Resume Guidebook: Kathryn Troutman. A thorough book covering the new procedures for applying for jobs with the federal government. JIST.

Using WordPerfect in Your Job Search: David Noble. A unique and thorough book that reviews how to use WordPerfect to create effective resumes, correspondence, and other job search documents including scannable and hypertext resumes. JIST.

100 Winning Resumes for $100,000+ Jobs: Enelow.

College Student's Resume Guide: Marino.

Complete Resume Guide: Faux. Some good ideas and examples.

Damn Good Resume Guide: Yana Parker. An irreverent title, but it has many good examples and an easy-to-follow process for creating resumes.

Developing a Professional Vita or Resume: McDaniels. Special resume advice for professionals with advanced education or experience.

Don't Use a Resume: Richard Lathrop. A booklet providing good examples and advice on a special resume that emphasizes skills.

Dynamic Cover Letters: Hanson. A very focused book, just on cover letters.

Dynamite Cover Letters: Ron and Carol Krannich. Good content.

Dynamite Resumes: Ron and Carol Krannich. Lots of good examples and advice.

Encyclopedia of Job Winning Resumes: Fournier and Spin. Lots of examples in a wide variety of jobs.

High Impact Resumes & Letters: Krannich and Banis. Good job search advice and lots of sample resumes and letters.

How to Write a Winning Resume: Bloch. Good examples for college grads, more experienced job seekers, and professionals.

Job Search Letters That Get Results: Ron and Carol Krannich. Good advice and over 200 sample letters.

Liberal Arts Power: Nadler. *How to sell it on your resume.*

Ready, Aim, Hired: Developing Your Brand Name Resume: Karson.

Resume Kit: Beatty. Better-than-average advice on putting together effective resumes and cover letters.

Resume Pro: The Professional Guide: Yana Parker. A how-to guide for those who help others write resumes.

Resumes for Computer Professionals: Shanahan. Many examples.

Resumes for Executives and Professionals: Shy and Kind.

Resumes for High School Graduates: VGM editors. An unusual but useful focus.

Resumes for Mid-Career Job Changes: VGM editors.

Resumes for Technicians: Shanahan. Examples, tips for use, and so on.

The No Pain Resume Workbook: Hiyaguha Cohen.

The Perfect Resume: Tom Jackson. Uses a workbook format, making it easy to identify job objective, skills, interests, and achievements. Good examples.

The Resume Catalog—200 Damn Good Resumes: Yana Parker. Organized by job objective. Good.

Writing a Job Winning Resume: John McLaughlin and Stephen Merman. A good book with examples showing how the resume covered a weakness.

Dress and Grooming Advice

One survey of employers I read found that about 40 percent of job seekers who made it through initial screening and got an interview then created a negative first impression based on dress and grooming. Another study found that candidates who made a negative impression within five minutes had virtually no chance of getting a job offer. So, put the two studies together, and you can see that a big problem exists with first impressions. How you dress and groom is only one issue, of course, but it is one that most people can easily change. So here are some books on that topic.

Always in Style with Color Me Beautiful: Pooser. By a noted color consultant, clothing styles, colors, and makeup for women. Many photos.

Big and Beautiful: Olds. Larger women can be gorgeous, too.

Color Me Beautiful: Jackson. Discover your "seasonal" colors and coordinate your look. Color photos. Well done.

Dress for Success: John Molloy. Some of the advice is dated, but this still gives good research-based advice on business attire.

Professional Image: Bixler. One of few on dress, grooming, body language, and details for both men and women.

Red Socks Don't Work: Karpinski. Dressing tips for men in formal corporate environments.

Women's Dress for Success: Molloy. Same thorough approach as for men.

Personal and Career Success and Advancement

There are thousands of personal and career success books and tapes. Some are very good, some are not. I include a selection of the better ones here.

Beat Stress with Strength—A Survival Guide for Work and Life: Stephanie Spera and Sandra Lanto. Includes a personal stress test and many tips for handling stress and achieving balance. JIST.

Career Satisfaction and Success—How to Know and Manage Your Strengths: Bernard Haldane. A complete revision of a classic by one of the founders of the modern career planning movement. It presents techniques for succeeding on the job and concepts that have changed many lives for the better, including defining your "motivated skills" and using them as a basis for career planning. JIST.

Dare to Change Your Job and Your Life: Carole Kanchier. Based on interviews with more than 5,000 adults, provides a proven self-help approach to developing a more meaningful career and more fulfilling life. JIST.

Job Savvy—How to Be a Success at Work: LaVerne Ludden. A workbook covering work-appropriate behaviors. JIST.

Jobscape—Career Survival in the New Global Economy: Colin Campbell. A well-written and fascinating book that presents the essential trends shaping the future workforce and how we can best prepare to benefit. JIST.

Networking for Everyone!: Michelle Tullier. More than for the job search, covers creating a network to help you through life—lots of motivational and practical tips. JIST.

Ready, Set, Organize!: Pipi Peterson. Time management strategies for your personal and work lives. Good advice and a fun read. JIST.

SuccessAbilities!—1,001 Practical Ways to Keep Up, Stand Out, and Move Ahead at Work: Paula Ancona. Short and motivational tips from Ancona's nationally syndicated column. JIST.

The Customer Is Usually Wrong!: Fred Jandt. Great tips for handling customers and doing the right thing. JIST.

The Perfect Memo!—Write Your Way to Career Success!: Patricia Westheimer. Good tips and activities for more effective business writing. JIST.

We've Got to Start Meeting Like This!: Roger Moskvick and Robert Nelson. An essential book for getting the most out of meeting time. JIST.

Brushing Up Your Clerical Skills: Steinberg. For new and returning office workers. Exercise on spelling, punctuation, typing, business letters, filing, and more.

Business Protocol: Yager. On-the-job manners.

Do What You Love, The Money Will Follow: Sinetar. For those who seek meaning as our first priority, there is hope that we can also make a living doing the things we really want to do.

Getting Things Done When You Are Not in Charge: Bellman.

How to Jump Start a Stalled Career: Prugh.

How to Make a Habit of Success: Bernard Haldane. Originally published many years ago, it was a best-seller and is still available. Many consider Haldane one of the founders of the career planning movement that began in the 1950s. This is an important book that has much good advice.

Improve Your Writing for Work: Chesla. Includes lots of samples and activities.

Love Your Work and Success Will Follow: Hirsch. For those who are not happy with their current career.

Moving Up—How To Get High Salaried Jobs: Djeddah. Techniques to get promoted or move out to a new job.

Not Just a Secretary: Morrow and Lebov. Techniques for doing well and getting ahead.

Secretary Today, Manager Tomorrow: How to Turn a Secretarial Job into a Managerial Position: Marrs.

Skills for Success: Scheele. Good advice on getting ahead in all sorts of careers.

Wish Craft: Barbara Sher. An upbeat book that provides activities and advice on setting goals and reaching your full potential.

Working Smart: Zehring. Advice on getting ahead, organizing time, dealing with people, developing leadership skills.

Would You Put That in Writing?: Booher. Good primer for improving your business communications.

Future Trends/Labor Market Information

Jobscape—Career Survival in the New Global Economy: Colin Campbell. A well-written and fascinating book that presents the essential trends shaping the future workforce and how we can best prepare to benefit. JIST.

Work in the New Economy: Robert Wegmann, Robert Chapman, and Miriam Johnson. A very well-researched book on where our economy is going and how we should adapt our career planning and job search methods to get better results.

While this is now an older book, I consider Wegman's work to be among the best on the topic and much of the advice remains current. JIST.

Emerging Careers: New Occupations for the Year 2000 & Beyond: Based on years of research; details hundreds of new careers. Very good.

Megatrends: Nesbitt. A best-seller that provides a review of where the economy is heading.

The Work Revolution: Schwartz and Neikirk. Thorough and well done. Predicts retraining, education, and other needs of rapid change.

Work Force 2020—Work and Workers in the 21st Century: Richard Judy and Carol D'Amico of the Hudson Institute. A well-researched book predicting likely trends in the workforce.

Work in the 21st Century: Isaac Asimov and others. Anthology of well-done articles on work trends for the future. Stimulating.

Self-Employment, Starting Your Own Business, Temporary, Part-Time, and Volunteer Jobs

More people are working for themselves, starting small businesses, or working in part-time, temporary, or volunteer jobs. There are hundreds of books on these topics, and a good library will have more resources than I can list. Here are a few suggestions.

Self-Employment: From Dream to Reality—An Interactive Workbook for Starting Your Small Business: Linda Gilkerson and Theresia Paauwe. A workbook to encourage "microenterprises," very small business started by those with little money or experience. Unique. JIST.

Mind Your Own Business—Getting Started as an Entrepreneur: LaVerne Ludden and Bonnie Maitlen. A good book for those considering their own business, with lots of good advice. JIST.

Be your Own Business—The Definitive Guide to Entrepreneurial Success: Marsha Fox and LaVerne Ludden. JIST.

Franchise Opportunities Handbook: LaVerne Ludden. Lists over a thousand franchise companies and provides tips on selecting one that makes sense for a business.

America's New Breed of Entrepreneurs: Presents collective experiences of 48 successful entrepreneurs and how they achieved their goals.

Beginning Entrepreneur: Matthews.

Best Home Businesses for the '90s: Edwards and Edwards.

Directory of Microenterprise Programs: Lists loans and programs for low-income entrepreneurs.

Getting Business to Come to You: Edwards and Edwards. Low-cost marketing tips.

Home Sweet Office: Meade. Telecommunicating from home to a regular job.

How to Build a Successful One Person Business: Bautista.

How to Run Your Own Home Business: Kern and Wolfgram.

How to Start, Run, and Stay in Business: Kishel. Good primer for the school of hard knocks.

Inc. Yourself: How to Profit from Setting Up your Own Corporation: Shows financial and other advantages, plus how to set up.

Job Sharing Handbook: Smith. Provides guidelines for setting up a shared job, case histories, and so on. Good.

Making It on Your Own—What to Know Before Starting Your Own Business: Feingold.

Opportunities in Your Own Service Business: McKay.

Part-Time Professional: Good information on finding part time jobs, benefits, negotiating with employers, converting full-time to part-time jobs, and other tips.

Running a One Person Business: Whitmeyer, Rasberry, Phillips. Practical.

Side by Side: Cuozzo and Graham.

Starting on a Shoe String: Building a Business Without a Bankroll: Goldstein.

Ten Best Opportunities for Starting a Home Business Today: Reed Glenn.

The Mid-Career Entrepreneur: Mancuso.

The Small Business Administration: The U.S. Small Business Administration (SBA) offers loans, training, and planning, and many useful publications. Its toll-free number is 1-800-U ASK SBA. In addition, its Service Corps of Retired Executives (SCORE) provides free help on how to set up and run a small business.

The Temp Track: Justice. *Reviews the many opportunities for temporary jobs.*

Volunteer America: Kipps. Lists over 1,400 organizations for training, service, and work experience.

Working from Home: Edwards and Edwards.

Places to Live or Move To

Some people will be unhappy wherever they live, but living in a place you like does make life more enjoyable. Here are a few books that provide details.

Best Towns In America: Bayless. 50 of the U.S.'s most desirable places plus ways to evaluate all communities.

Country Careers—Successful Ways to Live and Work in the Country: Rojak.

Finding Your Best Place To Live In America: Bowman and Guiliani. Another good book providing information on good places to live.

Greener Pastures Relocation Guide: Finding the Best State in the U.S. for You!

Places Rated Almanac: Richard Boyer and David Savagean. A thorough review of over 270 metropolitan areas with information on housing, education, climate, health services, recreation, arts, transportation, crime, and income.

Getting Information on Specific Employers

There are two basic reasons for you to be interested specific employers. The first has to do with identifying potential job search targets, and the second is to get more information on an employer prior to an interview.

Some books and businesses "sell" the idea of sending your resume to potential employers as a good thing. Some even sell lists in print or computer form, so you can mount a big mail campaign. And some sell the idea of having special lists of employers that you can buy from them. I do not think that sending unsolicited resumes to any list is a good idea. While any technique works for some people, you will be better off if your job search is more targeted and involves more direct contact.

You have to begin with knowing the type of job you want and the industries where you will find them. Then and only then can you intelligently begin your search for specific employers.

Free Resources

The yellow pages: The best resource you can get is probably free: it's the yellow pages of the phone book. Think about it: it lists all the organizations by type and gives you what you need to contact them. All of my job search books tell you how to use the yellow pages as an effective tool in your job search. The yellow pages for regions throughout the country is also now available on the Internet, as are many other sources of information on organizations.

Networking: Another free resource of information is networking. If you want to know more about a particular job or place of employment, ask the people who do that kind of work or who work in that place. This is often the only source of information for small organizations not listed in the directories. A good book on networking is *Networking for Everyone—Connecting with People for Career and Job Success* by Michelle Tullier. It provides lots of practical advice for personal and business success and is published by JIST.

Chambers of commerce: Most are not staffed to provide specific information to job seekers, but many do provide information such as new businesses in the area, larger employers, and other details.

Contact the organization directly: For large organizations, contact the human resources or public relations departments. In smaller ones the receptionist or manager may be able to help. Get brochures, an annual report, description of relevant jobs, and anything else that describes the organization.

Annual reports: All publicly owned and many smaller organizations provide annual reports detailing earnings, trends, strategies, and other information. If one is available, it is an excellent source of information.

A good bookstore or library has many sources of information on specific businesses and other organizations. While many of these resources were not specifically developed for use by job seekers, they can work just fine.

You can use resource materials in several ways. The first is to get information on a specific organization as background for an interview. You can also get names of organizations as well as background information to use in making direct contact lists. With so many potential sources of information, ask a librarian to help you once you have a good idea of what you are looking for.

Following are just a few of the many books and other resources for obtaining information on employers. Some are organized by industry or region or in other ways that may be of help to you. If you use the Internet, more and more information is now available there. I suggest you read one of the Internet job search books published by JIST for the most useful sites.

100 Best Companies to Work for in America: Levering and Moscowitz.

America's Corporate Families, The Billion Dollar Directory: Describes 2,500 large corporate "families" and their 28,000 subsidiaries; provides information on each; and cross references by location, business or product type, and other methods.

America's Fastest Growing Employers: Bob Adams. Lists more than 700 of the fastest-growing companies in the country.

American Business Information Inc. of Omaha Nebraska: Publishes business directories for many different industries. Phone (402) 593-4600.

Bay Area 500: Hoover. An example of a regional listing, this one providing profiles of the largest companies in the San Francisco area.

Business Newsbank: Newsbank, Inc. This service provides the narrative of articles from newspapers and business journals from 400 cities. Cross-references by company name, individual's name, industry, or product category.

Business Organizations and Agencies Directory: Gale Research Company. Provides useful information to look up by business name and types of activity. Provides contact information.

Business Periodicals Index: Cross-references business articles from over 300 periodicals by subject and company name.

Career Guide—Dun's Employment Opportunities Directory: Aimed specifically at the professional job seeker, lists more than 5,000 major U.S. companies and their personnel directors, career opportunities, and benefits packages.

Chamber of Commerce and local business associations: These often publish directories of local companies, available in libraries or by writing to the individual associations.

Contacts Influential: A series of directories providing information on smaller businesses. Allows look up by organization name or type to learn details of its operations and size.

Directory of Executive Recruiters: Joyce Lain Kennedy.

Directory of Executive Search Firms: Lists and cross-references 100s of these businesses, should they be appropriate for you.

Dun & Bradstreet Million Dollar Directory: Provides information on 180,000 of the largest companies in the country. Gives the type of business, number of employees, and sales volume for each. It also lists the company's top executives.

Hidden Job Market: A Guide to America's 2000 Little-Known Fastest Growing High-Tech Companies: Peterson's Guides. Concentrates on high-tech companies with good growth potential.

Hoover's Handbook of American Business: Profiles more than 750 larger companies.

Hoover's Handbook of Emerging Companies: Spain, Campbell, Talbot. Profiles of 250 entrepreneurial companies.

Job Bank Series: Bob Adams Inc. Series of books for job-seeking professionals, each covering a different large city or metropolitan area with details on economic outlook for the covered area, list of major companies, and positions within the company.

Job Hunter's Guide to 100 Great American Cities: Brattle Communications. Lists major employers for 100 of America's largest cities.

Little Known, Fastest Growing High-Tech Companies: Peterson's Guides.

Macrae's State Industrial Directories: Published for northeastern states, but similar volumes are produced for other parts of the country by other publishers. Each book lists thousands of companies, concentrating on those that produce products, rather than services. They include a large number of small firms, in addition to the larger ones listed in many other guides.

Million Dollar Directory: Dun's Marketing Services. Provides general information on over 115,000 businesses.

Moody's Industrial Manual: Provides detailed information on over 3,000 larger organizations.

Moody's Industrial News Reports: Provides articles related to each of the businesses listed in the related directory.

National Business Telephone Directory: Gale Research. An alphabetical listing of companies across the United States, with their addresses and phone numbers. It includes many smaller firms (20 employees minimum).

Peterson's Business and Management Jobs: An annual listing of 100s of employers plus essential background information on each.

Polk's Directories: R.L. Polk & Co. Each major city has its own Polk Directory created by door-to-door canvass of individuals and businesses in the area. Cross-references by name, address, type of business.

Reference Book of Corporate Management: Dun's Marketing Services. Provides information on the executives and officers of the 6,000 largest U.S. corporations.

Standard & Poor's Register of Corporations, Directors and Executives: Brief information on over 40,000 corporations and their key people cross-referenced by names, types of businesses, and other methods. Lists parent companies with subsidiaries and the interlocking affiliations of directors.

Thomas Register: Lists more than 100,000 companies across the country by name, type of product made, and brand name of product produced.

Yellow pages (the phone book): As I mentioned earlier, your best source is often the yellow pages of the phone book, because it lists virtually all business, government, and not-for-profit organizations in a given area—and even organizes them by type of business! And this book is free.

Many directories give information about firms in a particular industry. Here are just a few.

> *The Blue Book of Building and Construction*
>
> *Directory of Advertising Agencies*
>
> *Directory of Computer Dealers*
>
> *McFadden American Bank Directory*

School and Training Admissions, Financing, and Survival

Education pays. People with more education and training tend
to earn substantially more. Most of the rapidly-growing jobs require technical training beyond high school or a four- year college degree. While a four-year college degree makes sense for a lot of people, many occupations with high pay and rapid growth can be learned in two years or less.

More adults are going back to school to upgrade their career skills, and any young person should consider getting as much education and training as possible. Knowledge of computers is now important in most jobs and, if you have not kept up with the new developments in your field, it is important to do so as soon as possible. There are a wide variety of training options including technical schools, adult-education classes, workshops, formal college courses, and even classes you can take on the Internet.

You can finance post-secondary training or education in many ways, so don't let a lack of money be a barrier to getting what you need. If you want to do it, seek and ye shall find a way. Here are some resources.

Back to School: A College Guide for Adults: LaVerne Ludden. A comprehensive guide that includes self-assessment activities and good advice on setting goals, considering various degrees, selecting a college, juggling priorities, and much more. Includes a directory of 1,000 adult friendly degree programs. JIST.

Ludden's Adult Guide to Colleges and Universities: LaVerne and Marsha Ludden. Good advice for adults going back to school, plus information on more than 1,500 degree programs. Includes many nontraditional programs that can be used to reduce the time required to get a degree. JIST.

Career Connection for College Education—A Guide to College Education and Related Career Opportunities: Fred Rowe. Information on over 100 college majors and 1,000 related occupations. Includes details on salaries, course requirements, related high school courses, and other details useful in planning a college major. JIST.

Career Connection for Technical Education—A Guide to Technical Training and Related Career Opportunities: Fred Rowe. Similar to the above, describes over 60 technical education majors and the careers they lead to. JIST.

Bear's Guide to Finding Money For College: John Bear. Well written, readable, helpful.

But What if I Don't Want to Go to College?: Unger. Reviews alternative education or training needed for hundreds of jobs.

College 101: Farrar. Primer for getting along in college.

College Admissions Data Handbook: Orchard House. The most thorough and up-to-date source of information on colleges available, four volumes cover different sections of the country.

College Degrees by Mail: John Bear. Brief descriptions for 100 nonresident schools.

College Degrees You Can Earn from Home: Frey.

College Guide for Students with Learning Disabilities: Sciafini and Lynch. Covers over 500 programs.

College Majors and Careers: A Resource Guide for Effective Life Planning: Phifer. Good information on college majors, skills, related leisure activities, personal attributes, and additional resource materials for major occupational interests.

College Survival Guide: Mayer. Well-done, new student orientation to basics of making it.

Earn College Credit for What You Know: Simosko. On nontraditional college credit programs: types, application procedures, and so on.

Electronic University: A Guide to Distance Learning Programs: Peterson's Guides.

Free Dollars From the Federal Government: Blum.

Free Money for College: A Guide to More Than 1,000 Grants and Scholarships: Blum.

Guide to Non-Traditional College Degrees: John Bear. Fun to read, well done, thorough.

Guide to Technical, Trade, and Business Schools: A four-volume set with thorough profiles of 2,200 accredited schools.

Historically Black Colleges and Universities: Details on all 91 such schools.

How to Apply to American Colleges and Universities: Brennan and Briggs.

Internships: 50,000 On-The-Job Training Opportunities for Students and Adults: Rushing.

Liberal Education and Careers Today: Howard Figler. "I dropped out of pre-med in my junior year of college (a long story) and got a degree in liberal arts—and I turned out OK." Figler makes a case for a liberal arts education with research and advice on how liberal arts is a good way to go.

Major Decisions—A Guide to College Majors: Orchard House. Provides brief descriptions for all college majors.

Minority Student Enrollments in Higher Education: Provides information on 500 schools with the highest minority enrollments.

New Horizons—Education and Career Guide for Adults: Haponski. Methods of seeking and using education to get ahead.

Paying Less for College: Peterson's College Money Handbook: Provides costs, types of aid, and other details from over 1,700 schools.

Person's College Money Handbook.

Peterson's Colleges and Programs for Students with Learning Disabilities: Mangrum and Strichart. Lists over 1,000 colleges with these programs.

Peterson's Internships. Lists 40,000 positions to get experience as interns.

Peterson's Scholarships, Grants, and Prizes.

Peterson's Competitive Colleges: Tips on getting into the top 300 schools.

Peterson's Guide to College Admissions: Student workbook on preparing and competing. Well done.

Peterson's Guide to Four-Year Colleges: 1,900 schools and 400 majors. Organized to select by many criteria, plus tips on applying.

Peterson's Guide to Two-Year Colleges: Details on over 1,400 schools with associate degrees.

Peterson's Independent Study Catalog: Guide to over 12,000 correspondence and Internet courses.

Peterson's National College Databank: Data in over 350 categories, a major source of data for colleges of all descriptions.

Tech Prep Guide: Technical, Trade, & Business School Data Handbook: Orchard House. The most thorough reference of its kind, providing thorough information on over 1,600 schools plus summary information on another 3,000 schools. Four volumes cover different parts of the country.

Time for College—The Adult Student's Guide to Survival and Success: Siebert and Gilpin.

Who Offers Part-Time Degree Programs?: Peterson's Guides. Data on over 2500 institutions.

Winning Money for College: High school student's guide to scholarship contests.

You Can Make It Without a College Degree: Roesch.

Instructor and Trainer Resources

While you should be able to find books on public speaking in most bookstores and libraries, more specific materials such as instructor's guides for a job search workshop are very hard to find. JIST publishes or distributes a variety of these more specialized materials, should you be interested.

Career Exploration Groups: A Facilitator's Guide: Garfield and Nelson. Includes group activities and exercises to aid in self-knowledge, career information, and decision making.

Career Information Service: Norris. One of the few texts for university level career counseling and development courses. Thorough book for career counselors.

Career Planning Workshop Manual: Instructor's guide for life/work planning workshops. Includes group exercises, worksheets.

Developing Vocational Instruction: Mager and Beach. Easy to understand, step-by-step guidelines to developing good curriculum.

How to Organize and Manage a Seminar: What to Do and How to Do It: Murray. Budgets, plans, staffing, promotion, and more. Very good.

Louder & Funnier: A Practical Guide for Overcoming Stage Fright: Nelson. Getting over fear of groups is a major obstacle to success as a trainer or presenter. Excellent.

Making Successful Presentations: Smith. Good for the new or moderately experienced trainer.

Making Vocational Choices: A Theory of Careers: John Holland: There are few career theory books, and this is one of the most influential. In plain and readable English, it presents the research, rationale, and practical uses of his theory of six personality types.

The Business of Public Speaking: Good tips on business aspects of doing presentations.

Where To Start: An Annotated Career Planning Bibliography: Thorough, helpful. Organized by topic.

Work in the New Economy: Robert Wegmann, Robert Chapman, and Miriam Johnson. Well-researched and written review of the research on labor market trends and how a job seeker is affected. Though written some time ago, I consider this the best book of its kind. JIST.

Career Interest Tests and Books on Test-Taking

Too many people think a magical solution exists to their career planning problems that does not require effort. Tests are only tools to provide you with information and can't tell you what to do. I prefer assessment instruments that are self-scored and encourage you to participate in the career decision-making process.

If you have access to a career counselor, ask about taking a career interest test. But remember that it can only provide you food for thought, not an answer to what you should do. Following are a few of the self-administered and self-scored interest inventories that I like. Most are available from JIST but in packages. Individuals must get them through a counselor, though several inventories

are available as a package for individuals on JIST's Internet site at JIST.com. Test-related books are listed after the tests themselves.

Career Exploration Inventory (CEI): John Liptak. Uses a unique past/present and future orientation and results in scores that cross-references to major occupational interest areas. Includes a large chart of occupational information, an action plan, and recommends sources of additional information. Spanish version available. JIST.

The Guide for Occupational Exploration Inventory (GOEI): J. Michael Farr. Uses an intuitive process to lead to one or more of the 12 career interest areas from the ***Guide for Occupational Exploration.*** A related information chart then provides substantial information on the jobs in each area, related courses, and leisure activities. Includes an action plan and suggests additional sources of information. JIST.

Leisure/Work Search Inventory (LSI): John Liptak. Ties leisure activities to related jobs, making this a good test for young people with limited work experience or adults looking for more interesting career options. Includes substantial chart of career information, an action plan, and other useful elements. JIST.

Occupational Clues—A Career Interest Survey. A thorough book that includes checklists for values, interests, activities, school subjects. and work experience—all cross-referenced to related job clusters. JIST.

Barriers to Employment Success Inventory (BESI): John Liptak. Self-scored inventory that helps identify barriers to employment—very helpful for programs. JIST.

The Job Search Attitude Inventory: John Liptak. A self-scored that identifies potential problem areas for success in the job search. JIST.

Bibliography

Career Decision-Making System (CDM): Thomas Harrington and Arthur J. O'Shea. A popular interest test that is easy to use, self-scoring and interpreted. Records occupational preferences, school subjects, job values, abilities, plans for future education, and training.

College Majors Finder: Cross-references Holland codes (which can be obtained from the ***SDS*** and ***CDM*** described in this section as well as from other devices) to over 900 college majors.

Self-Directed Search (SDS): John L. Holland. Widely used, responses result in recommended jobs in six major clusters. A separate booklet cross-references over 1,100 jobs in a logical manner.

American College Testing Program (ACT): Over 450 pages of skills, reviews, sample questions, study tips, and tips to raise ACT scores.

Book of U.S. Postal Exams: Bautista. Sample exams for 44 job categories.

Career Aptitude Tests: Klein and Outerman. Series of self-scored tests measuring aptitudes against over 250 jobs.

Career Finder: The Pathways to Over 1500 Entry-Level Jobs: Schwartz and Breckner. Checklists result in recommended jobs for more exploration. List salary, openings, and more.

Civil Service Test Tutor: Practice drills and samples for government tests for beginning office jobs such as accounting, file clerk, telephone operator.

Counselor's Guide to Vocational Guidance Instruments: Kappes and Mastie. Reviews of many tests.

Fairness in Employment Testing: National Academy of Sciences.

Guide to 75 Tests for Special Education: Up-to-date guide covering major tests and how to select, interpret, and use.

How to Get a Clerical Job in Government: Hundreds of sample questions and answers covering major topics on federal, state, and local exams.

How to Pass Employment Tests: How to do well in tests you may encounter in your job search plus tests given to evaluate advancement potential.

Making the Grade: Study habits and techniques for getting good grades by doing well on all sorts of tests.

Practice for Clerical, Typing, Steno Tests: Sample questions, drills, exercises to improve scores on most clerical tests.

Practice For The Armed Forces Tests: Drills, sample questions, test-taking tips, general review for all service tests.

Preparation for the GED: Thorough preparation to increase scores.

Preparation for the SAT: Thorough preparation to increase scores.

Career-Oriented Software

I formerly listed software that you could find for reasonable prices in a retail software store, but changes occur so rapidly that any list is quickly out-of-date. A number of good resume preparation programs are quite helpful in preparing basic resumes, though you won't need them if you have access to a good word processing program and a good resume book. Two good resume programs that have been consistently available are ***WinWay Resume on CD-ROM*** and ***PFS Resume Pro***—both are popular and widely available.

The major word processing programs include resume formats, but they force you to use formats that may not be the best for your situation.

David Noble's book *Using WordPerfect in Your Job Search* shows you the many tricks you can do with a powerful word-processing program.

Another category of software that is very helpful in the job search is that of contact management programs such as ACT! or GoldMine. These are designed for individuals like sales people to follow up on their contacts and are well suited for any follow-up tasks including letters, schedules, and phone calls.

A growing number of career planning, occupational exploration, and related programs are becoming available. Some are poorly done while others seem helpful, so buyer beware.

JIST publishes a variety of software, but the software is priced for multiple users such as in schools or programs, and it is too expensive for individuals. JIST has a free job search program on its Internet site at www.JIST.com if you want to check it out.

To give you an idea of the types of information becoming available, here are some JIST-published programs followed by a few of the many available from other sources:

JIST's Career Explorer on CD-ROM: Answering a series of questions about your interests and other factors results in a list of the 20 jobs that best match your responses. The program then allows you to get information on each of these jobs. Takes about 15 minutes.

JIST's Multimedia Occupational Outlook Handbook: Very easy to use, includes descriptions for the 250 major jobs in the OOH, powerful search features, and color images and sounds.

Mike Farr's Get a Job Workshop on CD-ROM: Includes activities, text, video clips, and sound in an interactive format covering setting a job objective, details on all major jobs, identifying skills,

job search methods, resumes, job survival, and related topics. JIST.

The Electronic Enhanced Dictionary of Occupational Titles: This is a sophisticated CD-ROM program that includes the complete content of the ***Dictionary of Occupational Titles,*** the ***Occupational Outlook Handbook,*** the ***Complete Guide for Occupational Exploration,*** and over additional details on over 12,000 jobs. While it is easy to use, it provides access to detailed technical information on over 12,000 jobs that has not been readily available in the past. JIST.

Young Person's Electronic Occupational Outlook Handbook: A lively and simple-to-use format provides basic information on 250 major jobs.

Free Phone CD-ROM: Toll-free numbers for over 1,000 business categories covering the entire country. Allows lookup by region and other criteria.

Information USA: Provides substantial information on federal jobs, government resources, agencies, grants, loans, scholarships, statistics.

Lovejoy's College Counselor CD-ROM: Provides details on thousands of colleges and technical schools, 2,500 scholarships, and video clips of many schools. Excellent.

Scholarships 101: Information on over 5,000 scholarship sources. Sorts by various criteria and helps write letters asking for additional information.

Select Phone CD-ROM: Includes all listings in the white and yellow pages directories for the entire U.S. Search by name, region, business heading, and so on.

Recommended Internet and World Wide Web Sites

The information available on the Internet and World Wide Web is amazing, and the sites keep getting better. I still prefer old-fashioned books for many uses, but the Internet is clearly superior for certain tasks. If you have not already read Section 2, you should do so now, before you waste lots of hours on the Internet. That section gives you good advice on career planning and job seeking that will help you decide what, precisely, you want to look for before you dive into the cold deep waters of the Internet. At the end of that section, are a few brief cautions regarding the use of the Internet as well as tips for getting the most from it. Do use caution, as the Internet is addictive to some people. Remember, your objective is to get things done, not to play with your computer. Enough said.

The selection of Internet sites that follows is based on recommendations in a book by Anne Wolfinger titled *The Quick Internet Guide to Career and College Information*, published by JIST and used here with permission. I shortened comments and deleted sites that were primarily for professional counselors, educators, and the like. JIST's Internet site provides free access to the complete list, including many categories and sites that are not presented here. Anne's book has more detailed comments and many more entries, so you may want to buy the book as well.

Sites Providing Good Information on Careers, Job Search, Industries, and Related Subjects

These sites do a variety of useful things. Most provide good information as well as links to other career-related sites. Some have job listings or will accept your resume in a database for employers to search. You can start with almost any one of them and eventually get to what you want through links to other sites. With a few exceptions, I've arranged them in alphabetical order.

JIST Works
http://www.jist.com

JIST, the publisher of this book, maintains a site offering a variety of free information including career planning and job search advice, downloadable chapters from several books, an interactive job search workshop, (based on content provided by yours truly), and direct links to recommended career, education, and job search sites. They also have an online bookstore that includes many good books, assessment tests, and other products.

Careers On-Line
http://www.disserv.stu.umn.edu/TC/Grants/COL

This site has job search and employment information for people with disabilities.

Career Resource Center
http://www.careers.org

You'll find more than 11,000 links here to jobs, employers, business, education, and career services on the Web. This site also includes links to bibliographies, software lists, publications, resource evaluations, event calendars, and resources for small businesses and self-employed people. It even lists career resources by geographic location.

Career Resource Homepage, Rensselaer Polytechnic Institute

http://www.rpi.edu/dept/cdc/homepage.html

This lists commercial job databases and resume banks and employers who post job openings on their own Web sites. There are also links to professional associations, college career services, human resource management resources, alumni services, and various USENET newsgroups.

Career Toolbox

http://www.careertoolbox.com

Sponsored by Chevas Regal, this site features multimedia information on career planning, job search, entrepreneurship, professional development, and money management. While produced for recent college grads, it has useful information for anyone.

Catapult on JobWeb

http://www.jobweb.org/catapult/catapult.htm

From the National Association of Colleges and Employers, this site is aimed at career services professionals working with college students and alumni. It provides links to employment centers, colleges and universities, job search vehicles, industry information, relocation resources, and professional associations.

Definitive Guide to Internet Career Resources

http://phoenix.placement.oakland.edu/

From the Oakland University Career Services Office, this site boasts a thorough listing of career resources.

The Riley Guide: Employment Opportunities and Job Resources on the Internet

http://www.dbm.com/jobguide

One of the best career and job information clearinghouses, this site provides extensive information on using the Internet in your job search. Resources are organized into categories such as arts and humanities, computing and technology, and government jobs, with additional links for state, national, and international resources.

Emory Colossal List of Career Links

http://www.emory.edu/CAREER/Main/Links.html

From the placement office of Emory University, this site is oriented toward its student audience but contains links to and rates career and job search sites.

HomeFair

http://www.homefair.com

If you are relocating, you'll find here useful information on homes and cost of living in hundreds of U.S. and international cities. The site includes a salary calculator and many other resources.

Hoover's Online

http://www.hoovers.com

With information on more than 10,000 companies and a list of 4,000 specific corporate websites, this is a very useful site.

Job Search and Employment Opportunities: Best Bets

http://asa.ugl.lib.umich.edu/chdocs/employment

Best Bets includes only sites that meet the clearinghouse's standards and provides a lengthy description and evaluation of each. Links are organized by field, with additional information for beginners on the Web.

JobHunt
http://www.job-hunt.org

This is a comprehensive list of sites with descriptions and recommendations plus job listings and other job resources.

JobSmart
http://jobsmart.org/index.htm

From the Bay Area Library System, this site has links to job banks, job hotlines, career centers, and libraries—plus information on salary surveys, resume writing, the hidden job market, high tech, and career guides.

Military Career Guide Online
http://www.militarycareers.com

From the Department of Defense, this provides information on 152 enlisted and officer occupations, education, and other benefits. Browse the occupations by category or search occupations that meet your criteria.

National Occupational Information Coordinating Committee (NOICC)
http://www.noicc.gov

A federal agency addressing the needs of vocational education and the career development needs of youth and adults, NOICC provides links to job search assistance sites, career information, education and financial aid sites, and sources of occupational labor market information and educational statistics.

Peace Corps
http://www.peacecorps.gov

This site has comprehensive information on volunteering for the Peace Corps, including application information for agriculture, education, forestry, health, engineering, skilled trades, business, environmental, urban planning, youth development, and more. About 6,500 volunteers now serve in over 90 countries.

Public Register's Annual Report Service (PRARS)
http://www.prars.com

PRARS provides company financials, including annual reports, on more than 3,200 public companies. Listings are organized alphabetically or by industry.

Purdue University Placement Service
http://www.ups.purdue.edu/student/jobsites.htm

You'll find here well-organized links to job search sites, federal government and international job listings, classifieds, newsgroups, resume services, and professional recruiters. The *Reference and Resource Material* category links to helpful information on career planning, job search, resume writing, interviewing, and more.

What Color Is Your Parachute? Job Hunting Online
http://www.washingtonpost.com/parachute

This site provides an online version of Richard Bolles's *Parachute* book, plus his comments on Internet sites organized in useful groupings.

Sites with Online Listings of Job Openings, Want Ads, and Resume Banks

In addition to listing job openings, most of these sites provide substantial resources for job seekers. For example, some have interactive resume-writing software, and others offer tips for job seeking or a bookstore offering recommended books. Most allow free posting of your resume to their resume databanks for employers, who pay to view the resumes. They all make it easy to use their services and provide links to other sites that provide specialized information or services.

E-Span

http://www.espan.com

This is one of the largest resume banks and listings of job openings. Search for job openings by keyword or preferences; they will even e-mail you updates about openings that fit your needs. The site also offers well-organized links to additional resources on career assessment, job fairs, business indexes, education, relocation, and local, national and world newspaper want ads.

JIST maintains E-span's bookstore and free resource library of online career materials.

America's Job Bank

http://www.ajb.dni.us

Run by the U.S. Employment Service, this site lists all the job openings posted at the 1,800 state employment service offices throughout the country, searchable in a variety of ways. Free listings to employers and job seekers.

Best Jobs in the USA Today

http://www.bestjobsusa.com

Best Jobs lists wants ads from *USA Today* and from thousands of companies across the nation.

Search by state, category, job title, or company name, or enter your own resume. There is no fee for job seekers. The site also features corporate profiles, lists of career fairs, and recent issues of *Employment Review*.

Career City

http://www.careercity.com

Career City features a no-fee resume and job bank and informative articles on resumes and interviewing. Sponsored by Adams Media, the site sells their job search and career information books and software.

Career Magazine

http://www.careermag.com

This is an online career resource magazine with articles, job updates, employer profiles, discussion groups, a resume bank, and classified ads. It combines job postings from USENET newsgroups into a database searchable by preferred job locations, skills, and title, with a list ranked by best fit or most recent job postings.

CareerPath

http://www.careerpath.com

CareerPath allows a quick search of want ads from 25 major newspapers across the country. Search by specific newspaper, job category, keyword, or other criteria.

CareerSite

http://www.careersite.com

This unique site lets job seekers and employers create profiles of their credentials or job opportunities. You can search and respond to openings online or wait for them to e-mail you jobs that match your preferences. They only send your resume with your permission and only to employers with matching job needs.

CareerWeb

http://www.cweb.com

CareerWeb features a database of job openings, employer profiles, online career fairs, online bookstore, and links to other career sites. For a fee, they will
e-mail you openings that meet your preferences.

Federal Jobs Digest

http://www.jobsfed.com

This site claims to list more federal job vacancies than any other source. Organizes job openings by categories such as engineering, science and math, and trade and postal. For a fee, the matching service will
analyze which kinds of federal jobs you may be eligible for.

Internet Career Connection

http://www.iccweb.com

This site offers both a job bank and a resume/talent bank. Free to job seekers looking for openings, they do charge for posting your resume. The site also provides a computerized personality assessment and a list of career resources.

JobBank USA

http://www.jobbankusa.com

JobBank lets you search its own and other job databases for openings, making this a quick way to sort openings from a variety of sites. There is no fee for posting your resume.

JOBTRAK

http://www.jobtrak.com

A job and resume bank with access limited to students and alumni of the more than 400 colleges and universities, JOBTRAK includes employer profiles and full-time and part-time job listings. There is no charge to job seekers.

JobWeb

http://www.jobweb.com

JobWeb contains both job and employer databases with more than 450 employer links you can browse or search.

Online Career Center

http://www.occ.com

This large database of jobs is searchable by type, location, and other criteria, with no charge to job seekers to search the database or post their resumes. Also includes lots of career information.

Monster Board

http://www.monster.com

One of the largest, Monster Board allows you to search more than 50,000 job openings by location, discipline, or keywords, and delivers results to your personal in-box each time you log in to see your matches. Includes more than 4,000 employer profiles and lots of useful features.

Sites for Choosing a College or Training and for Getting Financial Aid

Many schools have their own Internet sites offering detailed information on their programs, student body, activities, admissions requirements, and more. Some of the sites listed here will help you sort through and then link to these schools, while others will help you select programs that meet your criteria or provide other information.

Adventures in Education
http://www.tgslc.org

This site covers financial aid resources with links to educational institutions, financial institutions, scholarship information, government agencies, standardized tests/admissions, and other resources.

Center for All Collegiate Information
http://www.collegiate.net

A clearinghouse for information on postsecondary education, this site links to almost all major college-related sites in a variety of useful ways.

College and University Home Pages
http://www.mit.edu:8001/people/cdemello/univ.html

This links to more than 3,000 college and university home pages worldwide, this site is sorted alphabetically and geographically. Also links to other school information Web sites around the world.

College Board Online
http://www.collegeboard.org

Run by an association of 3,000 two- and four-year colleges, universities, and education associations, this site offers many services for educators plus good searches for colleges, career searches, and scholarships.

CollegeNET
http://www.collegenet.com

CollegeNet lets you search for two-year and four-year schools and offers links to school home pages, scholarship searches, and education and financial aid resources.

CollegeView
http://www.collegeview.com

Here you can search colleges by criteria including field of study, state, student body size, athletics, and cost. The site also offers multimedia profiles of more than 3,500 colleges, e-mail connections to college admissions offices, and links to college home pages.

fastWEB
http://www.fastweb.com

This is a database of more than 180,000 private sector scholarships, fellowships, grants, and loans. There is no fee for matching with your profile of skills and abilities.

FinAid: The Financial Aid Information Page
http://www.finaid.org

With links to online scholarship databases and to many other financial aid resources, such as aid for students over 30 and other special groups, this is a good site.

Mapping Your Future
http://www.mapping-your-future.org

The main focus of this site is selecting a postsecondary school and applying for financial aid.

Peterson's Education and Career Center

http://www.petersons.com

You'll find substantial information here on K-12 schools, colleges and universities, graduate study, studying abroad, summer programs, language study, distance learning, financial aid, and other topics. Search colleges alphabetically, geographically, by major, or by keyword.

Project EASI (Easy Access for Students and Institutions)

http://easi.ed.gov/index.html

Run by the U.S. Department of Education to help parents and students get financial aid, this site covers planning for your education, applying, receiving financial aid, and repaying your loan, with links to related Web sites. Free download or online view of *Preparing Your Child For College: A Resource Book for Parents.*

The Princeton Review

http://www.review.com/index.cfm

Search databases for colleges, business schools, law schools, and medical schools, then link to the schools' home pages. This site offers information on admissions, testing, financial aid, and programs. Experts moderate discussion groups on related topics such as the SAT, the GRE, and the Bar Exam.

National Association of Colleges and Employers (NACE)

http://www.jobweb.org

NACE serves colleges, employer organizations, students, and alumni. The site includes employer/college surveys, salary surveys of newly hired college graduates, a quarterly journal, and a biweekly newsletter.

U.S. News & World Report Colleges & Careers Center

http://www.usnews.com/usnews/edu/home.htm

From *U.S. News & World Report*, this site features college rankings, admissions, articles on careers and self-employment, links to financial aid sites, online discussion forums, a parents' guide, and campus culture stuff.

The Very Quick Job Search, 2nd Edition

Get a Better Job in Half the Time!

By J. Michael Farr

A major revision of the most thorough career planning and job search book on the market, this is a "must have" for job seekers and career counselors!

ISBN: 1-56370-181-2 ■ **$14.95**
Order Code: J1812

Job Savvy, 2nd Edition

By LaVerne L. Ludden, Ed.D.

Job Savvy is a well-researched, step-by-step workbook for job survival and success. A practical guide to workplace readiness, it was written in response to requests from many employers, employment and training program instructors, and educators.

ISBN: 1-56370-304-1 ■ **$10.95**
Order Code: J3041

The Quick Resume & Cover Letter Book

Write and Use an Effective Resume in Only One Day!

By J. Michael Farr

Much more than a resume book. Includes a special "Same Day Resume" section, plus tips on searching for jobs, interviewing, cover and follow-up letters.

ISBN: 1-56370-141-3 ■ **$12.95**
Order Code: RCLQG

Back to School

A College Guide for Adults

By LaVerne L. Ludden, Ed.D.

An excellent two-part book for adults who are starting or returning to college! Although going back to school is not easy, this book will help you realize that it's easier than you think.

ISBN: 1-57112-070-X ■ **$14.95**
Order Code: P070X

America's Top Resumes for America's Top Jobs™

Good Advice Plus Hundreds of Professionally Written Resumes

By J. Michael Farr

Sample resumes for more than 200 major jobs! Nearly 400 of the best resumes submitted by members of the Professional Association of Resume Writers.

ISBN: 1-56370-288-6 ■ **$19.95**
Order Code: J2886

Luddens' Adult Guide to Colleges and Universities

By LaVerne L. Ludden, Ed.D., & Marsha J. Ludden, M.A.

This book is an excellent reference book with information on 1,500+ degree programs at more than 400 colleges and universities. These programs are not often mentioned in traditional college guides.

ISBN: 1-57112-076-9 ■ **$19.95**
Order Code: P0769

Networking for Everyone!

Connecting With People for Career and Job Success

By L. Michelle Tullier, Ph.D.

Networking is the key to business and professional success. And it's all here in this lively, entertaining book by a seasoned business professional, with many practical worksheets.

ISBN: 1-56370-440-4 ■ **$16.95**
Order Code: J4404

Cyberspace Resume Kit

How to Make a Snazzy Online Resume!

By Fred E. Jandt & Mary B. Nemnich

More than 80% of today's college graduates expect to use online resources to find jobs. This hands-on, how-to guide increases success rates with expert insight and information.

ISBN: 1-56370-484-6 ■ **$16.95**
Order Code: J4846

Job Search 101

Getting Started on Your Career Path

Edited by Pat Morton and Marcia R. Fox, Ph.D.

This book, edited by two long-time career guidance professionals, is filled with information and advice for first-time job seekers. Detailed sections on choosing the right career.

ISBN: 1-56370-314-9 ■ **$12.95**
Order Code: J3149

SuccessAbilities!

1,003 Practical Ways to Keep Up, Stand Out, and Move Ahead at Work

By Paula Ancona

With this book you can find more time in your busy day, handle conflicts like an old pro, balance work and family life, network, negotiate, and take charge of your career. A wonderful new book for the millions of people who want to succeed and get ahead.

ISBN: 1-56370-444-7 ■ **$14.95**
Order Code: J4447

Using the Internet & the World Wide Web in Your Job Search, 2nd Edition

The Complete Guide to Online Job Seeking and Career Information

By Fred E. Jandt & Mary B. Nemnich

There are thousands of job opportunities online, and this book shows you how to find them, with expert advice on everything from getting connected to getting the job.

ISBN: 1-56370-292-4 ■ **$16.95**
Order Code: J2924

Franchise Opportunities Handbook,
Revised Edition

A Complete Guide for People Who Want to Start Their Own Franchise

By LaVerne L. Ludden, Ed.D.

This reference book provides expert advice on selecting the right franchise—more than 1,500 listings by industry, with an alphabetical index for franchising participants.

ISBN: 1-57112-091-2 ■ **$16.95**
Order Code: P0912

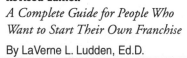